Communications in Computer and Information Science 3033

Series Editors

Rationale

The CCIS series is devoted to the publication of proceedings of computer science conferences. Its aim is to efficiently disseminate original research results in informatics in printed and electronic form. While the focus is on publication of peer-reviewed full papers presenting mature work, inclusion of reviewed short papers reporting on work in progress is welcome, too. Besides globally relevant meetings with internationally representative program committees guaranteeing a strict peer-reviewing and paper selection process, conferences run by societies or of high regional or national relevance are also considered for publication.

Topics

The topical scope of CCIS spans the entire spectrum of informatics ranging from foundational topics in the theory of computing to information and communications science and technology and a broad variety of interdisciplinary application fields.

Information for Volume Editors and Authors

Publication in CCIS is free of charge. No royalties are paid, however, we offer registered conference participants temporary free access to the online version of the conference proceedings on SpringerLink (http://link.springer.com) by means of an http referrer from the conference website and/or a number of complimentary printed copies, as specified in the official acceptance email of the event.

CCIS proceedings can be published in time for distribution at conferences or as post-proceedings, and delivered in the form of printed books and/or electronically as USBs and/or e-content licenses for accessing proceedings at SpringerLink. Furthermore, CCIS proceedings are included in the CCIS electronic book series hosted in the SpringerLink digital library at http://link.springer.com/bookseries/7899. Conferences publishing in CCIS are allowed to use our online conference service (Meteor) for managing the whole proceedings lifecycle (from submission and reviewing to preparing for publication) free of charge.

Publication process

The language of publication is exclusively English. Authors publishing in CCIS have to sign the Springer CCIS copyright transfer form, however, they are free to use their material published in CCIS for substantially changed, more elaborate subsequent publications elsewhere. For the preparation of the camera-ready papers/files, authors have to strictly adhere to the Springer CCIS Authors' Instructions and are strongly encouraged to use the CCIS LaTeX style files or templates.

Abstracting/Indexing

CCIS is abstracted/indexed in DBLP, Google Scholar, EI-Compendex, Mathematical Reviews, SCImago, Scopus. CCIS volumes are also submitted for the inclusion in ISI Proceedings.

How to start

To start the evaluation of your proposal for inclusion in the CCIS series, please send an e-mail to ccis@springer.com

Emmanuel G. Blanchard · Guanliang Chen ·
Min Chi · Seiji Isotani
Editors

Artificial Intelligence in Education

Late Breaking Results, WideAIED, Practitioners, Industry and Policies, Blue Sky, Doctoral Consortium, FoL Workshops and Tutorials, FoL Invited Papers

27th International Conference, AIED 2026
Seoul, South Korea, June 27 – July 3, 2026
Proceedings, Part III

Editors
Emmanuel G. Blanchard
Le Mans University
Le Mans, France

Guanliang Chen
Monash University
Clayton, VIC, Australia

Min Chi
North Carolina State University
Raleigh, NC, USA

Seiji Isotani
University of Pennsylvania
Philadelphia, PA, USA

ISSN 1865-0929 ISSN 1865-0937 (electronic)
Communications in Computer and Information Science
ISBN 978-3-032-29793-8 ISBN 978-3-032-29794-5 (eBook)
https://doi.org/10.1007/978-3-032-29794-5

This Springer imprint is published by the registered company Springer Nature Switzerland AG
The registered company address is: Gewerbestrasse 11, 6330 Cham, Switzerland

Preface

Welcome to the 27th International Conference on Artificial Intelligence in Education, taking place from June 27 – July 3rd, 2026 in Seoul, South Korea. AIED is ranked A in CORE[1] (top 13.09% of 825 ranked venues). AIED is clearly growing in scale and visibility, as evidenced by the 1,241 initial submissions received by the main track alone. For more than three decades, the AIED community has advanced a rich body of research at the intersection of computer science, learning sciences, cognitive science, and artificial intelligence. From early intelligent tutoring systems to contemporary data-driven and adaptive platforms, the field has consistently pushed the boundaries of how technology can support teaching and learning. These contributions have not only deepened our theoretical understanding of learning but have also shaped educational practice across diverse contexts worldwide. Today, we stand at a pivotal moment. The rapid emergence of Generative AI and increasingly capable learning technologies challenges long-standing assumptions about the role of AI in education. Systems are no longer confined to delivering content, scaffolding problem solving, or modeling student knowledge; they are now capable of engaging in dialogue, generating explanations, co-creating artifacts, and participating in complex, context-aware interactions. This transformation compels us to reconsider a fundamental question: what does it mean for AI to meaningfully participate in the learning process?

The theme of AIED 2026, "From Tools to Teammates: Human–AI Synergy for Augmented Learning", reflected this shift. Over decades of innovation, the AIED community has developed powerful tools and insights that have transformed learning worldwide. As these foundations continue to shape the field, emerging technologies, especially Generative AI, demand that we rethink how AI engages with learners and educators. Our field is entering a new era in which AI must evolve from simply supporting human learning to enabling richer human–AI collaboration. As AI becomes deeply embedded in everyday educational practice, AIED 2026 called for systems that foster genuine human–AI partnerships. This year's theme highlighted research on human and AI agency, collaborative intelligence, and the co-evolution of humans and AI. We invited work that reimagines AIED systems not merely as instruments, but as adaptive teammates that complement teachers and learners, align with human goals, and dynamically participate in shared educational processes. Such systems raise new opportunities and challenges: how to design for trust, transparency, and alignment; how to balance autonomy and control; how to support equity and inclusion; and how to rigorously evaluate learning in settings where humans and AI jointly construct knowledge.

AIED 2026 brought together a diverse and interdisciplinary community of researchers, practitioners, and policymakers to explore these questions. The contributions in these proceedings reflect a wide spectrum of perspectives—ranging from theoretical frameworks and empirical studies to system design, deployment, and real-world

[1] https://portal.core.edu.au/conf-ranks.

impact. Collectively, they illustrate a field that is both grounded in its intellectual heritage and boldly looking ahead.

AIED 2026 brought a rich program of keynote addresses, panel discussions, interactive demonstrations, and specialized sessions which are compiled in the supplementary CCIS volumes of the conference. Specifically, this year was part of the Festival of Learning, co-organized with sister conferences, Educational Data Mining (EDM 2026) and ACM Learning @ Scale (L@S 2026), which were co-located in Seoul, South Korea. Attendees had the opportunity to participate in the Doctoral Consortium, Late-Breaking Results sessions, and dedicated tracks for Practitioners, Industry, and Policy (PIP). The BlueSky track also invited visionary reflections on past progress and future trajectories in AIED, while the WideAIED track amplified perspectives from underrepresented regions and communities. Finally, several workshops and tutorials were organized in the context of the Festival of Learning. The conference program eventually comprised the following tracks:

- **The AIED 2026 Main Track** spanned three complementary areas: technical, human-centered, and societal aspects of AIED. Together, these tracks covered innovations in computational methods and system design, learning sciences and human–AI interaction, and the ethical, equitable, and policy implications of AI in education. The conference attracted 1,241 submissions, with 922 qualifying for review. From these, 143 full papers and 168 short papers were accepted, corresponding to acceptance rates of 16.5% and 15.3%, respectively. They are presented in their specific Springer LNAI proceedings.
- **The Doctoral Consortium Track** was chaired by Irene-Angelica Chounta (University of Duisburg-Essen, Germany), Yu Lu (Beijing Normal University, China), and Ido Roll (Technion – Israel Institute of Technology, Israel). It emphasized interactivity and provided opportunities for graduate students at critical stages of their professional development. Its primary objectives were to offer constructive mentorship from senior researchers and to foster a supportive peer community. To this end, the organizers facilitated connections between students and mentors aligned with their interests, complementing the traditional consortium sessions held during the conference. The consortium also promoted interdisciplinary research, underscoring the importance of integrating insights from the Learning Sciences and Computer Science in advancing AI in Education. By pairing students with mentors suited to their methodological and theoretical needs, the consortium aimed to strengthen research capacity in the field and support junior scholars in refining their work prior to dissertation completion. Out of 100 submissions, 44 were accepted to the Doctoral Consortium.
- **The Blue Sky Track** was chaired by Ivon Arroyo (University of Massachusetts Amherst, USA), Xiangen Hu (Hong Kong Polytechnic University, China), and H. Chad Lane (University of Illinois Urbana-Champaign, USA). The Blue Sky Track reflected on the progress of AI in Education while envisioning future directions for the field. In alignment with the AIED 2026 conference theme, "From Tools to Teammates," the track called for bold, forward-looking contributions that reconceptualize AI systems not merely as instructional tools, but as partners, collaborators, and amplifiers of human agency and thinking. Submissions underwent a rigorous double-blind review process by two to three program committee members, followed by further

evaluation by the co-chairs. The track received 76 submissions, of which 10 were administratively rejected due to misalignment with the track's scope. Of the remaining 66 submissions, 12 full papers (up to 14 pages) were accepted for inclusion in the proceedings, yielding an acceptance rate of 15.8%. The accepted papers articulate a broad and forward-looking research agenda for AIED, addressing themes such as reimagining human–AI collaboration in teaching, assessment, and embodied learning; advancing adaptive and meta-adaptive instructional architectures; emphasizing equity, cultural responsiveness, and inclusion in AI design; and critically examining the limitations, trade-offs, and unrealized potential of AI in supporting learner agency and motivation.

- **The Late Breaking Results (LBR) Track** was chaired by Davide Taibi (Consiglio Nazionale delle Ricerche, Italy), Renzhe Yu (Columbia University, USA), and Zheng Yuan (University of Sheffield, UK). The LBR Track was designed to provide a dynamic forum for presenting and discussing emerging ideas, preliminary findings, and innovative work in progress aligned with the overall conference theme. In 2026, the track received 350 submissions, highlighting strong and growing interest in rapidly evolving areas of Artificial Intelligence in Education. Of these, 283 submissions met formatting requirements and proceeded to a rigorous peer-review process. Ultimately, 81 papers were accepted for presentation and publication, corresponding to an acceptance rate of approximately 29%. The accepted contributions span a diverse range of technical, pedagogical, and societal perspectives, offering a rich snapshot of ongoing research in the field. Collectively, they foster dialogue on the co-evolution of human and AI agency within educational contexts and underscore the breadth and dynamism of current AIED research.
- **The Practitioners, Industry and Policy (PIP) Track** was chaired by Christian M. Stracke (University of Bonn, Germany), Lixiang Yan (Tsinghua University, China), and Diego Zapata-Rivera (Educational Testing Service, USA). The PIP Track, first introduced at AIED 2025, continued at AIED 2026 in response to strong interest and success in its inaugural year. Distinct from traditional research tracks, it focused on contributions that examine the role of AI in industry and society in relation to educational challenges and opportunities, rather than conventional scientific papers. The track invited practitioners and policymakers to share examples and initiatives of AI in Education across diverse contexts, including industry, schools, higher education, workplaces, and broader society. The PIP Track served as a platform for mutual exchange, enabling researchers to learn from real-world practice and policy, while also allowing these domains to be informed by rigorous, evidence-based research. It actively sought submissions that present implementations in education or industry, as well as strategies and policies related to AIED. Explicitly, the PIP Track welcomed descriptions and reflections of practical implementations, strategies, and policies, and analyses of personal experiences using AI in the educational domain from a practical perspective. This year, the PIP Track received again a record of 40 submissions from which 10 high quality contributions were selected after strict peer-review (acceptance rate of 25%). Therefore, it offered contributions from a range of different educational contexts and professions to reflect the manifold implementations and perspectives in AIED.

- **The WideAIED Track** was chaired by Alexandra I. Cristea (Durham University, UK) and Rafael Ferreira Mello (Federal Rural University of Pernambuco, Brazil). The WideAIED Track served as a global forum for AI in Education, with a particular focus on underrepresented contexts, global challenges, equity, and accessibility. It highlighted approaches that adapt AIED technologies and methodologies to diverse social, cultural, and technological settings. In 2026, the track experienced notable growth, receiving 61 submissions, reflecting the increasing importance and momentum of this area within the field. All submissions underwent a rigorous review process involving three program committee members per paper, followed by a meta-review conducted by the track chairs. From these, 17 high-quality papers were selected for inclusion, corresponding to an acceptance rate of 27%. Specifically, this year's papers reflect both a broad geographical coverage, as well as a broad topical coverage in the WideAIED area, exploring the AIED Unplugged perspective, GPT use for Filipino English, text accessibility, Latin American student success prediction, supporting novice programmers in India, participation inequality in AI agent learning communities, physical approaches for the Indian classroom, linguistic gatekeeping GenAI for legal education in Ghana, safe AI adoption, accessibility, participatory justice in Moroccan Darija-speaking autistic children, science learning in West Africa, and LLMs for Brazilian Portuguese Grammar.
- **The Festival of Learning - Workshops & Tutorials Track** was chaired by representatives of the three conferences: Engin Bumbacher (University of Teacher Education Vaud, Switzerland) and Shiyan Jiang (University of Pennsylvania, USA) for AIED2026, Jina Kang (University of Illinois Urbana-Champaign, USA) and Benjamin Paaßen (Bielefeld University, Germany) for the Educational Data Mining conference (EDM2026), and Roberto Martinez-Maldonado (Monash University, Australia) for the Learning@Scale conference (L@S2026). The track aimed to create opportunities for in-depth engagement with current and emerging topics in AI in Education and related fields, including Educational Data Mining, Learning Analytics, and large-scale instructional interventions. Particular emphasis was placed on fostering cross-community exchange, methodological and conceptual innovation, and active participation. Consistent with the collaborative philosophy of the Festival of Learning, proposals that integrated perspectives across AIED, EDM, and L@S, and that emphasized dialogue, hands-on engagement, and tangible participant outcomes beyond presentation-only formats, were especially encouraged. The track received 49 submissions, of which 28 were accepted following peer review.

Beyond the scholarly sessions and paper presentations compiled in these conference proceedings, the conference offered presentations on the latest publications in the International Journal of Artificial Intelligence in Education (IJAIED)[2]. As a member of the International Alliance to Advance Learning in the Digital Era (IAALDE)[3], AIED 2026 also hosts presentations of the best papers from other IAALDE conferences.

[2] https://www.sciencedirect.com/journal/international-journal-of-artificial-intelligence-in-education.

[3] https://alliancelss.com/.

This conference would not have been possible without the unwavering commitment of the International Artificial Intelligence in Education Society, the Organizing Committee, the Program and Senior Program Committees, the sponsors and partners who support our mission, and the Festival of Learning organizers. Their passion and dedication to advancing intelligent educational systems are the foundation of AIED's continued success and innovation.

We invite you to share your insights, spark new debates, and connect with peers to help drive the future of education. Together, we are exploring AI's potential as a powerful catalyst for inclusive, personalized, and ethical education globally. Welcome to AIED 2026: where we aren't just predicting the future; we are actively reimagining it through every new innovation.

June 2026

Emmanuel G. Blanchard
Guanliang Chen
Min Chi
Seiji Isotani

Organization

Conference General Co-chair

Seiji Isotani	University of Pennsylvania, USA

Program Co-chairs

Emmanuel G. Blanchard	Le Mans Université, France
Guanliang Chen	Monash University, Australia
Min Chi	North Carolina State University, USA

Workshop and Tutorials Co-chairs

Engin Bumbacher	University of Teacher Education Vaud, Switzerland
Shiyan Jiang	University of Pennsylvania, USA

Doctoral Consortium Co-chairs

Irene-Angelica Chounta	University of Duisburg-Essen, Germany
Yu Lu	Beijing Normal University, China
Ido Roll	Technion - Israel Institute of Technology, Israel

Late Breaking Results (Posters) Co-chairs

Davide Taibi	Consiglio Nazionale delle Ricerche, Italy
Renzhe Yu	Columbia University, USA
Zheng Yuan	University of Sheffield, UK

Blue Sky Co-chairs

Ivon Arroyo	University of Massachusetts Amherst, USA
Xiangen Hu	Hong Kong Polytechnic University, China

H. Chad Lane	University of Illinois Urbana-Champaign, USA

WideAIED Co-chairs

Alexandra I. Cristea	Durham University, UK
Rafael Ferreira Mello	Federal Rural University of Pernambuco, Brazil

Practitioners, Industry and Policy (PIP) Co-chairs

Christian M. Stracke	University of Bonn, Germany
Lixiang Yan	Tsinghua University, China
Diego Zapata-Rivera	Educational Testing Service, USA

Interactive Events (Demos) Co-chairs

Yuheng Li	Hong Kong Polytechnic University, China
Miguel Portaz	Universidad Nacional de Educación a Distancia, Spain
Sreecharan Sankaranarayanan	Extuitive Inc., USA

DEIA Fellowship Chairs

Ig Ibert Bittencourt	Federal University of Alagoas, Brazil
Valery Psyché	Université TÉLUQ, Canada

Lifetime Award Chair

Bruce M. McLaren	Carnegie Mellon University, USA

Awards Co-chairs

Gautam Biswas	Vanderbilt University, USA
Riichiro Mizoguchi	Japan Advanced Institute of Science and Technology, Japan
Olga C. Santos	Universidad Nacional de Educación a Distancia, Spain

Virtual Experiences Co-chairs

Patricia A. Jaques	Federal University of Paraná, Brazil
Huiyong Li	Kyushu University, Japan

Publicity Co-chairs

Cristian Cechinel	Universidade Federal de Santa Catarina, Brazil
Xinyuan Hao	University College London, UK

Proceedings Co-chairs

Matthieu Branthôme	University of Rennes, France
Diego Dermeval	Federal University of Alagoas, Brazil
Jionghao Lin	University of Hong Kong, China
Namrata Srivastava	Vanderbilt University, USA

Website Chair

Yuheng Li	Hong Kong Polytechnic University, China

Program Committees

Blue Sky Program Committee

Danielle Allessio	University of Massachusetts Amherst, USA
Pablo Arnau-González	Universitat de València, Spain
Ryan Baker	University of Pennsylvania, USA
Ig Ibert Bittencourt	Federal University of Alagoas, Brazil
Paulo Carvalho	Carnegie Mellon University, USA
Nick Degens	Hanze University of Applied Sciences, Netherlands
Toni Earle-Randell	University of Florida, USA
Sai Gattupalli	University of Massachusetts Amherst, USA
Jeff Ginger	University of Illinois rbana-Champaign, USA
Art Graesser	University of Memphis, USA
Sunčica Hadžidedić	Durham University, UK
Peter Hastings	DePaul University, USA
Neil Heffernan	Worcester Polytechnic Institute, USA
Krishna Chaitanya Rao	Ohio State University, USA
Kathala Christine Kwon	Carnegie Mellon University, USA
Andrew Lan	University of Massachusetts Amherst, USA
Blair Lehman	Brighter Research, USA
Gadea Lucas Pérez	University of Burgos, Spain
Collin Lynch	North Carolina State University, USA
Gordon McCalla	University of Saskatchewan, Canada
Bruce McLaren	Carnegie Mellon University, USA
Tanja Mitrovic	University of Canterbury, New Zealand
Kasia Muldner	Carleton University, Canada
Maria Mercedes T. Rodrigo	Ateneo de Manila University, Philippines
Ido Roll	Technion - Israel Institute of Technology, Israel
Nikol Rummel	Ruhr-Universität Bochum, Germany
Ana Serrano-Mamolar	Universidad de Burgos, Spain
Caitlin Tenison	Educational Testing Service, USA
Eric Tsui	Hong Kong Polytechnic University, China
Beverly Woolf	University of Massachusetts Amherst, USA
Chengxiang Zhai	University of Illinois, Urbana-Champaign, USA
Benedict du Boulay	University of Sussex, UK

WideAIED Program Committee

Aêda Sousa	CESAR School, Brazil
Newarney Torrezão da Costa	Instituto Federal Goiano, Brazil
Maomi Ueno	University of Electro-Communications, Japan
Giacomo Valente	University of L'Aquila, Italy
Thales Vieira	Federal University of Alagoas, Brazil
Mai Vuong	University of Pennsylvania, USA
Haoming Wang	East China Normal University, China
Siqi Wang	University of Edinburgh, UK
Adam Wynn	Durham University, UK
Cleon Xavier	Instituto Federal Goiano, Brazil
Luyao Zhang	Duke Kunshan University, China

Practitioners, Industry, and Policy (PIP) Program Committee

Burcu Arslan	Educational Testing Service, USA
Senad Becirovic	University College of Teacher Education Lower Austria, Austria
Beata Beigman Klebanov	Educational Testing Service, USA
Penghe Chen	Beijing Normal University, China
Robert Farrow	Open University, UK
Xiu Guan	Tsinghua University, China
Wenxin Guo	Tsinghua University, China
Eduardo Guzmán	Universidad de Málaga, Spain
Yueqiao Jin	Monash University, Australia
Dora Katsamori	NCSR 'Demokritos'/Institute of Informatics & Telecommunications, Greece
Lidija Kralj	EduConLK, Croatia
Xinyu Li	Monash University, Australia
Yuheng Li	Monash University, Australia
Zhiping Liang	Monash University, Australia
Qinyi Liu	University of Bergen, Norway
Jon Mason	Charles Darwin University, Australia
Teresa Ober	Educational Testing Service, USA
Simone Opel	FernUniversität in Hagen, Germany
Viktoria Pammer-Schindler	Graz University of Technology, Austria
Dimitra Pappa	NCSR Demokritos, Greece
Steve Ritter	Carnegie Learning, Inc., USA
Ron Salaj	University of Turin, Italy
Wanruo Shi	Tsinghua University, China
Tim Walther	University of Bonn, Germany
Sergej Zerr	Rhenish Friedrich Wilhelm University of Bonn, Germany

Liang Zhang	University of Michigan, USA
Linxuan Zhao	Monash University, Australia
Inge de Waard	EIT InnoEnergy, Belgium

Late Breaking Results (LBR) Program Committee

Sophie Abel	University of Wollongong, Australia
Hasan Abu-Rasheed	Goethe University Frankfurt, Germany
Luca Addiucci	Sapienza University of Rome, Italy
Imran Sharif Afizullah Khan	Laboratoire d'Informatique de l'Université du Mans (LIUM), France
Veljko Aleksić	University of Kragujevac, Serbia
Berk Atil	Boğaziçi University, Turkey
Damilola Babalola	North Carolina State University, USA
Ryan Baker	University of Pennsylvania, USA
Luca Benedetto	Télécom SudParis, France
Arne Bewersdorff	University of Georgia, USA
Indronil Bhattacharjee	New Mexico State University, USA
Cunling Bian	Ocean University of China, China
Franziska Bickel	North Carolina State University, USA
Diana-Laura Borza	Babeş-Bolyai University, Romania
Anis Boubaker	École de Technologie Supérieure, Canada
Ilona Buchem	Berlin University of Applied Sciences, Germany
Leon Camus	Leibniz Institute for Research and Information in Education, Germany
German Capdehourat	Ceibal, Uruguay
May Kristine Jonson Carlon	RIKEN Center for Brain Science, Japan
Cristian Cechinel	Universidade Federal de Santa Catarina, Brazil
Jeevan Chapagain	University of Memphis, USA
Angxuan Chen	Peking University, China
Eason Chen	Carnegie Mellon University, USA
Liangyu Chen	East China Normal University, China
Penghe Chen	Beijing Normal University, China
Xinghe Cheng	Jinan University, China
Yixin Cheng	Monash University, Australia
Jaroslaw A. Chudziak	Warsaw University of Technology, Poland
Tanya Churaman	University of Missouri, USA
Elizabeth Cloude	Michigan State University, Finland
Ruth Cobos	Universidad Autónoma de Madrid, Spain
Keith Cochran	DePaul University, USA
Jade Mai Cock	Lip6, Sorbonne Université, France
Cesar Collazos	Universidad del Cauca, Colombia

Evandro Costa	Federal University of Alagoas, Brazil
Jeffrey Cross	Tokyo Institute of Technology, Japan
Wei Dai	University of Hong Kong, China
Carrie Demmans Epp	University of Alberta, Canada
Yannis Dimitriadis	University of Valladolid, Spain
Konomu Dobashi	Aichi University, Japan
Isabela Drămnesc	West University of Timisoara, Romania
Anita Dąbrowicz-Tlałka	Gdańsk University of Technology, Poland
Yo Ehara	Tokyo Gakugei University, Japan
Bobbie Eicher	Georgia Institute of Technology, USA
Sabrina Eimler	Hochschule Ruhr West, Germany
Lukas Erle	Hochschule Ruhr West - University of Applied Sciences, Germany
Kelechi Ezema	University of Colorado Boulder, USA
Zhilin Fan	Beijing Normal University, China
Żywilla Fechner	Lodz University of Technology, Poland
Shihui Feng	University of Hong Kong, China
Zechu Feng	University of Hong Kong, China
Alessio Ferrato	Roma Tre University, Italy
Reva Freedman	Northern Illinois University, USA
Cristiano Galafassi	Universidade Federal do Pampa, Brazil
Jie Gao	McGill University, Canada
Sai Gattupalli	University of Massachusetts Amherst, USA
Gabrielle Gaudeau	University of Cambridge, UK
Jadon Geathers	Cornell University, USA
Thierry Geoffre	University of Luxembourg, Luxembourg
Dominik Glandorf	University of Tübingen, Germany
Sebastian Gombert	DIPF | Leibniz Institute for Research and Information in Education, Germany
Guher Gorgun	University of Georgia, USA
Beate Grawemeyer	Coventry University, UK
Jiong Guo	Northwest Normal University, China
Ashish Gurung	Carnegie Mellon University, USA
Fatma Betül Güreş	EPFL, Switzerland
Golnoush Haddadian	Georgia State University, USA
Ella Haig	University of Portsmouth, UK
Peter Hastings	DePaul University, USA
Xinyu He	University of Georgia, USA
Davinia Hernandez-Leo	Universitat Pompeu Fabra, Spain
John Hollander	Arkansas State University, USA
Langdon Holmes	Vanderbilt University, USA
Md Biplob Hosen	University of Maryland Baltimore County, USA

Federica Illuzzi	Università degli Studi di Bari Aldo Moro, Italy
Tsunenori Ishioka	National Center for University Entrance Examinations, Japan
Md Mirajul Islam	North Carolina State University, USA
Daneih Ismail	DePaul University, USA
Rositsa V. Ivanova	University of St. Gallen, Switzerland
Vimukthini Jayalath	Adelaide University, Australia
Yang Jiang	Columbia University, USA
Julian Marvin Jörs	Otto-von-Guericke-Universität Magdeburg, Germany
Soo Hyoung Joo	Teachers College, Columbia University, USA
Vishav Jyoti	IIT Gandhinagar, India
Shiming Kai	Columbia University, USA
Akihiro Kashihara	University of Electro-Communications, Japan
Mizue Kayama	Shinshu University, Japan
Priyanka Khare	North Carolina State University, USA
Selcuk Kilinc	University at Albany - State University of New York, USA
Yongnam Kim	Seoul National University, South Korea
Badmavasan Kirouchenassamy	LIP6 - Sorbonne Université, France
Aleksandra Klasnja-Milicevic	University of Novi Sad, Serbia
Jennifer Kleiman	University of Georgia, USA
Dan R. Kohen-Vacs	Holon Institute of Technology, Israel
Anna Korchak	Higher School of Economics, Russia
Sotiris Kotsiantis	University of Patras, Greece
Abhishek Kulkarni	University of Florida, USA
Mourya Teja Kunuku	Kennesaw State University, USA
Eleni Kyza	Cyprus University of Technology, Cyprus
Adnan Labib	King's College London, UK
Sébastien Lallé	Sorbonne University, France
Salima Lamsiyah	Université Sidi Mohamed Ben Abdellah Fès, Morocco
Min Lan	Zhejiang Normal University, China
H. Chad Lane	University of Illinois Urbana-Champaign, USA
Nguyen-Thinh Le	Humboldt Universität zu Berlin, Germany
Tai Le Quy	University of Koblenz, Germany
Hakeoung Hannah Lee	University of Virginia, USA
Jinsook Lee	Cornell University, USA
Morgan Lee	Worcester Polytechnic Institute, USA
Unggi Lee	Korea University, South Korea
Arun Balajiee Lekshmi	University of Pittsburgh, USA

Narayanan Pascal Leroux	Centre de Recherche en Education de Nantes, France
Hongming Li	University of Florida, USA
Huiyong Li	Kyushu University, Japan
Jane Hanqi Li	University of California, San Diego, USA
Lin Li	Monash University, Australia
Linlin Li	McGill University, Canada
Lynn Ling Li	Zhejiang Normal University, China
Tengju Li	Ocean University of China, China
Yuheng Li	Monash University, Australia
Zhaohui Li	Penn State University, USA
Zhi Li	University of California, Berkeley, USA
Changhao Liang	Kyoto University, Japan
Zhiping Liang	Monash University, Australia
Chang-Yen Liao	National Central University, Taiwan
Paul Libbrecht	IU International University of Applied Sciences, Germany
Lisa-Angelique Lim	University of Technology Sydney, Australia
Wen Chiang Lim	Worcester Polytechnic Institute, USA
Carla Limongelli	Università Roma Tre, Italy
Chang Liu	Colorado School of Mines, USA
Siyuan Liu	Nanyang Technological University, Singapore
Zifeng Liu	University of Florida, USA
Ziyuan Liu	Bank of China, China
Giosué Lo Bosco	Università di Palermo, Italy
Angelica Lo Duca	IIT-CNR, Italy
Min Lu	Akita University, Japan
Xinyi Lu	University of Michigan, USA
Yu Lu	Beijing Normal University, China
Bailing Lyu	University of Utah, USA
Boxuan Ma	Kyushu University, Japan
Netra Kumar Manandhar	Kathmandu University School of Education, Nepal
Massimiliano Mancini	Università degli Studi di Firenze, Italy
Luca Marconi	University of Milano-Bicocca, Italy
Ivana Marenzi	L3S Research Center, Germany
Joshua Marland	Cornell University, USA
Leonardo Brandão Marques	Federal University of Alagoas, Brazil
Tatsunori Matsui	Waseda University, Japan
Guilherme Medeiros Machado	ECE Paris, France
Het Darshan Mehta	Otto von Guericke University Magdeburg, Germany

Agon Memeti	State University of Tetovo, North Macedonia
Agathe Merceron	Berliner Hochschule für Technik - Berlin State University of Applied Sciences, Germany
Kamila Misiejuk	FernUniversität Hagen, Germany
Yoshimitsu Miyazawa	National Center for University Entrance Examinations, Japan
Riichiro Mizoguchi	Japan Advanced Institute of Science and Technology, Japan
Kiyrah Mowry	Texas A&M University, USA
Shatha N. Alkhasawneh	Pompeu Fabra University, Spain
Hunhui Na	Florida State University, USA
Takashi Nagai	Institute of Technologists, Japan
Tanya Nazaretsky	EPFL, Switzerland
Michael Neumann	University of Applied Sciences and Arts Hannover, Germany
Quan Nguyen	Thompson Rivers University, Canada
Hiran Nonato Macedo Ferreira	Universidade Federal de Uberlândia, Brazil
Ange Adrienne Nyamen Tato	Université Laval, Canada
Tadachika Ozono	Nagoya Institute of Technology, Japan
Mohan Kashyap P.	Children's Hospital of Philadelphia, USA
Abelardo Pardo	University of Adelaide, Australia
Zaki Pauzi	University College London, UK
Leisi Pei	Education University of Hong Kong, China
Yanping Pei	Worcester Polytechnic Institute, USA
Daniel Alberto Perez Perez	Durham University, UK
Yang Pian	Beijing Normal University, China
Eduard Pogorskiy	University College London, UK
Vijay Prakash	Indian Institute of Technology Bombay, India
Pipob Puthipiroj	Northwestern University, USA
Wang Qiao	Hosei University, Japan
Anna Radtke	Center for Advanced Internet Studies, Germany
Yuvaraj Rajamanickam	Anna University, India
Ramkumar Rajendran	IIT Bombay, India
Sowmya Ramachandran	Stottler Henke Associates Inc., USA
Manikandan Ravikiran	Thoughtworks AI Research Labs/IIT Mandi, India
Angelo Rega	Pegaso Telematic University, Italy
Valérie Renault	Le Mans University, France
José Raúl Romero	University of Cordoba, Spain
John Sabatini	University of Memphis, USA
Zeenar Salim	University of Georgia, USA
Rohit Saluja	IIT Mandi, India
Sreecharan Sankaranarayanan	Extuitive Inc. (Flagship Pioneering), USA

Michael Schellenbach	University of Applied Sciences Ruhr West, Germany
Daniele Schicchi	CNR ITD, Italy
Sabine Seufert	University of St. Gallen, Switzerland
Mohammed Seyam	Virginia Tech, USA
Vyom Sharma	Hippocratic AI, USA
Bruce Sherin	Northwestern University, USA
Yang Shi	Utah State University, USA
Kazutaka Shimada	Kyushu Institute of Technology, Japan
Machi Shimmei	Tohoku University, Japan
Anuradha Kumari Singh	Banaras Hindu University, India
Manpreet Singh	Education University of Hong Kong, China
Álvaro Sobrinho	Federal University of the Agreste of Pernambuco, Brazil
Christian M. Stracke	University of Bonn, Germany
Dan Sun	Hangzhou Normal University, China
Wenting Sun	Humboldt-Universität zu Berlin, Germany
Zhifan Sun	DIPF | Leibniz Institute for Research and Information in Education, Germany
Juan Andrés Talamás	Tecnológico de Monterrey, Mexico
Carvajal Xiangyu Tan	Shanghai Open University, China
Hao Tang	City University of New York, USA
Yan Tao	Cornell University, China
Maria Teleki	Texas A&M University, USA
Danielle R. Thomas	Carnegie Mellon University, USA
Jarne Thys	Hasselt University, Digital Future Lab - Flanders Make, Belgium
Sutapa Dey Tithi	North Carolina State University, USA
Anne Trumbore	University of Virginia, USA
Maomi Ueno	University of Electro-Communications, Japan
Onuralp Ulusoy	Utrecht University, Netherlands
Sam Urmian	University of Bergen, Norway
Masaki Uto	University of Electro-Communications, Japan
Giacomo Valente	University of L'Aquila, Italy
Kirk Vanacore	Cornell University, USA
Jessica Vandenberg	North Carolina State University, USA
Jobin Varughese	Texas A&M University, USA
Candace Walkington	Southern Methodist University, USA
Chengliang Wang	Australian Catholic University, Australia
Deliang Wang	Beijing Normal University, China
Haoming Wang	East China Normal University, China
Kenneth Wang	Yale University, USA

Ziwei Wang	University of Sydney, Australia
Carine Webber	Georgia Institute of Technology, USA
Zhanlan Wei	University of Pennsylvania, USA
Jacqueline Wong	Utrecht University, Netherlands
Kester Yew Chong Wong	University College London, UK
Eamon Worden	Worcester Polytechnic Institute, USA
Anna Wróblewska	Warsaw University of Technology, Poland
Adam Wynn	Durham University, UK
Ruiwei Xiao	Carnegie Mellon University, USA
Yu Xiong	Chongqing University of Posts and Telecommunications, China
Yaping Xu	Beijing Normal University, China
Yiqiao Xu	North Carolina State University, USA
Zhen Xu	Teachers College, Columbia University, USA
Saumya Yadav	IIIT-Delhi, India
Sedat Yalcin	Hisar School, Turkey
Sho Yamamoto	Kindai University, Japan
Hongxin Yan	Athabasca University, Canada
Lan Yang	Education University of Hong Kong, China
Pingjing Yang	University of Illinois Urbana-Champaign, USA
Weipeng Yang	Education University of Hong Kong, China
Yin Nicole Yang	Education University of Hong Kong, China
Chengyuan Yao	Teachers College, Columbia University, USA
Chung Yiu Richard Yeung	Education University of Hong Kong, China
Hideaki Yoshida	Morioka University, Japan
Nathaniel Taeho Yu	James Madison University, USA
Andres Felipe Zambrano	University of Pennsylvania, USA
Diego Zapata-Rivera	Educational Testing Service, USA
Di Zhang	Zhejiang Normal University, China
Jing Zhang	Dalian University of Technology, China
Nuodi Zhang	Florida State University, USA
Ryan Zhang	Johns Hopkins University, Canada
Shan Zhang	University of Florida, USA
Yimei Zhang	McGill University, Canada
Chloe Qianhui Zhao	Carnegie Mellon University, USA
Linxuan Zhao	Monash University, Australia
Weibing Zheng	University of Cincinnati, USA
Zhizi Zheng	Education University of Hong Kong, China
Yan Zhou	Zhejiang Normal University, China
Zhuqian Zhou	Teachers College, Columbia University, USA
Wangda Zhu	Cornell University, USA
Min Zhuang	North Carolina State University, USA

Doctoral Consortium Program Committee

International Artificial Intelligence in Education (IAIED) Society

IAIED Management Board

President

Secretary

Journal Editors

Finance Chair

Membership Chair

Benjamin D. Nye	University of Southern California, USA

Publicity Chair

Irene-Angelica Chounta	University of Duisburg-Essen, Germany

IAIED Officers

Xinyuan Hao	University College London, UK
Jionghao Lin	University of Hong Kong, China

IAIED Executive Committee

Ig Ibert Bittencourt	Universidade Federal de Alagoas, Brazil
Min Chi	North Carolina State University, USA
Irene-Angelica Chounta	University of Duisburg-Essen, Germany
Cristina Conati	University of British Columbia, Canada
Alexandra I. Cristea	Durham University, UK
Neil Heffernan	Worcester Polytechnic Institute, USA
Seiji Isotani	University of Pennsylvania, USA
Noboru Matsuda	North Carolina State University, USA
Bruce M. McLaren	Carnegie Mellon University, USA
Tanja Mitrovic	University of Canterbury, New Zealand
Andrew M. Olney	University of Memphis, USA
Erin Walker	University of Pittsburgh, USA
Beverly Park Woolf	University of Massachusetts Amherst, USA
Diego Zapata-Rivera	Educational Testing Service, USA

International Alliance to Advance Learning in the Digital Era (IAALDE)

The IAIED Society is a member of the International Alliance to Advance Learning in the Digital Era (IAALDE) and belongs to its board. IAIED is currently represented at IAALDE by Seiji Isotani (University of Pennsylvania, United States) as president of IAIED.

AIED 2026 Sponsors

Platinum

Gates Foundation

Silver

Bronze

VitalSource®

Best Paper Award Sponsorship

AIED 2026 Keynote

How Best to Harness AI's Great Potential to Improve Education?

Vincent Aleven

Human-Computer Interaction Institute, Carnegie Mellon University, USA

Abstract. AI has tremendous potential to improve education. For example, a substantial amount of scientific evidence shows that AI-based tutoring systems can help students learn better than other forms of instruction. Also, some scientific evidence suggests that AI-based tutoring systems can help reduce inequalities in the educational system, even if not all available evidence points in this direction.

Yet, in the USA, standardized test scores are stagnant, including in K-12 mathematics learning, where AI-based tutoring systems are often used. Nor is there evidence that existing inequalities within the educational system are shrinking. These results are beginning to lead to calls to outlaw the use of computers in classrooms, in the USA and elsewhere. How might we reconcile these seemingly opposing views from research and educational practice? More importantly, what might researchers do to help improve educational outcomes? We propose that it is important to focus on creating favorable circumstances for the use of AI-based tutoring systems. To this end, it is productive to view the smart classroom as a socio-technical ecosystem with many stakeholders: students, in the first place, and "facilitators" such as teachers, peers, human tutors, and parents/caregivers. By carefully designing human-AI interactions to support these stakeholders, we stand a good chance to harness AI's great potential to improve education and reduce educational inequalities. We illustrate this vision with several example projects and promising empirical results from our lab. In these projects, students use AI-based tutoring software and facilitators are helped by a variety of novel AI-based tools, including a mixed-reality analytics-based awareness tool for teachers, support for goal setting for students, and small-dosage AI-supported remote human tutoring.

Biography

Dr. Vincent Aleven is a Professor of Human-Computer Interaction at Carnegie Mellon University. As the head of the Creating Adaptive Tutoring Software (CATS) Lab, he investigates how AI can enhance education. His lab focuses on prototyping new designs for the smart classroom, with projects ranging from optimizing the design of AI-based tutoring systems, to a real-time mixed-reality teacher awareness tool, to easy-to-use authoring tools for creating AI-based tutoring systems. His work builds on cognitive theory and theories of self-regulated learning and helps extend the empirical science of how people learn with adaptive learning technologies. He has over 300 publications, is co-editor-in-chief of the International Journal of Artificial Intelligence in Education, received over 25 major research grants, and won 12 best paper awards at international conferences.

Contents

Festival of Learning - Invited Papers

Doctoral Consortium

Festival of Learning - Workshops and Tutorials

AI4CAREER: Responsible AI for STEM Career Development at Scale in K-16 Education

Sugana Chawla, Si Chen(✉), Julia Qian, Gina Svarovsky, Ying Alison Cheng, Rick Johnson, Nitesh V. Chawla, and Ronald Metoyer

University of Notre Dame, Notre Dame, IN, USA
schen34@nd.edu

Abstract. Rapid advances in artificial intelligence (AI) are reshaping how students imagine, explore, and prepare for STEM careers across K–16 education. As AI systems increasingly influence feedback, advising, and access to opportunity information, they are becoming part of the developmental infrastructure that shapes career identity formation and readiness. Yet uncertainty remains about how AI-supported career exploration tools should be designed, governed, and evaluated at scale—particularly across developmental stages and diverse institutional contexts. This half-day workshop convenes researchers, educators, practitioners, and policymakers to examine responsible AI for STEM career development. We focus on four themes: (1) how AI reshapes definitions and assessment of STEM career readiness; (2) appropriate roles and boundaries for AI in career decision-making; (3) developmental alignment of AI supports across the K–16 continuum; and (4) equity relevant issues and design to prevent the reproduction of structural disparities. Through lightning talks, structured group activities, and cross-sector dialogue, participants will surface design tensions, articulate governance principles, and identify research gaps. The workshop aims to advance shared language and actionable frameworks for responsible, developmentally grounded AI use in STEM career learning at scale.

Keyword: Career Readiness; STEM Pathways; K–16 Education

1 Motivation and Related Works

Artificial intelligence (AI) is rapidly becoming embedded in the infrastructure of K–16 education. Beyond tutoring or grading support, AI systems increasingly shape how learners receive feedback, interpret performance, explore academic options, and access information about future opportunities [12,14,16]. Across K–16 settings—from elementary inquiry tools to secondary advising platforms and postsecondary academic support systems—AI is influencing how students make sense of their abilities and imagine possible pathways [7]. Yet these systems

E. G. Blanchard et al. (Eds.): AIED 2026, CCIS 3033, pp. 3–8, 2026.
https://doi.org/10.1007/978-3-032-29794-5_1

are often introduced without sustained scaffolding for critical engagement or developmental alignment [19].

This shift is particularly consequential for STEM career development, which unfolds cumulatively across K–16 education. Early experiences in science and mathematics shape interest and participation, while later course-taking, specialization, mentoring, and advising translate emerging beliefs into structured educational and occupational options [6,8,11]. However, STEM preparation remains uneven due to persistent challenges in curriculum coherence, teacher capacity, advising resources, and fragmented implementation across districts and institutions [4,8]. As AI systems become embedded within instructional, exploratory, and advising infrastructures, they interact with these existing conditions and may either mitigate or amplify disparities depending on their design and deployment.

At scale, AI introduces both opportunities and risks for K–16 STEM career development. AI systems may broaden exposure to STEM pathways, personalize exploration, and surface relevant academic and career information [5,17]. At the same time, concerns arise regarding bias, inequitable access, over-personalization, and predictive labeling that may prematurely narrow students' perceived possibilities [10,14]. Family-facing AI use further highlights tensions between autonomy and over-reliance, as well as gaps in AI literacy that complicate responsible scaffolding across developmental stages [19]. As recommendation and predictive systems increasingly generate signals about performance and potential [1], it becomes critical to examine how these signals accumulate across K–16 transitions and shape STEM identities, aspirations, and trajectories.

Career readiness scholarship emphasizes that preparation extends beyond academic proficiency to include adaptability, exploratory behaviors, and evolving self-concepts [2,13,15]. If AI systems become part of the developmental infrastructure surrounding learners across K–16 education, they may influence not only short-term learning outcomes but also longer-term STEM career pathways—particularly when deployed at scale across diverse educational contexts.

This workshop centers Responsible AI for STEM Career Development at Scale in K–16 Education. We invite researchers, educators, designers, and policymakers to examine how AI systems can be designed, implemented, and governed to support cumulative STEM career development across K–16 pathways without reinforcing inequities or narrowing students' futures. Website can be found at https://ai4educationk-16.com/.

2 Organizers

The organizing team brings together complementary expertise at the intersection of responsible AI, STEM education, educational assessment, advising, data science, and community-engaged learning. Collectively, we work across K–16 education, higher education, and informal STEM ecosystems, with experience spanning human-centered AI design, psychometrics, career pathway development, educator professional learning, and institutional leadership. Our work bridges research and practice, including collaborations with schools, families, industry partners, and university teaching and learning units, enabling us to examine AI not only as a technical tool but as part of broader educational and developmental infrastructure. While the current team is primarily U.S.-based, our professional networks and collaborations extend internationally. To foster broader global representation and contextual diversity, we will actively engage scholars and practitioners through established AI-in-education and STEM networks, disseminate the call across international professional societies, and connect with regional education communities to ensure participation from varied policy and cultural contexts.

Sugana Chawla is Associate Professor of the Practice at the Lucy Family Institute for Data & Society at the University of Notre Dame and Data Science Education Program Director for iTREDS. With a background in Environmental Science and Education, she works at the intersection of STEM education and data science, preparing students and educators to engage meaningfully with data and emerging technologies while fostering STEM pathways.

Si Chen is a Postdoctoral Research Fellow at the University of Notre Dame, jointly affiliated with Notre Dame Learning and the Lucy Family Institute for Data & Society. Her research centers on human-centered and responsible AI in K–16 STEM education. With a background in Human–Computer Interaction and experience working with students with disabilities, she uses mixed-methods and design-based research to develop AI systems that support exploration while maintaining educator oversight.

Julia Qian is Associate Advising Professor and Director of Advising Strategy, Assessment, and Policy in Notre Dame's College of Engineering. Her work focuses on holistic student development and evidence-based advising. She is particularly interested in technology integration, personalized coaching, and assessment-driven policy to support student success.

Gina Svarovsky is Senior Executive Director for Research Engagement and Professor of the Practice at Notre Dame's Institute for Educational Initiatives. She studies how youth develop engineering interests and skills across formal and informal STEM environments, with a focus on authentic learning experiences and pathways into engineering.

Ying (Alison) Cheng is the Sweeney Sweeney Family Collegiate Professor of Quantitative Psychology and Education at Notre Dame. An expert in educational assessment and psychometrics, she integrates statistical modeling, data mining, and AI to design fair and interpretable measurement systems aligned with evolving demands in quantitative literacy.

Rick Johnson is Associate Professor of the Practice and Managing Director of the Applied Analytics and Emerging Technology Lab at the Lucy Family Institute. He leads applied AI initiatives with industry and community partners, including K–12 STEM pathway projects and a data-focused summer internship program.

Nitesh Chawla is the Frank M. Freimann Professor and Lucy Family Director of Data & AI Academic Strategy at Notre Dame. His research in AI and data science advances interdisciplinary innovation for societal impact. He is a Fellow of AAAI, ACM, AAAS, and IEEE and founder of multiple AI ventures.

Ronald Metoyer is Vice President and Associate Provost for Teaching and Learning and Professor of Computer Science and Engineering at Notre Dame. His work in human–computer interaction examines how data and emerging technologies can support learners and educators through responsible AI integration.

3 Themes of Interest

This workshop is structured around four distinct but complementary themes. First, AI and the Redefinition of STEM Career Readiness focuses on theory—how AI reshapes what counts as readiness and how it should be assessed. Second, AI Design Boundaries in Career Decision-Making centers on technology governance and human interactions —what AI systems should and should not do, and where human judgment must remain central. Third, AI Across the K–16 Continuum addresses developmental alignment—how AI-supported exploration should differ by age, stage, and institutional context. Finally, AI for Equity in STEM Pathways examines structural impact—how AI can broaden participation rather than reproduce disparities.

Redefining Career Readiness in the Age of AI *How does AI reshape how STEM career readiness is conceptualized and assessed?* We invite participants to examine how AI-mediated systems interact with developmental theories of STEM career exploration. Career readiness is multidimensional, encompassing attitudes (confidence, curiosity), knowledge (pathway awareness), and behaviors (exploration, planning) [13]. State and national frameworks similarly define readiness beyond content mastery [2,15]. As AI literacy becomes embedded in workforce strategies [18], preparation for STEM careers may increasingly include technical fluency, ethical reasoning, and human–AI collaboration. We encourage contributors to consider whether AI systems narrow readiness to measurable performance signals or expand how it is theoretically defined and longitudinally assessed.

AI Design Opportunities, Limits and Boundaries *What roles should AI play—and not play—in STEM career decision-making?* AI can surface pathways, prompt reflection, and provide formative feedback. However, responsible systems should not function as deterministic sorting mechanisms based on early performance signals. AI at scale must expand option spaces rather than predict "fit." Educators and advisors remain central in interpreting recommendations and supporting identity-relevant decisions. We invite discussion on governance and evaluation: What benchmarks define effective AI-supported career coaching? Should human advising serve as a gold standard? What data infrastructures are necessary to responsibly evaluate AI systems at scale while preserving student agency?

K–16 Differentiation and Continuum *How should AI-supported STEM career exploration vary across developmental stages and institutions?* Across K–16 education, AI-supported exploration must align with developmental readiness.

Early grades may emphasize identity expansion and exposure; middle school may scaffold exploratory behaviors; secondary and postsecondary levels may support structured decision-making tied to workforce pathways [6]. Because preparedness evolves iteratively [13], AI systems should shift from curiosity-building to informed planning without hardening trajectories. At scale, responsible systems must remain adaptable across institutional missions, disciplinary cultures, and regional workforce contexts.

Equity, Access, and Inclusion Pathways *How can AI systems broaden participation rather than reproduce historical inequities in STEM?* AI-driven career systems risk reproducing disparities embedded in historical data. Career development is shaped by contextual supports and access to opportunity [13], and perceptions of fairness vary across student populations [10]. We encourage discussion of bias auditing, transparent recommendation logic, diverse representation, and educator mediation [7,14]. Structural barriers in STEM—including those affecting students with disabilities—must also be considered; for example, deaf and hard-of-hearing learners often face cumulative access challenges in technical terminology [3]. Responsible AI for STEM career development should operate alongside sustained, equity-centered pipeline interventions such as #GOALS [9].

References

1. Bahalkar, P., Peddi, P., Jain, S.: Ai-driven career guidance system: a predictive model for student subject recommendations based on academic performance and aspirations. Front. Health Inform. **13**(3), 8216–8230 (2024)
2. Camara, W.: Defining and measuring college and career readiness: a validation framework. Educ. Meas. Issues Pract. **32**(4), 16–27 (2013)
3. Chen, S., Waller, J., Seita, M., Vogler, C., Kushalnagar, R., Wang, Q.: Towards co-creating access and inclusion: a group autoethnography on a hearing individual's journey towards effective communication in mixed-hearing ability higher education settings. In: Proceedings of the 2024 CHI Conference on Human Factors in Computing Systems, pp. 1–14 (2024)
4. Dickman, A., Schwabe, A., Schmidt, J., Henken, R.: Preparing the future workforce: Science, technology, engineering and math (stem) policy in k-12 education. Public Policy Forum. ERIC , (2009)
5. Duan, J., Wu, S., et al.: Beyond traditional pathways: Leveraging generative ai for dynamic career planning in vocational education. Inter. J. New Developm. Educ. **6**(2), 24–31 (2024)
6. Gandhi, S.J., Nandikolla, V.K., Youssef, G., Bishay, P.L.: Using career pathways to assimilate high school students into the engineering profession. In: 2016 ASEE Annual Conference & Exposition (2016)
7. Gillani, N., Eynon, R., Chiabaut, C., Finkel, K.: Unpacking the "black box" of ai in education. Educ. Technol. Soc. **26**(1), 99–111 (2023)
8. Kimmel, H.S., Burr-Alexander, L.E., Hirsch, L., Rockland, R.H., Carpinelli, J.D., Aloia, M.: Pathways to effective k-12 stem programs. In: 2014 IEEE Frontiers in Education Conference (FIE) Proceedings, pp. 1–6. IEEE (2014)

9. Kuskova, V., Chawla, S., Kress, R.B., Garrett-Ray, S., Jassem, K.R.: Fostering stem engagement: Evaluating the impact of the# goals program on middle-school students' interest and motivation in science and technology. In: 2025 ASEE Annual Conference & Exposition (2025)
10. Li, W., Sun, K., Schaub, F., Brooks, C.: Disparities in students' propensity to consent to learning analytics. Int. J. Artif. Intell. Educ. **32**(3), 564–608 (2022)
11. López, P., Simó, P., Marco, J.: Understanding stem career choices: a systematic mapping. Heliyon **9**(6) (2023)
12. Luckin, R., Holmes, W.: Intelligence unleashed: an argument for ai in education (2016)
13. Marciniak, J., Johnston, C.S., Steiner, R.S., Hirschi, A.: Career preparedness among adolescents: a review of key components and directions for future research. J. Career Dev. **49**(1), 18–40 (2022)
14. Mintz, J., Holmes, W., Liu, L., Perez-Ortiz, M.: Artificial intelligence and k-12 education: possibilities, pedagogies and risks (2023)
15. Mishkind, A.: Overview: state definitions of college and career readiness. College and career readiness and success center (2014)
16. Murphy, R.F.: Artificial intelligence applications to support k-12 teachers and teaching. Rand Corporation **10**(1), 1–20 (2019)
17. Sun, J.C., Pratt, T.L.: Navigating ai integration in career and technical education: diffusion challenges, opportunities, and decisions. Educ. Sci. **14**(12), 1285 (2024)
18. U.S. Department of Labor, Employment and Training Administration: Us department of labor releases ai literacy framework providing foundational content areas, delivery principles to guide nationwide efforts (Feb 2026). https://www.dol.gov/newsroom/releases/eta/eta20260213, release Number 26-199-NAT; published by the Employment and Training Administration, U.S. Department of Labor, Washington, DC
19. Xie, J., Wu, C., Wang, G., Yu, R., Zhang, H., Metoyer, R., Chen, S.: Understanding parents' perspectives on responsible ai for children's self-directed learning. In: Proceedings of the 2026 CHI Conference on Human Factors in Computing Systems, CHI 2026, pp. 1–20. ACM, New York (2026). https://doi.org/10.1145/3772318.3790479

Modeling Dynamics of Learning and Learners with the Transition Network Analysis Toolkit

Kamila Misiejuk[1(✉)], Sonsoles López-Pernas[2], Eduardo Araujo Oliveira[3], and Mohammed Saqr[2]

[1] CATALPA, FernUniversität in Hagen, 58097 Hagen, Germany
kamila.misiejuk@fernuni-hagen.de
[2] School of Computing, University of Eastern Finland, 80110 Joensuu, Finland
{sonsoles.lopez,mohammed.saqr}@uef.fi
[3] School of Computing and Information Systems, University of Melbourne, Parkville, VIC 3010, Australia
eduardo.oliveira@unimelb.edu.au

Abstract. This workshop introduces participants to Transition Network Analysis (TNA), a comprehensive framework for modeling learning processes through rigorous statistical methods. Participants will explore how TNA enables rigorous analysis of learning dynamics—with or without coding expertise. TNA includes a rich repertoire of tools and techniques for examining interaction data, including methods for visualizing and identifying recurring structural patterns such as dyads, triads, communities, and clusters. A key focus is TNA's integration of statistical validation techniques including bootstrapping, permutation testing, and case-dropping, allowing researchers to validate individual network edges with p-values and effect sizes, compare patterns across learner subgroups, and explain observed dynamics with edge-level significance. The workshop covers TNA's theoretical foundations and key variants: Frequency-based TNA, Attention Network Analysis, Heterogeneous TNA, and Co-occurrence Network Analysis. Through guided instruction and hands-on practice, attendees will learn to identify suitable data and research questions, perform data preprocessing, and apply TNA using both the tna R package and no-code platforms (tna-web and JTNA).

Keywords: Transition Network Analysis · Workshop · Learning analytics · Temporal Analysis · Learning Dynamics

1 Introduction and Background

Transition Network Analysis (TNA) is a novel framework for modeling learning dynamics and learner behavior, first presented at LAK 2025 [10]. At its core, TNA combines the temporal progression of learning events with relational modeling to capture how learners move through and interact within learning processes

E. G. Blanchard et al. (Eds.): AIED 2026, CCIS 3033, pp. 9–15, 2026.
https://doi.org/10.1007/978-3-032-29794-5_2

[12]. TNA provides a comprehensive toolset of analytical methods that enable researchers to address fundamental questions about how learning unfolds over time and how learners navigate educational activities.

TNA allows researchers to identify structural patterns in learning processes, such as cliques, communities, and sequential patterns that characterize how learners progress through tasks and activities. The framework helps pinpoint critical moments in learning by identifying central events and transitions, revealing which learning activities and pathways are most pivotal to learner success. Advanced clustering techniques within TNA capture recurring behavioral patterns, enabling researchers to understand the diverse tactics and strategies learners employ [6]. Importantly, TNA incorporates rigorous statistical validation techniques—including model reliability, bootstrapping, permutation testing, and case-dropping—ensuring that identified patterns represent genuine learning dynamics rather than random variations. TNA has been applied to analyze diverse learning contexts, including student prompts in generative AI interactions [4], small-group collaboration dynamics in project-based learning [10], learning processes during lab sessions using learning management system data [2], the development of performance, engagement, and problem-solving efficiency across blended learning phases [1], and student-chatbot interactions during active reading [14].

TNA encompasses several modeling approaches suited to different learning contexts: Markov-based models for sequential analysis, Frequency-based TNA (FTNA) for transition frequencies [11], Attention Network Analysis (ANA) with temporal decay functions to account for long memory events [7], Co-occurrence Network Analysis (CNA) for co-presence patterns [9], and Heterogeneous TNA (HTNA) for multi-layered learning interactions [8]. The framework also includes pattern mining methods for identifying differential learning behaviors across learner groups, as well as sequence analysis, comparison of sequences, and clustering. In this workshop, participants will gain hands-on experience applying TNA to analyze learning dynamics. We will demonstrate these methods using human-AI learning interactions as a contemporary example, though the analytical skills and techniques participants develop will be transferable to any learning context where understanding temporal patterns and learner pathways is essential.

2 Workshop

2.1 Organizational Details

This full-day interactive workshop will combine lectures, discussions, demonstrations, paper presentations, tutorials, and hands-on practice sessions to provide participants with both theoretical foundations and practical skills. We anticipate a maximum of 40 attendees, whom we will recruit through multiple channels to ensure diverse representation from all research communities attending the Festival of Learning. Our recruitment strategy includes outreach through

LinkedIn professional networks, the Learning Analytics Google Group, and Discord servers, such as IEEE TCLT and EATEL. This workshop represents the second edition in the TNA workshop series, with the inaugural workshop taking place at the LAK'26 conference in Bergen, Norway.

The workshop will begin with introductory content and advance to hands-on work. The morning session will focus on introducing core concepts, presenting real-world examples, and showcasing accepted papers, while the afternoon session will transition to hands-on practice activities where participants can apply learned techniques to their own contexts. To support knowledge dissemination beyond the event itself, we will issue a call for contributions with good quality, accepted and peer-reviewed papers to be published in Springer. A regular publication agreement with Springer for the proceedings was established in February 2026. The program committee for the workshop includes: Kamila Misiejuk and Daiana Rinja (FernUniversität in Hagen), Sonsoles López-Pernas and Mohammed Saqr (University of Eastern Finland), and Eduardo Araujo Oliveira (Melbourne University). All workshop materials, including presentation slides, tutorials, session highlights, and links to the proceedings, will be made permanently available on our dedicated workshop website, which will serve as a comprehensive resource hub accessible before, during, and after the event.

Our event will be a full-day interactive workshop combining lectures, discussions, demos, paper presentations, tutorials, and hands-on practice. We expect a maximum of 40 attendees.

2.2 Learning Objectives and Intended Audience

By the end of the workshop, attendees will have developed a comprehensive understanding of Temporal Network Analysis as a methodological approach, including its underlying mechanisms and various forms such as FTNA, ANA, CNA, and HTNA. Participants will be equipped to determine when TNA is the most suitable approach based on their data characteristics and research questions. Crucially, the workshop emphasizes practical application: participants will develop proficiency in applying TNA through hands-on work with available software tools, including the `tna` R package [13] and the no-code platforms tna-web [5] and JTNA [3]. This practical component will also build participants' capacity to interpret and make sense of TNA outputs.

This workshop is designed for participants across all three conferences (L@S, AIED, and EDM) who are investigating learning dynamics and learner interactions as they unfold over time. The methods presented are particularly valuable for researchers examining temporal patterns in learning processes, where understanding how learners progress, adapt, and engage moment-by-moment is essential. AIED researchers studying how learners develop through different phases of learning, how learner agency evolves during learning activities, and how collaborative learning emerges among peers or between learners and intelligent systems will find these analytical approaches directly applicable. EDM researchers focused on modeling learner cognition and behavior as it unfolds over time, tracing learning trajectories and developmental patterns, and analyzing collaborative learning dynamics will benefit from the temporal perspective these methods provide. L@S researchers exploring how learners engage with educational technologies and interventions at scale, including how learner experiences and interaction patterns evolve throughout learning sequences and how instructional dynamics shift across different learning contexts, will gain valuable tools for capturing these complex, temporal learning phenomena.

2.3 Communication of Information and Resources

A dedicated workshop website will serve as the primary platform for all communications and resource distribution. The site will offer open access to comprehensive information about the workshop's goals, agenda, and format, ensuring prospective attendees have a clear understanding of what the event will cover and how it will be conducted. Through this website, we will disseminate calls for participation, paper submission guidelines, software tools and resources, and program updates, establishing it as the definitive reference point throughout the entire workshop lifecycle. Prior to the event, registered participants will receive email communications with practical details and links to preparatory materials, including recommended readings and software installation guides. These materials will simultaneously be made available on the website, demonstrating our dedication to open access and open source principles . Following the workshop, the website will maintain its role as a knowledge repository. We will make all session materials publicly available, including presentation slides, tutorials, hands-on exercises, and links to the published proceedings, ensuring that both participants and the wider community can access and repurpose the workshop outputs (Table 1).

3 Workshop Schedule

Table 1. Workshop schedule.

Time	Item
9:00–9:15	Welcome & Workshop overview
9:15–10:00	Introduction to theoretical foundation and use cases in TNA
10:00–10:15	Coffee break
10:15–10:45	Capturing human-AI dynamics with TNA
10:45–12:00	Paper presentations with plenum discussions
12:00–13:00	Lunch break
13:00–14:00	Interactive demo of TNA Jamovi and TNA R package
14:00–14:45	Hands-on TNA and participatory exercises in small groups (I)
14:45–15:00	Coffee break
15:00–16:00	Hands-on TNA and participatory exercises in small groups (II)
16:00–17:00	Closing, reflections, discussions

4 Biographies

Kamila Misiejuk is a Postdoctoral Researcher in Learning Analytics at the FernUniversität, Hagen, Germany. Dr. Misiejuk has been an active member of the International Society for Quantitative Ethnography, where she served on the board and led the Resources Committee. She has developed extensive teaching and learning materials on Epistemic Network Analysis and has organized and conducted numerous workshops and data challenges on Quantitative Ethnography methods at international conferences and other venues. She has published methodological studies and empirical studies using network-based analytical methods, including Epistemic Network Analysis, Ordered Network Analysis, and methods in the TNA toolkit.

Sonsoles López-Pernas received the Ph.D. degree in engineering from the Universidad Politécnica de Madrid, Madrid, Spain, in 2021. She is currently an Academy Fellow with the University of Eastern Finland, Joensuu, Finland, funded by the Research Council of Finland. Her research focuses on developing learning analytics methods (including TNA), and tools for non-technical users (e.g., tna-web). Dr. López-Pernas received the IEEE Computer Society Technical Committee on Learning Technology Early Career Researcher Award in 2024 and the SoLAR Emerging Scholar Award in Learning Analytics in 2025. She is an Associate Editor for IEEE Transactions on Education, Smart Learning Environments, and PLoS One.

Eduardo Araujo Oliveira is a Senior Lecturer in the School of Computing and Information Systems at the University of Melbourne, Australia. His research focuses on learning analytics, AI in education, writing analytics, and self regulated learning. He leads large scale initiatives integrating AI into authentic assessment and software engineering education. Eduardo is a recipient of the University of Melbourne GEM Scott Teaching Fellowship and multiple university level awards for teaching excellence, recognising his leadership in advancing AI literacy and innovative pedagogical practice.

Mohammed Saqr is currently a Full Professor at the University of Eastern Finland. He has authored or coauthored extensively on learning analytics, education, and learning analytics methods in general. An important thread of his work is focused on temporal networks, complex dynamical systems and probabilistic networks. Most importantly, he has developed – with others–TNA and continues to expand the methods with other organizers of this workshop.

Acknowledgments. K.M. was partially funded by the *Development of the Ecosystem for Novel Learning Resources and Network Data Techniques* project (Postdoktorandinnenförderung: Eigenes Sachkostenbudget funding, FernUniversität in Hagen) and conducted this research in cooperation with the LEAD: FUH project funded by the Stiftung Innovation in der Hochschullehre (1001-3223).

References

1. Gao, Z., et al.: A complex system approach to decode different learning patterns in programming between majors: score, engagement, and problem-solving efficiency. Smart Learn. Environ. **13**(1), 5 (2026). https://doi.org/10.1186/s40561-026-00431-7
2. Kilanioti, I., Saqr, M., López-Pernas, S.: Exploring the process of students' learning in the laboratory with transition network analysis. In: Proceedings of the 13th Technological Ecosystems for Enhancing Multiculturality (TEEM) Conference (2025)
3. López-Pernas, S., Girault, D., Tikka, S., Saqr, M.: Jtna: a desktop software for transition network analysis. In: Proceedings of the 9th International Conference on Smart Learning Environments, ICSLE 2025(2026)
4. López-Pernas, S., Misiejuk, K., Kaliisa, R., Saqr, M.: Capturing the process of students' ai interactions when creating and learning complex network structures. IEEE Trans. Learn. Technol. **18**, 556–568 (2025). https://doi.org/10.1109/TLT.2025.3568599
5. López-Pernas, S., Tikka, S., Misiejuk, K., Saqr, M.: tna-web: advanced analytics just a few clicks away. In: Proceedings of the 13th Technological Ecosystems for Enhancing Multiculturality (TEEM) Conference (2025)
6. López-Pernas, S., Tikka, S., Saqr, M.: Mining patterns and clusters with transition network analysis: a heterogeneity approach. In: Advanced Learning Analytics Methods: AI, Precision and Complexity, pp. 447–468. Springer (2025). https://doi.org/10.1007/978-3-031-95365-1_17
7. López-Pernas, S., Tikka, S., Misiejuk, K., Oliveira, E.A., Saqr, M.: Modeling the dynamics and impact of human-AI interactions with attention transition network analysis. SSRN Preprint (2025). https://doi.org/10.2139/ssrn.6187958
8. López Pernas, S., Misiejuk, K., Tikka, S., Saqr, M.: Role dynamics in student-ai collaboration: A heterogeneous transition network analysis approach. In: Proceddings of the Transition Network Analysis Workshop, April 27-28, 2026 co-located at the 16th International Conference on Learning Analytics & Knowledge (LAK), Bergen, Norway (2026). https://doi.org/10.2139/ssrn.6082190
9. Misiejuk, K., Oliveira, E.A., Song, Y., López-Pernas, S., Saqr, M.: Modeling observation lens in co-occurrence network analysis: Four window approaches and implementations. In: Proceddings of the Transition Network Analysis Workshop, 27-28 April 2026 co-located at the 16th International Conference on Learning Analytics & Knowledge (LAK), Bergen, Norway (2026). https://doi.org/10.2139/ssrn.6189298
10. Saqr, M., López-Pernas, S., Törmänen, T., Kaliisa, R., Misiejuk, K., Tikka, S.: Transition network analysis: A novel framework for modeling, visualizing, and identifying the temporal patterns of learners and learning processes. In: Proceedings of the 15th International Conference on Learning Analytics & Knowledge (LAK), pp. 351–361 (2025). https://doi.org/10.1145/3706468.3706513
11. Saqr, M., Misiejuk, K., Törmänen, T., Kaliisa, R., Tikka, S., López-Pernas, S.: Frequency transition network analysis (ftna). In: Proceedings of the 18th International Conference on Computer-Supported Collaborative Learning-CSCL 2025, pp. 276–280 (2025). https://doi.org/10.22318/cscl2025.901997
12. Saqr, M., Nouri, J., Fors, U.: Time to focus on the temporal dimension of learning: a learning analytics study of the temporal patterns of students' interactions and self-regulation. Inter. J. Technol. Enhanced Learn. **11**(4), 398–412 (2019). https://doi.org/10.1504/IJTEL.2019.102549

13. Tikka, S., López-Pernas, S., Saqr, M.: tna: an r package for transition network analysis. Appl. Psychol. Meas. **49**(6), 326–328 (2025)
14. Woollaston, S., Flanagan, B., Ocheja, P., Ogata, H.: Archie: Efl learning processes in chatbot-supported active reading using transition network analysis. In: Proceedings of the 1st International Conference on Learning Evidence and Analytics (ICLEA) (2025)

Designing and Evaluating Next-Generation Learning Interfaces: Linking AI, HCI, and the Learning Sciences

Meng Xia[1(✉)], Yan Chen[2], Qiao Jin[3], Yang Shi[4], Paul Denny[5], Tiffany Barnes[3], Qingsong Wen[6], and Vincent Aleven[7]

[1] Texas A& M University, College Station, TX, USA
mengxia@tamu.edu
[2] Virginia Tech, Blacksburg, VA, USA
ych@vt.edu
[3] North Carolina State University, Raleigh, NC, USA
{qjin4,tmbarnes}@ncsu.edu
[4] Utah State University, Logan, UT, USA
yang.shi@usu.edu
[5] University of Auckland, Auckland, New Zealand
paul@cs.auckland.ac.nz
[6] University of Oxford, Oxford, UK
qingsongedu@gmail.com
[7] Carnegie Mellon University, Pittsburgh, PA, USA
aleven@cs.cmu.edu

1 Type of Event

This is a full-day, in-person workshop to be held at AIED 2026.

2 Theme and Goals

Recent advances in generative AI and immersive technologies, such as augmented and virtual reality, are transforming how people learn, teach, and collaborate across classrooms, homes, and workplaces. These technologies enable on-demand tutoring, adaptive content generation, multimodal interaction, and new forms of human–AI collaboration in shared environments. At the same time, their integration into education introduces critical challenges, including balancing efficiency with learner agency, ensuring accessibility in immersive settings, and addressing concerns related to bias, privacy, and over-reliance on AI. As a result, interaction design plays a central role in determining whether these technologies effectively support learning.

Prior work in intelligent tutoring systems has demonstrated the value of theoretically grounded educational technologies, with successful applications in domains such as mathematics and computer science [2,10]. These systems

E. G. Blanchard et al. (Eds.): AIED 2026, CCIS 3033, pp. 16–21, 2026.
https://doi.org/10.1007/978-3-032-29794-5_3

integrate cognitive theory [2], evidence-based practices [5], and data-driven approaches [3,6,10] to achieve measurable learning gains. However, they are typically built on fixed interaction paradigms, limiting their ability to support the open-ended, multimodal, and collaborative learning scenarios enabled by recent advances in AI and immersive technologies.

At the same time, research across AI, HCI, and the learning sciences has made significant progress in isolation. HCI contributes human-centered design principles and novel interaction techniques for educational interfaces [8,11,12]. AI provides methods for adaptive modeling, natural language interaction, and generative content creation [4,7,9]. Learning sciences offer theoretical and pedagogical foundations that ground technology design in evidence-based practice [1]. However, these perspectives are often not well integrated in the design and evaluation of next-generation learning interfaces.

This workshop addresses this gap by bringing together researchers and practitioners from AI, HCI, and the learning sciences to explore how interactive systems can better support learning. We focus on the design and evaluation of human–AI collaborative learning interfaces that are technically robust, human-centered, and pedagogically grounded. By fostering interdisciplinary dialogue, the workshop aims to identify shared challenges, design principles, and research directions for next-generation learning technologies.

The workshop has three specific aims, each accompanied by guiding questions to scaffold discussion and collaboration:

- **Engage AI and HCI researchers in educational design challenges.** We aim to encourage the application of novel interactive technologies (e.g., intelligent interfaces, immersive environments, and generative AI systems) to real learning contexts.
- **Introduce learning science theories and methods.** We aim to surface theories and approaches (e.g., student modeling, learning analytics, educational data mining) that can inform more data-driven and theoretically grounded interface and interaction design.
- **Bridge AI, HCI, and learning sciences communities.** We seek to inspire new collaborations and cross-community research agendas that advance both the design and the impact of educational technologies.

3 Workshop Planned Activities

A tentative schedule is shown in Table 1.

Introduction (9:00 - 10:00). The workshop will begin with an introduction, followed by participants' introductions. The host will play and introduce the slide deck about the participants' information.

Keynote (10:00 - 10:45): We will invite a keynote speaker to share insights related to the workshop theme.

Table 1. Workshop Day Schedule

Session	Time	Activity/Description
Introduction	09:00–10:00	Workshop introduction and participants introduction, including their background, current work, and potential contribution (e.g., dataset, tool, design method).
Keynote	10:00–10:45	Invited keynote aligned with the workshop theme.
Spotlight Presentations I	10:45–12:00	Selected submissions (short talks): 8 min talk + 4 min feedback; quick survey after each to surface connections (methods, collaborators, evaluation ideas).
Lunch Break	12:00–14:00	Organizer-hosted group lunch near the venue.
Spotlight Presentations II	14:00–14:45	Continuation of selected submissions with the same format (about 10 total across both sessions).
Thematic Breakouts	14:45–15:45	Curated themes with facilitation and note-taking: (1) controllability of educational interfaces; (2) scalable feedback; (3) data & privacy; (4) evaluation paradigms; plenary share-out.
Speed Collaboration Rounds	16:00–16:45	Paired 10-minute exchanges across disciplines; rotate to surface concrete collaboration opportunities.
Closing Reflections	16:45–17:00	Synthesis of insights and next steps for continued collaboration.

Paper Presentation (10:45 - 12:00, 2:00 - 2:45). Following the keynote, 10 selected workshop submissions will be invited to present in a short spotlight format in two sections. Each presenter will have 8 min to share their work, followed by 4 min of feedback from the audience. A quick feedback survey will be given after each talk, encouraging attendees to identify interdisciplinary connections and complementary methods that could improve the work, such as: potential collaborators, methods for improving data quality, expanded interface affordances or stakeholder considerations, or broader evaluation strategies.

Thematic Breakout Discussions: "Where Worlds Collide" (2:45 - 3:45). In the afternoon, we will organize a breakout session where participants will form small groups to discuss challenges and opportunities at the intersection of educational technology and user interface research. Each group will focus on one of several curated themes, including: (1) Controllability in educational interfaces - How we can enable educators or students to guide or refine AI behavior; (2) Scalable feedback mechanisms - How interface design can support timely and personalized feedback in large-scale learning environments; (3) Data and privacy - Balance the need for detailed educational data with transparency, consent, and trust; and (4) Evaluation paradigms - Understanding how HCI and EdTech communities approach evaluation differently, and what we can learn from each other. Each breakout group will be facilitated and will record key ideas to share in a whole-group reconvening session.

Speed Collaboration Rounds (4:00-4:45). To foster cross-community connections, we will host a speed collaboration activity. Participants from different disciplinary backgrounds will be paired for short, timed conversations. Each person will introduce their work and describe a specific problem they are trying to solve, followed by a short discussion of how their partner might contribute. For example, a participant working on educational data mining may offer a dataset and seek help designing an interface to visualize model output, while a HCI researcher may describe a novel interaction technique and ask for feedback on how it could be deployed in a classroom context. After each 10-minute round, the participants rotate to meet someone new.

Closing Reflections (4:45-5:00). We will conclude the workshop with a brief reflection session, where the organizers will summarize insights from the day and outline the next steps to continue the conversation beyond the workshop.

4 Prior or Related Work

This is the first edition of this workshop.

Recent years have seen increasing attention to AI-supported learning across multiple research communities. Major venues such as NeurIPS, AAAI, and KDD have hosted workshops on AI for Education[1][2][3] , while CHI has explored topics such as augmented educators and the future of work[4] . Learning sciences and learning analytics communities, including ICLS, CSCL, and LAK, have also advanced work on pedagogy and data-driven learning, with recent workshops on large language models for qualitative research and generative AI in learning analytics[5][6]. These efforts highlight growing interest in leveraging AI technologies to support learning. However, they are often fragmented across communities. AI research tends to focus on modeling and system capabilities, HCI emphasizes interaction design and user experience, and the learning sciences prioritize pedagogical theory and learning outcomes. As a result, there remains a lack of venues that explicitly integrate these perspectives to guide the design and evaluation of

---

[1] https://gaied.org/neurips2023/index.html.
[2] https://ai4ed.cc/workshops/aaai2022.
[3] https://ai-for-edu.github.io/workshop_kdd2024.html.
[4] https://sites.google.com/view/augemted-educators-and-ai/home.
[5] https://sites.google.com/view/lak-25-workshop-llms-for-qual/.
[6] https://sites.google.com/monash.edu/genai-la-workshop-lak25/.

next-generation learning interfaces. This workshop builds on these prior efforts while focusing on bridging AI, HCI, and the learning sciences. It aims to provide a dedicated space for interdisciplinary dialogue and collaboration around human–AI collaborative learning systems.

5 Program Committee

Our organizing committee brings together an interdisciplinary group of scholars spanning HCI, AI, and the learning sciences.

Meng Xia is an Assistant Professor in Computer Science and Engineering at Texas A&M University. Her research interests include Human–AI Interaction, Data Visualization, and Educational Technology, with a focus on human–AI collaboration for personalized education. She will serve as the General Chair and will coordinate all aspects of the workshop.

Yan Chen is an Assistant Professor of Computer Science at Virginia Tech. His work spans programming support tools, real-time learning analytics, and learning at scale, with a focus on interactive Human–AI systems for education. He will chair website development and technical infrastructure.

Qiao (Georgie) Jin is an Assistant Professor of Computer Science at North Carolina State University. Her research explores XR- and AI-driven mixed-reality tools to support teaching, learning, and social connection, particularly in real-world educational settings.

Yang Shi is an Assistant Professor of Computer Science at Utah State University. His research focuses on data-driven representations of program code for intelligent tutoring systems and student modeling in computing education, drawing on data mining and machine learning approaches.

Paul Denny is an ACM Distinguished Member and Professor at the University of Auckland whose work centers on collaborative learning and student-generated content in computing education. He is the creator of PeerWise, a large-scale platform used internationally, and brings extensive experience in building sustained research communities.

Tiffany Barnes is a Distinguished Professor of Computer Science at North Carolina State University. Her research focuses on computing education, educational data mining, and AI-supported learning environments. She will lead workshop outreach and community engagement, drawing on her extensive experience in inclusive computing initiatives.

Qingsong Wen is Head of AI and Chief Scientist at Squirrel Ai Learning and a PhD Supervisor at the University of Oxford. His research spans machine learning, time-series analysis, and AI for education, with extensive leadership experience across major AI conferences and professional societies.

Vincent Aleven is a Professor at Carnegie Mellon University's Human-Computer Interaction Institute and Director of the CATS Lab. His work focuses on intelligent tutoring systems, learning analytics, and authoring tools for educational technologies. He will co-lead workshop dissemination and outreach.

References

1. Aleven, V., Koedinger, K.R.: An effective metacognitive strategy: learning by doing and explaining with a computer-based cognitive tutor. Cogn. Sci. **26**(2), 147–179 (2002)
2. Aleven, V., McLaren, B.M., Sewall, J., Koedinger, K.R.: The cognitive tutor authoring tools (CTAT): preliminary evaluation of efficiency gains. In: Ikeda, M., Ashley, K.D., Chan, T.-W. (eds.) ITS 2006. LNCS, vol. 4053, pp. 61–70. Springer, Heidelberg (2006). https://doi.org/10.1007/11774303_7
3. Barnes, T.: The q-matrix method: mining student response data for knowledge. in: american association for artificial intelligence 2005 educational Data Mining Workshop, pp. 1–8. AAAI Press, Pittsburgh, PA, USA (2005)
4. Chu, Z., et al.: Llm agents for education: advances and applications. EMNLP (2025)
5. Koedinger, K.R.: Toward evidence for instructional design principles: examples from cognitive tutor math 6. In: Annual Meeting [of the] North American Chapter of the International Group for the Psychology of Mathematics Education (2002)
6. Koedinger, K.R., Stamper, J.C., McLaughlin, E.A., Nixon, T.: Using data-driven discovery of better student models to improve student learning. In: Lane, H.C., Yacef, K., Mostow, J., Pavlik, P. (eds.) AIED 2013. LNCS (LNAI), vol. 7926, pp. 421–430. Springer, Heidelberg (2013). https://doi.org/10.1007/978-3-642-39112-5_43
7. Koedinger, K.R., Stamper, J.C., McLaughlin, E.A., Nixon, T.: Using data-driven discovery of better student models to improve student learning. In: Lane, H.C., Yacef, K., Mostow, J., Pavlik, P. (eds.) AIED 2013. LNCS (LNAI), vol. 7926, pp. 421–430. Springer, Heidelberg (2013). https://doi.org/10.1007/978-3-642-39112-5_43
8. Pan, S., et al.: Tutorup: what if your students were simulated? training tutors to address engagement challenges in online learning. In: Proceedings of the 2025 CHI Conference on Human Factors in Computing Systems, pp. 1–18 (2025)
9. Piech, C., et al.: Deep knowledge tracing. In: Advances in Neural Information Processing Systems, vol. 28 (2015)
10. Price, T.W., Dong, Y., Lipovac, D.: isnap: towards intelligent tutoring in novice programming environments. In: Proceedings of the 2017 ACM SIGCSE Technical Symposium on Computer Science Education, pp. 483–488 (2017)
11. Tang, X., Wong, S., Pu, K., Chen, X., Yang, Y., Chen, Y.: Vizgroup: an ai-assisted event-driven system for collaborative programming learning analytics. In: Proceedings of the 37th Annual ACM Symposium on User Interface Software and Technology, pp. 1–22 (2024)
12. Zhang, G., Sun, G., Xia, M., Liang, R.: Classaid: a real-time instructor-ai-student orchestration system for classroom programming activities, arXiv preprint (2026). arXiv:2602.06734

10th Educational Data Mining in Computer Science Education (CSEDM) Workshop

Yang Shi[1](✉), Shan Zhang[2], Peter Brusilovsky[3], Thomas Price[4], Bita Akram[4], Juho Leinonen[5], Andrew Lan[6], Paulo F. Carvalho[7], Ken Koedinger[7], and Tiffany Barnes[4]

[1] Utah State University, Logan, UT, USA
yang.shi@usu.edu
[2] University of Florida, Gainesville, FL, USA
zhangshan@ufl.edu
[3] University of Pittsburgh, Pittsburgh, PA, USA
peterb@pitt.edu
[4] North Carolina State University, Raleigh, NC, USA
{twprice,bakram,tmbarnes}@ncsu.edu
[5] Aalto University, Espoo, Finland
juho.2.leinonen@aalto.fi
[6] University of Massachusetts Amherst, Raleigh, MA, USA
andrewlan@cs.umass.edu
[7] Carnegie Mellon University, Pittsburgh, PA, USA
{pcarvalh,kk1u}@andrew.cmu.edu

Abstract. We intend to host the workshop at the **EDM 2026** conference. There is a growing community of researchers at the intersection of data mining, AI, and computing education research. The objective of the CSEDM workshop is to facilitate a discussion among this research community, with a focus on how data mining can be uniquely applied in computing education research. For example, what new techniques are needed to analyze program code and CS log data? How can theoretical and empirical insights from computing education research inform the design, interpretation, and validation of data mining models? The workshop is meant to be an interdisciplinary event at the intersection of EDM and Computing Education Research. Researchers, faculty, and students are encouraged to share their AI- and data-driven methodologies, analytical frameworks, and empirical findings that demonstrate how data transforms and deepen out understanding of how students learn Computer Science (CS) skills. This **full-day** workshop will feature paper presentations and discussions to foster cross-disciplinary exchange and future partnerships.

Keywords: Computer Science Education · Educational Data Mining · AI in Education · Learning Analytics

E. G. Blanchard et al. (Eds.): AIED 2026, CCIS 3033, pp. 22–27, 2026.
https://doi.org/10.1007/978-3-032-29794-5_4

1 Workshop Goals

Computing is an increasingly fundamental skill for students across disciplines [1]. It enables them to solve complex, real, and challenging problems and make a positive impact on society [4]. As artificial intelligence (AI), automation, and data-driven decision-making continue to be integrated into every aspect of our lives, computational thinking is becoming essential for preparing students for future careers to participate meaningfully in the future of innovation [6]. Yet, the field of computing education is still facing a range of problems, from high failure and attrition rates to challenges in training and recruiting teachers to the under-representation of women and students of color.

Advanced learning technologies, which use data and AI, hold significant promise for addressing these challenges and improving student learning outcomes [2]. However, the domain of CS education presents novel challenges for applying these techniques. CS presents domain-specific challenges, such as helping students effectively use tools like compilers and debuggers and supporting complex, open-ended problems with many possible solutions [3]. CS also offers unique opportunities for developing learning technologies, such as abundant and rich log data, including code traces that capture each detail of how students' solutions evolved [5]. Providing researchers developing generative AI models with publicly available datasets of student coding behavior and how they respond to feedback can be highly impactful.

These domain-specific challenges and opportunities suggest the need for a specialized community of researchers working at the intersection of AI, data mining, and computing education research. The goal of this Educational Data Mining for Computer Science Education (CSEDM) is to bring this community together to share insights for supporting and understanding learning in the domain of CS using data. This field is nascent but growing, with research in computing education increasingly using data analysis approaches and researchers in the EDM community increasingly studying CS datasets. This workshop will help these researchers learn from each other and develop the growing sub-field of CSEDM.

Importantly, the workshop will build on eight successful prior CSEDM workshops at:

- the International Educational Data Mining Conference (EDM) in 2018[1],
- the International Learning Analytics and Knowledge Conference (LAK) in 2019[2],
- the International Conference on AI in Education (AIED) in 2019[3],
- the International Educational Data Mining Conference in 2020[4],
- the International Educational Data Mining Conference in 2021[5],

[1] http://sites.google.com/asu.edu/csedm-ws-edm-2018/.
[2] http://sites.google.com/asu.edu/csedm-ws-lak-2019/.
[3] http://sites.google.com/asu.edu/csedm-ws-aied-2019/.
[4] http://sites.google.com/ncsu.edu/csedm-ws-edm-2020/.
[5] http://sites.google.com/ncsu.edu/csedm-workshop-edm21/.

- the International Educational Data Mining Conference in 2022[6],
- the International Learning Analytics and Knowledge Conference in 2023[7].
- the International Educational Data Mining Conference in 2024[8].
- the International Educational Data Mining Conference in 2025[9].

Each of these workshops was productive and well-attended. Our past in-person workshops have been an interests for many participants, and our virtual events have had *over 100 people registered and over 70 simultaneous attendees.* The proceedings were published in CEUR[10] and Zenodo[11].

The CSEDM workshop is funded by the CS-SPLICE project[12]. The CSEDM workshop will serve as a hub for researchers in the EDM community to discuss potential collaborations and identify EDM challenges in computing education. **We plan to provide need-based funding support for participants, covering the cost of lodging on the workshop day and the registration fees.**

2 Workshop Activities

The workshop will be a **full day** workshop. It will primarily consist of paper presentations and discussions to facilitate collaboration. Interactive sessions include multiple parallel, short presentations, where participants can float around to the presentations they are interested in, similar to a poster session.

A tentative schedule is as follows:

- **09:00 - 09:30** Introductions and logistics
- **09:30 - 10:00** Networking
- **10:00 - 11:00** Paper Presentations
- **11:00 - 11:15** Coffee Break and Discussion
- **11:15 - 12:15** Paper Presentations
- **12:15 - 13:30** Lunch
- **13:30 - 14:30** Paper Presentations
- **14:30 - 14:45** Coffee Break and Discussion
- **14:45 - 15:45** Paper Presentations or Panel Discussion or Keynote
- **15:45 - 16:30** Wrap up Discussions

[6] http://sites.google.com/ncsu.edu/csedm-workshop-edm22/.
[7] http://sites.google.com/ncsu.edu/csedm-workshop-lak23/.
[8] https://sites.google.com/view/csedm-workshop-edm24/.
[9] https://sites.google.com/view/csedm-workshop-edm25/.
[10] Proceedings: 2021, 2024, 2025.
[11] Proceedings: 2022, 2023.
[12] http://cssplice.github.io/.

3 Relevant Topics

The workshop encourages contributions from the following topics of interest:

- Preserving explainability in the age of LLMs
- LLMs in Action: lessons learned for effective integration of LLMs in CS classrooms
- Generative AI and Computing Education
- Integrating the strength of classical ML with the power of LLMs
- Predictive and descriptive modeling for CS courses
- Adaptation and personalization within CS learning environments
- Intelligent support for collaborative CS problem solving
- Machine learning approaches to analyze massive CS datasets and courses
- Online learning environments for CS: implementation, design, and best practices
- Multimodal learning analytics and combination of student data sources in CS Education
- Affective, self-regulation, and motivational modeling of students as related to CS learning
- Adaptive feedback and adaptive testing for CS learning
- Discourse and dialogue research related to classroom, online, collaborative, or one-on-one learning of CS
- Teaching approaches using AI tools
- Visual Learning Analytics and Dashboards for CS
- Network Analysis for programming learning environments
- Classification of student program code
- Natural Language Processing for CS forums and discussions
- Analysis of programming design and trajectory paths
- Recommender systems and in-course recommendations for CS learning
- Adaptive educational technology and CS pedagogy for non-majors
- Deep learning approaches for analyzing, assessing, and scaffolding programming challenges

We will invite researchers who are interested in further exploring, contributing, collaborating, and developing data- and AI-driven techniques for building educational tools for Computer Science to submit papers on any of these topics.

4 Workshop Organization

The workshop will be organized by a team with a history of CSEDM research:

Yang Shi is an Assistant Professor at Utah State University. He has been working towards building data-driven methods for representing program code to enhance the ability of Intelligent Tutoring Systems and benefit student modeling processes for computing education.

Shan Zhang is a PhD Candidate in the educational technology program at the University of Florida. Before that, she gained her Ed.M. degree from Harvard

University. Her research focuses on multi-model AI Literacy assessment, learning analytics, educational data mining, and AI in education.

Peter Brusilovsky is a Professor of Information Science and Intelligent Systems at the University of Pittsburgh, where he also directs the Personalized Adaptive Web Systems (PAWS) lab. He has been working in the field of adaptive educational systems, user modeling, and intelligent user interfaces for more than 30 years.

Thomas Price is an Associate Professor of Computer Science at North Carolina State University. His primary research goal is to develop learning environments that automatically support students through AI and data-driven help features. His work has focused on the domain of computing education, where he has developed techniques for automatically generating programming hints and feedback for students in real-time by leveraging student data.

Bita Akram is an Assistant Professor with the Department of Computer Science at North Carolina State University. Her research lies at the intersection of artificial intelligence and advanced learning technologies with its application on improving access and quality of CS Education. She has been actively developing data-driven approaches for assessing students' CS competencies as demonstrated through their interactions with educational programming activities.

Juho Leinonen is an Assistant Professor and an Academy Research Fellow at Aalto University. His research focuses on creating better insight into students' learning with fine-grained learning analytics; using educational technology and artificial intelligence for personalizing course content; and using learnersourcing to create ample learning opportunities for distinct student needs.

Andrew (Shiting) Lan is an Associate Professor in the Manning College of Information and Computer Sciences, University of Massachusetts Amherst. His research focuses on the development of artificial intelligence (AI) and especially natural language processing (NLP) methods to enable scalable and effective personalized learning in education, covering areas such as learner modeling, personalization, content generation, and human-in-the-loop AI.

Paulo Carvalho is an Assistant Professor in the Human-Computer Interaction Institute at Carnegie Mellon University. His research explores how AI can revolutionize learning by creating engaging, practice-first environments. He uses data analytics and computational modeling to understand student learning, motivation, and meta-cognition and develop precise models for better learning experiences.

Ken Koedinger is the Hillman Professor of Computer Science with appointments in Human Computer Interaction and Psychology at Carnegie Mellon University. He focuses on understanding human learning processes and designing educational technologies to enhance student achievement. Dr. Koedinger has authored over 350 peer-reviewed publications and led over 45 funded research projects.

Tiffany Barnes is a Distinguished Professor of Computer Science at NC State University. She received the B.S. and M.S. degrees in Computer Science and Mathematics, and the Ph.D. degree in Computer Science from N.C. State.

Her research focuses on AI for education, educational data mining, serious games for education, health, and energy, computer science education, and broadening participation in computing education and research.

4.1 Program Committee

The 10th CSEDM Workshop's program committee will draw from members of prior program committees.

4.2 Timeline

The CFP will be released as soon as the workshop is accepted. An approximate timeline is as follows (all times AoE):

- May 1: Abstract Deadline for Papers from All Tracks.
- May 8: Paper Deadline for Papers from All Tracks.
- May 29: Notification of acceptance for Papers from All Tracks.
- June 12: Camera-Ready Deadline for Papers from All Tracks.

5 Solicitation Plan

Building on our growing network of contributors to prior workshops, we intend to solicit participation through a range of mailing lists and research networks, including ACM's Special Interest Group on Computer Science Education (SIGCSE), the Computer Science Education (CSED) research list from the ICER community, etc.

References

1. Denning, P.J., et al.: Computing as a discipline. Computer **22**(2), 63–70 (1989)
2. Denny, P., et al.: Computing education in the era of generative AI. Commun. ACM **67**(2), 56–67 (2024)
3. Franklin, D., Denny, P., Gonzalez-Maldonado, D.A., Tran, M.: Generative AI in Computer Science Education: Challenges and Opportunities, Cambridge University Press (2025)
4. Gallopoulos, E., Houstis, E., Rice, J.R.: Computer as thinker/doer: problem-solving environments for computational science. IEEE Comput. Sci. Eng. **1**(2), 11–23 (2002)
5. Ihantola, P., et al.: Educational data mining and learning analytics in programming: Literature review and case studies. In: Proceedings of the 2015 ITiCSE on Working Group Reports, pp, pp. 41–63 (2015)
6. Yadav, A., Good, J., Voogt, J., Fisser, P.: Computational thinking as an emerging competence domain. In: Mulder, M. (ed.) Competence-based Vocational and Professional Education. TVETICP, vol. 23, pp. 1051–1067. Springer, Cham (2017). https://doi.org/10.1007/978-3-319-41713-4_49

HAI-Agency: Workshop on Orchestrating Human and AI Agency for Proactive and Reflective Learning

Yiling Dai[1], Boxuan Ma[2], Huiyong Li[2(✉)], Patrick Ocheja[3], Kyoungwon Seo[4], and Brendan Flanagan[5]

[1] Hiroshima University, Hiroshima, Japan
[2] Kyushu University, Fukuoka, Japan
boxuan@artsci.kyushu-u.ac.jp, li.huiyong.194@m.kyushu-u.ac.jp
[3] Toronto, ON, Canada
[4] Seoul National University of Science and Technology, Seoul, Republic of Korea
kwseo@seoultech.ac.kr
[5] Ritsumeikan University, Kyoto, Japan
flanagan@fc.ritsumei.ac.jp

Abstract. As research momentum shifts toward the next evolution of generative AI (GenAI), Agentic AI, educational technologies are moving beyond reactive tools toward *proactive, teammate-like ecosystems* grounded in pedagogical principles. This transition raises a central challenge: how to design increasingly autonomous AI systems without diminishing learner agency or undermining teachers' professional judgment. This workshop introduces the concept of **HAI-Agency**, envisioning how human and AI agency can be orchestrated in learning and teaching. Foregrounding proactive and reflective learning, we aim to advance a shared research agenda spanning design methodologies, computational modeling, evaluation frameworks, and the classroom integration of agentic AI systems. This workshop is of particular interest to the AIED community, especially researchers and practitioners across human-AI interaction, learning analytics, AI-supported learning design, and learning sciences. Through an interactive, hybrid, half-day format, we will explore how to shape a future in which agentic AI contributes to more equitable, transparent, and pedagogically sound educational innovations.

Keywords: Proactive learning · Learner agency · Agentic AI · Human-AI interaction · AI-supported learning design

1 Introduction

Recent advances in large language models (LLMs) and multimodal generative AI (GenAI) have transformed educational systems across many areas, including automated feedback, content generation, and adaptive tutoring. However, two gaps are limiting

Patrick Ocheja—Independent Researcher.

E. G. Blanchard et al. (Eds.): AIED 2026, CCIS 3033, pp. 28–33, 2026.
https://doi.org/10.1007/978-3-032-29794-5_5

educational impact and motivating a new research agenda. First, most current GenAI applications remain reactive, relying on explicit prompts and continuous human guidance rather than autonomous, goal-directed support (Lee & Palmer, 2025). The AIED community also recognizes that GenAI is no longer just a "reactive tool" but is evolving toward "proactive teammate-like ecosystems". Second, GenAI adoption has outpaced the adoption of pedagogical design principles and evidence standards (Kostopoulos et al., 2025). The OECD emphasizes that GenAI can improve *task performance* without necessarily producing *learning gains* unless it is guided by clear pedagogical principles and designed to strengthen durable cognitive and metacognitive skills (OECD, 2026). In response, attention is shifting to the next evolution of GenAI: **Agentic AI**, a goal-directed AI system that not only responds but also perceives context, plans, and acts to pursue learning and teaching objectives.

This creates a core tension for human-AI collaboration in education: **increasing AI autonomy must not reduce learner agency or undermine teacher professional judgment**. Education succeeds when learners and teachers take initiative to set goals, monitor progress, reflect, and orchestrate complex social and classroom realities. As we move from single-chat interactions to multi-agent, co-adaptive systems, pedagogical alignment becomes more challenging: pedagogical principles must remain stable across agents, systems, and time while still preserving learner and teacher agency.

To address the technological and pedagogical gaps, we must rethink **design** (agent autonomy vs. human agency), **modeling** (human-AI co-orchestration, shared goals and initiative, pedagogical alignment), **evaluation** (new learning analytics that can distinguish overreliance from productive co-learning), and **integration** (fit with classroom practices, teacher workflows, and institutional governance). With AIED 2026 explicitly calling for a shift "from tools to teammates," this is the right moment for a community-level discussion that connects AIED with the wider edtech ecosystem. The workshop will therefore **network** researchers, practitioners, and policymakers participating in AIED 2026 and the Festival of Learning to address these gaps through an interactive, hybrid, half-day format.

2 Content and Themes

The call for participation will welcome theoretical or empirical submissions of position papers, case studies, or ongoing research on the following topics:

- **Learning goals and pedagogical foundations**:
  Proactive/reflective learning, self-regulated learning/co-regulation/learner agency, affective/cognitive/behavioral engagement, motivational orientations, competencies for the GenAI era (e.g., creativity, higher-order thinking, critical thinking).
- **Interaction, intervention & learning design**:
  Proactive/reflective prompts, scaffolds, and interventions, learning analytics-driven feedback and recommendations, teacher-facing design and support, human-centered and personalized interactions, creative AI-enhanced learning, human-computer interactions.

- **Modeling & analytics**:
  Student/teacher/context modeling, human-AI interaction modeling, learning sequence analysis, and process mining.
- **Evaluation & assessment**:
  Process-based assessment, outcome and process trade-offs, automated assessment, human-AI collaborative assessment, integrity-aware evaluation, assessment reinvention of GenAI-assisted competencies, and AI-powdered skills.
- **Agentic human-AI orchestration**:
  Agency/automation, negotiation and coordination, explainable/teachable/designable AI.
- **Ethics and social impact**:
  Safety/integrity/fairness/robustness/uncertainty/calibration/governance, challenges in classroom-level deployment, social infrastructure upgrading with AI agents, human-AI symbiosis.

3 Format and Activities

We propose a **half-day** workshop with a keynote talk, two presentation sessions, a hands-on demo, and group discussions in the afternoon. Online participants will also be supported if required. We have provided a detailed tentative schedule in Table 1.

Table 1. Schedule of activities

Time	Activity
14:00–14:10	**Opening Remarks** Welcome and overview of the workshop goals, theme, and expected outcomes.
14:10–14:30	**Keynote Talk** Invited keynote on the evolution from reactive GenAI tools to agentic AI teammates in education.
14:30–15:30	**Presentation Session 1** (4–6 talks)
15:30–15:45	Coffee Break
15:45–16:45	**Presentation Session 2** (4–6 talks)
16:45–17:15	**Hands-on Demo** Interactive demonstration of agentic AI concepts in practice, including example workflows using LLMs, agent architectures, tools, and orchestration frameworks.
17:15–17:45	**Group Discussion** (Opportunities and Challenges) Structured small-group and plenary discussion on key opportunities and risks of integrating agentic AI into educational ecosystems.
17:45–18:00	**Wrap Up and Closing**

4 Workshop Timeline

The plan to implement the workshop, including the CFP, spans three months before the conference and the month after. This is to allow sufficient time for the authors to submit their contributions and manage the conference registration on time.

Important dates (AOE):

- Publishing workshop's website: March 28, 2026
- Launch call for papers: April 3, 2026
- Paper submission deadline: April 24, 2026
- Notification of acceptance: May 15, 2026
- Paper camera-ready version: May 22, 2026
- Workshop: June 27 or 28, 2026
- Workshop proceedings submission to CEUR: July 31, 2026

5 Organizers and Advisors

The organizers and advisors are collaborators with interdisciplinary research backgrounds in AIED, EDM, LA, and HCI. Over the past several years, the organizers have conducted joint workshops at various international conferences and joint projects in AIED (Flanagan et al., 2022; Ma et al., 2025; Ocheja et al., 2024; Ogata et al., 2024; Yang et al., 2021). Those workshops spanned topics such as Learning Analytics Data Challenges at LAK (2018–2025), Learning Analytics workshops at ICCE (2018–2022), the GenAI in Education workshop at ICCE (2024), and the MiXai^learn workshop at AIED (2025).

5.1 Workshop Chairs

Dr. Yiling Dai is an Assistant Professor at the Graduate School of Advanced Science and Engineering, Hiroshima University, Japan. She has led and co-led four national research projects in Japan and serves as an active program committee member for leading international conferences (LAK, ICCE, and AIED), being awarded the best reviewer award at ICCE2024. Her research interests include knowledge representation, educational data mining, learning analytics, and educational recommendations, with a special focus on explainable AI-driven recommendations and interventions.

Dr. Boxuan Ma is an Assistant Professor in the Faculty of Arts and Science at Kyushu University and an adjunct member of the School of Interdisciplinary Science and Innovation at Kyushu University. His research lies at the intersection of Artificial Intelligence in Education, Educational Data Mining, Learning Analytics, Human-Computer Interaction, and Recommender Systems. He serves on the program committees of several leading international conferences in the field, including LAK, EDM, and AIED.

Dr. Huiyong Li is an Assistant Professor at the Research Institute for Information Technology, Kyushu University, Japan. His research focuses on learning analytics, educational data mining, and AI in education. He has led or co-led four national educational technology projects in Japan and serves as a Virtual Experience Co-Chair for AIED

2026. His work has received national and international recognition, including an Outstanding Research Award (Kyoto University) and the Best Short Paper Award (ICLEA 2025).

Dr. Patrick Ocheja is an AI, Data, and Cloud practitioner based in Canada and a former JSPS Postdoctoral Fellow at the Academic Center for Computing and Media Studies, Kyoto University, where he also earned his Ph.D. in Informatics. His research and professional work span Artificial Intelligence in Education (AIED), Learning Analytics, personalized and lifelong learning systems, and the design of scalable AI-driven infrastructure. He has previously served as a program committee member and workshop organizer at ICCE and LAK, and co-organized APSCE Student Wing activities from 2019 to 2023, serving as co-chair in 2021 and chair in 2022.

Prof. Kyoungwon Seo is an Associate Professor in the Department of Applied Artificial Intelligence at Seoul National University of Science and Technology, South Korea. His research focuses on Human-Centered AI, Artificial Intelligence, and intelligent interactive systems, integrating multimodal analytics, large language models, and multi-agent architectures to enhance human cognition and learning. He has led nationally funded research projects and interdisciplinary collaborations with industry partners, including Microsoft, Hyundai Motor Group, and healthcare organizations. His work has received international and national recognition, including the 2024 High Impact Award from the International Journal of Educational Technology in Higher Education and the 2023 Minister's Commendation from the Ministry of Trade, Industry and Energy (South Korea).

Prof. Brendan Flanagan is a Professor at the Graduate School of Information Science and Engineering at Ritsumeikan University. His research spans across the fields of Artificial Intelligence in Education (AIED), Learning Analytics, Educational Data Science, Educational Data Mining, NLP/Text Mining, and Computer-Assisted Language Learning. He is the principal investigator on three national-level research projects and also works as part of a Japanese government-funded large research project into educational symbiotic AI systems. He hosted and chaired LAK2024 in Kyoto and has organized workshops at LAK, AIED, and ICCE.

5.2 Workshop Advisors

Prof. Hiroaki Ogata is a Professor and Director at the Academic Center for Computing and Media Studies (ACCMS), Kyoto University, Japan. He has published more than 700 peer-reviewed papers in SSCI Journals and top international conferences. He has received APSCE (Asia-Pacific Society for Computers in Education) Distinguished Researcher Award in 2014, and several Best Paper Awards, and has given keynote lectures in several countries. Currently, he is the President of APSCE, an associate member of the Science Council of Japan, and the Director of Evidence-Driven Education Research Council, Japan.

Prof. Stephen J.H. Yang is Vice President at National Taiwan Normal University and was the first Director of the Department of Information and Technology Education at the Ministry of Education, Taiwan. He is a world-leading computer scientist and education scholar with over 100 journal articles, more than 16,000 Google Scholar citations, and an h-index of 56. His awards include Taiwan MOE's 2025 Excellent Teacher Award, the 69th Academic Award, and two National Science Council Outstanding Research Awards.

Prof. H. Ulrich Hoppe is an emeritus professor of the University of Duisburg-Essen (Germany). He is a fellow of the Asia-Pacific Society for Computers in Education (APSCE) and of the International Society of the Learning Sciences (ISLS). His research has focused on computer support for learning and knowledge building in various contexts, including higher education and vocational education and training. With his COLLIDE research group, founded in 1995, he has participated in more than ten EU projects on Technology-enhanced Learning with a special focus on intelligent, AI-based support for collaborative learning and scientific inquiry.

Acknowledgments. This workshop is partially supported by JSPS KAKENHI Grant Numbers JP23K25698, JP24K20903, JP24K20902, and JP25K17078.

References

Flanagan, B., Shimada, A., Okubo, F., Li, H., Majumdar, R., Ogata, H.: The 4th workshop on predicting performance based on the analysis of reading behavior. In: Companion Proceedings of the 11th International Conference on Learning Analytics and Knowledge, pp. 152–155 (2022). http://ceur-ws.org/Vol-3120/

Kostopoulos, G., Gkamas, V., Rigou, M., Kotsiantis, S.: Agentic AI in education: state of the art and future directions. IEEE Access **13**, 177467–177491 (2025)

Lee, D., Palmer, E.: Prompt engineering in higher education: a systematic review to help inform curricula. Int. J. Educ. Technol. High. Educ. **22**(1), 7 (2025)

Ma, B., et al.: Scaffolding metacognition in programming education: understanding student-AI interactions and design implications. arXiv preprint arXiv:2511.04144 (2025)

OECD: Digital Education Outlook 2026: Exploring Effective Uses of Generative AI in Education. OECD Publishing (2026). https://doi.org/10.1787/062a7394-en

Ogata, H., Flanagan, B., Takami, K., Dai, Y., Nakamoto, R., Takii, K.: EXAIT: Educational eXplainable Artificial Intelligent Tools for personalized learning. Res. Pract. Technol. Enhanc. Learn. **19**, 019 (2024). https://doi.org/10.58459/rptel.2024.19019

Yang, S.J., Ogata, H., Matsui, T., Chen, N.S.: Human-centered artificial intelligence in education: seeing the invisible through the visible. Comput. Educ. Artif. Intell. **2**, 100008 (2021)

Ocheja, P., Flanagan, B., Dai, Y., Ogata, H.: How good is ChatGPT in giving adaptive guidance using knowledge graphs in E-Learning environments? arXiv preprint arXiv:2412.03856 (2024)

I Workshop on AIED Unplugged

Ig Ibert Bittencourt[1,2], Seiji Isotani[1,3], Thomaz Veloso[1], Carlos Portela[1,4](✉), Emanuel Queiroga[1,5], Cristian Cechinel[1,6], Maúna Rocha[1], Elton Sarmanho[1,4], and Nicolas Pereira[1,2]

[1] National Institute of Science and Technology (INCT IA.Edu), Maceió, Brazil
sisotani@upenn.edu,
{thomaz.veloso,emanuel.queiroga,mauna.rocha}@nees.ufal.br
[2] Federal University of Alagoas (UFAL), Maceió, Brazil
{ig.ibert,nybsp}@ic.ufal.br
[3] University of Pennsylvania, Philadelphia, PA, USA
[4] Federal University of Pará (UFPA), Cametá, Brazil
{csp,eltonss}@ufpa.br
[5] Federal Technological University of Paraná (UTFPR), Dois Vizinhos, Brazil
[6] Federal University of Santa Catarina (UFSC), Araranguá, Brazil
cristian.cechinel@ufsc.br

Abstract. This workshop proposes a discussion of the AIED Unplugged framework as a lens for designing, implementing, and evaluating AI-in-Education solutions that operate offline-first, require low digital skill, support shared devices, and prioritize teacher mediation, with a focus on contexts of constrained infrastructure, especially in the Global South. Building on the diagnosis of educational inequalities exacerbated by gaps in connectivity, capacity building, and resources, the workshop aims to: (i) synthesize offline-first, low-skill, shared-device practices for equitable learning; (ii) examine evidence from real cases (e.g., mathematics and writing assessment via low-cost capture and offline analysis); (iii) connect leapfrogging and innovation to policy roadmaps; and (iv) co-create a prioritized research and policy agenda for underserved contexts. The program combines a keynote, contributed talks, a policy panel, and two thematic breakout blocks to produce practical artifacts, a public report, and comparable case vignettes. The main contribution of the I Workshop on AIED Unplugged is to consolidate a pragmatic pathway to "leapfrog" toward equity with educational AI in constrained environments.

Keywords: AIED Unplugged · Offline-first · Educational equity

E. G. Blanchard et al. (Eds.): AIED 2026, CCIS 3033, pp. 34–38, 2026.
https://doi.org/10.1007/978-3-032-29794-5_6

1 Title

I Workshop on AIED Unplugged

2 Type of Event and Duration

A full-day workshop.

3 Theme and Goals

Education inequality persists worldwide, especially in the Global South, due to infrastructure gaps, limited training, difficulties in serving remote areas, variability in material quality, and scarce resources [2,9]. The COVID-19 pandemic further derailed learning for 1.6 billion of students [6], while AI has become pivotal in reshaping education systems amid performance declines [1]. Yet many institutions lack adequate connectivity and devices to leverage AI in everyday educational interactions [3]; globally, two-thirds of children lack home internet [8]. The concentration of AI solutions in high-infrastructure regions risks widening disparities [7], undermining global commitments to quality education for all [5].

AIED Unplugged addresses these constraints by designing AI-powered workflows that do not depend on continuous internet access, accommodate limited digital skills and shared devices, and operate within existing school routines [4]. In this context, the theme emerges: The Use of AIED Unplugged To Reduce Learning Inequality in Resource-Constrained Environments.

The workshop aims to:

- synthesize offline-first, low-skill, shared-device practices for equitable learning;
- examine evidence from real cases (e.g., math and writing assessment via low-cost capture and offline analysis);
- connect leapfrogging and innovation to policy roadmaps;
- co-create a prioritized research and policy agenda for underserved contexts.

4 Prior or Related Work

This is the inaugural edition dedicated to AIED Unplugged.

5 Program Committee

5.1 Workshop Chairs

- **Ig Ibert Bittencourt Short Bio:** Professor at Federal University of Alagoas (Brazil) and UNESCO Unitwin Chair on AIED Unplugged. He co-founded the Center of Excellence in Social Technologies (NEES), which has played a key role in designing and implementing policies and programs for the digital transformation of education in Brazil and across Latin America, with a strong focus on the use of Artificial Intelligence. His academic career has been dedicated to advancing education through the design, development, and evaluation of educational technologies aimed at enhancing both learning outcomes and equity. He is also co-leading a global initiative on AIED Unplugged, which seeks to support underserved communities by enabling access to AI-driven solutions that can strengthen education systems worldwide. Professor Ig Ibert Bittencourt has been awarded the Order of Educational Merit, the highest educational honor in Brazil.

- **Seiji Isotani Short Bio:** Learning scientist and engineer internationally recognized for his contributions to artificial intelligence in education and the gamification of learning. His interdisciplinary work bridges computer science, the learning sciences, and public policy. For more than 15 years, he has led groundbreaking research on how people learn through interactive and intelligent educational technologies. His work also focuses on designing and implementing public policies that ensure all students receive the personalized support they need to experience fulfilling and meaningful learning, especially in underserved and resource-constrained contexts. Among his key accomplishments, Dr. Isotani pioneered "AIED Unplugged," a methodology that brings AI to schools in resource-constrained environments. He played a key role in shaping Brazil's national education policies, including leading the development of the K–12 computer science curriculum, which has impacted more than 40 million students. Dr. Isotani is the President of the International Artificial Intelligence in Education Society and serves on the boards of several institutions dedicated to advancing education.
- **Thomaz Edson Veloso Short Bio:** Brazilian researcher and entrepreneur in Artificial Intelligence in Education (AIED), founder of Educometrika, and Executive Director of the IA.Edu Institute. He holds a dual Ph.D. in Teleinformatics Engineering and Science at Federal University of Ceará, Brazil, and University of Copenhagen, Denmark, respectively, where he pioneered the applied field of Educometrics: the integration of psychometrics, learning analytics, and AI for evidence-based educational decision-making. His work focuses on large-scale assessment, AI-powered structured pedagogy, early-warning systems for dropout prevention, and the design of intelligent public education policies across Latin America in collaboration with ministries of education and international organizations. He has published in leading venues such as IJAIED, IEEE conferences, and national and international AIED forums. At AIED, his work bridges rigorous measurement models (IRT, PCA, CMF) with real-world implementation, offering scalable AI solutions that connect learning sciences, data science, and public policy to promote educational equity.
- **Carlos dos Santos Portela Short Bio:** Professor at Federal University of Pará (Brazil) and UNESCO Unitwin Institutional Representative on AIED Unplugged. Since 2021, he has been a member of the Center of Excellence in Social Technologies (NEES) at the Federal University of Alagoas, where

he conducts research at the intersection of Artificial Intelligence (AI), education, and public policy in Brazil. He has published in the field of AI in Education (AIED), focusing on solutions that do not rely on connectivity (AIED Unplugged), dropout prevention, and computer science education. Additionally, he participates in the Educational Equity Journey program, which operates within municipal education networks.

5.2 Organizing Committee

- **Emanuel Marques Queiroga**, Lead Technician at INCT IA.Edu, Federal Technological University of Paraná
- **Cristian Cechinel**, Specialist in School Dropout, Federal University of Santa Catarina
- **Maúna Soares de Baldini Rocha**, Director of Operations at INCT IA.Edu, Center for Excellence in Social Technologies
- **Elton Sarmanho Siqueira**, Specialist in Educational Data Mining, Federal University of Pará
- **Nicolas Yan Bittencourt Santana Pereira**, Specialist in Machine Learning, Federal University of Alagoas

Acknowledgements. The authors gratefully acknowledge the financial support by National Institute of Science and Technology in Artificial Intelligence in Education Unplugged (INCT IA.Edu) sponsored by Brazil's National Council for Scientific and Technological Development (CNPq), grant no. 408483/2024-5, and Alagoas Research Foundation (FAPEAL), grant no. 60030.0000001481/2025.

References

1. Chanduvi, J., et al.: Where are we on education recovery? taking the global pulse of a rapid response (2022). https://www.unicef-irc.org/publications/1391-where-are-we-on-education-recovery-taking-the-global-pulse-of-a-rapid-response.html
2. Chine, D.R., et al.: Educational equity through combined human-ai personalization: a propensity matching evaluation. In: 23rd International Conference on Artificial Intelligence in Education (2022)
3. Gašević, D.: Include us all! directions for adoption of learning analytics in the global south. Learning analytics for the global south, pp. 1–22 (2018)
4. Isotani, S., Bittencourt, I., Challco, G.C., Dermeval, D., Mello, R.F.: Aied unplugged: leapfrogging the digital divide to reach the underserved. In: International Conference on Artificial Intelligence in Education, pp. 772–779. Springer (2023)
5. Ossai, A.: Sustainable development goal four (sdg4): challenges and the way forward. Int. J. Adv. Res. Educ. Literat. **8**(2) (2022)
6. Pearson, H.: The school experiment. Nature **605**, 608–611 (2022)
7. Puigjaner, R.: Progressing toward digital equity. In: IFIP World Information Technology Forum, pp. 109–120. Springer (2016)

8. Thompson, G.: Two thirds of the world's school-age children have no internet access at home, new unicef-itu report says. https://www.unicef.org/press-releases/two-thirds-worlds-school-age-children-have-no-internet-/access-home-new-unicef-itu (2020)
9. Unesco: Latin american education systemsin response to covid-19:educational continuity and assessment (2020). https://unesdoc.unesco.org/ark:/48223/pf0000374018_eng

From Assessment to Human–AI Co-creation in Language Learning: Adaptive, Inclusive, and Game-Based Design in the Generative AI Era

Zheng Yuan[1(✉)], Okan Bulut[2], Thierry Geoffre[3], and Qiao Wang[4]

[1] The University of Sheffield, Sheffield, UK
zheng.yuan1@sheffield.ac.uk
[2] The University of Alberta, Edmonton, Canada
bulut@ualberta.ca
[3] University of Luxembourg, Luxembourg, Luxembourg
thierry.geoffre@uni.lu
[4] Hosei University, Chiyoda, Japan
judy.wang@hosei.ac.jp

Abstract. Recent advances in generative artificial intelligence (AI) and large language models (LLMs) are reshaping the design of intelligent language learning systems. While early AI-driven educational technologies primarily focused on automated assessment and feedback, emerging paradigms increasingly emphasise human–AI co-creation, adaptive scaffolding, and inclusive learning experiences. This *half-day tutorial* explores the transition from automated assessment pipelines to adaptive and inclusive game-based language learning ecosystems in which AI augments, rather than replaces, human agency. Grounded in educational natural language processing (NLP), psychometric modelling, and adaptive learning research, the tutorial provides a systems-level perspective on integrating generative AI into pedagogically aligned environments. We examine automated item generation, difficulty modelling, automated scoring, and feedback mechanisms, and connect these foundations to human–AI collaboration, adaptive scaffolding, and game-based design. Through lectures, demonstrations, and interactive activities, participants will gain practical design principles and conceptual frameworks for developing responsible, adaptive, and learner-centred AI systems for language education. The tutorial is primarily positioned within the AIED community, while also engaging complementary perspectives from EDM and L@S.

Keywords: AI in Education · Human–AI Collaboration · Adaptive Learning · Game-Based Language Learning · Generative AI · Automated Assessment

E. G. Blanchard et al. (Eds.): AIED 2026, CCIS 3033, pp. 39–43, 2026.
https://doi.org/10.1007/978-3-032-29794-5_7

1 Tutorial Theme & Goals

This tutorial explores the transition from automated assessment systems to human–AI co-management (adaptive-learning in classroom) or co-creation (Game-based design) in adaptive and inclusive education and game-based language learning. While early AI-driven educational systems focused primarily on automated scoring and feedback, recent advances in LLMs enable more interactive, collaborative, and learner-centered paradigms. The central theme of this tutorial is how different forms of AI can be integrated into coherent educational ecosystems that combine adaptive delivery, psychometric soundness, inclusive design, and scalable deployment.

The goals of the tutorial are threefold. First, to provide a principled overview of automated assessment pipelines, including item generation, difficulty modelling, automated scoring, and feedback generation. Second, to examine how human–AI collaboration can support adaptive scaffolding and inclusive learning experiences, positioning AI as a partner rather than a replacement. Third, to demonstrate how game-based language learning environments can integrate generative AI while maintaining validity, reliability, and pedagogical alignment.

2 Tutorial Theoretical Background

The tutorial builds on three complementary theoretical foundations. First, it draws on research in Educational NLP and AI-driven assessment, including automated item generation [4,13,14], adaptive delivery [19,29,32], automated essay scoring [2,6], automatic feedback generation [4,35], and grammatical error correction [3]. These approaches are grounded in established principles of validity, reliability, fairness, and interpretability in educational measurement.

Second, it connects to adaptive learning and educational data mining frameworks, including ontologies [1], item response theory [7], difficulty-controllable question generation [22,30], and process data modelling [9,12]. These methods provide the knowledgeable, statistical and analytical backbone for scalable and interpretable adaptive systems that can operate across diverse learner populations [11].

Third, the tutorial engages with emerging research on human-AI collaboration [16,27] and inclusive AI in education [10,17], particularly different forms of AI used for adaptive scaffolding, multimodal interaction, and co-creative learning environments. Rather than positioning AI as a substitute for teachers or learners, we emphasise co-creative and scaffolded interactions in which AI augments human agency, supports meta-cognitive development, and enables more equitable participation.

3 Schedule of Intended Activities

Proposed Length: Half-day session
Detailed Outline

1. **Introduction: Language Learning in the Generative AI Era**
   (a) Evolution of educational NLP: rule-based → feature-based → neural → LLM-driven systems [36]
   (b) From isolated AI tools to integrated adaptive learning ecosystems
2. **Automated Assessment Pipeline**
   (a) Automatic item and content generation [4,13,14]
   (b) Adaptive assessment delivery [19,29,32]
   (c) Automated scoring and feedback [2,4,35]
3. **Human–AI Collaboration for Inclusive Education**
   (a) Adaptive learning systems [5,11,15]
   (b) Adaptive scaffolding [8,18]
   (c) Case Study: Primary French classroom deployment [26]
4. **Game-Based Language Learning**
   (a) Commercial large-scale platforms and engagement design [20,21,28]
   (b) Designing self-built adaptive learning games [24,25]
   (c) Live demo: *GenQuest* – An LLM-powered multi-Modal interactive narrative game for language learners [33]
5. **Challenges and Moving Forward (25 mins)**
   (a) Risks and potential challenges [31,34,36]
   (b) Future directions [23,31,34,36]
   (c) Open research questions and community discussion

The session integrates lectures, live demonstrations, short hands-on activities, and structured discussions to promote active participation and cross-community exchange.

4 Previous Editions of then Tutorial Series

This tutorial builds upon our *AIED 2025 tutorial on NLP and Generative AI for Language Learning and Assessment* [36], which attracted strong engagement from researchers and practitioners across AI in Education and related communities. The proposed 2026 tutorial substantially extends this foundation by moving beyond automated assessment toward a human–AI co-creation paradigm centred on collaborative, learner-focused interaction.

References

1. Akhrif, O., El Fezazi, N.E., Saidi, Z., El Idrissi, Y.E.B.: A smart university ontology for educational data mining. In: 2025 11th International Conference on Optimization and Applications (ICOA), pp. 1–9 (2025)
2. Aydin, B., Kışla, T., Elmas, N.T., Bulut, O.: Automated scoring in the era of artificial intelligence: an empirical study with Turkish essays. System **133**, 103784 (2025). https://doi.org/10.1016/j.system.2025.103784

3. Bryant, C., Yuan, Z., Qorib, M.R., Cao, H., Ng, H.T., Briscoe, T.: Grammatical error correction: A survey of the state of the art. Comput. Linguist. **49**(3), 643–701 (2023). https://doi.org/10.1162/coli_a_00478
4. Bulut, O., Tan, B., Mazzullo, E.: Applications of large language models in automatic item and feedback generation for early elementary education. In: Papadakis, S. (ed.) AI Applications in Preschool and Primary Education – Teaching with Artificial Intelligence. Springer (In press)
5. Čep, A., Bernik, A., Tomičić, I.: Adaptive learning systems in higher education: Challenges, trends, and outcomes. In: Arai, K. (ed.) Proceedings of the Future Technologies Conference (FTC) 2025, vol. 4, pp. 1–17. Springer Nature Switzerland, Cham (2026)
6. Chen, S., Lan, Y., Yuan, Z.: A multi-task automated assessment system for essay scoring. Artificial Intelligence in Education (2024)
7. Chen, Y., Li, X., Liu, J., Ying, Z.: Item response theory–a statistical framework for educational and psychological measurement. Stat. Sci. **40**(2), 167–194 (2025)
8. Corbett, A.T., Anderson, J.R.: Knowledge tracing: Modeling the acquisition of procedural knowledge. User Model. User-Adap. Inter. **4**(4), 253–278 (1994)
9. Ersozlu, Z., Taheri, S., Koch, I.: A review of machine learning methods used for educational data. Educ. Inf. Technol. **29**(16), 22125–22145 (2024)
10. Fitas, R.: Inclusive education with ai: Supporting special needs and tackling language barriers. AI Ethics **5**(6), 5729–5757 (2025)
11. Geoffre, T.: An integration model for adaptive learning in primary language education. In: Choubsaz, Y., Díez-Arcón, P., Gimeno-Sanz, A., Morgana, V., Murphy, A.C., Seracini, F.L. (eds.) Advancing CALL: New research agendas - EUROCALL 2025 Short Papers (2025)
12. Geoffre, T., Geoffre, T.: Modeling grammatical hypothesis testing in young learners: A sequence-based learning analytics study of morphosyntactic reasoning in an interactive game (2026)
13. Gorgun, G., Bulut, O.: Exploring quality criteria and evaluation methods in automated question generation: A comprehensive survey. Educ. Inf. Technol. **29**, 24111–24142 (2024)
14. Gorgun, G., Bulut, O., Tan, B.: Designing classroom assessments with generative ai: A teacher-in-the-loop framework. In: Papadakis, S. (ed.) Teaching with Artificial Intelligence: A Guide for Primary and Elementary Educators, pp. 162–180. Routledge (2025)
15. Hariyanto, K., Maharani, F., R.: Artificial intelligence in adaptive education: a systematic review of techniques for personalized learning. Discov Educ 4(458) (2025)
16. Hemmer, P., Schemmer, M., Kühl, N., Vössing, M., Satzger, G.: Complementarity in human-ai collaboration: Concept, sources, and evidence. Eur. J. Inf. Syst. **34**(6), 979–1002 (2025)
17. Julien, G.: How artificial intelligence (ai) impacts inclusive education. Educ. Res. Rev. **19**(6), 95–103 (2024)
18. Koedinger, K.R., Corbett, A.T., C.P.: The knowledge-learning-instruction framework: Bridging the science-practice chasm to enhance robust student learning. Cogn. Sci. **36**(5), 757–798 (2012)
19. Khine, M.S.: In: Artificial intelligence in education: A machine-generated literature overview, pp. 341–466. Springer (2024). Using ai for adaptive learning and adaptive assessment
20. Li, K., Peterson, M., Wang, Q.: Out-of-school language learning through digital gaming: a case study from an activity theory perspective. Comput. Assist. Lang. Learn. **37**(5–6), 1019–1047 (2024)

21. Li, K., Peterson, M., Wang, Q., Wang, H.: Mapping the research trends of digital game-based language learning (dgbll): a scientometrics review. Comput. Assist. Lang. Learn. **38**(7), 1393–1422 (2025)
22. Li, K., Zhang, Y.: Planning first, question second: An LLM-guided method for controllable question generation. In: Ku, L.W., Martins, A., Srikumar, V. (eds.) Findings of the Association for Computational Linguistics: ACL 2024, pp. 4715–4729. Association for Computational Linguistics, Bangkok, Thailand (2024)
23. Mollick, E., Mollick, L., Bach, N., Ciccarelli, L., Przystanski, B., Ravipinto, D.: Ai agents and education: Simulated practice at scale (2024)
24. Naseer, F., Khan, M.N., Addas, A., Awais, Q., Ayub, N.: Game mechanics and artificial intelligence personalization: A framework for adaptive learning systems. Education Sciences **15**(3) (2025)
25. Pistono, A.M.A.d.A., dos Santos, A.M.P., Baptista, R.J.V., Mamede, H.S.: Framework for adaptive serious games. Comput. Appl. Eng. Educ. **32**(4), e22731 (2024)
26. Plessis-Ouzariah, I., Geoffre, T.: Using a digital visual dictionary to support reading comprehension: A single-case study with french-as-a-second language learners in primary school. In: Choubsaz, Y., Díez-Arcón, P., Gimeno-Sanz, A., Morgana, V., Murphy, A.C., Seracini, F.L. (eds.) Advancing CALL: New research agendas - EUROCALL 2025 Short Papers, (2025)
27. Song, B., Zhu, Q., Luo, J.: Human-ai collaboration by design. Proceedings of the Design Society **4**, 2247–2256 (2024)
28. Taguchi, N.: Technology-enhanced language learning and pragmatics: Insights from digital game-based pragmatics instruction. Lang. Teach. **57**(1), 57–67 (2024)
29. Thompson, N.A., Weiss, D.A.: A framework for the development of computerized adaptive tests. Pract. Assess. Res. Eval. **16**(1) (2011)
30. Tomikawa, Y., Uto, M.: Difficulty-controllable multiple-choice question generation for reading comprehension using item response theory. In: Olney, A.M., Chounta, I.A., Liu, Z., Santos, O.C., Bittencourt, I.I. (eds.) Artificial Intelligence in Education. Posters and Late Breaking Results, Workshops and Tutorials, Industry and Innovation Tracks, Practitioners, Doctoral Consortium and Blue Sky. pp. 312–320. Springer Nature Switzerland, Cham (2024)
31. Vajjala, S., Alhafni, B., Bannò, S., Maurya, K.K., Kochmar, E.: Opportunities and challenges of llms in education: An nlp perspective (2026)
32. Wainer, H., Dorans, N.J., Flaugher, R., Green, B.F., Mislevy, R.J.: Computerized adaptive testing: A primer. Routledge (2000)
33. Wang, Q., Labib, A., Swier, R., Hofmeyr, M., Yuan, Z.: Genquest: An llm-based text adventure game for language learners. In: Proceedings of the 5th Wordplay: When Language Meets Games Workshop, EMNLP 2025, November 2025
34. Wang, S., Xu, T., Li, H., Zhang, C., Liang, J., Tang, J., Yu, P.S., Wen, Q.: Large language models for education: A survey and outlook (2024)
35. Wongvorachan, T., Lai, K.W., Bulut, O., Tsai, Y.S., Chen, G.: Artificial intelligence: Transforming the future of feedback in education. Journal of Applied Testing Technology **23**, 95–116 (2022). Special Issue 1
36. Yuan, Z., Felice, M., Lan, Y., Wang, Q., Cristea, A.I., Walker, E., Lu, Y.: Artificial Intelligence in Education. Posters and Late Breaking Results, Workshops and Tutorials, Industry and Innovation Tracks, Practitioners, Doctoral Consortium, Blue Sky, and WideAIED. Presented at the (2025) Nlp and generative ai for language learning and assessment: Synergies between research and practice

AI Literacy For All: 2nd International Workshop on AI Literacy Education For All

Ruiwei Xiao[1](✉), Shan Zhang[2], Xinying Hou[3], Ying-Jui Tseng[1], Qianou Ma[1], Yash Tadimalla[4], Qing Xiao[1], Jionghao Lin[5], Bo Jiang[6], John Stamper[1], and Kenneth R. Koedinger[1]

[1] Carnegie Mellon University, Pittsburgh, PA 15213, USA
ruiweix@cs.cmu.edu
[2] University of Florida, Gainesville, FL 32608, USA
[3] University of Michigan, Ann Arbor, MI 48109, USA
[4] Computing Research Association, Washington DC 20036, USA
[5] The University of Hong Kong, Pok Fu Lam, Hong Kong
[6] East China Normal University, Shanghai 200062, China

Abstract. As artificial intelligence (AI) becomes increasingly embedded across societal and professional domains, AI literacy has emerged as a global educational priority. National and international policy initiatives underscore a growing consensus through executive orders and national plans equipping all individuals with the knowledge and critical capacity to engage with AI is essential for fostering equitable, ethical, and future-ready societies. Therefore, we propose the second International Workshop on AI Literacy Education for All (ALIT4ALL), aimed to advance research and practice on AI literacy education for non-technical learners, including K–12 students, educators across disciplines, and workforce professionals. By convening researchers, practitioners, policymakers, and industry stakeholders, the workshop seeks to address persistent challenges such as limited teacher preparation, inaccessible learning resources, fragmented upskilling programs, and the absence of validated assessment frameworks. Key topics include the design and evaluation of AI literacy curricula, professional development models for educators, inclusive pedagogical strategies, and innovative assessment methodologies. By fostering interdisciplinary collaboration, this workshop aims to generate actionable insights and strategies for equipping all learners with the necessary knowledge and skills to navigate an AI-driven world and contributing to the global effort to democratize AI understanding and participation across diverse educational and professional contexts.

Keywords: AI Literacy · Teaching and Learning about AI · Curriculum Design · AI Policy · Professional Development · AI in Education (AIED)

E. G. Blanchard et al. (Eds.): AIED 2026, CCIS 3033, pp. 44–50, 2026.
https://doi.org/10.1007/978-3-032-29794-5_8

1 Motivation and Theme

As artificial intelligence increasingly shapes how people learn, work, and communicate, governments and international organizations are prioritizing AI literacy as a central educational objective. Global and national policy initiatives, including UNESCO's Guidance for GenAI in Education [7], the U.S. Executive Order on Advancing AI Education for American Youth [6], and the National Artificial Intelligence Initiative [3] reflect a shared recognition that AI literacy is now a critical 21st-century competency for preparing learners to engage responsibly and effectively in an AI-infused world. As generative AI (GenAI) tools become increasingly embedded in everyday educational and professional practices [4], the urgency of developing developmentally appropriate AI literacy has intensified.

Despite this growing momentum, substantial gaps remain in how AI and GenAI literacy should be conceptualized, implemented, and evaluated. Numerous frameworks and curricula have emerged to support instruction [9], yet questions persist regarding what should be taught, how it should be taught, and how AI literacy develops across different populations across learning and working contexts. Existing studies frequently emphasize the technical affordances of GenAI tools, but far fewer examine how teachers and students cultivate conceptual understanding, critical judgment, ethical awareness, and creative capacity through sustained classroom use [9]. Although recent efforts have advanced the co-design of AI-focused professional development [1] and curricula [5], empirical evidence regarding their long-term impact on instructional practice, student learning, and classroom dynamics remains limited. Moreover, integrating AI literacy meaningfully into non-STEM domains (e.g., humanities, arts, and social sciences) continues to present challenges, as many educators lack domain-specific strategies for embedding AI into existing curricular structures [9]. Advancing the field therefore requires coordinated, design-based, classroom- and workforce-integrated research that produces objective evidence of how teachers and learners engage with GenAI systems to support inquiry, creativity, ethical reasoning, and problem solving. Equally important is cultivating a collaborative research community that systematically shares empirical evidence, rigorously evaluates effectiveness, and advances the field beyond framework development toward demonstrable, measurable impact. In light of the above, this workshop will engage with the following themes:

K–12 Students and Teachers: Early exposure to foundational AI concepts can spark long-term interest, cultivate critical thinking, and empower the next generation to participate thoughtfully in an AI-driven society. Meanwhile, K-12 teachers also require sustained professional development and accessible resources to confidently integrate AI concepts into the classroom [2] across disciplines, while also guiding students to critically, ethically examine AI's societal impact.

Higher Education Students and Faculty: Universities and colleges play a critical role in preparing both technical and non-technical students to engage with AI systems. We invite work that examines curriculum design, interdisciplinary integration, domain-specific AI literacy, and the development of critical, ethical, and creative competencies related to GenAI across undergraduate programs, graduate programs and faculty training programs.

Workforce Training: In a rapidly evolving labor market, professionals at varying skill levels require continuous upskilling to use AI tools responsibly and effectively. This includes addressing ethical challenges such as bias, data privacy, transparency, and algorithmic accountability, as well as evaluating the effectiveness of AI literacy initiatives in workplace settings.

Policy Frameworks and Institutional Guidelines/Strategies: We welcome contributions that examine approaches for integrating AI literacy into existing educational systems, policy guidelines, standards, and evaluation frameworks at local, national, and international levels.

Through collaboration among educators, researchers, policymakers, and industry partners, this workshop seeks to foster a shared agenda for scalable, innovative, and ethically grounded AI literacy initiatives that empower learners, regardless of background, to navigate and shape an AI-enabled future.

2 Objectives

This **full-day** workshop aims to bring together researchers, educators, industry professionals, and policymakers to explore comprehensive strategies for AI Literacy education that serve non-technical learners: including students and teachers in K-12 and higher education, and the broader workforce. The objectives of the workshop are to explore the design and evaluation of AI literacy programs, examine educational technologies that support AI literacy development, advance approaches to AI literacy assessment, discuss pedagogical strategies for diverse learners, and address issues of diversity, equity, and inclusion in AI literacy.

3 Call for Submission

While submission is not required to attend, we strongly encourage scholars, educators, practitioners, and industry professionals to submit Work-in-progress Papers (6 pages); full papers: 12 pages, posters: 3 pages (including references) related to AI Literacy. Submissions may include research on K–12 curricula, teacher training programs, workforce upskilling strategies, ethical frameworks, policy considerations, or novel assessment and educational technology approaches. Please see our website for more details[1].

We particularly invite submissions that:

- Investigate frameworks and methodologies for implementing AI literacy, ensuring broad accessibility and meaningful impact across diverse contexts.
- Highlight and evaluate emerging tools and platforms that enable hands-on AI experiences and conceptual understanding for non-technical audiences.

[1] https://sites.google.com/view/ai-literacy-for-all-2026/home.

- Advance new paradigms for measuring AI literacy, including project-based tasks, reflective portfolios, and performance-based evaluations that capture both practical skills and ethical considerations.
- Explore inclusive teaching approaches that demystify core AI concepts for K–12 students, educators, and professionals seeking upskilling, regardless of subject-area expertise.

We welcome papers presenting empirical research, theoretical discussions, design prototypes, or reflections on work-in-progress, and encourage diverse methodological approaches (qualitative, quantitative, design-based, or mixed methods). Submissions must follow the workshop's paper template; accepted papers will be published in the workshop proceedings.

By gathering a wide range of perspectives, from researchers and educational technologists to policymakers, teachers, and industry stakeholders, this workshop aims to generate actionable insights that make AI literacy more inclusive, engaging, and impactful. We look forward to your contributions as we work together to shape the future of AI Literacy Education for non-technical learners in an equitable and ethically grounded manner.

4 Workshop Format and Activities

This workshop will be an interactive full-day event designed to engage participants in hands-on exploration, discussion, and collaboration around AI literacy. It will be held in a hybrid format to welcome in-person and online participants (via Zoom with a moderator). We will advertise our event through social media (e.g., Linkedin) posts relevant listservs (e.g., ai4k12@lists.aaai.org), and will also reach out to authors of previous related submissions to share our workshop Call for Papers. We expect to receive 20–30 submissions and anticipate approximately 150–200 participants for attendance. All accepted workshop papers will be published in a CEUR proceedings volume. A tentative schedule is as follows:

- **09:00 - 09:30** Introductions and logistics
- **09:30 - 10:00** Invited Guest Speaker
- **10:00 - 15:00** Paper Presentations
- **15:00 - 16:00** Round-Table Discussions
- **16:00 - 17:30** Mini-Hackathon

5 Organization

5.1 Organizing Committee

Ruiwei Xiao is a PhD student at Carnegie Mellon University (CMU) and co-founder of Active AI. Her research and startup experience are focused on AI Literacy Education. She organized the largest workshop at AIED 2025 (the previous edition of this proposed workshop). The AI literacy materials she developed have reached over 10k active users and 100k total users worldwide.

Shan Zhang is a PhD candidate in Educational Technology at the College of Education, University of Florida. Her research centers on multimodal AI literacy assessment and the design of theory-driven AI-powered learning technologies that foster AI literacy, enhance student engagement, and support meaningful interactions for sustained learning gains. Her recent work examines AI integration in K–12 education, collaborative learning and affect in STEM+C+AI contexts, and learner modeling.

Xinying Hou is a PhD candidate at the School of Information, University of Michigan. Her research focuses on two key facets of AI and education: Educational Actors with AI and AI for Education. Her AI-powered computing learning tool has been integrated into Runestone Academy, a widely used online computing platform serving over 80,000 students annually. The AI literacy activities she created have also gained significant global reach.

Ying-Jui Tseng is a Carnegie Mellon University alumnus and Co-Founder of ActiveAI, a learning platform dedicated to advancing equitable AI literacy in K–12 education. Through ActiveAI, he has led the development and large-scale implementation of AI literacy programs that have empowered over 20k learners and more than 200 educators, translating research into measurable classroom impact.

Qianou Ma is a PhD student at the Human-Computer Interaction Institute, Carnegie Mellon University. Her research focuses on training AI literacy, especially for non-experts in programming. She designs, builds, and evaluates LLM applications to help humans adapt and thrive in AI-infused development environments and optimize human-AI collaboration.

Yash Tadimalla is a Computing Research Association (CRA) AI Education Fellows supporting research and outreach across multiple NSF-funded initiatives and serves as the lead Fellow for the NAIRR Pilot Expansion AI EDU RCN. As a passionate advocate for global STEM equity, Yash holds leadership roles with the United Nations Major Group for Children and Youth and the International Federation of Engineering Education Societies.

Qing Xiao is a PhD student at Carnegie Mellon University. His research focuses on AI literacy in workplace settings, with a particular emphasis on helping professionals collaborate with increasingly capable AI systems and on designing AI to function as a more responsible collaborator at work. Before beginning his doctoral studies, he worked as an award-winning journalist and researcher in newsrooms such as the Financial Times and China Media Group.

Jionghao Lin is currently an Assistant Professor in Learning Technologies at the Faculty of Education, University of Hong Kong. His research interests include learning analytics, artificial intelligence in education, educational data mining, educational feedback, dialogue-based intelligent tutoring systems, and natural language processing.

Bo Jiang is currently a professor at the Shanghai Institute of Artificial Intelligence for Education, East China Normal University, Shanghai, China. His research interests focus on educational large models, learner modeling, and K-12 AI education. He led the development of the first Chinese K–12 AI Curriculum

Guideline and authored a seven-volume AI textbook series adopted by over 100 schools nationwide. He serves on the Executive Committee of APSCE and the editorial boards of journals including IEEE TLT, RPTEL, and IJBIC, and has chaired major conferences such as ICCE and GCCCE. He received the APSCE Early Career Research Award in 2021.

John Stamper is an Associate Professor at the Human-Computer Interaction Institute at Carnegie Mellon University and the Technical Director of the Pittsburgh Science of Learning Center DataShop. His work involves leveraging educational data mining techniques and the creation of data tools.

Ken Koedinger is the Hillman University Professor of Computer Science with appointments in Human Computer Interaction and Psychology. His research has contributed to an understanding of student thinking and learning that has implications for educational technology and teaching. He has created cognitive models that have been used to create educational materials and technologies, including intelligent tutoring systems that adapt to student needs. His work combines cognitive science, artificial intelligence, and educational practice.

5.2 Previous Editions of the Workshop

The 1st *AI Literacy for All (ALIT4ALL)* Workshop [8] was held in the hybrid format in conjunction with AIED 2025 in Palermo, Italy. The workshop brought together an international community of researchers, educators, policymakers, and practitioners committed to advancing AI literacy across diverse contexts and populations. Overall, the ALIT4ALL Workshop attracted over 100 attendees, making it one of the largest workshops at AIED 2025. More details of the previous edition of the proposed workshop are available on https://ai-literacy-for-all-aied2025-activeai.vercel.app/.

References

1. Hutchins, N.M., Zhang, S., Barrett, J.R., Isreal, M.: Empowering educators in ai: Insights from co-designing an ai microcredential with and for k-12 educators. In: Proceedings of the AAAI Conference on Artificial Intelligence, vol. 39, pp. 29137–29144. (2025)
2. Lee, I., Zhang, H., Moore, K., Zhou, X., Perret, B., Cheng, Y., Zheng, R., Pu, G.: Ai book club: An innovative professional development model for ai education. In: Proceedings of the 53rd ACM Technical Symposium on Computer Science Education-Volume 1, pp. 202–208 (2022)
3. National Artificial Intelligence Initiative Office: Presidential ai challenge. https://www.ai.gov/initiatives/presidential-challenge (2025). Accessed 6 Jan 2026
4. Prather, J., et al.: Beyond the hype: A comprehensive review of current trends in generative ai research, teaching practices, and tools. 2024 Working Group Reports on Innovation and Technology in Computer Science Education, pp. 300–338 (2025)
5. Tatar, C., Jiang, S., Rosé, C.P., Chao, J.: Exploring teachers' views and confidence in the integration of an artificial intelligence curriculum into their classrooms: A case study of curricular co-design program. Int. J. Artif. Intell. Educ. **35**(2), 702–735 (2025)

6. The White House: Advancing artificial intelligence education for american youth. https://www.whitehouse.gov/presidential-actions/2025/04/advancing-artificial-intelligence-education-for-american-youth/ (April 2025), executive Order
7. UNESCO: Guidance for generative ai in education and research. https://www.unesco.org/en/articles/guidance-generative-ai-education-and-research (2023), ethical Guidance Report
8. Xiao, R., Tseng, Y.J., Li, H., Liao, G., Stamper, J., Koedinger, K.R.: Ai literacy for all: 1st international workshop on ai literacy education for all. In: International Conference on Artificial Intelligence in Education, pp. 255–260. Springer (2025)
9. Zhang, S., Ganapathy Prasad, P., Schroeder, N.L.: Learning about ai: a systematic review of reviews on ai literacy. J. Educ. Comput. Res. **63**(5), 1292–1322 (2025)

AI-Enabled Learning at Scale: Integrating Theory, Implementation, and Impact
Full-Day Tutorial

Linlin Li(✉), Mingyu Feng, and I. Yelee Jo

WestEd, San Francisco, CA 94107, USA
{lli,mfeng,yjo}@wested.org

1 Tutorial Theme and Goals

As AI-enabled learning systems scale across districts, states, and online platforms, researchers are increasingly asked to evaluate their effectiveness under authentic, high-variability conditions. Unlike static curricular interventions, AI-enabled systems introduce algorithmic personalization, dynamic model updates, evolving feature sets, and heterogeneous user pathways. In these environments, the definition of "treatment," exposure, and fidelity is often non-uniform across learners and sites. As a result, impact findings are only as credible as the implementation evidence and analytic alignment that support them.

Large-scale deployments of adaptive and data-intensive learning platforms generate substantial behavioral and system-level data, yet interpreting impact requires more than sophisticated modeling. Product iteration during deployment, variation in local usage models, differences in institutional supports, and staggered rollouts can all complicate causal inference and the interpretation of heterogeneous effects. Producing credible, scalable evidence in such contexts requires coherence across the intervention's theory of action, implementation processes, platform instrumentation, and analytic strategy.

This full-day tutorial addresses that coherence challenge directly. Grounded in real constraints encountered in large-scale efficacy and effectiveness studies of AI-enabled interventions, we focus on how to design a study in alignment with the theory-of-change within real-world constraints, and implement interventions as designed while rigorously examining their impact. Rather than treating theory, implementation, and impact estimation as separate phases, we demonstrate how alignment across these components strengthens internal validity, supports interpretable modeling of variation, and advances cumulative knowledge building in AI-mediated learning at scale.

2 Theoretical Background and Relevance to the Community

2.1 Logic Model as a Testable Theory of Action in AI-Enabled Learning

Designing an AI-enabled intervention does not ensure that it will be implemented as intended—or that its impact can be interpreted rigorously at scale. While guidance exists for designing technology-supported interventions, fewer resources address how to systematically connect learning theory, implementation processes, and impact estimation in large-scale deployments of adaptive systems.

E. G. Blanchard et al. (Eds.): AIED 2026, CCIS 3033, pp. 51–54, 2026.
https://doi.org/10.1007/978-3-032-29794-5_9

In this tutorial, we position the logic model as a testable theory of action that structures both implementation and analysis. Drawing on Vygotsky's Sociocultural Theory [6], learning is understood as mediated development occurring through scaffolded participation and eventual internalization. In AI-enabled environments, mediation is enacted not only through human interaction but also through algorithmic mechanisms—such as adaptive sequencing, automated feedback, and recommendation systems—that shape learner pathways. Evaluating impact in these systems therefore requires clarity about how theoretical mechanisms are operationalized in platform features, instructional routines, and measurable indicators.

The logic model [3] makes these linkages explicit. It specifies:

- **Inputs**: AI-enabled tools, instructional supports, data systems, and partnership structures necessary for implementation.
- **Activities**: Enacted interactions with AI-mediated scaffolds, including adaptive practice, feedback cycles, and instructional responses to system-generated data and reports.
- **Outputs**: Observable indicators of engagement and participation, such as usage patterns, interaction traces, and emerging instructional practices.
- **Short- and Medium-Term Outcomes**: Developmental changes as learners and educators internalize practices initially supported through mediated interaction with technology.
- **Impact**: Sustained system-level changes in learning outcomes, instructional routines, or institutional capacity.

By mapping theoretical mechanisms (e.g., mediation, scaffolding, internalization) to measurable constructs, the logic model provides a framework for defining exposure, fidelity, and outcome variables in analytically coherent ways. In AI-enabled systems—where personalization, dosage, and even system versions may vary across users—implementation divergence is not merely noise but a source of analytic leverage. The logic model thus functions as both an implementation guide and a structure for modeling variation in impact. For researchers and developers working within the AI and education communities, this approach supports tighter alignment between theory, platform instrumentation, implementation measurement, and statistical modeling, enabling more interpretable and scalable impact evaluation.

2.2 Integrating Iterative Development and Experimental Evaluation

Sociocultural theory provides conceptual grounding, but large-scale implementation requires methodological structures that translate theory into operational research designs. Design-Based Research (DBR) and Design-Based Implementation Research (DBIR) emphasize iterative refinement in authentic contexts, partnership structures, and responsiveness to emerging findings [1, 2, 4]. These approaches are particularly common in the early development of AI-enabled systems, where features, user feedback and supporting strategies, and usage flows evolve through cycles of testing and revision.

When interventions move into large-scale effectiveness testing, researchers often adopt randomized controlled trials (RCTs) or quasi-experimental designs to establish causal evidence. This shift introduces a tension: iterative refinement and contextual responsiveness can appear misaligned with the standardization and treatment stability required for causal inference in such studies. Rather than treating these paradigms as incompatible, this tutorial demonstrates how coherence can be maintained across phases. For example, a theory-informed logic model anchors both iterative refinement and experimental testing by specifying stable mechanisms of action, even when some system features evolve. Implementation data, such as dosage—often captured systematically by the platform in the backend—can be incorporated into analytic models rather than treated solely as compliance indicators. For AI-enabled interventions, this integration is essential. Algorithmic updates and platform-level changes may occur during multi-site studies. Maintaining alignment between system evolution, implementation measurement, and analytic strategy allows researchers to generate credible and interpretable evidence.

2.3 Aspects of Implementation in Large-Scale Efficacy Studies

Implementing and evaluating AI-enabled interventions at scale requires coordinated systems for recruitment, onboarding, communication, and data management across multiple sites. Even when an intervention is well specified, variation in scheduling, staffing, technology infrastructure, and local priorities can introduce meaningful differences in exposure and fidelity. Without deliberate structures to manage and document these factors, analytic interpretation becomes difficult.

In large-scale deployments of adaptive systems, implementation is not simply a matter of providing users access to the systems. Differences in device access, classroom routines, local instructional priorities, and technical configurations can alter how learners interact with the system. In addition, feature updates or configuration changes may result in non-uniform exposure across users or sites. These realities require explicit coordination and documentation to ensure that "treatment" is consistently defined and measurable.

Collaboration with participating schools and districts is therefore central to rigorous evaluation [5]. Clear agreements around recruitment, onboarding, scheduling, and data-sharing protocols help stabilize implementation conditions. Ongoing communication allows researchers to identify operational shifts—such as staffing changes, policy adjustments, or platform updates—that may affect usage patterns or fidelity during the study period.

Implementation research distinguishes among adherence, dosage, quality of delivery, participant responsiveness, and contextual influences. These dimensions provide a practical framework for measuring fidelity in large-scale studies. For AI-enabled systems, they must be operationalized using multiple data sources, including platform telemetry, administrative records, and observational or survey data. Coordinated data systems are essential to ensure that these sources can be linked and interpreted coherently.

Drawing on multi-year efficacy studies of technology-enabled learning systems, this tutorial illustrates how site coordination, operational alignment, and systematic documentation shape the validity and interpretability of impact findings. Participants will analyze case materials that demonstrate how implementation decisions influence exposure definitions, analytic modeling, and the interpretation of heterogeneous effects.

References

1. Cobb, P., Confrey, J., DiSessa, A., Lehrer, R., Schauble, L.: Design experiments in educational research. Educ. Res. **32**(1), 9–13 (2003)
2. Fishman, B.J., Penuel, W.R., Allen, A.R., Cheng, B.H., Sabelli, N.O.R.A.: Design-based implementation research: an emerging model for transforming the relationship of research and practice. Teach. Coll. Rec. **115**(14), 136–156 (2013)
3. Kao, Y.S., Matlen, B.J., Tiu, M., Li, L.: Logic models as a framework for iterative user research in educational technology: illustrative cases. In: End-User Considerations in Educational Technology Design, pp. 52–75. IGI Global Scientific Publishing (2018)
4. Penuel, W.R., Fishman, B.J., Haugan Cheng, B., Sabelli, N.: Organizing research and development at the intersection of learning, implementation, and design. Educ. Res. **40**(7), 331–337 (2011)
5. Sperling, J., Gray, M., Lee, V., Schmid, L., Malinowski, N.: Where community-engaged research and randomized controlled trials align: lessons from implementation of an experimental evaluation in partnership with a community-based afterschool program. Am. J. Eval. **46**(3), 446–469 (2025)
6. Vygotsky, L.S.: Mind in Society: Development of Higher Psychological Processes. Harvard University Press (1978)
7. What Works Clearinghouse: What Works Clearinghouse procedures and standards handbook, version 5.0. U.S. Department of Education, Institute of Education Sciences, National Center for Education Evaluation and Regional Assistance (NCEE) (2022)

The First International Workshop on Pedagogical Evaluation of Automated Feedback (PEAF 2026)

Marcus Messer[1(✉)], Peter B. Johnson[1], Alexandra Neagu[1], Camille Kandiko Howson[1], Jaromir Savelka[2], and Simon Woodhead[3]

[1] Imperial College London, London, UK
{m.messer,peter.johnson,alexandra.neagu20,c.howson}@imperial.ac.uk
[2] Carnegie Mellon University, Pittsburgh, USA
jsavelka@andrew.cmu.edu
[3] Eedi, London, UK
simon.woodhead@eedi.com

Abstract. Providing effective feedback to students can greatly increase learning, and what makes feedback effective depends on the norms and objectives of the student, teacher, institution, and discipline. To facilitate feedback at scale and increase opportunities for teacher-student interactions, automated feedback is becoming increasingly commonplace, especially since the broad adoption of generative artificial intelligence tools in education. While automated feedback can be beneficial for learning by providing timely feedback at scale, evaluating its pedagogical quality is often limited to accuracy and small-scale student surveys. This full-day workshop aims to explore in more depth how to evaluate the pedagogical quality of automated feedback. Attendees will share practical applications of education theory across different learning contexts, engage with lightning talks on work-in-progress and position papers, and establish future research directions, study designs, and collaborations from interdisciplinary and international backgrounds.

Keywords: Automated Feedback · Automated Assessment · Pedagogy · Feedback Quality

1 Background and Motivation

Feedback is fundamental to education [9,10]. Formative feedback, which informs students about a goal, their progress towards the goal, and how they should progress [4,17], and summative feedback, which evaluates learning against a set of standards, is provided after the task is complete and often consists of the achievement report, or grade [6,7]. Summative and formative feedback are both effective for learning, and they are commonly used in conjunction to support students' learning.

E. G. Blanchard et al. (Eds.): AIED 2026, CCIS 3033, pp. 55–60, 2026.
https://doi.org/10.1007/978-3-032-29794-5_10

What makes feedback effective depends on both general principles [18] and the learning context, such as the norms and objectives of the student, teacher, institution, and disciplinary community [5,11]. Shute [18] conducted a review of education literature and derived guidelines for providing formative feedback, including elements that can enhance and diminish learning, when to deliver feedback and how different learner characteristics affect the feedback that educators should provide.

Feedback can take many forms, from text to visual to verbal feedback, and while typically conducted by human educators, automated feedback is becoming increasingly commonplace. Broadly, the feedback process can be defined as either transactional or dialogic. A transaction is a single exchange of student work that receives a reply [15]; multiple transactions may take place, such as resubmissions, but they are typically independent. Dialogic refers to a multi-turn conversation [13]; this can be oral between two people, or a more abstract interchange over prolonged periods, or it can be an interaction between a human student and a computer agent (chatbot). We refer to 'feedback' hereafter to cover both the transactional and dialogic modes.

Automated feedback has been used in education for decades [1,12,19], and consists of a broad set of approaches, from students submitting work for instant feedback [1,14,16], to intelligent tutor systems that incorporate student modelling to guide student-tutor interactions contained by student and instructional agenda [8]. Generative AI has accelerated and expanded the delivery of automated feedback to students; recent research has investigated how large language models can be used for assessment, dialogic feedback, and for providing feedback on multimedia tasks, such as videos and images [2].

Automated feedback can benefit student learning by providing timely feedback and freeing educators to provide direct in-person support [16]. However, the evaluation of the pedagogical quality of automated feedback remains an open question, with a predominant focus on the accuracy of the feedback, especially when using generative AI tools, and student surveys [3,14]. These methods of evaluation only scratch the surface of how to evaluate pedagogically effective feedback.

The primary purpose of this workshop is to establish community approaches that encourage and facilitate research to address the current gap in evaluating pedagogical quality across different contexts and learning domains. The organisers envision that this workshop, the resulting collaborative and interdisciplinary discussions, and subsequent research will enable context-aware automatic evaluation of the pedagogical quality of automated feedback in a multitude of domains.

2 Workshop Organisation

The inaugural Pedagogical Evaluation of Automated Feedback (PEAF) workshop will run as a full-day workshop, with an aim of 20 to 40 attendees. Section 2.1 presents the core themes and goals of the PEAF workshop. Section 2.2

provides an overview of the proposed schedule, followed by details of each activity. Section 2.3 introduces how to submit, the publication of the proceedings, and the advertisement of the workshop.

2.1 Themes, Goals and Outcomes

The primary target audience for PEAF is members of the AIED, EDM and Learning@Scale communities. All communities conduct research into automated feedback, whether that be using AI to provide automated feedback, using data to explore the effects of automated feedback on learning, or exploring how automated feedback can facilitate learning at scale. In our inaugural year, the workshop will cover a set of themes across the wider education domain, and welcome submissions and discussions on the following, and other related topics:

- Establish shared practical applications of *education theory* to evaluate the pedagogical quality of feedback, beyond accuracy.
- Methods for *evaluating* the pedagogical quality of feedback, including computable metrics and qualitative methods.
- How *personalising* feedback to the learner, and to their preferences on how to interact with automated feedback, can affect the pedagogical quality of the feedback.
- How *culture and disciplines* factor into the pedagogical quality of automated feedback, especially accounting for biases in generative AI tools.
- *Ethical and societal considerations* of automating feedback in education, including, but not limited to, fairness, bias and equity across learner populations, socialisation, sense of belonging, curiosity and critical thinking.
- How automated feedback *impacts* teaching and learning. Examples include, but are not limited to, classroom activities, learning objectives, attitudes to learning, and societal and cultural changes.

These themes, supported by our participants and attendees, will help achieve our goals and expected outcomes, which are to:

- Share and discuss how education theory can be applied to the evaluation of the pedagogical quality of automated feedback.
- Generate discussion on how to research and evaluate the pedagogical quality of automated feedback for learning, to produce a set of research priorities.
- Explore and identify key challenges and limitations on the pedagogical quality of automated feedback.
- Facilitate initial collaboration opportunities for our attendees to then conduct cross-institutional and interdisciplinary research on the pedagogical quality of automated feedback.
- Publish proceedings of extended abstracts on work-in-progress and position papers on the topic of evaluating the pedagogical quality of automated feedback.

Specifically, attendees can expect to leave with an interdisciplinary understanding of how to approach the evaluation of the pedagogical quality of feedback and new connections with potential collaborators. Post-workshop, the organisers will create a mailing list to enable easy communication between potential collaborators and to inform attendees of future iterations of this workshop.

In the future, this workshop plans to continue exploring these themes by facilitating discussion and collaboration and by running a dataset challenge in which participants evaluate the pedagogical quality of automated feedback across the same set of tasks.

2.2 Schedule

A preliminary schedule can be found in Table 1, split into the morning and the afternoon. The morning focuses on defining standard terms, presentations and discussions on evaluating automated feedback from a pedagogical perspective. The afternoon is an opportunity to develop avenues of research and collaborations with like-minded researchers.

Table 1. Summary of Workshop Schedule

Session	Description
Morning	
Welcome and Introduction	Introduction to the workshop, including defining shared terms, an overview of current work, and emerging challenges of evaluating the pedagogical quality of automated feedback.
Interactive Session	A short interactive activity, where workshop attendees in small groups evaluate and discuss real-world examples of automated feedback from various disciplines.
Lightning Talks	Short presentations from participants on their submitted work.
Discussion of Presentations	Attendees will have a further opportunity to discuss the submitted work with the presenters.
Morning Summary	Summarise key elements of the lightning talks, discussion and interactive sessions.
Afternoon	
Afternoon Opening	Introduction to the afternoon's objectives and structure.
Structured Research Design	Attendees are provided a set of topics, provided by the organisers and the attendees, on potential avenues of research. Attendees are then split into groups based on their topic of interest to discuss potential avenues of research.
Research Design Report and Collaboration Discussion	Groups feedback on the potential avenues of research for each topic, and then have the chance to discuss future collaboration opportunities.
Closing	Organisers close the workshop by summarising the discussions throughout the day.

2.3 Submissions and Proceedings

Prior to the workshop, members of the AIED, EDM, Learning@Scale and associated communities will have the opportunity to submit up to four-page extended abstracts through EasyChair, following the CEUR-WS[1] format. We particularly welcome submissions from early-stage work and encourage shorter submissions within the four-page limit. These extended abstracts will address the workshop themes described in Sect. 2.1, and can include work-in-progress or position papers. After the workshop, all accepted submissions will be published in CEUR-WS proceedings, a free open-source publishing service.

References

1. Ala-Mutka, K.M.: A survey of automated assessment approaches for programming assignments. Comput. Sci. Educ. **15**(2), 83–102 (2005). https://doi.org/10.1080/08993400500150747
2. Bahroun, Z., Anane, C., Ahmed, V., Zacca, A.: Transforming education: A comprehensive review of generative artificial intelligence in educational settings through bibliometric and content analysis. Sustainability 15(17) (2023)
3. Belkina, M., Daniel, S., Nikolic, S., Haque, R., Lyden, S., Neal, P., Grundy, S., Hassan, G.M.: Implementing generative ai (genai) in higher education: A systematic review of case studies. Comput. Educ. Artif. Intell. **8**, 100407 (2025)
4. Black, P., Wiliam, D.: Assessment and classroom learning. Assessment in Education: principles, policy & practice **5**(1), 7–74 (1998)
5. Dawson, P., Henderson, M., Mahoney, P., Phillips, M., Ryan, T., Boud, D., Molloy, E.: What makes for effective feedback: staff and student perspectives. Assessment Eval. High. Educ. **44**(1), 25–36 (2019)
6. Dixson, D.D., Worrell, F.C.: Formative and summative assessment in the classroom. Theory Into Practice **55**(2), 153–159 (2016). https://doi.org/10.1080/00405841.2016.1148989
7. Glazer, N.: Formative plus Summative Assessment in Large Undergraduate Courses: Why Both? Int. J. Teach. Learn. High. Educ. **26**(2), 276–286 (2014)
8. Graesser, A.C., Conley, M.W., Olney, A.: Intelligent tutoring systems, (2012)
9. Hattie, J.: Visible Learning: A Synthesis of Over 800 Meta-analyses Relating to Achievement. Routledge (2009)
10. Hattie, J., Timperley, H.: The power of feedback. Rev. Educ. Res. **77**(1), 81–112 (2007)
11. Henderson, M., Ryan, T., Phillips, M.: The challenges of feedback in higher education. Assessment Evaluat. High. Educ. **44**(8), 1237–1252 (2019)
12. Hollingsworth, J.: Automatic graders for programming classes. Commun. ACM **3**(10), 528–529 (1960)
13. Maheshi, B., Dai, W., Martinez-Maldonado, R., Tsai, Y.S.: Dialogic feedback at scale: Recommendations for learning analytics design. J. Comput. Assist. Learn. **40**(6), 2790–2808 (2024)
14. Messer, M., Brown, N.C.C., Kölling, M., Shi, M.: Automated grading and feedback tools for programming education: A systematic review. ACM Trans. Comput. Educ. **24**(1) (Feb 2024). https://doi.org/10.1145/3636515

[1] CEUR-WS: https://ceur-ws.org/.

15. Nicol, D.J., Macfarlane-Dick, D.: Formative assessment and self-regulated learning: a model and seven principles of good feedback practice. Stud. High. Educ. **31**(2), 199–218 (2006)
16. Paiva, J.C., Leal, J.P., Figueira, A.: Automated assessment in computer science education: A state-of-the-art review. ACM Trans. Comput. Educ. **22**(3) (Jun 2022). https://doi.org/10.1145/3513140
17. Sadler, D.R.: Formative assessment and the design of instructional systems. Instr. Sci. **18**(2), 119–144 (1989)
18. Shute, V.J.: Focus on formative feedback. Rev. Educ. Res. **78**(1), 153–189 (2008). https://doi.org/10.3102/0034654307313795
19. Yang, Y., Buckendahl, C.W., Juszkiewicz, P.J., Bhola, D.S.: A review of strategies for validating computer-automated scoring. Appl. Measur. Educ. **15**(4), 391–412 (2002)

Open Learner Models in the Age of Generative AI

Irene-Angelica Chounta[1(✉)], Kaimao Sheng[1], Mohamed Abdelmagied[1], Tomohiro Nagashima[2], and Diego Zapata-Rivera[3]

[1] University of Duisburg-Essen, Duisburg, Germany
{irene-angelica.chounta,kaimao.sheng}@uni-due.de, mohamed.abdelmagied@stud.uni-due.de

[2] Saarland University, Saarbrücken, Germany
nagashima@cs.uni-saarland.de

[3] Educational Testing Service, Princeton, USA
DZapata@ets.org

Abstract. Research in Open Learner Models (OLMs) has long explored how enabling learners to review and interact with a learner model can support learner metacognition and agency by making learner representations transparent and inspectable. Nowadays, Generative AI, and in particular, Large Language Models (LLMs) create both an opportunity and a challenge for OLMs: while LLMs can generate rich, naturalistic explanations of learner states and lower the cost of OLM development, they lack the structured, inspectable representations that give OLMs their epistemic integrity. This half-day interactive workshop aims to bring together researchers and practitioners to critically examine this tension and explore how OLMs can leverage the communicative power of LLMs without sacrificing transparency, validity, and learner agency. Through opening provocations, a state-of-the-art presentation, and a hands-on design challenge, participants will surface open research questions, identify non-negotiable principles for LLM-enhanced OLMs, and collectively develop a research agenda. The workshop targets the AIED, learning analytics, and user modeling communities, and will produce a shared position paper and design guidelines as concrete outputs.

Keywords: Open Learner Models · Explainable AI · Generative AI · Large Language Models

1 Type of Event and Duration

This event takes place as an interactive, half-day, in-person workshop[1] at the Festival of Learning 2026, and aims to trigger "*difficult*" discussions through various activities.

[1] https://colaps-research.github.io/OLM-GENAI/.

E. G. Blanchard et al. (Eds.): AIED 2026, CCIS 3033, pp. 61–65, 2026.
https://doi.org/10.1007/978-3-032-29794-5_11

2 Theme and Goals

The workshop explores the intersection of Open Learner Models (OLMs) and Generative AI (GenAI), with a particular focus on Large Language Models (LLMs).

The emergence and wide spreading of Generative AI (GenAI), and in particular Large Language Models (LLMs), creates both a challenge and opportunity for Open Learner Models (OLMs). LLMs can generate rich, naturalistic explanations of learner states but without the structured, inspectable representations that make OLMs meaningful [9]. The workshop aims to bring together researchers and practitioners to critically examine this tension and explore how OLMs can leverage the communicative power of LLMs without sacrificing transparency, validity, and learner agency. The workshop targets the artificial intelligence in education(AIED), learning analytics, and user modeling communities, including system developers and educational researchers. Concretely, the workshop raises and aims to address the following questions:

- What are the requirements for an LLM-generated explanation of a learner's state to "*count*" as an genuinely open model?
- How do we evaluate whether LLM-mediated OLMs are accurate, fair, and trusted by learners?
- What safeguards are needed when natural language explanations can be fluent but wrong?
- How might collaborative and group-level learner modeling change when LLMs mediate the representation?

To that end, the workshop proceeds through five activities: opening provocations by invited speakers presenting deliberately contrasting positions; a state-of-the-art presentation on learner modeling and OLM–LLM approaches; a hands-on design challenge in which mixed small groups design LLM-enhanced OLM explanations for a realistic learner scenario while explicitly addressing core OLM principles (accuracy, inspectability, learner agency, contestability); a synthesis session mapping findings onto a collectively-owned research agenda; and a closing session in which groups nominate non-negotiable principles for LLM-enhanced OLMs and identify concrete follow-on actions. Expected outputs include a shared position paper or research agenda document and a curated set of design principles or guidelines for LLM-enhanced OLMs, to be submitted to a relevant venue such as IJAIED or JEDM, or carried forward to a follow-up workshop.

3 Related Work

Despite AIED's long history, the recent proliferation of Generative AI (GenAI) has intensely amplified the interest in AI's role in education. In public discourse, the term AI is now used almost interchangeably with GenAI—and with good reason: anyone with an internet connection can access capable generative models for personal use, without any specialist knowledge or institutional affiliation. Large

Language Models and generative content tools, especially ones without educational orientation, have captured the attention of educators and policy-makers alike, intensifying discussions about what AI can and should do in educational settings [6]. Therefore, one – naively – could propose the following: "*Instead of a traditional open learner model, we could use an LLM that has received as input the learner's interaction history, dialogue, artifacts, and behavior*". Then, the LLM practically becomes the OLM. The learner can proceed to interact with it using natural language and ask: "*what is the topic I struggle the most with?*", "*what exercise should I solve next?*", or "*how can I improve my contribution to the groupwork?*". The LLM will consequently reason over the accumulated context.

The AIED community has for a long time embraced OLMs as a method to improve the diagnostic ability of learner models, to engage learners in reflective activities, to offer formative assessment opportunities and to prompt learners' metacognition processes such as self-regulation [2–4,9]. The effectiveness of OLMs is well-established across different domains, such as mathematics [7], language learning [5], and programming [1]. Over the years, there have been different types of OLMs according to how they interact with learners and are classified accordingly, they can be only inspectable where a learner can only view their model, editable where a learner can impose their assessment on the model, persuadable where a learner has to answer some challenges from the system to change their proficiency and negotiable where the learner and the learner and the system maintain the same level of control ([2]). Despite being effective, OLM systems generally require high effort and cost to develop and maintain them especially if they provide learners with more interactivity options which makes their adoption in general difficult [8].

The emergence of LLMs offer new opportunities for OLMs, as their ability to understand and reason with natural language can help simplify OLMs both in terms of development and use. For example, in a negotiable OLM, an LLM can be used to provide explanations to a learner about their state, reason about the evidence provided to a learner, design challenges or questions for a learner, or it can accept or reject a learner's advances to change their state. While these features were previously there in different OLMs, LLMs can help simplify the development process of such features, support scaling up and at the same time provide learners and teachers with a more natural and expressive interface for these interactions with the system.

Despite the opportunities, LLMs present OLMs with a new set of challenges as they might require rethinking the existing frameworks for developing OLMs. This workshop will document such opportunities and challenges towards rethinking existing practices for the design and implementation of OLMs and establish reference guidelines and requirements for enabling the effective and appropriate integration of GenAI as support for OLMs.

This is the first edition of the workshop. The organizers envision it as the inaugural event in a recurring series at future AIED and relevant venues.

4 Workshop Organizers

The organizing team is multidisciplinary and includes experts from the fields of learning analytics and AIED, learning sciences, and computer science with experience in the organization of workshops and other events:

Prof. Dr. Irene-Angelica Chounta holds a Professorship on Computational Methods in Modeling and Analysis of Learning Processes in the Department of Human-Centered Computing and Cognitive Science, University of Duisburg-Essen and she is the head of the research group colaps (https://www.uni-due.de/colaps/). Her research focuses on computational learning analytics (LA) for technology-enhanced learning (TEL), artificial intelligence in education (AIED) and educational technologies. Her main research interest is to model learners' behavior to provide evidence-based, adaptive and personalized feedback, in a variety of contexts: from intelligent tutoring systems and computer-supported collaborative learning environments to hackathons and makerspaces. Irene serves as an expert consultant in topics about the use of Artificial Intelligence in Education for the Council of Europe and as a member of the Executive Board of the IAIED Society. In the past, she served as the Communications Co-Chair for the International Society of the Learning Sciences (ISLS).

Prof. Dr. Tomohiro Nagashima is a Tenure-Track Junior (Assistant) Professor of Technology-Enhanced Learning in the Department of Computer Science at Saarland University, Germany, and Faculty Associate at Harvard University's Berkman Klein Center for Internet and Society in the US. He conducts interdisciplinary research at the intersection of the Learning Sciences and Human-Computer Interaction to better understand and support school students' cognitive and self-regulated learning processes in STEM domains using AI-based learning technologies and learning analytics. He holds a Ph.D. in Human-Computer Interaction from Carnegie Mellon University and M.A. in Education from Stanford University.

Dr. Diego Zapata-Rivera is Distinguished Presidential Appointee at ETS in Princeton, NJ. He earned a Ph.D. in computer science (with a focus on artificial intelligence in education) from the University of Saskatchewan in 2003. His research at ETS has focused on the areas of innovations in reporting assessment results and technology-enhanced assessment including work on personalized learning and assessment environments, conversation-based assessment, caring assessment, Bayesian student modeling, open learner modeling, and game-based assessment. Dr. Zapata-Rivera is a Co-PI and research co-director of the NSF AI INVITE Institute (invite.illinois.edu). He was elected as a member of the International AI in Education Society Executive Committee (2022–2027). He is a member of the Editorial Board of User Modeling and User-Adapted Interaction, an Associate Editor for the International Journal of Artificial Intelligence in Education, AI for Human Learning and Behavior Change, and a former Associate Editor of the IEEE Transactions on Learning Technologies. Dr. Zapata-Rivera has been invited to contribute his expertise to projects sponsored by the National Research Council, the National Science Foundation, NASA, and the US Army Research Laboratory.

Kaimao Sheng is a PhD candidate in Human-Centered Computing and Cognitive Science at the University of Duisburg-Essen. His research focuses on computational representations of learning processes, with particular interest in designing AI-based models that formalize and operationalize theoretical paradigms of how learning occurs. He explores how artificial intelligence can bridge cognitive theory and computational implementation to better understand learning dynamics. He holds a master's degree in Robotics from RWTH Aachen University (Germany).
Mohamed Abdelmagied is an M.Sc candidate in Computer Engineering at the University of Duisburg-Essen, Germany. His research focuses on how generative AI can support learners in intelligent learning environments through transparent and interactive approaches with a particular focus on negotiable OLMs. He explores how Large language Models (LLMs) can be embedded into existing (Open) Learner Modeling frameworks to promote learner-agency and metacognition processes such as self-reflection and exploration in learners. He also currently works as a Teaching Assistant at the University of Duisburg-Essen and a Research Intern in Agentic AI at Bayer AG. He holds B.Sc degree in Computer Engineering with distinction from the University of Duisburg-Essen.

References

1. Barria-Pineda, J., Guerra-Hollstein, J., Brusilovsky, P.: A fine-grained open learner model for an introductory programming course. In: Proceedings of the 26th Conference on User Modeling, Adaptation and Personalization, pp. 53–61. UMAP '18, ACM (Jul 2018). https://doi.org/10.1145/3209219.3209242
2. Bull, S.: There are open learner models about! IEEE Trans. Learn. Technol. **13**(2), 425–448 (2020). https://doi.org/10.1109/tlt.2020.2978473
3. Bull, S., Kay, J.: Open Learner Models as Drivers for Metacognitive Processes, pp. 349–365. Springer New York (2013). https://doi.org/10.1007/978-1-4419-5546-3_23
4. Dimitrova, V.: Style-olm: Interactive open learner modelling. Int. J. Artif. Intell. Educ. **13**(1), 35–78 (2003). https://doi.org/10.3233/irg-2003-13(1)06
5. Ginon, B., Boscolo, C., Johnson, M.D., Bull, S.: Persuading an Open Learner Model in the Context of a University Course: An Exploratory Study, pp. 307–313. Springer International Publishing (2016). https://doi.org/10.1007/978-3-319-39583-8_34
6. Mavrikis, M., Topali, P., Gkreka, C., Chounta, I.A.: Polarisation and potential: Reframing the generative ai in education discourse. Conferences of the Hellenic Scientific Association of Information and Communication Technologies in Education, pp. 1193–1197 (Jan 2026). https://doi.org/10.12681/cetpe.9393
7. Sosnovsky, S., Müter, L., Valkenier, M., Brinkhuis, M., Hofman, A.: Detection of Student Modelling Anomalies, pp. 531–536. Springer International Publishing (2018). https://doi.org/10.1007/978-3-319-98572-5_41
8. Yuan, A., Fang, A., Liu, D., Kay, J.: OLiMent: Conversations About Open Learner Modelling to Help Learners Understand and Self-assess Learning Goals, pp. 132–145. Springer Nature Switzerland (2025). https://doi.org/10.1007/978-3-031-98420-4_10
9. Zapata-Rivera, D., Greer, J.E.: Exploring Various Guidance Mechanisms to Support Interaction with Inspectable Learner Models, pp. 442–452. Springer, Heidelberg (2002). https://doi.org/10.1007/3-540-47987-2_47

GenAI as Semantic Sensors for Collaborative Learning

Daniel Spikol[1(✉)], Andy Nguyen[2], Kester Wong[3], Richard Lee Davis[4], Olga Viberg[5], Namrata Srivastava[6], Sa'ar Karp Gershon[9], Roberto Martinez-Maldonado[7], Marcelo Worsley[8], Qi Zhou[3], and Xavier Ochoa[10]

[1] Center for Digital Education, University of Copenhagen, Copenhagen 2200, Denmark
ds@gdi.ku.dk

[2] Learning and Educational Technology, Oulu University, Oulu 90014, Finland
andy.nguyen@oulu.fi

[3] UCL Knowledge Lab, University College London, London WC1N 3QS, UK
yew.wong.21@ucl.ac.uk, qtnvqz3@ucl.ac.uk

[4] Digital Learning, KTH Royal Institute of Technology, Stockholm 10044, Sweden
rldavis@kth.se

[5] Media Technology and Interaction Design, KTH Royal Institute of Technology, Stockholm 10044, Sweden
oviberg@kth.se

[6] Institute for Software Integrated Systems, Vanderbilt University, Nashville, TN 37212, USA
namrata.srivastava@vanderbilt.edu

[7] Faculty of Information Technology, Monash University, Melbourne 3800, Australia
Roberto.MartinezMaldonado@monash.edu

[8] McCormick School of Engineering, Northwestern University, Evanston, IL 60208, USA
marcelo.worsley@northwestern.edu

[9] Data Science Section, IT University, Copenhagen 2300, Denmark
skge@di.ku.dk

[10] Steinhardt School, New York University, New York 10003, USA
xavier.ochoa@nyu.edu

Abstract. Generative Artificial Intelligence (GenAI) is reshaping Multimodal Learning Analytics (MMLA) by augmenting and extending the semantics of learning interactions. While recent systematic research indicates that GenAI is currently used primarily for individual learners' tasks such as tutoring or co-programming, its application in collaborative learning environments remains largely underdeveloped and overlooked. This half-day workshop invites researchers to explore how Large Language Models (LLMs) and multimodal generative learning and teaching architectures can serve as additional sources of semantic sensors to decode meaning, motivation, coherence, and learning performance in group learning. By enhancing and extending simple behaviour tracking, we aim to envision systems and tools that foster meaningful reciprocal human-GenAI educational interaction, supporting teams in sustain-

E. G. Blanchard et al. (Eds.): AIED 2026, CCIS 3033, pp. 66–73, 2026.
https://doi.org/10.1007/978-3-032-29794-5_12

ing and further developing higher-order thinking skills such as problem-solving and critical thinking without falling into the trap of cognitive "replacement" or over-reliance.

Keywords: Multimodal Learning Analytics, GenAI, Semantic Features, Collaborative Learning

1 Workshop Background and Motivation

Learning Analytics is transitioning from descriptive dashboards toward an AI-empowered paradigm in which technology serves as a tool to augment human intelligence and provide new tools for supporting education [8–11]. In active learning, which encompasses Problem-Based Learning (PBL) and Collaborative Learning (CL), the challenge lies in facilitating the social construction of knowledge [5]. While current research identifies five key interaction roles—Tutoring, Co-creating, Processing, Coaching, and Simulating these are overwhelmingly situated in individual learning spaces [9]. The challenge is to develop technology-mediated support systems that augment collaborative learning and to examine the opportunities and challenges these new approaches may create.

This workshop addresses this gap by leveraging the rise of LLMs to unlock the semantics frontier of MMLA [1,8]. Historically, tools have focused on observable behaviours such as gaze patterns and gestures [2,3,8]. However, when paired with speech-to-text models such as Whisper, LLMs can extract high-level semantic representations from classroom dialogue, mapping transcripts into meaningful codes in real time [7,14,15]. Furthermore, advances in multimodal LLMs now make it feasible to analyse the semantic content of non-verbal cues, such as physical interactions, group and individual behaviours, facial expressions, and gaze sequences [6,8,12]. By treating LLMs as semantic sensors integrating discourse and behaviour, we can support the orchestration of more active, collaborative, and context-sensitive learning environments that address the "black box" of student collaboration [9,13]. More importantly, they unlock one of the most challenging and exciting frontiers of MmLA: semantics [1]

The CROSSMMLA workshop series has been pivotal in advancing MMLA research across the LAK, ICLS, and AIED communities over the last decade [4,8]. This year's workshop invites the MMLA community to come together, share, explore, and reflect on harnessing Generative AI to explore the semantics frontier for collaborative learning. Through presentations, collective discussion and hands-on activities, we aim to envision a new generation of multimodal learning analytics tools and methods that go beyond behaviour tracking to interpret meaning, motivation, and coherence across modalities. Additionally, the workshop brings forward to the community the current challenges and opportunities of adopting these state-of-the-art methods and tools.

2 Workshop Details

2.1 Event Type and Structure

The workshop will be a half-day workshop designed to foster knowledge exchange and collective reflection among researchers and developers. An open call for extended abstracts will be disseminated to the community prior to the event.

2.2 Schedule and Activities

- **Introduction to the Symposium (15 min):** Overview of goals and how GenAI intersects with MMLA to support semantic analysis in group settings.
- **Flash Presentations with Q&A (1.5 h):** Short, focused presentations from researchers sharing emerging tools, experimental results, or conceptual frameworks for analysing collaborative semantics.
- **Plenary Guided Discussion (1 h):** A structured discussion to identify key challenges (e.g., algorithmic bias, privacy, ethics and information reliability) and opportunities for unlocking semantic insights.
- **Affinity Groups for Post-Symposium Work (30 min):** Participants will organise into groups based on shared interests—such as co-programming support or social-emotional sensing—to lay the groundwork for ongoing collaborations.

2.3 Call for Extended Abstracts

We plan to invite the community to submit extended abstracts (500-word limit) that address the transformative potential of Generative AI in unlocking the "semantics frontier" of Multimodal Learning Analytics. As the education field transitions toward an AI-empowered paradigm that prioritises human-AI synergy and cognitive augmentation, we seek contributions that move beyond existing behaviour tracking to decode meaning, motivation, and coherence within complex group learning interactions.

The workshop will welcome submissions detailing the latest research, emerging tools, experimental results, or conceptual frameworks. We are particularly interested in work that explores the use of Large LLMs as "semantic sensors" capable of processing multimodal data (e.g., dialogue, gestures, gaze sequences) to support higher-order thinking skills (HOTS) such as problem-solving, critical thinking, and computational thinking within STEM active learning environments.

- **Demos & Emerging Tools:** Novel applications or prompt-based pipelines leveraging GenAI for automated transcribing, coding, or real-time feedback.
- **Original Research:** Empirical studies examining how human-GenAI interactions (such as Tutoring, Co-creating, Processing, Coaching, or Simulating) influence student agency and learning outcomes.

- **Practitioner Reports:** Insights and challenges from implementing GenAI-powered tools in real-world classrooms or collaborative group settings.
- **New Methods & Theories:** Conceptual frameworks for analysing social knowledge construction, fostering hybrid intelligence, and mitigating the risks of student overreliance.

By contributing to this symposium, you will help shape a collaborative research agenda to envision the next generation of context-sensitive, semantic-driven analytics tools.

2.4 Recruitment and Dissemination

Participants will be recruited from the AIED, Educational Data Mining (EDM), Learning at Scale, and from SoLAR communities (specifically the MMLA SIG). Outreach will target those working with multimodal data and educators interested in applying semantic analytics in collaborative learning contexts.

3 Intended Outcomes

The workshop aims to produce three tangible outcomes to extend its impact beyond the conference:

1. **Collaborative Research Agenda:** A summary of the symposium's priorities and open challenges for leveraging GenAI and LLMs as semantic sensors, specifically focusing on overcoming student over-reliance in collaborative settings.
2. **Independent Publication of Workshop Proceedings:** A compilation of extended submissions to the symposium, made openly accessible to the community.
3. **Special Issues Proposal:** A proposal for a special section in the International Journal of Artificial Intelligence in Education titled "GenAI as Semantic Sensors for Collaborative Learning," planned for 2026/2027.

4 Relevance to the Community

This workshop aligns with the shift from a "replacement" to an "augmentation" perspective. By exploring how GenAI can enhance every stage of the learning analytics pipeline from data collection to communication, we can ensure that AI serves as a powerful partner in shaping the future of collaborative learning in education.

5 Organizing Team

Daniel Spikol is Associate Professor at the University of Copenhagen's Centre for Digital Education, a joint research group between the departments of Computer Science and Science Education. With over 15 years of experience, his research bridges human-computer interaction, multimodal learning analytics, and AI in education, with a particular focus on collaborative learning and design for STEM contexts. He designs and develops sensor-integrated systems that analyse human behaviour and generate insights into group interaction in educational settings. He has supervised 11 PhD students, contributed to the coordination of PhD programmes, and served on the editorial boards of international journals and conferences. A driving force behind the MMLA SIG at SoLAR for over a decade, he also served as local chair of Learning@Scale 2023.

Andy Nguyen is an Associate Professor in the Hybrid Intelligence profiling project at the Learning & Educational Technology (LET) Research Lab, Faculty of Education and Psychology, University of Oulu, Finland. He also holds a Research Council of Finland Fellowship and an Adjunct Professorship in Applied AI at the Faculty of Information Technology and Electrical Engineering at the same university. His research has achieved strong international visibility, with recognition as a top-cited and most-read author in leading journals including the British Journal of Educational Technology and Studies in Higher Education, and he is listed among the world's top 2% of researchers in the 2025 Stanford-Elsevier global ranking. He serves on the editorial boards of several leading journals and is the recipient of the 2025 IEEE TCLT Early Career Researcher Award in Learning Technologies.

Olga Viberg is an Associate Professor and docent in Media Technology with a specialisation in Technology-Enhanced Learning at the Department of Human-Centred Technology (EECS) at KTH Royal Institute of Technology. Her research focuses on the design and evaluation of AI and learning analytics tools to improve digital learning experiences, with particular interests in human-AI support for literacy development, autonomous learning, digital assessment, and the responsible use of student data in STEM education. She currently serves as Editor-in-Chief of the International Journal of Learning Analytics, as president of the European Association of Technology-Enhanced Learning (EATEL) from 2025, and previously as vice-president of the Society for Learning Analytics Research (SoLAR).

Qi Zhou is a Postdoctoral Researcher in the UCLAIT team at the UCL Knowledge Lab, University College London, UK. His PhD research focused on utilising MMLA to analyse non-verbal behaviours in collaborative learning contexts. He is currently developing teacher-facing AI tools, based on MMLA models trained in collaborative learning settings, to support teaching practice in real-world scenarios.

Kester Wong is a PhD student and part of the UCLAIT team at the UCL Knowledge Lab, University College London, UK. His research focuses on AI-based support for Collaborative Problem Solving (CPS). Kester is also a Teaching Assistant at the Nanyang Technological University, National Institute of Education (NTU/NIE) in Singapore under the Learning Sciences and Assessment Academic Group (LSA AG).

Richard Lee Davis is an Assistant Professor in the Division of Digital Learning at KTH Royal Institute of Technology. He holds a PhD in Learning Sciences and Technology Design and an MSc in Computer Science from Stanford University. He completed a postdoctoral fellowship at EPFL under Pierre Dillenbourg, where he also co-directed the ETHz-EPFL Joint Doctoral Program in the Learning Sciences. His research draws on constructionist theory to design educational tools that expand "learning by making" through technologies like AI, digital fabrication, haptics, and XR. His work has been recognised with the Stanford Interdisciplinary Graduate Fellowship, best paper awards, and grants supporting AI-driven creativity in education.

Namrata Srivastava is an R&D Scientist and Adjunct Assistant Professor in the Department of Computer Science at Vanderbilt University, where she designs and studies human-centered AI systems and multimodal learning analytics to support equitable STEM+C education. Her research focuses on understanding students' inquiry, collaboration, and self-regulated learning processes through multimodal data, including eye-tracking, dialogue, interaction logs, and classroom analytics. She holds a PhD in Computer Science from the University of Melbourne, where she pioneered non-invasive sensor-based approaches to detecting cognitive load, and has held postdoctoral and adjunct research positions at the University of Pennsylvania and Monash University. Her work contributes to federally funded initiatives such as the EngageAI Institute and SPICE, as well as collaborations with international organisations including the OECD. She is a recipient of the 2024 SoLAR Emerging Scholar Award.

Roberto Martinez-Maldonado is Senior Lecturer of Learning Analytics and Human-Computer Interaction at Monash University's Faculty of Information Technology. He holds a doctorate from the University of Sydney and previously held research and teaching positions at the University of Technology Sydney. His research sits at the intersection of learning analytics, HCI, and AI, with a focus on teamwork analytics—developing multimodal methods and tools such as dashboards, warning systems, and data storytelling applications to assess and support collocated team performance in classrooms and healthcare settings. More recently, his work has pioneered co-design approaches at the intersection of education and data science.

Sa'ar Karp Gershon is a researcher and consultant specialising in advanced statistical methodologies, with a focus on their application in learning analytics and educational measurement. His expertise spans the rigorous analysis of complex behavioural and cognitive constructs, program evaluation, and data-driven decision-making. He holds a PhD in Mathematical Statistics from the Hebrew University of Jerusalem, where his dissertation developed a novel functional regression approach using kernel estimation and LASSO-based bandwidth selection, with implications for multimodal and image-based data analysis.

Marcelo Worsley is an Associate Professor in Computer Science and Learning Sciences, and director of the Technological Innovations for Inclusive Learning and Teaching (TIILT) Lab. His research advances equity in education by designing and studying multimodal technologies that support diverse learners in hands-on, collaborative environments. He combines multimodal signal processing and AI to analyse how learning unfolds across modalities and time scales, and to develop interfaces and analytical tools that promote inclusivity and support reflection for both students and teachers.

Xavier Ochoa is an Associate Professor of Learning Analytics whose work integrates learning sciences, multimodal sensing, and human-centered AI to design educational systems that make complex skills visible, measurable, and continuously improvable. His research focuses on AI-augmented technologies that support communication, collaboration, and creativity while amplifying human capabilities rather than replacing them.

References

1. Cukurova, M.: The interplay of learning, analytics and artificial intelligence in education: a vision for hybrid intelligence. Br. J. Edu. Technol. **56**(2), 469–488 (2025). https://doi.org/10.1111/bjet.13514
2. Davalos, E., et alk.: LLMs as educational analysts: transforming multimodal data traces into actionable reading assessment reports. In: International Conference on Artificial Intelligence in Education, pp. 191–204 (2025). https://doi.org/10.1007/978-3-031-98417-4_14
3. Di Mitri, D., Schneider, J., Specht, M., Drachsler, H.: From signals to knowledge: a conceptual model for multimodal learning analytics. J. Comput. Assist. Learn. **34**(4), 338–349 (2018). https://doi.org/10.1111/jcal.12288
4. Mitri, D., et al.: The second international workshop on multimodal artificial intelligence in education (MAIEd 2025). In: International Conference on Artificial Intelligence in Education, pp. 292–299. Springer (2025). https://doi.org/10.1007/978-3-031-99267-4_38
5. Doolittle, P., Wojdak, K., Walters, A.: Defining active learning: a restricted systemic review. Teac. Learn. Inquiry **11** (2023). https://doi.org/10.20343/teachlearninqu.11.25
6. Fonteles, J.H., et al.: Analyzing embodied learning in classroom settings: a human-in-the-loop AI approach for multimodal learning analytics. Learn. Instruction **103**, 102274 (2026). https://doi.org/10.1016/j.learninstruc.2025.102274
7. Li, Z., Yamaguchi, S., Spikol, D.: OpenMMLA: an IoT-based multimodal data collection toolkit for learning analytics. In: Proceedings of the 15th International Learning Analytics and Knowledge Conference, LAK 2025, pp. 872–879 (2025). https://doi.org/10.1145/3706468.3706525
8. Ochoa, X., Di Mitri, D., Zamecnik, A., Spikol, D., Srivastava, N., Cobos, R.: CROSSMMLA: exploring the frontier of multimodal semantic features with the help of generative AI. In: Workshop Proposal for LAK26 (2025)
9. Otto, S., Lavi, R., Bertel, L.B.: Human-GenAI interaction for active learning in STEM education: state-of-the-art and future directions. Comput. Educ. **239**, 105444 (2025). https://doi.org/10.1016/j.compedu.2025.105444
10. Ouyang, F., Jiao, P.: Artificial intelligence in education: the three paradigms. Comput. Educ. Artifi. Intell. **2**, 100020 (2021). https://doi.org/10.1016/j.caeai.2021.100020

11. Srivastava, N., Jain, S., Cohn, C., Mohammed, N., Timalsina, U., Biswas, G.: LearnLens: An AI-enhanced dashboard to support teachers in open-ended classrooms. In: International Conference on Artificial Intelligence in Education Workshop on Advances in Artificial Intelligence for Exploratory Learning (AI4EXL) (2025). https://doi.org/10.48550/arXiv.2509.10582
12. Whitehead, R., Nguyen, A., Järvelä, S.: Utilizing multimodal large language models for video analysis of posture in studying collaborative learning: a case study. J. Learn. Analy. **12**(1), 186–200 (2025). https://doi.org/10.18608/jla.2025.8595
13. Yan, L., Martinez-Maldonado, R., Gasevic, D.: Generative artificial intelligence in learning analytics: contextualising opportunities and challenges through the learning analytics cycle. In: Proceedings of the 14th Learning Analytics and Knowledge Conference, pp. 101–111 (2024). https://doi.org/10.1145/3636555.3636856
14. Zhang, J et al.: Using Large Language Models to Detect Socially Shared Regulation of Collaborative Learning (2026). https://doi.org/10.48550/arXiv.2601.04458
15. Zhao, L., et al.: Towards automated transcribing and coding of embodied teamwork communication through multimodal learning analytics. Br. J. Edu. Technol. **55**(4), 1673–1702 (2024). https://doi.org/10.1111/bjet.13476

Build and Deploy Microservices for Automated Feedback

Alexandra Neagu[1(✉)], Peter B. Johnson[1], Marcus Messer[1], and Fun Siong Lim[2]

[1] Imperial College London, London, UK
{alexandra.neagu20,peter.johnson,m.messer}@imperial.ac.uk
[2] Nanyang Technological University, Singapore, Singapore
LIM_Fun_Siong@ntu.edu.sg

Abstract. E-learning platforms are growing increasingly complex, embedding automated assessment and feedback tools to support learning at scale. Yet such tools are usually tightly tied – locked-in – to the platforms for which they were built, limiting the pedagogical flexibility of teachers adopting such tools and platforms. One approach to addressing this 'lock-in' challenge is to source discipline-specific education *microservices* – modular, independent software or plugins that can be connected to e-learning platforms to perform a specialised task. This modular architecture allows educational logic to be developed by domain experts and be reused across the entire sector, regardless of the platform employed. This tutorial will introduce participants to education microservices for automated feedback using an active e-learning platform. Working in mixed-ability groups, participants will design, implement, and deploy a live microservice to evaluate student submissions on a specific learning task. By the end of the tutorial, participants will have contributed a working, publicly accessible automated feedback tool to an open-source education microservice ecosystem and engaged in community discussion on shared education microservice architecture and infrastructure.

Keywords: Automated Feedback · Automated Assessment · Microservice · E-Learning Platform

1 Key Information

We present a half-day (4-hour) hands-on tutorial to design, implement, and deploy an education microservice to evaluate student submissions to learning tasks and provide automated feedback. The tutorial targets up to 30 participants from the Learning@Scale and AIED communities, welcoming domain experts regardless of programming experience.

The tutorial is motivated by the need for domain-specific knowledge when automating feedback. To source the necessary expertise within each domain, feedback automation must be developed at a granular level within each discipline and be informed by experts. We conceive of each discipline-specific feedback

E. G. Blanchard et al. (Eds.): AIED 2026, CCIS 3033, pp. 74–79, 2026.
https://doi.org/10.1007/978-3-032-29794-5_13

automation logic as a *microservice*—a modular, independently deployed software service that communicates via standard protocols and performs a specialised role. These microservices can be re-used by different e-learning platforms across the sector.

The tutorial has three goals:

1. Enable participants to build and deploy an education microservice for feedback on learning tasks;
2. Generate community discussion and collaboration on shared education microservice architecture and infrastructure;
3. Contribute to an open-source education microservice ecosystem that persists beyond this tutorial.

The tutorial will use the public, platform-independent μEd API [4] to make microservices available across e-learning platforms. The Lambda Feedback platform [1] will be provided as an example e-learning platform where teachers curate learning tasks, students submit answers, and automated feedback is delivered by calling specialist microservices that evaluate the student submission against a criteria or expected solution.

The microservice model employed by the μEd API and the Lambda Feedback platform addresses the 'platform lock-in' challenge [2,3][5, p. 140], where teacher agency over the automations made available to their students is limited by the learning platforms employed. By sourcing automation from platform-agnostic sources (microservices), teachers may maintain a free choice of automated feedback algorithms or tools regardless of their primary learning platform. This tutorial aims to introduce the microservice model through hands-on development and deployment.

Tutorial participants will be divided in groups of 3–5 of mixed expertise, with each member encouraged to adopt one of three proposed roles: the *Task Designer* who defines the learning task and its evaluation criteria, the *Implementer* who codes the evaluation microservice, and the *Test Author* who creates sample student submissions and judges feedback quality.

To minimise the 'blank-page' burden, we provide example tasks and evaluation strategies for the participants to choose or get inspired from. Boilerplates[1] of an evaluation microservice will be provided and will include deployment pipelines using cloud functions (such as AWS Lambda). No prior knowledge of microservices, REST APIs, or the platforms involved is assumed, and participation does not necessary require previous coding experience. The only prerequisite is a GitHub account for at least one member per group—which can be created during the tutorial if necessary.

2 Education Microservices in Action: Lambda Feedback

Lambda Feedback [1] is an e-learning platform developed at Imperial College London, UK, built around the microservice architecture concept for automated

[1] Available in Python, Wolfram, and Lean; other languages can be added.

feedback. Lambda Feedback is used by thousands of students each year across undergraduate studies in Engineering, Natural Sciences, Medicine, and Business, as well as in secondary schools, for example in Essay writing. The platform facilitates teachers to curate self-study tasks for students.

To provide automated feedback on domain-specific learning tasks, Lambda Feedback connects to independent *evaluation functions*—microservices that evaluate student submissions and return timely feedback (see Fig. 1). Each evaluation function is invoked via the μEd API [4], an open HTTP API specification for education microservices. The μEd API enables subject experts to contribute feedback algorithms to any platform without engaging with the full platform stack[2]. The μEd API is initially being adopted into the education microservice design of four institutions—Imperial College London, TU Munich, ETH Zürich, and Nanyang Technological University—with the ambition to serve the whole sector in future.

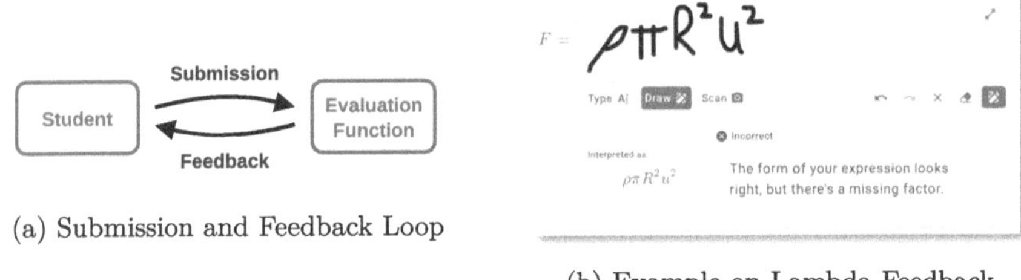

(a) Submission and Feedback Loop

(b) Example on Lambda Feedback

Fig. 1. Student submits a task solution on Lambda Feedback (e-learning platform). The submission is reviewed by an evaluation function (microservice) and is provided automated feedback.

3 Tutorial Goals and Outcomes

The tutorial aims to:

1. Enable participants to build and deploy an *evaluation function* (a working microservice to evaluate student submissions and return feedback) to a learning task of own choice on Lambda Feedback.
2. Generate community discussion and collaboration on the adoption and design of education microservices architecture and infrastructure for scaling pedagogical innovation (such as discussion on how the service might accommodate automated feedback design for formative vs summative contexts; domain-specific heuristics vs LLM-based approaches.). Community feedback gathered during the discussion session will inform future versions of the μEd API [4] specification.

[2] μEd API specification: https://www.mued.org/.

3. Contribute to an open-source education microservice ecosystem that persists beyond this tutorial. Participants will be able to continue improving and using the created microservice after the tutorial. After the tutorial ends, groups' repositories can remain public under the `lambdafeedback` GitHub organisation or be moved to own repositories, contributing directly to the open-source microservice ecosystem community.

4 Tutorial Schedule

The session runs for four hours and is structured in three phases. The *Introduction Phase* covers the motivation for the tutorial, a technical introduction with a live demo of Lambda Feedback and its connected evaluation functions, and a live survey to form groups for the following phase. The *Hands-on Phase* involves groups creating sample tasks on Lambda Feedback and building their own evaluation function, deploying and connecting it to the platform. The *Closing Phase* comprises the group live demos where groups test each other's evaluation functions, an open discussion on μEd API and the education microservice architecture, and a wrap-up.

5 Participant Group Roles

To ensure all participants can contribute during the *Hands-on Phase*, regardless of programming background, each member within the group adopts one of the three suggested roles shown in Table 1.

Table 1. Participant Group Roles

Role	Description	Suggested Expertise
Task Designer	Defines the task domain, evaluation criteria, and what constitutes as good feedback; judges the feedback output from the evaluation function.	Educators, Domain Experts, Learning Designers
Implementer	Takes charge in adopting the team ideas into code for the evaluation function	Programming, EdTech, AI-Assisted Coding
Test Author	Creates sample student submissions (correct, partially correct, incorrect), stress-tests the evaluation function.	Educators, Domain Experts

Groups may have members with overlapping roles, but there must be at least one *Implementer* per group.

6 Microservice Development and Deployment Process

Throughout the tutorial, groups will follow the same development and deployment process split per role designed to minimise setup and debugging friction. The group will first decide on the domain and learning task they want to provide automated feedback on then start working on the development, with each member focusing on the tasks appointed to each role.

The tutorial provides boilerplates[3] for an evaluation function which are publicly available on GitHub[4]. Each team will fork the boilerplate of the preferred programming language into the `lambdafeedback` GitHub organisation and develop their evaluation function on the forked repository. When pushing new code onto the group's repository, a deployment CI/CD pipeline triggers automatically and deploys the microservice to Lambda Feedback's AWS infrastructure. After a successful deployment the evaluation function will be made available into Lambda Feedback for the team to use on their agreed sample learning task.

For post-tutorial use, participants are not restricted to Lambda Feedback's AWS deployment infrastructure. Developers may move the evaluation function repository to their own organisation and deploy the microservice on any infrastructure of their choice. Developers will then still be able to register the publicly accessible microservice API URL with Lambda Feedback. This illustrates the power of a provider-agnostic microservices model: an evaluation microservice built during the tutorial can later be moved to an institution's own servers but still be in use by Lambda Feedback.

7 Example Tasks and Evaluation Strategies

To avoid idea paralysis, during the *Introduction Phase* we introduce four example task and evaluation strategies for the groups to get inspiration from. Groups can select one of the example strategies or pursue their own ideas.

- **Keyword/Concept Check:** Evaluate a text submission for expected words or concepts (example tasks: definition of physics phenomena, components of a chemical substance, ...)
- **Numerical Value Comparison:** Evaluate whether the numerical submission is within acceptable bounds (example tasks: verify a rounding of decimal places, estimate pressure value at 100m under the sea, ...)
- **Criteria Comparison:** Map student submission against a given criteria (e.g., by using large language models (LLMs)) and return per-criterion feedback (example tasks: review an explanation of why the urban heat island effect forms, verify the time and space complexity of a code snippet, ...)

[3] Available in Python, Wolfram, and Lean; other languages can be added.
[4] Python Boilerplate GitHub repository: https://github.com/lambda-feedback/evaluation-function-boilerplate-python.

- **Image Analysis:** Evaluate an uploaded image for specific patterns (e.g., by using machine learning models) and return observational feedback (example tasks: verify existence of specific electrical components in an image of a breadboard, analyse a hand-drawn visualisation of Roman bath ruins, ...)

The organiser will provide a limited amount of API credits for LLMs, if they are chosen as a methodology for evaluation.

Acknowledgements. In accordance with the author policy, we disclose that we used AI tools for grammar and stylistic editing. The authors carefully reviewed all content.

References

1. Johnson, P.B., Fenton, J., Ramsden, P., Chatley, R., Ribera-Vicent, M., Lundengård, K.: Formative feedback on engineering self-study: Towards 1 million times per year per cohort. In: 2025 IEEE Global Engineering Education Conference (EDUCON), pp. 1–3. IEEE (2025)
2. Kerssens, N., Van Dijck, J.: Governed by edtech? valuing pedagogical autonomy in a platform society. Harv. Educ. Rev. **92**(2), 284–303 (2022)
3. Pangrazio, L., Selwyn, N., Cumbo, B.: A patchwork of platforms: mapping data infrastructures in schools. Learn. Media Technol. **48**(1), 65–80 (2023). https://doi.org/10.1080/17439884.2022.2035395
4. Sölch, M., et al.: muEd-api (Feb 2026). https://doi.org/10.17605/OSF.IO/FET3U
5. Thomas, D.A., Laterza, V.: Critical perspectives on edtech in higher education: Varieties of platformisation (2026)

Seventh Annual Workshop on A/B Testing and Platform-Enabled Learning Engineering

April Murphy[1(✉)], Stephen E. Fancsali[1], Steve Ritter[1], Neil Heffernan[2], Debshila Basu Mallick[3], Jeremy Roschelle[4], Danielle McNamara[5], Joseph Jay Williams[6], John Stamper[7], Norman Bier[7], and Jeff Carver[8]

[1] Carnegie Learning, Pittsburgh, PA 15219, USA
amurphy@carnegielearning.com
[2] Worcester Polytechnic Institute, Worcester, MA 01609, USA
[3] SafeInsights-OpenStax, Houston, TX 77005, USA
[4] Digital Promise, Redwood City, CA 94063, USA
[5] Arizona State University, Tempe, AZ 85287, USA
[6] University of Toronto, Toronto M5S 3H2, Canada
[7] Carnegie Mellon University, Pittsburgh, PA 15213, USA
[8] University of Alabama, Tuscaloosa, AL 35487, USA

Abstract. Learning engineering applies data and learning science principles to better understand outcomes and support improvement research. One important approach is A/B testing–common in large software companies and also represented academically at conferences like the Annual Conference on Digital Experimentation (CODE), and the International Consortium for Innovation and Collaboration in Learning Engineering (IEEE ICICLE). Several systems supporting A/B testing in educational applications are in active use, including UpGrade, E TRIALS, and Terracotta. Although A/B testing can help improve educational platforms and inform learning science research, there are challenging issues unique to conducting such work in these contexts. In response, a number of digital learning platforms have opened their systems to learning-improvement research by instructors and/or third-party researchers, with specific supports necessary for education-specific research designs. This workshop will explore how A/B testing is conducted in educational contexts, how digital learning platforms are accelerating education research, and how empirical approaches can be used to drive powerful gains in student learning. It will also discuss opportunities for funding to conduct platform-enabled learning engineering.

Keywords: A/B Testing · Learning Engineering · Educational Technology · Digital Experimentation

1 Theme and Goals

The conference organizers have deep practical experience building learning engineering platforms for educational software. We will solicit presentations through the call for participation and, upon acceptance, organize those presentations into themes that will form the basis of the workshop.

E. G. Blanchard et al. (Eds.): AIED 2026, CCIS 3033, pp. 80–83, 2026.
https://doi.org/10.1007/978-3-032-29794-5_14

This will be a half-day workshop. The workshop will be devoted to presentations and discussions of accepted papers. We will organize presentations according to major themes (e.g., "adaptive algorithms", "school communication strategies"), with the expectation that we will have 2–3 themes addressed during the workshop.

We will accept both full papers (5–10 pages) and short submissions for papers or demos (up to 4 pages). Accepted presenters for full papers will have 25 min to present, followed by 5 min for questions. Accepted short submissions will present their work as 15 min talks or demo sessions following the long presentations.

2 Background and Relevance to L@S

"There is no simple path that will take us immediately from the contemporary amateurism of the college to the professional design of learning environments and learning experiences. The most important step is to find a place on campus for a team of individuals who are professionals in the design of learning environments—learning engineers, if you will" [7].

Learning engineering applies data and learning science principles to better understand outcomes and support improvement research, often by adding tools and processes to learning platforms [8]. One important approach is A/B testing [2], which is common in large software companies and also represented academically at conferences like the Annual Conference on Digital Experimentation (CODE) and the International Consortium for Innovation and Collaboration in Learning Engineering (IEEE ICICLE). Several A/B testing systems focused on educational applications are in current use, including UpGrade [4], E-TRIALS [5], and Terracotta [6]. A/B testing can be part of the puzzle of how to improve educational platforms and inform learning research, but challenging issues in education go beyond the generic paradigm. For example, the importance of teachers and instructors to learning means that students not only connect with software as individuals, but as part of a shared classroom experience. Further, learning patterns in topics like mathematics can be highly dependent on prior experiences, and thus condition assignments such as A or B may support improvement only in interaction with prior knowledge [1]. In response to these challenges, a set of learning platforms has opened their systems to improvement research by instructors and/or third-party researchers, with specific supports necessary for education-specific research designs. This workshop will explore how A/B testing in educational contexts is different, how learning platforms offer new possibilities, and how these empirical approaches can be used to drive powerful gains in student learning. It will also discuss forthcoming opportunities for funding to conduct platform-enabled learning engineering research.

Issues to be addressed are expected to include:

- The role of A/B testing systems in complying with SEER principles (https://ies.ed.gov/seer/), which set a high bar for the goals of empirical studies of educational improvement
- Awareness of opportunities to use existing learning platforms to conduct research (http://seernet.org)
- Using adaptive experimentation methods (e.g., multi-armed bandits) in education research

- Managing unit of assignment issues, as arise when students are in classrooms with a shared teacher
- Practical considerations related to experimenting in school settings, MOOCs, and other contexts
- A/B testing within adaptive learning software
- Ethical, data security, and privacy issues
- Relating experimental results to learning-science principles
- Understanding use cases (core, supplemental, in-school, out-of-school, etc.)
- Accounting for interactions between the intended contrast (A vs. B) and learners' prior knowledge, aptitudes, background, or other important variables
- Attrition and dropout
- Stopping criteria
- User experience issues
- Educator involvement and public perceptions of experimentation
- Balancing practical improvements with open and generalizable science

Six previous instances of this workshop (2020–2025) at the Learning at Scale conference were very successful, some with the highest registrations of any workshops at the conference. We welcome participation from researchers and practitioners who have either practical or theoretical experience related to running A/B tests and/or randomized trials as well as platform-enabled learning engineering research. This may include researchers with backgrounds in learning science, computer science, economics and/or statistics.

3 Expected Outcomes and Contributions

Papers and demos from this workshop will be published as Proceedings on the OA Works portal (https://oa.works/) to support open access to scientific knowledge. We will continue to develop and deploy systems in this area. We expect to conduct this workshop yearly, as it has become part of the basis for a community of researchers and learning engineers conducting A/B tests at scale.

Acknowledgments. This workshop was supported by grants from the Institute of Education Sciences, the Gates Foundation, and the National Science Foundation.

Disclosure of Interests. The authors have no competing interests to declare that are relevant to the workshop and content of this article.

References

1. Fyfe, E.R.: Providing feedback on computer-based algebra homework in middle-school classrooms. Comput. Hum. Behav. **63**, 568–574 (2016)
2. Kohavi, R., Deng, A., Frasca, B., Walker, T., Xu, Y., Pohlmann, N.: Online controlled experiments at large scale. In: Proceedings of the 19th ACM SIGKDD International Conference on Knowledge Discovery and Data Mining, pp. 1168–1176 (2013)

3. Ostrow, K., Heffernan, N., Williams, J.J.: Tomorrow's EdTech today: establishing a learning platform as a collaborative research tool for sound science. Teach. Coll. Rec. **119**(3), 1–36 (2017)
4. Ritter, S., Murphy, A., Fancsali, S.E., Fitkariwala, V., Patel, N., Lomas, J.D.: UpGrade: an open source tool to support A/B testing in educational software. In: Proceedings of the First Workshop on Educational A/B Testing at Scale (at Learning@ Scale 2020) (2020)
5. Siedahmed, A., et al.: E-TRIALS: empowering data-driven decisions to enhance computer-based learning platforms. arXiv preprint arXiv:2502.10545 (2025)
6. Motz, B.A., et al.: Terracotta: a tool for conducting experimental research on student learning. Behav. Res. Methods **56**(3), 2519–2536 (2024)
7. Simon, H.: The job of a college president. Educ. Rec., 68–78 (1967)
8. Uncapher, M.R.: From the science of learning (and development) to learning engineering. Appl. Dev. Sci. **23**(4), 349–352 (2019)
9. Stamper, J.C., Lomas, D., Ching, D., Ritter, S., Koedinger, K.R., Steinhart, J.: The rise of the super experiment. Int. Educ. Data Mining Soc. (2012)

Fair4AIED 2026: Second International Workshop on Fairness in AI-Assisted Decision-Making for Education

Frank Stinar[1(✉)], Chengyuan Yao[3], Mirko Marras[2], Renzhe Yu[3], and Nigel Bosch[1]

[1] University of Illinois Urbana–Champaign, Champaign, USA
fstinar2@illinois.edu, cy2706@tc.columbia.edu
[2] University of Cagliari, Cagliari, Italy
mirko.marras@unica.it
[3] Columbia University, New York, NY, USA
pnb@illinois.edu, renzheyu@tc.columbia.edu

Abstract. As AI tools increasingly reshape educational activities through applications such as intelligent tutoring systems, early warning systems, and automated essay scoring, ensuring fairness in these AI-assisted decision-making scenarios remains a critical challenge. While researchers have been addressing AI fairness in education, existing efforts remain largely algorithmically focused and less integrated with broader socio-political ideas of fairness. As generative AI enables significantly more diverse and dynamic applications in education, research on fairness needs to take more holistic and collaborative perspectives. The Fair4AIED 2026 workshop aims to bring together researchers, practitioners, and policymakers from the AIED, EDM, and L@S communities to foster interdisciplinary dialogues and develop a joint vision on fairness in decision-making for education. The half-day workshop features a keynote presentation from outside the education community, research talks on fairness-focused research, and a moderated panel discussion on emerging themes such as technical bias, downstream harms, unfairness mitigation, and fairness in generative AI. The workshop welcomes both experts and novices in fair AI. Thus, providing a platform for translating theoretical fairness frameworks into actionable strategies for educational systems. The workshop website is available at https://fair4aied.github.io/2026/.

Keywords: AI-Assisted Decision-Making · Bias in AI · AI Fairness · Responsible AI · Educational Equity

1 Type of Event

This is a half-day workshop.

E. G. Blanchard et al. (Eds.): AIED 2026, CCIS 3033, pp. 84–89, 2026.
https://doi.org/10.1007/978-3-032-29794-5_15

2 Theme and Goals

Education is being reshaped due to artificial intelligence (AI) tools. AI is being used in intelligent tutoring systems [11], risk detection [13], personalization [7], and even for unstructured learning with large language models [9].

While significant progress has been made, achieving fairness in educational AI continues to pose substantial challenges that draw attention from academic researchers, policymakers, and industry professionals. These challenges stem from an increasing dependence on algorithmic decision-making systems and large data ecosystems that are often unrepresentative of diverse student populations [1]. Biases within training data can be magnified by AI systems, which can result in harm and discrimination [5]. Furthermore, the fast adoption of generative AI in educational contexts has created many new fairness and ethical challenges that are still being explored in the AI in education field [8].

Current research in AI and education addresses fairness concerns through various approaches, including algorithmic auditing techniques [14], unfairness mitigation strategies [10], and fairness-aware model development [12]. Researchers are exploring methods to detect and quantify bias in educational datasets, developing debiasing algorithms tailored to educational contexts [3], and investigating how different fairness metrics apply to learning environments. However, these efforts remain fragmented across subcommunities and often lack integration with broader fairness frameworks from the machine learning community [1,4,6].

This workshop bridged these gaps by fostering interdisciplinary dialogue and knowledge exchange among researchers, practitioners, and policymakers working at the intersection of AI and education. Through presentations and panel discussions, participants can share practical experiences and identify research questions that require attention. The workshop provides a platform for translating fairness frameworks into actionable strategies for real-world educational systems, while also providing opportunities to discuss challenges posed by generative AI technologies. Thus, the workshop can advance socio-technical, interdisciplinary appraaches to AI fairness, moving beyond largely algorithmic and technical efforts. The workshop brings together researchers, practitioners, policymakers, and those in industry whose expertise is essential for creating AI-powered educational systems with fairness and ethics at the forefront.

The `Fair4AIED` workshop is extremely relevant to each community in the Festival of Learning (AIED, EDM, and L@S), since the communities are critical in developing state-of-the art educational tools and AI-driven interventions. Thus, perspectives from these research communities are integral to having fair educational tools for learners. By bringing together these communities, the workshop can build upon established foundations and research norms to ensure that fairness in considered in the AIED, EDM, and L@S communities.

2.1 Schedule

The workshop is structured into sessions throughout a half-day (Table 1). First, we involve a keynote speaker to present on state of the art research in handling

Table 1. Summary of Workshop Organization.

Session	Description
Keynote Talk	A presentation and Q/A session highlighting advances and emerging challenges concerning fairness in AIED.
Participant Talks	Short presentations delivered by participants based on either their submitted abstracts or their published research at the Festival of Learning.
Moderated Panel	A panel with attendees centered around themes of the participant talks.

challenges of fairness and harm in machine learning and AI, prioritizing a speaker from outside the AI and education community to provide a novel viewpoint for the participants as many different fields are handling ethical and fairness challenges. The keynote is then followed by a Q&A session. Second, following the keynote, we hold short, fairness-focused talks from the participants. These talks can be from two sources: (1) Presenters who submitted an abstract of their talk to the organizers prior to the workshop, or (2) presenters who are presenting their work at the Festival of Learning and wish to give a talk specifically about fairness or ethical aspects of the research. These aspects can either be at the forefront of their publication or an aside that was not the main contribution of their publication. The presenters have 5–7 minutes to present slides related to their abstract or research. Depending on the number of talks, there is a short Q&A session after each presentation or after groups of participant presentations. Finally, after the talks from participants, we hold a moderated panel with the attendees centered around themes from the participant talks. While themes are dependent on the submissions, we predict that possible themes can be technical bias, downstream harms, unfairness mitigation, and fairness in generative AI.

2.2 Publishing Workshop Output

After the workshop sessions, we post the outputs of the workshop onto the workshop website. This includes the accepted abstracts and presentations for the participant talks (for those willing to share their presentations) and the themes/topics discussed during the keynote and moderated panel.

2.3 Advertising

All workshop information is hosted on a dedicated website, which serves as the central hub for submission guidelines, important dates, and program details. Abstract submissions are accepted through the website before the workshop and advertised through social media platforms and relevant mailing lists to maximize outreach. Participants receive notification of their acceptance status through an online submission system on the website. The workshop website also handles submissions of already published work, which can be promoted through the same communication channels. We plan to accommodate approximately 50 attendees for this event, based on attendance last year and the growth trajectory of conferences making up the Festival of Learning.

3 Prior Work

Building upon the experience and insights developed in its inaugural 2025 edition, `Fair4AIED` 2026 represents a new edition of a workshop on fairness in algorithmic decision-making for education [2].

4 Organizing Committee

Frank Stinar is a Doctoral Candidate at the University of Illinois Urbana–Champaign in the school of Information Sciences. His research focuses on how normative ethics, algorithmic fairness, and student modeling interact. Broadly, his research aims to improve equity in education.

Chengyuan Yao is a Doctoral Candidate in the Measurement, Evaluation, and Statistics program at Teachers College, Columbia University. His research focuses on trustworthy transfer learning in educational predictive modeling and psychometric approaches to evaluating large language models. Broadly, his work examines fairness, validity, and generalizability of AI systems across diverse educational contexts.

Nigel Bosch is an Associate Professor at the University of Illinois Urbana–Champaign, with a joint appointment in Information Sciences and Educational Psychology. His research include machine learning methods for measurement and intervention, especially in educational contexts where both fair processes and fair outcomes are essential.

Renzhe Yu is an Assistant Professor at Teachers College, Columbia University, and faculty member of the Data Science Institute. His research takes a sociotechnical lens to study responsible AI in education, addressing issues like algorithmic bias and digital divides in real-world contexts.

Mirko Marras Mirko Marras is a Tenure-Track Assistant Professor at the University of Cagliari, specializing in responsible AI, with a strong focus on AI in education and fairness. He has published over 120 papers in top conferences and journals and serves on program committees for major venues, including AIED, EDM, LAK, ICALT, EC-TEL, and UMAP. He has co-chaired multiple workshops, including BIAS (ECIR 2020-2023), FATED (EDM 2022), L2D (WSDM 2021), and RKDE (ECML-PKDD 2023-24). He has been General Co-Chair of ACM UMAP 2024, Blue Sky Track Co-Chair at AIED 2024, Proceedings Co-Chair at EDM 2023-25, and IR for Good Track Co-Chair at ECIR 2024.

References

1. Baker, R.S., Hawn, A.: Algorithmic bias in education. Inter. J. Artifi. Intell. Educ., 1–41 (2022)
2. Belitz, C., et al.: Fair4AIED 2025: first international workshop on fairness in algorithmic decision-making for education. In: Cristea, A.I., Walker, E., Lu, Y., Santos, O.C., Isotani, S. (eds.) Artificial Intelligence in Education. Posters and Late Breaking Results, Workshops and Tutorials, Industry and Innovation Tracks, Practitioners, Doctoral Consortium, Blue Sky, and WideAIED, pp. 308–314. Springer Nature Switzerland, Cham (2025). https://doi.org/10.1007/978-3-031-99267-4_40
3. Cock, J., Stinar, F., Kizilcec, R., Kaser, T.: Applying DebiasEd: a package for mitigating unfairness in educational data. In: Mills, C., Alexandron, G., Taibi, D., Bosco, G.L., Paquette, L. (eds.) Proceedings of the 18th International Conference on Educational Data Mining. pp. 695–698. International Educational Data Mining Society, Palermo, Italy (Jul 2025). https://doi.org/10.5281/zenodo.15870322
4. Fenu, G., Galici, R., Marras, M.: Experts' view on challenges and needs for fairness in artificial intelligence for education. In: AIED, pp. 243–255. Springer (2022). https://doi.org/10.1007/978-3-031-11644-5_20
5. Friedman, B., College, C.: Bias in computer systems. ACM Trans. Inform. Syst. **14**(3) (1996)
6. Heuer, L.: What's just about the criminal justice system - a psychological perspective. J. Law Policy **13**(1), 209–228 (2005). https://brooklynworks.brooklaw.edu/jlp/vol13/iss1/11
7. Hutt, S., Mills, C., Bosch, N., Krasich, K., Brockmole, J., D'Mello, S.: "Out of the Fr-Eye-ing Pan": towards gaze-based models of attention during learning with technology in the classroom. In: Proceedings of the 25th Conference on User Modeling, Adaptation and Personalization, pp. 94–103. ACM, Bratislava Slovakia (Jul 2017). https://doi.org/10.1145/3079628.3079669, https://dl.acm.org/doi/10.1145/3079628.3079669
8. Li, Y., Du, M., Song, R., Wang, X., Wang, Y.: A survey on fairness in large language models (2024). https://arxiv.org/abs/2308.10149
9. Razafinirina, M.A., Dimbisoa, W.G., Mahatody, T.: Pedagogical Alignment of Large Language Models (LLM) for personalized learning: a survey, trends and challenges. J. Intell. Learn. Syst. Appl. **16**(04), 448–480 (2024). https://doi.org/10.4236/jilsa.2024.164023
10. Stinar, F., et al.: Fairness of Bayesian Knowledge Tracing for Math Learners of Different Reading Ability. In: Mills, C., Alexandron, G., Taibi, D., Bosco, G.L., Paquette, L. (eds.) Proceedings of the 18th International Conference on Educational Data Mining, pp. 170–181. International Educational Data Mining Society, Palermo, Italy (Jul 2025). https://doi.org/10.5281/zenodo.15870165
11. Toth, A., Roch, N., Zufferey, N., Zimmermann, V.: "I Would Share It, But..." exploring ways to optimize the privacy-personalization trade-off in intelligent tutoring systems. In: Cristea, A.I., Walker, E., Lu, Y., Santos, O.C., Isotani, S. (eds.) Artificial Intelligence in Education, pp. 68–76. Springer Nature Switzerland, Cham (2025). https://doi.org/10.1007/978-3-031-98462-4_9
12. Verger, M., Lallé, S., Bouchet, F., V, Luengo, a.: Is Your Model "MADD"? A Novel Metric to Evaluate Algorithmic Fairness for Predictive Student Models. In: Proceedings of the 16th International Conference on Educational Data Mining, pp. 91–102. International Educational Data Mining Society (Jul 2023). https://doi.org/10.5281/zenodo.8115786, https://doi.org/10.5281/zenodo.8115786

13. Wang, W., Zhao, Y., Wu, Y.J., Goh, M.: Factors of dropout from MOOCs: a bibliometric review. Library Hi Tech **41**(2), 432–453 (2023). https://doi.org/10.1108/LHT-06-2022-0306
14. Zambrano, A.F., Zhang, J., Baker, R.S.: Investigating algorithmic bias on bayesian knowledge tracing and carelessness detectors. In: Proceedings of the 14th Learning Analytics and Knowledge Conference, pp. 349–359. ACM, Kyoto Japan (Mar 2024). https://doi.org/10.1145/3636555.3636890, https://dl.acm.org/doi/10.1145/3636555.3636890

8th International Workshop on Culturally-Aware Tutoring Systems (CATS2026)

Ivon Arroyo[1], Emmanuel G. Blanchard[2], Christine Kwon[3](✉), and Maria Mercedes T. Rodrigo[4]

[1] University of Massachusetts Amherst, Amherst, USA
ivon@cs.umass.edu, emmanuel.blanchard@univ-lemans.fr
[2] Le Mans Université, Le Mans, France
ckwon2@andrew.cmu.edu
[3] Carnegie Mellon University, Pittsburgh, USA
mrodrigo@ateneo.edu
[4] Ateneo de Manila University, Quezon City, Philippines

1 Content and Theme

In her work in multicultural education, Margaret Pusch [18] defines culture as "a system of shared beliefs, values, norms, behaviors and artifacts that members of a group use to make sense of their world and relate to others". Prior educational technology research has shown the importance of culturally-aware educational practices [8,13] as well as in many learning-related domains such as cognition, motivation, and emotions [7,11,14,15]. Hence, with the growing adoption of educational technologies, culture has become an increasingly important consideration for the AIED community. With the rapid advancement and development of AI, prior work has shown the potential for AI-mediated educational technologies to bridge educational and digital divides worldwide [4,9,20]. Although most AI and educational technological systems have been primarily designed for the Developed World [2,5,16], an increasing number of these systems are designed with different contexts in mind [10,13], and more and more intercultural evaluations are reported [1,6,17,19].

Moreover, this year's AIED conference calls for AI to co-evolve with learners, enabling richer human-AI interaction and synergy. As prior work has mainly focused on general technology adoption for education, greater attention is needed to understand how learners can draw on their lived experiences, contexts, culture, and realities in their interactions with AI-mediated technologies. Additionally, as recent publications have focused on large-scale efforts using AI to reach students in under-resourced, and marginalized contexts [9,12], there is a need to better understand how insights from their culture and contexts can drive culturally responsive human-AI partnerships in learning.

The 2026 edition of the CATS workshop aims to engage interested researchers in a conversation on how to take culture and context into account in the design and operations of learner-AI interactions and to address these questions:

E. G. Blanchard et al. (Eds.): AIED 2026, CCIS 3033, pp. 90–96, 2026.
https://doi.org/10.1007/978-3-032-29794-5_16

- What features of culture are important to consider in the design process of AIED systems?
- Can educational technologies designed and developed in a specific cultural context transfer to other parts of the World and remain effective?
- How can we embed culturally-adaptive mechanisms into intelligent educational technologies?

2 Format

CATS2026 is a workshop proposal that primarily targets the AIED community but welcomes contributors and participants from the L@S and EDM communities. CATS2026 is envisioned as a half-day workshop event. Based on previous editions, we expect the audience to be between 40 and 60 participants. Participation in CATS2026 will be advertised through mailing lists, social media, and professional and academic networks to reach a diverse global audience.

3 Past Editions

The CATS workshop has been held seven times to date, in conjunction with the ITS and AIED conferences: ITS2008, AIED2009, ITS2010, AIED2013, ITS2014, AIED2015, and AIED2024. It has grown in popularity since its first edition –a trend reflected in the increasing number of submissions and steady participation from researchers in the community. During its most recent edition (at AIED 2024 in Brazil), 94 people registered, with around 65 researchers attending on site (the remainder participating online), which made CATS2024 one of the most popular workshops –if not the most popular– of the conference.

This demonstrates that many researchers in our community clearly recognize the relevance of this workshop and the importance of having a venue to discuss culture and AIED in a transversal manner. For many colleagues, it is becoming increasingly crucial to understand and integrate diverse cultural perspectives to ensure that developments, technologies, and methods arising from AIED research are inclusive, equitable, and globally relevant.

4 Organizers

The 8th CATS workshop will be organized by Ivon Arroyo, Emmanuel G. Blanchard, Christine Kwon, and Maria Mercedes T. Rodrigo. Maria and Emmanuel contributed to the creation of the workshop, Ivon has been involved on several occasions (and led similar workshops on Cross-Cultural Differences and Learning Technologies for the Developing World at AIED2013 and ICALT2011), and Christine is bringing fresh ideas to the table. Below, you will find paragraphs summarizing their professional biographies. The four co-organizers are equally involved in the preparation of the workshop; therefore, their information is presented in alphabetical order.

Ivon Arroyo is Professor in the College of Education and the College of Information and Computer Sciences, at the University of Massachusetts Amherst, Massachusetts, USA. Her research in Artificial Intelligence in Education examines how intelligent tutoring systems can support personalized learning through affect modeling, adaptive feedback, and culturally responsive design. Her work explores how AI-driven educational technologies can better account for learners' diverse cultural backgrounds, identities, and contexts to promote equity and meaningful learning. For instance, Dr. Arroyo designs educational technologies that make STEM learning more engaging and accessible for English language learners. In collaboration with colleagues at UMass, she is developing a bilingual digital math tutoring system that allows students to switch between English and Spanish, supporting learners who navigate dual linguistic identities. Funded by the Institute of Diversity Sciences, the project addresses the underrepresentation of Hispanic students in STEM by providing linguistically and culturally responsive resources. That tutoring system integrates bilingual instruction and culturally-sensitive avatars, helping students strengthen math skills while fostering a sense of belonging in STEM. More broadly, Prof. Arroyo has served as PI or co-PI on more than 20 research projects involving the design, development, and research of Advanced Learning Technologies for K-12 and higher education. She has been supported on these projects by the National Science Foundation (including an NSF CAREER award), the Institute of Education Sciences, the Gates Foundation, and seed funding awards from UMass Amherst.

Emmanuel G. Blanchard is an Associate Professor at Le Mans Université, France, and a member of its computer science research laboratory. He is also an Adjunct Professor in the Department of Surgery at McGill University, Canada. He holds a PhD in Computer Science from the Université de Montral and completed a postdoctoral fellowship in the Department of Educational and Counselling Psychology at McGill University. He has previously been a Visiting Researcher at Osaka University, where he focused on formal ontology engineering; a Senior Lecturer in Software Engineering at the Polytechnic of Namibia; and an Assistant Professor in the Department of Architecture, Design and Medialogy at Aalborg University, Denmark. From 2014 to 2023, he was active in the startup ecosystem in Montreal, Canada. His research interests include, but are not limited to, human factors (cognition, motivation, affect, and culture) in relation to technology, expert-centered design, formal ontology engineering, virtual simulations for training and education, and humancomputer interaction more broadly. He co-created the series of international workshops on Culturally-Aware Tutoring Systems, was an invited participant in a Dagstuhl Seminar on Computational Models of Cultural Behaviors for Human-Agent Interactions[1] and served as principal editor of the Handbook of Research on Culturally-Aware Information Systems [3], one of the first publications to examine the links between culture and technology.

[1] See https://www.dagstuhl.de/en/seminars/seminar-calendar/seminar-details/14131.

Christine Kwon is a PhD student in the Human-Computer Interaction Institute at Carnegie Mellon University, advised by Dr. John Stamper and Dr. Amy Ogan. Her research interests center on educational technologies and learning sciences. Her work explores how to improve access to meaningful learning opportunities through educational technologies for marginalized learners. Her research primarily focuses on how low-infrastructure and contextually aligned technologies can support out-of-school learning for learners in underrepresented communities. Her current research investigates learner interactions and experiences with educational courses delivered via radio and mobile phones in Uganda.

Maria Mercedes T. Rodrigo is a professor at the Department of Information Systems and Computer Science, Ateneo de Manila, the Philippines. Her research interests include learning analytics, artificial intelligence in education, technology in education, and educational games. She is the head of the Ateneo Laboratory for the Learning Sciences (ALLS). Since 2007, she has received approximately US$800,000 in research grants from government and non-government organizations. In collaboration with colleagues and students, Dr. Rodrigo has published on computers and related technologies in education, human-computer interaction, computer science education and others. Her current research projects include the establishment of a virtual, augmented, and mixed reality laboratory at the Ateneo de Manila University, analyses of learning management systems logs collected during the pandemic, deployment of Minecraft to increase STEM interest among Filipino learners, and an eye tracking study on programmer reading and debugging skills. She serves on the editorial boards of several high-impact journals including Internet and Higher Education and Research and Practice in Technology-Enhanced Learning. Dr. Rodrigo is on the Executive Committee of the Artificial Intelligence Education Society. In 2021, Dr. Rodrigo received the Distinguished Researcher Award from the Asia-Pacific Society for Computers in Education (APSCE).

5 Program Committee

CATS program committees have always been tailored to express cultural diversity through their members, which is a prerequisite for the workshop's credibility given its theme (culture and AIED). The CATS2026 program committee is no exception and includes researchers not only from the leading countries in the AIED community, but also academics from less present countries. Similarly, this committee is made up mainly of members of our community (senior and emerging scholars) as well as a few researchers from related disciplines (e.g., HCI). Finally, several of these PC members have been involved in previous editions of CATS. The list of program committee members is presented below:

- Danielle Allessio, University of Massachusetts Amherst, USA
- Faisal Bin Badar, EDvantage Digital Learning System, Australia
- Geoffray Bonnin, University of Nancy, France

- Charibeth Cheng, De La Salle University, Philippines
- Bruce McLaren, Carnegie Mellon University, USA
- Isabela Gasparini, Santa Catarina State University, Brazil
- Sai Gattupalli, University of Massachusetts Amherst, USA &India
- Gahgene Gweon, Seoul National University, South Korea
- Seiji Isotani, University of Pennsylvania, USA
- Shimin Kai, Ministry of Education, Singapore
- Shamya Karumbaiah, University of Wisconsin-Madison, USA
- Vwen Yen Alwyn Lee, National Institute of Education, Singapore
- Paul Libbrecht, IU International University of Applied Science, Germany
- Xiner (Rachel) Liu, University of Pennsylvania, USA
- Shitanshu Mishra, UNESCO MGIEP, India
- Riichiro Mizoguchi, Japan Advanced Institute of Science and Technology, Japan
- Phaedra Mohammed, University of the West Indies, Trinidad and Tobago
- Benjamin Nye, University of Southern California, USA
- Jaclyn Ocumpaugh, University of Houston, USA
- Amy Ogan, Carnegie Mellon University, USA
- Prajakt Pande, Aarhus University, Denmark
- Genaro Rebolledo-Mendez, AffectSense, Mexico
- Davide Taibi, National Research Council of Italy, Italy
- May Marie Talandron-Felipe, University of Science and Technology of Southern Philippines, Philippines
- Beverly Woolf, University of Massachusetts Amherst, USA

6 Conclusion

The CATS workshop has been designed as a half day face-2-face event with remote facilitations to help participants (especially newcomers) develop a richer, and more nuanced understanding of the challenges and opportunities of taking culture into account in AIED.

With its different sessions with complementary formats and objectives, this event will help AIED researchers deepen their knowledge and understanding of existing CATS initiatives and perspectives. We hope that new ideas will be sparked by these engaging discussions, and that international collaborations will emerge from this event.

References

1. Banawan, M., Rodrigo, M.M., Andres, J.M.: An investigation of frustration among students using physics playground. In: International Conference on Computers in Education (2015)
2. Blanchard, E.G.: Socio-cultural imbalances in AIED research: investigations, implications and opportunities. Int. J. Artif. Intell. Educ. **25**(2), 204–228 (2015)

3. Blanchard, E.G., Allard, D.: Handbook of Research on Culturally-aware Information Technology (2011)
4. Blanchard, E.G., Mohammed, P.: On cultural intelligence in LLM-based chatbots: implications for artificial intelligence in education. In: Olney, A.M., Chounta, IA., Liu, Z., Santos, O.C., Bittencourt, I.I. (eds.) AIED 2024. LNCS, vol. 14829, pp. 439–453. Springer, Cham (2024). https://doi.org/10.1007/978-3-031-64302-6_31
5. Blanchard, E.G., Ogan, A.: Infusing cultural awareness into intelligent tutoring systems for a globalized world. In: kambou, R., Bourdeau, J., Mizoguchi, R. (eds.) Advances in Intelligent Tutoring Systems. SCI, vol. 308, pp. 485–505. Springer, Heidelberg (2010). https://doi.org/10.1007/978-3-642-14363-2_24
6. Esclamado, M.A., Rodrigo, M.M.T.: Are all who wander lost? An exploratory analysis of learner traversals of minecraft worlds. In: Rodrigo, M.M., Matsuda, N., Cristea, A.I., Dimitrova, V. (eds.) AIED 2022. LNCS, vol. 13356, pp. 263–266. Springer, Cham (2022). https://doi.org/10.1007/978-3-031-11647-6_48
7. Henrich, J., Heine, S.J., Norenzayan, A.: Most people are not weird. Nature **466**(7302), 29–29 (2010)
8. Hofstede, G.: Cultural differences in teaching and learning. Int. J. Intercult. Relat. **10**(3), 301–320 (1986)
9. Isotani, S., Bittencourt, I.I., Challco, G.C., Dermeval, D., Mello, R.F.: AIED unplugged: leapfrogging the digital divide to reach the underserved. In: Wang, N., Rebolledo-Mendez, G., Dimitrova, V., Matsuda, N., Santos, O.C. (eds.) AIED 2023. CCIS, vol. 1831, pp. 772–779. Springer, Cham (2023). https://doi.org/10.1007/978-3-031-36336-8_118
10. Karumbaiah, S., Ocumpaugh, J., Baker, R.S.: Context matters: differing implications of motivation and help-seeking in educational technology. Int. J. Artif. Intell. Educ. **32**(3), 685–724 (2022)
11. Linch, M., Salikhova, N., Eryemeeva, A.: Basic needs in other cultures: using qualitative methods to study key issues in self-determination theory research. Psychology. J. High. Sch. Econ. **17**(1), 133–144 (2020)
12. McReynolds, A.A., Naderzad, S.P., Goswami, M., Mostow, J.: Toward learning at scale in developing countries: lessons from the global learning XPRIZE field study. In: Proceedings of the Seventh ACM Conference on Learning@ Scale, pp. 175–183 (2020)
13. Melis, E., Goguadze, G., Libbrecht, P., Ullrich, C.: Culturally aware mathematics education technology. In: Handbook of Research on Culturally-Aware Information Technology: Perspectives and Models, pp. 543–557. IGI Global Scientific Publishing (2011)
14. Mesquita, B.: Between us: How Cultures Create Emotions. WW Norton & Company (2022)
15. Nisbett, R.E., Norenzayan, A.: Culture and cognition. In: Stevens' Handbook of Experimental Psychology, vol. 2, pp. 561–597 (2002)
16. Nye, B.D.: Intelligent tutoring systems by and for the developing world: a review of trends and approaches for educational technology in a global context. Int. J. Artif. Intell. Educ. **25**(2), 177–203 (2015)
17. Ogan, A., Yarzebinski, E., Fernández, P., Casas, I.: Cognitive tutor use in Chile: understanding classroom and lab culture. In: Conati, C., Heffernan, N., Mitrovic, A., Verdejo, M.F. (eds.) AIED 2015. LNCS (LNAI), vol. 9112, pp. 318–327. Springer, Cham (2015). https://doi.org/10.1007/978-3-319-19773-9_32
18. Pusch, M.D.: Multicultural Education: A Cross Cultural Training Approach. ERIC (1979)

19. Rodrigo, M.M.T., Baker, R.S., Rossi, L.: Student off-task behavior in computer-based learning in the Philippines: comparison to prior research in the USA. Teach. Coll. Rec. **115**(10), 1–27 (2013)
20. Saal, P.E., Chetty, K., Ntshayintshayi, N., Moosa, T., Masuku, N.: A scoping review of the integration of artificial intelligence in primary and secondary schools from 2020 to 2024: policy implications for South Africa. J. Educ. (98), 62–85 (2025). University of KwaZulu-Natal

Small Language Models for Education: Opportunities, Challenges, and a Shared Research Agenda

Yumou Wei[1(✉)], Steven Moore[2], Paulo F. Carvalho[1], John Stamper[1], Christopher Brooks[3], and Michael Liut[4]

[1] Carnegie Mellon University, Pittsburgh, PA 15213, USA
smoore59@gmu.edu , jstamper@andrew.cmu.edu, brooksch@umich.edu
[2] George Mason University, Fairfax, VA 22030, USA
pcarvalh@andrew.cmu.edu
[3] University of Michigan, Ann Arbor, MI 48109, USA
michael.liut@utoronto.ca
[4] University of Toronto Mississauga, Mississauga, ON L5L 1C6, Canada

Abstract. Small language models (SLMs) are emerging as a promising alternative to large language models for educational applications. This workshop aims to explore the potential of SLMs in education, focusing on their unique advantages and the challenges they present. By bringing together researchers from the AIED, EDM, and L@S communities, we hope to foster interdisciplinary collaboration and identify new research directions that leverage the strengths of each community to improve learning outcomes. The expected results of the workshop include a comprehensive understanding of the current state of small language models, the identification of key research challenges and opportunities, and the development of a shared research agenda that guides future work.

Keywords: Small Language Models · Accessible EdTech · Shared Agenda

1 Introduction

We plan to organize a **full-day workshop**[1] that brings researchers from the Artificial Intelligence in Education (AIED), Educational Data Mining (EDM), and Learning at Scale (L@S) communities to **explore the potential of small language models (SLMs) in education**. We define SLMs as open-weight language models with fewer than 10 billion parameters [12], in contrast to large language models (LLMs) with hundreds of billions of parameters that have dominated recent discussions in the field. Capable of being deployed locally on consumer-grade hardware, SLMs offer a unique opportunity for research communities to develop personalized, accessible, and privacy-preserving educational

[1] Workshop website: https://slm4ed-workshop.github.io/

E. G. Blanchard et al. (Eds.): AIED 2026, CCIS 3033, pp. 97–101, 2026.
https://doi.org/10.1007/978-3-032-29794-5_17

technologies. The purpose of this workshop is to foster interdisciplinary collaboration and develop a shared research agenda that takes advantage of the strengths of each community to address the unique challenges and opportunities presented by SLMs in education. By focusing on the intersection of these three communities, we hope to identify innovative applications of SLMs, develop new methodologies for their evaluation and deployment, and ultimately contribute to the development of effective educational technologies accessible to a wide range of learners.

We welcome researchers and practitioners from all three communities: AIED, EDM, and L@S. We believe that the integration of SLMs in education presents a multifaceted challenge that requires the combined expertise of these communities to address effectively. AIED researchers will bring insights into instructional design and the development of intelligent tutoring systems, while EDM researchers will contribute their expertise in data mining and analysis to understand how SLMs can be fine-tuned and evaluated using educational data. L@S researchers will provide valuable perspectives on the scalability and deployment of SLMs in large-scale educational settings. We expect to attract around 30 participants, including researchers, educators, and industry professionals interested in the emerging applications of SLMs in education. This workshop will provide a unique opportunity for attendees to engage in interdisciplinary discussions, share their research, and collaborate to develop a shared research agenda for SLMs in education.

2 Theme and Goals

It is an exciting time for the AIED, EDM, and L@S communities, as rapid advances in natural language processing (NLP) have opened up new possibilities for personalized learning, intelligent tutoring systems, and educational content generation. However, the integration of NLP technologies into education has largely been dominated by large language models (LLMs) with hundreds of billion parameters. The GPT model family [3], for example, has become nearly synonymous with "LLM" in public discourses, and the AIED community has been no exception [12]. A quick, conservative search of "large language model" or "LLM" in the AIED 2025 proceedings [1] reveals that 157 of 259 full and short papers (60.6%) contained these two keywords and that 93 of those 157 papers (59.2%) also mentioned "GPT". Although these LLMs have demonstrated impressive NLP capabilities, they are often proprietary and require significant computational resources to deploy. In addition, their adoption in education is constrained by privacy concerns, high inference costs, and latency issues, which can limit their accessibility and effectiveness in educational settings, especially in environments with limited resources [12].

In contrast, small language models, which we define as **open-weight language models with fewer than 10 billion parameters**, have only recently begun to gain attention in the community. SLMs offer several advantages over LLMs, including lower computational requirements, reduced inference costs, and the ability to be deployed locally on consumer-grade hardware [12]. This makes SLMs particularly attractive for educational applications [10], where privacy concerns and resource constraints are often significant barriers to adoption [9]. In addition, SLMs can be efficiently fine-tuned on high-quality domain-specific educational data to provide accurate curriculum-aligned responses [5] and have great potential to build flexible AI agents [2].

This workshop aims to explore the potential of SLMs in education, focusing on their unique advantages and the challenges they present. By bringing together experts from the AIED, EDM, and L@S communities, we hope to foster interdisciplinary collaboration and identify new research directions that leverage the strengths of SLMs to improve learning outcomes. The expected results of the workshop include a comprehensive understanding of the current state of SLMs in education, the identification of key research challenges and opportunities, and the development of a shared research agenda that can guide future work.

3 Expected Outcomes and Contributions

The expected outcomes of this workshop include:

- A comprehensive understanding of the current state of SLM research in education, including recent advancements, ongoing challenges, and potential applications.
- Identification of key research challenges and opportunities related to SLMs in education, informed by interdisciplinary discussions among AIED, EDM, and L@S researchers.
- Development of a shared research agenda that can guide future work in this area, which will be documented in a white paper co-authored by all participants.
- Strengthened interdisciplinary collaborations between researchers from the AIED, EDM, and L@S communities, as well as with participants from related fields such as human-computer interaction and machine learning.
- Dissemination of the workshop's findings and outputs through publications in the CEUR Workshop Proceedings[2] and a relevant journal, as well as through the workshop's website.

We believe that these outcomes will make significant contributions to the research communities by providing a clear agenda for the integration of SLMs into education. The insights gained from this workshop will help inform the design, development, and deployment of SLM-based educational applications accessible to a wide range of learners. In addition, the interdisciplinary collaborations that are fostered by this workshop will help drive innovation and advance research in this burgeoning area.

[2] https://ceur-ws.org/

4 Program Committee

The program committee of this workshop includes a PhD student, an early-career researcher, and four senior researchers from the AIED, EDM, and L@S communities. We have a track record of organizing successful workshops at major conferences in the field [4,6–8], and we are committed to fostering an inclusive and collaborative environment that encourages participation from researchers at all stages of their career. Our combined expertise in educational technology, data mining, and learning analytics will enable us to facilitate meaningful discussions and guide the development of a comprehensive research agenda for SLMs in education. The biographies of the organizers are as follows:

- **Yumou Wei** (Workshop Chair) is a PhD student in the Human-Computer Interaction Institute at Carnegie Mellon University. His research focuses on building educational technologies that support mastery learning at scale. He has published papers in the EDM and Learning Analytics and Knowledge (LAK) conferences describing innovative uses of SLMs for KC modeling [11] and question generation [13].
- **Steven Moore** is an Assistant Professor in the Department of Information Sciences and Technology at George Mason University. He studies how to design educational technologies that improve student learning and how people use AI to learn.
- **Paulo F. Carvalho** is an Assistant Professor in the Human-Computer Interaction Institute at Carnegie Mellon University. His research sits at the intersection of learning science and educational technology, investigating how the cognitive, metacognitive, and motivational processes of learners can inform the design of more effective, practice-first learning technologies.
- **John Stamper** is an Associate Professor in the Human-Computer Interaction Institute at Carnegie Mellon University. His research focuses on using big data collected from educational systems to improve student learning.
- **Christopher Brooks** is an Associate Professor in the School of Information at the University of Michigan. He builds and studies the effects of educational technologies in higher education and informal learning environments, with a particular domain focus on data science education and methodological interests in predictive modeling, learning analytics, and collaborative learning.
- **Michael Liut** is an Assistant Professor, Teaching Stream (Computer Science) in the Department of Mathematical and Computational Sciences, University of Toronto Mississauga. His research focuses on the design and development of educational technologies that support learning in computer science, with a particular interest in the use of AI and machine learning to enhance student learning outcomes.

This is the first edition of the workshop, and we hope to establish it as an annual event that continues to foster interdisciplinary collaboration and advance research on small language models in education.

References

1. Artificial Intelligence in Education: 26th International Conference, AIED 2025, Palermo, Italy, 22–26 July 2025, Proceedings, Part VI. Springer, Heidelberg (2025)
2. Belcak, P., et al.: Small language models are the future of agentic AI (2025). https://doi.org/10.48550/arXiv.2506.02153. https://arxiv.org/abs/2506.02153
3. Brown, T., et al.: Language models are few-shot learners. In: Larochelle, H., Ranzato, M., Hadsell, R., Balcan, M., Lin, H. (eds.) Advances in Neural Information Processing Systems, vol. 33, pp. 1877–1901. Curran Associates, Inc. (2020)
4. Kizilcec, R.F., et al.: Applications of generative AI to support teaching and learning in higher education: a half-day workshop. In: Cristea, A.I., Walker, E., Lu, Y., Santos, O.C., Isotani, S. (eds.) Artificial Intelligence in Education. Posters and Late Breaking Results, Workshops and Tutorials, Industry and Innovation Tracks, Practitioners, Doctoral Consortium, Blue Sky, and WideAIED, pp. 267–274. Springer, Cham (2025)
5. Koutcheme, C., Woodrow, J., Piech, C.: Aligning small language models for programming feedback: towards scalable coding support in a massive global course. In: Proceedings of the 57th ACM Technical Symposium on Computer Science Education V.1, SIGCSE TS 2026, pp. 610–616. Association for Computing Machinery, New York (2026). https://doi.org/10.1145/3770762.3772539
6. Moore, S., Singh, A., Khosravi, H., Denny, P., Brooks, C., Stamper, J.: Partnerships for cocreating educational content. In: LAK23 Workshop on Partnerships for Cocreating Educational Content (2023). https://stevenjamesmoore.com/assets/papers/lak23_workshop_moore.pdf
7. Moore, S., et al.: LearnerSourcing: student-generated content @ scale: 3rd annual workshop. In: Proceedings of the Twelfth ACM Conference on Learning @ Scale, L@S 2025, pp. 410–413. Association for Computing Machinery, New York (2025). https://doi.org/10.1145/3698205.3733963
8. Moore, S., et al.: Empowering education with LLMs - the next-gen interface and content generation. In: Wang, N., Rebolledo-Mendez, G., Dimitrova, V., Matsuda, N., Santos, O.C. (eds.) Artificial Intelligence in Education. Posters and Late Breaking Results, Workshops and Tutorials, Industry and Innovation Tracks, Practitioners, Doctoral Consortium and Blue Sky, pp. 32–37. Springer, Cham (2023)
9. Reich, J., Ito, M.: From good intentions to real outcomes: equity by design in learning technologies. In: Fitzgerald, W., Burns, J., Sonwalkar, N., Urry, J. (eds.) The Digital Learning Challenge: Obstacles to Educational Uses of Copyrighted Material in the Digital Age, pp. 1–42. The Digital Media and Learning Research Hub, Irvine (2017). https://clalliance.org/publications/good-intentions-real-outcomes-equity-design-learning-technologies/
10. UNESCO: Small language models (SLMs): a cheaper, greener route into AI (2024). https://www.unesco.org/en/articles/small-language-models-slms-cheaper-greener-route-ai. Accessed 11 Nov 2025
11. Wei, Y., Carvalho, P., Stamper, J.: Kcluster: an LLM-based clustering approach to knowledge component discovery. In: Proceedings of the 18th International Conference on Educational Data Mining, pp. 228–240. International Educational Data Mining Society (2025). https://doi.org/10.5281/zenodo.15870197
12. Wei, Y., Carvalho, P., Stamper, J.: Small but significant: on the promise of small language models for accessible AIED (2025). https://arxiv.org/abs/2505.08588
13. Wei, Y., Stamper, J., Carvalho, P.F.: Generate-then-validate: a novel question generation approach using small language models (2026). https://arxiv.org/abs/2512.10110

Advancing the Science of Human and AI Tutoring Through Shared Infrastructure: A Collaborative Workshop

Kirk Vanacore[1,6(✉)], Danielle R. Thomas[2,6,11], Ana Ribeiro[3,7], Julian Bernado[3,7], Chelsea Chandler[4], Candida Crawford[12], Doug Pietrzak[6,8], John Whitmer[9], Jason Godfrey[10], Susanna Loeb[3,7], Kenneth R. Koedinger[2,6,11], Justin Reich[5,6], Rachel Slama[1,6], and René F. Kizilcec[1,6]

[1] Cornell University, Ithaca, NY, USA
kpv27@cornell.edu
[2] Carnegie Mellon University, Pittsburgh, PA, USA
[3] Stanford University, Stanford, CA, USA
[4] University of Colorado Boulder, Boulder, CO, USA
[5] Massachusetts Institute of Technology, Cambridge, MA, USA
[6] National Tutoring Observatory, New York, USA
[7] SCALE Initiative, Stanford, USA
[8] FreshCognate, Teaneck, USA
[9] Learning Data Insights, Davis, USA
[10] Accelerate, Houston, USA
[11] Personalized Learning Squared, Pittsburgh, USA
[12] Third Space Learning, London, UK

Abstract. High-quality tutoring is among the most impactful instructional interventions in education. However, these programs remain difficult to scale effectively, and the specific "moves" underlying quality tutoring are understudied due to historical data scarcity. Despite extensive research, progress is hindered by challenges in data de-identification, multimodal analysis, and the predictive modeling of student outcomes. The emergence of Artificial Intelligence is fundamentally shifting the capacity to scale and study tutoring, offering transformative potential alongside significant pitfalls. This workshop, led by the National Tutoring Observatory, the SCALE Initiative, and the LEVI HAT project, brings together researchers, providers, and practitioners to explore human and AI tutoring systems. Featuring sessions on open-source data, infrastructure benchmarks, and synthetic students, the workshop aims to foster collaboration that ensures the future of instruction is grounded in rigorous empirical science.

Keywords: Tutoring · Learning Analytics · Science of Teaching · Open Science · AI Annotation · AI Tutors · AI Infrastructure

E. G. Blanchard et al. (Eds.): AIED 2026, CCIS 3033, pp. 102–110, 2026.
https://doi.org/10.1007/978-3-032-29794-5_18

1 Significance and Relevance

Interest in tutoring is surging across the AIED, EDM, and L@S communities [1–4], yet a systemic understanding of the granular instructional "moves" that define effective teaching remains elusive [5,6]. While high-impact educators significantly alter student trajectories [7], the specific interactional mechanisms facilitating these outcomes are insufficiently theorized and currently buried within disparate, unanalyzed datasets. As the field shifts toward conversational AI, robust evaluation and quality assurance systems are essential to ensure the next generation of intelligent tutoring platforms achieves maximal impact [8].

Historically, scientific breakthroughs have relied on shared observation infrastructure; just as the Kepler Space Telescope rendered the invisible visible for astronomers [9], learning scientists now require comparable "data observatories" to allow researchers access to difficult-to-unlock the principles of impactful teaching. By systematically capturing improvisational instructional moves and linking them to longitudinal learning outcomes, the field can transition from anecdotal evidence toward a rigorous, predictive science of instruction. The potential for such discovery cannot be realized through existing, isolated data, but requires a unified framework for collaborative analysis.

Building last year's *Advancing the Science of Teaching with Tutoring Data: A Collaborative Workshop with the National Tutoring Observatory* at Learning@Scale [10], this workshop convenes a multi-disciplinary cohort of researchers, developers, and practitioners who are building and leveraging large-scale datasets and scalable AI infrastructure. Our collective objective is to catalyze a paradigm shift in the tutoring landscape, using empirical evidence to inform the architectural design of the next generation of AI-driven instructional tools. By bridging the gap between research and practice, we aim to transform millions of untapped tutoring interactions into a shared foundation for advancing the science of teaching at scale.

2 AI Infrastructure Projects

2.1 The National Tutoring Observatory (NTO)

The NTO is pioneering research infrastructure designed to advance the science of teaching by providing large-scale, real-time data on tutoring interactions. Identified as a strategic priority in the 2022 Learning@Scale Decadal Survey, the NTO addresses the long-standing need for fine-grained data on educators in-the-moment actions linked to student outcomes [11]. At its core is the Million Tutoring Moves (MTM) repository, a comprehensive, multimodal pool of datasets that capture the dynamic, improvisational teaching strategies that drive effective student engagement. The NTO utilizes a multi-tier AI infrastructure designed to transform fragmented tutoring sessions into a unified, research-ready repository. For example, the NTO recently released *Sandpiper*[1], an open-source middleware

[1] https://app.nationaltutoringobservatory.org/.

that ingests data from educational dialogue, like tutoring sessions, and normalizes them into a standardized format, allowing optimized AI systems to flexibly annotate the data based on specific user parameters. This system leverages AI orchestration innovations, which improve classification accuracy [12]. To expand this capability, the NTO is developing advanced multimodal ingestion pipelines that employ a modular system of audio and video processing to extract relevant instructional features. Because the NTO seeks to release data in the MTM dataset, it employs de-identification technology that ensures strict compliance with the Family Educational Rights and Privacy Act (FERPA) and the General Data Protection Regulation (GDPR) by removing sensitive identifiers while preserving the pedagogical body language and prosody essential for studying effective instructional moves [13].

2.2 SCALE Initiative

Housed at Stanford Universitys Graduate School of Education and part of the Stanford Accelerator for Learning, the Systems Change Advancing Learning and Equity (SCALE) Initiative is dedicated to transforming educational opportunity by leveraging knowledge for better education decision-making [14]. SCALE conducts rigorous research, identifies and supports promising solutions, and engages decision makers to integrate research, policy, and practice across critical issues in K12 education. A key strand of SCALEs work focuses on tutoring through the National Student Support Accelerator (NSSA). In collaboration with tutoring providers and school districts, SCALE carries out research "with the field" and translates evidence into practical tools and strategic advising. More than 20 research partnerships nationwide support this work and provide insights into both the tutoring program features that drive impact and common implementation challenges districts face and how to overcome those challenges. SCALE is also at the forefront of exploring AI applications for tutoring: alongside districts, providers, and technology companies, SCALE researchers study how AI tools shape tutors practices with the aim of improving tutoring effectiveness and student learning. Central to this effort is developing new, research-rooted measures of instructional practice, student engagement, and learning using natural language data from educatorstudent interactions that can validate effective tutor moves and enable faster research cycles that keep pace with rapid AI advancement.

2.3 LEVI HAT Project

The LEVI HAT project is a University of Colorado Boulder-led initiative that advances Hybrid Human-AI Tutoring (HAT) to improve the quality and scalability of high-dosage math tutoring for middle school students from underserved communities [15,16]. Developed within the context of the Learning Engineering Virtual Institute (LEVI) Math program, HAT addresses a central barrier to scale: maintaining consistent tutoring quality across a large workforce. The platform uses secure, AI-supported analysis of tutoring session discourse to generate structured feedback for instructional coaches, tutors, and students. According to their theory of change, providing coaches with AI-based feedback can strengthen tutors' capacity to lead academically rich and rigorous mathematical discussions while build caring and equitable learning environments, which will result in improved student engagement and learning outcomes. LEVI HAT has been developed in close collaboration with Saga Education, a national tutoring provider serving predominantly low-income students in Title I schools. By embedding AI-generated analytics into tutor and coaching routines, HAT functions as an assistant, reducing variability in tutor practice while preserving the relational core of human tutoring. Through ongoing implementation studies, the University of Colorado Boulder team is evaluating whether this hybrid human-AI infrastructure can sustain tutoring quality and student learning gains with programs at scale.

3 Tutoring Partners

These AI Infrastructure projects operate on a partnership model that bridges the gap between educational service providers and academic research by acting as a trusted intermediary. These mutually beneficial partnerships grant researchers access to diverse, large-scale datasets to uncover effective instructional principles, while providing tutors with actionable insights and AI tools to enhance pedagogical impact across various subjects and socioeconomic contexts. The following tutoring providers present key partners who will participate in this workshop:

Carnegie Learning. A pioneer in AI-driven instruction that provides data from its MATHia, which also provides students with access to remote human tutoring.

Eedi. A diagnostic assessment and adaptive learning platform that allows students to access human tutoring while working to resolve misconceptions.

Littera. An edtech company that provides a comprehensive platform and services for K-12 school districts to implement, manage, and scale high-impact, virtual, and in-person tutoring.

Personalized Learning Squared (PLUS). A Carnegie Mellon University initiative that offers data on "human-in-the-loop" tutoring models, where human educators augment intelligent tutoring systems.

Saga Education. A national leader in high-dosage remote tutoring at scale that provides high-fidelity data from professional and near-peer mentors working in high-needs K-12 environments.

StepUp. A non-profit organization providing free, one-on-one virtual tutoring and mentorship to students in grades 26, primarily focusing on math and reading for underserved communities, using a hybrid model of trained volunteers/college students and AI-powered, adaptive learning software to provide two sessions per week.

Third Space Learning. A large-scale online provider contributing a vast longitudinal record of 1-on-1 audio and text interactions focused on primary and secondary numeracy.
UPchieve. A non-profit platform providing on-demand, 24/7 tutoring that helps the NTO study "just-in-time" learning interactions for low-income high school students.

4 Full-Day Workshop

Table 1 presents the tentative schedule for this full day workshop.

Table 1. Tentative Workshop Schedule: Demos, Presentations, and Panels

Time	Session Topic	Speaker/Chair
09:00–09:45	Welcome & Introductions	NTO
AI Infrastructure Projects Overviews & Interactive Sessions		
9:45–10:30	Finding Impactful Tutor Moves	NTO
10:30–11:15	A/B Testing Tutor Moves	SCALE Initiative
11:15–12:00	AI-Enabled Tutor Coaching	LEVI HAT Project
12:00–1:00	Lunch	
Tutoring Provider Research & Demos		
1:00–1:30	Human to AI Tutoring	Third Space Learning
1:30–3:00	Interactive Sessions & Demos	Tutoring Providers
Panel Discussions		
3:00–3:30	K-12 AI Infrastructure	Learning Data Insights
3:454:15	Practitioner Needs Panel	NTO
4:15–4:45	Funder Panel	NTO
4:45–5:00	Closing Remarks	SCALE Initiative

4.1 AI Infrastructure Projects Overviews and Interactive Sessions

The NTO, SCALE Initiative, and LEVI HAT will provide overviews of their projects, their current research, and the infrastructure. This will lead to interactive sessions after lunch, which will include annotation of the MTM using the NTO's *Sandpiper* application, developing measure schemas, iterating, and producing predictive diagnostics from classifiers with SCALE, and live demonstrations of the LEVI HAT project's AI-enabled tutoring discourse analytics pipeline.

4.2 Tutoring Provider Research and Demos

This session will begin with a presentation on approaches to moving from human tutoring at scale to conversational AI tutoring from Candida Crawford, Third Space Learning's Chief Learning Officer and Director of AI Learning Design. Then, leading tutoring organizations, including Saga Education, UPchieve, and Carnegie Learning, will lead interactive demos and presentations alongside research partners. Providers will showcase their current digital platforms, highlight recent impactful research projects, and describe the unique challenges of delivering high-quality tutoring at scale. Presentations will focus on the data capture mechanisms used in real-world settings and the specific pedagogical strategies—such as scaffolding and error correction—that these organizations prioritize. These demos serve to ground the technical infrastructure discussions in the practical realities of K-12 and higher-education tutoring environments.

4.3 Panel Discussions

The workshop concludes with three strategic panel discussions focusing on the future of educational AI. First, Learning Data Insights and Digital Promise will lead a session on current and future AI infrastructure projects. This is followed by an NTO-moderated panel of tutors and administrators addressing "usability-in-the-loop," specifically how AI can support human educators through real-time pedagogical prompts and culturally responsive feedback while reducing administrative burdens. The final session brings together representatives from the Bill & Melinda Gates Foundation, the Chan Zuckerberg Initiative, and Accelerate to explore the strategic funding landscape. This closing discussion will highlight how shared repositories, open-source benchmarks, and cross-sector collaboration can transition educational research from small-scale pilots to national-level infrastructure.

4.4 Intended Audience and Expected Participation

This full-day workshop is designed for researchers and practitioners across the AIED, EDM, and L@S communities who are engaged in studying or building human and AI-supported tutoring systems. The intended audience includes learning scientists, educational data miners, AI and machine learning researchers, tutoring providers, instructional designers, district leaders, and funders interested in scalable instructional infrastructure. The NTO is providing funding to support tutoring providers' travel. The workshop aims to foster cross-community dialogue around shared data standards, benchmarks, and research infrastructure. Based on the previous workshop and the broad relevance of AI-supported tutoring across these venues, we anticipate approximately 5070 participants.

5 Outcomes and Contributions

This workshop will generate actionable insights and catalyze collaboration to advance large-scale tutoring research. Participants will refine methods for capturing and analyzing tutoring interactions at scale, strengthening frameworks for data collection, annotation, and predictive modeling. By convening experts in AI, learning analytics, and education, the workshop will surface concrete strategies for improving tutoring effectiveness, integrating data into interoperable systems, and addressing challenges of standardization, accessibility, and bias. Through focused, interdisciplinary exchange, the workshop aims to shape both the research agenda and practical implementation of AI-driven tutoring.

Author Biographies

Kirk Vanacore is an Assistant Research Professor at Cornell University and the Research Director of the NTO, focusing on studying impactful AI and human tutoring.
Danielle R. Thomas is a System Scientist at Carnegie Mellon University and Director of Research to Practice at the NTO, specializing in the design and implementation of AI-driven tutoring systems within the PLUS initiative.
Ana Riberio is a Senior Research Associate at Stanford Universitys SCALE Initiative, dedicated to improving educational equity through scalable instructional practices.
Julian Bernado is a Senior Research Data Analyst at the SCALE Initiative at Stanford University, applying traditional causal inference methods with AI methods for text analysis.
Chelsea Chandler is a doctoral student at the University of Colorado Boulder whose work explores natural language processing and its applications in educational environments.
Candida Crawford serves as Third Space Learning's Chief Learning Officer and Director of AI Learning Design.
Doug Pietrzak is the founder of FreshCognate and a Technical Director with the NTO, focusing on technical architecture for learning data systems.
John Whitmer is Senior Researcher and Founder of Learning Data Insight and Senior Fellow with the Federation of American Scientists, who specializes in using large-scale analytics to improve student outcomes.
Jason Godfrey is a Director of Data Science at Accelerate, working on data science and AI projects that shape institution, state, and federal policy.
Susanna Loeb is a professor at Stanford University and Director of the SCALE Initiative, renowned for her research on education policy and its impact on student trajectories.
Kenneth R. Koedinger is a professor at Carnegie Mellon University and a pioneer in the development of cognitive tutors and the study of human-computer interaction.
Justin Reich is an Associate Professor at the Massachusetts Institute of Technology and Director of the Teaching Systems Lab, focusing on the future of learning in a networked world.
Rachel Slama is the Associate Director of the Future of Learning Lab at Cornell University and the Partnership Director of the NTO who investigates the implementation and efficacy of large-scale tutoring interventions.

Ren F. Kizilcec is an Associate Professor at Cornell University, Director of the Future of Learning Lab, and Primary Investigator of the NTO, where he studies the impact of technology on equity and performance in education.

References

1. Borchers, C., Yang, K., Lin, J., Rummel, N., Koedinger, K.R., Aleven, V.: Combining dialog acts and skill modeling: what chat interactions enhance learning rates during AI-supported peer tutoring?. Int. Educ. Data Min. Soc. (2024)
2. Pal Chowdhury, S., Zouhar, V., Sachan, M.: Autotutor meets large language models: a language model tutor with rich pedagogy and guardrails. In: Proceedings of the 11th ACM Conference on Learning @ Scale, pp. 5–15 (2024)
3. Chen, E., et al.: VTutor for high-impact tutoring at scale. In: Proceedings of the 12th ACM Conference on Learning @ Scale, pp. 320–324. ACM, New York (2025). https://doi.org/10.1145/3698205.3733948
4. Scarlatos, A., Baker, R.S., Lan, A.: Exploring knowledge tracing in tutor-student dialogues using LLMs. In: Proceedings of the 15th International Learning Analytics and Knowledge Conference, pp. 249–259 (2025)
5. Demszky, D., Hill, H.: The NCTE transcripts: a dataset of elementary math classroom transcripts, arXiv:2211.11772 (2022)
6. Suresh, A., Jacobs, J., Harty, C., Perkoff, M., Martin, J.H., Sumner, T.: The TalkMoves dataset: K-12 mathematics lesson transcripts annotated for teacher and student discursive moves. In: Proceedings of the 13th Language Resources and Evaluation Conference, pp. 4654–4662 (2022)
7. Hattie, J.: Teachers make a difference, what is the research evidence? In: ACER Research Conference, pp. 1–17 (2003)
8. Vanacore, K., Baker, R.S., Closser, A.H., Roschelle, J.: The Path to Conversational AI Tutors: Integrating Tutoring Best Practices and Targeted Technologies to Produce Scalable AI Agents (2026). http://arxiv.org/abs/2602.19303
9. Borucki, W.J., et al.: Kepler planet-detection mission: introduction and first results. Science **327**(5968), 977–980 (2010)
10. Thomas, D.R., et al.: Advancing the science of teaching with tutoring data. In: Proceedings of the 12th ACM Conference on Learning @ Scale, pp. 404–406 (2025). https://doi.org/10.35542/osf.io/kcqb9
11. Kizilcec, R.F., Reich, J.: Learning@Scale Inaugural Decadal Survey: Summary of Findings. OSF (2024). https://osf.io/preprints/edarxiv/kcqb9_v1
12. Ahtisham, B., Vanacore, K., Lee, J., Zhou, Z., Pietrzak, D., Kizilcec, R.F.: AI Annotation Orchestration: Evaluating LLM verifiers to Improve the Quality of LLM Annotations in Learning Analytics (2025). http://arxiv.org/abs/2511.09785
13. Vanacore, K., Thomas, D.R., Smith, D., Groot, B., Reich, J., Kizilcec, R.: A Causal Framework for Estimating Heterogeneous Effects of On-Demand Tutoring. arXiv:2602.19296 (2026)
14. Systems Change Advancing Learning and Equity: Stanford SCALE Initiative (2026). https://scale.stanford.edu/. Accessed 01 Mar 2026

15. Booth, B.M., Jacobs, J., Bush, J.B., Milne, B., Fischaber, T., D'Mello, S.K.: Human-tutor Coaching Technology (HTCT): automated discourse analytics in a coached tutoring model. In: Proceedings of the 14th Learning Analytics and Knowledge Conference, pp. 725–735. ACM, New York (2024). https://doi.org/10.1145/3636555.3636937
16. Sawaya, S., et al.: Improving tutor discourse practices via AI-enhanced coaching: a piecewise latent growth curve modeling approach. In: Cristea, A.I., Walker, E., Lu, Y., Santos, O.C., Isotani, S. (eds.) AIED 2025. LNCS, vol. 15880, pp. 76–89. Springer, Cham (2025). https://doi.org/10.1007/978-3-031-98459-4_6

Multimodal Affect in AI for Education: Design, Application, and Ethical Implications Website: https://multimodal-affect-ai4ed.github.io/

Xiaoshan Huang[1(✉)], Andy Nguyen[2(✉)], Jie Gao[1,3], Haolun Wu[1,3], Yimeng Wang[4], Tony Ahn[5], Tiantian Jin[6], Roger Azevedo[7], and Susanne Lajoie[1]

[1] McGill University, Montreal, Canada
{xiaoshan.huang,jie.gao3,haolun.wu}@mail.mcgill.ca, susanne.lajoie@mcgill.ca
[2] University of Oulu, Oulu, Finland
andy.nguyen@oulu.fi
[3] Quebec Artificial Intelligence Institute (Mila), Montreal, Canada
[4] Yale University, New Haven, USA
[5] University of British Columbia, Vancouver, Canada
tony.ahn@ubc.ca
[6] Teachers College, Columbia University, Manhattan, USA
[7] University of Central Florida, Orlando, USA
Roger.Azevedo@ucf.edu

Abstract. As artificial intelligence becomes increasingly embedded in educational contexts, the ability of AI systems to perceive, interpret, and respond to learners' affect has shifted from a niche research interest to a central necessity. This workshop introduces Multimodal Affect in AI for Education (MAAI4Ed), bringing advances in multimodal analytics, affective computing, and learning theories. The workshop focuses on (1) AI-driven approaches in detecting and interpreting affective states through multimodal data streams and (2) designing affect-aware AI systems to support emotional regulation and human well-being. By fostering dialogue among researchers, designers, and practitioners, the workshop aims to advance ethically responsible affect-aware AI for Education.

Keywords: Affective Computing · Multimodal Learning Analytics · Human-AI Collaboration · Emotion in Education · AI Ethics

1 Introduction

As Artificial Intelligence (AI) becomes fundamentally embedded in educational ecosystems, the capacity for these systems to perceive, interpret, and adapt

E. G. Blanchard et al. (Eds.): AIED 2026, CCIS 3033, pp. 111–115, 2026.
https://doi.org/10.1007/978-3-032-29794-5_19

to learners' emotional states has transitioned from a specialized research interest to a central necessity [6,11]. The *Multimodal Affective in AI for Education* (MAAI4Ed) workshop addresses the critical synergy between AI-driven multimodal analytics including physiological signals, facial expressions, and verbal data, and contemporary educational theories such as Self-Regulated Learning (SRL) and Socially Shared Regulation of Learning (SSRL) [8]. While traditional research has prioritized "cold" cognitive processes, affect represents the "hot" functional dimension that is intrinsically intertwined with learning outcomes [9]. By leveraging the pervasive rise of Generative AI and Large Language Models (LLMs), we now have unprecedented opportunities to map complex "affective trajectories" and provide just-in-time scaffolding to fosters emotional regulation and learner well-being [6,10]. This workshop helps bridge the gap between affective science and the AIED community, fostering an interdisciplinary dialogue on the design, application, and ethical implications of truly affect-aware intelligent systems [1].

1.1 Theme and Goals

As AI systems become increasingly ubiquitous in educational settings, the capacity to perceive and respond to learners' emotional states has transitioned from a theoretical interest to a critical necessity. The MAAI4Ed workshop explores the technical and pedagogical synergy between AI-driven analytics and interventional approaches and established educational theories.

The workshop's mission is structured around two central pillars:

Pillar 1: Detection and Interpretation of Affect in Learning Settings Leveraging advanced AI techniques to decode complex affective states in real-time by identify "pivotal moments" of learning, providing the empirical data necessary to support both teaching and learning processes.

Pillar 2: Affect-Aware Design Moving beyond detection to the creation of AI interventions that actively scaffold emotional regulation and promote learner well-being. This involves designing intelligent facilitators that foster supportive emotional states to optimize cognitive load and engagement.

The workshop aims to emphasize affect as a core component of AI-enhanced learning, promote interdisciplinary exchange, and foster community collaboration for future development of affect-aware educational technologies.

1.2 Event Type and Duration

Type: Workshop

Length: Half-day

Intended Audience: AIED/EDM/Learning@Scale communities

Expected Participants: 30–45 (researchers, designers, practitioners)

2 Background

Affective states are psycho-physiological, conscious or subconscious phenomena encompassing emotions, moods, and feelings. They serve as a core component of the human mind [11] and are often described as the "hot" functional dimension, contrasting with the "cold" cognitive processes traditionally emphasized in educational research [9]. Affect is integral to teaching and learning, fundamentally intertwined with cognitive processes [6]. While cognition is well-documented, a significant gap remains in understanding the nuanced role of affect in situ.

Without regulation, high-arousal negative states such as anxiety impair performance by consuming cognitive resources needed for information processing [10]. Contemporary research suggests affect drives engagement, not merely reflects it [5]. Affective states can be captured and interpreted through multimodal channels: behavioral interactions (facial expressions), physiological signals (heart rate/BVP), and verbal data (think-aloud protocols and forum discourse) [4,5,7]. By capturing emotions from these diverse sources, researchers have identified "pivotal moments" where critical cognitive exchanges occur. As well, certain levels of "productive frustration" or arousal can signify higher cognitive engagement and expertise-level performance [2,7].

Contemporary theories of Self-Regulated Learning (SRL) and Socially Shared Regulation (SSRL) highlight the dynamic interplay among affective, cognitive, motivational, and behavioral dimensions [3,4,8]. Yet, the interconnections among these constructs often obscure the distinct role of affect, leaving it a "black box" in many adaptive systems.

The pervasive rise of Generative AI (GenAI) and Large Language Models (LLMs) offers a transformative opportunity to distinguish and categorize affective states with unprecedented efficiency [12]. Multimodal analytics provides a pathway for capturing these "affective trajectories" in complex, large-scale online settings [1,6]. Within AIED, the role of AI is two-fold: 1) **Detection and Interpretation:** Identifying emotional cues to pinpoint critical knowledge acquisition moments and inform just-in-time scaffolding. 2) **Affective Scaffolding:** Designing AI facilitators that actively foster supportive emotional states to reduce cognitive load and promote community interaction.

3 Workshop Schedule

3.1 Workshop Format and Participation

The MAAI4Ed workshop is formatted as a half-day session (approx. 4 h) aimed at bringing together a diverse cohort of learning scientists, AI specialists, and UX designers. To ensure high-quality interactions, we anticipate a capacity of 30–45 participants. Attendees are encouraged to submit 2–6 page papers detailing recent empirical research, design-based study, or theoretical frameworks regarding multimodal affective analytics in education. These submissions will undergo a peer-review process by the organizing committee to ensure relevance and academic rigor.

3.2 Workshop Activities

The workshop activities are structured into three distinct phases to move from theoretical inspiration to collaborative application:

1. **Opening and Keynote (75 min):** The session begins with the chairs' welcome to define the workshop's vision, followed by two keynote speeches from Profs. Roger Azevedo and Kshitij Sharma.
2. **Lightning Talks (60 min):** Authors of accepted papers will present their work in a dynamic "Lightning Talk" format. Each presenter is allocated 10 min (7 min for presentation and 3 min for Q&A).
3. **Interactive Design Seminar (45 min):** Participants will engage in a hands-on group activity where they are divided into small groups based on shared interests (e.g., early childhood education vs. large-scale online communities) and tasked with "Designing the Ideal Affect-Aware Tool". Each group will identify specific learners, data streams, and affective scaffolding interventions and will give a demo at the workshop.
4. **Panel Discussion (45 min):** The following hour will feature a panel discussion focused on the design, application, and ethical implication of affect-aware AI. We will debate about whether AI should always reduce negative states like confusion – since they can lead to productive learning – and how to address negative emotions caused by AI overuse (AI fatigue). Furthermore, drawing from the HCI theory of Value-Sensitive Design (VSD), the discussion will explore how to safeguard learner autonomy while fostering supportive, "warm" learning environments.

3.3 Dissemination and Logistics

All accepted papers will be published in a dedicated digital repository. We will establish a persistent communication channel to maintain the network after the conference concludes. We will explore opportunities for a post-workshop special issue or collaborative publication depending on participant interest. The physical

Table 1. Workshop Schedule

Time	Activity
15 min	Opening Remarks: Introduction to the MAAI@AIED Workshop vision and goals.
60 min	Keynote Speeches by Profs Roger Azevedo & Kshitij Sharma.
60 min	Lightning Talks: Paper presentations to spark ideas.
15 min	Coffee Break: Networking and informal discussion.
45 min	Interactive Design Seminar: "Designing the Ideal Affect-Aware Tool."
45 min	Penal Discussion: Design, Applications and Ethics.
15 min	Wrap-up & Next Steps: Closing remarks and information on publishment.

venue will require flexible seating to accommodate the transition from plenary presentations to collaborative design circles (Table 1).

References

1. Blikstein, P., Worsley, M.: Multimodal learning analytics and education data mining: using computational technologies to measure complex learning tasks. J. Learn. Anal. **3**(2), 220–238 (2016)
2. D'Mello, S., Graesser, A.: Dynamics of affective states during complex learning. Learn. Instr. **22**(2), 145–157 (2012)
3. Giannakos, M., et al.: The promise and challenges of generative AI in education. Behav. Inf. Technol. **44**(11), 2518–2544 (2025)
4. Huang, X., Huang, L., Lajoie, S.P.: Exploring teachers' emotional experience in a tpack development task. Educ. Tech. Res. Dev. **70**(4), 1283–1303 (2022)
5. Huang, X., Nguyen, A., Lajoie, S.P.: Examining socially shared regulation of learning in medical training: the interplay of heart rate change points on regulatory interactions: Huang, et al.: Eur. J. Psychol. Educ. **40**(3), 93 (2025)
6. Huang, X., Wu, H., Liu, X., Lajoie, S.: Examining the role of peer acknowledgements on social annotations: unraveling the psychological underpinnings. In: Proceedings of the 2024 CHI Conference on Human Factors in Computing Systems, pp. 1–9 (2024)
7. Huang, X., et al.: Linking facial recognition of emotions and socially shared regulation in medical simulation. In: Companion Publication of the 2025 Conference on Computer-Supported Cooperative Work and Social Computing, pp. 239–243 (2025)
8. Järvelä, S., Nguyen, A., Hadwin, A.: Human and artificial intelligence collaboration for socially shared regulation in learning. Br. J. Edu. Technol. **54**(5), 1057–1076 (2023)
9. Metcalfe, J., Mischel, W.: A hot/cool-system analysis of delay of gratification: dynamics of willpower. Psychol. Rev. **106**(1), 3 (1999)
10. Plass, J.L., Kaplan, U.: Emotional design in digital media for learning. In: Emotions, Technology, Design, and Learning, pp. 131–161. Elsevier (2016)
11. Russell, J.A.: Core affect and the psychological construction of emotion. Psychol. Rev. **110**(1), 145 (2003)
12. Wu, X., et al.: A deep learning approach to emotionally intelligent AI for improved learning outcomes. Sci. Rep. (2026)

Stakeholder-Driven Contextual Evaluation of Language Models in Education

Shamya Karumbaiah(✉), Ananya Ganesh, and Anurag Maravi

University of Wisconsin Madison, Madison, USA
shamya.karumbaiah@wisc.edu

Abstract. With the increasing reliance of AIED on opaque, black-box scaffolds such as large language models to support student learning, there is a growing concern about their limitations when used in diverse pedagogical contexts. This opacity often undermines stakeholders' trust and shapes their perceptions, contributing to resistance toward the adoption of AI scaffolds in schools. To address these challenges, we developed AIBAT, a workflow and system designed to support stakeholders in auditing and critically evaluating the potential benefits and harms of AI systems within their specific pedagogical contexts (e.g., subject matter, grade level, English proficiency). With AIBAT, stakeholders can specify expected behaviors—i.e., what they anticipate the AI scaffold should do—and test the system against those expectations. In this half-day tutorial, participants will use AIBAT to identify and make sense of AI-related risks and use evidence to calibrate their trust in AI scaffolds. At the end of the tutorial, we will deliberate on AI auditing processes and discuss broader implications for promoting responsible and effective stakeholder participation in the evaluation and deployment of AI systems in educational settings.

Keywords: Large Language models · Evaluation · Stakeholders · Context · Behavior analysis · Responsible AI in education

1 Expected Outcome

In this **half-day tutorial**, participants will explore a new evaluation method (behavior analysis [2]; Sect. 2) and a corresponding tool (AIBAT [1]; Sect. 4) to learn how they can analyze AI system behaviors to contextually evaluate AI and identify the benefits and harms of using AI with diverse student data.

With the advent of generative AI, stakeholders are faced with the difficult choice of trusting advanced technologies to take advantage of them (e.g., NLP systems for writing feedback, conversational agents). Trusting such systems is especially difficult as they become less transparent and raise equity concerns for minoritized students. Hence, we ask: How do we equip educational stakeholders

E. G. Blanchard et al. (Eds.): AIED 2026, CCIS 3033, pp. 116–123, 2026.
https://doi.org/10.1007/978-3-032-29794-5_20

with tools that build their expertise and agency in trustworthy and equitable AI use in classrooms?

Responsible use of AI in classrooms must acknowledge differences in pedagogical contexts. However, AI evaluation typically assumes universal deployment. Indeed, the dominant approach for AI evaluation (i.e., generalization estimation on test data) often tends to be an overestimation of real-world performance [16,22]. In most cases, the test data used to evaluate generalization poorly represent the range of real-world scenarios and often contain the same biases as the training data. Even when tested with data from the deployment context, the population distribution may shift over time [15].

Recent research in natural language processing (NLP)—a kind of AI system involving computational models of text—has shown that engaging stakeholders to analyze NLP model behaviors (in conditions relevant to their context) was effective in identifying failures that are likely to go unnoticed in tests for generalization [6,7]. Stakeholders with limited prior experience in AI were able to identify failures in key capabilities such as fairness (e.g., biases against linguistic minorities), robustness to perturbations (e.g., spelling errors), and domain-specific vocabulary when evaluating NLP systems used for language translation, content moderation, and question-answering.

2 Theoretical Background

We first show how system failures differ by pedagogical context in ways not captured by generalization estimates. Then, we explain how allowing stakeholders such as researchers, teachers, developers, and practitioners to evaluate AI system behaviors in their pedagogical context fosters trust and agency for an equitable use of AI.

2.1 The Need to Go Beyond Generalization Estimates for Equitable AI

Despite significant differences in the pedagogical contexts in which educational AI systems are used, AI evaluation is often limited to generalization estimates (e.g., overall accuracy, mean squared error) that inherently assume universal deployment [24]. Moreover, AI systems are known to systematically fail on rare groups not obvious in aggregate evaluation [20], such as minoritized student populations. Past research demonstrates how ignoring learner context in the design of AI tutors could introduce harmful biases in them [3]. Despite a recent spike in efforts to identify and mitigate bias in educational AI [8], significant challenges remain. A common approach to fairness is ensuring that the system performs well for student subgroups. In addition to oversimplified or politically influenced categorizations of student demographics, these approaches fall short in considering the myriad of ways in which student identities intersect [13]. Moreover, technical conceptions of bias are often vague, lack normative grounding, and diverge from how bias is socially understood [21]. Hence, answers to the question of "what kinds of system behaviors are harmful, in what ways, to whom, and why?" [18] need to be contextually grounded in the lived experiences of the stakeholders.

2.2 Stakeholder-Driven Contextual Evaluation of Behaviors for Human–AI Trust

There has been an increasing call for contextual evaluation [9] that recognizes differences in the lived experiences of stakeholders, which in turn define system failures differently [11]. Specifying desired system behavior serves an important role in transparency and trust, opening the AI system for stakeholder scrutiny [6]. Prior work has formalized human–AI trust as contractual, i.e., trust is built on explicit, context-specific contracts that stakeholders specify based on the expected behaviors of the AI system [5]. System *behaviors* defined through testing can act as components of such contracts—particularly when they incorporate stakeholders' contextual expertise to translate implicit expectations (e.g., fairness) into explicit, testable criteria. In addition to better-informed trust, contextual evaluation of AI scaffold behaviors can improve AI transparency [4]. With improved awareness of both the benefits and limitations of using AI scaffolds in their context—as well as the associated equity concerns—stakeholders can more effectively situate AI scaffolds within their broader system of scaffolding distributed across tools and social supports. This may involve adjusting scaffolding practices to amplify the benefits and mitigate the limitations of the AI scaffold.

3 Tutorial Description

In this tutorial, participants will learn about behavior analysis and use AIBAT (Fig. 1) to specify *behaviors* (i.e., what they expect the AI scaffold to do) and test large language models (LLMs) against those expectations. For example, to analyze how fairly an LLM treats bilingual students, participants can define a target LLM behavior (e.g., tag incorrect student response for feedback) and test whether that behavior stays invariant based on a specified condition (e.g., no change in assessment when a relevant Spanish idiom is added to the response).

3.1 Intended Activities with AIBAT

Contextualize Evaluation With Custom Topics and Behaviors. By default, the platform includes two sample middle-school science topics—how Potential Energy (PE) varies with height and how mass affects total energy—along with a set of predefined student responses. For each topic, users are presented with 20 predefined statements on the main panel, each accompanied by an AI-generated assessment indicating whether the statement is deemed acceptable or unacceptable. Users can review these assessments and provide feedback by agreeing or disagreeing with the AI's decision with a single click. To provide adaptability to different subject areas and grading criteria, AIBAT offers a Custom Topic Definition feature, allowing users to define and evaluate new topics dynamically.

This feature comprises two configurable options to support varied evaluation needs. First, Custom Topics allow participants to create their own topics by defining assessment prompts and adding up to 10 test statements tailored to their subject matter. These user-defined topics function as prompts that help AIBAT generate a bookmarkable topic page, similar to the default Height/PE and Mass/Energy topics, allowing users to switch between them. If participants wish to augment their evaluation with additional, auto-generated test statements, they can select "Generate More Statements", prompting AIBAT to produce new statements under the defined topic.

Second, User-Defined Statements allow users to manually input specific statements under an existing topic for AI evaluation. Users can either edit an existing statement and save it, prompting the LLM to regrade the modified statement, or input a completely new statement instead of modifying a predefined one, indicating whether they consider it acceptable or unacceptable. Once submitted, the statement appears in the panel under the selected topic, accompanied by the LLM-generated assessment (acceptable/unacceptable) and an indication of whether the AI's assessment aligns with the participant's decision (agree/disagree). Together, these options allow stakeholders to tailor AIBAT's evaluation system to a range of grading needs, ensuring flexibility beyond its default topics and statements.

Scale Up Behavior Analysis with Relevant Linguistic Variations. AIBAT incorporates a Linguistic Variation feature to account for the diverse ways a given statement can be expressed. When participants enable this feature by clicking the Analyze AI Behavior button, each statement expands into a dropdown menu displaying multiple linguistically modified versions. These variations include adjustments such as spelling modifications, negation, synonyms, paraphrasing, acronyms, antonyms, and translations into Spanish by default. Additionally, users can access the Criteria Editor Panel to define custom linguistic variations, providing key information that helps fine-tune the model's responses. Taken holistically, this feature aims to enhance scalability by allowing participants to assess AI-graded patterns across multiple linguistic forms with their previous decisions populated automatically, rather than manually reviewing each case in isolation. In real-world classroom settings, student responses naturally vary in wording, grammar, and phrasing, yet traditional AI evaluation methods often rely on fixed expressions, limiting the scope of assessment. By automating the generation of systematic linguistic variations, AIBAT enables stakeholders to efficiently examine how AI models handle diverse inputs at scale.

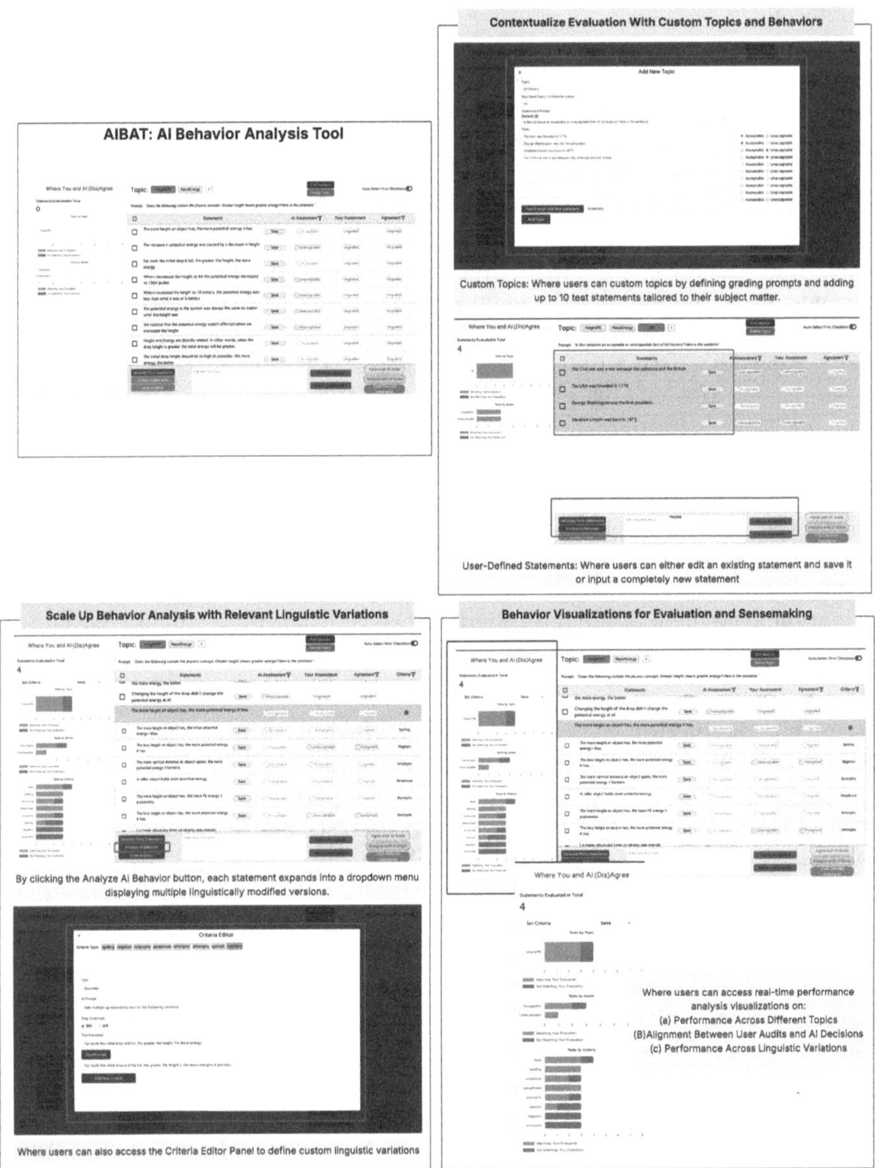

Fig. 1. AIBAT's Interface and Key Features. The interface includes default status (top left), Contextualize Evaluation with Custom Topics and Behaviors (top right), Scale Up Behavior Analysis with Relevant Linguistic Variations (bottom left), and Behavior Visualizations for Evaluation and Sensemaking (bottom right).

Behavior Visualizations for Evaluation and Sensemaking. AIBAT includes a real-time AI performance analysis panel that provides dynamic insights into the AI model's evaluation accuracy through bar charts. The visualization is structured around three key dimensions: (a) Performance Across Different Topics—The system evaluates AI behaviors across various subject areas, enabling users to assess whether the model generalizes effectively or struggles with certain topics. This feature helps identify subject-specific biases and inconsistencies that may impact grading fairness. (b) Alignment Between User Audits and AI Decisions—This metric measures the extent to which users' auditing decisions align with the AI's assessment. It distinguishes between true positives (correct acceptances), true negatives (correct rejections), false positives (incorrect acceptances), and false negatives (incorrect rejections). This allows users to identify patterns in the AI's errors and assess its reliability in different grading scenarios. (c) Performance Across Linguistic Variations—AIBAT also analyzes how the AI responds to different linguistic variations, such as changes in grammar, spelling, and negation. By tracking performance across these variations, users can detect potential biases or weaknesses in the model's ability to handle diverse linguistic expressions.

LLM Model Specifications. AIBAT leverages various LLMs throughout the application to perform different tasks effectively. For grading the default topics, the platform utilizes a fine-tuned RoBERTa classification model, specifically trained to evaluate responses related to the default subjects. When it comes to grading new, user-defined topics, AIBAT switches to a general-purpose, pre-trained Llama 3 model, which provides flexibility for a broader range of grading tasks. For generating new test cases, AIBAT relies on a Mistral model, which helps create diverse and relevant test scenarios. Linguistic perturbations are generated using Mistral. Through these carefully selected models, AIBAT ensures accurate grading, efficient test case generation, and robust perturbation handling for various educational needs.

3.2 Organizers

Shamya Karumbaiah is an assistant professor in the Department of Educational Psychology, where she directs The Responsible AI for Learning (TRAIL) Lab. Her lab's research, at the intersection of learning sciences, learning analytics, AI, and human-centered design: (1) supports students to bring diverse linguistic and cultural assets into their learning, (2) enables K–12 teachers to develop equitable practices, and (3) improves methods to identify and mitigate AI biases.

Ananya Ganesh is a postdoctoral researcher at the University of Wisconsin Madison. She received her Ph.D. in Computer Science from the University of Colorado Boulder where she developed new natural language processing techniques for educational dialog understanding in collaboration with the NSF-funded National AI Institute for Student-AI Teaming.

Anurag Maravi is a software engineer with the TRAIL Lab at the University of Wisconsin–Madison. He designs and builds AI-enabled learning technologies that support educators and students in K–12 settings. His work involves developing full-stack systems that integrate natural language processing and machine learning into practical educational applications.

4 Intended Audience, Schedule, and Plans for Advertising

Intended Audience. 20–30 educational AI stakeholders such as researchers, teachers, developers, and practitioners participating in AIED, EDM, or L@S.

A Rough Schedule of Intended Activities.

1. (30 min) Opening remarks on evaluation crisis with LLMs
2. (30 min) Small group deliberation and share-out on current approaches to AI evaluation
3. (15 min) Introduction to behavior analysis
4. (15 min) Individual think time on relevant linguistic variations
5. (15 min) Whole group demo of AIBAT with participant use case
6. (15 min) Break
7. (60 min) Small group work with AIBAT
8. (30 min) Fishbowl demo of small group to whole group
9. (30 min) Closing reflection on effective stakeholder participation in the evaluation and deployment of AI

Plans for Advertising the Event. We will share our tutorial in relevant listservs, professional organizations, newsletters, and social media.

References

1. Karumbaiah, S., Yin, Y., Bharadwaj, A.: AIBAT: AI behavior analysis tool for teacher-driven contextual evaluation of language models in education. In: Cristea, A.I., Walker, E., Lu, Y., Santos, O.C., Isotani, S. (eds.) AIED 2025. LNCS, vol. 15877, pp. 63–76. Springer, Cham (2025). https://doi.org/10.1007/978-3-031-98414-3_5
2. Karumbaiah, S., Ganesh, A., Bharadwaj, A., Anderson, L.: Evaluating behaviors of general purpose language models in a pedagogical context. In: Olney, A.M., Chounta, I.A., Liu, Z., Santos, O.C., Bittencourt, I.I. (eds.) AIED 2024. LNCS, vol. 14830, pp. 47–61. Springer, Cham (2024). https://doi.org/10.1007/978-3-031-64299-9_4
3. Karumbaiah, S., Ocumpaugh, J., Baker, R.S.: Context matters: differing implications of motivation and help-seeking in educational technology. Int. J. Artif. Intell. Educ. **1**, 1–40 (2021)
4. Bommasani, R., Liang, P., Lee, T.: Holistic evaluation of language models. Ann. N.Y. Acad. Sci. (2023)

5. Jacovi, A., Marasović, A., Miller, T., Goldberg, Y.: Formalizing trust in artificial intelligence: prerequisites, causes, and goals of human trust in AI. In: Proceedings of the ACM Conference on Fairness, Accountability, and Transparency, pp. 624–635 (2021)
6. Suresh, H., et al.: Kaleidoscope: semantically-grounded, context-specific ML model evaluation. ACM Hum. Factors Comput. Syst. **1**, 1–13 (2023)
7. Ribeiro, M.T., Wu, T., Guestrin, C., Singh, S.: Beyond accuracy: behavioral testing of NLP models with CheckList. arXiv preprint arXiv:2005.04118 (2020)
8. Baker, R.S., Hawn, A.: Algorithmic bias in education. Int. J. Artif. Intell. Educ. **1**, 1–41 (2021)
9. Raji, D., Denton, E., Bender, E.M., Hanna, A., Paullada, A.: AI and the everything in the whole wide world benchmark. In: Neural Information Processing Systems (2021)
10. Corbett, A.T., Anderson, J.R.: Knowledge tracing: modeling the acquisition of procedural knowledge. User Model. User-Adapt. Interact. **4**, 253–278 (1994)
11. D'Ignazio, C., Klein, L.F.: Data Feminism. MIT Press, Cambridge (2020)
12. Dillenbourg, P.: The evolution of research on digital education. Int. J. Artif. Intell. Educ. **26**, 544–560 (2016)
13. Crenshaw, K.W.: On Intersectionality: Essential Writings, The New Press (2017)
14. Puntambekar, S.: Distributed scaffolding: scaffolding students in classroom environments. Educ. Psychol. Rev. **34**(1), 451–472 (2022)
15. Quinonero-Candela, J., Sugiyama, M., Schwaighofer, A., Lawrence, N.D. (eds.): Dataset Shift in Machine Learning. MIT Press (2008)
16. Recht, B., Roelofs, R., Schmidt, L., Shankar, V.: Do ImageNet classifiers generalize to ImageNet? In: International Conference on Machine Learning, pp. 5389–5400. PMLR (2019)
17. Engelbart, D.C., English, W.K.: A research center for augmenting human intellect. In: Proceedings of the December 9–11, 1968 Fall Joint Computer Conference, Part I, pp. 395–410 (1968)
18. Blodgett, S.L., Barocas, S., Daumé, I., Wallach, H., H.: Language (technology) is power: a critical survey of "bias" in NLP. arXiv preprint arXiv:2005.14050 (2020)
19. Shneiderman, B.: Human-Centered AI. Oxford University Press (2022)
20. Rajani, N., Liang, W., Chen, L., Mitchell, M., Zou, J.: SEAL: interactive tool for systematic error analysis and labeling. arXiv preprint arXiv:2210.05839 (2022)
21. Birhane, A.: Algorithmic injustice: a relational ethics approach. Patterns **2**(2) (2021)
22. Patel, K., Fogarty, J., Landay, J.A., Harrison, B.: Investigating statistical machine learning as a tool for software development. In: Proceedings of the SIGCHI Conference on Human Factors in Computing Systems, pp. 667–676. ACM, New York (2008)
23. Martin, N.D., Tissenbaum, C.D., Gnesdilow, D., Puntambekar, S.: Fading distributed scaffolds: the importance of complementarity between teacher and material scaffolds. Instr. Sci. **47**(1), 69–98 (2019)
24. Paquette, L., Ocumpaugh, J., Li, Z., Andres, A., Baker, R.: Who's learning? Using demographics in EDM research. J. Educ. Data Min. **12**(3), 1–30 (2020)
25. Kozulin, A.: Psychological tools and mediated learning. In: Kozulin, A., Gindis, B., Ageyev, V.S., Miller, S.M. (eds.) Vygotsky's Educational Theory in Cultural Context, pp. 15–38. Cambridge University Press (2003)

2nd Annual Workshop on Human-AI Teaming: From Tools to Teammates II: Designing AI That Belongs

Nia Nixon[1(✉)], Jennifer Meyer[2], Srecko Joksimovic[3], Andrew Zamecnik[3], Mohammad Amin Samadi[1], Jaeyoon Choi[1], Seehee Park[1], and Pedro Martins de Bastos[1]

[1] University of California, Irvine, Irvine, CA 92618, USA
{dowelln,masamadi,jaeyooc3,seeheep,pedrom4}@uci.edu
[2] University of Vienna, Vienna, Austria
jennifer.meyer@univie.ac.at
[3] University of South Australia, Adelaide, SA 5001, Australia
{srecko.joksimovic,andrew.zamecnik}@unisa.edu.au

Abstract. This second annual **half-day, in-person workshop** explores opportunities and challenges in Human-AI teaming for collaborative learning. As AI systems shift from passive tools to active teammates, the workshop asks how learners perceive AI as a social and relational partner, and how these perceptions shape coordination, trust, participation, and inclusion. Grounded in the Machines as Teammates framework, it brings together researchers, educators, designers, and technologists to examine how learning analytics can inform the design and evaluation of AI teammates. Rather than focusing on traditional paper presentations, the workshop emphasizes interactive engagement through design sprints, structured brainstorming, and conceptual mapping. Participants will identify key opportunities, risks, research questions, and methodological approaches for designing equitable and inclusive Human-AI teams.

Keywords: Human-AI Teaming · Collaborative Learning · Learning Analytics · AI in Education · Equity and Inclusion

This proposal is for a **half-day, in-person workshop**. This is the second edition of the workshop series; the first edition was held at AIED 2025 [7].

1 Organizers and Contact Information

Dr. Nia Nixon, Associate Professor, School of Education & Department of Cognitive Science, University of California, Irvine, USA; Distinguished International Professor, Hector Research Institute for Education Sciences and Psychology, University of Tübingen (dowelln@uci.edu).

E. G. Blanchard et al. (Eds.): AIED 2026, CCIS 3033, pp. 124–129, 2026.
https://doi.org/10.1007/978-3-032-29794-5_21

Dr. Nia Nixon's research examines AI as a socio-technical actor within collaborative systems, experimentally studying how human–AI interaction shapes collective intelligence, epistemic participation, and inclusive team dynamics in STEM problem-solving contexts through computational discourse analytics. She has held leadership roles in the research community, including serving as Vice President of the Society for Learning Analytics Research (SoLAR). Her work advances equity-focused, AI-driven approaches to collaborative learning.

Dr. Jennifer Meyer, Assistant Professor, Educational Diagnostics and Counselling in Schools, Centre for Teacher Education, University of Vienna, Austria (jennifer.meyer@univie.ac.at).

Dr. Jennifer Meyer's research focuses on determinants of the effective use of artificial intelligence in education, particularly in formative feedback contexts. She investigates how students' individual learning prerequisites and differences influence the effectiveness of AI-supported educational technologies. Dr. Meyer is a 2024–2026 Jacobs Foundation Research Fellow.

Dr. Srecko Joksimovic, Associate Professor & Co-Director, Centre for Change and Complexity in Learning (C3L), University of South Australia, Australia (srecko.joksimovic@unisa.edu.au).

As Co-Director of the Centre for Change and Complexity in Learning (C3L), Dr. Srecko Joksimovic's work explores how technology and AI can enhance learning, foster collaboration, and support human development through meaningful human-AI interaction. His research informs policy and practice through partnerships with governments, schools, and industry stakeholders. He co-leads the SIG on Responsible and Equitable AI within EATEL and has played a key role in shaping the field of learning analytics through leadership within SoLAR and ASCILITE's Learning Analytics SIG, as well as editorial roles in major journals and conferences.

Dr. Andrew Zamecnik, Researcher, Centre for Change and Complexity in Learning (C3L), University of South Australia, Australia (andrew.zamecnik@unisa.edu.au).

With a PhD in Learning Analytics, Dr. Andrew Zamecnik's research focuses on team behaviors such as cohesion and trust in collaborative learning. He develops real-time analytics systems with AI agents that provide instructors dynamic feedback to enhance team processes and student problem-solving. His work integrates user-centered design to improve usability and impact in collaborative learning technologies. He collaborates with international research centers and industry partners and contributes actively to the global learning analytics community.

Mohammad Amin Samadi, PhD Candidate, School of Education, University of California, Irvine, USA (masamadi@uci.edu). Mohammad Amin Samadi is a PhD candidate specializing in Artificial Intelligence, Natural Language Processing, and Learning Analytics. His research focuses on leveraging machine learning and large language models to analyze human interaction and collaborative learning behaviors. He leads research initiatives investigating human-AI collaboration in team settings and develops AI teammates that support and analyze collaborative interactions. His research bridges AI and human collaboration while advancing responsible and effective AI deployment.

Jaeyoon Choi, PhD Student, School of Education, University of California, Irvine, USA (jaeyoon.choi@uci.edu).

Jaeyoon Choi is a doctoral student at UC Irvine whose research examines fairness, bias, and theoretical foundations of AI in collaborative learning environments. His work explores how AI systems influence team dynamics, equity, and epistemic participation. She contributes to the design and evaluation of human-AI teaming systems with a focus on responsible and equitable AI integration.

Seehee Park, PhD Candidate, School of Education, University of California, Irvine, USA (seeheep@uci.edu).

Seehee Park is a doctoral student at UC Irvine whose research focuses on collaborative learning, socio-cognitive discourse processes, and the integration of AI in team-based learning environments. Her work investigates how communication dynamics shape inclusion and learning outcomes in hybrid human-AI teams. She contributes to the development of analytic frameworks for understanding equitable participation in collaborative settings.

Pedro Martins de Bastos, PhD Student, University of California, Irvine, USA (pedrom4@uci.edu).

Pedro Martins de Bastos is a doctoral student at UC Irvine whose research focuses on Human-AI teaming in educational contexts. His work investigates how AI systems can support collaborative learning while remaining sensitive to student motivation, engagement, and enjoyment. He brings prior industry experience in educational technology to bridge practical innovation with theoretical grounding in learning sciences.

2 Intended Audience and Number of Participants

This workshop is intended for an interdisciplinary audience spanning **Artificial Intelligence in Education (AIED)**, **Educational Data Mining (EDM)**, and **Learning at Scale** communities. We welcome researchers, designers, and practitioners working at the intersection of learning analytics, AI, and collaborative learning, including:

- **AIED researchers and designers** exploring Human–AI teaming, socially aware AI systems, and the role of AI as an active partner in collaborative learning environments.
- **EDM and learning analytics scholars** investigating discourse, multimodal interaction, team processes, and scalable measurement of collaboration, equity, and inclusion.
- **Learning at Scale researchers and practitioners** interested in deploying AI-supported collaboration and belonging-centered interventions in large-scale or digitally mediated settings.
- **Educators, instructional designers, and technologists** developing human-centered AI tools that augment coordination, participation, and peer learning.

Based on engagement in the previous year's workshop, we anticipate approximately **30–40 participants**, creating a focused yet interactive setting that promotes cross-community dialogue, methodological exchange, and opportunities for future collaboration across AIED, EDM, and Learning at Scale perspectives.

3 Theme and Goals

This second annual half-day in-person workshop explores the potentials and challenges of Human–AI teaming in collaborative learning contexts. As AI systems evolve from passive tools into active teammates, a central open question is **how learners perceive AI as a social and relational partner, and how these perceptions shape team processes such as coordination, trust, participation, and inclusion**. Grounded in the Machines as Teammates (MaT) framework [2], the workshop brings together researchers, educators, designers, and technologists to examine how learning analytics can inform the design and evaluation of AI teammates whose social signals, interaction styles, and relational positioning influence equity, belonging, and collaboration, particularly in STEM and team-based learning environments [1,3–9]. Rather than emphasizing paper submissions, the workshop centers on interactive, activity-driven participation, including design sprints, group brainstorming, and conceptual mapping activities focused on understanding and shaping Human–AI team dynamics.

This workshop directly embodies AIED 2026's theme of *From Tools to Teammates*, providing a dedicated space to operationalize this vision within collaborative learning. We move beyond *whether* AI can function as a teammate to examine *how* such positioning shapes learner experiences, team dynamics, and educational outcomes.

The transition from tools to teammates raises questions about agency, trust, and relational dynamics that technical innovation alone cannot address. Our workshop bridges this gap by bringing together perspectives from learning sciences, AI design, and equity research to develop shared frameworks for understanding AI teammates.

3.1 Key Topics and Themes

The workshop explores questions at the intersection of human-AI teaming and collaboration, education, design, and inclusion:

Perception and Conceptualization: How is AI perceived as a teammate rather than a tool? Which social and relational attributes shape these perceptions, and how can AI be conceptualized, operationalized, and evaluated as an active teammate?

Team Dynamics and Collaboration: How do learners' perceptions of AI influence core team processes such as coordination, trust, participation, and psychological safety? How does AI inclusion alter the nature and dynamics of collaboration in learning teams?

Equity and Inclusion: How can AI systems support belonging and voice for underrepresented learners? What analytic approaches can capture equitable participation and detect bias in Human–AI teams?

Design and Ethics: What design principles ensure AI augments, rather than disrupts, group processes and agency? What ethical and power-related challenges arise when positioning AI as a teammate, and how can innovation align with responsible, equity-oriented design?

4 Activities and Program

The workshop blends expert insights with collaborative design activities and demonstrations. The following is a tentative schedule (subject to change):

- **Welcome and Introduction** (15 min): Framing Human-AI teaming and its relevance to teams in education
- **Invited Talks** (30 min): Brief presentations from leaders in AI, learning analytics, and DEI
- **Panel Discussion** (30 min): Exploring challenges and opportunities in Human-AI collaboration
- **Coffee Break** (15 min)
- **Human-AI Teaming Vignette Challenge** (45 min): Analyze short scenarios of human-AI interaction and identify inclusion opportunities
- **Design Your AI Teammate** (45 min): Small-group sprint to prototype inclusive AI teammate concepts
- **Interactive Demonstrations** (30 min): Showcasing tools and platforms that foster equitable collaboration
- **Roundtable Reflection** (30 min): Synthesizing principles, frameworks, and open questions for future work

5 Publishing Workshop Outcomes

As this workshop is discussion-driven rather than paper-centered, key insights and recommendations will be synthesized and disseminated through accessible formats to maximize impact and reach.

Specifically, we plan to:

- **Publish a publicly available summary** outlining key discussions, emerging research questions, design tensions, and recommendations on an open-access platform.
- **Pursue dissemination through practitioner-facing venues**, including potential collaboration with BOLD (Blog on Learning and Development) and AI-focused education networks to extend the workshop's impact beyond the academic community.

- **Maintain a dedicated workshop website**, where session materials, speaker contributions, activity outputs, and follow-up discussions will be archived to support ongoing engagement and collaboration.

These dissemination efforts aim to translate workshop dialogue into actionable insights for researchers, designers, educators, and policymakers working at the intersection of learning analytics and Human–AI teaming.

Acknowledgments. This research was supported in part by the Jacobs Foundation (Grant No. 2024-1533-00), the Spencer Foundation Vision Grant (Grant No. 202600129), and the Bill & Melinda Gates Foundation (Grant No. INV-068818).

Disclosure of Interests. The authors have no competing interests to declare that are relevant to the content of this article.

References

1. Samadi, M.A., JaQuay, S., Gu, J., Nixon, N.: The AI collaborator: bridging human–AI interaction in educational and professional settings. arXiv preprint arXiv:2405.10460 (2024)
2. Seeber, I., et al.: Machines as teammates: a research agenda on AI in team collaboration. Inf. Manag. **57**(2), 103174 (2020)
3. Samadi, M.A., Nixon, N.: Personalities at play: probing alignment in AI teammates. arXiv https://arxiv.org/abs/2603.00429 (2026)
4. Choi, J., Samadi, M.A., JaQuay, S., Park, S., Nixon, N.: Read the room or lead the room: understanding socio-cognitive dynamics in human-AI teaming. In: Proceedings of the 16th International Conference on Learning Analytics and Knowledge (LAK '26) (2026)
5. Graesser, A.C., Dowell, N., Hampton, A.J., Lippert, A.M., Li, H., Shaffer, D.W.: Building intelligent conversational tutors and mentors for team collaborative problem solving: guidance from the 2015 Program for International Student Assessment (2018)
6. Language and Learning Analytics Lab, UC Irvine: TRAIL: Team Research and AI Integration Lab (2026). https://the-language-and-learning-analytics-lab.github.io/TRAIL-landing-page/
7. Nixon, N., et al.: Human-AI collaboration and culture for equity and inclusion (half-day workshop). In: Cristea, A.I., Walker, E., Lu, Y., Santos, O.C., Isotani, S. (eds.) AIED 2025. CCIS, vol. 2592, pp. 241–248. Springer, Cham (2025). https://doi.org/10.1007/978-3-031-99267-4_30
8. Nixon, N., Joksimovic, S., Zamecnik, A., Choi, J., Park, S., Samadi, M.A.:Beyond tools, toward teammates: human-AI teaming for inclusive learning analytics [Workshop]. In: The 16th International Conference on Learning Analytics and Knowledge (LAK26), Bergen, Norway (2026)
9. Choi, J., Nixon, N.: Measuring inclusion in interaction: inclusion analytics for human-AI collaborative learning. arXiv preprint arXiv:2602.09269 (2026)

IRAISE 2026: Impactful and Responsible AI Systems for Education

Muktha Ananda[1], Debshila Basu Mallick[2(✉)], Jill Burstein[3], April Murphy[4], Zichao Wang[5], and Simon Woodhead[6]

[1] Google, 1600 Amphitheater Pkwy, Mountain View, CA 94043, USA
[2] SafeInsights-OpenStax, 6500 Main St, Houston, TX 77005, USA
debshila@rice.edu
[3] Duolingo, 5900 Penn Ave, Pittsburgh, PA 15206, USA
[4] Carnegie Learning, 436 Seventh Ave, Pittsburgh, PA 15219, USA
[5] Adobe Research, 345 Park Avenue, San Jose, CA 95110, USA
[6] Eedi Labs, 86-90 Paul Street, London EC2A 4NE, England

Abstract. We propose IRAISE (Impactful and Responsible AI Systems for Education), a one-day workshop at the Festival of Learning 2026 (in Seoul, South Korea). Building on two successful AAAI workshops (2024 and 2025) on responsible innovation in AI for education, IRAISE is organized around three pillars that address the most pressing challenges facing AI in education today. From static to continuous: the field must move beyond one-time evaluations toward continuous improvement cycles that keep pace with AI's rapid evolution while respecting education's slower, evidence-based rhythms. From tech-first to learning theory-driven: AI tools must be grounded in learning science, cognitive science, and psychometric theory—not merely technically sophisticated. From labs to classrooms: translating research into deployable products requires multi-stakeholder co-design with teachers, students, and policymakers. Through a keynote, invited talks, posters, roundtables, and a panel, IRAISE will convene researchers, practitioners, policymakers, and industry leaders to catalyze best practices at the intersection of responsible AI innovation and real-world educational impact.

Keywords: AI for Education · continuous improvement · real-world deployment · AI evaluation · responsible AI · learning theory-driven AI

1 Description and Motivation

The landscape of AI in education has transformed rapidly since our first AAAI 2024 workshop "AI for Education: Bridging Innovation and Responsibility" [1], which attracted over 60 submissions and 100+ registrants, and our follow-up AAAI 2025 workshop on "Responsible Innovation in AI for Education". The emergence of agentic AI systems, autonomous agents capable of planning, tool use, and multi-step reasoning [24], raises profound questions about learner autonomy, educator authority, and accountability. Simultaneously, advances in multimodal foundation models [4] that process and generate text, images, audio, and video open new frontiers for accessible and engaging learning, while amplifying concerns around bias [2], hallucinations [12], and privacy.

E. G. Blanchard et al. (Eds.): AIED 2026, CCIS 3033, pp. 130–137, 2026.
https://doi.org/10.1007/978-3-032-29794-5_22

Yet the field's most pressing challenge may be neither technical nor ethical in isolation: it is the growing disconnect between the pace of AI innovation, weeks and months, and the deliberate, evidence-based pace of educational change, where curricula take years to adopt and learning impact requires longitudinal study. Many AI-for-education innovations remain confined to conference papers, never reaching the learners who need them most.

IRAISE addresses this disconnect head-on by organizing the workshop around three pillars that together define what it means to build AI systems that are both impactful and responsible in educational contexts (Table 1):

Table 1. Three pillars that are the core of the IRAISE workshop.

From Static to Continuous	From Tech-First to Learning Theory-Driven	From Labs to Classrooms
Moving beyond one-time evaluations toward continuous improvement cycles that keep pace with AI's rapid evolution while respecting education's evidence-based timelines and academic cycles.	Ensuring AI tools are grounded in learning science, cognitive science, and psychometric theory—not merely technically sophisticated.	Translating research into deployable products through multi-stakeholder co-design with teachers, students, policymakers, and communities.

This proposal complements related workshops (GAIED at NeurIPS 2023, LLM4EDU at AIED 2023, AI4EDU at SIGKDD 2024, AI4ED at AAAI 2025–2026), but is distinctive in its dual emphasis on responsible practice and real-world impact—seeking concrete pathways to translate research into tools, policies, and practices that benefit learners and educators worldwide.

2 Pillar I: From Static to Continuous

The pace mismatch between AI development [24] and educational adoption [25] is more than an operational inconvenience—it has substantive implications for evaluation validity.

An AI tool validated one semester may run on a substantially different underlying model the next, with changed capabilities, failure modes, and biases the original evaluation could not anticipate. Rigorous evidence in this fast-moving landscape is rare, but a recent exploratory RCT in UK classrooms [23] shows that high-quality evidence of safety and effectiveness can be gathered in situ—offering a model to replicate and build on. IRAISE argues that the field must move decisively beyond one-time evaluations toward continuous evaluation and improvement as a foundational principle of AI-for-education product development.

2.1 The Case for Continuous Evaluation

Traditional evaluation paradigms—RCTs, pre/post assessments, usability studies—remain essential but insufficient for AI systems that change continuously. Jurenka et al. [13] argue for an evaluation-driven approach that treats assessment not as a one-time gate but as an ongoing process across the product lifecycle; the OECD framework for trustworthy AI [18] similarly emphasizes lifecycle governance, with monitoring, auditing, and improvement throughout operational life.

Three factors make continuous evaluation imperative in education: (1) learner populations shift, so a system validated on one cohort may perform differently as demographics and prior knowledge change [8, 15]; (2) foundation-model updates introduce drift, altering feedback quality, question difficulty, or scoring fairness in downstream applications; and (3) educational contexts themselves evolve, making the criteria for "effective" AI support a moving target [15].

2.2 A Framework for Continuous Improvement

Drawing on learning engineering [10], responsible AI standards [6, 19], and quality improvement science [5], we propose that AI-for-education products adopt an iterative cycle of:

- **Ongoing monitoring.** Real-time or near-real-time tracking of key performance indicators, including learning outcomes, fairness metrics across demographic groups, system reliability, and user satisfaction, to detect degradation or drift before it affects learners at scale.
- **Periodic bias and fairness auditing.** Regular, structured assessments of whether the AI system produces equitable outcomes across student subgroups defined by race, gender, disability status, language background, and socioeconomic status. These audits must be repeated whenever the underlying model or data pipeline changes [4].
- **Longitudinal impact evaluation.** Studies that track learner outcomes over months and years, not just within a single session or semester, to understand the cumulative effects of AI-mediated learning and to detect late-emerging harms or benefits.
- **Stakeholder feedback loops.** Structured mechanisms for teachers, students, and administrators to report issues, suggest improvements, and participate in prioritization decisions, ensuring that the people closest to the learning process have a voice in shaping the technology.
- **Transparent reporting.** Public or semi-public documentation of system performance, known limitations, and improvement actions taken, building trust and accountability with the educational communities served [6, 18].

2.3 Bridging the Pace Gap

The workshop will examine strategies for bridging the pace gap: (1) modular evaluation frameworks allowing rapid re-assessment of components without full-system re-evaluation; (2) automated pipelines running continuous benchmarks against validated educational criteria, flagging regressions before they reach learners [13]; (3) educator-in-the-loop monitoring that empowers teachers as frontline evaluators [11]; and (4) adaptive governance that updates policies in response to technological change without multi-year legislative cycles [18].

3 Pillar II: From Tech-First to Learning Theory-Driven

Too often, AI tools for education are technically sophisticated but ungrounded in established theories of how people learn. IRAISE advocates for learning theory-driven AI development—the principled application of cognitive science, learning science, and psychometric theory to the design and evaluation of AI systems [14, 15, 21]—ensuring that technological innovation serves pedagogical goals rather than the inverse [8].

This pillar encompasses three interconnected frontiers that define the current state of AI in education:

Agentic AI Grounded in Pedagogy. AI agents that autonomously plan, reason, use tools, and act [24] enable personalized tutoring, automated curriculum design, and adaptive assessment—but without pedagogical grounding risk optimizing narrow metrics rather than genuine learning, and raise open questions of accountability and human oversight. IRAISE will examine responsible design patterns for educational AI agents, including guardrails informed by scaffolding and the zone of proximal development, transparency mechanisms, and human-in-the-loop architectures [9].

Multimodal AI Informed by Cognitive Science. Models like GPT-4o [17], Gemini, and open-source systems now process and generate content across text, image, audio, and video—enabling richer assessment and more accessible content. But these capabilities must be designed with attention to cognitive load theory [7]: multimodal presentations aid learning when they reduce extraneous load, and harm it when they add complexity. The workshop will address how theory can guide the design and evaluation of multimodal educational AI.

Principled Learning Models. We advocate AI systems explicitly grounded in established frameworks: cognitive load theory [7], spaced and retrieval practice [20], the Knowledge-Learning-Instruction framework [14], formative assessment, multimedia learning [16], motivation, and metacognition. This grounding ensures AI tools are pedagogically sound, not merely technically impressive, and provides a principled basis for evaluating whether interventions genuinely support learning—including theory-informed knowledge tracing that integrates psychometric models with deep learning [22].

4 Pillar III: From Lab to Classroom

A distinctive feature of IRAISE is its explicit focus on connecting academic research to practical applications in education technology. This pillar addresses the full pipeline from research prototype to classroom-deployed product, emphasizing that translation requires not just engineering but multi-stakeholder co-design [11], educator-in-the-loop systems, and continuous improvement practices [5, 6].

4.1 Multi-stakeholder Co-design

Responsible AI for education cannot be developed by technologists alone. IRAISE champions a co-design approach in which educators, learners, families, researchers, developers, policymakers, and community members actively participate in the design, evaluation, and governance of educational AI [5, 10]. The workshop's roundtables will model this approach, producing recommendations that reflect the full range of stakeholder needs.

4.2 Bridging Research and Practice

Specifically, IRAISE will:

- **Prioritize practitioner voices.** We will reserve lightning talk and poster slots for educators, learning engineers, and edtech developers who have deployed AI systems in real classrooms and can speak to implementation challenges.
- **Showcase classroom-deployed projects.** Invited speakers have been selected for their track record of translating research into tools used by real learners—from Duolingo's AI-driven assessment to Eedi's human-in-the-loop tutoring system [23].
- **Facilitate dataset and benchmark sharing.** A sub-track for open datasets and evaluation benchmarks will encourage shared infrastructure for reproducible AI-in-education research.
- **Produce actionable outputs.** Roundtables are designed to generate concrete recommendations for researchers, developers, policymakers, and educators, compiled into a post-workshop report for the broader community.

4.3 Responsible AI Standards and Policy

Translating research into classroom practice requires supportive policy. IRAISE will address responsible AI guidelines, fairness auditing, privacy-preserving techniques, and governance frameworks at institutional, national, and international levels [4, 18]. The panel will convene practitioners, funders, policymakers, industry, and educators to identify mechanisms for bridging the research-practice gap.

5 Call for Contributions

IRAISE will solicit submissions across the three pillars: continuous evaluation, monitoring, and lifecycle governance of AI for education (Pillar I); learning theory-driven design of agentic and multimodal AI, including theory-informed knowledge tracing, item response theory, and cognitive load theory (Pillar II); and case studies, multi-stakeholder co-design, classroom deployments, shared benchmarks and open datasets, and responsible AI standards and policy (Pillar III). Many themes cut across pillars. Submissions will undergo peer review by an international program committee; we welcome both research and practitioner contributions.

6 Workshop Format and Tentative Schedule

We propose a one-day (~8-h) workshop structured to maximize interaction and actionable outcomes. The format combines a keynote, four invited talks, a poster spotlight, a poster session with networking time, and roundtables that directly inform a closing panel—ensuring audience perspectives shape the conversation. Based on prior workshop attendance, we expect 60–100 participants (Table 2).

Table 2. Tentative Agenda.

Time	Session	Speaker/Details
9:00–9:15	**Opening Remarks**	Simon Woodhead and Muktha Ananda
9:15–10:00	**Keynote Address**	Irina Jurenka (Google) and Bibi Groot (Eedi)
10:00–10:30	**Invited Talk 1**	Kevin Yancey (Duolingo)
10:30–11:00	*Coffee Break & Poster Session I*	
11:00–11:30	**Invited Talk 2**	Temple Lovelace (Assessment for Good), YJ Kim (University of Adelaide)
11:30–12:00	**Invited Talk 3**	Stephen Fancsali (Carnegie Learning) and Ana Ribeiro (SCALE, Stanford U)
12:00–12:20	**Poster Spotlight**	10 contributed poster-spotlight session (90 s each). Selected from an open call. Focus on classroom-deployed AI projects, new datasets, and practitioner perspectives.
12:20–13:45	**Lunch Break & Poster Session II**	Extended poster viewing and networking
13:45–14:15	**Invited Talk 4**	Shashank Sonkar (University of Central Florida), Neil and Christina Heffernan (ASSISTments)
14:15–14:45	**Small-Group Roundtables**	Themed roundtables facilitated by organizers. Topics: agentic AI safety, multimodal assessment, co-design methods, and bridging research-practice gaps. Output feeds directly into the panel discussion.
14:45–15:15	*Coffee Break & Poster Session III*	
15:15–16:15	**Panel Discussion**	Moderator: Jeremy Roschelle Panelists: TBD
16:15–16:30	**Closing Remarks & Next Steps**	Debshila Basu Mallick

7 Organizers and Roles

Muktha Ananda (mukthananda@google.com), Director of Engineering at Google, leads the LearnX team building AI learning capabilities across Google surfaces and improving Gemini for learning. Role: Travel scholarship oversight.

Debshila Basu Mallick (debshila@rice.edu), Scientific Director of SafeInsights and Director of Research at OpenStax, Rice University; oversees cross-cutting learning research from K-12 to higher education on generative AI for educational applications. Role: Overall workshop lead and primary contact.

Jill Burstein (jill@duolingo.com), Principal Assessment Scientist at Duolingo, leads validity and efficacy research for the Duolingo English Test and authored its RAI Standards; co-founded SIGEDU and the BEA Workshop. Role: Speaker recruitment and program coordination.

April Murphy (amurphy@carnegielearning.com), Senior Director of Learning Engineering at Carnegie Learning, oversees UpGrade, an open-source platform for field testing in educational software. Role: Review management.

Zichao Wang (jackwa@adobe.com), Research Scientist at Adobe Research focused on AI for education. Role: Oversees workshop proceedings.

Simon Woodhead (simon.woodhead@eedi.com), Co-Founder and Chief Scientist at Eedi Labs (UK math edtech). Role: Outreach, social media, and on-site compère.

8 Expected Participation and Logistics

Based on our prior workshops (60+ submissions, 100+ registrants at AAAI 2024), we anticipate 60–100 participants for this one-day workshop. We will solicit contributions through a call for papers and posters distributed via major AI and education mailing lists (SIGEDU, EDM, IAIED, Learning@Scale), social media, and direct outreach. Submissions will undergo peer review by an international program committee.

We will work with the conference organizers to set up at least one scholarship to broaden the participation of students and emerging scholars from underrepresented backgrounds. Two recipients will be selected as panelists.

8.1 Plans for Publishing the Workshop's Proceedings

For lasting scholarly impact, we will publish our proceedings as archival Proceedings of Machine Learning Research (PMLR) volumes. The organizing team has done so for the previous two workshops (see [1, 3]) and has extensive experience compiling, preparing, and publishing the proceedings.

8.2 Plans for Advertising the Event

We will leverage channels used for prior workshops—Learning Engineering and Learning Analytics Google groups, Women in Machine Learning, AERA/NCME, ACL, SIGEDU, and AAAI email lists, LinkedIn, BlueSky, and university mailing lists—to attract diverse audiences and submissions.

9 Disclosure of Interests.

The authors have no competing interests to declare that are relevant to the workshop and content of this article.

Acknowledgments. The organizers thank the IRAISE program committee and partner institutions for their support.

References

1. Ananda, M., et al.: AI for education at AAAI 2024: bridging innovation and responsibility. In: Proceedings of the 2024 AAAI Conference on Artificial Intelligence, pp. 1–2. PMLR, Vancouver (2024)
2. Baker, R.S., Hawn, A.: Algorithmic bias in education. Int. J. Artif. Intell. Educ. **32**(4), 1052–1092 (2022)
3. Basu Mallick, D., Burstein, J., Woodhead, S., Sharpnack, J., Wang, Z.: Preface: innovation and responsibility in AI-supported education. In: Proceedings of the Innovation and Responsibility in AI-Supported Education Workshop (2025)
4. Belzak, W.C.M., Naismith, B., Burstein, J.: Ensuring Fairness of Human- and AI-Generated Test Items, pp. 701–707. Springer, Cham (2023)
5. Bryk, A.S., Gomez, L.M., Grunow, A., LeMahieu, P.G.: Learning to Improve: How America's Schools Can Get Better at Getting Better. Harvard Education Press, Cambridge (2015)
6. Burstein, J.: Responsible AI Standards. Technical report, Duolingo, Inc. (2023)
7. Chandler, P., Sweller, J.: Cognitive load theory and the format of instruction. Cogn. Instr. **8**(4), 293–332 (1991)
8. National Academies of Sciences: Engineering, and Medicine: How People Learn II: Learners, Contexts, and Cultures. National Academies Press, Washington, DC (2018)
9. Gabriel, I., et al.: The Ethics of Advanced AI Assistants. arXiv:2404.16244 (2024)
10. Goodell, J., Kolodner, J. (eds.): Learning Engineering Toolkit. Routledge, New York (2023)
11. Holstein, K., McLaren, B.M., Aleven, V.: Co-designing a real-time classroom orchestration tool to support teacher–AI complementarity. J. Learn. Anal. **6**(2) (2019)
12. Ji, Z., et al.: Survey of hallucination in natural language generation. ACM Comput. Surv. **55**(12), 1–38 (2023)
13. Jurenka, I., et al.: Towards Responsible Development of Generative AI for Education: An Evaluation-Driven Approach. Google Research. Technical report (2024)
14. Koedinger, K.R., Corbett, A.T., Perfetti, C.: The knowledge-learning-instruction framework: bridging the science-practice chasm to enhance robust student learning. Cogn. Sci. **36**(5), 757–798 (2012)
15. Liu, N., et al.: Learning Context: a unified framework and roadmap for adaptive learning systems. arXiv (2025)
16. Mayer, R.E.: Applying the science of learning: evidence-based principles for the design of multimedia instruction. Am. Psychol. **63**(8), 760–769 (2008)
17. OpenAI: Hello GPT-4o. https://openai.com/index/hello-gpt-4o/. Accessed 03 June 2024
18. Perset, K.: Advancing accountability in AI: Governing and managing risks throughout the lifecycle for trustworthy AI. In: OECD Artificial Intelligence Papers (2023)
19. Porayska-Pomsta, K.: A manifesto for a pro-actively responsible AI in education. Int. J. Artif. Intell. Educ. **34**(1), 73–83 (2024)
20. Roediger, H.L., Butler, A.C.: The critical role of retrieval practice in long-term retention. Trends Cogn. Sci. **15**(1), 20–27 (2011)
21. Sonkar, S., Liu, N., Mallick, D., Baraniuk, R.: CLASS: a design framework for building intelligent tutoring systems based on learning science principles. In: Findings of the Association for Computational Linguistics: EMNLP 2023 (2023)
22. Sonkar, S., Waters, A.E., Lan, A.S., Grimaldi, P.J., Baraniuk, R.G.: qDKT: Question-centric Deep Knowledge Tracing. arXiv:2005.12442 (2020)
23. LearnLM Team, Eedi: Exploratory Randomised Controlled Trial of AI Tutoring in UK Classrooms. arXiv (2025)
24. Wang, L., et al.: A survey on large language model based autonomous agents. Front. Comput. Sci. **18**(6), 186345 (2024)
25. UNESCO: Guidance for Generative AI in Education and Research. UNESCO (2023)

Open Adaptive Tutor 2.0: Chatbot Integration, Community Deployments, and Future Directions

Yerin Kwak, Allison Wang, Ioannis Anastasopoulos, and Zachary A. Pardos(✉)

University of California, Berkeley, CA, USA
{kwak,allison-wang,ioannisa,pardos}@berkeley.edu

Abstract. This workshop builds on tutorials at AIED '23 and L@S '23 to introduce the open-source, GenAI-enabled version of Open Adaptive Tutor (OATutor). OATutor is a fully open-source (MIT License) and Creative Commons adaptive tutoring system grounded in Intelligent Tutoring Systems principles. The workshop will debut a chatbot integration framework for exploring educational system prompt design, along with the latest features of the platform. It will also feature guest speakers who will share their independent use of OATutor for research and instructional purposes, followed by hands-on activities in which participants design, test, and interact with GenAI-supported chatbot prompts. Through these activities, the workshop aims to lower the barrier to rapid research and development with adaptive tutors.

Keywords: OATutor · Intelligent Tutoring Systems · Learning Sciences · Chatbots

1 Theme and Goals

Adaptive learning systems based on Intelligent Tutoring Systems (ITS) principles have long been established as effective tools for improving learning gains compared to conventional classroom instruction [5]. Prior work has shown positive results across multiple randomized controlled trials, including studies conducted in middle school mathematics and reading contexts [8,12,16].

Recent advances in generative AI (GenAI) introduce new opportunities to extend these systems. In particular, GenAI-supported assistants and chatbots offer new ways to support both teachers and students, potentially reducing instructor workload while enabling more responsive and personalized learning interactions.

Open Adaptive Tutor[1] is a fully open-source (MIT License) and Creative Commons adaptive tutoring system based on ITS principles intended to serve as

[1] http://OATutor.io.

E. G. Blanchard et al. (Eds.): AIED 2026, CCIS 3033, pp. 138–144, 2026.
https://doi.org/10.1007/978-3-032-29794-5_23

a tool for learning sciences researchers and engineers to engage in rapid experimentation with the features and HCI of computer tutors [9]. In this workshop, which builds on tutorials at AIED '23 [10] and L@S '23 [2], we will introduce OATutor 2.0, which includes a chatbot integration framework designed to support experimentation with LLM agent behavior and efficacy, including a hands-on activity customizing the chatbot using our system prompt design. In addition, guest speakers will share their experience with independent deployments of the tutor as well as best practices on chatbot design from the field.

2 Related Work

A number of movements in digital education have promoted openness in one form or another. Opening up resources, courses, datasets, and algorithms has enabled the large-scale adoption of digital learning materials and accelerated progress in learning sciences research. Open Educational Resources (OERs), which are openly provisioned for reuse and adaptation [7], have broadened access to instructional content and facilitated knowledge sharing. Various GenAI applications themselves can be framed as a form of OER, due to their similarities in how they adhere to long-standing OER challenges [1]. Massive Open Online Courses (MOOCs) gave an open access glimpse into university-level instructional materials [4] and the release of anonymized open datasets from tutoring system has supported replication and generalization in educational data mining [6]. Public datasets from platforms such as Carnegie Learningś MATHia (formerly Cognitive Tutor) [15] and ASSISTments [13] have been widely used in research. Finally, open source code reduce barriers to expanding and replicating research. For example, pyBKT [3] provides an open source Python implementation of Bayesian Knowledge Tracing, a widely used model for cognitive mastery estimation.

Despite these advances and movements, platforms that integrate open content, data, and algorithms remain rare. OATutor is the first open-source adaptive tutoring system, enabling accessible rapid experimentation and continuous improvement from the community.

3 OATutor 2.0

3.1 UI Features and Redesign

Since the first public release of OATutor 1.5, the platform has undergone UI/UX changes to update its design and functionality, as seen in Fig. 1. The platform redesign introduces an interactive Table of Contents sidebar to navigate to any lesson. Each lesson includes a progress ring indicator for three status modes (not started, in progress, and completed/mastered). The overall progress percent of the textbook displayed adjacent to the textbook name is calculated based on the number of lessons completed. Per lesson mastery is also now displayed in a dynamic progress bar above the problems with a branded avatar that advances when lesson mastery increases. The per lesson mastery is further specified for each learning objective (i.e., knowledge component) in the lesson and can be viewed by hovering over the progress bar.

In the default configuration, the student supports are now integrated into the AI hinting agent, although this can be switched back to the OATutor 1.5 design at the textbook or lessons level. The avatar defaults to collapsed when the lesson is first navigated to, and can be clicked open to view hints and scaffolds for the particular problem card open. Any hints, explanations, and scaffolds that are AI generated also specify the AI model used (defaulting to OpenAI o1).

A text-to-speech pipeline has also been developed that reads problem bodies, steps, and hints aloud using AWS Polly via Lambda. The feature is off by default for all lessons and can be turned on by setting the *"allowTTS"* to equal true in the coursePlans file. Once initialized, the play, pause, and replay buttons are integrated into the problem titles, step titles, and hints.

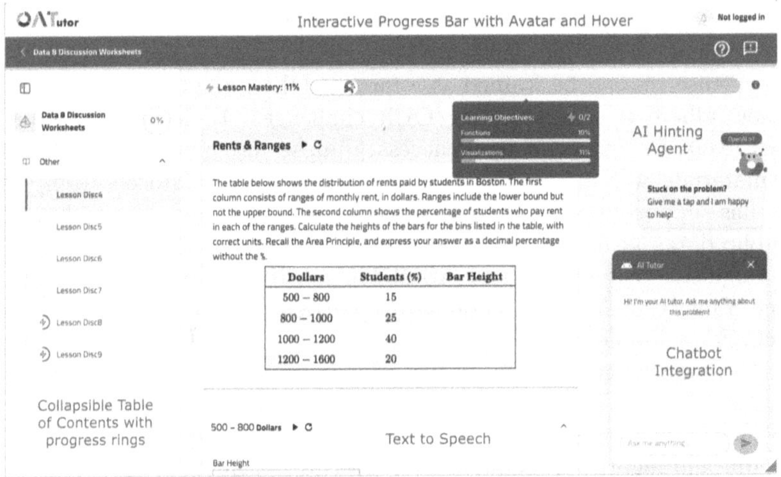

Fig. 1. Notable new features in the early alpha OATutor 2.0 Interface

3.2 General Platform Updates and Language Localization

A completion-based mode for lessons has also been added as an alternative to the default mastery mode, with the lesson-level toggle between mastery and completion as the *"enableCompletionMode"* meta tag within the coursePlans file. Instead of completing the lesson upon reaching a BKT-calculated mastery threshold, the lesson is finished when all problems in the lesson are exhausted. Finishing the lesson in completion mode depends on the problems being completed regardless of first-try correctness.

Content equivalent to OpenStax Calculus has been added to the content library in Swedish, in addition to a new localization framework for language specification. OATutor currently supports English, Spanish, and Swedish, with the ability to specify any interface language through a locale file. Language is specified in the content spreadsheets, and remains localized within each course independently. If a language is not specified, the platform will use the default language specified in the config file, which is currently set to English.

This new version also includes significant upgrades to platform Cloud infrastructure (see Fig. 2), migrating a majority of the code base to be hosted via an AWS backend integration with AWS Lambda functions and API Gateway. Amazon DynamoDB is used for back-end data storage, and Google Firebase stores front-end data. We have also transitioned to a cloud-based LTI support system for improved integration of the platform with Canvas courses.

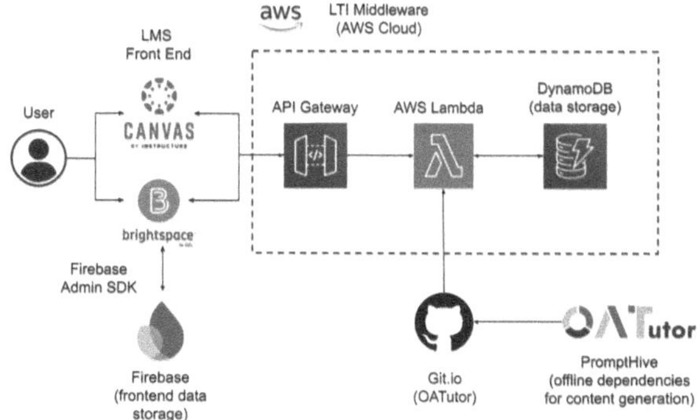

Fig. 2. Diagram for revised platform flow with AWS integration

3.3 Chatbot Integration

A new feature that is being introduced in this version and is a focus of the workshop is the new AI chatbot integration. The chatbot can be seen as a resizable window and a text chat between the agent and student, and is also configurable per lesson using the *"enable_ai_chat"* meta tag in coursePlans.

Chatbot content is generated through a set prompt in the prompt.txt file, and can be uniquely customized to the chatbot behavior desired. The default prompt the chatbot uses to generate responses includes an engineered data pipeline to aggregate context on the student's current knowledge and mastery state, which allows the LLM to have full visibility into student's progress, struggles, and current problem context. Context currently includes the course, problem topic, current step, correctness, and mastery, prior attempt history, relevant BKT skill levels, and a set of critical rules and universal teaching guidelines.

4 Use of GenAI in Authoring

Traditionally, ITS content authoring takes place in either GUI or programmatic interfaces. OATutor itself relies on a spreadsheet interface for the creation of content [9]. However, a comparison of both GUI and programmatic interfaces demonstrated that both types of interfaces have low usability (with System Usability Scale scores of 62 and 40 respectively) with content authors preferring the less accurate interface of the two (GUI) [14]. These results highlighted a gap in opportunity for productive and usable content authoring platforms.

In response to this need, the PromptHive interface was created [11]. PromptHive utilizes GenAI to empower subject matter experts through a platform that allows content authors to collaborate with GenAI. PromptHive supports content creation by previewing content and sharing prompts directly within its interface, paired with the capability of exporting content in a desired file format (spreadsheets in the case of OATutor). The interface also features a prompt notepad, to allow for editing and iterating content prompts. Once content has been exported, it can be edited in the traditional interface as normal.

OATutor has transitioned to now use GenAI for purposes of content authoring through PromptHive's interface. PromptHive was found to be much more usable than previous alternatives (a System usability Scale score of 89) while also demonstrating learning gains similar to those of completely human authored content [11]. Furthermore, PromptHive significantly reduced content authoring time, transforming the OATutor content ecosystem by supporting content authors through GenAI applications.

5 Workshop Structure

This half-day workshop centers on OATutor and is organized into three main parts: (1) an introduction to the system, (2) guest talks, and (3) a hands-on working session.

Introduction. We begin with participants introducing themselves and briefly sharing their research interests. This helps foster discussion throughout the workshop and supports connections among participants with related research agendas. We then provide an overview of OATutor, including its core functionalities, its latest GenAI-enhanced features, and a demonstration of the chatbot integration framework.

Guest talks. Guest speakers will present how they have independently used OATutor in both research and instructional settings, highlighting diverse applications such as course integration, research studies, and adaptations across different contexts. We will also feature speakers who share best practices for chatbot design from the field.

Hands-On Activity. The final part of the workshop will be an interactive, hands-on session. Participants will engage directly with a GenAI-supported chatbot by designing and refining prompts and observing how these changes influence system behavior. The session will conclude with a group discussion on opportunities and challenges for integrating such tools into educational practice, along with future directions for OATutor.

6 Organizers

- **Zach Pardos** – Lab director of the Computational Approaches to Human Learning research group at UC Berkeley, with over 20 years of experience in intelligent tutoring systems research.
- **Yerin Kwak** – PhD student in Social Research Methodology at UC Berkeley, exploring multilingual interfaces and generative AI approaches that bridge subject matter expertise and automation in education.
- **Allison Wang** – Undergraduate student in Data Science at UC Berkeley and development team lead for OATutor.

References

1. Anastasopoulos, I., Pardos, Z.A.: Generating change: AI as an opportunity to address long-standing OER challenges. In: European Conference on Technology Enhanced Learning, pp. 3–16. Springer, Cham (2025). https://doi.org/10.1007/978-3-032-03873-9_1
2. Anastasopoulos, I., Sheel, S., Pardos, Z., Bhandari, S.: Introducing an open-source adaptive tutoring system to accelerate learning sciences experimentation. In: Proceedings of the Tenth ACM Conference on Learning@ Scale, pp. 251–253 (2023)
3. Badrinath, A., Wang, F., Pardos, Z.: pyBKT: an accessible python library of bayesian knowledge tracing models. arXiv preprint arXiv:2105.00385 (2021)
4. Baturay, M.H.: An overview of the world of MOOCs. Procedia. Soc. Behav. Sci. **174**, 427–433 (2015)
5. Corbett, A.T., Koedinger, K.R., Anderson, J.R.: Intelligent tutoring systems. In: Handbook of Human-Computer Interaction, pp. 849–874. Elsevier (1997)
6. Fischer, C., et al.: Mining big data in education: affordances and challenges. Rev. Res. Educ. **44**(1), 130–160 (2020)
7. Johnstone, S.: Forum on the impact of open courseware for higher education in developing countries-final report. Educ. Q. **3**, 15–18 (2005)
8. Pane, J.F., Griffin, B.A., McCaffrey, D.F., Karam, R.: Effectiveness of cognitive tutor algebra I at scale. Educ. Eval. Policy Anal. **36**(2), 127–144 (2014)
9. Pardos, Z., Tang, M., Anastasopoulos, I., Sheel, S., Zhang, E.: Oatutor: an open-source adaptive tutoring system and curated content library for learning sciences research. In: Proceedings of the 2023 CHI Conference on Human Factors in Computing Systems. ACM, Hamberg, Germany (2023)
10. Pardos, Z.A., Anastasopoulos, I., Sheel, S.K.: Conducting rapid experimentation with an open-source adaptive tutoring system. In: International Conference on Artificial Intelligence in Education, pp. 38–43. Springer, Cham (2023). https://doi.org/10.1007/978-3-031-36336-8_5
11. Reza, M., Anastasopoulos, I., Bhandari, S., Pardos, Z.A.: Prompthive: bringing subject matter experts back to the forefront with collaborative prompt engineering for educational content creation. In: Proceedings of the 2025 CHI Conference on Human Factors in Computing Systems, pp. 1–22 (2025)
12. Roschelle, J., Feng, M., Murphy, R.F., Mason, C.A.: Online mathematics homework increases student achievement. AERA Open **2**(4), 2332858416673968 (2016)

13. Selent, D., Patikorn, T., Heffernan, N.: Assistments dataset from multiple randomized controlled experiments. In: Proceedings of the Third (2016) ACM Conference on Learning@ Scale, pp. 181–184 (2016)
14. Sheel, S., Anastasopoulos, I., Pardos, Z.A.: Comparing authoring experiences with spreadsheet interfaces vs GUIs. In: Proceedings of the 14th Learning Analytics and Knowledge Conference, pp. 598–607 (2024)
15. Stamper, J., Pardos, Z.A.: The 2010 KDD cup competition dataset: engaging the machine learning community in predictive learning analytics. J. Learn. Anal. **3**(2), 312–316 (2016)
16. Wijekumar, K., et al.: Multisite randomized controlled trial examining intelligent tutoring of structure strategy for fifth-grade readers. J. Res. Educ. Effect. **7**(4), 331–357 (2014)

Scenario-Based Learning Through and with AI: Evidence-Informed Simulations for Education Leaders

Ella Hamonic[1](✉), Candy Lugaz[2], Annina Demirag[2], Rémi Sharrock[3], Agustina Thailinger[2], Maria Victoria Picchio[2], Vinitra Swamy[4], and Paola Mejia[4]

[1] International Institute for Educational Planning (IIEP-UNESCO), Paris, France
e.hamonic@unesco.org
[2] IIEP-UNESCO, Paris, France
{c.lugaz,a.demirag,a.thailinger,v.picchio}@unesco.org
[3] LTCI, Télécom Paris IMT, IP Paris, Paris, France
remi.sharrock@telecom-paris.fr
[4] Scholé AI, EPFL, Lausanne, Switzerland
{vinitra,paola}@schole.ai

Abstract. This workshop explores how generative AI can strengthen scenario-based learning for the professional development of school and district leaders. Building on IIEP-UNESCO's work in online and blended learning and Télécom Paris' expertise in AI-supported learning, we present an approach in which AI not only helps generate context-aware scenarios, but also delivers simulations, prompts reflection, and provides evidence-informed feedback during leadership practice. Participants will experience how AI can place leaders in realistic school situations, invite them to analyse challenges, take decisions, justify their reasoning, and receive coaching-style feedback informed by literature on school leadership, educational planning and management. The workshop also introduces an AI literacy strand for school and district leaders, focused on responsible use, critical judgement, ethics, and leadership for AI integration in education systems. Participants will examine design principles, test simulation formats, and co-design scenarios for leadership learning.

Keywords: scenario-based learning · generative AI · school leadership · AI coaching · professional development · AI literacy · ethics

1 Introduction

Education systems increasingly need school and district leaders who can make sound decisions in complex environments. Leadership development programmes have used cases and scenarios to foster critical thinking, problem-solving, reflection, and transfer to practice. Such approaches allow participants to work through realistic dilemmas rather than simply absorb abstract principles (Yin, 2015) [1]. However, such approaches often depend on intensive facilitation and are therefore difficult to scale across contexts and languages.

E. G. Blanchard et al. (Eds.): AIED 2026, CCIS 3033, pp. 145–152, 2026.
https://doi.org/10.1007/978-3-032-29794-5_24

Recent advances in generative AI create new possibilities for scenario-based professional learning. AI can now support the creation of context-aware leadership cases, simulate stakeholders through text or voice interactions, adapt prompts to participants' responses, and provide timely feedback that encourages reflection rather than simply giving an answer. A key challenge is therefore to design AI tools in ways that encourage participants to justify decisions, consider alternatives, and connect their choices to evidence-informed leadership principles. This opens new opportunities for more interactive, personalised, and scalable leadership training. At the same time, international guidance stresses that such uses of AI should remain human-centred, ethically governed, and designed to augment rather than replace professional judgement (UNESCO, 2023) [2].

In this workshop, we will explore how AI can be used not only for designing learning scenarios but also to deliver them: as a simulation partner, reflective coach, and structured feedback tool. We focus on leadership challenges faced by school and district leaders, such as instructional supervision, health and wellbeing in schools, or communication with parents. We also argue that such approaches must be accompanied by explicit AI literacy training for leaders, so that they can use AI critically, responsibly, and strategically in school management and improvement.

2 Theme and Goals

The workshop explores how AI can support scenario-based learning and coaching for leadership and management in education. It has four interrelated goals.

First, it aims to show how AI can deliver scenario-based learning through simulations in which school and district leaders respond to realistic cases and receive structured feedback. Second, it examines AI as a training tool that supports reflection, professional judgement, and iterative decision-making rather than simply evaluating performance. Third, it introduces an AI literacy component for education leaders, focused on critical use, ethical judgement, governance, and responsible institutional adoption. Fourth, it invites participants to co-design practical formats and research questions for future use of AI-enabled simulations in leadership development. These goals are aligned with wider work in AI in education, which highlights both the pedagogical opportunities of AI-supported interaction and the need for careful human oversight and sound design (UNESCO, 2023) [2].

By the end of the workshop, participants will be able to:

- identify key design principles for AI-supported leadership simulations,
- analyse how AI-generated prompts and feedback can support reflective practice,
- articulate core AI literacy needs for school and district leaders,
- and co-design a short leadership scenario with an accompanying AI-supported feedback sequence.

3 Theoretical Background and Relevance

This proposal draws on scenario-based and case-based learning that treat learning as situated, experiential, and rooted in the interpretation of complex professional situations. From a case-based reasoning perspective, cases allow learners to work through analogies, compare situations, and build richer decision repertoires over time (Kolodner, 1997) [3]. From a situated learning perspective, professional learning is strengthened when it resembles the social and contextual features of authentic practice (Lave & Wenger, 1991) [4]. Scenario-based learning has similarly been shown to offer a productive bridge between theory and action, especially in leadership and professional education, where judgement, and context-sensitive response are central (Errington, 2011; Yin, 2015) [1, 5].

Scenario-based learning seems particularly relevant to school leadership development. Leadership learning is not only about knowing policies or management tools; it is about interpreting tensions, balancing values, making decisions under uncertainty, and understanding how actions influence teaching, school culture, and improvement processes. Research on successful school leadership has repeatedly highlighted the significance of leadership for learning, especially when leadership practices are closely tied to teaching quality, professional support, and student-centred improvement (Leithwood et al., 2020; Robinson, 2011) [6, 7]. The UNESCO GEM Report 2024/5 further reinforces this rationale by reviewing evidence that leadership contributes to better educational outcomes and improved teaching practices (UNESCO, 2024) [8].

This perspective is also reinforced by work on the role of the middle tier in educational improvement. Leading teaching and learning is not only the responsibility of individual principals, but also depends on the actors and structures that support schools between the central system and the school level. Tournier et al., (2023) [9] show that the middle tier plays an important role in connecting policy, professional learning, instructional support, and school improvement efforts. This is particularly relevant for the present workshop, which includes both school and district leaders and emphasizes leadership as a practice of support, coordination, and improvement.

This rationale is further supported by research on leadership education showing the value of case-based instruction for leadership learning. Drawing on the Norwegian National School Leadership Program, Vennebo and Aas (2023) show that case-based instruction creates promising opportunities for leadership learning by engaging participants in authentic dilemmas, connecting theory and practice, and fostering reflection through dialogue. This is especially relevant for school leadership development, where learning depends on interpreting complex situations rather than applying fixed technical solutions (Vennebo & Aas, 2023) [10].

AI extends these pedagogical traditions in three important ways. First, AI can support the creation and adaptation of realistic scenarios across contexts, languages, and participant profiles, drawing on research literature or contextualized source material, such as interviews with school and district leaders. Second, it can simulate interaction by taking on the role of teachers, parents, students, district officers, or community representatives, thereby making leadership practice more immersive. Third, it can provide immediate feedback that encourages explanation, reconsideration, and deeper reflection. This potential aligns with research on AI in education, which has identified opportunities for AI to support personalised interaction, adaptive feedback, and richer learning processes when pedagogically well designed (Pereyra et al., 2025) [11].

At the same time, the workshop adopts a deliberately cautious stance: AI feedback should not be treated as authoritative judgement. Instead, it should function as a prompt for professional reflection. This position is consistent with dialogic understandings of feedback, which frame effective feedback as a process that develops learner judgement, encourages active interpretation, and supports iterative improvement rather than passive reception of feedback (Boud & Molloy, 2013) [12].

4 Use Case: AI-Enabled Leadership Simulations and Coaching

The workshop presents use cases in which participants engage with AI-mediated simulations built around common leadership challenges faced by school and district leaders. Rather than reading a static case, participants enter a simulated situation in which they must interpret the problem, ask questions, make decisions, explain their reasoning, and respond to evolving developments.

The emphasis on simulation is also supported by research on immersive learning for aspiring principals. Gilbert found that immersive simulation can strengthen participants' self-efficacy and that the design of the simulation experience is a crucial factor in its educational value. This is highly relevant to AI-enabled leadership simulations, suggesting that the quality of scenario design, interaction structure, and feedback cycles is likely to shape whether simulations meaningfully support professional confidence and decision-making (Gilbert, 2017) [13].

Examples of cases may include a school leader responding to incidents of cyber gender-based violence among students; a school leader planning and facilitating teacher training on AI literacy and responsible AI use; a school leader managing tensions between staff and families around a sensitive school issue; a district leader supporting a school after a decline in student performance and community trust; or a district leader developing a district-wide health and wellbeing plan (UNESCO, 2025) [14]. These situations are especially appropriate for scenario-based learning because they involve incomplete information, multiple perspectives, and no single predetermined answer.

In these simulations, AI can play several roles: it can serve as a scenario generator, producing realistic and context-sensitive cases; as an interactive actor, simulating the voices of teachers, families, students, or supervisors; as a reflection prompt engine, asking participants to justify or reconsider their decisions; and as a feedback coach, offering responses informed by literature on leadership, communication, ethics, norms and laws, and educational planning guidelines, among others. Used in this way, AI becomes a tool for rehearsal and reflection rather than simple automation. This is compatible with the broader argument that AI in education should be designed to augment human learning processes while preserving agency, oversight, and professional judgement (UNESCO, 2023) [2].

The emphasis in these simulations is not on scoring leaders against a fixed correct answer. Instead, the emphasis is on supporting structured reflection. Feedback may invite participants to ask: What assumptions am I making? What information is still missing? Whose perspective has not been heard? How might this decision affect trust, equity, or teaching quality? Such questions align with reflective and organisational learning that treat professional growth as a process of examining underlying assumptions, surfacing tacit theories of action, and improving judgement through inquiry (Argyris and Schön, 1996) [15].

5 AI Literacy for School and District Leaders

A dedicated strand of the workshop focuses on AI literacy for educational leaders. In this proposal, AI literacy is understood not as technical expertise in building AI systems, but as the capacity to critically evaluate AI technologies, communicate and collaborate effectively with them, and make informed decisions about their responsible use. This understanding is consistent with work defining AI literacy as a set of competencies for critical evaluation, use, and engagement with AI systems (Long & Magerko, 2020) [16]. It also resonates with education-specific competency frameworks, including UNESCO's *AI competency framework for teachers* (UNESCO, 2024) [17] and the *IIEP competency framework for educational planning and management* (UNESCO, 2024) [18].

For school and district leaders, AI literacy has at least four dimensions. The first is foundational understanding: knowing what generative AI can and cannot do, why outputs may be inaccurate or biased, and what this means for educational use. The second is critical and ethical judgement: assessing reliability, fairness, privacy implications, and the need for human oversight. The third is professional and organisational use: exploring how AI might support leadership tasks such as planning and communication, while remaining aligned with educational goals. The fourth is governance and change leadership: leading institutional conversations on acceptable use, risk mitigation, staff capacity-building, and responsible adoption. UNESCO's ethics recommendation and guidance on generative AI both emphasize the importance of human-centred design, governance, rights, transparency, and capacity development in educational settings, making them particularly relevant to leadership-focused AI literacy (UNESCO, 2021; UNESCO, 2023; UNESCO, 2025) [19, 20].

6 Workshop Format

We propose an interactive, hands-on half-day workshop format (Table 1).

Table 1. Workshop Timetable

Activity	Time	
Welcome & framing	15 min	Introduction to the workshop rationale, with a focus on AI-enabled scenario-based learning for the professional development of school and district leaders and its relevance to current debates on AI in education and leadership for learning
Live demonstration of an AI-delivered leadership case	20 min	Participants observe or actively engage in simulated leadership scenarios involving a realistic school or district dilemma. The AI plays multiple roles, including generating scenarios, stakeholder interaction and reflective feedback

(*continued*)

Table 1. (*continued*)

Activity	Time	
Deconstruction of the simulation	20 min	Unpack the pedagogical design of the simulation, including the leadership competencies targeted, the structure of prompts, the role of reflection, and the ethical safeguards guiding the use of AI
AI literacy for education leaders	20 min	Introduction to key dimensions of AI literacy for school and district leaders, including critical use, responsible decision-making, governance, and ethical considerations for AI adoption in schools and districts
Break	15 min	
Co-design activity: creating a leadership simulation case	60 min	In small groups, participants design a short leadership scenario and an accompanying AI coaching sequence. They define the dilemma, identify stakeholder roles, formulate prompts, and decide what kind of feedback the AI should provide in line with the current literature and latest research and evidence
Group synthesis	20 min	Participants share their draft scenarios and discuss recurring design choices, tensions, and opportunities for AI-supported scenario-based learning
Closing discussion and next steps	10 min	Final reflection on implementation challenges, research priorities, and opportunities for future use of AI-enabled simulations in leadership development

7 Intended Audience and Expected Participants

The workshop is intended for researchers in AI in education (AIED), learning sciences, educational leadership, and professional development; instructional designers and faculty involved in leadership training; ministries of education and district support teams; school leadership academies; and companies and practitioners involved in the development or interested in AI-supported coaching and reflective simulation.

It is designed for participants who are interested in both the pedagogical possibilities and the governance implications of using generative AI in education leadership professional development.

8 Expected Outcomes and Contributions

First, it offers a clearer pedagogical model for using AI to deliver scenario-based leadership learning. Second, it demonstrates how AI-supported feedback can be used in a coaching-oriented way to strengthen reflective judgement and rehearsal for complex professional situations. Third, it proposes a leadership-oriented framing of AI literacy that is directly relevant to school and education leaders. Fourth, it creates space for a research and design agenda around AI-enabled simulations for education leadership professional development.

More broadly, the workshop contributes to conversations about how AI can support critical thinking skill development for education professionals while preserving human agency, contextual sensitivity, and ethical responsibility.

9 Ethical Considerations

The workshop emphasizes human-in-the-loop design and responsible AI use throughout. This includes transparency about the role of AI in simulations and feedback, attention to bias and stereotyping in scenario design, protection of privacy and data minimisation, and explicit recognition that AI outputs should serve as prompts for reflection rather than as authoritative decisions. These commitments align with UNESCO's ethics framework for AI and with wider work on AI ethics that stresses principles such as human agency, accountability, transparency, and fairness (UNESCO, 2021; UNESCO, 2023).

This is especially important in leadership development, where participants often work through sensitive interpersonal, organisational, and ethical dilemmas. For that reason, the workshop treats AI not as a replacement for facilitation or leadership expertise, but as a structured support for reflective learning.

References

1. Yin, R.K.: Case Study Research: Design and Methods, 5th edn. SAGE Publications, Thousand Oaks (2015)
2. UNESCO: Guidance for Generative AI in Education and Research. UNESCO, Paris (2023)
3. Kolodner, J.L.: Educational implications of analogy: a view from case-based reasoning. Am. Psychol. **52**(1), 57–66 (1997)
4. Lave, J., Wenger, E.: Situated Learning: Legitimate Peripheral Participation. Cambridge University Press, Cambridge (1991)
5. Errington, E.P.: Preparing Graduates for the Professions Using Scenario-Based Learning. Post Pressed, Teneriffe (2011)
6. Leithwood, K., Harris, A., Hopkins, D.: Seven strong claims about successful school leadership revisited. School Leadersh. Manage. **40**(1), 5–22 (2020)
7. Robinson, V.M.J.: Student-Centered Leadership. Jossey-Bass, San Francisco (2011)
8. UNESCO: Global education monitoring report 2024/5: Leadership in education: Lead for learning. UNESCO, Paris (2024). https://unesdoc.unesco.org/ark:/48223/pf0000391406
9. UNESCO IIEP: Education Development Trust: Leading teaching and learning together: The role of the middle tier. UNESCO IIEP, Paris (2023). https://doi.org/10.54675/WBUO9725

10. Vennebo, K.F., Aas, M.: Case-based instruction for leadership learning in the Norwegian national school leadership program. J. Res. Leadersh. Educ. **18**(1), 63–79 (2023)
11. Akrasi, A.-E., Pereyra, J., Kosteridou, I., Lake, S.: Mainstreaming AI in the training cycle: Insights from designing capacity development learning experiences. In: Ninth European MOOCs Stakeholders Summit 2025 (EMOOCS 2025), Télécom Paris, Palaiseau, France. Zenodo (2025). https://doi.org/10.5281/zenodo.15766152
12. Boud, D., Molloy, E. (eds.): Feedback in Higher and Professional Education: Understanding It and Doing It Well. Routledge, London (2013)
13. Gilbert, K.A.: Investigating the use and design of immersive simulation to improve self-efficacy for aspiring principals. J. Inf. Technol. Educ. Innov. Pract. **16**(1), 127–169 (2017). https://doi.org/10.28945/3726
14. UNESCO, Global Partnership for Education, Research Consortium on School Health and Nutrition, UNESCO Chair in Global Health and Education, UNICEF, World Food Programme, World Bank, World Health Organization: Integrating health and well-being into education policy and planning: A handbook. UNESCO, Paris (2025). https://unesdoc.unesco.org/ark:/48223/pf0000396442
15. Argyris, C., Schön, D.A.: Organizational Learning II: Theory, Method, and Practice. Addison-Wesley, Reading (1996)
16. Long, D., Magerko, B.: What is AI literacy? Competencies and design considerations. In: Proceedings of the 2020 CHI Conference on Human Factors in Computing Systems, pp. 1–16. ACM, New York (2020)
17. UNESCO: AI competency framework for teachers, Paris (2024). https://unesdoc.unesco.org/ark:/48223/pf0000391104
18. UNESCO: IIEP competency framework for educational planning and management. UNESCO, Paris (2024) https://unesdoc.unesco.org/ark:/48223/pf0000389048
19. UNESCO: Recommendation on the ethics of artificial intelligence. UNESCO, Paris (2021). https://unesdoc.unesco.org/ark:/48223/pf0000381137
20. UNESCO: AI and the future of education: disruptions, dilemmas and directions. UNESCO, Paris (2025). https://unesdoc.unesco.org/ark:/48223/pf0000395236

From Tools to Teammates? Examining Human–AI Synergy in Educational Design Fictions Through the Lens of Extended Cognition

Florence Lehnert[1](✉), Maka Eradze[2], and Marcus Specht[1]

[1] FernUniversität in Hagen, Universitätsstraße 47, 58097 Hagen, Germany
{florence.lehnert,marcus.specht}@fernuni-hagen.de
[2] University of L'Aquila, Viale Nizza, 14, 67100 L'Aquila (AQ), Italy
maka.eradze@univaq.it

Abstract. Artificial Intelligence (AI) in education is evolving from a supportive tool into a system that increasingly shapes how learners think, reason and learn. As AI systems take on roles in writing, problem-solving, and decision-making, educational discourse is shifting from viewing AI merely as a tool toward understanding it as a potential "teammate." Yet, meaningful human–AI synergy requires clear understanding of the underlying cognitive roles AI plays in learning and raises a critical question: under what conditions does AI remain a support tool, and when does it become part of the learner's cognitive process? This participatory workshop addresses this question through Andy Clark's extended mind theory. Drawing on Clark's extension conditions – reliable availability, easy accessibility, automatic endorsement, and integration into cognitive routines – participants will analyse educational design fiction scenarios that depict diverse forms of Human–AI collaboration in learning contexts. These scenarios serve as shared analytical artefacts, enabling participants to surface hidden assumptions and examine how AI's integration shapes epistemic responsibility, cognitive effort, and reflective engagement. The workshop will result in a collaboratively developed, theory-informed set of design and evaluation guidelines to support researchers and educators in (1) assessing the degree to which AI becomes cognitively integrated into the learning processes, (2) designing learning activities that foster deliberate rather than automatic endorsement of AI outputs, and (3) structuring human–AI interaction to enable a productive distribution of cognitive effort. By linking theory, speculative design, and participatory analysis, the workshop contributes to a deeper understanding of human–AI synergy and advances a shared research and design agenda for responsible and reflective AI integration in education.

Keywords: Human–AI Interaction · Extended Cognition · Speculative Design · Artificial Intelligence in Education · Learning Science

E. G. Blanchard et al. (Eds.): AIED 2026, CCIS 3033, pp. 153–160, 2026.
https://doi.org/10.1007/978-3-032-29794-5_25

1 Theoretical Background

1.1 Generative AI and Epistemic Transformation

Enlightenment thinkers such as Descartes and La Mettrie conceptualised the mind as a system of interacting parts that could, in principle, be reproduced artificially. In the twentieth century, this perspective evolved into computational models of intelligence. Alan Turing's "imitation game" reframed intelligence in behavioural terms, suggesting that if a machine's responses were indistinguishable from those of a human, it could be considered intelligent [1]. This framing paved the way for systems that not only appear intelligent but also increasingly participate in human epistemic practices. Search engines represent an earlier stage of this transformation: they retrieve ranked documents and present a landscape of sources, while evaluation remains the user's responsibility. Large language models (LLMs), by contrast, synthesise information into a single response, collapsing searching, selecting, and explaining into one authoritative output [2], often privileging highly cited, frequently accessed, or otherwise prominent sources embedded in their training data. As a result, users receive answers ready for immediate consumption. This constitutes an epistemological transformation, as the interpretive labour previously performed by the individual becomes partially or fully delegated to the system. While this compression increases efficiency (e.g., by reducing the need to consult multiple sources), it may also reduce epistemic transparency and foster overreliance on fluent but opaque outputs.

These epistemic asymmetries become particularly significant when human and artificial systems are tightly coupled. Andy Clark and David Chalmers' (1998) theory of extended cognition offers a framework for examining such coupling [3]. Clark later generalises this argument, suggesting that humans are "natural-born cyborgs" whose cognitive systems routinely incorporate external artefacts [4]. This perspective resonates with related frameworks, such as N. Katherine Hayles' notion of cognitive assemblages, which conceptualises human–AI "teaming" as a form of distributed, agentic cognition rather than a simple human–tool relation [5]. Clark and Chalmers illustrate the extended mind thesis through the example of Otto, who relies on a notebook to compensate for memory impairment [3]. Under certain conditions, the notebook does not merely assist cognition – it becomes part of Otto's cognitive system. According to the extended mind thesis, external artefacts may count as components of cognition when four conditions are satisfied: reliable availability, easy accessibility, automatic endorsement, and integration into cognitive routines. *Reliable availability* means that the resource is consistently present when needed. Otto's notebook is reliably carried and consulted whenever memory is required. Applied to generative AI, this implies a persistent presence across drafting, revising, searching, or problem-solving, rather than occasional consultation. *Easy accessibility* concerns the effort required to retrieve information. Otto consults his notebook with minimal friction. Similarly, when AI systems are embedded directly within writing interfaces or learning platforms, the threshold for consultation becomes minimal, increasing the likelihood of incorporation into ongoing reasoning.

Automatic endorsement is more demanding. Otto typically trusts the notebook's contents as he would biological memory; he does not constantly re-verify them. For generative AI, the critical question becomes: when are AI-generated outputs critically evaluated, and when are they incorporated without reconstruction? Finally, *integration* into cognitive routines refers to the artefact's stable role in shaping habitual patterns of thought and action. Otto's notebook is not an occasional aid, but part of the structure of his cognitive activity. Applied to educational AI, the question is whether AI systems function as intermittently consulted tools or become stably embedded in learners' problem-solving practices. When learners routinely organise their reasoning around AI-generated suggestions or drafts, AI may shift from external support to a structurally integrated component of the cognitive process. Taken together, Otto's notebook illustrates how external artefacts can become constitutive parts of cognition. The central question for generative AI is whether similar conditions are increasingly being met – and, if so, what this implies for epistemic agency, responsibility, and the architecture of learning.

1.2 AI-Mediated Learning

In educational contexts, generative AI is increasingly embedded in everyday learning practices. Students use AI systems to summarise readings, generate arguments, structure essays, and refine drafts. Recent work in AI in Education and Learning at Scale has begun to examine these emerging practices, particularly regarding hybrid intelligence and human–AI collaboration [6]. While much of this literature focuses on performance gains, efficiency, or instructional design, fewer studies address the structural implications of AI becoming deeply integrated into learners' cognitive processes. When AI is reliably available and easily accessible, learners may delegate retrieval, synthesis, and explanation. Cognitive offloading has long been recognised as a functional strategy for managing cognitive load [7]. External tools can reduce extraneous load and enable more complex reasoning. However, research on generative learning and retrieval practice suggests that active reconstruction, elaboration, and effortful processing are central to durable understanding [8]. If AI increasingly performs these generative functions, opportunities for learning effort may be reduced. Clark's condition of automatic endorsement is particularly salient in educational contexts. Generative systems produce fluent, coherent and linguistically plausible [9] responses that may invite uncritical acceptance, and a partial or full elimination of human judgment. Research on automation bias shows that individuals tend to over-trust automated systems, even when errors are present [10]. Similarly, studies on the illusion of explanatory depth demonstrate that perceived fluency can be mistaken for genuine understanding [11]. When learners incorporate AI-generated reasoning without reconstruction, epistemic responsibility may subtly shift from the learner to the system. As AI becomes integrated into drafting, revision, and argumentation routines, it may also reshape metacognitive regulation. Metacognition – monitoring and controlling one's own understanding – is central to self-regulated learning [12]. AI tools can scaffold reflection by suggesting counterarguments or highlighting inconsistencies. Yet they may also displace internal monitoring processes if learners rely on automated feedback without developing their own evaluative skills. The central issue is therefore not whether AI is inherently beneficial or harmful, but how its integration reshapes cognitive architecture and epistemic agency. Clark's theory of the extended mind offers a clear framework for examining how deeply AI is integrated into learning processes and whether it functions as a tool or becomes part of the learner's cognitive system. However, these structural shifts are not easily captured in short-term performance studies or isolated system evaluations. Because cognitive integration develops gradually in everyday practice, its implications require methods that make assumptions about human–AI interaction visible. Instead of focusing only on whether AI improves outcomes, we must examine how different forms of integration reshape responsibility, cognitive effort, and understanding. This calls for approaches that enable systematic and reflective exploration of alternative configurations of human–AI learning.

1.3 Design Fiction for Reflection Inquiry

Design fiction offers such an approach by employing speculative narrative scenarios to explore possible technological futures and provoke critical reflection [13]. Rather than predicting developments, design fiction constructs plausible yet imagined situations that surface implicit assumptions, tensions, and value conflicts embedded in emerging technologies. Narrating how technologies become embedded in everyday practices, it renders visible what often remains implicit in policy discourse and system design. As such, design fiction functions not as forecasting but as a reflective and discursive method. In educational research, design fiction and speculative pedagogy have been used to interrogate AI-enabled futures of learning, assessment, and governance [14, 15]. Scholars have applied speculative narratives to examine themes such as automation, personalisation, surveillance, learner agency, and institutional power [14, 16, 17]. These works demonstrate how imagined futures can reveal dominant imaginaries and ethical tensions surrounding AI in education. Rather than offering immediate technical solutions, they create structured spaces for questioning what kinds of educational futures are desirable and whose values are embedded in technological design. Design fiction is particularly suited to the present workshop for three reasons. First, it allows participants to examine structural [re]configurations of human–AI interaction without relying on existing systems, thereby avoiding premature assumptions influenced by technological determinism. By manipulating narrative elements, such as the reliability, accessibility, authority, or integration of AI, participants can explore varying degrees of cognitive coupling and dependency. Second, speculative scenarios externalise cognitive processes; They make visible how reasoning unfolds within sociotechnical arrangements, enabling systematic analysis of how AI is positioned relative to learner cognition. Third, design fiction supports collaborative interpretation and redesign, aligning well with participatory workshop formats and enabling the co-construction of design principles. In this workshop, design fictions serve as shared analytical artefacts. When examined through Clark's conditions for extended cognition, these narratives provide a structured framework for analysing how different [re]configurations of AI integration reshape epistemic responsibility, cognitive effort, and reflective engagement. Design fiction thus bridges philosophy of technology, cognition and education design practices, enabling systematic reflection on human–AI synergy and cognitive coupling within AIED contexts.

2 Workshop Outline

2.1 Workshop Goals and Relevance for AIED

This interactive half-day workshop invites participants to critically examine the growing metaphor of AI as a "teammate" in education. Drawing on Andy Clark's extended cognition framework, participants will analyse how AI is positioned in learning processes by applying four conditions – reliable availability, accessibility, automatic endorsement, and integration into cognitive routines – to design fiction scenarios of AI-mediated learning. In structured small-group sessions, participants will identify patterns of human–AI cognitive coupling and key opportunity–risk tensions, such as cognitive support versus reduced effort or enhanced creativity versus uncritical acceptance of fluent outputs. In a subsequent design phase, these insights will be translated into concrete principles for AIED systems and learning activities (e.g., interrupting automatic endorsement, configurable AI access, or prompts requiring critical engagement). At a meta-level, participants will reflect on the strengths and limitations of extended cognition as a lens for understanding hybrid intelligence in education. The workshop will culminate in collaboratively developed principles that function as shared heuristics for responsible, reflective, and agentive human–AI collaboration. Ethical and equity considerations – including bias, surveillance, unequal access, and epistemic injustice – will be addressed throughout.

3 Expected Outputs Include:

- A shared analytical template for examining the AI "teammate" metaphor in design fiction scenarios using Clark's four conditions.
- Theory-informed design principles for reflective and responsible AI integration in learning.
- A collaboratively developed advanced research agenda and theorisation on human–AI cognitive coupling and epistemic responsibility.
- Publicly available workshop materials and a brief synthesis report for the AIED community.

The workshop is intended for researchers in AIED and Learning at Scale (L@S), scholars working on generative AI and hybrid intelligence, designers of AI-supported learning systems, and doctoral students. We anticipate 20–30 participants to enable interactive discussion and cross-disciplinary exchange. No prior knowledge of extended cognition is required. By grounding the "AI teammate" metaphor in a structured conceptual framework, the workshop strengthens theoretical clarity within AIED and connects speculative educational futures with concrete research and design practice in responsible AI-supported learning.

3.1 Workshop Structure

The workshop is designed as a structured, interactive half-day session (4 h), combining theoretical framing, collaborative analysis, and collective synthesis. The format balances short conceptual inputs with small-group work and plenary reflection.

- **0:00–0:30 | Framing: From Tools to Teammates**
  The workshop opens with a concise theoretical introduction to extended cognition and Clark's four conditions. Participants are introduced to the analytical lens and its relevance for examining AI-mediated learning. A short design fiction vignette is presented to ground the discussion.
- **0:30–1:15 | Small-Group Analysis of AI "Teammate" Narratives**
  Participants work in small interdisciplinary groups to analyse selected design fiction scenarios. Using Clark's conditions, groups examine how AI is positioned within the learning process, identify integration depth, and discuss tensions between augmentation and dependency.
- **1:15–1:30 | Break**
- **1:30–2:15 | Synthesis: Patterns of Cognitive Coupling**
  Groups report back key observations. Facilitators synthesise recurring patterns of human–AI cognitive coupling, including issues related to endorsement, offloading, and metacognitive regulation. Emerging themes are documented collaboratively.
- **2:15–3:15 | Design Principles for Reflective AI Integration**
  Participants shift from analysis to constructive redesign. In groups, they translate their insights into design principles for AI-mediated learning environments that support epistemic responsibility and sustained critical engagement.
- **3:15–3:30 | Break**
- **3:30–4:00 | Meta-Reflection and Research Agenda**
  The workshop concludes with a plenary discussion on the usefulness and limitations of extended cognition as an analytical lens. Participants collectively outline open research questions and potential collaborative next steps.

3.2 Workshop Organizers

Florence Lehnert is a Postdoctoral Researcher in Learning Sciences at the Center of Advanced Technology for Assisted Learning and Predictive Analytics (CATALPA), FernUniversität in Hagen, Germany. Her research explores how generative AI reshapes learning processes and human–AI collaboration in educational contexts. She examines AI-mediated learning through theoretical and design-oriented lenses, including extended cognition and speculative methods, with the aim of developing conceptually grounded frameworks and practical guidelines for responsible AI integration in higher education. She completed her PhD at the University of Luxembourg in 2024, focusing on user experience evaluation in digital assessment contexts, and has been active in the HCI and educational technology communities.

Maka Eradze is Associate Professor of educational research and teaching methodologies at the University of L'Aquila, where she leads research on educational technologies, learning design, and digital education in school and higher-education contexts. She has authored numerous international publications, and she serves as editor, reviewer, and committee member for international journals and conferences in technology-enhanced learning and digital education. Currently, her main interest is in educational innovation and its sociotechnical dimensions, futures of education, speculative methods and Human-GenAI co-creative processes.

Marcus Specht is Scientific Director of CATALPA and Head of the research professorship Learning Sciences in Higher Education. With an interdisciplinary background and over 30 years of experience across computer science and psychology, he also holds a chair in Digital Education at TU Delft's Faculty of Electrical Engineering, Mathematics and Computer Science (EEMCS). In addition, he is affiliated with Erasmus University Rotterdam (Erasmus School of Social and Behavioural Sciences) and Leiden University's Institute for Advanced Computer Science (LIACS). His recent research focuses on Learning Analytics, AIED, Digital Skills, and Computational Thinking. His future work will primarily explore how Learning Analytics, AI, and Mixed Reality technologies can support teaching and learning processes.

3.3 Previous Editions and Outreach

This workshop is offered in this format for the first time and builds on the organizers' research on AI futures, extended cognition, and human–AI collaboration in education. It draws on prior design fiction workshops (e.g., EADTU Conference 2025; JTEL Summer School 2025), where participants created and analyzed AI-related design fictions using a structured heuristic framework. Insights from these sessions inform the participatory structure and analytical scaffolding of this workshop. Materials and outcomes – including collaboratively developed guidelines and thematic summaries – will be made openly available (e.g., via Zenodo or a workshop website) to support ongoing community engagement. Participants will be invited to contribute to a collaborative reflection, with potential follow-up publications (e.g., joint articles or special issues).

The workshop will be promoted through AIED and Learning at Scale (L@S) networks, mailing lists, and social platforms. Additional outreach will target underrepresented regions and practitioner communities (e.g., teachers, learning designers, student support staff) to ensure diverse participation. Design fiction scenarios will be developed to reflect varied educational, cultural, and infrastructural contexts.

Disclosure of Interests. The authors have no competing interests to declare that are relevant to the content of this article.

References

1. Turing, A.M.: Computing machinery and intelligence. In: Epstein, R., Roberts, G., Beber, G. (eds.) Parsing the Turing Test, pp. 23–65. Springer, Dordrecht (2009). https://doi.org/10.1007/978-1-4020-6710-5_3
2. Li, X., et al.: From matching to generation: a survey on generative information retrieval. ACM Trans. Inf. Syst. **43**, 1–62 (2025). https://doi.org/10.1145/3722552
3. Clark, A.: The extended mind. Analysis **58**, 7–19 (1998). https://doi.org/10.1093/analys/58.1.7
4. Clark, A.: Natural-Born Cyborgs: Minds, Technologies, and the Future of Human Intelligence. Oxford University Press, Oxford New York (2003). https://doi.org/10.1093/mind/113.450.326
5. Hayles, N.K.: Cognitive assemblages: technical agency and human interactions. Crit. Inq. **43**, 32–55 (2016). https://doi.org/10.1086/688293

6. Cukurova, M.: The interplay of learning, analytics and artificial intelligence in education: a vision for hybrid intelligence. Br. J. Edu. Technol. **56**, 469–488 (2025). https://doi.org/10.1111/bjet.13514
7. Sweller, J.: Cognitive load during problem solving: effects on learning. Cogn. Sci. **12**, 257–285 (1988). https://doi.org/10.1207/s15516709cog1202_4
8. Bjork, E.L., Bjork, R.A.: Making things hard on yourself, but in a good way: creating desirable difficulties to enhance learning. Psychol. Real World Essays Illustrating Fundam. Contrib. Soc. **2**, 56–64 (2011)
9. Quattrociocchi, W., Capraro, V., Perc, M.: Epistemological fault lines between human and artificial intelligence. arXiv preprint arXiv:2512.19466 (2025)
10. Parasuraman, R., Riley, V.: Humans and automation: use, misuse, disuse. Abuse. Hum Fact. **39**, 230–253 (1997). https://doi.org/10.1518/001872097778543886
11. Rozenblit, L., Keil, F.: The misunderstood limits of folk science: an illusion of explanatory depth. Cogn. Sci. **26**, 521–562 (2002). https://doi.org/10.1207/s15516709cog2605_1
12. Zimmerman, B.J.: Becoming a self-regulated learner: an overview. Theory Into Pract. **41**, 64–70 (2002). https://doi.org/10.1207/s15430421tip4102_2
13. Dunne, A., Raby, F.: Speculative Everything, With a New Preface by the Authors: Design, Fiction, and Social Dreaming. MIT press (2024)
14. Bozkurt, A., Xiao, J., Lambert, S., et al.: Speculative Futures on ChatGPT and Generative Artificial Intelligence (AI): A Collective Reflection from the Educational Landscape. **18**, 53–130 (2023)
15. Bayne, S., Ross, J.: Speculative futures for higher education. Int. J. Educ. Technol. High. Educ. **21**, 39 (2024). https://doi.org/10.1186/s41239-024-00469-y
16. Cox, A.M.: Exploring the impact of artificial intelligence and robots on higher education through literature-based design fictions. Int. J. Educ. Technol. Higher Educ. **18**, 3 (2021). https://doi.org/10.1186/s41239-020-00237-8
17. Gidiotis, I., Hrastinski, S.: Imagining the future of artificial intelligence in education: a review of social science fiction. Learn. Media Technol. 1–13 (2024). https://doi.org/10.1080/17439884.2024.2365829

User-Driven Explainable AI in Education and Its Implications for Human Agency

Hasan Abu-Rasheed[1(✉)], Jakub Kuzilek[2], Mutlu Cukurova[3], Hassan Khosravi[4], Luc Paquette[5], Tanja Käser[6], Benjamin Paaßen[7], Christian Weber[8], Vinitra Swamy[6,9], and Qianhui Sophie Liu[5]

[1] Goethe University Frankfurt, Frankfurt, Germany
rasheed@sd.uni-frankfurt.de
[2] FernUniversität in Hagen, Hagen, Germany
[3] University College London UCL, London, UK
[4] The University of Queensland, Brisbane, Australia
[5] University of Illinois Urbana-Champaign, Illinois, USA
[6] EPFL, Lausanne, Switzerland
[7] Bielefeld University, Bielefeld, Germany
[8] University of Siegen, Siegen, Germany
[9] Scholé AI, Lausanne, Switzerland

Abstract. The rapid integration of artificial intelligence (AI) into educational contexts has intensified concerns regarding transparency, accountability, fairness, and stakeholder agency. Explainable AI (XAI) research has the potential to advance methods for interpreting complex machine learning models, revealing opportunities to utilize explainability to enable safe, sustainable, and user-driven implementation of AI-supported systems in authentic educational settings. This half-day interdisciplinary workshop addresses this potential by focusing on explainability by design as a mechanism for strengthening the agency of teachers, learners, and institutions. Bringing together researchers and practitioners from AIED, EDM, and L@S, we aim to develop a shared understanding of design principles, XAI frameworks, technical challenges, and a research agenda for embedding transparency across the entire AI life cycle, from data pipelines and modeling to classroom integration and governance. We utilize targeted discussions, engaging talks and group activities to emphasize collaborative and cross-disciplinary exchange and long-term community building. By re-framing explainability as a socio-technical design challenge rather than solely a technical feature, this workshop advances the field toward more accountable, equitable, and agency-supportive AI in education.

Keywords: Explainable AI · Artificial Intelligence in Education · Learning Analytics · Stakeholder Agency · Sustainable AI Implementation

E. G. Blanchard et al. (Eds.): AIED 2026, CCIS 3033, pp. 161–166, 2026.
https://doi.org/10.1007/978-3-032-29794-5_26

1 Introduction and Workshop Motivation

Artificial intelligence (AI) systems are increasingly embedded in educational infrastructures, influencing assessment, feedback, recommendation, and instructional decision-making [10,12]. Predictive analytics, adaptive learning environments, and generative AI tools are now routinely deployed in schools and higher education. While these systems promise personalization and scalability, they also introduce risks related to opacity, bias, over-reliance, erosion of professional judgment, and the redistribution of agency among learners, educators, and automated systems.

Explainable AI (XAI) has emerged as a response to the opacity of complex machine learning models, seeking to make their behavior understandable to humans [1,5]. However, educational settings raise questions that extend beyond technical interpretability or one-off explanations of classification decisions. Educational AI systems participate in socio-technical environments, characterized by pedagogy, institutional accountability, and long-term human development.

The recent emergence of large language models (LLMs) and generative AI systems introduces new challenges and opportunities for explainability in education [11]. Unlike traditional predictive models, LLM-based systems can produce natural language explanations on demand, creating an appearance of transparency that may not correspond to the actual reasoning processes underlying model outputs [2]. Explanations generated by such systems may be incomplete, post-hoc, or even hallucinated, potentially misleading learners and educators if interpreted as faithful representations of model decision-making. Moreover, the rise of agentic AI systems, supposedly capable of autonomous planning, tool use, and multi-step reasoning further complicates explainability by distributing decision-making across dynamic and partially observable processes. These developments highlight the need to move beyond explanation as interface-level output toward life-cycle oriented approaches that address reliability, epistemic uncertainty, and human oversight as central components of safe and sustainable educational AI design, similar to the notion of social explainable AI (sXAI) [13].

This workshop argues that a safe and sustainable pathway for AI in education requires moving beyond post-hoc explanation interfaces toward *explainability-by-design* as a socio-technical approach that treats explanations as a core design constraint shaped by stakeholder goals, decision rights, and educational values. In this view, explanations are not merely model artifacts, but rather mechanisms embedded across the AI life cycle, from data collection and preprocessing to model development, interface design, deployment, and institutional governance. The aim is to promote educational stakeholders' agency, supporting them to understand and contest automated inferences, calibrate reliance, adapt or override recommendations, and have an active role in governing pipelines and model updates.

2 Theoretical Background and Relevance

XAI has emerged as a response to the opacity of complex machine learning systems, aiming to provide interpretable insights into model decisions [1,5]. In educational contexts, explainability is particularly critical because AI systems directly influence learners' recommendations, feedback, assessment, and learning trajectories. The increasing integration of predictive analytics and generative AI into everyday learning environments further amplifies the stakes of opacity [7,11].

Research in Artificial Intelligence in Education (AIED) and Educational Data Mining (EDM) increasingly points out the need for explainability in educational tasks, learner modeling, decision support, and learning analytics, reflecting on the autonomy and accountability of educational stakeholders [8,14]. Literature show that concrete explanation mechanisms (e.g. visualised reasoning, clear provenance, separation of human-assigned and AI-recommended tasks) shape how teachers and students calibrate trust, contest recommendations, and maintain control over teaching and learning processes [11]. However, recent AI-driven systems, especially deep learning architectures and generative models, reintroduce opacity at scale, challenging established model interpretability and system explainability.

Feldman-Maggor et al. [4] show that carefully designed explanation schemes can strengthen teachers' understanding and trust when they align with domain needs and decision contexts. Likewise, Kim et al. [9] work on learner-facing GenAI tools demonstrates that interface features can be designed to protect learner agency by making planning, monitoring, and AI-reliance visible and actionable.

Recent work by Cukurova [3] argues that agency in AI-mediated education is best understood as a property of the humanAI system, emerging from interaction designs, task structures, and institutional arrangements rather than residing solely in individual learners or teachers. Conceptual and empirical work on hybrid intelligence and teacherAI teaming distinguishes between automation that replaces human judgment and higher-agency configurations in which AI externalises patterns while humans retain goal-setting, evaluation, and governance roles.

This resonates well with the work of Viberg et al. [14] that points out that the interpretability of human-AI interactions, prioritizing choice, customization and learner control, as well as designing for long-term development rater than short-term efficiency, is essential to counteract the risks of generative AI on educational contexts and stakeholders. This is because the growing involvement of those system in educational tasks is introducing significant shifts in the distribution of autonomy and control between the educational stakeholders and the AI-supported system.

To correspond to such influences, the involvement of educational stakeholders in the early staged of the design of AI-supported systems, as we ll as the transparency of their developments, becomes essential to ensure sound autonomy and accountability in education. Holstein et al. [6] highlight the need for human-centered AI in education, emphasizing co-design with teachers to ensure that AI tools align with classroom realities and professional judgment. This is meant to augment, not replace human actors in the mechanisms of human-AI interaction and support actionable insight and helps prevent over-reliance on black-box predictions and preserve human oversight.

Therefore, we position explainability-by-design not only as an interface characteristic but as a property of the broader socio-technical system in which AI operates. This perspective guides the discussions and outcomes of the workshop, raising research questions for the AIED, EDM, and L@S communities concerning governance, accountability, professional agency, and the life cycle integration of AI technologies.

This workshop contributes to the AIED, EDM, and L@S communities by:

- Integrating technical XAI research with participatory design and implementation research.
- Addressing explainability at the level of data infrastructures, not only model architectures.
- Framing explainability as a mechanism for agency and governance, rather than merely interpretability.
- Bridging algorithmic transparency with pedagogical alignment and organizational sustainability.

3 Goals, Theme, and Prior Work

Our aim is to explore how educational AI systems can be co-designed to preserve meaningful human agency while benefiting from advances in automation and data-driven modeling. Rather than concentrating on specific explanation techniques, we focus on the conditions under which explainability contributes to responsible adoption and sustained educational value, aiming to:

- Articulate an agency-oriented design perspective: Develop a shared vocabulary for understanding explainability as a mechanism that enables stakeholders to question, adapt, and guide AI-supported processes.
- Connect technical transparency to educational practice: Examine how interpretable models, data documentation, and interface design translate into actionable understanding for teachers and learners.
- Identify life cycle challenges: Map where opacity emerges across the AI life cycle, including procurement, data governance, deployment, and classroom integration.
- Develop a cross-disciplinary research agenda: Define open problems that require collaboration among AIED, EDM, HCI, learning sciences, and policy research.

These goals orient the workshop toward concrete outcomes. A central deliverable is a **conceptual framework**, co-developed with participants to links technical explainability to organizational and pedagogical contexts. The framework will describe how transparency must be addressed at multiple layers, including data practices, modeling choices, user interaction, and institutional oversight. The framework will also point out **actionable design principles** for aligning AI functionality with educational values, including maintaining teacher authority in decision loops, documenting data provenance, and designing explanations that support deliberation rather than automation bias. Moreover, we aim to discuss a **research agenda** discussing priority research directions such as evaluating human-AI collaboration in classrooms, designing tools that support contestability, and studying long-term institutional integration of explainable systems. Overall, the workshop extends thematic offering to a continued **community building** process, by connecting researchers across AIED, EDM, and L@S, establishing a network focused human agency dimensions of explainable educational AI.

While this is the first edition of this workshop under the present framing, it is grounded in a mature line of prior community work. The HEXED[1] and XAI-ED[2] workshops, which have been held over the last three years, constitute direct predecessors and serve as the community foundation for this initiative. These prior editions established an active research network and validated the demand for dedicated venues addressing explainability in educational AI.

Safe and sustainable AI implementation requires collaboration across these domains. Therefore, this workshop extend this trajectory by foregrounding stakeholder agency and systemic, life cycle-oriented sustainability which are dimensions that complement the more technically focused contributions of earlier editions.

Acknowledgments. The work in this paper is supported by the LEAD:FUH project funded by the Stiftung Innovation in der Hochschullehre (1001-3223), the Swiss State Secretariat for Education, Research and Innovation (SERI), and InnoSuisse.

References

1. Adadi, A., Berrada, M.: Peeking inside the black-box: a survey on explainable artificial intelligence. IEEE Access **6**, 52138–52160 (2018). https://doi.org/10.1109/ACCESS.2018.2870052
2. Barez, F., et al.: Chain-of-thought is not explainability (2025)
3. Cukurova, M.: The interplay of learning, analytics and artificial intelligence in education: a vision for hybrid intelligence. Br. J. Edu. Technol. **56**(2), 469–488 (2025). https://doi.org/10.1111/bjet.13514
4. Feldman-Maggor, Y., Cukurova, M., Kent, C., Alexandron, G.: The impact of explainable ai on teachers' trust and acceptance of ai edtech recommendations: the power of domain-specific explanations. Int. J. Artif. Intell. Educ. **35**, 2889–2922 (2025). https://doi.org/10.1007/s40593-025-00486-6
5. Gunning, D., Aha, D.: Darpa's explainable artificial intelligence (XAI) program. AI Mag. **40**(2), 44–58 (2019). https://doi.org/10.1609/aimag.v40i2.2850

[1] https://hexed-workshop.github.io/.
[2] https://sites.google.com/view/xai-ed.

6. Holstein, K., McLaren, B.M., Aleven, V.: Co-designing a real-time classroom orchestration tool to support teacher–AI complementarity. In: Proceedings of the 2019 CHI Conference on Human Factors in Computing Systems, pp. 1–14 (2019). https://doi.org/10.1145/3290605.3300844
7. Kasneci, E., et al.: ChatGPT for good? On opportunities and challenges of large language models for education. Learn. Individ. Differ. **103**, 102274 (2023). https://doi.org/10.1016/j.lindif.2023.102274
8. Khosravi, H., et al.: Explainable artificial intelligence in education. Comput. Educ. Artif. Intell. **3**, 100074 (2022). https://doi.org/10.1016/j.caeai.2022.100074
9. Kim, S., So, H.J., Park, K.: Supporting learner agency in collaborative writing with generative AI. Br. J. Educ. Technol. 1–25 (2025). https://doi.org/10.1111/bjet.70015
10. Matos, T., Santos, W., Zdravevski, E., Coelho, P.J., Pires, I.M., Madeira, F.: A systematic review of artificial intelligence applications in education: emerging trends and challenges. Decis. Anal. J. **15**, 100571 (2025). https://doi.org/10.1016/j.dajour.2025.100571
11. OECD: OECD Digital Education Outlook 2026: Exploring Effective Uses of Generative AI in Education. OECD Publishing, Paris (2026). https://doi.org/10.1787/062a7394-en
12. Rismanchian, S., Doroudi, S.: The evolution of research on ai and education across four decades: insights from the AIxEd framework. Int. J. Artif. Intell. Educ. **35**(5), 2797–2820 (2025)
13. Rohlfing, K.J., et al.: Explanation as a social practice: toward a conceptual framework for the social design of ai systems. IEEE Trans. Cogn. Dev. Syst. **13**(3), 717–728 (2021). https://doi.org/10.1109/TCDS.2020.3044366
14. Viberg, O., Poquet, O., Kovanovic, V., Khosravi, H.: Fostering human agency in age of AI: a learning analytics perspective. J. Learn. Anal. **12**(3), 1–7 (2025). https://doi.org/10.18608/jla.2025.9485

Ethical Artificial Intelligence and Education: The Need for International Regulation to Foster Human Rights, Democracy and Equity

Christian M. Stracke[1,7](✉), Beth Havinga[2,7], Wayne Holmes[3,7], Ron Salaj[4,7], Daniel Burgos[5], and Jon Mason[6]

[1] University of Bonn, Bonn, Germany
stracke@uni-bonn.de
[2] European EdTech Alliance, Marienfelde, Germany
[3] University College London, London, UK
[4] University of Torino, Turin, Italy
[5] Universidad Internacional La Rioja, Logroño, Spain
[6] Charles Darwin University, Darwin, Australia
[7] Council of Europe AI&ED Expert Group, Strasbourg, France

Abstract. The growing implementation of Artificial Intelligence in education (AIED) raises pressing ethical, legal, and political questions. Unlike other sectors, education affects minors and youth, shapes societal values and civic participation, and plays a foundational role in upholding democratic principles. Education cannot, therefore, be treated as a standard application domain for AI technologies because the relationship between AI and Education (AI&ED) is very complex and special. The introduction of AI systems in educational environments risks reinforcing inequality, diminishing democratic oversight, and displacing core human functions in pedagogy. This paper introduces the concept of the workshop held at the international 27th AIED Conference 2026. It responds to these concerns by focusing on the development of binding international regulations and organisational safeguards to govern the complex relationship between AI and education (AI&ED). Grounded in the work of the Council of Europe's AI&ED Expert Group, it aims to identify specific legal requirements and structural measures necessary to protect human rights, democracy, and the rule of the law in educational contexts. A special focus will be on formal education for all including AI use and policies for assessment to foster and improve human rights, democracy and equity. Through interactive formats, the workshop will critically examine existing policy proposals, identify omissions, and propose principles for effective regulation that serve the common good. The results can feed into the design of international AI policies and regulations for education including the Council of Europe's development of international AI&ED laws and conventions: The key focus is on a binding convention for the AI use in education (AIED) and on a recommendation for the education about AI (AI literacy).

Keywords: Artificial Intelligence and Education (AI&ED) · regulation · human rights · democracy · equity · formal education · assessment · international laws and conventions · AI use in education (AIED) · education about AI (AI literacy) · Council of Europe

E. G. Blanchard et al. (Eds.): AIED 2026, CCIS 3033, pp. 167–174, 2026.
https://doi.org/10.1007/978-3-032-29794-5_27

1 Introduction

Education is a Human Right and a Sustainable Development Goal for the common good and improvement of our society [23]. Thus, education is a special sector that requires specific regulation of Artificial Intelligence (AI) [22, 27]. The adoption of AI technologies in education is proceeding rapidly, often with minimal public debate or not sufficient regulatory scrutiny [5, 6, 24, 25]. This expansion brings with it not only technical challenges, but also ethical and societal concerns [16, 19, 21]. The domain of education is distinct from other sectors because it deals with users of systems who have limited agency over the tools that they use and it is mandatory in school education [15, 18]. Education environments play a vital role in the safeguarding and enactment of societal values and development of democratic awareness and principles [13, 15].

Unregulated AI use in education risks exacerbating social inequalities, displacing critical pedagogical roles, undermining essential principles of democracy and further limiting the agency of learners and educators with regard to safe data practices [4, 14]. Standard regulatory approaches that treat AI as a neutral tool are insufficient to address the power asymmetries and institutional vulnerabilities specific to education [15].

This context demands a targeted, rights-based regulatory framework that prioritises transparency, public accountability, and democratic control [22, 27]. Not the commercial interests by AI providers but the common good of our society should be the goals for education with and about AI [22, 23].

1.1 Background

In 2021, the Council of Europe (COE) established an expert group exploring the application of AI in education (AIED), the teaching of AI in education (AI Literacy) and the regulatory needs associated with these areas [7]. The goal of the group is to develop actionable insights and recommendation for CoE Member States, which cover 46 countries within wider Europe and are responsible for a population of approximately 675 million people. These recommendations are intended to guide the application of AI in education for the common good and aligned with the essential focus areas of the CoE: Human rights, democracy and the rule of the law [8].

In 2022, the CoE expert group on education prepared the report, *Artificial Intelligence and Education: A critical view through the lens of human rights, democracy and the rule of law* [11]. This report highlighted the need for education-specific safeguarding, AI governance structures, and was designed to further critical discourse. The report served as an important step towards developing two policy instruments as requested by the Member States: a binding legal instrument regulating the use of AI in education, and a recommendation covering AI literacy across educational systems specifically focusing on human-centred approaches [7]. After receiving a mandate in September 2023 from all Member States, work began on drafting these international instruments [8].

This workshop provides an opportunity for critical scrutiny and stakeholder engagement to inform these developments and ensure their democratic legitimacy.

2 Workshop Objectives and Importance

2.1 Workshop Objectives

This workshop at the AIED 2025 in Palermo, Italy [26] is the continuation of the very successful discussions held at the AIED 2023 in Tokyo, Japan [1, 12], AIED 2024 in Recife, Brazil [2, 17] and AIED 2025 in Palermo, Italy [3, 20]. The aim of the workshop is to continue important global discourse on regulatory practices regarding AI and education whilst at the same time providing important and ongoing updates and raising awareness for the important topic of ethical AI&ED. Additionally, the workshop discussions are intended to contribute to the CoE's current developments of an international AI regulation in education as binding law in Europe and design of comprehensive AI literacy recommendations.

The workshop is designed to help participants:

- Think through what kinds of ethical and legal guidelines are necessary for the responsible use of AI in education and critically examine how these could be applied in real contexts.
- Discuss how AI might influence the future of education, learning design and assessment, including questions of trust, fairness, and responsibility, and bring together different perspectives to better understand the consequences.
- Work collaboratively to explore how rules and policies for ethical AI use can be created, focusing on what legal and institutional structures are needed and how they might be developed.
- Consider how to keep up with the rapid pace of AI development while still ensuring that regulation remains effective and meaningful over time.

These goals are tied to a set of guiding concerns:

- What steps are needed to put in place legal and organisational systems that support ethical use of AI in educational settings?
- In what ways can AI be introduced without weakening, but instead, and ideally, strengthening human rights, democracy, equal access to education, and the rule of law?
- And how can we make sure that stakeholders at all levels of the education system, from individual learners to national policymakers, are involved in shaping these decisions and ensuring AI is used in fair and transparent ways?

The main focus of the workshop will be on the legal and organizational requirements to achieve a regulation in the fields of AI and Education (AI&ED). The discussions will be based on the work and activities of the CoE and its appointed AI&ED expert group. In particular, the most recent work of this group regarding the preparation of the legal instrument and recommendation for AI literacy will form the basis of the workshop. In addition to a fundamental exploration of these themes, open and urgent issues will be addressed, and next steps in relation to these requirements and goals will be defined.

2.2 Workshop Relevance and Importance to the AIED Community

In preparation of the CoE Council of Ministers meeting in 2025 [7, 8], during which the proposed texts for the legal instruments on AI in education will be discussed and the final report from the expert group will be presented, the CoE expert group is currently collecting feedback. It is essential that this feedback reflects different stakeholder perspectives. These include those of students, teachers, industry representatives, NGOs, and academia.

The AIED research community plays an important role within this process, bringing valuable knowledge and experience to the discussions and ensuring that future legal instruments and guidelines reflect the realities of education. It is imperative that these perspectives are considered in the work of the CoE.

This workshop also gives members of the AIED community a chance to get directly involved and is closely aligned with the AIED 2025 conference theme, "AI as a Catalyst for Inclusive, Personalised, and Ethical Education". During the workshop, participants will learn about the work of the CoE that has already been conducted. This includes the results of the CoE AI&ED Expert conferences "Artificial Intelligence and Education" held on 21st / 22nd of November 2023 [9] and on 24th / 25th of October 2024 in Strasbourg [10]. Furthermore, the workshop will draw on the group's first report [11] in viewing AI in education from the perspective of human rights, democracy, and the rule of law and on the results from the two former AIED workshops [12, 17].

Through an active discussion, the workshop will also facilitate the formation of a wider community of practice within the AIED community with the goal of considering the wider societal implication of AIED.

3 Workshop Format and Methodology

This half-day workshop will be run in an interactive, hybrid format, encouraging active participation throughout. It is divided into two parts, each building on the other. The first part focuses on small group work, where participants will collaborate on four key questions.

- What issues have to be addressed in AIED regulations by CoE and beyond?
- What types of legal and institutional mechanisms are needed to uphold rights?
- Which real-world examples best illustrate the risks and regulatory needs?
- And how have learning design and assessment to change due to AI challenges?

In the second part, the workshop will use the World Café approach, where participants can choose from up to ten prepared questions and explore them in rotating group discussions. The discussions will be documented, synthesised, and structured into categories that reflect actionable regulatory needs.

The workshop will take place with both in-person and online groups working in parallel. After each round of discussion, participants will come together in plenary sessions to share insights and reflect on the results. This format ensures that ideas and perspectives from all groups are exchanged and taken forward collectively.

3.1 Workshop Programme

In the first section, the interactive Workshop will begin with a brief introduction to the workshop and a keynote by the Council of Europe. It is followed by a summary of the key messages from the initial report on AI&ED and the current work by the CoE Expert Group (20 min). The core part of the first section will centre on four key questions (the length will be dependent on the total time available). Each question will be introduced by a 5-min presentation. Participants will then work in small groups, to respond to the issues introduced, before reporting back their views and ideas to the whole workshop. The first section will conclude with a discussant summarising the workshop participants' input (15 min) followed by a wrap up (5 min).

In the second section, the interactive Workshop follows the World Café method and consists of four parts:

1. In the first short part (5 min), we will briefly present the World Café method and the topic "Requirements for international conventions to ensure ethical AI introduction and usage in education strengthening democracy building".
2. In the second core part (the length will be dependent on the total time available), we will discuss different and pre-prepared themes and aspects in groups of ideally 4 to 10 participants. We will prepare 10 themes before the conference and will decide depending on the number of participants how many group tables we will offer during the workshop. The procedure will be identical on all group tables:
    - The theme will be read that always consists of an open question and clarified.
    - Afterwards, the contributions (= answers on the open question of the theme) will be collected as post-it at a flipchart next to the group table.
    - Finally, all collected contributions will be sorted in open discussion and be clustered according defined categories or criteria so that they can be presented. That can be done independently or using the categories or criteria from the other rounds before.
3. In the third part (30 min), the results from the group tables will be presented in the plenary and critically discussed and reflected. These can then be provided as summaries for publication after the event.
4. In the fourth part, we will collect all issues that the workshop participants wish to discuss and bring to the attention of the CoE Expert Group (15 min). Finally, we will define next steps and activities and conclude with a wrap up of the whole Workshop (10 min).

3.2 Target Audience

The workshop is open to all members of the AIED community, regardless of their level of experience. It welcomes both newcomers who may be exploring these issues for the first time and experienced experts who are already engaged in the field. By using a hybrid format that includes both in-person and online participation, the workshop aims to create space for inclusive and diverse discussions across the global AIED community.

4 Expected Outcomes and Next Steps

The workshop will collect and discuss key legal and organisational ideas that can help shape future strategies and guidelines for ethical and trustworthy AI. This includes identifying what is needed to ensure that AI use supports democratic values, both in education and in other areas. Participants will work together to explore what kinds of rules and frameworks are required and how they might be applied in practice.

The results of these discussions will be shared with the Council of Europe's expert group on AI and Education. They will help inform the group's final report and the legal texts that will be considered by the Council of Ministers at the end of 2026.

Furthermore, all results will be published on the workshop website [3] and contribute to ongoing AI policy and research activities such as the ASSAI project on AI-driven assessment in education that is shaping AI policies for responsible and ethical implementation of formative and summative assessment with AI support in formal (higher) education [28].

Additionally, there are plans to develop a joint publication based on the outcomes of the workshop. This will document the ideas and recommendations that emerge and make them available to a wider audience.

5 Conclusion

The unchecked use of AI in education threatens to undermine key societal values. As education plays a unique role in shaping democratic culture, it must be protected through deliberate, transparent, and enforceable regulation. This workshop seeks to move beyond abstract discussions and contribute concrete input to international governance processes.

We hope that the exchanges, collaboration and results of the workshop will strengthen the public awareness and required AIED regulation to facilitate responsible, fair and ethical AI use in education as well as they will foster AI literacy in all sectors and disciplines to enable education about AI and AI competence building at large-scale.

Disclosure of Interests. The authors have no competing interests to declare that are relevant to the content of this article.

References

1. AIED 2023 Workshop Website. https://aied2023.learning-innovations.eu. Accessed 30 Mar 2026
2. AIED 2024 Workshop Website. https://aied2024.learning-innovations.eu. Accessed 30 Mar 2026
3. AIED 2025 Workshop Website. https://aied2025.learning-innovations.eu. Accessed 30 Mar 2026
4. Bond, M., et al.: A meta systematic review of artificial intelligence in higher education: a call for increased ethics, collaboration, and rigour. Int. J. Educ. Technol. High. Educ. **21**(4) (2024). https://doi.org/10.1186/s41239-023-00436-z
5. Bozkurt, A., et al.: The Manifesto for Teaching and Learning in a Time of Generative AI: A Critical Collective Stance to Better Navigate the Future. Open Praxis **16**(4), 487–513 (2024). https://openpraxis.org/articles/10.55982/openpraxis.16.4.777
6. Bozkurt, A., et al.: Speculative futures on ChatGPT and generative artificial intelligence (AI): a collective reflection from the educational landscape. Asian J. Distance Educ. **18**(1), 53–130 (2023). https://www.asianjde.com/ojs/index.php/AsianJDE/article/view/709/394

7. Council of Europe: Regulating Artificial Intelligence in education (2023a). https://rm.coe.int/regulating-artificial-intelligence-in-education-26th-session-council-o/1680ac9b7c
8. Council of Europe: The transformative power of education: universal values and civic renewal. In: Resolutions of the 26th Session of the Council of Europe Standing Conference of Ministers of Education (28–29 September 2023). MED-26(2023)06 final (2023b). https://rm.coe.int/resolutions-26th-session-council-of-europe-standing-conference-of-mini/1680abee7f
9. CoE Report on Working Conference (2023). https://www.coe.int/en/web/education/-/working-conference-on-regulating-the-use-of-ai-systems-in-education. Accessed 06 May 2025
10. CoE Report on Working Conference (2024). https://rm.coe.int/artificial-intelligence-and-education-2nd-working-conference-provision/1680b314a3. Accessed 06 May 2025
11. Holmes, W., Persson, J., Chounta, I.-A., Wasson, B., Dimitrova, V.: Artificial intelligence and education: A critical view through the lens of human rights, democracy and the rule of law. Council of Europe (2022). https://rm.coe.int/artificial-intelligence-and-education-a-critical-view-through-the-lens/1680a886bd
12. Holmes, W., et al.: AI and education. A view through the lens of human rights, democracy and the rule of law. Legal and organizational requirements. In: Artificial Intelligence in Education. Communications in Computer and Information Science, vol. 1831. pp. 79–84 (2023). https://doi.org/10.1007/978-3-031-36336-8_12
13. Holmes, W., Tuomi, I.: State of the art and practice in AI in education. Eur. J. Educ. **57**, 542–570 (2022). https://doi.org/10.1111/ejed.12533
14. Nguyen, A., Ngo, H.N., Hong, Y., Dang, B., Nguyen, B.-P.T.: Ethical principles for artificial intelligence in education. Educ. Inf. Technol. **28**, 4221–4241 (2023). https://doi.org/10.1007/s10639-022-11316-w
15. Stracke, C.M.: Artificial intelligence and education: ethical questions and guidelines for their relations based on human rights, democracy and the rule of law. In: Burgos, D. et al. (eds.), Radical Solutions for Artificial Intelligence and Digital Transformation in Education. Lecture Notes in Educational Technology, pp. 97–107 (2024). https://doi.org/10.1007/978-981-97-8638-1_7
16. Stracke, C.M., et al.: What is Artificial Intelligence (AI)? How can I use AI ethically at university? Ethical Use of AI (2024a). https://doi.org/10.5281/zenodo.10995669
17. Stracke, C.M., Chounta, I.-A., Dimitrova, V., Havinga, B., Holmes, W.: Ethical AI and education: the need for international regulation to foster human rights, democracy and the rule of law. Artificial intelligence in education. Commun. Comput. Inf. Sci. **2151**, 439–445 (2024). https://doi.org/10.1007/978-3-031-64312-5_55
18. Stracke, C.M., Chounta, I.-A., Holmes, W.: Global trends in scientific debates on trustworthy and ethical artificial intelligence and education. Artificial intelligence in education. Commun. Comput. Inf. Sci. **2150**, 254–262 (2024). https://doi.org/10.1007/978-3-031-64315-6_21
19. Stracke, C.M., et al.: Analysis of artificial intelligence policies for higher education in Europe. Int. J. Interact. Multimedia Artif. Intell. **9**(2), 124–137 (2025). https://doi.org/10.9781/ijimai.2025.02.011
20. Stracke, C.M., Havinga, B., Holmes, W., Salaj, R.: Ethical artificial intelligence and education: the need for international regulation to foster human rights, democracy and equity. Artificial intelligence in education. Commun. Comput. Inf. Sci. **2592**, 284–291 (2025). https://doi.org/10.1007/978-3-031-99267-4_37
21. Stracke, C.M., et al.: Artificial intelligence policies for higher education: manifesto for critical considerations and a roadmap. MAP Educ. Humanit. **6**, 61–73 (2025c). https://doi.org/10.53880/2744-2373.2025.6.61
22. Stracke, C.M.: Education is a special sector: why we need ethical regulation of artificial intelligence and education (AI&ED) and how we benefit from it. AI and Ethics (accepted, in print) (2026). Preprint: https://doi.org/10.5281/zenodo.17279562

23. Stracke, C.M.: Artificial intelligence and education (AI&ED). In: Manzeschke, A., Wittenberg, T. (eds.), Ethical Perspectives on Artificial Intelligence in Biomedical Engineering, pp. 145–158 (2026). https://doi.org/10.1515/9783111586458-011
24. Tlili, A., et al.: Taming the monster: how can open education promote the effective and safe use of generative AI in education? J. Learn. Dev. **11**(3), 398–413 (2024). https://doi.org/10.56059/jl4d.v11i3.1657
25. Xiao, J., et al.: Venturing into the unknown: critical insights into grey areas and pioneering future directions in educational generative AI research. TechTrends (2025). https://doi.org/10.1007/s11528-025-01060-6
26. AIED 2026 Workshop Website. https://aied2026.learning-innovations.eu. Accessed 30 Mar 2026
27. Holmes, W.: AI, education, and children's rights. Front. Educ. **10**, 1656736 (2025). https://doi.org/10.3389/feduc.2025.1656736
28. ASSAI website. https://www.assai-project.eu

Intelligent Textbooks 2026: The Seventh International Workshop

Sergey Sosnovsky[1(✉)], Peter Brusilovsky[2], Andrew S. Lan[3], and Isaac Alpizar-Chacon[1]

[1] Utrecht University, Princetonplein 5, 3584 CC Utrecht, The Netherlands
{s.a.sosnovsky,i.alpizarchacon}@uu.nl
[2] University of Pittsburgh, 135 North Bellefield Avenue, Pittsburgh, PA 15260, USA
peterb@pitt.edu
[3] University of Massachutsetts Amherst, 140 Governors Dr., Amherst, MA 01003, USA
andrewlan@cs.umass.edu

Abstract. Textbooks have evolved over the last several decades in many aspects. Most textbooks can be accessed online, many of them freely. They often come with libraries of supplementary educational resources or online educational services built on top of them. As a result of these enrichments, new research challenges and opportunities emerge that call for the application of AIED methods to enhance digital textbooks and learners' interaction with them. Therefore, we ask: How can we use intelligent and adaptive technologies to facilitate access to digital textbooks and improve the learning process? What new insights about knowledge and learning can be extracted from textbook content and data-mined from the logs of students interacting with it? How can these insights be leveraged to develop improved intelligent texts? How can we leverage new language technology to manage and augment textbooks? This workshop will feature research contributions addressing these and other research questions related to intelligent textbooks. It will bring together researchers working on different aspects of learning technologies to establish intelligent textbooks as a new, interdisciplinary research field.

Keywords: intelligent textbooks · digital and online textbooks · open educational resources (OER) · modelling and representation of textbook content · assessment generation · adaptive presentation and navigation · content curation and enrichment · interactive textbooks · generative AI · LLM

1 Introduction

Textbooks remain one of the main methods of instruction, but – just like other educational tools – they have been evolving over the last several decades in many aspects (how they are created, published, formatted, accessed, and maintained). Most textbooks these days have digital versions and can be accessed online. Plenty of textbooks (and similar instructional texts, such as tutorials) are freely available as open educational resources (OERs). Many commercial textbooks come with libraries of supplementary

E. G. Blanchard et al. (Eds.): AIED 2026, CCIS 3033, pp. 175–180, 2026.
https://doi.org/10.1007/978-3-032-29794-5_28

educational resources or are even distributed as parts of online educational services built on top of them. The transition of textbooks from printed copies to digital and online formats has facilitated numerous attempts to enrich them with various kinds of interactive functionalities, including search and annotation, interactive content modules, automated assessments, chatbots (especially given the capabilities of models like ChatGPT), and more.

As a result of these enrichments, new research challenges and opportunities emerge that call for the application of artificial intelligence (AI) methods to enhance digital textbooks and learners' interaction with them. There are many research questions associated with this new area of research; examples include:

- How can one facilitate access to textbooks and improve the reading process?
- How can one process textbook content to infer knowledge underlying the text and use it to improve learning support?
- How can one process increasingly more detailed logs of students interacting with digital textbooks and extract insights on learning?
- How can one find and retrieve relevant content "in the wild", i.e., on the web, that can enrich the textbooks?
- How can one leverage advanced language technology, especially chatbots, to make textbooks more interactive?
- How can one better understand both textbooks and student behaviors as they learn within the textbook and create personalized learner experiences?

In particular, this year's workshop will put an emphasis on the potential of generative AI techniques in intelligent textbooks. Many recent works on intelligent textbooks have started to incorporate these technologies, especially large language models (LLMs). Since LLMs are pre-trained on textbooks, they have acquired some information on knowledge and structure in textbooks. Therefore, one can use LLMs to power automated question-answering tools for learners, especially using retrieval-augmented generation techniques to mitigate intrinsic hallucination in LLMs. One can also use LLMs to power more interactive experiences around textbooks, e.g., chatbots, when learners browse textbooks. These interactions can also go beyond text to handle multiple modalities, such as text and images and/or diagrams, based on vision-language models.

Our workshop will seek research contributions addressing these and other research questions related to the idea of intelligent textbooks. While the pioneer work on various kinds of intelligent textbook technologies has already begun, research in this area is still rare and has spread over several different fields, including AI, human-computer interaction, natural language processing, information retrieval, intelligent tutoring systems, educational data mining, and user modeling. This workshop will bring together researchers working on different aspects of intelligent textbook technologies in these fields and beyond to establish intelligent textbooks as a new, interdisciplinary research field.

2 Content, Themes and Potential Audience

This workshop will build upon the success of the six workshops on Intelligent Textbooks (iTextbooks) that we organized in conjunction with AIED'2019, AIED'2020, AIED'2021, AIED'2022, AIED'2023 and AIED'2025. Additionally, we have edited a special issue on Intelligent Textbooks recently published in the International Journal of AI in Education. We aim to continue developing the iTextbooks community as an active group of researchers with a wide range of backgrounds who are interested in all aspects of intelligent textbooks.

The workshop has accumulated an active audience over the years, which has been reflected both in the number of submissions and the number of attendants. This year, we expect the workshop audience to grow even further given the joint nature of the event. All three sister communities – AIED, L@S and EDM – conduct research relevant to the themes of the workshop.

The workshop themes include but are not limited to:

- Modelling and representation of textbooks: examining the prerequisite and semantic structure of textbooks to enhance their readability;
- Analysis and mining of textbook usage logs: analyzing the patterns of learners' use of textbooks to obtain insights on learning and the pedagogical value of textbook content;
- Collaborative technologies: building and deploying social components of digital textbooks that enable learners to interact with not only content but other learners;
- Generation, manipulation, and presentation: exploring and testing different formats and forms of textbook content to find the most effective means of presenting different knowledge;
- Assessment and personalization: developing methods that can generate assessments and enhance textbooks with adaptive support to meet the needs of every learner using the textbook;
- Content curation and enrichment: sorting through external resources on the web and finding the relevant resources to augment the textbook and provide additional information for learners.
- Interactive textbooks: leveraging chatbot technology to support and facilitate learner-textbook dialogues.

Figure 1 visualizes chronologically how these topics were represented in the workshop proceedings over the years and how the community interests have gradually evolved. The numbers in the table indicate how many papers covered a particular topic in a particular year. The area of a topic zone in the diagram visualizes the corresponding ratio of this topic. Since many papers covered more than one topic, these areas do not reflect the direct percentage of papers covering the topic but rather the relative focus of the topic compared to all other topics covered that year.

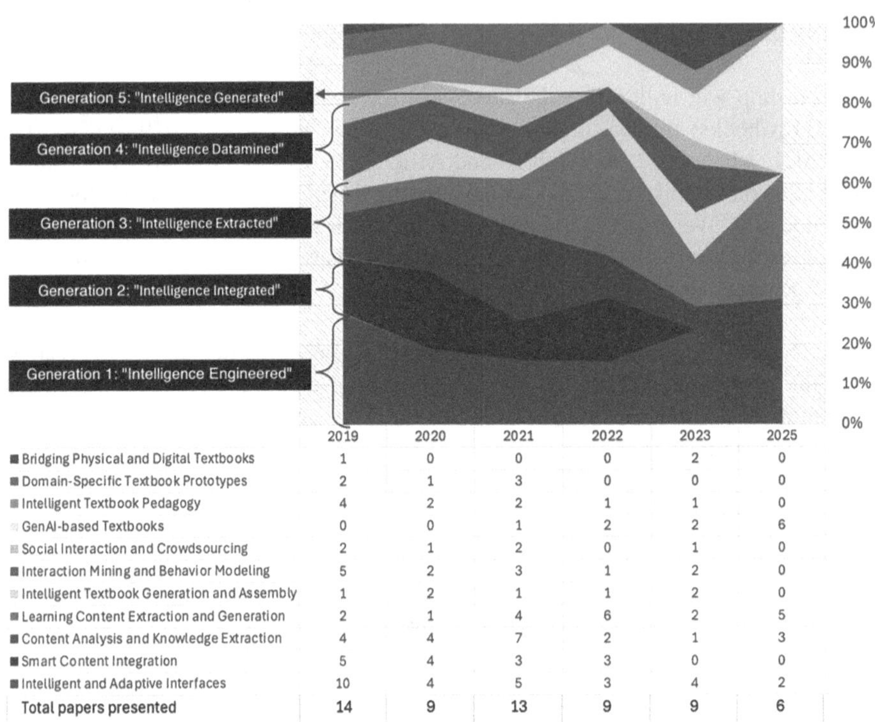

	2019	2020	2021	2022	2023	2025
Bridging Physical and Digital Textbooks	1	0	0	0	2	0
Domain-Specific Textbook Prototypes	2	1	3	0	0	0
Intelligent Textbook Pedagogy	4	2	2	1	1	0
GenAI-based Textbooks	0	0	1	2	2	6
Social Interaction and Crowdsourcing	2	1	2	0	1	0
Interaction Mining and Behavior Modeling	5	2	3	1	2	0
Intelligent Textbook Generation and Assembly	1	2	1	1	2	0
Learning Content Extraction and Generation	2	1	4	6	2	5
Content Analysis and Knowledge Extraction	4	4	7	2	1	3
Smart Content Integration	5	4	3	3	0	0
Intelligent and Adaptive Interfaces	10	4	5	3	4	2
Total papers presented	14	9	13	9	9	6

Fig. 1. Intelligent textbooks topics distribution in the workshop proceedings over the years.

3 Organizers

Sergey Sosnovsky is an Associate Professor of Software Technology for Learning and Teaching at the Department of Information and Computing Sciences, Utrecht University. His research interests include various aspects of designing, developing, and evaluating adaptive educational systems and personalized information systems in general. Dr. Sosnovsky holds a PhD degree in Information Sciences from the University of Pittsburgh (Pittsburgh, PA, USA). Before joining Utrecht University, Dr. Sosnovsky worked as the head of the e-Learning lab at the German Center for Artificial Intelligence (DFKI) and as a senior researcher at Saarland University (Germany).

Peter Brusilovsky is a Professor of Information Science and Intelligent Systems at the University of Pittsburgh, where he directs the Personalized Adaptive Web Systems (PAWS) lab. Peter Brusilovsky has been working in the field of adaptive educational systems, user modeling, and intelligent user interfaces for more than 30 years. He published numerous papers and edited several books on adaptive hypermedia, adaptive educational systems, user modeling, and the adaptive Web. Peter is the past Editor-in-Chief of IEEE Transactions on Learning Technologies and a board member of several journals, including User Modeling and User Adapted Interaction and ACM Transactions on Social Computing. Peter has been exploring the topic of intelligent textbooks for over 20 years. Together with G. Weber, he developed one of the first online intelligent textbooks ELM-ART, which received the 1998 EU Academic Software award.

Andrew S. Lan is an Assistant Professor in the College of Information and Computer Sciences, at the University of Massachusetts Amherst. His research focuses on the development of human-in-the-loop machine learning methods to enable scalable, effective, and fail-safe personalized learning in education by collecting and analyzing massive and multi-modal learner and content data. Prior to joining UMass, Andrew was a postdoctoral research associate in the EDGE Lab at Princeton University. He received his M.S. and Ph.D. degrees in Electrical and Computer Engineering from Rice University in 2014 and 2016, respectively. He has also co-organized a series of workshops on machine learning for education; see http://ml4ed.cc/ for details.

Isaac Alpizar-Chacon is an Assistant Professor in the Software Technology for Learning and Teaching group at the Department of Information and Computing Sciences, Utrecht University. In addition to his primary role, he is also an associate professor at the Instituto Tecnológico de Costa Rica. His research interests focus on the impact of GenAI tools in computing education, the integration of these tools into the classroom, the teaching and learning of computational thinking skills, and knowledge extraction. He earned his PhD degree in Information and Computing Sciences from Utrecht University in the Netherlands, where his research focused on extracting knowledge from digital textbooks.

4 Program Committee

- Isaac Alpizar-Chacon (Utrecht University)
- Peter Brusilovsky (University of Pittsburgh)
- Vinay Chaudhri
- Scott Crossley (Vanderbilt University)
- Brendan Flanagan (Kyoto University)
- Reva Freedman (Northern Illinois University)
- Benny Johnson (VitalSource Technologies)
- Andrew Lan (University of Massachusetts Amherst)
- Noboru Matsuda (North Carolina State University)
- Roger Nkambou (Université du Québec à Montréal)
- Hiroaki Ogata (Kyoto University)
- Benjamin Paaßen (Bielefeld University)
- Philip I. Pavlik Jr. (University of Memphis)
- Cliff Shaffer (Virginia Tech)
- Sergey Sosnovsky (Utrecht University)
- Francesco Sovrano (University of Italian-speaking Switzerland)
- Khushboo Thaker (University of Pittsburgh)
- Ilaria Torre (University of Genoa)
- Brian Wright (University of Virginia)

References

1. Sosnovsky, S., Brusilovsky, P., Baraniuk, R., Agrawal, R., Lan, A. (eds.) Proceedings of the 1st Workshop on Intelligent Textbooks at 20th International Conference on Artificial Intelligence in Education (AIED 2019). CEUR Workshop Proceedings, Vol. 2384, Chicago, USA: CEUR (2019)

2. Sosnovsky, S., Brusilovsky, P., Baraniuk, R., Lan, A. (eds.) Proceedings of the 2nd Workshop on Intelligent Textbooks at 21st International Conference on Artificial Intelligence in Education (AIED 2020). CEUR Workshop Proceedings, Vol. 2674, Chicago, USA: CEUR (2020)
3. Sosnovsky, S., Brusilovsky, P., Baraniuk, R., Lan, A. (eds.) Proceedings of the 3rd Workshop on Intelligent Textbooks at 22nd International Conference on Artificial Intelligence in Education (AIED 2021). CEUR Workshop Proceedings, Vol. 2895, CEUR (2021)
4. Sosnovsky, S., Brusilovsky, P., Lan, A. (eds.) Proceedings of the 4th Workshop on Intelligent Textbooks at 23rd International Conference on Artificial Intelligence in Education (AIED 2022). CEUR Workshop Proceedings, Vol. 3192, CEUR (2022)
5. Sosnovsky, S., Brusilovsky, P., Lan, A. (eds.) Proceedings of the 5th Workshop on Intelligent Textbooks at 24th International Conference on Artificial Intelligence in Education (AIED 2023). CEUR Workshop Proceedings, Vol. 3444, CEUR (2023)
6. Sosnovsky, S., Brusilovsky, P., Lan, A. Alpizar Chacon, I. (eds.) Proceedings of the 6th Workshop on Intelligent Textbooks at 25th International Conference on Artificial Intelligence in Education (AIED 2025). CEUR Workshop Proceedings, Vol. 4010, CEUR (2025)
7. Sosnovsky, S., Brusilovsky, P., Lan, A.: Intelligent textbooks. Int. J. Artif. Intell. Educ. **35**(3), 967–986 (2025)

Festival of Learning - Invited Papers

Learning Components as Intermediary for Educational Standards Crosswalks

Rabia Turan, Sadie Gill, Desirée Stanley, and Parva Thakkar(✉)

Learning Commons, Redwood City, CA, USA
{rturan,sgill,dstanley,pthakkar}@learningcommons.org

Abstract. Educational standards crosswalks are the interoperability backbone of educational technology, supporting curriculum discovery, reporting, and compliance, yet they remain a persistent operational bottleneck. In the U.S., edtech systems must contend with fifty evolving state standards frameworks, the District of Columbia standards, the Common Core, and other multi-state frameworks. Learning Components (LCs) are granular representations of skills or concepts that decompose broad standards into teachable parts. We describe a scalable approach that uses learning components as an intermediary representation for crosswalking heterogeneous educational standards frameworks. Instead of constructing pairwise standard-to-standard crosswalks, each framework is independently aligned to a shared set of learning components in a hub-and-spoke architecture. This enables crosswalks to be derived through directional overlap and Jaccard similarity, revealing asymmetric coverage. This representation supports weighted crosswalks that quantify gaps and asymmetries, rather than obscuring them behind binary mappings. We apply this approach to crosswalking Common Core State Standards (CCSS) with both nominally aligned frameworks (New York) and non-Common Core frameworks (Texas, Florida). Analysis shows learning component-mediated crosswalks reveal systematic coverage differences that are masked by traditional approaches, while reducing crosswalk maintenance complexity from quadratic (51^2 pairwise alignments) to linear (51 framework-to-LC alignments). Bidirectional coverage analysis identifies three distinct crosswalk patterns (shown as framework→CCSS/CCSS→framework): high-overlap implementations (New York: 96%/84%), divergent smaller frameworks (Texas: 62%/35%), and moderately divergent frameworks (Florida: 63%/47%), exposing coverage relationships that binary mappings cannot express. These results demonstrate learning components provide a practical and shared intermediary layer for crosswalking in large-scale educational systems.

Keywords: Standards crosswalk · Standards Alignment · Learning Components

E. G. Blanchard et al. (Eds.): AIED 2026, CCIS 3033, pp. 183–196, 2026.
https://doi.org/10.1007/978-3-032-29794-5_29

1 Introduction

Educational standards crosswalks are the interoperability backbone of educational technology systems, enabling curriculum discovery, reporting, and compliance across jurisdictions by mapping learning expectations across standards frameworks so that content, assessments, and reports aligned to one framework can be interpreted in terms of another. In practice, however, crosswalks remain a persistent operational bottleneck. In the United States, educational technology providers must support more than fifty state standards frameworks, the District of Columbia standards, the Common Core, and other multi-state frameworks, all of which evolve over time. Maintaining reliable crosswalks across this landscape requires significant expert effort, making scalability and long-term sustainability an ongoing challenge.

Most standards crosswalks are constructed as pairwise mappings between frameworks. While effective at small scale, pairwise crosswalks are not sustainable as the number of frameworks grows or as standards are updated. Beyond maintenance cost, pairwise mappings fail to surface important structural properties of standards relationships. Binary alignments provide limited visibility into partial coverage and directional asymmetries between frameworks, making it difficult to reason about equivalence, gaps, or divergence in curricular scope.

This paper proposes learning components as an intermediary representation for standards crosswalking. Learning components (LCs) are granular representations of teachable and measurable skills or concepts that decompose broad educational standards into smaller units. Rather than aligning standards frameworks directly to one another, we independently align each framework to a shared set of learning components. This representation induces a **hub-and-spoke topology**, with learning components serving as the intermediary hub. In contrast, pairwise crosswalks create a fully connected mesh requiring n^2 alignments. Crosswalks are derived analytically through comparisons of learning component coverage, enabling directional overlap and asymmetry to be measured explicitly rather than inferred from binary mappings.

Framing crosswalking as a coverage inference problem over a shared intermediary representation yields both analytical and operational benefits. Coverage-based comparisons reveal partial alignments and asymmetric relationships masked by binary mappings. At the same time, maintaining alignments to a shared learning component set reduces crosswalk maintenance complexity from quadratic to linear in the number of frameworks, making the approach more sustainable as standards evolve. The scalability benefit applies to crosswalk maintenance, not initial framework alignment—which remains a hybrid process requiring expert validation. Operational savings accrue when standards evolve or new frameworks are added: updates affect only a single framework's LC alignment rather than all pairwise relationships. We have applied this approach to 44 state frameworks; this paper focuses on three representative cases.

We focus our evaluation here on an empirical case study crosswalking the Common Core State Standards for Mathematics (CCSS) with both nominally aligned frameworks (New York) and non-Common Core frameworks (Texas and

Florida). Our analysis identifies distinct crosswalk patterns, including high-overlap implementations with moderate asymmetry, divergent smaller frameworks, and moderately divergent frameworks, and quantifies directional asymmetries that range from minimal to substantial. For instance, New York exhibits 96% forward but only 84% backward overlap with CCSS, revealing incomplete adoption despite nominal alignment. Learning component-mediated crosswalks provide a practical and analytically meaningful foundation for standards interoperability. The contributions of this paper are threefold:

- We introduce learning components as an intermediary representation, reframing crosswalking as coverage inference.
- We quantify overlap, asymmetry, and coverage gaps using learning component coverage metrics.
- We provide an empirical analysis across Common Core and non-Common Core frameworks, showing both analytical insight and improved scalability over traditional pairwise approaches.

2 Related Work

2.1 Standards Alignment and Crosswalking

Educational standards alignment has long been a foundational task in K-12 education, supporting curriculum development, assessment, and reporting, and has become increasingly important as states emphasize standards-based instruction. Standards-to-standards alignment studies have a well-established history in educational measurement, including expert-based evaluations [1], comparisons of state framework to Common Core [6], and bidirectional coverage analyses. In practice, standards crosswalks are most often constructed as pairwise mappings between frameworks, typically through manual expert review or semi-automated text-matching approaches.

Automated and semi-automated approaches have applied keyword and rule-based heuristics to support standards alignment, relying on structured descriptors and categorical overlap to compute alignment between frameworks [4,7,8]. More recently, embedding-based and language-model based approaches have been explored to support semantic similarity-driven alignment [2,3,9]. Although these methods can surface candidate alignments, they often conflate semantic similarity with curricular equivalence and provide limited support for identifying coverage gaps, overgeneralization, or asymmetric relationships. For instance, embedding-based methods may align *'Count a mixed collection of coins'* with *'Solve word problems involving dollar bills, quarters.'* based on surface semantic similarity, despite these representing distinct instructional sequences and prerequisite structures. As a result, crosswalks derived from these approaches often fail to capture prerequisite relationships, differences in granularity, and asymmetric coverage patterns that are critical for determining instructional equivalence.

2.2 Positioning and Present Work

Prior work highlights the importance of instructional representations for alignment but leaves unresolved the challenge of scalable, maintainable crosswalking across heterogeneous standards frameworks. In contrast, the present work treats crosswalking as a coverage inference problem over a shared intermediary representation. By aligning each framework to a common set of learning components, crosswalks can be derived analytically rather than constructed directly, enabling quantification of overlap, asymmetry, and coverage gaps while reducing maintenance complexity. This allows new crosswalks (e.g., New York-Texas) to be computed without additional alignment effort.

3 Learning Component as an Intermediary Representation

This section introduces learning components as a shared intermediary representation for standards crosswalking and formalizes how crosswalks are derived from learning components.

3.1 Learning Components

Learning Components (LCs) are granular representations of teachable and measurable skills or concepts that decompose broad educational standards into smaller units. Each learning component captures a single instructional idea at a level of granularity that is more specific than the full standard, but more stable and generalizable than individual assessment items. As such, learning components provide a balance between the coarseness of standards and the granularity of the item level representations.

Learning components are not intended to replace standards frameworks. Instead they serve as a shared analytical layer that supports comparison across heterogeneous frameworks. Because learning components abstract over differences in phrasing, sequencing, and grouping, they provide a stable basis for comparing standards that differ in structure or decomposition. This property is particularly important when crosswalking frameworks that are nominally aligned but differ in implementation, as well as when comparing Common Core-aligned and non-Common Core standards.

3.2 Representing Standards with Learning Component Coverage

Each standards framework is represented as a mapping from standards to sets of learning components. This induces a bipartite graph between standards and learning components, where edges indicate coverage relationships. Importantly, each framework is aligned independently to the shared learning component set, rather than being aligned directly to other frameworks.

This representation contrasts with traditional pairwise crosswalks, which implicitly induce a mesh topology in which each framework must be directly aligned to every other framework. In contrast, aligning frameworks to a shared set of learning components induces a hub-and-spoke topology, with learning components acting as the intermediary hub. This structural shift enables crosswalks to be derived analytically rather than constructed and maintained explicitly. A key benefit of this representation is that crosswalks between any pair of frameworks can be derived without additional expert alignment effort. For example, a crosswalk between New York and Texas can be computed by comparing their respective learning component coverage sets, neither of which was aligned with reference to the other framework.

Formally, let L denote the set of learning components, and let S_i and S_j denote two standards frameworks. Each framework is represented by a coverage function mapping standards to subsets of L. Crosswalk relationships between frameworks are then derived by comparing their respective learning component coverage sets.

3.3 Deriving Crosswalks from Learning Component Coverage

Given two standards frameworks aligned to the same learning component set, crosswalks are derived by computing overlap between their learning component coverage. We measure overlap using **directional coverage** and **set-based similarity metrics**.

Directional coverage captures asymmetry in crosswalk relationships by measuring the extent to which the learning components covered by one framework are contained within another. Specifically, the proportion of learning components covered by framework S_i that are also covered by framework S_j may differ from the reverse comparison. Such asymmetries reflect differences in scope that are not visible with pairwise mappings.

Figure 1 illustrates this situation. Two standards share a single learning component, but differ in their overall coverage. Standard *MA.7.AR.4.4* is aligned with two learning components, whereas standard *7.RP.A.2.c* is aligned with only one. As a result, the directional coverage from *MA.7.AR.4.4* to *7.RP.A.2.c* is 0.5, while the directional coverage from *7.RP.A.2.c* to *MA.7.AR.4.4* is 1. This asymmetry indicates that one standard represents a narrowed or more specific realization of the other, rather than a symmetric correspondence.

Directional coverage from standard S_i to standard S_j is defined as:

$$\text{Coverage}(S_i \rightarrow S_j) = \frac{|L(S_i) \cap L(S_j)|}{|L(S_i)|}$$

where $L(S_i)$ denotes the set of learning components aligned with S_i.

Such asymmetric relationships are common in standards crosswalks, particularly when one standard decomposes concepts more finely or omits instructional constraints present in another. At the framework level, coverage is aggregated from standard-to-standard alignments (see Sect. 4.3).

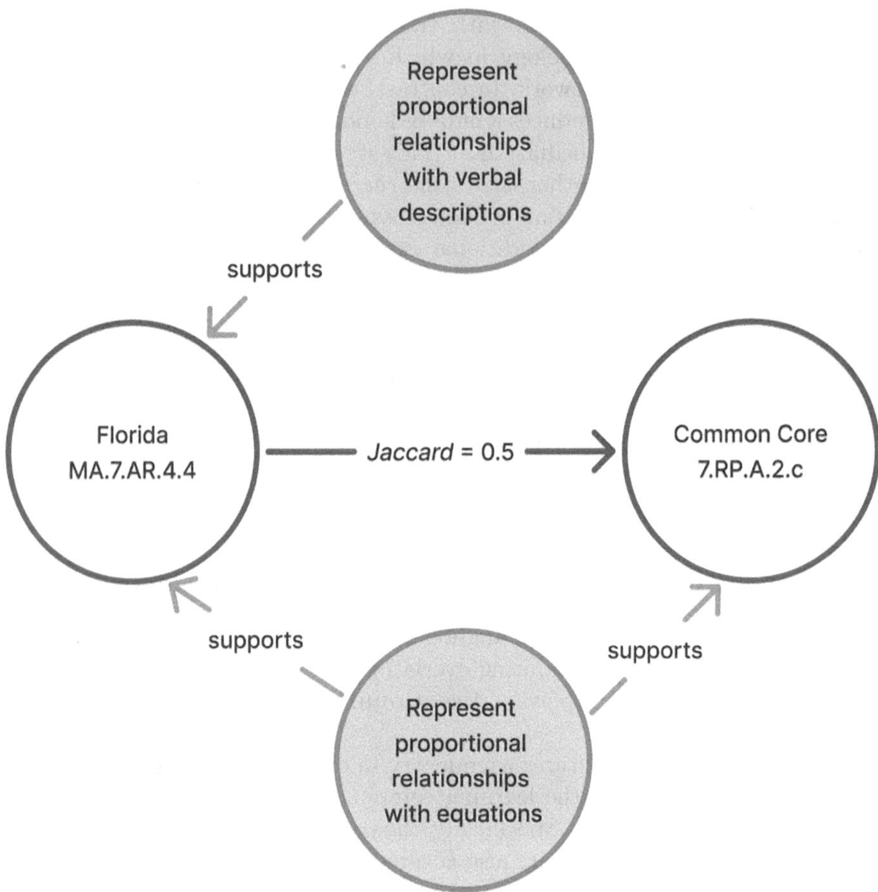

Fig. 1. Example standard pair with shared learning components. Crosswalk relationships are derived from learning component overlap, including directional coverage and Jaccard similarity.

While directional coverage captures asymmetry between standards, it does not summarize overall overlap. To provide a symmetric measure of correspondence, we additionally compute Jaccard similarity over learning component coverage sets, defined as the ratio of shared learning components to the total number of learning components covered by either standard:

$$\text{Jaccard}(S_i, S_j) = \frac{|L(S_i) \cap L(S_j)|}{|L(S_i) \cup L(S_j)|}$$

While Jaccard similarity provides a simple instantiation, the representation itself is agnostic to the specific similarity function used. Weighted variants can incorporate confidence, expert validation, or instructional importance, allowing crosswalks to reflect the degrees of relationships rather than binary equivalence.

By deriving crosswalks from learning component coverage, the representation explicitly supports the identification of partial alignments, coverage gaps, and directional asymmetries. These properties are difficult to capture with traditional pairwise crosswalks that treat alignment as a binary relation between standards.

3.4 Scalability and Maintenance Implications

The intermediary representation yields significant scalability benefits. Traditional pairwise crosswalks require maintaining alignments between every pair of frameworks, resulting in quadratic growth in maintenance effort as the number of frameworks increases. In contrast, aligning each framework independently to a shared learning component set reduces maintenance complexity to linear in the number of frameworks.

When standards evolve, updates are localized to the affected framework's alignment to learning components, and derived crosswalks can be recomputed without revisiting all pairwise relationships. This property is especially important in real-world settings where standards are revised incrementally and crosswalks must be updated regularly.

Taken together, learning components provide a shared intermediary representation that reframes standards crosswalking as a coverage inference problem. This reframing enables both richer analytical comparisons across frameworks and more sustainable maintenance in large-scale educational systems.

In the following section, we apply these coverage-based measures to analyze crosswalks between the Common Core State Standards and multiple state frameworks, illustrating how asymmetric and partial relationships emerge in practice.

4 Empirical Case Study

We evaluate learning component-mediated crosswalks through an empirical case study comparing Common Core State Standards (CCSS) with multiple state frameworks. Rather than assessing standard quality, we examine how frameworks relate to one another when represented through shared learning components, revealing structural relationships hidden by traditional pairwise crosswalks.

4.1 Standards Frameworks

Our analysis compares mathematics standards across the following frameworks.

- **Common Core State Standards for Mathematics (CCSS)**
- **New York State Mathematics Standards**, a nominally aligned Common Core implementation
- **Texas Essential Knowledge and Skills (TEKS) - Mathematics**, a non-Common Core framework
- **Florida Benchmarks for Excellent Student Thinking (B.E.S.T.) - Mathematics**, a non-Common Core framework

These frameworks span both nominally aligned (NY) and divergent (TX, FL) implementations, enabling comparison of structural differences manifest in learning component coverage.

4.2 Learning Component Alignment

Learning components were developed iteratively by mathematics education experts, beginning with Common Core and expanding as additional frameworks were aligned as described below. The final shared set contains 4,010 learning components covering K-12 mathematics; CCSS uses 1,616 of these, NY uses 1,564, while other frameworks draw from different subsets including framework-specific components. The dataset and learning component alignments used in this study are publicly available [5].

To create the learning components for the first two frameworks (Common Core and Texas), a small team of tenured mathematics education experts decomposed each standard and approved learning components by consensus. To align each standards framework to this set, we used a hybrid approach combining automated and expert methods. Semantic similarity using *all-MiniLM-L6-v2* sentence embeddings with cosine similarity identified candidate LC matches for each standard. Subject matter experts then reviewed these candidates, validating high-confidence matches, manually identifying additional alignments for standards where automated methods had low confidence or where high semantic similarity masked substantive instructional differences. Each framework was independently aligned without reference to other frameworks. A standard may align to one or more learning components, reflecting its scope and level of decomposition. This ensures derived crosswalks reflect the structural relationships rather than assumptions from direct pairwise comparison.

4.3 Coverage-Based Crosswalk Metrics

Crosswalk relationships between frameworks are derived using the coverage-based metrics defined in Sect. 3. For any pair of standards or aggregated framework-level coverage sets, we compute:

- **Directional coverage**, measuring the proportion of learning components aligned to one framework that are also aligned to the other
- **Jaccard similarity**, summarizing symmetric overlap between learning component coverage sets

Directional coverage captures asymmetric containment relationships, while Jaccard similarity provides a complementary measure of overall overlap. Together, these metrics support analysis of partial alignment and differences in scope between mathematics standards frameworks.

Framework-level coverage metrics are computed by aggregating standard-to-standard alignments. For each standard in framework S_i, we identify all standards in framework S_j that share at least one learning component, calculate directional overlap as the proportion of the standard's LCs that appear in S_j, then compute the weighted mean across all standards in S_i, weighted by each standard's LC count. This approach reflects how well individual standards map across frameworks, with broader-scoped standards naturally contributing greater weight to overall coverage. Similarly, confidence distributions (Table 2) are based on Jaccard similarity calculated for each standard-to-standard pair.

Three distinct crosswalk patterns emerge (Table 1):

- **High-overlap implementations with grade-level reorganization**: Framework maintains high bidirectional overlap but shows moderate asymmetry, potentially reflecting content sequencing differences rather than scope reduction. New York exhibits high directional overlap with CCSS (96%/84%), indicating selective adoption with reorganization. NY standards represent a 2017 revision of Common Core ("Next Generation Learning Standards") that reorganized content across grade levels, particularly moving concepts in statistics, probability, and algebra to different grades while maintaining overall K-12 scope.

  Evidence of reorganization: Analysis reveals some learning components appear in multiple NY courses (e.g., both Algebra I and Algebra II) where CCSS treats them as single-year content. Framework-level metrics count each LC once, potentially undercounting content that NY teaches across multiple years for mastery. This supports documented claims that NY emphasizes "fewer topics with greater depth" through multi-year spiraling rather than content reduction.
- **Divergent smaller frameworks**: Texas exhibits moderate coverage of CCSS (62%) but substantially lower reverse coverage (35%). This asymmetry reflects both reduced scope and differences in how mathematical concepts are decomposed.
- **Moderately divergent frameworks**: Florida shows moderate bidirectional overlap with CCSS (63%/47%), with 16-point asymmetry indicating a framework of intermediate scope. Florida maintains partial CCSS coverage while incorporating substantial framework-specific content, falling between New York's tight alignment and Texas's extreme divergence.

These patterns distinguish varying degrees of alignment and divergence through coverage-based analysis. Traditional binary crosswalks hide these distinctions. For example, a binary crosswalk may label New York as "CCSS-aligned," and Texas as "non-CCSS", obscuring that NY shows 16% asymmetry (potentially from grade-level reorganization) while TX exhibits 27 point asymmetry from genuine structural divergence. Learning component-mediated crosswalks make structural properties (omission and asymmetry) explicit while providing greater analytical precision and reducing maintenance complexity.

4.4 Alignment Confidence Distribution

Learning component-mediated crosswalks support confidence-aware alignment by quantifying the strength of standard-to-standard correspondences. We use

Table 1. Bidirectional overlap and Jaccard similarity for state mathematics frameworks with CCSS. Asymmetry (difference between forward and backward coverage) distinguishes high-overlap implementations (NY), moderate divergence (FL), and substantial divergence (TX).

Framework Pair	Coverage (State to CCSS)	Coverage (CCSS to State)	Jaccard Similarity
NY - CCSS	0.96	0.84	0.82
TX - CCSS	0.62	0.35	0.30
FL - CCSS	0.63	0.47	0.37

Jaccard similarity as a proxy for alignment confidence, categorizing standard pairs as high confidence ($J > 0.7$), medium confidence ($0.3 \leq J \leq 0.7$), or low confidence ($J < 0.3$). Table 2 shows the distribution of confidence levels across framework pairs.

Confidence distributions correlate with the crosswalk patterns identified earlier. New York exhibits 82% high-confidence alignments (median Jaccard of 1.00), indicating that most NY standards have exact LC matches in CCSS, validating its high-overlap implementation classification. In contrast, Texas shows only 13.9% high-confidence matches and 39.8% low-confidence matches (median Jaccard: 0.33), reflecting genuine framework divergence rather than measurement noise. Florida (20.9%, median: 0.45), falls between NY's tight alignment and TX's substantial divergence.

Table 2. Confidence distribution of standard-to-standard alignments by framework pair. NY's 82% high-confidence matches (median Jaccard: 1.00) validate its high-overlap implementation classification, while TX and FL show majority medium-to-low confidence, reflecting genuine divergence.

Framework Pair	% High Conf (J>0.7)	% Medium Conf (0.3–0.7)	% Low Conf (J <0.3)	Median Jaccard
NY - CCSS	82.0%	14.6%	3.4%	1.00
TX - CCSS	13.9%	46.3%	39.8%	0.33
FL - CCSS	20.9%	49.6%	29.5%	0.45

High-confidence matches indicate standards requiring minimal adaptation, while low-confidence signals genuine curricular differences. For example, Florida standard **MA.1.GR.1.2** (*"Sketch two-dimensional figures when given defining attributes"*) shares only one LC with **CCSS 1.G.A.1** (Jaccard: 0.25). While both address geometric attributes, CCSS emphasizes conceptual understanding: differentiating defining from non-defining attributes, using these distinctions to identify shapes. Florida, on the other hand, focuses on procedural sketching. This low confidence correctly signals different instructional goals (procedural vs. conceptual) rather than equivalent content.

Traditional binary crosswalks would map these as "aligned geometry standards," obscuring this pedagogical difference.

4.5 Domain Level Patterns: Contrasting High-Overlap vs Divergent Implementations

Domain-level analysis reveals how crosswalk patterns manifest in content structure. New York and Florida, both showing framework-level asymmetry, exhibit fundamentally different domain patterns.

New York Pattern: New York preserves CCSS's 34-domain structure with eighteen domains at 100% alignment, including all K-8 core content. Observed gaps concentrate in advanced high school topics (Making Inferences: 40%, Geometric Properties: 67%), but multiple lines of evidence suggest these reflect content reorganization rather than omission.

Framework-level analysis cannot distinguish content taught at different grade levels from missing content. Further, NY distributes some learning components across multiple courses that CCSS treats as single-year content. For example, certain LCs appear in both Algebra I and Algebra II in NY but only one course in CCSS, consistent with NY's emphasis on fewer topics with greater depth.

The observed pattern reflects comprehensive reorganization for deeper treatment that framework-level and domain-level analysis cannot resolve. Grade-by-grade and course-by-course analysis would be needed to determine the nature of these gaps.

Florida Pattern: Florida reorganizes mathematics into seven broader domain categories, fundamentally restructuring CCSS's conceptual organization. No domain achieves 100% alignment, with coverage ranging from 86% (Fractions) to 32% (Data Analysis and Probability). Florida's "Algebraic Reasoning" (52%) and "Number Sense and Operations" (49%) aggregate content CCSS distributes across multiple specialized domains. This coarser granularity produces moderate coverage across all domains rather than concentrated gaps in specific areas, indicating comprehensive reorganization rather than selective omission.

Implications: These domain patterns validate framework-level classifications through structural evidence. NY's high-overlap implementation requires targeted supplementation in 2–3 advanced high school domains while maintaining direct CCSS correspondence elsewhere. FL's divergent framework demands comprehensive remapping: vendors must translate between fundamentally different organizational schemes (34 fine-grained domains $\leftrightarrow$ 7 broad categories), even where content overlap exists. A standard in FL's "Algebraic Reasoning" may map to CCSS domains in Expressions, Equations, Functions, or Operations, requiring nuanced understanding beyond simple coverage percentages.

5 Discussions and Conclusions

Learning component-mediated crosswalks reveal three distinct patterns: high-overlap implementations with reorganization (NY: 96%/84%, 82% high confidence), moderate divergence (FL: 63%/47%, 20.9% high confidence), and substantial divergence (TX: 62%/35%, 13.9% high confidence). Domain analysis validates these classifications structurally: NY preserves CCSS's 34-domain organization with 18 domains at 100% alignment, while FL reorganizes into 7 broader categories with no perfect alignment domains. Traditional binary crosswalks often fail to express the distinction between NY's 16-point asymmetry (high overlap with potential reorganization) and TX's 27-point asymmetry (substantial structural divergence).

Practical Implications: LC-mediated crosswalks enable differentiated adaptation strategies based on crosswalk patterns. NY's 95–100% K-8 coverage and high confidence (82%) suggest minimal elementary modification is needed, though the 16-point asymmetry warrants investigation of whether gaps reflect grade-level shifts or genuine omissions. FL's reorganization demands comprehensive remapping between different domain structures ($34 \leftrightarrow 7$), even where content overlaps. TX's substantial divergence (35% backward coverage, 13.9% high confidence) signals the need for extensive curriculum development. Confidence distributions guide resource allocation: high-confidence matches support automated mapping, while low-confidence matches require expert review.

The hub-and-spoke architecture reduces maintenance from $O(n^2)$ to $O(n)$. For 51 frameworks, this eliminates 2,550 pairwise operations, replacing them with 51 independent alignments, substantially reducing maintenance overhead as standards evolve over time.

Limitations: Framework-level analysis pools content across all grades and courses, making it difficult to distinguish content taught at different grade levels or distributed across multiple courses from genuinely omitted content. For example, New York distributes certain learning components across both Algebra I and Algebra II, while CCSS treats them as single-year content. Framework-level metrics undercount such multi-year spiraling. The approach does not capture pedagogical sequence, cognitive demand, or instructional emphasis. Results depend on expert-designed LC sets and work best when frameworks have comparable scope.

Governance of the LC set itself is a practical concern that deserves acknowledgment. While the hub-and-spoke architecture reduces crosswalk maintenance complexity, the LC set is not static. Standards will evolve, new frameworks will introduce novel content, and definitions may drift over time if left unmanaged. LC governance requires a versioning strategy including stable identifiers for LCs, a logged record of additions and deprecations, and a review process for proposed changes analogous to the initial construction process. Because all derived crosswalks flow from the same LC set, versioned releases ensure that crosswalk consumers can pin to a stable LC version while updates are reviewed, preventing inconsistencies from propagating silently through dependent systems. Periodic audits to detect near-duplicate or overly broad LCs would further mitigate conceptual drift. Our LC set is a product that will be maintained and managed by Learning Commons and available under a permissive license for the community.

Contributions: This work demonstrates learning components provide scalable intermediary representation for large-scale crosswalking. Coverage metrics quantify asymmetry and partial alignment hidden by binary mappings, while domain analysis reveals organizational patterns framework-level metrics cannot detect. LC-mediated crosswalks transform standards alignment from labor-intensive exercises into maintainable foundations for educational technology interoperability.

6 Future Work

Validation of learning component (LC) quality through inter-rater reliability studies and comparison of LC-mediated crosswalks against expert-constructed pairwise crosswalks remains an important direction for future work.

The present study is limited to mathematics, a domain with relatively well-defined and hierarchically organized content. Extending the LC approach to less structured domains, such as social studies, arts, or health education, raises additional challenges. In these domains, standards are often written at higher levels of abstraction, content boundaries are less clearly defined, and expert consensus on appropriate LC granularity may be harder to achieve.

While the proposed framework is expected to generalize, the construction, validation, and governance of LC sets in such domains require dedicated investigation.

Acknowledgments. We would like to thank Sean Johnson from Achievement Network (ANet) for his contributions to the learning component design and alignment process. We also thank the Steve Perella and Michelle Pustilnik for their support and feedback on this work. Finally, we thank the anonymous reviewers for their thoughtful comments and suggestions.

References

1. Bowzer, A., Dyke, E.: Standards alignment and evaluation study. Tech. rep., WestEd, San Francisco, CA (2023). https://csaa.wested.org/wp-content/uploads/2023/08/Bowzer-and-Dyke-2023.pdf
2. Butterfuss, R., Doran, H.: An application of text embeddings to support alignment of educational content standards. Educ. Meas. Issues Pract. (2024)
3. Camilli, G.: An NLP crosswalk between the Common Core State Standards and NAEP item specifications (2024)
4. Common Core/Next Generation Learning Standards Crosswalk (2018). https://resources.finalsite.net/images/v1685711926/esbocesorg/pbhla4bb4t9qyqsgh6le/ccss-nglscrosswalk.pdf

5. Learning Commons: Knowledge graph. https://github.com/learning-commons-org/knowledge-graph (2026)
6. Petrilli, M.J., Wright, B.L.: Are state standards still aligned to the Common Core? Tech. rep., Thomas B. Fordham Institute, Washington, DC (2018). https://fordhaminstitute.org/national/research/state-state-standards-post-common-core
7. Porter, A.C., Smithson, J.L.: Alignment of assessments, standards, and instruction using curriculum indicator data. In: Proceedings of the Annual Meeting of the American Educational Research Association (AERA '02). New Orleans, LA (2002). https://curriculumanalysis.org/Reference/PorterSmithson-AlignmentNCME02.pdf
8. Webb, N.L.: Criteria for alignment of expectations and assessments in mathematics and science education, Madison, WI (1997). Tech. rep
9. Xu, Q., Jiao, H., Zhou, T.: Automated alignment of math items to content standards using language models. In: Proceedings of the International Conference on Educational Data Mining (EDM '25) (2025)

Doctoral Consortium

Building Regulation Capacity in Human–AI Collaborative Learning: A Human-Centred GenAI System

Yujing Zhang and Jionghao Lin(✉)

The University of Hong Kong, Hong Kong SAR, China
zhangyujing@connect.hku.hk, jionghao@hku.hk

Abstract. Collaborative learning works when groups regulate together by setting shared goals, coordinating participation, monitoring progress, and responding to breakdowns through co-regulation (CoRL) and socially shared regulation (SSRL). As generative AI (GenAI) enters group work, however, it remains unclear whether and how it supports these socially distributed regulation processes. This doctoral project proposes a GenAI-supported collaborative learning system grounded in CoRL and SSRL to strengthen groups' *socially distributed regulation capacity*. The system links three components: (1) group activity generation; (2) an in-group support agent that provides process-focused prompts without giving solutions; (3) and an embedded learning analytics dashboard that turns interaction traces into timely summaries for monitoring and decision making. The project progresses from mechanism to design to impact: it first identifies how GenAI reshapes regulation patterns and which patterns indicate more effective HumanAI collaboration, then builds an integrated GenAI system that targets these patterns, and finally evaluates whether the GenAI system improves regulation capacity and group performance across varying levels of GenAI involvement. Expected contributions include a teacher-in-the-loop system for HumanAI collaboration and process-level evidence on how GenAI reconfigures CoRL and SSRL in group work.

Keywords: Generative AI · Learning analytics · Socially Shared regulation · Co-Regulation · Computer-Supported Collaborative Learning

1 Introduction

As collaboration becomes a critical 21st-century competency, Computer-Supported Collaborative Learning (CSCL) has emerged as a key pedagogical approach that leverages digital technologies to support group reasoning and shared knowledge construction [1]. In parallel, the rise of generative AI (GenAI) introduces new design possibilities for CSCL. GenAI refers to AI models that generate content (e.g., text, images, or video) from natural-language prompts

E. G. Blanchard et al. (Eds.): AIED 2026, CCIS 3033, pp. 199–204, 2026.
https://doi.org/10.1007/978-3-032-29794-5_30

and can engage in natural back-and-forth conversation by interpreting context and producing coherent responses [2]. It can also follow structured instructions and summarise complex information into concise, usable outputs [2]. Thus, these capabilities make GenAI well suited to support an integrated CSCL cycle. As illustrated in Fig. 1A, GenAI can, in principle, support an integrated workflow across three phases of a CSCL activity that closes the loop from group activity design to in-group support and learning analytics, and back to evidence-informed redesign. In the *Before the activity* phase, GenAI can support teachers in generating and adapting a structured group activity design based on their goals and constraints [6]. This design is then deployed to the group activity. In the *During the activity* phase, GenAI supports collaboration in two coordinated ways: it can prompt groups with process-focused messages that encourage peer sensemaking [9,10]; and it can support real-time learning analytics by interpreting unstructured data such as collaborative dialogues and text records to produce simple indicators of group progress, engagement, and performance [7]. These indicators guide both teacher attention and the timing and type of the next prompt. The activity produces interaction traces, which are captured for analysis. In the *After the activity* phase, GenAI summarises these traces into teacher-facing learning analytics feedback, which directly informs revisions to the next activity design [7,9]. However, existing research and tools often separate activity generation, in-activity support, and learning analytics, with few systems integrating them into a single loop. Consequently, teachers face high coordination costs to use these tools together, which can prevent them from iteratively improving and reusing collaborative activities in authentic classroom contexts.

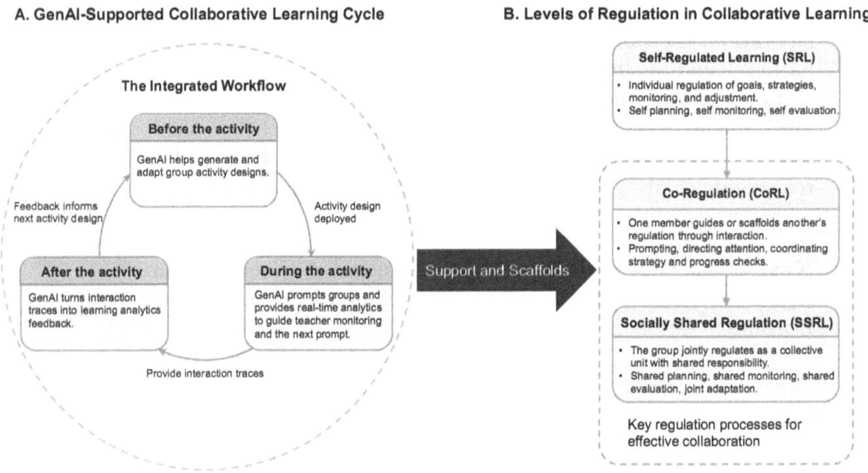

Fig. 1. Focus of the doctoral study: (A) a GenAI-supported CSCL cycle to strengthen socially distributed regulation; (B) SRL, CoRL, and SSRL theory as its foundation.

Additionally, to unlock the full potential of our proposed integrated workflow (Fig. 1B), it is necessary to strengthen the processes that make collaboration effective. In CSCL, productive collaboration is defined by more than participation alone; it depends on whether groups can sustain joint work over time through shared planning, monitoring, evaluation, adaptation, and repair when obstacles arise [5]. To explain these processes, current research extends self-regulated learning (SRL) beyond the individual to socially distributed forms of regulation, including co-regulation (CoRL), where learners guide one another's regulation through interaction, and socially shared regulation (SSRL), where regulation is enacted collectively at the group level [4] (Fig. 1B). As such, these socially distributed forms of regulation are central to effective collaboration because they emerge through coordination, mutual orientation, and shared responsibility among group members. Nevertheless, much GenAI-mediated collaboration research has paid limited attention to these regulation capacities, leaving open the question of how GenAI should be designed to strengthen, rather than displace, shared regulation in group work.

To address these gaps, this doctoral research aims to build an integrated GenAI-supported CSCL system to strengthen socially distributed regulation (CoRL and SSRL). The research is organised around three **Research Questions** that progress from mechanism to design to evaluation:

- **RQ1:** How does GenAI reconfigure socially distributed regulation (CoRL and SSRL) and group interaction patterns in group work, and which patterns distinguish more effective Human–AI collaboration?
- **RQ2:** How can we design and implement an integrated GenAI-supported CSCL system that links group activity generation, in-group support during the activity, and a real-time learning analytics dashboard?
- **RQ3:** To what extent can this GenAI-supported system strengthen socially distributed regulation (CoRL and SSRL) and improve group performance?

Figure 2 summarises the **RQ1–RQ3** progression (top) and the proposed teacher-in-the-loop system linking activity generation, in-group support, and real-time learning analytics in an evidence-informed loop (bottom).

2 Background and Theoretical Basis

This study is grounded in regulation learning theory, especially co-regulation (CoRL) and socially shared regulation (SSRL) (See Fig. 1B), to guide the design of the proposed GenAI-supported system. CoRL captures moments when one learner scaffolds another's regulation, while SSRL refers to regulation enacted collectively at the group level [4]. Together, these constructs explain how groups coordinate goals, strategies, monitoring, evaluation, and adaptation over time [4,8]. Therefore, this project treats GenAI system as *bounded support*, constrained to regulation-oriented moves intended to strengthen CoRL and SSRL. Accordingly, CoRL and SSRL serve both as evaluation targets and as design specifications for what the system prompts, when it intervenes, and which trace-based indicators it surfaces to teachers for monitoring and improvement [3].

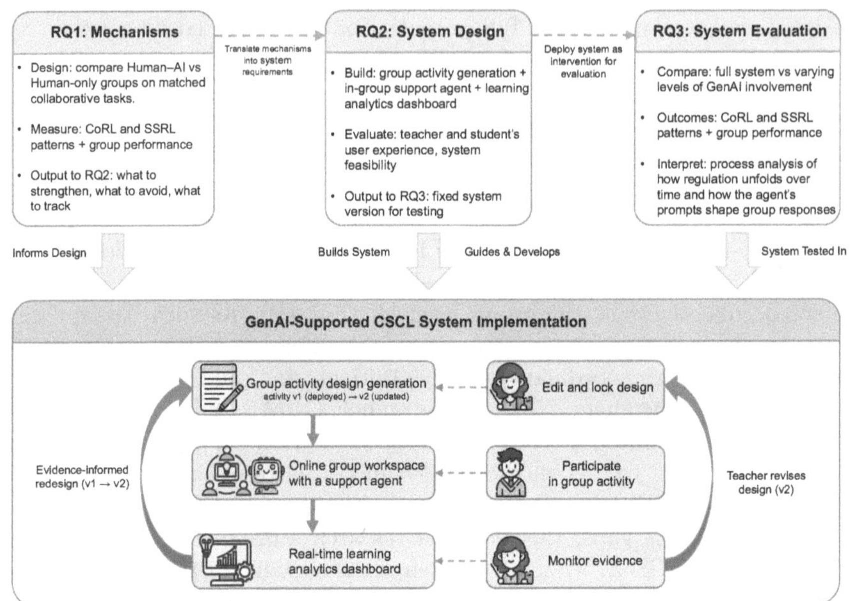

Fig. 2. Overview linking RQ1RQ3 to the GenAI collaboration system.

3 Methodology and Research Plan

3.1 Overview

Figure 2 summarises the staged plan linking **RQ1RQ3** to system implementation. **RQ1** identifies regulation mechanisms and yields design targets and indicators. **RQ2** builds and pilots the integrated system, producing a fixed configuration for evaluation. **RQ3** evaluates system impact.

3.2 Current Progress: RQ1 Regulation Mechanisms in Human–AI Group Work

To date, we have completed the empirical work for RQ1, with some findings reported in [10]. We conducted a parallel-group randomised experiment with university students ($N = 71$), working in triads, comparing Human-only and Human–AI groups on matched collaborative tasks. In the Human-only condition, groups used Microsoft Teams with no GenAI. In the HumanAI condition, groups used an online CSCL platform with an embedded GenAI agent (`OpenAI GPT-4o mini`) for real-time text collaboration. The agent did not give content or solutions; it delivered process-focused prompts to elicit explanation, encourage perspective-taking, and support planning and monitoring. We used statistical comparisons and network analysis to examine group-level regulation and how regulatory processes were enacted through participation moves across conditions.

Key Findings. GenAI availability reconfigured collaborative regulation. Compared with Human-only groups, Human–AI groups shifted from predominantly socially shared regulation towards more hybrid co-regulatory forms, with selective increases in directive, obstacle-oriented, and affective processes. While overall participation-focus distributions were broadly similar across conditions, Human–AI groups exhibited a more differentiated regulatory structure, with regulation more tightly coupled to monitoring, evaluative reasoning, and reporting. By contrast, Human-only groups centred regulation on shared strategic negotiation and shared action change, supported by a wider range of participatory actions. Group performance did not differ by condition; however, only high-performing Human–AI teams showed a coherent obstacle-driven plan–monitor pattern.

Implications. Together, these findings suggest that GenAI can reshape where regulatory responsibility lies and how group regulation is coordinated. Consequently, effective HumanAI collaboration is unlikely to emerge by default. GenAI should therefore scaffold shared regulation by prompting joint planning, progress checks, and coordinated action when obstacles arise. During group work, learning analytics can use indicators such as missing or weak coupling patterns to trigger targeted support and reorient groups towards effective regulation.

3.3 Future Work

Human-Centred System Design and Feasibility (RQ2). Building on **RQ1**, **RQ2** translates the identified targets into system requirements for activity structure, bounded in-group prompting, and trace-based indicators for teachers. We will answer **RQ2** by building GenAI-supported CSCL system and piloting it with teachers and students to assess usability and feasibility. This system has three components: group activity generation, an in-group support agent during the activity, and a real-time learning analytics dashboard (See Fig. 2). We will assess feasibility and perceived value through teacher and student feedback, including semi-structured interviews, alongside interface logs and system metrics (e.g., bound compliance and dashboard latency). These findings will guide system refinement and finalise the indicators used in RQ3.

System Impact Under Different Levels of GenAI Involvement (RQ3). We will answer **RQ3** by conducting a quasi-experimental, between-groups comparison with matched tasks and settings, varying the level of GenAI involvement. Study 3 will compare three conditions: (i) *baseline*, with unstructured chatbot-only access during group work; (ii) *in-group support only*, where the GenAI agent provides bounded, process-focused prompts during the activity; and (iii) *in-group support plus teacher-monitoring learning analytics dashboard*, where the same in-group support is paired with a dashboard for teacher monitoring and decision making. Outcomes will include trace-based indicators of collaborative regulation capacity and group performance, supplemented by process analysis of group responses to prompts and regulation dynamics over time to interpret differences across conditions.

4 Expected Contributions

This project will contribute to Artificial Intelligence in Education (AIED) in three ways. *First*, it will deliver a closed-loop GenAI-supported CSCL system aligned with the collaborative learning cycle (see Fig. 1A), linking teacher-facing group activity generation, an in-group support agent during the activity, and trace-based learning analytics feedback for monitoring and improvement.

Second, it will contribute human-centred design knowledge by keeping teachers in the loop through key control points before, during, and after class, clarifying how control and evidence presentation support appropriate trust (see Fig. 2).

Third, it will advance AIED theory of HumanAI collaboration by providing process-level evidence on how GenAI reconfigures CoRL and SSRL, and when these shifts support productive collaboration.

References

1. Baker, M., Reimann, P.: CSCL: a learning and collaboration science? Int. J. Comput.-Support. Collaborative Learn. **19**(3), 273–281 (2024)
2. Cao, Y., et al.: A comprehensive survey of AI-generated content (AIGC): A history of generative AI from GAN to ChatGPT. arXiv preprint (2023)
3. Edwards, J., et al.: Human-ai collaboration: designing artificial agents to facilitate socially shared regulation among learners. Br. J. Edu. Technol. **56**(2), 712–733 (2025)
4. Hadwin, A., Järvelä, S., Miller, M.: Self-regulation, co-regulation, and shared regulation in collaborative learning environments. In: Schunk, D.H., Greene, J.A. (eds.) Handbook of Self-Regulation of Learning and Performance, pp. 83–106. Routledge/Taylor & Francis Group, 2 edn. (2018)
5. Järvelä, S., et al.: Socially shared regulation of learning in CSCL: understanding and prompting individual-and group-level shared regulatory activities. Int. J. Comput.-Support. Collab. Learn. **11**(3), 263–280 (2016)
6. Karaman, M.R., et al.: Are lesson plans created by ChatGPT more effective? An experimental study. Int. J. Technol. Educ. **7**(1), 107–127 (2024)
7. Ouyang, F., Zhang, L.: AI-driven learning analytics applications and tools in computer-supported collaborative learning: a systematic review. Educ. Res. Rev. **44**, 100616 (2024)
8. Rogat, T.K., Linnenbrink-Garcia, L.: Socially shared regulation in collaborative groups: an analysis of the interplay between quality of social regulation and group processes. Cogn. Instr. **29**(4), 375–415 (2011)
9. Yan, L., Greiff, S., Teuber, Z., Gašević, D.: Promises and challenges of generative artificial intelligence for human learning. Nat. Hum. Behav. **8**, 1839–1850 (2024)
10. Zhang, Y., Meng, X., Feng, S., Lin, J.: Human-AI collaboration reconfigures group regulation from socially shared to hybrid co-regulation. In: International Conference on Artificial Intelligence in Education, Springer (2026)

Designing a Lightweight AI Tutor for Pedagogically Grounded Classroom Use

Erica Perseghin(✉) and Gian Luca Foresti

Department of Mathematics, Computer Science and Physics, University of Udine, Udine, Italy
perseghin.erica@spes.uniud.it, gianluca.foresti@uniud.it

Abstract. This doctoral research investigates how curriculum-based generative AI (GenAI) tutors can be designed for responsible classroom integration in secondary education. Adopting a design-based research (DBR) approach, the study builds on prior work on teachers' and students' AI literacy to inform the iterative design of a lightweight Retrieval-Augmented Generation (RAG) tutor guided by three theory-informed principles: curriculum alignment, delayed feedback as temporal scaffolding, and explicit signaling of system limitations. An exploratory classroom pilot (n = 10, ages 18–19) in SQL learning provides preliminary indications that deferring responses creates temporal space for peer discussion, while content grounding and limitation signaling may support instructional coherence and more reflective engagement with AI. The expected contribution is empirically grounded design knowledge on how GenAI tutors can function as pedagogical structures that support collaborative sensemaking, informing research and practice in AI in Education (AIEd).

Keywords: Collaborative Learning · GenAI Learning · RAG-based Tutoring

1 Introduction and Problem Statement

The rapid diffusion of GenAI has expanded educational technology toward interactive and multimodal architectures [17]. Although AI-assisted feedback shows potential for participation and formative learning [10,13], classroom adoption remains limited due to persistent concerns about privacy, transparency, and uncritical reliance on automated responses [5,20]. Educators face barriers including limited trust, concerns about reliability, and insufficient alignment with instructional materials [1]. These challenges highlight the need for AI systems that augment rather than replace human cognition, supporting metacognitive regulation and learner agency through curated instructional content and temporal structures that support peer-mediated reasoning [5,21]. RAG architectures [2] offer a promising pathway to constrain AI behavior and maintain curriculum

E. G. Blanchard et al. (Eds.): AIED 2026, CCIS 3033, pp. 205–210, 2026.
https://doi.org/10.1007/978-3-032-29794-5_31

coherence, yet empirical evidence in secondary education remains scarce and the interactional consequences of design choices such as feedback timing and transparency signaling are underexplored. This doctoral research investigates how lightweight, curriculum-grounded RAG-based tutors can be designed for classroom use, focusing on collaborative learning and trust calibration. Adopting a DBR approach [18], this preliminary work aims to contribute empirically grounded design knowledge for pedagogically responsible AI tutoring systems. The research is guided by the following questions: (RQ1) How can lightweight, curriculum-grounded GenAI tutors be designed as pedagogical structures for classroom use in secondary education? (RQ2) How do design features such as delayed feedback and transparency signaling shape collaborative learning and trust in AI tutors?

2 Proposed Architecture and Methodology

Unlike general-purpose conversational agents that lack curriculum alignment, or proprietary ITS systems [19] that require extensive data and infrastructure, RAG-based tutors offer a middle ground: generation grounded in instructional materials, with the possibility of local deployment on school-controlled infrastructure. Across design iterations [18], the proposed tutor was shaped by empirical investigations of teachers' AI literacy and students' AI interaction competencies. It is conceptualized as a pedagogical artifact evaluated through its design features (curriculum grounding, transparency, and temporal regulation of feedback) and their influence on collaborative classroom practices.

Phase 1: Teacher AI Literacy and Design Requirements. To inform system design, we examined teachers' AI literacy in Italian secondary education [15]. Despite growing institutional attention, classroom adoption remains limited by insufficient training and concerns about opaque AI behavior [6,22]. This motivated a curriculum-grounded RAG architecture constrained to teacher-authored materials and the inclusion of transparency features such as source exposure.

Phase 2: Student Baseline Competencies in AI Interaction. We analyzed students' baseline competencies in AI interaction by examining the prompt formulation of 32 upper-secondary computer science students using the CLEAR framework [7,16]. Despite intermediate programming knowledge, students' prompts lacked technical specificity and contextual clarity, revealing a gap between domain competence and AI interaction skills that risks cognitive offloading and superficial learning [3]. Observations from collaborative settings suggest that AI use is more pedagogically effective when embedded in peer discussion and critical evaluation [21], informing the tutor design.

These phases directly shaped the design principles (Sect. 3). Phase 1 motivated curriculum grounding and source exposure to address teachers' distrust of opaque AI. Phase 2 highlighted students' limited AI interaction skills, motivating small-group collaboration and non-immediate response timing to support peer-mediated reasoning. The classroom pilot constitutes the third iteration, providing preliminary observations of these design principles in practice.

3 Design Principles for Pedagogical AI Tutoring

Building on the identified constraints and informed by sociocultural learning theory [21] and dialogic learning theory [14], we implemented a lightweight RAG tutor guided by three interconnected design principles: curriculum grounding, transparent limitation signaling, and non-immediate response timing as temporal scaffolding [4]. Curriculum grounding promotes instructional coherence by constraining generations to teacher-provided materials, reducing conceptual misalignment with classroom content. Transparent limitation signaling externalizes system boundaries and encourages verification practices, mitigating over-reliance on AI. When retrieved evidence is insufficient to generate a grounded response, the tutor directs students to consult the teacher rather than attempting to generate potentially unreliable content. Finally, the tutor introduces non-immediate response timing as a deliberate pedagogical feature rather than a technical limitation [4] aligned with [21], creating temporal space for student interaction and collaborative reasoning [11]. In classroom use, these delays foster hypothesis generation, peer consultation, and engagement with instructional materials rather than passive waiting. These three principles operate synergistically to create learning settings in which students: (a) receive consistent responses aligned with instructional materials, (b) engage in peer discussion during delay intervals rather than depending continuously on AI, (c) consult original sources when system confidence is low, and (d) recognize situations in which AI assistance is intentionally unavailable. Together, these principles shape interaction patterns rather than positioning the tutor as an immediate answer provider.

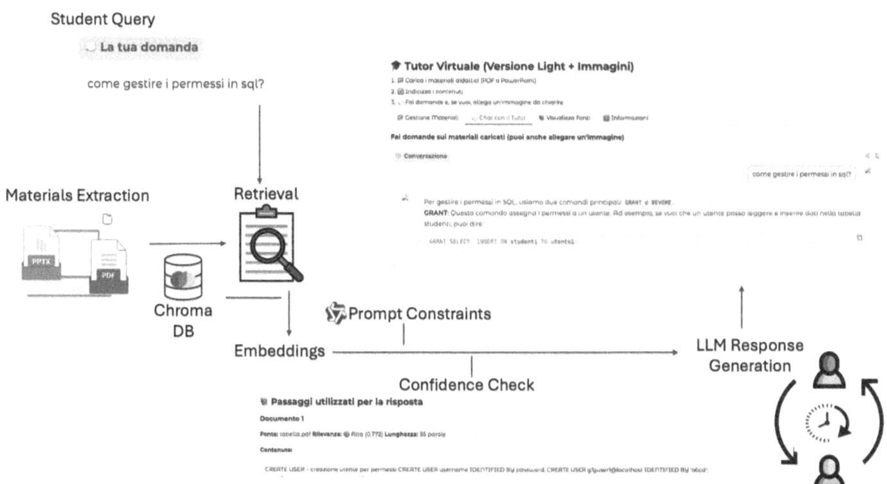

Fig. 1. RAG-based tutoring architecture with teacher-authored material grounding and delayed feedback supporting peer negotiation. Available at https://huggingface.co/spaces/erica92/tutor-rag-scuola.

Pilot Implementation and Deployment. To examine how the proposed design principles function in authentic classroom practice, we conducted an exploratory pilot study in a 2-hour lesson with 10 Italian final-year secondary school students (ages 18–19) working on previously unseen SQL content. Data collection comprised interaction logs (queries, timestamps, similarity scores) and observation notes on peer discussion patterns.

The tutor was used as a supplementary classroom tool in small-group settings, integrated within a teacher-mediated workflow. The teacher assigned DCL query tasks to the whole class on topics not explicitly covered in prior lessons and set a fixed time window for task completion. During this phase, students worked in groups using the tutor alongside preloaded instructional materials, while the teacher remained available for guidance when needed. This study focuses specifically on SQL instruction in computer science secondary education; while scope is intentionally narrow, it enables controlled examination of design principles before broader generalization. All interactions were logged for analysis; queries were in Italian to avoid linguistic confounds, e.g.:

- "Come gestire i permessi in SQL?" → *"How to manage permissions in SQL?"* (avg. score: 0.80, reply time: ∼1 m 10 s)
- "Come faccio a creare utente1?" → *"How do I create user1?"* (avg. score: 0.79, reply time: ∼1 m 14 s)
- "Come faccio a inserire i permessi di lettura, inserimento e aggiornamento?" → *"How do I insert read, insert and update permissions?"* (avg. score: 0.80, reply time: ∼1 m 36 s)

Technically, the tutor implements a RAG pipeline designed to preserve data control and minimize privacy risks, with the current prototype also available as a hosted demonstration (Fig. 1). It is lightweight relative to conventional ITS architectures, relying on small open-weight model, teacher-provided materials, and no labelled training data, supporting deployment on school-controlled infrastructure, with feasibility varying across educational settings depending on available resources. The system comprises three components: (i) a multilingual-e5-small embedding model for retrieval supporting Italian-language queries natively, (ii) a Chroma vector database indexing teacher-provided PDF/PowerPoint materials, and (iii) a 1.5B open-weight instruction-tuned LLM generating responses from retrieved passages. The architecture is modular, allowing the LLM component to be replaced with larger or domain-specific models as institutional resources permit. Dual guardrails enforce grounding: a similarity threshold filters low-relevance passages, and a response-level confidence check triggers abstention when evidence is insufficient. Transparent limitation signaling is further supported through source exposure and relevance indicators (high/medium/low).

4 Preliminary Results

During the classroom pilot, students interacted with the tutor through a chat interface where queries were submitted in natural language; responses were delayed and accompanied by source excerpts and confidence indicators. Delay intervals were used for peer discussion, consultation of instructional materials, and distributing cognitive labor (e.g., parallel drafting of SQL queries and material review), rather than waiting passively for AI responses. First author's observation notes document that when one group queried "Come faccio a creare utente1?", delay was used by one student to draft a preliminary CREATE USER statement while other partner reviewed the PDF handout for syntax details. When feedback became available, groups compared AI-generated explanations with their own reasoning, often identifying discrepancies that prompted further discussion, mirroring the evaluative dialogue characteristic of [9]. Although delayed responses initially elicited mild frustration (e.g., "How long do we need to wait?"), they created temporal space for peer negotiation and resource consultation that immediate feedback would likely have foreclosed. Across all interactions, generated responses achieved similarity scores (avg. score) between 0.77 and 0.80, indicating consistent curriculum grounding and no observed ungrounded outputs. Feedback timing research suggests that even brief delays can support deeper processing [12], yet optimal duration remains context-dependent [8]: it varies with educational level, task design, and learning domain, while excessively long delays may induce anxiety or disengagement. In the current implementation, given the moderate complexity of SQL tasks and the collaborative laboratory setting, a delay of approximately one minute was adopted as a task-compatible compromise to create temporal space for peer interaction and collaborative reasoning. This temporal structuring enabled what we term "negotiation windows" in which students engage in hypothesis generation, peer discussion, and evaluative comparison before receiving AI feedback. Adaptive timing strategies, scaling latency to query complexity and group dynamics, remain an open direction for future investigation. Students treated the tutor as an episodic resource embedded in peer collaboration rather than a central authority. Groups successfully completed the 15-minute post-lesson tasks, indicating that delayed feedback did not hinder task completion. Taken together, these observations provide preliminary evidence addressing RQ2, suggesting that delayed feedback and transparent limitation signaling can shape collaborative interaction patterns and support more calibrated and reflective engagement with AI tutors.

5 Future Work and Expected Contribution

Building on these preliminary findings, which provide exploratory evidence without systematic measures of trust or learning outcomes, planned studies will examine pedagogical effects and design transferability: (Spring/Summer 2026) cross-domain validation with multimodal materials; (Fall 2026) a structured comparison of immediate versus delayed feedback using pre/post assessments and coded interaction analysis. Expected contributions include: (1) design principles for trust calibration and metacognitive scaffolding, operationalized through post-session 5-point Likert questionnaires on perceived reliability and confidence in the tutor, complemented by log-based indicators such as verification against materials, acceptance of AI responses, and integration into peer discussion; (2) evidence on how temporal feedback regulation shapes collaborative learning; and (3) practical frameworks for lightweight, privacy-aware AI adoption in resource-constrained secondary schools, contributing to broader AIED discussions on AI literacy, trust, and human–AI collaboration.

References

1. An, Y., Yu, J.H., et al.: Investigating the higher education institutions' guidelines and policies regarding the use of GenAI in teaching, learning, research, and administration. Int. J. Educ. Technol. High. Educ. **22**, 10 (2025)
2. Barenji, R.V., Salimi, N.: An LLM-powered assessment retrieval-augmented generation (RAG) for higher education (2026). arXiv:2601.06141
3. Cain, W.: Prompting change: exploring prompt engineering in large language model AI and its potential to transform education. TechTrends **68**(1) (2024)
4. Corral, D., et al.: The effects of immediate versus delayed feedback on complex concept learning. Q. J. Exp. Psychol. **74**(4), 786–799 (2021)
5. Denny, P., Prather, J., Becker, B.A., et al.: Computing education in the era of generative AI. Commun. ACM **67**(2), 56–67 (2024)
6. Feldman-Maggor, Y., Cukurova, M., Kent, C., et al.: The impact of explainable AI on teachers' trust and acceptance of AI EdTech recommendations. Int. J. Artif. Intell. Educ. (2025)
7. Hsu, H.P.: From programming to prompting: developing computational thinking through large language model-based generative AI (2025). TechTrends
8. Kandemir, E.N., et al.: A meta-analysis of the impact of feedback timing on learning outcomes in computer-assisted learning. Educ. Psychol. Rev. **38**, 13 (2026)
9. Kapur, M.: Examining productive failure, productive success, unproductive failure, and unproductive success in learning. Educ. Psychol. **51**(2), 289–299 (2016)
10. Kiesler, N.: Exploring the potential of large language models to generate formative programming feedback. In: Proceedings of IEEE FIE, pp. 1–5 (2023)
11. Lehmann, M.: AI meets the classroom: when do LLMs harm learning? (2025)
12. Mai, H.: The comparative effect of immediate and delayed feedback on EFL learners' engagement. PsyCh J. **14**(6), 1008–1017 (2025)
13. Maity, S., Deroy, A., Sarkar, S.: Can large language models meet the challenge of generating school-level questions? Comput. Educ. Artif. Intell. **8**, 100370 (2025)
14. Mercer, N.: Words and Minds. Routledge, London (2000)
15. Perseghin, E., Foresti, G.L.: Empowering teachers with AI literacy. In: Proceedings of edu4AI 2025 (co-located with ECAI (2025))
16. Perseghin, E., Foresti, G.L.: Educational promptization in secondary school. In: Proceedings of IEEE EDUCON (2026). to appear
17. Rajesh, P., et al.: Multimodality in Online Education. Multimed, Tools Appl (2025)
18. Sawyer, R.K.: The Cambridge Handbook of the Learning Sciences. Cambridge Univ. Press, Cambridge (2014)
19. Silva, L.R., Fior, C., Rodrigues, L.: Use of feedback in intelligent tutoring systems: a systematic literature review. Interact. Learn. Environ. 1–22 (2025)
20. Vogt, M., Ferraioli, V.: Teachers' perspectives on using and teaching artificial intelligence in early primary education. In: Proceedings of AIED (2025)
21. Vygotsky, L.S.: Mind in Society. Harvard Univ. Press, Cambridge (1978)
22. Wut, T.M., Sum, C., Wong, H.: Does Perceived Risk of AI Matter? Teachers' AI literacy and institutional support. Educ. Inf, Technol (2025)

Relatable Pedagogical Agents: Teacher-Informed Design for Learner Characteristics

Samuel Hum(✉)

University of Illinois at Urbana-Champaign, Champaign, IL 61820, USA
hum3@illinois.edu

Abstract. Pedagogical agents (PAs) have been applied in a variety of research contexts with positive results when designed and implemented in ways consistent with good pedagogical practice. Teachers have unique relationships with students that would enable them to design relatable PAs; however, to date, there has been no research that has explored the effects of such designs. My research will investigate the role of teachers in designing the pedagogy for relatable PAs that leverage GenAI for feedback and build upon prior literature that has focused on the importance of agent appearance. Ultimately, I seek to make contributions around centering the voice of teachers in the design of PAs and developing theory-driven, modernized design principles for the use of relatable PAs in educational systems.

Keywords: Pedagogical agents · Participatory design · Learner-centered design · Design-based research · Relatable agents

1 Introduction

The rapid evolution of Artificial Intelligence (AI), particularly advancements in Generative AI (GenAI) and Large Language Models (LLMs), has accelerated the development of intelligent pedagogical agents (PAs) [2]. PAs are characters that cohabit virtual learning environments with students to aid instruction. Grounded in the "computers are social actors" (CASA) paradigm and the media equation, PA research is based on the premise that people respond to computers similarly to how they would with social partners, attributing to them qualities that are typically reserved for human-human interactions [7]. This work is guided by the Cognitive-Affective-Social Theory of Learning in digital Environments (CASTLE) framework. CASTLE is the culmination of previous PA theories and emphasizes the importance of triggering social processes to mediate information processing [9]. Interactions with PAs, however, are not a replacement for human-human interactions. Educational technologies leveraging AI are most effective when utilized to augment teacher capabilities to support learners. Thus, PAs in this study will be designed as knowledgeable peers that extend the teacher's

E. G. Blanchard et al. (Eds.): AIED 2026, CCIS 3033, pp. 211–216, 2026.
https://doi.org/10.1007/978-3-032-29794-5_32

ability to provide personalized one-on-one support enabling teachers to instead focus on broader classroom challenges.

Although PAs are a promising educational support, the design of these tools is typically driven by researchers or "experts" who are often disconnected from the lived realities of teachers and students [1]. There are open questions about how learners receive PAs and the role of teachers in implementing AI educational technologies. Participatory design explores the collaboration of stakeholders and designers to jointly shape educational interventions and is a vehicle to leverage teacher insights into designs [3]. I propose that by incorporating teacher perspectives into the creation of relatable PAs, PAs will attend on a deeper level to learner perceptions, identities, and needs. Although "relatable agent" is not a term commonly used in the field, I define it as agents that share meaningful qualities with their student, which is dependent on how learners receive their agent. By meaningful, I mean agent features that learners can identify with that elicit social connections and familiarity.

1.1 Relatable Pedagogical Agents

Recent work has begun exploring teacher involvement in the design of PAs. These are, however, preliminary studies without empirical findings for learner outcomes. Including teachers in the design of PAs could be a powerful direction for the field. Participatory design highlights the importance of taking a learner-centered approach to designing educational systems [3]. This is particularly relevant for PA design, as their usefulness depends on the context in which they are deployed and whether they align with student needs and expectations [4]. Participatory design addresses this weakness with PA research through the co-creation of educational systems that prioritize the needs of the people who use them [3]. Previous work in the field for designing PAs for diverse learners in STEM has typically focused on the external features of agents and in particular agent ethnicity and gender. Research has shown that learners can project stereotypes or characteristics onto their agents based on perceived features [4]. Kim and Wei [5] found that students may prefer to work with agents that match their ethnicity and gender and they hypothesize that matched agents can potentially serve as powerful motivators and role models.

Incorporating teacher perspectives into design takes effort and time for designers, researchers, and stakeholders. This study will investigate how teachers can effectively inform the design of relatable PAs and in particular the agent pedagogy and appearance, which I hypothesize are factors of relatability. This study will use a 2×2 design: a teacher-informed pedagogy (TP) and a researcher-designed pedagogy (RP) condition for agent pedagogy and a teacher-informed appearance (TA) and a researcher-designed appearance (RA) condition for agent appearance. I seek to demonstrate the added value of engaging with teachers and enhancing social interactions with relatable agents through CASTLE. My work will be guided by the following research questions:

RQ1: To what extent does teacher expertise emerge in how teachers design a pedagogical agent?

RQ2: How does learner reception of their agent depend on agent pedagogy and agent appearance?

RQ3: How do student learning outcomes depend on agent pedagogy and agent appearance?

2 Methods

2.1 Participants

Teachers and students will be recruited through ongoing relationships with school and community partners. Learners must be enrolled in one of our teachers' fall programs and will be 11 to 13 years old. Teachers and students will be from the West, Midwest, and Southeast United States. Informed written consent will be obtained from teachers and at least one parent/guardian of each student through signing printed consent forms. Assent will be obtained from each participant on the first day of data collection. I conducted a power analysis (power = .80), resulting in a target sample size of 128 participants. Participants will be randomly assigned to one of the pedagogy and appearance PA conditions.

2.2 Materials

Teacher Participatory Design Activities. *VEXcode VR* is a drag-and-drop block coding environment where students program robots to perform tasks in virtual playgrounds (see Fig. 1). In *VEXcode VR*, users have access to pre-defined blocks that can be dragged into their code. The code runs sequentially and modifies how their robot in a playground behaves when their program is run. A playground is a virtual environment where the students try to solve tasks using the robot that they code. On the sidebar there will be a PA and chat window. Users can communicate with the PA using the chat window to type messages. Agents will respond using text in the same chat window and will have gestures to facilitate communication.

To design agent pedagogy, teachers will engage with a role-playing activity. They will be given a link to a researcher-designed *VEXcode VR*-like interface similar to the one that their students will interact with. In the chat window of the interface, Gemini 2.5 Flash will be system prompted to generate a goal in the playground, buggy code, and a question about their code. Teachers will be prompted to provide feedback to their virtual student agent by typing in the same chat window. LLM-generated messages and teacher-generated responses will be automatically logged in a secure, anonymous SQL database. The data generated from this activity will be used with LLM-generated synthetic data to fine-tune a local frontier small language model (SLM) from Hugging Face. The teachers will also be given access to the pedagogical agent toolkit (PATK) to design the physical characteristics of their relatable PAs. The PATK is a website where novice designers can select the visual characteristics of pedagogical agents and can export their PA designs into the *VEXcode VR* environment (see Fig. 1).

Fig. 1. PATK interface (left) and *VEXcode VR* interface with block menu, code window, playground, and agent sidebar (right).

Learner Activities. Middle school participants in our *VEXcode VR* programming will all be provided with a laptop, mouse, and class and student ID to use the *VEXcode VR* environment (see Fig. 1). They will be tasked with working through three playgrounds, one per day. Each time the student modifies their code, presses the play button, an event from the playground is fired, or interacts with their agent, log data will be stored in an anonymized and secure database. They will also complete a pre- and post-test measure for computer science knowledge growth. The knowledge assessment will be the previously validated Middle Grades Computer Science Concept Inventory (MG-CSCI) [6]. The measure consists of 24 multiple-choice questions that utilize block code and computer science knowledge [6].

2.3 Procedure

Procedures regarding teachers participating in the design of the relatable agent and the *VEXcode VR* programming will be identical across locations. The researcher will meet with each participating teacher individually in hour-long sessions via Zoom. The teacher will first participate in a think-aloud activity. They will brainstorm priorities for individualizing instruction for their students. The researcher will then introduce the role-playing activity to the teacher and remind the teacher not to mention sensitive data. The teachers will then have 45 minutes to provide feedback to a series of synthetic student simulated behavior and will be instructed to provide personalized feedback based on their own teaching experience and understanding of their students. After the activity, the researcher and teacher will spend the remaining time iterating the researcher-designed system prompt to consolidate and incorporate ideas from the think-aloud and role-playing activity to capture their intended PA pedagogical behaviors.

After meeting with all teachers, a researcher on the team will fine-tune the SLMs. The researcher will then schedule additional meetings with each teacher. For the first 30 minutes, the teacher will interact with the model fine-tuned using their pedagogy data. If the teacher is satisfied with the functionality of the model, the researcher will send them a link to the PATK and will instruct the teacher to design the appearance of a knowledgeable peer PA. They will have 30 minutes to complete the appearance. If the teacher is not satisfied with the model, the researcher and teacher will set up another meeting and continue to iterate the pedagogy of the agent. The following session will repeat the activity from the first session and modify the system prompt to align more with the teacher's expectations. The researcher will then fine-tune the model using the additional data and will set up another meeting with the teacher to test the new design. This process will continue until all teachers are satisfied with the pedagogy. Once all teachers have designed their relatable PAs, the researcher will set up a final session with each teacher to reflect on their design of their PA and go over the *VEXcode VR* curriculum for their students.

The data collection with the learners will consist of three days based in a classroom. On the first day, teachers will introduce the research and ask each student for verbal assent. All participants who have parental consent and verbal assent will be given the *VEXcode VR* knowledge pre-test. They will have 25 minutes to complete the assessment. For all three days, learners will be introduced to the *VEXcode VR* playground and relevant blocks for 10 minutes and will be given 20 minutes to interact with their playground and assigned agent. On the final day, they will be given the *VEXcode VR* knowledge post-test and a reflection prompt on their experience with their agent after playing in the environment. They will have the rest of the session to complete the task.

3 Data Analysis

To answer the first research question regarding the role of teachers in the design of relatable PAs, I will conduct topic modeling on the feedback they provided in the role-playing activity and inductive coding of the think-aloud activity with the teachers. For the second research question regarding the influence of relatability on agent reception, I will assess learner engagement and code their reflections on their interactions with their agent. I hypothesize that engagement aligns with relatability and specifically how learners affectively, behaviorally, and cognitively respond to agents. I will use a bottom-up approach to identify different types of engagement using sequential pattern mining (SPM). The SPM dataset will consist of log data and thematic codes from the student-agent dialogues to identify differences in how learners receive their agents between groups. I will use a hybrid approach to code learner reflections on their interactions with their agent. Self-determination theory (SDT) will inform the coding of how agents satisfy or do not satisfy learner autonomy, competence, or relatedness [8]. Additional codes that emerge will give a more nuanced perspective to how learners receive their agents. To answer the third research question regarding the role of relatability on learning outcomes, I will conduct a 2×2 ANCOVA for the effect of pedagogy and appearance on *VEXcode VR* knowledge post-test scores with a covariate of pre-test scores. This approach will demonstrate whether there is a cumulative effect of different designs for relatability and will build upon prior literature regarding the importance of appearance with more modern technology.

4 Contributions to the Field

My proposed work seeks to define relatability in the field of PAs. It will demonstrate the role of teachers in the design of PAs, how they affect how agents are received, and the implications for relatability for learning. This work will also contribute to the understanding of the effort, time, and technical requirements needed for teachers to effectively contribute to PA design. Findings that support relatability would signify that greater teacher involvement leads to more responsive and relatable tools for their students. I would like to caution, however, that non-significant or even results that contradict relatability should not be interpreted as teacher involvement not being relevant for the design of AI technologies. Instead, these results would signify that modifying system prompts or focusing teacher involvement on other aspects of design is just as effective as the more labor-, technical-, and time-intensive fine-tuning approach or designing PA appearance. As such, future interventions could be solely designed by teachers who would be able to design their own PAs with the PATK and shape their pedagogy through prompting without the need for researchers or technical designers.

Acknowledgments. The materials used in this study are based upon work supported by the National Science Foundation and Institute of Education Sciences under Grant 2229612.

References

1. Bang, M., Vossoughi, S.: Participatory design research and educational justice: Studying learning and relations within social change making (2016)
2. Chu, Z., et al.: LLM agents for education: Advances and applications, vol. 2 (2025). arXiv:2503.11733 arXiv preprint
3. DiSalvo, B., Yip, J., Bonsignore, E., Carl, D.: Participatory design for learning. In: Participatory Design for Learning, pp. 3–6. Routledge (2017)
4. Haake, M., Gulz, A.: A look at the roles of look & roles in embodied pedagogical agents-a user preference perspective. Int. J. Artif. Intell. Educ. **19**(1), 39–71 (2009)
5. Kim, Y., Wei, Q.: The impact of learner attributes and learner choice in an agent-based environment. Comput. Educ. **56**(2), 505–514 (2011)
6. Rachmatullah, A., et al.: Development and validation of the middle grades computer science concept inventory (MG-CSCI) assessment. EURASIA J. Math. Sci. Technol. Educ. **16**(5), em1841 (2020)
7. Reeves, B., Nass, C.: The media equation: how people treat computers, television, and new media like real people. Cambridge, UK **10**(10), 19–36 (1996)
8. Ryan, R.M., Deci, E.L.: Self-determination theory and the facilitation of intrinsic motivation, social development, and well-being. Am. Psychol. **55**(1), 68 (2000)
9. Schneider, S., Beege, M., Nebel, S., Schnaubert, L., Rey, G.D.: The cognitive-affective-social theory of learning in digital environments (CASTLE). Educ. Psychol. Rev. **34**(1), 1–38 (2022)

AI-Supported Regulation Processes in Collaborative Writing

Stella Kolarik(✉)

FernUniversität Hagen, Universitätsstraße 11, 58097 Hagen, Germany
stella.kolarik@fernuni-hagen.de

Abstract. Collaborative learning can be beneficial but not always successful, especially in digitally mediated group work requiring coordination, monitoring, and regulation. Socially Shared Regulation of Learning (SSRL) provides a theoretical framework for understanding these group-level processes. Recent advances in artificial intelligence offer new possibilities for supporting collaborative processes; however, most existing systems focus on individual learning rather than group regulation. This doctoral project investigates how AI-supported technologies can be designed to facilitate group-level regulatory processes in collaborative writing in higher education. The research follows a design-based research approach consisting of three phases: (1) a systematic review and empirical baseline analysis of collaborative writing processes, (2) iterative design and development of conversational agent prototypes informed by learning analytics, and (3) evaluation of their effects in authentic course contexts. The project integrates CSCL theory, regulation models, and AI design to derive principles for technologies supporting group collaboration and regulation. Expected contributions include a framework for AI-supported collaborative regulation, empirical evidence on group processes, and design guidance for educational technologies.

Keywords: Collaborative learning · regulation · pedagogical conversational agent · artificial intelligence

1 Theoretical Background

Group work has become a cornerstone of higher education, where it can aid students in developing skills for their careers and personal development [7]. However, group work does not always lead to successful collaborative learning [7]. When students encounter problems in their collaboration, they oftentimes do not know how to cope with them [5]. Computer-Supported Collaborative Learning (CSCL) conceptualizes collaboration as a socio-technical process that integrates cognitive, social, and material dimensions [14], emphasizing the importance of regulation—how groups jointly plan, monitor, and adapt their learning.

Socially Shared Regulation of Learning (SSRL) describes these processes at the group level [5]. Studies on collaborative writing demonstrate that regulation strategies are central to group success [15]. When groups fail to establish effective SSRL, negative emotions and lost learning opportunities often follow [7]. Both motivation and

E. G. Blanchard et al. (Eds.): AIED 2026, CCIS 3033, pp. 217–222, 2026.
https://doi.org/10.1007/978-3-032-29794-5_33

engagement have been connected to SSRL in a dual role. They act both as a condition influencing regulatory actions and as an outcome of successful SSRL [1, 7, 21]. Further, they are connected to learning outcomes and behaviors, such as academic achievement and persistence [9, 21].

Collaborative writing requires sustained coordination, negotiation of meaning, and joint decision-making [16], making it an authentic testbed for studying regulation and technological support. Yet there are limited works on regulation in a collaborative writing context [7]. Digital writing environments generate trace data (e.g., logs, revisions) enabling analysis of otherwise hard-to-observe group processes [12]. Learning Analytics (LA) offers methodological and technical means to observe and interpret such processes [2]. By linking CSCL and LA, we can identify when and how learners struggle and design data-driven interventions to enhance collaboration.

Advances in artificial intelligence, particularly pedagogical conversational agents (PCAs), create new opportunities to scaffold collaboration. Current research indicates the potential of AI to support SSRL, also in connection with LA [8]. Most AI-based writing support focuses on content-related feedback or correctness [17, 19], rather than on group processes. PCAs may adopt roles such as facilitator or collaborator [6, 8] and can be conceptualized as socio-cognitive participants influencing group regulation.

SSRL has been evaluated in the context of collaborative writing, where findings show different strategies and factors leading to successful regulation as well as situations where SSRL fails [7, 15]. Collaborative writing is also a relevant context for LA, where past studies developed methods to understand the collaborative writing process [12]. Past studies also connected collaborative writing with AI support, focusing on topics such as Social Response Theory and corrective feedback [17, 18].

While individual strands of research connect CSCL, SSRL, LA, or AI, there is a lack of integrative approaches. This project addresses this gap by combining regulation theory, learning analytics, and AI-based conversational agents to support SSRL in collaborative writing. By studying mixed human-AI groups in authentic higher education contexts, the project aims to contribute to a deeper psychological understanding of group regulation and to derive design principles for AI-supported collaboration.

2 Research Questions

Although collaborative learning is well studied, most technologies support individuals or provide static collaboration tools [5, 13]. At the same time, recent work on AI-assisted writing and conversational agents demonstrates their potential to enhance engagement and provide feedback [19]. However, these systems are typically designed for individual use and rarely address SSRL as a collective psychological process [8].

This project investigates how PCAs can support shared regulation in higher education by integrating CSCL theory, SSRL models, and learning analytics. The research questions are structured across three phases:

RQ1.1: Which challenges and strategies related to SSRL emerge at the group level in large-scale collaborative writing scenarios in higher education?

RQ1.2: How is existing technological support designed to facilitate collaborative writing, and which design gaps can be identified regarding facilitating regulation?

RQ2: How can PCAs be designed to support SSRL in collaborative writing tasks, and how are they accepted by human group members?

RQ3: How does the integration of pedagogical conversational agents affect (a) socially shared regulation processes, (b) learner engagement and motivation, and (c) perceived collaboration quality in collaborative writing groups compared to groups without agent support?

3 Methodology

The PhD project will take on a design-based research (DBR) approach. DBR is focused on improving both education and learning, through setting an objective for collecting data, creating the intervention and the final analysis regarding progress towards the objective [4]. The project is structured into three phases, each addressing distinct research questions. Across all phases, the focus lies on understanding and supporting group-level processes, rather than on optimizing writing outcomes alone.

Phase 1: Baseline Analysis of SSRL in Collaborative Writing

The first phase aims to establish an empirically grounded understanding of existing support for collaborative writing, as well as SSRL challenges and strategies in large-scale collaborative writing scenarios in higher education (RQ1.1, RQ1.2). This phase combines a systematic literature review, secondary data analysis and qualitative inquiry. The data sources include:

- A systematic literature review, using the Preferred Reporting Items for Systematic Reviews and Meta Analyses [11], focusing on technological support for collaborative learning and writing
- Existing datasets from FernUniversität in Hagen (1,292 collaborative writing groups from winter 2021/22 to summer 2025) including revision histories, interaction log data, and self-report questionnaire data
- Qualitative interviews and/or focus groups with students and instructors involved in collaborative writing courses

Quantitative learning analytics methods and qualitative analysis will be combined to capture both observable regulatory behavior and subjective experiences [5]. To capture temporal dynamics, Transition Network Analysis (TNA) will be used to model transitions between SSRL challenges and strategies, identifying recurring regulation patterns over time. *Outcomes*: collaboration indicators and metrics, design requirements for PCAs, identification of critical moments for support.

Phase 2: Prototype Design and Development

Based on the findings from phase 1, PCAs will be designed within an LLM-powered multi-agent system architecture. The prototypes will support group regulation processes, for example, by facilitating coordination tasks, prompting reflection, or helping groups reach consensus. These agents will cooperate to interpret group processes and connect them with previous knowledge (Fig. 1). Iterative user testing and redesign will refine implementation. The prototypes will be developed in collaboration with the CATALPA research center, where technical development will be supported and existing infrastructure such as Moodle plugin for Etherpad Lite [2] and LLM infrastructure [20] can be used. The conceptual design, theoretical grounding, definition of intervention logic and empirical evaluation and interpretation constitute the doctoral candidate's main contribution. *Outcomes*: Functional PCA prototypes, refined design principles for AI support of SSRL.

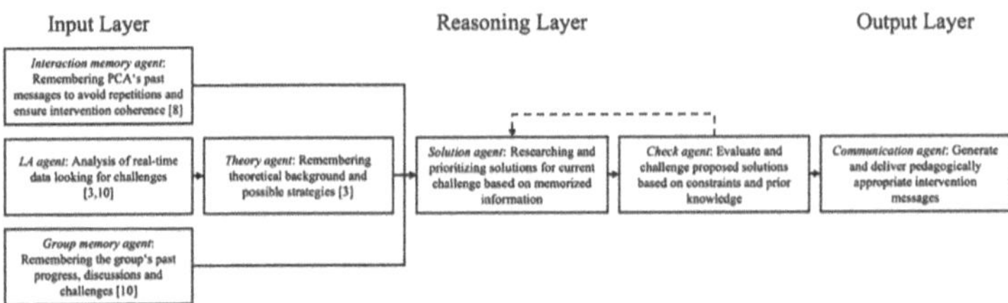

Fig. 1. Conceptual architecture of the multi-agent system supporting socially shared regulation in collaborative writing

Phase 3: Evaluation in authentic learning contexts

The final phase will evaluate the effects of the developed prototypes in authentic course settings through summative testing. Agents will be integrated into the existing Moodle/Etherpad environment for real-time group interaction. A randomized controlled trial will be conducted in an introductory psychology module at the FernUniversität in Hagen, where students complete a collaborative writing assignment. Groups with and without PCA support will be compared. The following data will be collected:

- Self-report questionnaires assessing SSRL, engagement, motivation and perceived collaboration quality.
- Changeset data capturing, for example, participation balance and revision behavior.
- Trace data from written interactions, analyzed with coding schemes

Through this multi-layered analysis, the study will explore how the inclusion of conversational agents influences engagement, motivation and SSRL processes. Additionally, TNA will be used to compare regulatory transition patterns between groups with and without PCA support. *Outcomes:* Empirical evidence of PCA effects on SSRL, engagement and motivation, validation and refinement of theoretical assumptions about mixed human-AI regulation.

The project is still in early stages. The systematic review is underway, and the analysis of secondary data has started.

4 Implications of the Doctoral Procedure

Drawing on CSCL and educational psychology, this project investigates how PCAs support SSRL in collaborative writing. By integrating learning analytics with the design of AI agents, the project contributes to a deeper understanding of group-level regulatory processes in digitally mediated learning environments.

From a *theoretical perspective*, the project advances research on SSRL by examining regulation as an emergent group-level process that unfolds over time and is shaped by socio-technical conditions. By studying mixed human–AI groups, the research extends existing SSRL frameworks and contributes to CSCL theory by conceptualizing AI agents as socio-cognitive participants that can influence collaboration without replacing human agency. *Methodologically*, the project demonstrates how LA can be combined with psychological theory to analyze collaborative learning processes using trace data, self-reports, and discourse analyses. It further contributes a process-oriented analysis of SSRL by modeling its temporal dynamics. The design-based research approach enables the iterative development and evaluation of theoretically grounded interventions in authentic educational contexts. From a *practical perspective*, the project aims to derive design principles for scalable, ethically responsible PCAs that support collaboration and regulation in large-scale online courses.

Disclosure of Interests. The authors have no competing interests to declare that are relevant to the content of this article.

References

1. Bakhtiar, A., Hadwin, A.F.: Motivation from a self-regulated learning perspective: application to school psychology. Can. J. Sch. Psychol. **37**(1), 93–116 (2021). https://doi.org/10.1177/08295735211054699
2. Burchart, M., Haake, J.M.: Supporting collaborative writing tasks in large-scale distance education. IEEE Trans. Learn. Technol. **17**, 1051–1068 (2024). https://doi.org/10.1109/TLT.2024.3355791
3. Dias De Araujo Junior, A.: Could you elaborate more on what your partner just said? Guiding dialogue in science education using a conversational agent. University of Twente (2024). https://doi.org/10.3990/1.9789036563154
4. Euler, D., Sloane, P.F.E. (eds.): Design-based research. Franz Steiner Verlag, Stuttgart (2014)
5. Hadwin, A.F., Bakhtiar, A., Miller, M.: Challenges in online collaboration: effects of scripting shared task perceptions. Intern. J. Comput.-Support. Collab. Learn. **13**(3), 301–329 (2018). https://doi.org/10.1007/s11412-018-9279-9
6. Jung, Y., Jin, S.-H.: Questioning the role of AI as collaborator: a systematic literature review of generative AI-supported knowledge construction. Interact. Learn. Environ. 1–20 (2025). https://doi.org/10.1080/10494820.2025.2556808
7. Khuder, B., Negretti, R.: Collaborative writing regulation: a comparative case study of co-regulation and socially shared regulation in higher education. High. Educ. **91**, 677–699 (2025). https://doi.org/10.1007/s10734-025-01437-9
8. Kim, J., Detrick, R., Yu, S., Song, Y., Bol, L., Li, N.: Socially shared regulation of learning and artificial intelligence: opportunities to support socially shared regulation. Educ. Inf. Technol. **30**(9), 11483–11521 (2025). https://doi.org/10.1007/s10639-024-13187-9
9. Manwaring, K.C., Larsen, R., Graham, C.R., Henrie, C.R., Halverson, L.R.: Investigating student engagement in blended learning settings using experience sampling and structural equation modeling. Internet High. Educ. **35**, 21–33 (2017). https://doi.org/10.1016/j.iheduc.2017.06.002
10. Ortega-Ochoa, E., Arguedas, M., Daradoumis, T.: Empathic pedagogical conversational agents: a systematic literature review. Brit. J. Educ. Technol. **55**(3), 886–909 (2024). https://doi.org/10.1111/bjet.13413

11. Page, M.J., et al.: The PRISMA 2020 statement: an updated guideline for reporting systematic reviews. BMJ **372** (2021). https://doi.org/10.1136/bmj.n71
12. Seidel, N., Burchart, M., Haake, J.M., Schumacher, C., Kuzilek, J.: Detecting interaction patterns in educational collaborative writing. Proc. ACM Hum.-Comput. Interact. **9**, 7 (2025). https://doi.org/10.1145/3757467
13. Sharma, K., Nguyen, A., Hong, Y.: Self-regulation and shared regulation in collaborative learning in adaptive digital learning environments: a systematic review of empirical studies. Brit. J. Educ. Technol. **55**(4), 1398–1436 (2024). https://doi.org/10.1111/bjet.13459
14. Stahl, G., Hakkarainen, K.: Theories of CSCL. In: Cress, U. et al. (eds.) International Handbook of Computer-Supported Collaborative Learning, pp. 23–43. Springer International Publishing, Cham (2021). https://doi.org/10.1007/978-3-030-65291-3_2
15. Stell, A., Iwashita, N.: Enhancing collaboration: exploring regulated learning strategies in the co-regulatory processes of collaborative L2 writing. System **125** (2024). https://doi.org/10.1016/j.system.2024.103410
16. Storch, N.: Collaborative writing in L2 contexts: processes, outcomes, and future directions. Annu. Rev. Appl. Linguist. **31**, 275–288 (2011). https://doi.org/10.1017/S0267190511000079
17. Wiboolyasarin, W., Wiboolyasarin, K., Suwanwihok, K., Muenjanchoey, R.: Synergizing collaborative writing and AI feedback: an investigation into enhancing L2 writing proficiency in wiki-based environments. Comput. Educ.: Artif. Intell. **6** (2024). https://doi.org/10.1016/j.caeai.2024.100228
18. Wiethof, C., Tavanapour, N., Bittner, E.: Implementing an intelligent collaborative agent as teammate in collaborative writing: toward a synergy of humans and AI. In: Proceedings of the 54th Hawaii International Conference on System Sciences, pp. 400–409 (2021). https://doi.org/10.24251/HICSS.2021.047
19. Yuan, A., Coenen, A., Reif, E., Ippolito, D.: Wordcraft: story writing with large language models. In: Proceedings of the 27th International Conference on Intelligent User Interfaces, pp. 841–852 Association for Computing Machinery, New York, NY, USA (2022). https://doi.org/10.1145/3490099.3511105
20. Zesch, T., Hanses, M., Seidel, N., Aggarwal, P., Veiel, D., De Witt, C.: Flexible LLM Experimental infrastructure (Flexi) – enabling experimentation and innovation in higher education through access to open LLMs. In: 2024 21st International Conference on Information Technology Based Higher Education and Training (ITHET), pp. 1–8, Paris, France (2024). https://doi.org/10.1109/ITHET61869.2024.10837635
21. Zhou, X., Tsai, C.-W.: The effects of socially shared regulation of learning on the computational thinking, motivation, and engagement in collaborative learning by teaching. Educ. Inf. Technol. **28**, 8135–8152 (2023). https://doi.org/10.1007/s10639-022-11527-1

An LLM-Powered Embodied VR Tutor for Smoking Cessation: SRL via Reflective Dialogue

Fatimah D. M. Alshahrani(✉) and Alexandra I. Cristea

Durham University, Durham, UK
{fatimah.d.alshahrani,alexandra.i.cristea}@durham.ac.uk

Abstract. Many people who want to quit smoking struggle not because they lack information, but because they need support to develop self-regulation skills for managing cravings, triggers, and setbacks. While prior work has explored virtual reality (VR) smoking interventions (often via cue-exposure) and text-based cessation chatbots, most systems treat quitting primarily as motivation/behaviour change support; comparatively few explicitly frame it as *skills learning*. To the best of our knowledge, we have not identified prior smoking-cessation work that combines an *LLM-driven, motivational interviewing (MI)-consistent embodied tutor in immersive VR* to explicitly teach and assess cessation-relevant self-regulation skills. This PhD frames smoking cessation as a skills-learning challenge and proposes an LLM-powered embodied VR tutor that delivers MI-consistent reflective dialogue, to help learners identify triggers, formulate implementation intentions (`if--then` coping plans), strengthen self-efficacy, and reflect after difficult moments. The evaluation will compare an audio-visual embodied VR tutor (avatar + spoken dialogue) with a content-matched non-VR embodied agent (avatar + the same spoken dialogue) delivered on a standard screen; both use the same LLM back-end, differing only in immersive VR delivery. Outcomes will focus on learning process and learning outcomes (coping-plan quality, reflective depth, and self-efficacy), alongside engagement and perceived support, with auditing for MI-consistency and safety. The work aims to produce design and evaluation guidance for pedagogically-controlled, MI-consistent conversational tutoring in immersive settings.

Keywords: embodied conversational agent · VR · large language models · motivational interviewing · self-regulated learning · smoking cessation

1 Introduction

Smoking remains a major global public health burden. The World Health Organization estimates that tobacco kills more than 7 million people each year, including around 1.6 million non-smokers due to second-hand smoke [17].

E. G. Blanchard et al. (Eds.): AIED 2026, CCIS 3033, pp. 223–228, 2026.
https://doi.org/10.1007/978-3-032-29794-5_34

Digital smoking-cessation support increasingly uses chatbots and conversational agents to provide behavioural help at scale, yet the evidence base remains mixed, as interventions vary widely in features, outcomes, follow-up, and study quality [16]. Many systems still rely on scripted or constrained dialogue, which can improve controllability, limiting naturalness and sustained engagement [6].

Recent advances in large language models (LLMs) promise more responsive and personalised dialogue, but raise concerns about safety, fidelity, and consistency in counselling-style support. A pilot integrating a ChatGPT-based cessation chatbot into a text-messaging programme illustrates both feasibility and ongoing fidelity/safety questions [2]. Motivational Interviewing (MI) is frequently referenced in this space, yet reviews emphasise the need to specify MI strategies clearly and assess MI-consistency in implemented dialogue [16].

Cessation chatbots span social messaging, SMS, mobile apps, and web interfaces [6,14]. Virtual reality (VR) offers a more embodied, tutor-like delivery context; however, smoking-related VR research has largely focused on cue-exposure and cue-reactivity rather than sustained motivational conversation.

Research Idea and Gap. We frame smoking cessation as *self-regulated learning (SRL)* skills training via MI-consistent dialogue (e.g., triggers, if–then plans, lapse reflection). **Gap:** Prior work focuses on VR cue-exposure [13] or text-based cessation chatbots [6,16]; we have not identified an *embodied* VR tutor that trains and assesses MI-consistent SRL skills while isolating the effect of *VR immersion* under real-time constraints. We therefore compare VR against a content-matched non-VR embodied agent (same avatar + speech; same LLM) (Table 1).

Aim and Research Questions. This PhD designs and evaluates an embodied VR tutor powered by an LLM to teach smoking-cessation self-regulation skills through MI-consistent reflective dialogue. It addresses three research questions:

1. **RQ1 (Design and fidelity):** How can an embodied VR tutor be designed to deliver MI-consistent reflective dialogue for teaching cessation-relevant self-regulation skills, while maintaining safety and an MI-consistent conversational style?
2. **RQ2 (Learning outcomes):** Compared with a content-matched non-VR embodied agent (same avatar + spoken dialogue; same LLM), does the embodied VR tutor improve learning outcomes relevant to smoking cessation (e.g., coping-plan quality, self-efficacy, and depth of reflection)?
3. **RQ3 (Real-time constraints):** How do response delays/interruptions affect turn-taking, perceived support, and SRL skill uptake in the embodied VR condition?

2 Related Works

Conversational Tutoring, Reflection, and SRL: Dialogue-based tutoring supports learning when interaction is structured around clear pedagogical goals and guided feedback [11]; SRL prompts scaffold planning, monitoring, and reflection over time [18]. However, these scaffolds are rarely framed as repeatable smoking-cessation skills practice. We adapt them for trigger identification, `if--then` coping plans, and lapse reflection via an MI-consistent LLM tutor.

Computational MI in Digital Agents: MI requires a consistent reflective, autonomy-supportive style and should be assessed via fidelity checks rather than surface terminology [7]; MI quality can be operationalised using computational signals [7]. Yet MI-consistency for real-time, open-ended LLM dialogue remains under-specified. We define and evaluate explicit MI fidelity criteria (computational and/or annotation-based) for live LLM-generated coaching.

Embodiment, VR, and Contextualised Skills Practice: Immersive systems can increase engagement via social presence and enable contextualised practice [12]; in smoking cessation, VR cues can elicit craving and support safe coping rehearsal [13]. However, VR work often prioritises cue exposure over structured, dialogue-based SRL rehearsal. We link in-situ cues to guided planning and reflective review through an embodied VR tutor.

LLMs under Pedagogical Control: LLMs enable responsive dialogue but raise safety and controllability concerns in sensitive domains [8]; prior work bounds interaction via session structure and prompt scaffolding and evaluates fidelity explicitly [5]. Building on this, we implement an auditable orchestration layer for spoken, audio-visual embodied coaching and evaluate whether immersive VR adds value beyond a content-matched non-VR embodied delivery when the avatar, spoken dialogue, and LLM back-end are held constant (including under latency/interruptions).

3 LLM-Powered Embodied VR Tutor: System and Learning Design

The system uses a three-layer pipeline: a cloud LLM with MI-style guidance generates candidate responses; an edge orchestrator enforces session structure, SRL prompts, personalisation, and safety; and an embodied teacher delivers

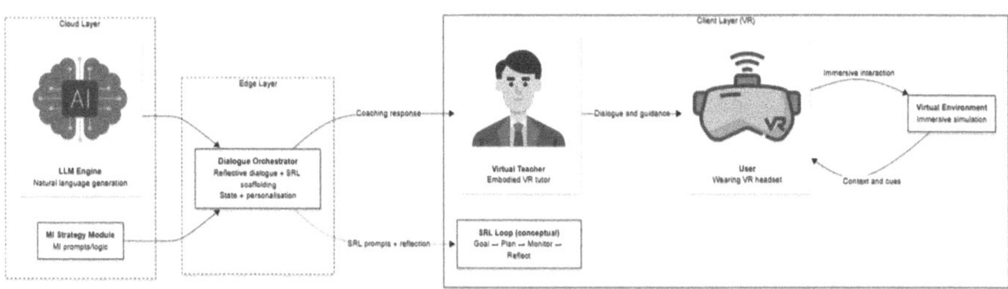

Fig. 1. Proposed architecture of the LLM-powered embodied VR tutor. Cloud-based LLM and MI strategy modules feed an edge-level dialogue orchestrator, which delivers personalised coaching via a VR teacher and supports an SRL loop (goal–plan–monitor–reflect) within an immersive virtual environment.

spoken dialogue in immersive VR. The orchestrator logs turns, choices, and latency/interruptions for fidelity and real-time analysis (Fig. 1).

4 Methodology

Theoretical Grounding. We frame smoking cessation as a *skills-learning* problem, operationalised as *self-regulated learning (SRL)* and structure sessions around a brief plan–monitor–reflect cycle that provides instructional *scaffolding* to practice and elicit assessable implementation intentions (`if--then` coping plans) [18]. Skills-learning components in smoking cessation have been operationalised through coping-skills training (including VR-based practice), behavioural rehearsal via games/apps, craving-regulation training, relapse-prevention programmes, and action planning [3,4,9,10,15]. MI-consistent reflective dialogue acts as the core pedagogical mechanism and is audited for fidelity, while VR provides a *situated* context for practising coping skills [7,13,14] (see Introduction).
System Design and Implementation. The tutor is implemented in Unity; the system pipeline and orchestration components are detailed in Sect. 3 (Fig. 1).
Study Design and Conditions. We will run a comparative study with adult university students (18+) who currently smoke and are interested in quitting or reducing smoking. Participants will complete sessions in either an immersive VR condition or a content-matched non-VR embodied condition (Table 1).
Procedure and Measures. Participants will complete one or more short tutoring sessions; we will record response latency and interruptions, followed by brief post-session measures using short validated scales [12,14]. Primary outcomes focus on skills learning: coping-plan quality (rubric-scored `if--then` plans adapted from prior work), self-efficacy, and reflective depth. Secondary outcomes include urge ratings, engagement (e.g., completion, time-on-task, turn counts), and perceived support/presence [6,7,12,13].
Fidelity, Safety, Analysis, and Ethics. MI-consistency will be assessed on a sampled set of dialogues using a brief MI-fidelity checklist [7,14]. Unsafe outputs will trigger refusal and signposting to approved cessation resources [8]. Quantitative analyses will compare conditions on primary outcomes and engagement, complemented by targeted qualitative inspection of dialogue excerpts. Participants will provide informed consent and may withdraw at any time; data will be minimised and de-identified.
Progress to Date. We are conducting a systematic review of digital smoking-cessation interventions and have implemented an initial Convai prototype [1] as feasibility evidence for the intended MI-consistent SRL flow (Fig. 2).

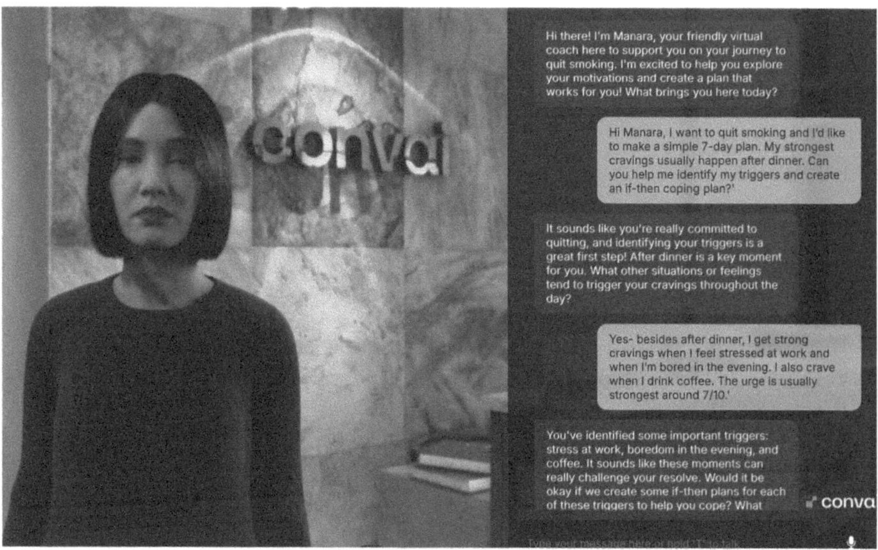

Fig. 2. Convai embodied-coaching prototype illustrating Motivational Interviewing (MI) through reflective listening, affirmations, and permission seeking, while scaffolding SRL planning by summarising triggers and initiating an if–then coping plan.

5 Planned PhD Work and Expected Contributions

Planned Work Summary. Table 1 summarises RQ1–RQ3, the planned evaluation, and expected outputs.

Table 1. Research questions and planned evaluation summary.

RQ	What we test/do	Measures/outputs
RQ1	Define MI-fidelity criteria; assess via automated measures and sampled human annotation.	MI-fidelity scores; safety audit; refusal/signposting events.
RQ2	Compare VR vs non-VR audio-visual agents (same avatar + speech; same LLM; content-matched).	Plan quality (`if--then`); reflective depth; self-efficacy; engagement; support/presence.
RQ3	Test effects of latency/interruptions on SRL skill uptake; refine orchestration policies.	Latency/interruptions; turn-taking; perceived support; SRL uptake; updated orchestration rules.

Expected Contributions. This work will provide (i) a protocol to check whether **LLM-generated** spoken coaching in an embodied tutor follows MI while supporting smoking-cessation self-regulation skills practice, (ii) evidence on whether immersive VR improves **LLM-based** skills practice and engagement compared with a matched non-VR embodied version, and (iii) design guidance for running **real-time LLM interactions** effectively under delays or interruptions.

References

1. Convai documentation. https://docs.convai.com/. Accessed 3 Apr 2026
2. Abroms, L.C., Wysota, C.N., Yousefi, A., Wu, T.C., Broniatowski, D.A.: ChatGPT-based chatbot for help quitting smoking via text messaging: an interventional study. JMIR Formative Res. (2025)
3. Bordnick, P.S., Traylor, A.C., Carter, B.L., Graap, K.M.: A feasibility study of virtual reality-based coping skills training for nicotine dependence. Res. Soc. Work. Pract. (2012)
4. Brendryen, H., Drozd, F., Kraft, P.: A digital smoking cessation program delivered through internet and cell phone without nicotine replacement (happy ending): randomized controlled trial. J. Med. Internet Res. (2008)
5. Giannakos, M., Azevedo, R., Brusilovsky, P., et al.: The promise and challenges of generative AI in education. Behav. Inf. Technol. (2025)
6. He, L., Balaji, D., Wiers, R.W., Antheunis, M.L., Krahmer, E.: Effectiveness and acceptability of conversational agents for smoking cessation: a systematic review and meta-analysis. Nicotine Tobacco Res. (2023)
7. Imel, Z.E., et al.: Design feasibility of an automated, machine-learning based feedback system for motivational interviewing. Psychotherapy (2019)
8. Kasneci, E., Sessler, K., et al.: ChatGPT for good? On opportunities and challenges of large language models for education. Learn. Individual Differences (2023)
9. Krebs, P., et al.: The QUITIT coping skills game for promoting tobacco cessation among smokers diagnosed with cancer: pilot randomized controlled trial. JMIR Mhealth Uhealth (2019)
10. Lopez, R.B., Ochsner, K.N., Kober, H.: Brief training in regulation of craving reduces cigarette smoking. J. Subst. Abuse Treat. (2022)
11. Nye, B.D., Graesser, A.C., Hu, X.: AutoTutor and family: a review of 17 years of natural language tutoring. Int. J. Artif. Intell. Educ. (2014)
12. Oh, C.S., Bailenson, J.N., Welch, G.F.: A systematic review of social presence: definition, antecedents, and implications. Front. Robot. AI (2018)
13. Pericot-Valverde, I., Secades-Villa, R., Gutierrez-Maldonado, J., et al.: Effects of Systematic Cue Exposure Through Virtual Reality on Cigarette Craving. Nicotine & Tobacco Research (2014)
14. Perski, O., Crane, D., Beard, E., Brown, J.: Does the addition of a supportive chatbot promote user engagement with a smoking cessation app? An experimental study. Digit. Health (2019)
15. de Vries, H., Eggers, S.M., Bolman, C.: The role of action planning and plan enactment for smoking cessation. BMC Public Health (2013)
16. Whittaker, R., Dobson, R., Garner, K.: Chatbots for smoking cessation: scoping review. J. Med. Internet Res. (2022)
17. WHO: Tobacco. Tech. rep. (2025). https://www.who.int/news-room/fact-sheets/detail/tobacco
18. Wong, J., Baars, M., Davis, D.: Supporting self-regulated learning in online learning environments and MOOCs: a systematic review. Int. J. Hum. Comput. Interact. (2019)

Toward Multi-signal Dropout Prediction in Work-Study Programs: Integrating Behavioral and Attitudinal Signals Through NLP

Duaa Baig[1,2](✉), Diana Nurbakova[1], Sylvie Calabretto[1], and Baba MBaye[2]

[1] INSA Lyon, CNRS, Université Claude Bernard Lyon 1, LIRIS, UMR5205, 69621 Villeurbanne, France
{diana.nurbakova,sylvie.calabretto}@insa-lyon.fr
[2] EffetB SAS, Lyon, France
duaa.baig@insa-lyon.fr, baba@effetb.com

Abstract. The dropout in apprenticeships is a major challenge in vocational education and training (VET), with approximately 30% of contracts prematurely terminated in France. Existing dropout prediction models overlook tri-stakeholder dynamics (apprentice, workplace master, and training provider) inherent to apprenticeship. In this study, we propose a multi-phase approach to address this challenge. In the first phase, we developed an ensemble stacking model (ESPM) that encodes tri-stakeholder (triad) engagement patterns. The approach achieves 72.21% F1 and demonstrates that the engagement signals outweigh performance metrics (56.1% vs. 43.9%) in dropout predictions. In the second phase, we plan to apply NLP to 210K+ multi-stakeholder French questionnaire responses to extract attitudinal signals complementing behavioral features. To the best of our knowledge, this work is the first study to combine behavioral engagement data with NLP-based sentiment features for multi-stakeholder dropout prediction in French apprenticeships, addressing the limited use of unstructured text in existing VET analytics.

Keywords: Dropout Prediction · AI in Education · Sentiment Analysis

1 Introduction

VET systems play a crucial role in preparing a skilled workforce aligned with the labor market. Apprenticeship programs facilitate the study-to-work transition effectively across multiple countries by combining the experience of the workplace training with theoretical studies [1]. In 2023, the number of active apprenticeship contracts in France exceeded 800,000 [2]. However, the dropout rate remains a concerning challenge, with approximately 30% of apprenticeship

E. G. Blanchard et al. (Eds.): AIED 2026, CCIS 3033, pp. 229–235, 2026.
https://doi.org/10.1007/978-3-032-29794-5_35

contracts ending prematurely [3]. The premature contract terminations create multiple negative effects for stakeholders. The allocated resources of companies experience interruptions, and they face rehiring expenses [4]. The educational institutes face challenges to maintain program standards and bear reductions in funding [5]. The apprentice faces prolonged joblessness, reduced motivation, and lasting career impacts [6]. Modeling the predictive system for educational dropout has noticeably advanced using machine learning (ML) in recent years [7], particularly gradient boosting approaches shows the consistent effectiveness on structured datasets [8]. However, current approaches reveal three important limitations for apprenticeship dynamics. (1) Most of the existing work focuses on students in a university environment [12], overlooking the collaborative structure of VET. (2) The majority of studies emphasize behavioral signals (evaluation frequency, attendance logs, and performance data) while not fully utilizing the qualitative stakeholder feedback. (3) The learning dynamics of the workplace and the stakeholders' engagement remain under-explored [10]. This study addresses these challenges using a two-phase design. In phase 1, we developed a tri-stakeholder ensemble architecture, which shows that engagement factors signal dropout risk before performance decline. In phase 2 (in progress), we plan to extract sentiments using NLP on triad questionnaire data to capture attitudinal indicators that can complement behavioural features. Based on our previous work with language models [11], this work extends NLP from knowledge tracing (KT) into the VET dropout prediction. The work contributes through French sentiment analysis and multi-signal fusion, while providing proactive dropout prevention. It advances AIED by demonstrating how AI-driven educational modeling can address a multi-stakeholder learning environment. It extends the student modeling paradigm from individual learners to collaborative workplace-based contexts.

2 Related Work

As ML has been adopted for dropout prediction, boosting techniques have repeatedly shown strong performance on structured data. In a recent work [7], the CatBoost with a synthetic oversampling approach is used on the logs of the learning management system (LMS), while [8] demonstrates that optimized LightGBM and CatBoost surpass conventional approaches on university educational data. Using 13 years of longitudinal data, [12] broadens the time horizon of prediction and shows that signs of dropout risk are visible as early as the completion of elementary school. However, their study is situated in a university context and relies mainly on student-level variables. In contrast, the review in [10] of 70 VET dropout studies points out a key gap: while most research focuses on individual factors, it largely overlooks the workplace, which plays a central role in apprenticeship supervision and training. Overall, studies specifically on apprenticeships remain limited. Evidence from England [6], Switzerland [4], and Australia [13] shows that workplace training quality, changes in job satisfaction, and access to apprenticeship positions all affect retention of apprentices. However, these studies rely mostly on self-reported surveys and rarely combine behavioural platform data with qualitative feedback from multiple stakeholders.

The NLP for dropout prediction is a promising approach that is still underexplored in VET contexts. In [9], the authors demonstrate in their work that combining sentiment analysis on student comments with demographic and behavioural data improves dropout prediction in online education, establishing correlations between expressed emotions, language patterns, and dropout risk. Current NLP work mostly analyzes text from a single party, like students or instructors, rather than multi-stakeholder feedback from a triad. French-language sentiment analysis in education is also limited and underrepresented. Applying French NLP to apprenticeship questionnaires addresses three gaps: dropout research mostly focuses on universities [12], behavioural signals dominate while multi-stakeholder attitudinal feedback remains underexplored, and workplace engagement dynamics lack systematic ML analysis in the VET context [10]. The study addresses these gaps through a tri-stakeholder framework that integrates behavioural and attitudinal indicators using ensemble learning and French NLP.

3 Research Context and Dataset

The Apprenticeship System: sometimes called alternating training, where apprentices spend around 60 to 75% of their time at a workplace. The system is regulated by the National Directory of Professional Certifications (RNCP), which sets the skills or competency standards for each program. Three key stakeholders involved in this program: apprentice, workplace supervisor (master), and training provider (Centre de Formation d'Apprentis (CFA)) or tutor. **Dataset:** The study is based on a dataset collected from a French CFA that uses a digital platform to manage its apprenticeship programs. The dataset includes 3,511 apprenticeship contracts (triads) from 2020 to 2023, with a dropout rate of 10.5%. The lower dropout rate compared to the national 30% average is potentially due to the CFA's retention practices or regional variation. Along with demographic data, the overall dataset also comprises: (1) Behavioural data (143,550 skill evaluations/ assessments across triads), (2) Questionnaire response data (over 313,000 questionnaire responses across triads). (3) RNCP certification metadata (extracted features from the *RNCP*[1]). In response data, approximately 210,000 responses contain free-text French narratives authored by all three stakeholders.

4 Proposed Approach

4.1 Phase 1: Behavioural Tri-Stakeholder Dropout Prediction

A triad engagement modeling that has multi-stakeholder interactions involving asymmetric information, divergent expectations, and variable engagement

[1] https://www.francecompetences.fr/.

is established as a conceptual foundation. The approach is different from traditional university dropout models that focus on student characteristics and academic metrics [12]. The experiment results of this model show that dropout risks first manifest through the disengagement factors (evaluation frequency or stakeholder participation, etc.) before emerging in the performance factors (evaluation score). **Methodology:** The Ensemble Stacking with Perception-aware Meta-learning (ESPM) is designed to encode the triad dynamics. The ESPM architecture integrates three base learners built on gradient boosting approaches (Hist-GradientBoosting, Gradient-Boosting, XGBoost) with a neural meta-learner. The meta-learner processes three specialized inputs: (1) base model predictions, (2) perception gap features (difference between apprentice self-assessment scores and supervisor evaluation scores), and (3) stakeholder presence or participation indicators. The feature engineering yielded 53 features across the data. An Engagement Asymmetry Index (EAI) module is also used to generate seven engagement-derived features. The generated features enable the model to provide SHAP-based interpretability analysis, decomposing stakeholder-specific and engagement-versus-performance contributions. **Results:** The ESPM achieved 72.21% F1 and 71.92% recall, surpassing the nine baseline models. The ablation study confirms that both perception gap encoding and stakeholder presence patterns contribute to enhance model performance. **Key Findings:** The SHAP-based interpretability revealed three important patterns. (1) Most of the predictive signals come from engagement features (56.1%) while performance features contribute 43.9% only. (2) The workplace supervisor features contribute 52.2% of total predictive importance, which is more than the combined contribution of apprentice (39.0%) and training provider (8.8%). (3) Engagement patterns analysis highlights that triads with "apprentice-only" evaluation exhibited 41.7% dropout rate, which is nearly 5 times higher than the triads with complete stakeholder engagement (8.5%). **Limitations:** The experiments performed in phase 1 are mainly based on behavioural factors such as evaluation frequency and scores. They haven't used any qualitative comments that can explain how apprentices are actually progressing during their contracts. Moreover, the evaluation data is available only in aggregated form at the contract level, which lacks temporal granularity and prevents any time-based analysis or early identification of risk.

4.2 Phase 2: NLP-Based Multi-Stakeholder Sentiment Analysis

In phase 2, we incorporate a plan with phase 1 to address phase 1's attitudinal signal limitation by extracting the questionnaire data and applying French NLP sentiment analysis on that data. The study focuses on four research questions. **RQ1.** Can sentiment signals from multi-stakeholder questionnaire data predict dropout better than the ESPM's behavioural features? **RQ2.** Does the divergence in cross-stakeholders increase the performance of dropout risk prediction, like the concept of Phase 1's perception gap? **RQ3.** Can early-contract questionnaire sentiment (first 90 days) help us to generate temporal early warning before behavioural disengagement emerges? **RQ4.** Do attitudinal signals (questionnaire responses) provide better predictive value compared with behavioural signals, or both capture redundant information?

Planned Methodology: Step 1 - French NLP Sentiment Analysis: In the first step, a sentiment extraction will be performed by using transformer-based French sentiment models. There are two candidate approaches planned: (1) using a zero-shot approach to apply to multilingual sentiment models (XLM-RoBERTa) directly on questionnaire response text. This allows rapid deployment and has proven effective on French text in cross-lingual settings. (2) using a fine-tuned approach by fine-tuning CamemBERT, which is a RoBERTa-based model pretrained on French corpora. For this, we need a French labeled sentiment data creation or acquisition before using the model on our questionnaire data. Both approaches extract sentiment scores for each response, then aggregate to the triad level by producing mean sentiment score features for all stakeholders, sentiment divergence (cross-stakeholder standard deviation), and sentiment trajectory (temporal slope). In **Step 2 - Domain-Specific Linguistic Feature Extraction:** Beyond generic sentiment analysis, we will apply richer text analysis to capture underlying patterns. Topic modeling will identify recurring themes in feedback (e.g., autonomy development, task complexity, etc.). Intent recognition will be applied to classify questionnaire responses by communicative purpose. Domain-specific linguistic patterns will extract workplace integration status, skill development trajectories, and relationship quality indicators. The approach moves beyond sentiment scores to capture the nuanced content of what stakeholders communicate about apprentice progress. **Step 3 - Temporal Windowing:** In this step, questionnaire timestamps will allow us to perform early warning analysis. All the available responses in the dataset will be partitioned into temporal windows (first 90, 90–180, or 180+ days) to identify whether early sentiment can predict subsequent dropout. Analysis is targeted to evaluate whether early sentiment mean alone can predict dropout or not. And how does the predictive performance evolve as temporal data accumulates? **Step 4 - Model Integration and Evaluation:** In the final step, three model configurations will be evaluated and compared. (1) ESPM only (baseline), (2) Sentiment only, and (3) Combined setting to use both behavioural and sentiment features. The combined model is expected to maximize interpretability and enable direct comparison with phase 1. The combined approach will help SHAP analysis to decompose contributions by both feature and stakeholder type. Simple baselines (bag-of-words, keyword-based) will be included for NLP comparison.

4.3 Key Questions and Main Contributions

The study contributes to both learning and computer science dimensions of the AIED community. The framework advances the interpretability and understanding of the dropout mechanism in the VET environment. It demonstrates that employer disengagement precedes academic performance decline, and that employer engagement signals dominate (52.2%) in predictions, which conflicts with the traditional student-centered models and distinguishes behavioural engagement (participation frequency) from attitudinal engagement (expressed sentiments). The phase 2 study will extend the contributions by establishing multi-stakeholder sentiment divergence as a dropout signal. It will help to validate temporal early-warning using first-quarter questionnaire sentiment and provide empirical evidence on whether attitudinal signals add predictive value beyond behavioural patterns. Along with contributions, several decisions are still open in our work, which include (a) model selection for sentiment analysis, (b) identification of a labeled French educational dataset, (c) decision on the optimal temporal window size, (d) managing sparse or low-participation stakeholders in sentiment analysis, and (e) addressing the sentiment class imbalance issue.

5 Conclusion

Apprenticeship dropout remains an important challenge across VET, which affects not only learners but also employers and training providers. This study addresses a gap by modeling apprenticeships' triad structure and combining behavioural engagement factors with attitudinal signals derived from text. Results from our Phase 1 study show that stakeholders' disengagement, particularly on the employer side, tends to appear before any decline in performance. The finding indicates that disengagement features could be used as an early warning signal. Phase 2 will extend this approach by applying French sentiment analysis of multi-stakeholder questionnaires to complement behavioural data. The project aims to examine dropout trajectories and translate model explanations into practical tools for providers. From an AIED perspective, the work extends AI-driven student modeling beyond traditional settings. It also demonstrates how ML and NLP can capture complex tri-stakeholder educational interactions.

References

1. Wolter, S.C., Ryan., P.: Apprenticeship. In: Handbook of the Economics of Education, vol. 3, pp. 521–576. Elsevier (2011)
2. DARES. L'apprentissage en 2023. Dares Résultats, No. 72 (2024). https://dares.travail-emploi.gouv.fr/sites/default/files/fbfd8c7ae119e0a9f62abff38f4bc6b6/Dares%20R%C3%A9sultats_apprentissage_2023.pdf
3. Plé, A.: L'apprentissage en 2024. Dares Résultats, No. 3, 1-4 (2026). https://dares.travail-emploi.gouv.fr/publication/lapprentissage-en-2024
4. Mohrenweiser, J., Backes-Gellner, U.: Apprenticeship training: for investment or substitution? Int. J. Manpow. **31**(5), 545–562 (2010)
5. Billett, S.: Vocational Education: Purposes, Traditions and Prospects. Springer Science & Business Media (2011)
6. Gambin, L., Hogarth, T.: Factors affecting completion of apprenticeship training in England. J. Educ. Work. **29**(4), 470–493 (2016)
7. Rebelo Marcolino, M., et al.: Student dropout prediction through machine learning optimization: insights from moodle log data. Sci. Rep. **15**(1), 9840 (2025)

8. Villar, A., de Andrade, C.R.V.: Supervised machine learning algorithms for predicting student dropout. Discov. Artif. Intell. **4**(1), 2 (2024)
9. Zerkouk, M., et al.: Predicting online education dropout. Int. J. Artif. Intell. Educ. **35**(4), 2345–2371 (2025)
10. Böhn, S., Deutscher, V.: Dropout from initial vocational training: a meta-synthesis. Educ. Res. Rev. **35**, 100414 (2022)
11. Baig, D., et al.: Enhancing knowledge tracing with large language models (LLMs). In: Proceedings of AIED 2025, pp. 459–471. Springer (2025). https://doi.org/10.1007/978-3-031-99261-2_41
12. Psyridou, M., et al.: Machine learning predicts upper secondary education dropout as early as the end of primary school. Sci. Rep. **14**(1), 12956 (2024)
13. Powers, T.E., Watt, H.M.G.: Understanding why apprentices consider dropping out. Empir. Res. Vocat. Educ. Train. **13**(1), 9 (2021)

Teachers' Repairs of Artificial Conversations in Superdiverse Adult Education

Enrico Vignando[1,2](✉)

[1] University of Udine, via Margreth, 3 33100 Udine, Italy
enrico.vignando@unimore.it
[2] University of Modena-Reggio Emilia, Reggio Emilia, Italy

Abstract. This paper presents a participatory action research project on AI literacy conducted in Italian Adult Education Centers (CPIAs) with in-service teachers. Drawing on sociomaterial approaches to adult learning and education, it researches teacher-GenAI interactions as artificial conversations, by highlighting teachers' repairs of AI-generated content when it does not align with their pedagogical and ethical considerations. Qualitative data on teachers' maintenance of AI-generated content in complex and heterogeneous educational environments are collected and thematically analyzed. Expected contributions to AIED research include empirical insights into teachers' practices of using GenAI tools both as examples of situated AI literacy and sites where their agency is enacted.

Keywords: AI literacy · Participatory action research · In-service teachers' professional development · Artificial communication · Maintenance

1 Teachers' AI Literacy: More Than Prompting

Discussions about the role of Generative Artificial Intelligence (GenAI) in education have been intensifying due to increasing scholarly research and policy recommendations for teachers to become AI-literate and develop AI competencies [1, 2]. Despite this, few publications address in-service teachers' professional development in AI literacy [3, 4], and even fewer focus on adult education [5, 6]. Generally, it is agreed that critical, ethical, and even creative approaches should be prioritized; however, in practice, teachers' professional development may result in activities focused on knowledge of GenAI and training in prompting competencies [2, 7]. Alternatively, some authors [8] recommend action research as an underexplored opportunity to shift away from one-off workshops or short-impact courses on AI competencies. Recent reflections on AI literacy in educational contexts [9] caution against offering teachers only technically oriented professional development, which privileges abstract knowledge and skills related to using specific GenAI tools over critical reflection and responsible adoption of GenAI for teaching and learning.

This study is positioned at the intersection of these considerations by presenting a participatory action research project situated in Italian Adult Education Centers (CPIAs) and involving in-service teachers.

E. G. Blanchard et al. (Eds.): AIED 2026, CCIS 3033, pp. 236–241, 2026.
https://doi.org/10.1007/978-3-032-29794-5_36

It addresses the following research questions:

RQ1: Which contextual characteristics of CPIAs situate and shape in-service teachers' professional development in AI literacy?

RQ2: Beyond prompting, what practices of interaction and repair emerge in teachers' professional practice with GenAI tools?

2 Situating AI Literacy in Postdigital, Superdiverse, AI-Entangled Educational Environments

An Adult Education Center in Italy, or CPIA (*Centro per l'Istruzione degli Adulti*), is a publicly funded school, part of the formal Italian education system, which functions as territorial service for promoting lifelong learning. Most of the adult students attending CPIAs come from different migratory backgrounds and are enrolled in basic Italian courses. Due to their biographical and educational backgrounds, students' learning needs and profiles are highly diverse, and much of teachers' work involves planning and personalizing significant and effective learning activities while taking into account such superdiversity [10]. Furthermore, these highly heterogeneous educational environments can be described as postdigital [11], given the blurring boundaries between online and offline activities enabled by pervasive digital technologies and widespread Internet access. Within this intertwining of postdigital and superdiverse characteristics [12], AI comes in as a complex socio-technical assemblage of technological components, human actions performed with and through AI systems, and material artifacts and narratives related to AI [13]. Situating teachers' AI literacy within CPIAs entails overcoming a distinction between AI tools and their contextualized use, that is, the separation of AI competence from its socio-cultural contexts. Rather than promoting teachers' upskilling in AI competence alongside the adoption of GenAI tools, AI literacy should foster teachers' capabilities, empowerment, and agency [14] in a society where GenAI is increasingly used.

Sociomaterial approaches [15] contribute to this holistic understanding of AI literacy by reconfiguring GenAI tools as more than "mere instruments to advance educational performance" [15, p. 50] and as actors with which teachers interact when performing teaching tasks. In the postdigital webs of actions and artifacts, sociomaterial approaches suggest investigating teachers' capabilities by tracing teachers' improvisations and tinkering [16] with GenAI tools in their daily practices [17]. A privileged space where teachers' capabilities emerge is during artifact malfunctions and AI system breakdowns, which prompt teachers' repair [18] and maintenance of AI-generated content they judge good enough [19] to be integrated in their professional practice and educational environments.

3 Teachers' Postdigital Practices of Artificial Communication

As most of the GenAI tools provide chat-based interfaces for user multimodal interaction [20], teachers' practices with GenAI occur in what Esposito [21] conceptualizes as artificial communication, i.e., interactions between human users and an artificial agent, which acts according to an algorithm that lacks full access to users' contextual information (i.e., teachers and their classrooms) and is designed by somebody who does not participate in agent-user conversations. Artificial conversations [22] are thus the result of teachers' prompting GenAI tools to perform tasks (e.g., generating learning materials), GenAI responses to users' prompts, and teachers' reception of GenAI output. As in any conversational exchange, misunderstandings may arise during this process [23].

We argue that such misunderstandings in artificial conversations represent mismatches between teachers' expectations and the AI-generated outputs. Teachers' expectations are shaped on teachers' pedagogical expertise, their situated experience of educational contexts, and the assumption and expectation that GenAI will follow instructions and produce appropriate (e.g., unbiased, targeted) outputs. When inaccuracies and mismatches occur, teachers may modify or reject AI-generated outputs, taking into account the peculiar characteristics of their educational environments. As shown by recent research [24, 25], such practices of repair include modifications or adjustments made by teachers either on their own prompts (e.g., reformulations and iterations to refine AI output) or on AI-generated content by editing, simplifying, adapting, and critically evaluating it in relation to learners' linguistic and cultural backgrounds, as well as correcting biases and inaccuracies.

4 Preliminary Findings

The action research involved 28 teachers, half of whom working at CPIAs. All of them have experience in working in superdiverse educational contexts. Qualitative data were collected through individual interviews, focus groups, diary-keeping or other monitoring instruments co-designed with participants. The anonymized data were analyzed thematically using an inductive-deductive approach [26].

Interviews, particular those focused on the explicitation of professional practices [27], could provide rich descriptions of practices of repair in their artificial conversations. One of the emerging themes concerns the generation of learning materials as complementary or alternative to textbooks. As one teacher noted, in her classrooms "the competencies to be developed change every year, depending on the students' skills, languages, and educational backgrounds, and textbooks [...] are either too simple or too complex", thus being inadequate for adult learners at CPIAs. By using GenAI tools, she was able to "create learning materials [...] tailored for the students in my classroom". However, she also observed that GenAI tools tend to represent "migrant students at CPIAs as disadvantaged learners facing significant difficulties. You need to stay on top of [GenAI tools] to make them understand that it's not just this. Their descriptions are factual but [students at CPIAs] are not just economic migrants who have undertaken a desperate journey, lacking economic resources and constantly looking for a job: this must be corrected, I mean, it is a bias. So I keep on asking, I explain that this is not the reality, and I hope that, in a couple of months, [GenAI] will answer back differently". Similarly, as another teacher noted that GenAI tools can also generate "stereotyped" or "simplistic" materials, which require teachers' mediation. As she claimed, "I always modify them, and I select only what I need". Teachers' interactions with GenAI therefore involve either careful prompt construction or direct instructions, but consistently require critical reading and constant modification before teachers could integrate AI-generated content into their teaching activities.

The participatory action research [28] builds on these individual reflections and provide a space where teachers can elaborate and expand on their uses of GenAI tools, by co-designing small interventions with GenAI tools in small groups per school institution. During the discussions within each community, teachers could describe in detail and co-analyze their practices of repairs, reflect on their lived experienced [29] with GenAI, and share solutions to and experiences with GenAI malfunctions.

5 Expected Contributions

This participatory action research is expected to contribute to AIED research at an empirical level, by providing additional insights and details into how teachers enact AI literacy within postdigital and superdiverse educational environments like CPIAs, by highlighting the constant repairs in teachers' artificial conversations, performed according to their professional judgment [19], pedagogical responsibility, and context-sensitive agency. In this sense, prompting emerges not as a purely technical skill, but as situated professional practices, embedded in educational processes and situations where GenAI does not work as expected and, although useful, requires to be adjusted or mediated [30] by teachers. This study contributes also on a conceptual level, by framing AI competence and literacy as critical and situated interaction with GenAI tools, which unfolds dialogically and through iterative prompting [31], modifications, and repairs [24] to align AI-generated outputs with ethical and pedagogical expectations of users. This perspective foregrounds teachers' agency and, at times, resistance as integral to AI assemblages, whose educational implications unfold over time [32] and through teachers' maintenance of AI-generated content as harmless and educationally relevant as possible. Teachers' professional development in AI literacy becomes meaningful when it positions teachers not as users of GenAI tools, but as agents capable of shaping how AI is integrated into teaching and learning.

Acknowledgments. The Ethics Committee for Safeguarding of Ethical Principles in Research Involving Human Participants at the Department of Languages and Literature, Communication, Education and Society of the University of Udine approved the research project (CGPER-2025-05-13-01).

References

1. Tan, X., Cheng, G., Ling, M.H.: Artificial intelligence in teaching and teacher professional development: a systematic review. Comput. Educ. Artif. Intell. **8**, 100355 (2025). https://doi.org/10.1016/j.caeai.2024.100355
2. Chiu, T.K.F., Ahmad, Z., Ismailov, M., Sanusi, I.T.: What are artificial intelligence literacy and competency? A comprehensive framework to support them. Comput. Educ. Open. **6**, 100171 (2024). https://doi.org/10.1016/j.caeo.2024.100171
3. Ding, A.-C.E., Shi, L., Yang, H., Choi, I.: Enhancing teacher AI literacy and integration through different types of cases in teacher professional development. Comput. Educ. Open. **6**, 100178 (2024). https://doi.org/10.1016/j.caeo.2024.100178

4. Miao, F., Cukurova, M.: AI competency framework for teachers. UNESCO (2024). https://doi.org/10.54675/ZJTE2084
5. Sperling, K., Stenberg, C.-J., McGrath, C., Åkerfeldt, A., Heintz, F., Stenliden, L.: In search of artificial intelligence (AI) literacy in teacher education: a scoping review. Comput. Educ. Open. **6**, 100169 (2024). https://doi.org/10.1016/j.caeo.2024.100169
6. Laupichler, M.C., Aster, A., Schirch, J., Raupach, T.: Artificial intelligence literacy in higher and adult education: a scoping literature review. Comput. Educ. Artif. Intell. **3**, 100101 (2022). https://doi.org/10.1016/j.caeai.2022.100101
7. Moorhouse, B.L., Wan, Y., Wu, C., Kohnke, L., Ho, T.Y., Kwong, T.: Developing language teachers' professional generative AI competence: an intervention study in an initial language teacher education course. System **125**, 103399 (2024). https://doi.org/10.1016/j.system.2024.103399
8. Zhou, X., Lavicza, Z., Chiu, T.K.F.: Developing teacher AI competence: a systematic review of beliefs, professional learning, and cultural factors. Teach. Teach. Educ. **172**, 105384 (2026). https://doi.org/10.1016/j.tate.2026.105384
9. Sperling, K., Stenliden, L., Mannila, L., Hallström, J., Nordlöf, C., Heintz, F.: Perspectives on AI literacy in middle school classrooms: an integrative review. Postdigit Sci Educ. **7**, 719–749 (2025). https://doi.org/10.1007/s42438-025-00560-1
10. Vertovec, S.: Super-diversity and its implications. Ethn. Racial Stud. **30**, 1024–1054 (2007). https://doi.org/10.1080/01419870701599465
11. Jandrić, P., Knox, J., Besley, T., Ryberg, T., Suoranta, J., Hayes, S.: Postdigital science and education. Educ. Philos. Theory **50**, 893–899 (2018). https://doi.org/10.1080/00131857.2018.1454000
12. Pasta, S., Zoletto, D.: Postdigital Intercultures. Interculture Postdigitali. Postdigital Intercultures. **2**, 19–46 (2023)
13. Lindgren, S.: Critical Theory of AI. Polity Press, Cambridge Hoboken (2023)
14. Markauskaite, L., et al.: Rethinking the entwinement between artificial intelligence and human learning: what capabilities do learners need for a world with AI? Comput. Educ. Artif. Intell. **3**, 100056 (2022). https://doi.org/10.1016/j.caeai.2022.100056
15. Fenwick, T., Edwards, R.: Performative ontologies. Sociomaterial approaches to researching adult education and lifelong learning. Eur. J. Res. Educ. Learn. Adults **4**, 49–63 (2013). https://doi.org/10.25656/01:7706
16. Bardone, E., Mõttus, P., Eradze, M.: Tinkering as a complement to design in the context of technology integration in teaching and learning. Postdigit. Sci. Educ. **6**, 114–134 (2024). https://doi.org/10.1007/s42438-023-00416-6
17. Pink, S., Sumartojo, S., Lupton, D., Heyes La Bond, C.: Mundane data: the routines, contingencies and accomplishments of digital living. Big Data Soc. **4**, 2053951717700924 (2017). https://doi.org/10.1177/2053951717700924
18. Denis, J., Pontille, D.: Before breakdown, after repair: the art of maintenance. In: Mica, A., Pawlak, M., Horolets, A., Kubicki, P. (eds.) Routledge international handbook of failure, pp. 209–222. Routledge, Abingdon New York (N.Y.) (2023)
19. Biesta, G.: What is education for? On good education, teacher judgement, and educational professionalism. Eur. J. Educ. **50**, 75–87 (2015). https://doi.org/10.1111/ejed.12109
20. Zhao, W.X., et al.: A survey of large language models (2025). http://arxiv.org/abs/2303.18223. https://doi.org/10.48550/arXiv.2303.18223
21. Esposito, E.: Artificial Communication: How Algorithms Produce Social Intelligence. The MIT Press, Cambridge (2022)
22. Rivoltella, P.C.: Talking to machines: semiotic analysis, implications for teaching and media literacy. AN-ICON. **3**, 17–35 (2024). https://doi.org/10.54103/ai/23944
23. Albert, S., De Ruiter, J.P.: Repair: the interface between interaction and cognition. Top. Cogn. Sci. **10**, 279–313 (2018). https://doi.org/10.1111/tops.12339

24. Selwyn, N., Ljungqvist, M., Sonesson, A.: When the prompting stops: exploring teachers' work around the educational frailties of generative AI tools. Learn. Media Technol. **50**, 310–323 (2025). https://doi.org/10.1080/17439884.2025.2537959
25. Wang, X., Suo, X., Ji, Y.: Beyond the algorithm: unpacking the hidden labour and professional expertise in 'automated' special education technologies. Learn. Media Technol., 1–18 (2026). https://doi.org/10.1080/17439884.2026.2642201
26. Fereday, J., Muir-Cochrane, E.: Demonstrating rigor using thematic analysis: a hybrid approach of inductive and deductive coding and theme development. Int J Qual Methods **5**, 80–92 (2006). https://doi.org/10.1177/160940690600500107
27. Vermersch, P.: L'entretien d'explicitation. ESF sciences humaines, Paris (2019)
28. McTaggart, R.: Principles for participatory action research. Adult Educ. Q. **41**, 168–187 (1991). https://doi.org/10.1177/0001848191041003003
29. Medrado, A., Verdegem, P.: Participatory action research in critical data studies: Interrogating AI from a south-north approach. Big Data Soc. **11**, 20539517241235868 (2024). https://doi.org/10.1177/20539517241235869
30. Shieh, E., Vassel, F.-M., Sugimoto, C., Monroe-White, T.: Laissez-faire harms: algorithmic biases in generative language models (2024). https://arxiv.org/abs/2404.07475. https://doi.org/10.48550/ARXIV.2404.07475
31. Cain, W.: Prompting change: exploring prompt engineering in large language model AI and Its potential to transform education. TechTrends **68**, 47–57 (2023). https://doi.org/10.1007/s11528-023-00896-0
32. Steinert, S.: Maintenance of value and the value of maintenance. In: Maintenance and Philosophy of Technology, pp. 215–239. Routledge, New York (2024). https://doi.org/10.4324/9781003316213-11

Towards Trustworthy Accessible STEM Learning: A Comprehensive Research Framework for Formula Vocalization

Xueyi Li and Zitao Liu(✉)

Guangdong Institute of Smart Education, Jinan University, Guangzhou, China
liuzitao@jnu.edu.cn

Abstract. Accessible learning in online STEM education often depends on spoken access for blind or low-vision learners, which makes reliable formula vocalization essential. However, converting formulas into unambiguous speech while preserving symbol semantics and structure remains challenging. In this paper, we present a comprehensive research framework for trustworthy formula vocalization in accessible STEM learning. Specifically, we define the task using standardized inputs paired with reference audio and transcripts. We then introduce an evaluation protocol that combines symbolic-level and semantic-level metrics to handle multiple acceptable vocalizations. Finally, we propose a standardized dataset construction pipeline, along with a formula-aware training strategy that leverages special boundary tokens. Preliminary results on a small set confirm a reliability gap in existing models, motivating a standardized framework to guide model development for accessible STEM learning.

Keywords: Accessible Learning · Formula Vocalization · Online Learning

1 Introduction

Accessible learning seeks to ensure that learners with diverse abilities can participate meaningfully and equitably in education, and it has become a central goal of modern online learning environments [5,12]. Many online learning systems provide spoken guidance and feedback, which is particularly critical for blind or low-vision learners who primarily access instructional content via audio (as shown in Fig. 1) [2]. In science, technology, engineering, and mathematics (STEM) learning, where formulas encode dense and precise meanings, learners often rely on the system's spoken rendering to interpret the expression. This makes accurate and consistent formula vocalization a foundational requirement for trustworthy accessible STEM learning [1].

Formula vocalization translates compact symbolic expressions into an unambiguous spoken form while preserving structural information, which can easily be lost or distorted in natural speech. Existing research has largely addressed this problem through cascaded pipelines that first recognize the expression, then

E. G. Blanchard et al. (Eds.): AIED 2026, CCIS 3033, pp. 242–247, 2026.
https://doi.org/10.1007/978-3-032-29794-5_37

apply language based correction, and finally synthesize speech, with representative systems integrating automatic speech recognition (ASR), language model based correction, and text-to-speech (TTS) to produce spoken outputs [6]. In contrast, the rapid progress of large language models (LLMs) [13] has motivated end-to-end large speech language models (LSLMs) that align language and speech representations through multimodal alignment techniques [14], offering practical advantages such as reduced system complexity and low-latency streaming generation. However, when facing formula-rich STEM content, current end-to-end LSLMs still exhibit reliability issues in formula vocalization and often generate inconsistent verbal forms or symbol-level misreadings, which undermines trustworthiness in accessible learning settings and leaves trustworthy formula vocalization as an open challenge.

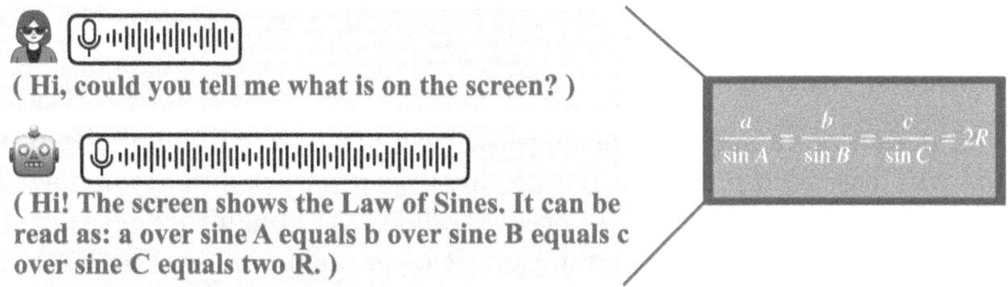

Fig. 1. Illustration of a blind learner accessing online course content.

To address this challenge, we present a comprehensive research framework for trustworthy formula vocalization in accessible STEM learning. We first provide a clear task definition and organize training data with paired formulas, reference audio, and standardized transcripts. We then introduce an evaluation protocol that combines symbolic-level and semantic-level metrics to account for multiple acceptable vocalizations. Finally, we describe a standardized pipeline for dataset construction and a formula-aware training strategy that uses special boundary tokens to explicitly separate formulas from ordinary language during training. This standardized framework helps improve the trustworthiness of formula vocalization to better support blind and low-vision learners in accessible STEM learning.

2 Related Work

2.1 Formula Vocalization

Formula vocalization studies how to render symbolic expressions such as LaTeX formulas into spoken language that is clear and consistent with the underlying structure, which is especially important in learning settings where learners cannot rely on visual content. Early efforts largely approached this problem with conventional speech and language processing techniques, including hidden

Markov models and rule based systems that depend on handcrafted normalization and grammars [11]. To improve robustness, subsequent work introduced more structured formalism and domain knowledge, for example by developing unified grammars based on finite-state transducers to support both recognition and synthesis and to encourage consistent cross-lingual rendering [9]. Text-side verbalization models such as dictionary-guided generation were explored and shown to outperform purely rule based baselines on mathematical expressions [3]. More recently, research has increasingly favored cascaded pipelines that decompose the problem into recognition, correction, and synthesis stages, with representative systems combining ASR and language model based symbolic correction to improve formula transcription [6]. Dedicated evaluations of TTS systems further suggest that pronunciation quality degrades as structural complexity increases, indicating that preserving formula semantics and structure remains challenging for current speech generation models [10].

2.2 Speech Models

Speech interaction in many online learning systems has traditionally been implemented with cascaded pipelines that separate speech recognition, language modeling, and speech synthesis into different modules. Although this modular design is straightforward to build and maintain, it often incurs noticeable latency and can amplify errors when mistakes made in earlier stages propagate to later ones [4]. Motivated by these limitations, recent work has explored end-to-end LSLMs that bring speech understanding and speech generation into a unified modeling framework, aiming to support more seamless and low-latency spoken interaction. Zeng et al. proposed interleaved speech-text training together with a supervised speech tokenizer, demonstrating strong spoken question answering and conversational capabilities [14]. Liu et al. proposed Text-to-Talk, a unified audio-language framework that integrates autoregressive modeling for text with non-autoregressive discrete diffusion for audio, based on the observation that text and audio exhibit fundamentally different dependency structures [7]. To further reduce response delay, Long et al. proposed a fast interleaved token generation mechanism that enables near-instant audio responses through efficient token prediction modules [8].

Please note that a related full paper by the authors, titled "Benchmarking Scientific Formula Vocalization in Large Speech Language Models Toward Accessible Learning", has been accepted at AIED 2026. That paper focuses on benchmark construction and empirical evaluation, whereas this doctoral consortium paper presents a broader research framework for trustworthy formula vocalization in accessible STEM learning.

3 Methodology

3.1 Problem Definition

We study formula vocalization for trustworthy accessible STEM learning, where the input is a formula written in standardized LaTeX and the output is a correct spoken reading of the formula. We adopt LaTeX as the canonical representation because it is the most common format for storing, exchanging, and rendering formulas in digital STEM resources, and normalization reduces superficial variation introduced by different authoring conventions. Formally, a formula is denoted as $x \in \mathcal{X}$, where $x = (z_1, z_2, \ldots, z_n)$ is a token sequence of length n and each z_i is a token from a vocabulary $\mathcal{V}$. We define a dataset as a collection of triplets $\mathcal{D} = \{(x_i, a_i, t_i)\}_{i=1}^{N}$, where x_i is the input LaTeX formula, $a_i \in \mathcal{A}$ is the reference audio that correctly reads the formula, and $t_i \in \mathcal{T}$ is the corresponding transcript that specifies the standardized spoken form aligned with a_i. Given $\mathcal{D}$, the goal is to learn a model that generates a spoken output $\hat{a}$ for an input formula x.

3.2 Research Pipeline

Evaluation Metrics. Formula vocalization takes a LaTeX formula $x \in \mathcal{X}$ as input and generates a spoken output $\hat{a}$. Although this resembles a TTS task, a single formula can have multiple acceptable vocalizations, so evaluating only by surface-form matching can be misleading. We therefore use two complementary metrics. First, we report a symbolic-level word error rate (WER) by transcribing the generated audio with an ASR model $\psi(\hat{a}) = \hat{t}$ and computing $\mathrm{WER}(\hat{t}, t)$ against the reference transcript $t \in \mathcal{T}$, where lower is better. Second, we report a semantic-level score that focuses on meaning preservation by asking an LLM judge to score the pair $(x, \hat{t})$, denoted as $\mathrm{SemScore}(x, \hat{t})$, where higher indicates that the vocalization better preserves the intended semantics and structure of the input formula.

Dataset Construction. To support trustworthy formula vocalization, we adopt a standardized pipeline for building text-audio paired data. To achieve broad coverage of STEM formula patterns, we collect large-scale formula-rich content from STEM courses on online learning platforms, and then normalize the extracted formulas into canonical LaTeX to reduce superficial variation and filter malformed or low-quality samples. Next, standardized vocalization transcripts are produced to preserve symbol semantics and structural relations, and are reviewed to ensure correctness and consistency. Finally, a TTS model synthesizes speech from the verified transcripts, followed by audio quality checks with regeneration when necessary. Overall, this is designed to produce aligned triples (x, a, t), where x is the normalized LaTeX formula, t is the standardized vocalization transcript, and a is the corresponding reference audio.

Model Training. To train a formula-aware speech model to support accessible STEM learning, it is important to distinguish formula text from ordinary language during training, since the two types of inputs follow very different syntactic and semantic regularities. We achieve this by introducing special boundary tokens that explicitly mark the LaTeX formula sequence, for example

$\langle$FML$\rangle$ x $\langle$/FML$\rangle$, and training the model to generate the corresponding transcript t and the audio a from the triples (x, a, t). From a modeling perspective, these markers act as a conditioning signal that partitions the input distribution into mode-specific subspaces, so the model can learn different internal representations and attention patterns for symbolic segments versus natural language segments. Equivalently, the special tokens provide an inductive bias that encourages the learned mapping to be piecewise structured, improving sample efficiency and reducing spurious correlations between literal characters and mathematical operators.

4 Current Progress

In our preliminary study, we curated a small set of formula instances and evaluated several representative end-to-end speech models on formula vocalization. The results suggest that current models remain unreliable when reading structure-sensitive formulas, even though they can produce fluent speech. We observe that these models often drift into free-form explanations, hallucinate non-existent symbols, or spell out fragments that do not correspond to the input formula. We attribute these errors to the lack of formula-speech supervision and the weak grounding between LaTeX tokens and speech units in general-purpose speech models, where tokenization and multimodal alignment are primarily optimized for natural language rather than hierarchical symbolic syntax. As a result, formula tokens may be treated as ordinary text, leading to unstable symbol mapping and structural information loss during generation.

5 Conclusion

This paper proposes a comprehensive research framework for trustworthy formula vocalization in accessible STEM learning, including task definition, evaluation, dataset construction, and formula-aware training. Our preliminary experiments on a small set show that current end-to-end speech models often misread symbols and lose structural information when vocalizing formulas, which confirms that reliable formula vocalization remains a challenging problem. In future work, we will scale up data collection and standardization to build high-quality paired formulas, transcripts, and audio, and refine the evaluation protocol to better reflect both symbolic accuracy and meaning preservation under multiple acceptable readings. We will then train formula-aware speech models with explicit formula markers and conduct iterative error analysis to improve robustness and consistency. Ultimately, our goal is to deliver an end-to-end model that can read formulas accurately and reliably for accessible STEM learning.

References

1. Abram, N.: Personalized learning in action: Exploring AI and robotics for early childhood education. In: Proceedings of the 39th Annual AAAI Conference on Artificial Intelligence, Philadelphia, PA, USA (2025)

2. Anderer, K., Muller, K., Strobel, L., Wolfel, M., Niehues, J., Gerling, K.: Making lecture videos accessible for students who are blind or have low vision through AI-assisted navigation and visual question answering. In: Proceedings of the 27th International ACM SIGACCESS Conference on Computers and Accessibility, New York, NY, USA (2025)
3. Dong, S., Liu, S., Liu, S., Tang, B.: Chinese spelling text generation of mathematical formulas. In: Proceedings of the 2022 IEEE International Conference on Acoustics, Speech and Signal Processing. Singapore (2022)
4. Fang, Q., Guo, S., Zhou, Y., Ma, Z., Zhang, S., Feng, Y.: Llama-omni: seamless speech interaction with large language models. In: Proceedings of the 13th International Conference on Learning Representations, Singapore (2025)
5. Hadi Mogavi, R., Hoffman, J., Deng, C., Du, Y., Haq, E.U., Hui, P.: Envisioning an inclusive metaverse: student perspectives on accessible and empowering metaverse-enabled learning. In: Proceedings of the 10th ACM Conference on Learning @ Scale, Copenhagen, Denmark (2023)
6. Hyeon, S., et al.: MathSpeech: leveraging small LMS for accurate conversion in mathematical speech-to-formula. In: Proceedings of the 39th Annual AAAI Conference on Artificial Intelligence, Philadelphia, PA, USA (2025)
7. Liu, T., et al.: From text to talk: Audio-language model needs non-autoregressive joint training. In: Proceedings of the 14th International Conference on Learning Representations. Rio de Janeiro, Brazil (2026)
8. Long, Z., et al.: Vita-audio: fast interleaved cross-modal token generation for efficient large speech-language model. arXiv preprint arXiv:2505.03739 (2025)
9. Ritchie, S., et al.: Unified verbalization for speech recognition & synthesis across languages. In: Proceedings of the 20th Annual Conference of the International Speech Communication Association. Graz, Austria (2019)
10. Roychowdhury, S., Ranjani, H., Soman, S., Paul, N., Bandyopadhyay, S., Iyengar, S.: Intelligibility of text-to-speech systems for mathematical expressions. In: Proceedings of the 26th Annual Conference of the International Speech Communication Association, Rotterdam, Netherlands (2025)
11. Sak, H., Beaufays, F., Nakajima, K., Allauzen, C.: Language model verbalization for automatic speech recognition. In: Proceedings of the 2013 IEEE International Conference on Acoustics, Speech and Signal Processing, Vancouver, BC, Canada (2013)
12. Shi, Z., et al.: Build your own robot friend: an open-source learning module for accessible and engaging ai education. In: Proceedings of the 38th AAAI Conference on Artificial Intelligence. Vancouver, Canada (2024)
13. Vaswani, A., et al.: Attention is all you need. In: Proceedings of the 31st Conference on Neural Information Processing Systems, Long Beach, CA, USA (2017)
14. Zeng, A., et al.: Scaling speech-text pre-training with synthetic interleaved data. In: Proceedings of the 13th International Conference on Learning Representations, Singapore (2025)

AI Among Secondary Vocational Education Teachers

Veronika Štolfová[1](✉), Jirí Zounek[1], and Libor Juhaňák[2]

[1] Department of Educational Sciences, Faculty of Arts, Masaryk University, Brno, Czechia
481714@mail.muni.cz

[2] Interdisciplinary Research Team on Internet and Society, Faculty of Social Studies, Masaryk University, Brno, Czechia

Abstract. This dissertation examines how teachers in secondary vocational education and training (VET) perceive, adopt, and implement artificial intelligence (AI) tools in school learning environments. Although research on AI in education is expanding, evidence from authentic VET teaching contexts remains limited, despite the growing need for AI literacy in technologically evolving industries. Building on established technology-adoption and knowledge-integration frameworks (TAM and UTAUT), the dissertation addresses the overarching question of how VET teachers implement AI tools and what factors influence this process. So far, it is organized into two phases: (1) a scoping review mapping existing studies on teacher use of AI and related digital technologies in school-based settings; (2) a quantitative survey of vocational teachers in the Czech Republic measuring adoption-related constructs (e.g., performance expectancy, effort expectancy, and social influence), AI literacy, AI self-efficacy, attitudes toward AI, institutional support, and the frequency and purposes of AI use, with demographic moderators (age, gender, teaching experience, and specialization).

Keywords: vocational education and training · VET teachers · artificial intelligence in VET education · AI adoption

1 Introduction to the Research Problem

The integration of artificial intelligence (AI) and digital technologies in education has become a key area of interest in current pedagogical research. While academic discourse on AI in education is growing rapidly, much of the existing work has focused on higher or general K–12 education, and studies examining how vocational education teachers engage with AI tools in real-world teaching contexts remain limited. This represents a significant gap, given that vocational education and training (VET) schools prepare students for technologically evolving industries in which AI literacy is increasingly critical.

E. G. Blanchard et al. (Eds.): AIED 2026, CCIS 3033, pp. 248–253, 2026.
https://doi.org/10.1007/978-3-032-29794-5_38

There are several theoretical frameworks—including the Technology Acceptance Model (TAM) and the Unified Theory of Acceptance and Use of Technology (UTAUT) [12], as well as the Technological Pedagogical Content Knowledge (TPACK) framework [11] and more recent AI-oriented extensions such as Intelligent-TPACK [5]—that have been used to analyze technology adoption and integration in education. However, these frameworks have not yet been sufficiently applied to the vocational education context. This dissertation addresses the gap by exploring how vocational education teachers perceive, adopt, and implement AI technologies.

1.1 State of the Art in AIED

AI in Education research covers a wide range of AI-enabled learning technologies (e.g., intelligent tutoring systems, adaptive learning environments, and learning analytics) as well as the emerging area of AI education (i.e., teaching about AI). Within the AIED community, the *International Journal of Artificial Intelligence in Education* (IJAIED) has published work on K–12, including a dedicated Special Issue on K–12 AI Education [8]. As summarized by Lane, this special issue includes two contributions explicitly focused on the high school level: one presenting an Erasmus+ two-year AI curriculum that integrates mobile learning and Python [3], and another describing a learner-informed educational game (ARIN-561) for teaching core AI techniques and roles [9]. Notably, IJAIED has not (to our knowledge) published a special issue dedicated specifically to secondary education or vocational upper-secondary (VET) contexts, which further motivates the present dissertation's focus on VET teachers' adoption and implementation of AI tools in practice.

2 Theoretical Framing and Proposed Approach

2.1 Technology Adoption Framework and AI-Related Constructs

To examine teachers' adoption and use of AI tools, this dissertation draws on established technology-acceptance frameworks, particularly UTAUT [12] and related TAM constructs [7]. These models offer a set of predictors (e.g., perceived usefulness/performance expectancy, perceived ease of use/effort expectancy, and social influence) that are well suited for explaining why teachers decide to try, continue using, or avoid new technologies. In the present study, these constructs are operationalized through a structured questionnaire and are used to model both self-reported AI use (frequency and purposes) and teachers' intentions and attitudes toward AI-supported educational practice.

Because AI tools introduce novel opportunities and risks for teaching, the acceptance constructs are complemented with AI-specific and school-contextual variables. In particular, the study considers (a) AI literacy as a prerequisite for informed use, (b) AI self-efficacy—teachers' confidence in their ability to use AI competently [6]—and (c) attitudes toward AI as a broader evaluative orientation, which can be measured with validated scales such as GAAIS [10]. In addition, we include perceived school/leadership support as an enabling condition that may shape whether teachers feel permitted and supported to experiment with AI in formal schooling contexts. Together, these variables allow us to distinguish between *can I use AI?* (literacy, self-efficacy), *do I want to use AI?* (attitudes, acceptance), and *am I supported to use AI?* (institutional support).

2.2 Research Questions and Objectives

This research aims to answer the overarching question: *How do upper-secondary vocational education teachers implement AI tools in school learning environments, and what factors influence this process?* The dissertation is guided so far by the following research objectives: (1) to examine the current state of attitudes and AI usage among vocational education teachers through a scoping literature review; and (2) to quantitatively measure constructs influencing AI use through a structured survey grounded in UTAUT and TAM.

2.3 Progress Already Made

Progress to date covers both the evidence-mapping and empirical component of the dissertation. First, a scoping review is being conducted to map what is currently known about AI use by vocational education teachers in formal education. The primary research question is: "What is known about the use of artificial intelligence (AI) by vocational education teachers in formal education?" Following the PCC framework (Population: secondary vocational education teachers, ISCED 3–4; Concept: use/adoption/integration/perception of AI in education; Context: formal vocational secondary schooling), searches were conducted in Scopus, ERIC, and Web of Science using a search string developed with support from a university librarian. After deduplication, 1,469 records were screened; 32 articles advanced to full-text screening, and 5 studies were included for data extraction. At the time of writing, the extracted studies are being coded. The scoping review protocol has been preregistered on OSF (currently under embargo) and submitted to *Campbell Systematic Reviews*, where it has been under review for several weeks.

Second, the quantitative survey examines the key factors that influence AI adoption among upper-secondary (primarily vocational) teachers in the Czech Republic. The questionnaire measures *AI literacy* (items adopted from a broader project in which I participate and developed by colleagues in that project), *attitudes toward AI* [1,10], *AI acceptance* adapted from a combined UTAUT+TAM framing [7,12] (performance expectancy, effort expectancy, social influence, and facilitating conditions; with behavioural intention operationalised as willingness to integrate AI [13] and attitude toward use reflected in attitudes toward AI in education), *AI self-efficacy* [6], perceived *school/leadership support*, and *AI use* (frequency and purposes), with age, gender, and teaching subject considered as moderators. The instrument was pilot tested in spring 2025, and the first wave of data collection was completed in autumn 2025 (approximately 350 upper-secondary teachers, mostly from vocational schools).

Building on these data, we plan quantitative analyses suitable for (future) longitudinal research designs, including correlations, linear regression models, and group-difference tests (e.g., between teacher subgroups). The study design anticipates three waves of data collection; however, we expect that participation may decline in later waves, as teachers are often reluctant to complete repeated surveys. The topic and early methodological work have been presented at the ECER Conference (Serbia) and an EDUC seminar (France).

2.4 Proposed Solutions and Methodology

To extend the core scoping review and survey, we propose several optional methodological strands that can be used either as follow-up studies or as triangulation of the quantitative findings.

Online Experiment on Multi-agent GenAI Support. We are considering an online, two-condition randomized experiment to test whether a multi-agent generative AI tool can better support upper-secondary vocational (VET) teachers in designing learning activities than a conventional single-agent (chatbot-style) GenAI tool.

Teachers would be randomly assigned to (A) a traditional GenAI chatbot without agents or (B) a multi-agent GenAI system with specialized roles supporting activity design (e.g., subject-matter expert, pedagogy/didactics coach). Participants would complete a pretest capturing technology-acceptance constructs (UTAUT), attitudes toward and prior experience with GenAI, receive brief tool training, and then complete a time-limited design task based on a standardized prompt. Outcomes would include the quality of the resulting activity design (rated by two independent evaluators using predefined criteria, including the extent to which technological, pedagogical, and content components are integrated in line with TPACK), and interaction traces (tool logs and number of revisions), complemented by a posttest and a think-aloud protocol. The study would be conducted in collaboration with a research team in Rennes using their own GenAI tool.

Scenario-Based Web Study on Teachers' AI-Related Decisions. As a second possible extension, we are considering a scenario-based web study inspired by MIT's *Moral Machine* [2], adapted to educational practice and distributed primarily among secondary school teachers. Visitors would be presented with short classroom scenarios involving the use of AI and asked to choose between two response options. Before or after completing a set of scenarios, participants would complete a brief, anonymous questionnaire collecting demographics (e.g., age, gender, highest completed education, and school type) and selected belief measures (e.g., pedagogical philosophy, attitudes towards AI and related constructs). Data would be collected in an unmoderated manner over a fixed time window (e.g., several weeks), logging timestamps and IP addresses to support basic deduplication heuristics while acknowledging that duplicates cannot be fully ruled out. After participation, the website would provide feedback by showing aggregated results for each scenario, allowing participants to compare their choices with those of other visitors; optionally, participants could be offered a way to share their results (e.g., on social media), which may help increase website traffic and, in turn, the number of survey respondents.

Participatory Qualitative Inquiry Using Photovoice. As a third possible extension, we are considering a participatory qualitative study using the photovoice method [4]. Teachers would document their real-life experiences with classroom AI use through photographs and short written narratives, which would then be discussed in in-depth semi-structured interviews. The resulting visual and textual materials would be analyzed thematically (and, where appropriate, visually) to deepen understanding of how teachers translate their beliefs, competencies, and institutional conditions into everyday AI-related pedagogical practices. This qualitative strand would also help interpret and contextualize the quantitative findings by examining how perceived competencies and challenges are experienced in practice and by identifying novel or unanticipated factors that may not be captured by survey measures. To support dissemination beyond academic venues, we plan a public-facing visual exhibition (digital and/or physical) showcasing teachers' experiences and key themes emerging from the data.

3 Expected Contributions and Impact

This dissertation contributes to the AIED community by providing a teacher- and context-sensitive account of AI adoption and implementation in vocational upper-secondary education.

From a Learning Sciences perspective, it offers evidence on how teachers' beliefs, AI literacy and self-efficacy, and institutional conditions shape everyday pedagogical practices with AI, thereby refining adoption and integration accounts in an underrepresented sector (VET).

From a Computer Science perspective within AIED, the dissertation can contribute by translating these teacher- and context-level insights into system-level implications: it identifies measurable human factors that can be operationalised as requirements and evaluation criteria for teacher-facing AI systems (e.g., which aspects of acceptance, self-efficacy, and support need to be addressed for a system to be usable in schools.

Although substantial progress has been made (scoping review screening and the first survey wave completed), key analytical and design decisions remain open, and the dissertation is still at a stage where feedback can be incorporated. In particular, while the survey instrument itself is already finalized, I seek advice on (1) appropriate quantitative analysis strategies for the current dataset and planned follow-up waves, and (2) choosing the proposed extensions (multi-agent GenAI experiment, scenario-based web study, and/or photovoice) to maximize theoretical contribution, feasibility, and relevance for the AIED community; importantly, I also welcome suggestions for alternative directions or study designs that we may not have considered.

References

1. Alshorman, S.: The readiness to use AI in teaching science: science teachers' perspective. J. Balt. Sci. Educ. **23**(3), 432–448 (2024)
2. Awad, E., Dsouza, S., Kim, R., et al.: The moral machine experiment. Nature **563**, 59–64 (2018). https://doi.org/10.1038/s41586-018-0637-6
3. Bellas, F., Guerreiro-Santalla, S., Naya, M., et al.: AI curriculum for European high schools: an embedded intelligence approach. Int. J. Artif. Intell. Educ. **33**, 399–426 (2023). https://doi.org/10.1007/s40593-022-00315-0
4. Breny, J.M., McMorrow, S.: Photovoice for Social Justice: Visual Representation in Action. SAGE Publications, Inc., Thousand Oaks, CA (2021). https://doi.org/10.4135/9781071938966
5. Celik, I.: Towards Intelligent-TPACK: an empirical study on teachers' professional knowledge to ethically integrate artificial intelligence (AI)-based tools into education. Comput. Hum. Behav. **139**, 107468 (2023). https://doi.org/10.1016/j.chb.2022.107468
6. Chiu, T.K.F., Ahmad, Z., Çoban, M.: Development and validation of teacher artificial intelligence (AI) competence self-efficacy (TAICS) scale. Educ. Inf. Technol. **30**(5), 6667–6685 (2025). https://doi.org/10.1007/s10639-024-13094-z
7. Davis, F.D.: Perceived usefulness, perceived ease of use, and user acceptance of information technology. MIS Q. **13**(3), 319–340 (1989). https://doi.org/10.2307/249008
8. Lane, H.C.: Commentary for the international journal of artificial intelligence in education special issue on K-12 AI education. Int. J. Artif. Intell. Educ. **33**, 427–438 (2023). https://doi.org/10.1007/s40593-023-00359-w
9. Leitner, M., Greenwald, E., Wang, N., et al.: Designing game-based learning for high school artificial intelligence education. Int. J. Artif. Intell. Educ. **33**, 384–398 (2023). https://doi.org/10.1007/s40593-022-00327-w
10. Schepman, A., Rodway, P.: The General Attitudes towards Artificial Intelligence Scale (GAAIS): confirmatory validation and associations with personality, corporate distrust, and general trust. Int. J. Hum. Comput. Interact. **39**(13), 2724–2741 (2023). https://doi.org/10.1080/10447318.2022.2085400
11. Schmidt, D.A., Baran, E., Thompson, A.D., Mishra, P., Koehler, M.J., Shin, T.S.: Technological Pedagogical Content Knowledge (TPACK): the development and validation of an assessment instrument for preservice teachers. J. Res. Technol. Educ. **42**(2), 123–149 (2009). https://doi.org/10.1080/15391523.2009.10782544
12. Venkatesh, V., Morris, M.G., Davis, G.B., Davis, F.D.: User acceptance of information technology: toward a unified view. MIS Q. **27**(3), 425–478 (2003). https://doi.org/10.2307/30036540
13. Yang, Y., Xia, Q., Liu, C., Chiu, T.K.F.: The impact of TPACK on teachers' willingness to integrate generative artificial intelligence (GenAI): the moderating role of negative emotions and the buffering effects of need satisfaction. Teach. Teach. Educ. **154**, 104877 (2025). https://doi.org/10.1016/j.tate.2024.104877

Bridging Explainable Modeling and Actionable Feedback: Multimodal AI-Augmented Pedagogical Interventions for Developing Active Listening Skills in Collaborative Problem Solving

Xiaomeng Huang(✉) and Xavier Ochoa

New York University, New York City, NY, USA
{xiaomeng.huang,xavier.ochoa}@nyu.edu

Abstract. Active listening—the ability to move beyond hearing to interpret diverse perspectives and build on others' contributions during collaboration—is a foundational skill in collaborative problem solving (CPS). Yet it is rarely explicitly taught because teachers lack scalable ways to observe, assess, and support its development during group work. This research addresses this longstanding challenge in CPS by leveraging multimodal AI to create new pedagogical interventions for active listening skill development. These interventions bridge explainable learner modeling and dialogic, actionable feedback. We introduce the Theory—Measurement—Evaluation (TME) framework, an explainable modeling architecture that operationalizes theory-informed behavioral indicators into interpretable multimodal learner models using uncertainty-aware probabilistic modeling. Rather than producing black-box evaluations, ***explainability*** is achieved by linking observable multimodal evidence directly to theoretically grounded constructs. These explainable evaluations are then translated into pedagogical feedback grounded in feedback theories, where ***actionability*** is achieved through structured dialogic guidance that promotes reflection and skill learning while preserving learner agency. This work contributes to AIED by advancing pedagogically grounded explainable AI and demonstrating how multimodal AI can augment pedagogical interventions to support the development of complex collaboration skills.

Keywords: Multimodal AI · Active Listening Skills · Collaborative Problem Solving

1 Introduction

Collaborative learning is central to education, not only as a way to build understanding across perspectives, but also as preparation for civic life, where collaboration is essential [4]. Yet participation in collaboration is rarely equal [2,12].

E. G. Blanchard et al. (Eds.): AIED 2026, CCIS 3033, pp. 254–260, 2026.
https://doi.org/10.1007/978-3-032-29794-5_39

Studies consistently show that some students dominate while others are sidelined, which limits both individual learning and group outcomes. Most interventions to date have focused on efforts to design equitable conditions—structuring tasks, scripting activities, or assigning group roles [2]. Far less attention, however, has been given to students' own capacity to notice and regulate unequal participation within their groups. A promising but underdeveloped pathway for building such capacity is active listening. The National Communication Association defines active listening as "the process of receiving, constructing meaning from, and responding to spoken and/or nonverbal messages" [13]. This definition highlights core skills such as hearing, understanding, remembering, interpreting, evaluating, and responding [1]. In collaborative learning settings, active listening requires interpreting and responding to peers' contributions in ways that make space for diverse voices and foster shared understanding. Despite its importance, active listening is rarely taught in schools. Teachers often lack the time and resources to observe subtle interactional dynamics and provide feedback, and even research has largely emphasized regulating speaking (e.g., turn-taking, talk time) [10] over listening [12]. As a result, one of the most critical levers for improving equitable collaboration—students' ability to listen actively—has remained underdeveloped.

Recent advances in multimodal learning analytics (MmLA) and multimodal AI models offer new opportunities to observe and model collaborative interaction through rich multimodal data [9]. However, our prior semi-systematic review of collaborative analytics systems [5] identified persistent limitations, including insufficient operationalization of theory-informed indicators, limited use of interpretable modeling approaches, and a lack of pedagogical grounding in analytics-supported feedback design. Many systems rely on black-box modeling techniques [11] or static dashboards that provide limited actionable guidance for learners [8]. To address these challenges, this research adopts an explainable modeling approach inspired by Evidence-Centered Design (ECD) and integrates dialogic feedback principles [14] to translate the explainable learner models into pedagogical feedback.

Two design principles guide this work: *explainability* and *actionability*. Explainability is conceptualized not merely as model transparency, but as a pedagogical bridge between automated assessment and instruction. Bayesian Skill Tracing is used to estimate theory-informed constructs from multimodal behavioral evidence while preserving uncertainty. Rather than assigning global labels (e.g., "good" or "poor" listener), the system models multiple sub-constructs (e.g., understanding checks) together with confidence estimates. These estimates are derived from aggregated multimodal evidence (e.g., clarifying questions or head nodding) detected using multimodal AI models. In this approach, AI supports evidence extraction, while evaluative interpretations remain theory-aligned and transparent. *Actionability* extends this bridge by structuring feedback across cognitive, structural, and social-affective dimensions [14], ensuring that learners not only receive guidance on what to do next but also understand the rationale, feel capable of acting, and retain agency in the learning process. For example, instead of presenting behavioral metrics (e.g., counts of clarifying questions) through dashboards, the system presents estimated levels of the "understanding checks" construct together with examplary moments (e.g., showing video clips when learners asked clarifying questions, or other understanding check behaviors). Learners are then invited to reflect on their intentions at these specific moments, their perspectives are acknowledged, and actionable guidance (e.g., strategies for inviting peers' contributions) is provided in context. Guided by these principles, this research addresses the following questions:

- ***RQ1***: How can theory-informed behavioral indicators of active listening be translated into explainable multimodal learner models, and to what extent do these models produce faithful and pedagogically useful assessments?
- ***RQ2***: Does dialogic and actionable feedback derived from explainable learner models support changes in learners' active listening skill development, including self-awareness, motivation, and observable listening behaviors, in collaborative problem solving?

2 Theoretical Frameworks

This research integrates two complementary theoretical framework: the HURIER active listening model [1] to operationalize active listening as measurable constructs, and the PEARLS framework [3] to structure dialogic, pedagogically grounded feedback.

The HURIER model conceptualizes listening as a set of interrelated processes (e.g., understanding, interpreting, evaluating, and responding) that can be manifested through observable verbal and nonverbal behaviors. While originally developed for dyadic communication and self-report assessment, this research adapts HURIER for small-group collaborative problem solving by translating listening processes into multimodal behavioral indicators suitable for computational modeling. These theory-informed constructs provide the foundation for explainable learner modeling of active listening.

To turn assessment into pedagogically meaningful intervention, this work draws on the PEARLS framework, a structured dialogic debriefing model widely used in simulation-based learning. PEARLS organizes feedback around guided reflection, facilitated discussion, and targeted instructional support. Adapted for AI-mediated feedback, it provides a pedagogical structure for transforming explainable assessments into dialogic guidance that supports reflection, learner agency, and skill development.

3 Proposed Solution and Current Progress

Figure 1 illustrates the overall approach. An initial empirical study has been completed to develop and validate the explainable modeling approach, and a second study is planned to evaluate the effectiveness of the dialogic feedback intervention within the same experimental context: small-group, in-person collaborative problem-solving tasks. In these settings, groups of 3–4 college students engage in information-distribution challenges that require integrating unique pieces of knowledge held by each participant, creating conditions that necessitate active listening and shared understanding. Group interactions are captured through multimodal audio and video recordings. Interaction data are processed during collaboration, while feedback is delivered after the session to avoid disrupting natural group dynamics. The system generates explainable evaluations from multimodal data and pedagogical feedback aligned with the modeling and pedagogical principles described earlier.

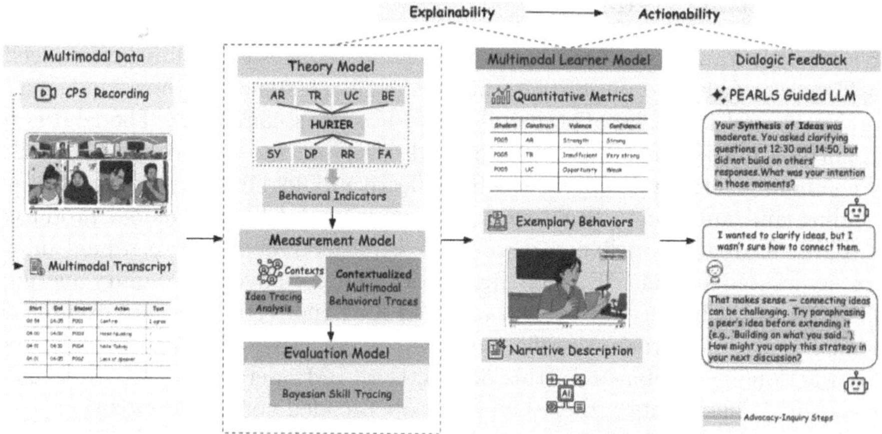

Fig. 1. System Overview: Bridging Explainable Modeling and Actionable Feedback

3.1 Explainable Modeling

To address RQ1, this work introduces the Theory-Measurement-Evaluation (TME) framework [7], an explainable modeling architecture (Fig. 1). TME transforms multimodal interaction data into interpretable learner models by explicitly linking theoretical constructs, observable behavioral evidence, and uncertainty-aware probabilistic evaluation.

TME consists of three stages. The **Theory Model** operationalizes HURIER-informed listening processes into theory-aligned behavioral indicators, including 19 verbal and 3 nonverbal behaviors (e.g., paraphrasing, clarifying questions, integrating peers' ideas, head nodding, note-taking) organized across eight sub-constructs. The **Measurement Model** extracts and contextualizes multimodal behavioral traces, incorporating collaboration context through Idea Tracing Analysis (ITA) [6]. Multimodal AI techniques (e.g., language and vision models) are used to detect behavioral indicators aligned with theory-informed constructs.

The **Evaluation Model** applies Bayesian Skill Tracing, inspired by Bayesian Knowledge Tracing but adapted for collaborative discourse. Rather than treating observations as binary correctness events, behavior-in-context evidence is modeled as weighted probabilistic updates that estimate each learner's latent proficiency while preserving uncertainty. The resulting multimodal learner model supports both evaluation and downstream pedagogical intervention, producing (1) quantitative construct estimates, (2) exemplary interaction moments linked to those estimates, and (3) LLM-supported natural-language summaries derived from structured evidence. Preliminary evaluation indicates high faithfulness and usefulness of model outputs (mean ratings $> 4.4/5$ across components).

3.2 Actionable Feedback

To address RQ2, this work conceptualizes *actionability* as extending beyond feedback content (what to improve) to include feedback structure (how guidance is organized) and its social-affective delivery (how it is conveyed). The goal is to support learners' agentic and self-regulated development of active listening skills by combining actionable guidance with reflective dialogue that promotes understanding and autonomy. Building on the multimodal learner model produced by TME, feedback is delivered through a LLM-mediated conversational interface structured by the PEARLS framework and its advocacy-inquiry method [3], as shown in Fig. 1. The system presents construct estimates and exemplary moments, invites learners to reflect on their perspectives, and provides personalized actionable guidance. In this design, the LLM operates within predefined pedagogical constraints rather than as an open-ended generative agent.

To evaluate the effectiveness of this intervention, a randomized between- and within-subjects experiment with 90 college students is planned for Spring 2026. Participants will be randomized at the group level to either an active control condition involving prompted self-reflection or an experimental condition receiving the dialogic feedback intervention. All groups will complete two comparable collaborative sessions; the first session serves as baseline, and feedback or self-reflection is delivered between sessions. Outcomes will assess pre-post changes between conditions in (1) self-awareness of active listening [1], (2) motivation toward active listening [13], and (3) behavioral change measured through TME across tasks.

4 Expected Contributions

This work contributes to AIED and CPS research by advancing pedagogically grounded multimodal AI for supporting complex collaboration skills. *Theoretically,* it operationalizes active listening as a measurable construct linking active listening theory with multimodal behavioral indicators. *Methodologically,* it introduces the Theory-Measurement-Evaluation (TME) framework, connecting theory-informed indicators, multimodal evidence, and uncertainty-aware learner modeling. *Pedagogically,* it demonstrates how explainable assessments can be translated into actionable dialogic interventions that support self-regulated collaboration skill development.

References

1. Brownell, J.: Listening: Attitudes, Principles, and Skills. Routledge, New York, 7 edn. (2023). https://doi.org/10.4324/9781003316794, https://www.taylorfrancis.com/books/9781003316794
2. Cress, U., Rosé, C., Wise, A.F., Oshima, J. (eds.): International Handbook of Computer-Supported Collaborative Learning, Computer-Supported Collaborative Learning Series, vol. 19. Springer, Cham (2021). https://doi.org/10.1007/978-3-030-65291-3
3. Eppich, W., Cheng, A.: Promoting excellence and reflective learning in simulation (pearls): development and rationale for a blended approach to health care simulation debriefing. Simul. Healthcare: J. Soc. Simul. Healthcare **10**(2), 106–115 (2015). https://doi.org/10.1097/SIH.0000000000000072
4. Graesser, A.C., Fiore, S.M., Greiff, S., Andrews-Todd, J., Foltz, P.W., Hesse, F.W.: Advancing the science of collaborative problem solving. Psychol. Sci. Public Interest **19**(2), 59–92 (2018)
5. Huang, X., Ochoa, X.: Charting the development of collaboration skills through collaborative learning analytics systems. J. Learn. Anal. **12**(1), 338–366 (2025). https://doi.org/10.18608/jla.2025.8523
6. Huang, X., Ochoa, X., Gopalakrishnan, M., Zhang, S.: Idea tracing analysis (ITA):a temporal-structural methodology for modeling collaborative discourse and contextualizing multimodal interactions. In: Proceedings of the International Conference on Computer Supported Collaborative Learning (CSCL) (2026)
7. Huang, X., Ochoa, X., Hiterer, D.: The TME framework: multimodal learner modeling for active listening skills in collaborative problem solving. In: Proceedings of the 27th International Conference on Artificial Intelligence in Education(AIED) (2026)
8. Kaliisa, R., Misiejuk, K., López-Pernas, S., Khalil, M., Saqr, M.: Have learning analytics dashboards lived up to the hype? a systematic review of impact on students' achievement, motivation, participation and attitude. In: Proceedings of the 14th learning analytics and knowledge conference, pp. 295–304 (2024)
9. Ochoa, X.: Multimodal learning analytics-rationale, process, examples, and direction. Handbook Learn. Anal. **2**, 54–65 (2022)
10. Ochoa, X., Huang, X., Charlton, A.: Unpacking the complexity: why current feedback systems fail to improve learner self-regulation of participation in collaborative activities. J. Learn. Anal. **11**(2), 246–267 (2024)

11. Rosé, C.P., McLaughlin, E.A., Liu, R., Koedinger, K.R.: Explanatory learner models: why machine learning (alone) is not the answer. Br. J. Edu. Technol. **50**(6), 2943–2958 (2019)
12. Strauß, S., Rummel, N.: Promoting regulation of equal participation in online collaboration by combining a group awareness tool and adaptive prompts. but does it even matter? Int. J. Comput.-Support. Collab. Learn. **16**(1), 67–104 (2021)
13. Worthington, D.L., Bodie, G. (eds.): The Sourcebook of Listening Research: Methodology and Measures. Wiley, Hoboken, NJ (2017)
14. Yang, M., Carless, D.: The feedback triangle and the enhancement of dialogic feedback processes. Teach. High. Educ. **18**(3), 285–297 (2013). https://doi.org/10.1080/13562517.2012.719154, http://www.tandfonline.com/doi/abs/10.1080/13562517.2012.719154

Teach to Learn AI Literacy: A Teachable Agent with Evaluator-Guided Scaffolding and Analytics

Zhihan Guo and Jionghao Lin(✉)

The University of Hong Kong, Pok Fu Lam, Hong Kong
zhihang330@connect.hku.hk, jionghao@hku.hk

Abstract. Developing AI literacy has become increasingly urgent for students as AI becomes an integral part of learning and work. This doctoral study posits that learning-by-teaching principles can help students build AI literacy by prompting them to articulate what AI can and cannot do, justify claims with evidence, and reflect on responsible use. Learning by teaching can strengthen conceptual understanding by leading learners to explain and refine ideas to tutees, yet such interactions can drift into superficial explanations without scaffolding and timely feedback. Thus, we aim to develop an LLM-based teachable agent for AI literacy, where learners teach a deliberately low-competence AI student through dialogue, while an evaluator agent provides detailed feedback with revision suggestions and the system records fine-grained interaction traces for process analysis. Using these trace data, we will identify which teaching moves and reflection behaviours are associated with learners' learning gains and confidence changes, and then we will evaluate the framework in an online prepost study measuring conceptual understanding, self-efficacy and learner experience. Expected contributions include a scalable teachable agent design for AI literacy education and an analytic pipeline that links process traces to learning impacts.

Keywords: Teachable Agent · Learning by Teaching · Large Language Models · AI Literacy

1 Introduction

AI literacy has become increasingly important as generative AI (GenAI) is embedded in learning and work [9]. In this study, we focus on AI literacy as learners' conceptual understanding and responsible use of AI, including what AI can and cannot do, how to evaluate outputs, and how to use AI appropriately. Prior work has used a range of approaches to build AI literacy, such as AI-led explanations with guided practice and feedback, as well as activities that prompt learners to critique AI outputs and reflect on responsible use [9]. In this doctoral study, we focus on learning-by-teaching because it requires human learners to take responsibility for improving a novice tutee, which elicits diagnosis, correction

E. G. Blanchard et al. (Eds.): AIED 2026, CCIS 3033, pp. 261–267, 2026.
https://doi.org/10.1007/978-3-032-29794-5_40

and iterative refinement of explanations [1,3]. In our study, we used LLM-based teachable agent to simulate student's misconceptions and questions. Prior work suggests that learning-by-teaching activities benefit from explicit structure and timely feedback that reduce superficial explanations and help learners notice and repair misconceptions, like sequencing prompts from misconception correction to "why" explanation and then to an applied judgment task [1,3]. Earlier teachable agent systems often relied on manually built expert knowledge models and constrained interaction formats, which made it difficult to scale learning-by-teaching to open-ended dialogue [5]. Recent LLM-based teachable agents make dialogue-based learning-by-teaching more feasible, and they motivate interaction designs that both support learners during the teaching process and capture process traces (e.g., revision counts and key-idea coverage) for analysis [2,6].

The goal of this doctoral study is to design and evaluate an LLM-based teachable agent system to support AI literacy learning through learning-by-teaching. The system integrates a virtual student (an AI-simulated novice learner) with an automated agent evaluator (We called it "*Clara*"), which provides detailed feedback and revision suggestion, and the system records interaction traces for process analysis. We define learning progress as completing a short sequence of teaching tasks for each AI literacy concept, moving from misconception correction to rationale explanation and applied judgment [9]. In this study, the target concepts include distinguishing traditional software from AI systems, appropriate human oversight, bias and fairness, explainability, and data drift and system maintenance. We will examine how *Clara*'s feedback shapes learners' knowledge retention and learning experience, and develop quantitative measures of interaction quality, instructional quality and learner engagement. Within the scope of doctoral research, we aim to explore the following **R**esearch **Q**uestion (**RQ**s):

- **RQ1**: Do students show significant learning gains in their conceptual understanding of AI literacy after interacting with a teachable agent?
- **RQ2**: Do students show significant gains in self-efficacy regarding their conceptual understanding of AI literacy after interacting with a teachable agent?
- **RQ3**: How do students perceive learning AI literacy through interaction with teachable agent?
- **RQ4**: What interaction processes and teaching behaviors are associated with students' learning gains and self-efficacy gains in learning-by-teaching with a teachable agent?
  - **RQ4.1** Which process indicators (e.g., number of interactions, time-on-task, coverage of knowledge points) best explain or predict gains?
  - **RQ4.2** Do these associations differ across rounds and knowledge points?

2 Background and Related Work

2.1 AI Literacy Education with AI Systems

AI literacy education has become increasingly urgent as AI is integrated into education and society, and recent work emphasizes competencies for understanding and responsible use rather than simple tool operation [9]. Prior work has used AI systems to build students' AI literacy mainly by having AI explain concepts and provide guided practice with feedback, or by guiding learners to evaluate AI outputs and improve prompts through hands-on activities [4,7]. A common limitation of these approaches is that learners may focus on getting correct answers or interacting at a shallow level, and evidence often relies primarily on outcome measures rather than examining how learners' reasoning and misconceptions change during interaction [9].

2.2 Learning by Teaching with Teachable Agents

Learning-by-teaching positions learners as tutors, and the *protégé effect* suggests that learners invest more effort when they feel responsible for helping a tutee improve, which encourages them to articulate ideas in their own words, monitor gaps in understanding, and refine explanations [1,3]. From a cognitive engagement perspective, generating and revising explanations is associated with stronger learning than primarily receiving information [8].

Teachable agents support this pedagogy by providing an artificial student that learners can instruct and assess [1]. Classic systems such as Betty's Brain show that learners can benefit from repeatedly explaining to and correcting a simulated student, and recent work shows that LLMs can also be positioned as teachable students that prompt learners to explain and revise in natural language [2,6]. Prior work notes that learners may still provide brief or superficial teaching responses unless the activity structure and feedback encourage reflection and revision [3]. Accordingly, we address this by prompting a low-competence AI student and adding an evaluator agent that checks key ideas and requests revisions, which enables process measurement while supporting actionable guidance.

3 Method

Study Design. This study adopts a staged evaluation plan. **Stage 1.** We will run a small-scale online pilot on Prolific to validate the end-to-end procedure, assess and balance the difficulty of the pre- and post-tests, and refine interaction burden and data-quality controls. **Stage 2.** We will conduct the main evaluation with an authentic classroom cohort (target $N \approx$ 30–50, depending on course enrollment) using the same pre–post procedure. An initial power analysis for the pre–post design suggests that this sample size can detect medium-sized gains and we will increase the sample if the pilot indicates smaller effects or higher variability than expected. Participants will complete a fixed sequence consisting of a brief pre-survey, a conceptual pre-test, the teachable agent teaching interaction, a conceptual post-test and a short post-survey. The pre-survey collects background information to characterize the sample. The experiment targets five AI literacy knowledge points and uses an identical structure to ensure procedural consistency and minimize extraneous cognitive load. Where feasible, we will include a delayed post-test to assess retention and strengthen validity.

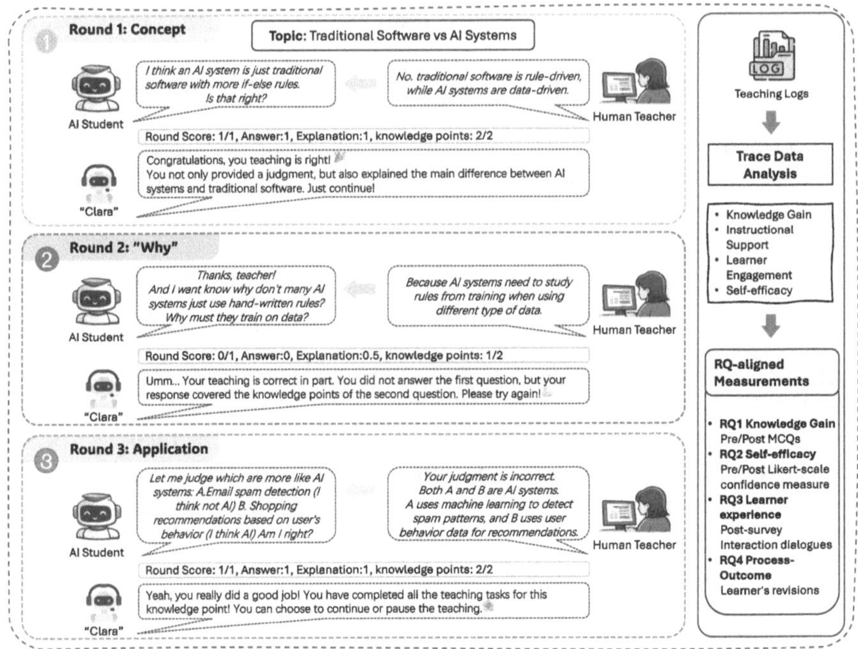

Fig. 1. Simulating a three-round teachable agent interaction with *Clara* evaluation and RQ-aligned measurement design.

Figure 1 summarizes the overall teaching interaction and measurement pipeline used in this study. Throughout this process, the participant acts as the human teacher. For each knowledge point, the interaction unfolds as a three-role dialogue among the teacher, the AI student and the evaluator agent (*Clara*). We implement the AI student by prompting as a deliberately low-competence learner who exhibits fragile mastery of the target concept and is prone to common misconceptions. This student is guided to present common misconceptions, ask a "why" question and provide a judgment-style statement with intentionally incorrect points, while *Clara* offers timely scaffolding throughout the interaction. Each knowledge point follows a fixed three-round sequence from misconception correction to rationale explanation and then to applied judgment, followed by a self-check summary. After each response, *Clara* applies a staged decision process. It first checks for critical factual errors or contradictions and then checks whether the response covers the required ideas. If the response is incomplete or unclear, *Clara* returns missing points and requests a revision; otherwise, the interaction proceeds. Previously covered ideas are treated as background in later rounds to reduce repetition.

Conceptual understanding is assessed with multiple-choice tests aligned with the same five knowledge points. To mitigate practice effects, we use two equivalent test forms (A/B) with counterbalancing, so that half of participants complete A then B and the other half complete B then A. The post-survey captures learners' perceived usefulness and burden of learning-by-teaching, with brief reflections on the most helpful and challenging rounds. The overall session is designed to last about 1–1.5 h, with short surveys (3–5 min each), pre/post tests (10–15 min each), and the teaching interaction (approximately 25–45 min depending on revisions).

Data Collection and Analysis. We will collect complementary data from surveys, pre–post assessments and system interaction traces. The instruments include a brief background questionnaire, a short Likert-scale confidence measure administered immediately after the pre- and post-tests, and a post-interaction survey that assesses perceived usefulness and cognitive load of learning-by-teaching and also includes open-ended prompts about helpful features, encountered difficulties and suggestions for improvement. The system also logs interaction traces between human teacher and the AI student, including the knowledge point and round, participants' responses, *Clara*'s verdicts and reasons, semantic coverage indicators, missing points, revision counts and time spent per round.

To address RQ1–RQ3, we will compare pre–post performance and confidence using paired analyses and report effect sizes. Survey responses will be summarized with descriptive statistics and open-ended responses will be analyzed with a lightweight thematic analysis to characterize perceived benefits and challenges. To address RQ4, we will examine associations between process indicators from the interaction traces and learners' gains and confidence changes.

4 Current Progress

Working Prototype. We have implemented a teachable agent prototype that supports a complete learning-by-teaching workflow in which participants teach an AI student across AI literacy concepts. The interface includes a task-focused teacher mode, a reading material panel and a *Clara* feedback panel.

Stabilized Three-turn Interaction Script. We have stabilized a three-turn script for each knowledge point, progressing from misconception correction to reason explanation and applied judgment, followed by the AI student self-summary to check its understanding.

Operational Evaluator Agent. The evaluator agent (*Clara*) is integrated into the interaction loop. After each response, *Clara* checks correctness and key-idea coverage and prompts revision when needed. To reduce unnecessary rework, *Clara* accepts answers with similar meaning as long as they convey the required content, rather than relying on exact wording.

Curated Content and Learning Materials. We prepared bilingual reading materials for five AI literacy knowledge points, covering traditional software versus AI systems, over-reliance and human oversight, bias and fairness, explainability, and data drift and system maintenance.

Prepared Assessments. We developed multiple-choice pre- and post-tests for each knowledge point and iteratively improved distractor design and difficulty calibration to reduce obvious guessing and strengthen measurement validity.

Pilot Study and Iteration. We are conducting a small-scale pilot to validate the workflow and identify usability and evaluation issues. Early traces suggest several areas for improvement, such as reducing overly strict matching in earlier *Clara* versions, which has informed the current rubric and feedback strategy.

5 Expected Contributions and Future Directions

This work is expected to contribute to Artificial Intelligence in Education (AIED) in three ways. *First*, it proposes a structured learning-by-teaching interaction paradigm for AI literacy that guides learners to teach an AI student through misconception correction, reason explanation, and applied judgment. *Second*, it introduces a scalable teachable agent design that instantiates a low-competence AI student via prompting and uses an evaluator agent (*Clara*) to flag missing key ideas and revisions. *Third*, we aim to design a measurement approach that links interaction indicators to learning gains and confidence changes.

Next, we will complete a small-scale pilot to analyze the difficulty of pre- and post-tests, cognative load and evaluator behavior. Then we will conduct a larger-sample study in real classroom to examine learning and confidence outcomes and their process correlates. Aligned with the AIED 2026 conference theme of moving from tools to teammates, extend the system toward an adaptive learning partner that provides timely and detailed feedback while preserving learner agency. We will also test a bilingual version and tune prompt and feedback specificity for learners with different language proficiency levels. These studies will yield practical design guidelines for teachable agents on what feedback to provide, how specific it should be and when to remind revision.

References

1. Chase, C.C., Chin, D.B., Oppezzo, M.A., Schwartz, D.L.: Teachable agents and the protégé effect: increasing the effort towards learning. J. Sci. Educ. Technol. **18**(4), 334–352 (2009)
2. Chen, A., Wei, Y., Le, H., Zhang, Y.: Learning by teaching with chatgpt: The effect of teachable chatgpt agent on programming education. Br. J. Edu. Technol. **57**(1), 163–184 (2026)
3. Debbané, A., Lee, K.J., Tse, J., Law, E.: Learning by teaching: key challenges and design implications. Proc. ACM Hum.-Comput. Interact. **7**(CSCW1), 1–34 (2023)
4. Dennison, D.V., et al.: From consumers to critical users: prompty, an ai literacy tool for high school students. In: Proceedings of the AAAI Conference on Artificial Intelligence, vol. 38, pp. 23300–23308 (2024)
5. Leelawong, K., Biswas, G.: Designing learning by teaching agents: the betty's brain system. Int. J. Artif. Intell. Educ. **18**(3), 181–208 (2008)

6. Rogers, K., Davis, M., Maharana, M., Etheredge, P., Chernova, S.: Playing dumb to get smart: creating and evaluating an llm-based teachable agent within university computer science classes. In: Proceedings of the 2025 CHI Conference on Human Factors in Computing Systems, pp. 1–22 (2025)
7. Tseng, Y.J., et al.: Activeai: the effectiveness of an interactive tutoring system in developing k-12 ai literacy. In: European Conference on Technology Enhanced Learning, pp. 452–467. Springer (2024)
8. Vosniadou, S., Lawson, M.J., Bodner, E., Stephenson, H., Jeffries, D., Darmawan, I.G.N.: Using an extended icap-based coding guide as a framework for the analysis of classroom observations. Teach. Teach. Educ. **128**, 104133 (2023)
9. Yang, Y., Zhang, Y., Sun, D., He, W., Wei, Y.: Navigating the landscape of ai literacy education: insights from a decade of research (2014–2024). Human. Soc. Sci. Commun. **12**(1), 1–12 (2025)

Theory-Informed Design of Personalized Computational Proxies for Learning in Intelligent Learning Environments

Kaimao Sheng[(✉)]

University of Duisburg-Essen, Duisburg, Germany
kaimao.sheng@uni-due.de

Abstract. This research aims to explore the design of computational representations using artificial intelligence of theoretical paradigms of how learning happens. Understanding when a student is ready to learn and when intervention is most effective is critical to improving learning outcomes, yet this remains an open challenge. Most existing systems rely on surface-level performance signals without grounding their decisions in established learning theories, limiting their ability to capture meaningful learning states. To address this, I reviewed current student modeling approaches and examined how established learning theories have been incorporated into these models. Building on this review, I aim to design computational proxies for Zone of Proximal Development. I expect to produce a validated computational model of optimal learning and a theory-informed adaptive support mechanism evaluated in a real world setting. I aim to contribute to bridging the gap between learning science and artificial intelligence in education, providing a principle foundation for building systems that support students more effectively.

Keywords: Artificial Intelligence · Computational methods in education · Learning Theory · Student Modeling · Reinforcement Learning

1 Introduction

Intelligent Tutoring Systems (ITSs) rely on student models to monitor learning and guide two core functions: selecting the next problem and providing support when needed [11]. However, the effectiveness of these decisions depends on how well the underlying model captures where a student truly is in their learning process. Theories such as the Zone of Proximal Development (ZPD) [14], which describes a learners cognitive state where growth occurs through guided assistance, offers another possibility to inform modeling of learning: rather than simply classifying student as having mastered or not mastered a concept, we can model learning as occurring within a dynamic range where challenge and support (delivered through hints and other forms of assistance, which are understood as integral to the learning process itself) must be carefully balanced. This

E. G. Blanchard et al. (Eds.): AIED 2026, CCIS 3033, pp. 268–273, 2026.
https://doi.org/10.1007/978-3-032-29794-5_41

research investigates how Zone of Proximal Development can be translated into computational representations and used to improve adaptive decision-making in ITSs. Specifically, I aim to explore:

- **RQ1** How can the Zone of Proximal Development be translated into computational proxies to inform adaptive scaffolding in ITSs?
- **RQ2** How can this proxy be embedded into an ITS to guide adaptive support delivery?

2 Related Work

2.1 Learning Theories and Optimal Learning

For optimal learning, the Zone of Proximal Development (ZPD) defines the space between what a learner can do independently and what they can achieve with guidance from a more knowledgeable other [14]. Flow theory similarly describes an optimal state of engagement that arises when challenge and skill are well matched [5]. Both theories converge on the same principle: there exists an optimal learning zone, and identifying it dynamically for each learner is essential for effective instruction.

2.2 Student Modeling in Intelligent Tutoring Systems

Student models represent learners' knowledge, skills, and misunderstandings. They support personalized learning by predicting performance and informing instructional decisions [11]. Over time, a range of modeling approaches have been developed, from rule-based systems and knowledge tracing methods [4] that track concept mastery, to knowledge space models that map relationships between concepts, to dialogue-based models that monitor understanding in real time conversations [7].

3 Method

This research follows a mixed-methods design structured in two phases[1], each addressing a distinct research question. In the first phase, I reviewed existing student modeling approaches to understand what information current models rely on and how this information shapes instructional decisions. From this review, I identified how the current approaches modeling ZPD area and use these insights to design a new computational proxy for ZPD. In the second phases, I will integrate this proxy into an adaptive tutoring system to guide when and how support is delivered to students. I plan to evaluate the approach in two ways: first, through a field study within a real university course, including interviews with students to understand their learning experiences; and second, through a controlled experiment comparing the system with the proxy against a baseline system without it. Together, the two phases move from understanding how optimal learning can be represented computationally to actively using that representation to support students.

[1] See the CQOCE PhD planning: Link.

4 Proposed Research

4.1 RQ1 Modeling the Optimal Learning Zone

RQ1 is addressed through a systematic literature review followed by a simulation study.

This systematic literature review was conducted following the PRISMA guidelines, with a structured search across six databases (ACM, EBSCO, Scopus, IEEE, Web of Science, and DIM) covering publications from 2015 to 2025. I reviewed how prior computational models have attempted to represent the ZPD and related constructs. It identified a subset of models that specifically attempt to operationalize the ZPD, including Bayesian Belief Networks [8], hint-based metric windows [10], Grey Area (GA) approaches [2], and reinforcement learning methods [6]. Despite their differences, these models share a common goal: keeping students in a state of productive challenge by adjusting task difficulty based on evolving indicators of knowledge and performance.

Building on this findings, the simulation study extended the GA approach by introducing the Personalized Grey Area (P-GA) approach (Fig. 1) [12]. The P-GA incorporates students' help-seeking behavior–specifically, whether a student requests hints and whether those hints lead to success– as an additional signal for estimating their learning zone. When a student performs above the center of their estimated zone, hint usage and consecutive incorrect responses causes the upper boundary to expand. When a student performs below the center, hint usage reduces the lower boundary, reflecting reduced need for support on easier material, while consecutive non-correct responses (only consider first attempt types here) shift that boundary upward, narrowing the zone. This personalization allows the model to adapt its estimates of each student's optimal zone as their behavior evolves.

To assess whether this extension improves zone estimation, the P-GA was compared against the original GA approach on its ability to identify correct-after-support sequences, that is, instances where a student succeeded on a problem only after receiving a hint, which serves as a behavioral indicator that the students was operating within their ZPD.

4.2 RQ2 - Guiding Adaptive Support Delivery Through Proxy-Informed Tutoring

RQ2 investigates whether the P-GA concept can be used to improve the timing and quality of support within an ITS. This phase has two objectives: a) refining zone estimation using rich features such as student performance data and help-seeking behaviors, and b) training an reinforcement learning agent that learns to assign students to the appropriate P-GA zone based on indirect outcome. Course content is drawn from an introduction to Python programming course used at University of Duisburg-Essen, designed for novice learners with no programming experience. The content is organized into a knowledge graph, where each node represents a skill and edges encode prerequisite relationships [1]. Each

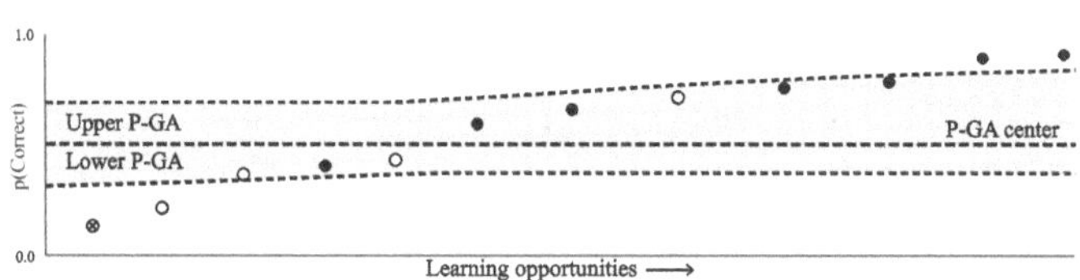

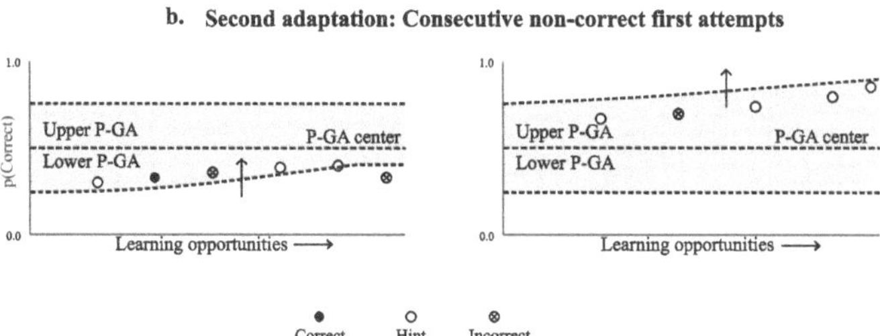

Fig. 1. Personalization of the Grey Area (P-GA). (Color figure online)

skill will be associated with multiple difficulty levels. The learning state is represented as a feature vector for each knowledge component, where each dimension encodes various indicators (for example, current mastery estimate, recent error rate, help-seeking behaviors [12], time one task, and task difficulty level). Because the true P-GA zone of a student cannot be directly observed–it is a latent theoretical construct derived from ZPD–supervised classification is not applicable, as no ground truth labels exist for which zone a student occupies at any given moment. Reinforcement learning is therefore used to learn this mapping through indirect feedback [13]. The agent observes the student's feature vector and assigns the student to one of four zones: below P-GA, lower P-GA, upper P-GA, or above P-GA. Each zone is associated with a predefined set of support actions designed in collaboration with domain experts. Once a zone is assigned, the corresponding support is delivered to the student (Fig. 2). The reward function will be defined to encourage outcomes consistent with ZPD-based learning: a reward of +1 for a correct answer after a hint (indicating the student was in the ZPD and benefited from support); a penalty of −0.5 for a hint followed by an incorrect answer (indicating the student was below the ZPD and support was insufficient); a reward of 0 for an unaided correct answer (indicating the student was above the ZPD and did not need help); and a penalty of −1 for an unnecessary hint when prior performance suggests mastery (indicating over-scaffolding). This formulation encodes the ZPD intuition: support should be given when it bridges the gap between unaided failure and guided success, and penalized when it is redundant or ineffective.

Because no prior interaction data will be available at deployment, the agent will be initialized with a rule-based warm-start policy: begin with no hint, and escalate only if the student continues to struggle [3]. After each iteration, the

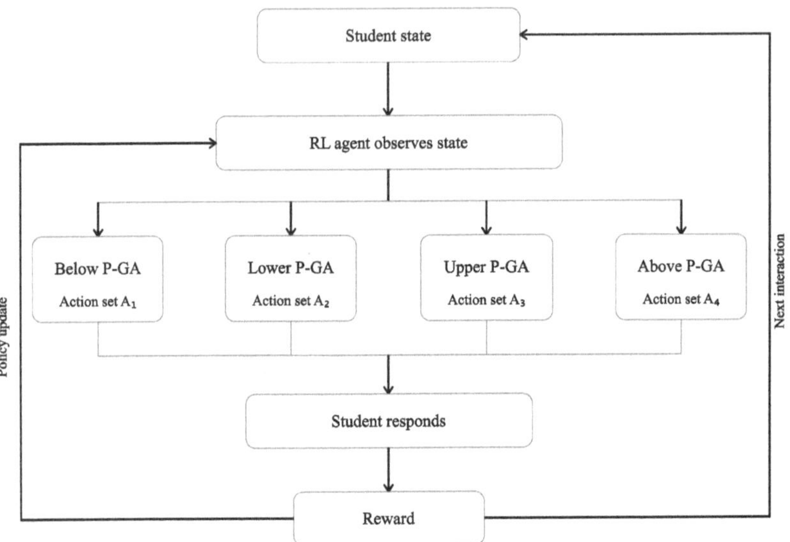

Fig. 2. RL-based adaptive support loop.

agent will update its policy based on observed outcomes, allowing it to improve through real classroom use [9].

The system will be evaluated in two ways. First, it will be deployed in a real course and supplemented with student interviews to assess usability and perceived support quality. Second, it will be compared against a baseline system that delivers hints according to a fixed rule, specifically, a hint after every incorrect response.

5 Expected Contributions

This research aims to make contributions to both theory and practice in Intelligent Tutoring Systems. It will introduce improved computational representations of students' optimal learning zones, grounded in established learning theories. It will also advance adaptive support design by embedding ZPD-informed scaffolding into a reinforcement learning approach, producing hint-selection policies that balance guidance and independent struggle for individual learners. Further this work aim to support transparency and interpretablity for educators and researchers. Finally, it will offer practical guidelines and empirical evidence for theory-informed ITS design, demonstrating how computational proxies of optimal learning zones can improve personalization and learning outcomes.

Overall, this research seeks to bridge learning theory and computational practice, contributing to tutoring systems that are both adaptive and pedagogically grounded.

References

1. Chen, P., Lu, Y., Zheng, V.W., Chen, X., Yang, B.: Knowedu: a system to construct knowledge graph for education. IEEE Access **6**, 31553–31563 (2018). https://doi.org/10.1109/ACCESS.2018.2839607
2. Chounta, I.A., Albacete, P., Jordan, P., Katz, S., McLaren, B.M.: The "grey area": a computational approach to model the zone of proximal development. In: European Conference on Technology Enhanced Learning, pp. 3–16. Springer (2017). https://doi.org/10.1007/978-3-319-66610-5_1
3. Clément, B., Roy, D., Oudeyer, P.Y., Lopes, M.: Multi-armed bandits for intelligent tutoring systems. J. Educ. Data Min. **7**(2), 20–48 (2015). https://inria.hal.science/hal-00913669
4. Corbett, A.T., Anderson, J.R.: Knowledge tracing: modeling the acquisition of procedural knowledge. User Model. User-Adap. Inter. **4**(4), 253–278 (1994)
5. Csikszentmihalyi, M., Csikszentmihalyi, I.: Beyond Boredom and Anxiety: The Experience of Play in Work and Games. Jossey-Bass, San Francisco (1975)
6. Fenza, G., Orciuoli, F., Sampson, D.G.: Building adaptive tutoring model using artificial neural networks and reinforcement learning. In: 2017 IEEE 17th International Conference on Advanced Learning Technologies (ICALT), pp. 460–462. IEEE (2017). https://doi.org/10.1109/ICALT.2017.124
7. Graesser, A.C., Person, N.K.: Question asking during tutoring. Am. Educ. Res. J. **31**(1), 104–137 (1994)
8. Luckin, R., Du Boulay, B., et al.: Ecolab: the development and evaluation of a vygotskian design framework. Int. J. Artif. Intell. Educ. **10**(2), 198–220 (1999)
9. Mandel, T., Liu, Y.E., Levine, S., Brunskill, E., Popovic, Z.: Offline policy evaluation across representations with applications to educational games. In: AAMAS, vol 1077 (2014)
10. Murray, T., Arroyo, I.: Toward measuring and maintaining the zone of proximal development in adaptive instructional systems. In: International Conference on Intelligent Tutoring Systems, pp. 749–758. Springer (2002)
11. Pavlik, P., Brawner, K., Olney, A., Mitrovic, A.: A review of student models used in intelligent tutoring systems. Des. Recommendations Intell. Tutoring Syst. **1**, 39–68 (2013)
12. Sheng, K., Chounta, I.A.: Beyond one-size-fits-all: personalizing computational proxies of the zone of proximal development through help-seeking behaviors. In: The 27th International Conference on Artificial Intelligence in Education (AIED 2026). Lecture Notes in Computer Science (LNCS), Springer Nature Switzerland AG (2026) to appear
13. Sutton, R.S., Barto, A.G.: Reinforcement Learning: An introduction, MIT Press Cambridge (1998)
14. Vygotsky, L.S.: Interaction between learning and development. In: Gauvain, M. (ed.) Readings on the Development of Children, pp. 34–40. Scientific American Books, New York (1978)

AI-Driven Analytics of Team Teaching: Understanding and Supporting Teachers' Spatial Pedagogy Behaviours

Yuchen Liu(✉), Roberto Martinez-Maldonado, Dwi Rahayu, Dragan Gasevic, and Sadia Nawaz

Monash University, Melbourne, Australia
{Yuchen.Liu1,Roberto.MartinezMaldonado,dwi.rahayu,dragan.gasevic,sadia.nawaz}@monash.edu

Abstract. Higher education classrooms are becoming increasingly complex due to massification, increasing student diversity, and interdisciplinary teaching demands. Team-teaching has emerged as a pedagogical response to these challenges, yet it introduces substantial enactment challenges. Spatial pedagogy offers a theoretically grounded lens to characterise these micro-level enactments. However, empirical examination of team-teaching enactment still relies on manual observation and video-based coding, which is costly and difficult to scale and therefore limits timely support. Recent AIED research has demonstrated the promise of teacher-facing orchestration support through dashboards and low-attention interfaces, yet most feedback remains student-centric and evidence is limited for supporting teachers' own behaviours in team-teaching classrooms. This study proposes an AI-driven multimodal classroom analytics system to understand and support teachers' spatial pedagogy behaviours in team-teaching classrooms.

Keywords: Spatial Pedagogy · Team Teaching · Classroom Analytics

1 Introduction

As higher education faces growing pressures from massification, increased student diversity, and the rise of interdisciplinary teaching, university classrooms have become more complex [13]. Teachers are expected to manage multiple responsibilities simultaneously, including delivering content, monitoring student engagement, and managing classroom interactions, while continuously adapting their teaching strategies to meet student needs [14,17]. In this context, team-teaching has emerged as a pedagogical response to these challenges [15]. Team-teaching refers to situations when two or more teachers collaboratively plan and co-lead the same classroom session, sharing responsibility for instruction in real-time [3]. When well-executed, team-teaching can enable distributed expertise and differentiated support [3,8]. However, team teaching also introduces substantial

E. G. Blanchard et al. (Eds.): AIED 2026, CCIS 3033, pp. 274–280, 2026.
https://doi.org/10.1007/978-3-032-29794-5_42

enactment challenges: teachers must coordinate their actions in shared classroom spaces while dynamically shifting between whole-class instruction, monitoring student activity, and interacting with groups, often without fixed scripts or stable role divisions [6]. These challenges may be exacerbated in higher education, where team teaching is frequently adopted as an ad hoc strategy [2].

A theoretically grounded way to examine these enactment challenges is through *spatial pedagogy* [11]. This perspective treats classroom space as a pedagogical resource: where teachers position themselves, how they move, and how close they are to students and learning resources can signal different instructional functions. Lim et al. [11] distinguish four classroom space types—*Authoritative*, *Interactional*, *Supervisory*, and *Personal*—which can be operationalised as observable *spatial pedagogy behaviours* to capture the micro-level enactment of teaching [12]. In practice, however, empirical examination of team-teaching enactment still typically relies on manual observation and video-based coding, which is costly and difficult to scale [1,4]. This limits opportunities to generate timely support for teachers.

Providing teachers with timely, actionable feedback about classroom dynamics remains a practical challenge. This has motivated a growing body of AIED work on teacher-facing orchestration support that aims to translate real-time classroom state estimates into timely, actionable cues while keeping teachers in the loop [5,7,9,16]. Across this line of research, teacher-facing interfaces span a spectrum from screen-based dashboards [5,7] to lower-attention-cost designs, including wearable mixed-reality displays [10]. Despite these advances, most existing teacher-facing feedback remains primarily student-centric: real-time indicators are typically inferred from students' learning traces and then surfaced to teachers, rather than being grounded in teachers' own teaching behaviours. In addition, most existing tools have been designed and evaluated primarily in single-teacher classrooms, leaving limited evidence on how analytics can be used to understand and support teaching behaviours in team-teaching classrooms. Due to these challenges, this study aims to explore following main research question and four sub-questions:

To what extent can AI-driven analytics based on multimodal classroom data be used to understand and support teachers' spatial pedagogy behaviours in team-teaching classrooms?

- **RQ1:** What does existing research on multimodal classroom analytics reveal about teachers' practices in classrooms?
- **RQ2:** To what extent can multimodal classroom analytics reveal variations in teachers' spatial pedagogy behaviours within team-teaching classrooms?
- **RQ3:** How can visual interfaces be designed to support teachers' reflection ***on*** the team-teaching classroom?
- **RQ4:** How can visual interfaces be designed to support teachers' reflection ***in*** the team-teaching classroom?

2 Methodology

To address the four research questions, this PhD project adopts a staged research programme that transitions from theoretical synthesis to empirical modeling and system evaluation (Fig. 1). First, to address RQ1, we will conduct a systematic literature review to synthesise how multimodal classroom analytics has been used to represent and support teachers' practices, identify common modalities and analytic approaches, and clarify gaps in linking analytics to collaborative teaching and reflective practice.

Second, we will leverage a previously collected multimodal dataset from authentic higher-education team-teaching sessions to develop and validate interpretable indicators of spatial pedagogy behaviours (RQ2-3). The dataset includes 36 two-hour sessions taught by triads of teachers, with indoor-positioning trajectories, individual headset audio, and human-coded spatial pedagogy behaviours, complemented by post-class teacher interviews. To answer RQ2, behavioural dynamics will be modelled using Transition Network Analysis on coded behaviours and compared across key contextual factors (e.g., teacher experience, cohort characteristics, and learning task design), while speech features (prosodic and discourse indicators) will be extracted and aligned to behavioural segments to provide multimodal evidence for behavioural variation. To address RQ3, interview transcripts will be analysed to understand how teachers interpret analytics, what makes indicators trustworthy and actionable, and what representations best support post-hoc reflection, producing a set of teacher-grounded design requirements. These outputs will be integrated into a teacher-facing visual interface prototype that translates multimodal indicators into concise reflection cues.

Finally, to address RQ4, the interface will be implemented and evaluated in new team-teaching classrooms to examine reflection-in-action. Teachers will access low-attention visual snapshots at natural transition points (e.g., short breaks), and the evaluation will triangulate (i) field observation and usage traces to examine appropriation, (ii) behavioural comparisons across adjacent teaching segments to assess immediate adjustment following consultation, and (iii) stimulated recall interviews to probe teachers' in-the-moment interpretation and perceived practicality.

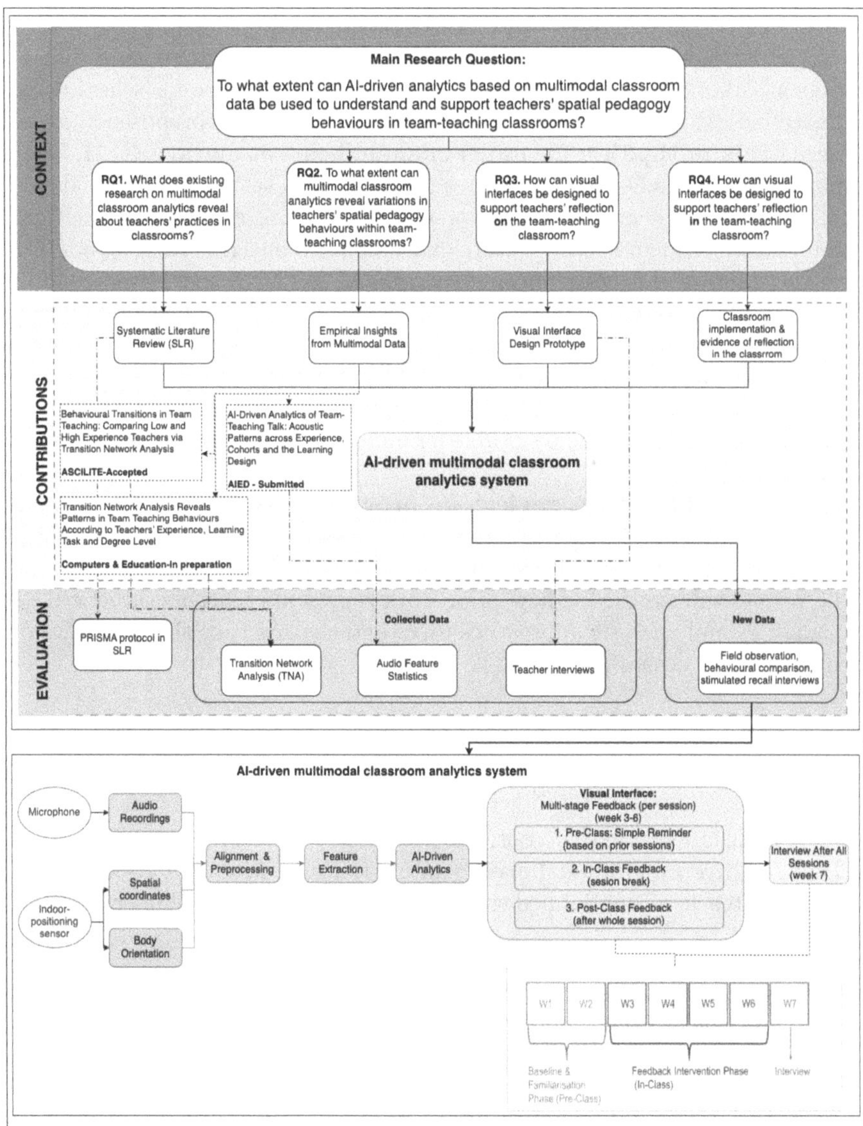

Fig. 1. Overview of the PhD thesis, linking RQ1-RQ4 to the planned contributions and evaluation.

3 Current Progress

- **Preliminary analyses on contextual variation (RQ2).** Using the previously collected sessions in which teachers wore the same sensing setup, we conducted initial analyses to examine how teachers' behaviours vary across contextual factors (e.g., teaching experience, learning design, and different student cohorts). These results provide formative evidence for selecting candidate indicators and feedback to be implemented in the proposed system.
- **Cross-talk mitigation for multi-channel headset audio (RQ2).** Due to multi-channel headset recordings in a team-teaching setting, substantial cross-talk (bleed across channels) was present, which can compromise transcription and subsequent speech-feature extraction. To mitigate this, we applied a weighted fusion of spectral masking and ECAPA-TDNN speaker-embedding–based masking to reduce cross-channel interference. We verified suitability for downstream analysis by transcribing audio using WhisperX and computing word error rate (WER). After cross-talk mitigation, WER decreased from 158% to 21%, indicating a substantial improvement in transcript quality and making the processed audio suitable for our subsequent speech feature extraction and analyses.
- **Systematic literature review in progress (RQ1).** We are currently conducting a PRISMA-guided systematic literature review on multimodal classroom analytics and teacher practices. Initial screening is underway, and the review will synthesise how prior work represents teachers' practices, the modalities and analytic approaches used, and the key gaps that motivate our empirical and design phases (RQ2–RQ4).

4 Expected Contributions

This research is expected to contribute to the AIED community by advancing how AI-driven multimodal classroom analytics can be used to understand and support teachers' spatial pedagogy behaviours in team-teaching classrooms. Specifically:

- **Theory contribution.** This study extends spatial pedagogy beyond its predominant single-teacher operationalisation by conceptualising spatial pedagogical behaviours as observable, time-varying patterns that can be enacted by multiple teachers within the same classroom. Crucially, it proposes an AI-enabled operationalisation that characterises these patterns from multimodal classroom data (e.g., positioning and speech), enabling spatial pedagogy to be studied at scale without relying solely on manual observation. This conceptual shift specifies a multi-teacher unit of analysis for spatial pedagogy research and supports systematic investigation of how instructional space is enacted in team-teaching classrooms.

- **Educational practice contribution.** This study aims to demonstrate how AI-driven multimodal sensing and analytics can be integrated into team-teaching classrooms to provide teachers with interpretable insights into their spatial pedagogical behaviours. The system applies AI-based preprocessing and modelling to translate raw positioning and audio streams into behaviour-grounded indicators and concise feedback cues. Specifically, we will design and implement a teacher-facing visual interface with two feedback modes: (1) a low-attention, rapid-feedback view (e.g., pre-class reminders and brief in-class snapshots during session breaks) that surfaces one AI-generated actionable cue without information overload to support in-the-moment instructional adjustment; and (2) a richer post-class report that summarises and visualises session-level patterns of spatial pedagogical behaviours to support post-lesson reflection. By making implicit spatial patterns more visible and actionable, the system aims to support reflective practice and coordination among team-teachers.

References

1. Alfredo, R., et al.: Teamteachingviz: benefits, challenges, and ethical considerations of using a multimodal analytics dashboard to support team teaching reflection. In: Proceedings of the International Conference on Learning Analytics & Knowledge, pp. 58–69 (2025). https://doi.org/10.1145/3706468.3706475
2. Álvarez, I., Fuertes Gutiérrez, M., Gallardo Barbarroja, M.: Team teaching in languages: a scoping review of approaches and practices in higher education. Innov. Lang. Learn. Teach. **18**(1), 59–77 (2024). https://doi.org/10.1080/17501229.2023.2229798
3. Baeten, M., Simons, M.: Student teachers' team teaching: models, effects, and conditions for implementation. Teach. Teach. Educ. **41**, 92–110 (2014). https://doi.org/10.1016/j.tate.2014.03.010
4. Decuyper, A., Simons, M., Vanderlinde, R.: Teachers' effective teaching behaviour during team teaching: a video-based observation study. Stud. Educ. Eval. **86**, 101494 (2025). https://doi.org/10.1016/j.stueduc.2025.101494
5. Dickler, R., et al.: Examining the use of a teacher alerting dashboard during remote learning. In: International Conference on AI in Education, pp. 134–138. Springer (2021). https://doi.org/10.1007/978-3-030-78270-2_24
6. Do, M.L., Hascher, T.: Peer cooperation during teaching in paired field placements: forms and challenges. Front. Learn. Res. **11**(1), 94–122 (2023). https://doi.org/10.14786/flr.v11i1.1305
7. Gupta, A., et al.: Affective teacher tools: affective class report card and dashboard. In: International Conference on AI in Education, pp. 178–189. Springer (2021). https://doi.org/10.1007/978-3-030-78292-4_15
8. Hellier, S., Davidson, L.: Team teaching in nursing education. J. Continuing Educ. Nursing **49**(4), 186–192 (2018). https://doi.org/10.3928/00220124-20180320-09
9. Holstein, K., McLaren, B.M., Aleven, V.: Student learning benefits of a mixed-reality teacher awareness tool in ai-enhanced classrooms. In: International Conference on on AI in Education, pp. 154–168. Springer (2018). https://doi.org/10.1007/978-3-319-93843-1_12

10. Jin, Q., et al.: Lumilo 2: a scalable mixed reality system for real-time teacher analytics and intervention (2025)
11. Lim, F.V., O'Halloran, K.L., Podlasov, A.: Spatial pedagogy: mapping meanings in the use of classroom space. Camb. J. Educ. **42**(2), 235–251 (2012). https://doi.org/10.1080/0305764X.2012.676629
12. Liu, Y., et al.: Behavioural transitions in team teaching: comparing low and high experience teachers via transition network analysis. In: Proceedings of the ASCILITE 2025 Conference on Future-Focused: Educating in an Era of Continuous Change (2025). https://doi.org/10.65106/apubs.2025.2634
13. Maringe, F., Sing, N.: Teaching large classes in an increasingly internationalising higher education environment: pedagogical, quality and equity issues. High. Educ. **67**, 761–782 (2014)
14. Reinke, W.M., Herman, K.C., Copeland, C.B.: Student engagement: the importance of the classroom context. In: Handbook of Research on Student Engagement, pp. 529–544 (2022). https://doi.org/10.1007/978-3-031-07853-8_25
15. Roberts, M., Bissett, M., Wilding, C.: Team teaching as a strategy for enhancing teaching about theory-into-practice. Innov. Educ. Teach. Int. **60**(1), 26–36 (2023). https://doi.org/10.1080/14703297.2021.1966490
16. Segal, A., et al.: Keeping the teacher in the loop: technologies for monitoring group learning in real-time. In: International Conference on AI in Education, pp. 64–76. Springer (2017)
17. Thompson, G., Creagh, S., Stacey, M., Hogan, A., Mockler, N.: Researching teachers' time use: complexity, challenges and a possible way forward. Aust. Educ. Res. **51**(4), 1647–1670 (2024). https://doi.org/10.1007/s13384-023-00657-1

Design and Evaluation of an AI-Mediated Oral Interview System for Authorship Evidence: An Evidence-Centered Validity-By-Design Approach

Karen Haeng-A. Kim(✉)

The University of Queensland, St. Lucia, QLD 4072, Australia
haenga.kim@uq.edu.au

Abstract. The widespread use of Generative Artificial Intelligence (GenAI) has complicated the interpretation of authorship in student work, as written submissions no longer reliably mirror student understanding. Text-matching tools cannot verify authorship, and human-led oral interviews, although effective, are difficult to implement at scale. Therefore, this doctoral research addresses this challenge by developing a conversational AI system that conducts a structured oral interview for students to explain and justify their submitted work. The system combines Evidence-Centered Assessment Design (ECD) with Human-AI Shared Regulation in Learning (HASRL) to realize learning-oriented assessment. A Finite-State Machine (FSM) prompt architecture probes conceptual reasoning, writing process awareness, and written-oral alignment, producing a structured report card. Methodologically, the research uses a two-phase design and evaluation study. In phase 1, ECD-based interview process is translated into AI prompt, which will then be iteratively refined through scenario-based red teaming. In phase 2, students will engage with the AI system while educators will evaluate the quality of AI-generated questions and report cards, followed by interviews from both stakeholders about perceived validity and usability of the system. The study is expected to contribute a clear authorship construct, a pedagogically informed AI prompting approach, and a scalable working prototype for eliciting evidence of students' understanding of their own work in the AI era.

Keywords: academic integrity · Evidence-Centered Design · Human-AI Shared Regulation in Learning · Finite-State Machine AI prompting · red teaming

1 Introduction

1.1 Current Issues: AI, Assessment, and Academic Integrity

Generative Artificial Intelligence (GenAI) is disrupting entrenched assessment practices in higher education, particularly those relying on written submissions, due to its abilities to respond to user prompts and generate human-like text (Lodge et al., 2023). Such capabilities undermine the reliability of assessment scores when students use GenAI

E. G. Blanchard et al. (Eds.): AIED 2026, CCIS 3033, pp. 281–287, 2026.
https://doi.org/10.1007/978-3-032-29794-5_43

throughout the task completion process. Not only does it weaken accurate measurement of students' current level of understanding, but, when used haphazardly, it also threatens the development of accountable practices expected in professional contexts after graduation (Guerrero-Dib et al., 2020). Banning the use of AI cannot be a solution as AI is already pervasive in daily life. Educators are, therefore, confronted with a fundamental conundrum.

How can academic integrity in assessment be maintained in the AI era when written submissions alone can no longer guarantee authorship or student understanding?

In response to this question, Viva Voce (Vivas, Latin for 'living voice'), mainly used in doctoral thesis defence, has been proposed. It supplements written thesis with verbal explanation, requiring students to articulate their knowledge about their own thesis (Brogan et al., 2024). Despite its benefits for academic integrity, it is time- and labor-intensive, limiting scalability, especially in large-cohort contexts (O'Riordan et al., 2025). Also, interviewer variability and power imbalances between assessor and student lead to reliability and fairness (Crossouard, 2011). Therefore, this thesis proposes an AI-mediated viva system that may reduce those challenges of human-led vivas for eliciting authorship evidence.

1.2 Proposed Solution (the State of the Art in AIED)

Recent advances in AI offer new possibilities for addressing the limitations of human-led vivas. Rather than functioning as plagiarism detectors, AI systems can support vivas by (1) Automatic Questions Generation (AQG) (Ebrahimzadeh et al., 2025), (2) Spoken Dialogue System (SDS) and Intelligent Personal Assistants (IPAs), which help maintain adaptive dialogue contingent on students' responses (Ericsson & Johanson, 2023), and (3) Natural Language Processing (NLP)-based feedback report for offering personalized, criterion-referenced feedback based on semantic alignment between students' oral explanations and their written work (Karatay & Xu, 2025).

Building on these capabilities, this PhD project conceptualizes an AI-mediated dialogic assessment system. Figure 1. Illustrates how human and AI collaboration works in the proposed AI-mediated oral interview system.

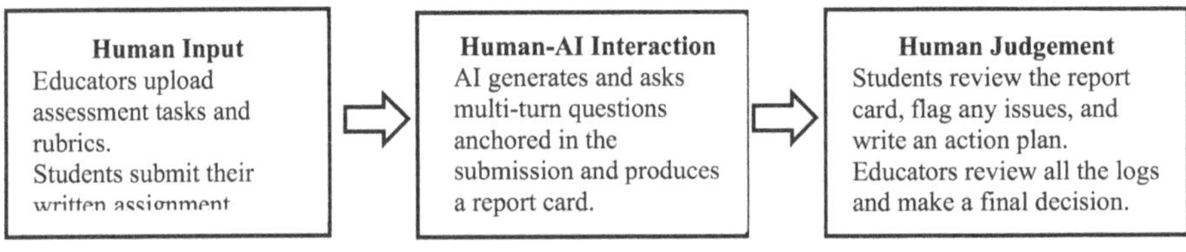

Fig. 1. Human-AI collaboration in the AI-mediated viva system

First, educators upload course information, assessment tasks, and rubrics to establish the context, and students are asked to submit their written work. The AI tool then (1) generates questions anchored in the submitted text, (2) conducts a multi-turn dialogic interview contingent on students' responses, and (3) produces a structured report card. After engaging with the AI tool, students can review the report card. If issues are found, students can flag issues for educators to review, followed by an action plan writing activity. The aim of such activity is to encourage students to build metacognitive awareness, by reflecting on their interactions, and evaluative judgement, by evaluating their own performance for further improvement. All the information generated by the AI and students will be reviewed by educators, who will be the final decision maker.

2 Theoretical Framework

The overarching theory behind the study is Socio Cognitive Theory (SCT) in that dialogic assessment inherently engages social interactions between assessor and student. Moreover, authorship-focused questions aim to reveal students' cognitive and metacognitive awareness of their own submitted work. Therefore, I employed SCT as the backbone of this study both for assessment design and as underpinning learning theory.

2.1 Socio Cognitive Assessment Theory: Evidence-Centered Design (ECD)

The proposed assessment framework is based on Mislevy's (2018) Evidence-Centered Assessment Design (ECD) principle, which provides a principled structure of student model, evidence model, and task model. Student model proposes the claim that the student is the author of the submitted work. This claim requires evidence, such as their ability to articulate rationale behind the selection of the theories. As this evidence is not observable, measurable tasks should be formulated, such as asking students to explain why a particular theory was chosen, not the others, to address a given problem. These tasks, the resulting evidence, and the underlying construct must be explicitly aligned through a coherent chain of inference. Therefore, the first aim of the study is to design questions by identifying what constitutes authorship.

2.2 Socio Cognitive Learning Theory: Human-AI Shared Regulation in Learning (HASRL)

Building on the theory-informed assessment design, a conversational AI system is added to complete the human-AI collaborative learning-oriented assessment logic to efficiently and validly trace evidence of student understanding of their submitted work through oral explanations. Based on Järvelä at el.'s (2023) Human-AI Shared Regulation in Learning (HASRL) framework, this thesis introduces an abridged-version of HASRL model linking to ECD-based conceptualized assessment logic. The aim of this condensed model is to clearly identify the elements of evidence that should be gathered during human-AI interactions to support the authorship claim (Fig. 2).

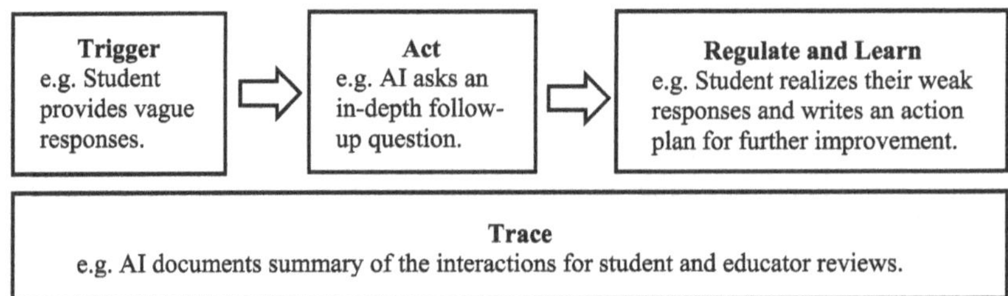

Fig. 2. An abridged-version of Human-AI Share Regulation in Learning (HASRL) model

2.3 Implementation of the Conceptualized Design in the AI System

Prompting is understood as the practice of providing structured input to a large language model (LLM) to shape its behavior, outputs, and reasoning. In this sense, prompting functions as an interface between human intent and model inference, underscoring the central role of human-defined logic in purposeful AI operation.

The conversational behaver of the AI system is guided by rule-based conditional prompting principles while flexible, personalised interaction is performed by LLM. Conditional branching (IF-THEN) was a critical design feature, as the system delivers assessment rather than instruction, thereby underscoring the controlled logical sequence of interaction (e.g. IF vague responses detected, THEN Follow-up question MUST be asked). Also, behavioral constraints (e.g. Do not repeatedly probe the same issue), anchoring rule (e.g. Always ask questions by referring to a sentence from the submission), and safeguards (e.g. Do not treat limited English skills as weak evidence by default) are added to minimize conversational drift and hallucinations.

Two complementary assessment logics were implemented: (1) Cognitive Performance Assessment through Verbalization (CPAV), which elicits evidence of conceptual reasoning underlying the written work, and (2) a Process-Based Verification Layer (PBVL), which probes process awareness through questions targeting authorial intention and writing decisions. These logics were refined through iterative interaction with ChatGPT, during which the system was tested on diverse writing samples, including simulated ghostwriter cases and weak-writer but genuine-author cases, in order to mitigate potential false positives and false negatives in authorship inference.

These design principles were subsequently formalized into a Finite-State Machine (FSM) AI prompting, which strictly follows the logical sequence of assessment process, with constraints and safeguards added, ensuring consistent, rule-bound execution of the assessment process.

3 Methodology

3.1 Research Questions

This two-phase design and evaluation study examines the validity of an AI-mediated oral interview system as an authorship evidence-generating tool. Phase 1 aims to check internal system validation to ensure stable AI behavior when students are engaging with the system. Scenario-based red teaming is applied to refine the system's vulnerability by identifying breakdown elements when attached.

***RQ1. Red teaming**: Which breakdown elements emerge from the AI and what strategies are used to resolve the issues?*

To respond to RQ1, two AI experts will be invited for a think-aloud session to diagnose and come up with solutions for prompt refinement. Four scenarios will be used: (1) a real author with limited English skills, (2) a real author with extremely minimal responses, (3) a fake author reading the submitted work, and (4) a fake author responding with generic answers.

With the finalized prompt after Phase 1, Phase 2 aims to analyze (1) evidence gathered from the interaction logs to address the revised HASRL framework and (2) stakeholder evaluation of the system's perceived validity and usability.

***RQ2. Trigger and Act**: Are there any patterns of students' responses that lead to follow-up questions?*

***RQ3. Trace**: To what extent are the defined construct elements shown from students' responses?*

***RQ4. Regulate and Learn**: Which evaluative judgement elements emerge from action plan writing logs?*

***RQ5. Perceived validity**: To what extent do AI-generated interview questions and report cards represent the authorship construct, as judged by human experts?*

***RQ6. User acceptability**: How do students and educators feel about using the AI system as a learning-oriented assessment tool for authorship integrity and student understanding?* (Table 1)

3.2 Research Design Overview

Table 1. Research design overview

Phase	RQ	Data collection	Data analysis
Phase 1. Design and Development	RQ1. System validation through AI prompting investigation	Think-aloud audio during scenario-based red teaming by experts (n = 2)	Codebook thematic analysis Frequency descriptive statistics
Phase 2. Evaluation Students: Lab study Instructors: Think-aloud and interview	RQ2–4. Evidence evaluation RQ 5. Perceived validity	1. Students' submissions (n = 30) 2. Students' oral interaction logs including questions, report cards, and action plans 3. Educators' think-aloud (n = 4)	Construct-evidence mapping thematic analysis

(continued)

Table 1. *(continued)*

Phase	RQ	Data collection	Data analysis
	RQ6. Usability and pedagogical implication	1.Student survey (n = 30) 2. Student (n = 4) and educator (n = 4) interview	Frequence descriptive statistics Reflexive thematic analysis

4 Expected Contributions and Impact of the Research

This research reconceptualizes authorship in AI-permissive assessment contexts as students' ability to understand and explain their own submitted work, positioning AI as a tool for evidence elicitation rather than outcome verification. It has practical implications for higher education, particularly in academic writing, where oral interviews can supplement written submissions to evidence student contribution. In terms of application, the proposed AI-mediated oral interview system functions as both a learning tool for academic communication and a scalable method for gathering authorship evidence. Furthermore, it provides a structured prompting approach for generating adaptive follow-up questions in multi-turn dialogue designed to elicit evidence.

Acknowledgments. This study was funded by an Australian Government Research Training Program Scholarship.

Disclosure of Interests. The author has no competing interests to declare that are relevant to the content of this article.

References

Brogan, M., Gooding, B., Feld, F.: The viva voce: a post-pandemic assessment. Law Teacher **58**(4), 442–468 (2024)
Crossouard, B.: The doctoral viva voce as a cultural practice: the gendered production of academic subjects. Gend. Educ. **23**, 313–329 (2011)
Ebrahimzadeh, M., Shibani, A., Buckingham Shum, S.: Coauthorship integrity: reconceptualizing assessment validity for the age of generative AI (2025)
Ericsson, E., Johansson, S.: English speaking practice with conversational AI: lower secondary students' educational experiences over time. Comput. Educ. Artif. Intell. **5**, 100164 (2023)
Guerrero-Dib, J.G., Portales, L., Heredia-Escorza, Y.: Impact of academic integrity on workplace ethical behaviour. Int. J. Educ. Integr. **16**, 2 (2020)
Karatay, Y.: Using spoken dialog systems to assess L2 learners' oral skills in a local language testing context. In: Yan, X., Dimova, S., Ginther, A. (eds.) Local language testing, vol. 61, pp. 231–252. Springer (2023)
Lodge, J.M., Howard, S., Bearman, M., Dawson, P., et al.: Assessment reform for the age of artificial intelligence. Tertiary Education Quality and Standards Agency (2023)

Mislevy, R.: Sociocognitive Foundations of Educational Measurement. Routledge, New York, NY (2018)

O'Riordan, F., Thangaraj, J., Girme, P., Ward, M.: Interactive oral assessment: staff perceptions, challenges and benefits of this robust, authentic assessment design approach. Innov. Educ. Teach. Int. **63**(2), 494–507 (2026)

Järvelä, S., Ngueyn, A., Hadwin, A.: Human and artificial intelligence collaboration for socially shared regulation in learning. Br. J. Edu. Technol. **54**(5), 1057–1076 (2023)

What Calculus Should We Teach in the Age of AI? Identifying and Improving Higher-Order Thinking in College Math

Qianou Ma[(✉)], Sherry Tongshuang Wu, and Kenneth R. Koedinger

Carnegie Mellon University, Pittsburgh, PA, USA
{qianoum,sherryw,krk}@cs.cmu.edu

Abstract. In the age of AI, procedural calculus skills (e.g., symbolic differentiation) are increasingly automated. However, higher-order reasoning—formulating mathematical models, articulating assumptions, and evaluating solutions—remains essential for effective humans. Traditional calculus instruction emphasizes execution over interpretation and validation, leaving students underprepared to use mathematics meaningfully in real-world contexts. This proposed research aims to develop and evaluate an AI-powered Calculus Teachable Agent that re-centers instruction around mathematical model communication and model evaluation. Human students will teach AI students to solve contextual calculus problems and construct rubrics to diagnose AI-generated errors. A randomized controlled study will compare higher-order-focused instruction with traditional practice, measuring learning, transfer, motivation, and AI collaboration ability. We aim to identify learnable higher-order calculus skills and empirically test whether an AI-supported teachable agent improves students' reasoning in authentic problem-solving contexts.

Keywords: GenAI Literacy · Calculus Teaching · Teachable Agent

1 Problem Statement and Research Questions

Calculus education has long emphasized procedural fluency, focusing on students' ability to compute derivatives, integrals, and limits accurately. Yet these are precisely the skills most easily automated by AI systems. As large language models (LLMs) and symbolic engines increasingly handle algebraic manipulation, the human role in mathematical problem solving shifts toward specifying problems clearly, articulating assumptions, interpreting outputs, and evaluating whether results are meaningful. Nonetheless, many introductory calculus curricula still prioritize computation over interpretation and validation [4].

Instructors rarely have time to design realistic contexts or evaluate reasoning quality, leading to a focus on easily gradable procedural accuracy over sense-making and transfer. Efforts to make mathematics more meaningful include

E. G. Blanchard et al. (Eds.): AIED 2026, CCIS 3033, pp. 288–293, 2026.
https://doi.org/10.1007/978-3-032-29794-5_44

storytelling [7] and personalization [1], which help learners make sense of complex information and increase motivation. Projects like Calculus in Context [4], RME [6], and SimCalc [12] help a wide range of students (from middle school to college) connect calculus with real-world scenarios such as population growth or motion. However, these curricula could require years of expert design, and primarily support concept understanding rather than higher-order reasoning.

Meanwhile, LLMs create opportunities for adaptive scaffolding on reasoning exercises and automatic generation of math word problems (e.g., MATHWELL; [5]). ChatGPT deployments in college calculus classrooms [3,13] show that AI can personalize practice and offer instant feedback. However, GenAI has mainly been supporting execution, not reasoning. As prior work found, students often copy AI outputs without critique, highlighting the need for guided evaluation [8]. Nonetheless, deliberate practice that drives expertise is largely absent for modeling and validation skills in calculus.

Research Questions. Our proposed project aims to address the gap between traditional calculus instruction and the demands of AI-mediated quantitative reasoning by exploring these questions:

RQ1 **Discovery:** What higher-order thinking skills are needed and learnable in AI-mediated calculus problem solving?
RQ2 **Learning:** Does a teachable-agent intervention improve students' model formulation and evaluation skills?
RQ3 **Human-AI Collaboration:** Does training on higher-order reasoning improve students' ability to use LLMs for contextual calculus tasks?
RQ4 **Basic vs. Higher-Order Skills:** How do procedural skills interact with higher-order reasoning gains?

2 Theoretical Framing and Proposed Solution

This work is grounded in learning-by-teaching paradigms and emerging frameworks of human-AI collaboration. Prior teachable-agent systems, such as Betty's Brain [2] and SimStudent [11], demonstrate that students deepen their understanding when they must teach or diagnose an artificial learner. In other STEM domains, our prior work in computer science education demonstrates how LLMs can support higher-order cognitive processes. When students taught an AI to debug code in a teachable agent [10] or wrote natural-language requirements for programs in an interactive tutor [9], they developed stronger skills in communicating inputs and evaluating outputs, core abilities for human-AI collaboration.

A parallel could be drawn to identify which skills matter most for effective mathematical usage when AI tools are available (Fig. 1). No prior work provides control comparisons between traditional versus AI-assisted instructions' effectiveness on real-world math-solving abilities, which we aim to address.

Proposed Solution: The Calculus Teachable Agent. Our system-in-development consists of three interacting components:

1. **Human Student** (role-play a tutor): Creates and critiques calculus problems based on real-world scenarios or datasets to practice mathematical problem formulation and evaluation skills.

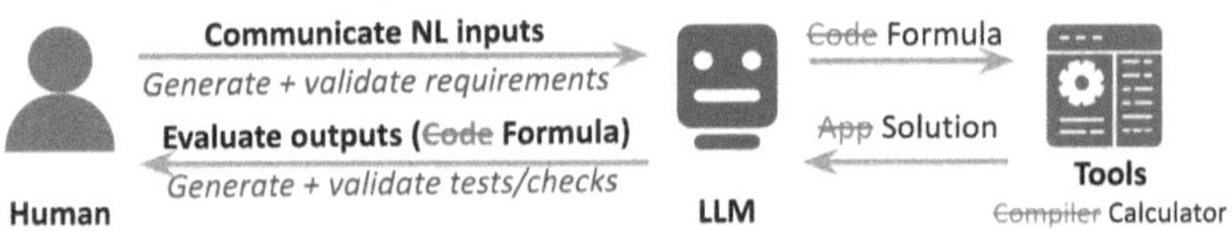

Fig. 1. The fundamental human-LLM workflow with a parallel between computer science (our prior work, greyed out) and math (this proposed work).

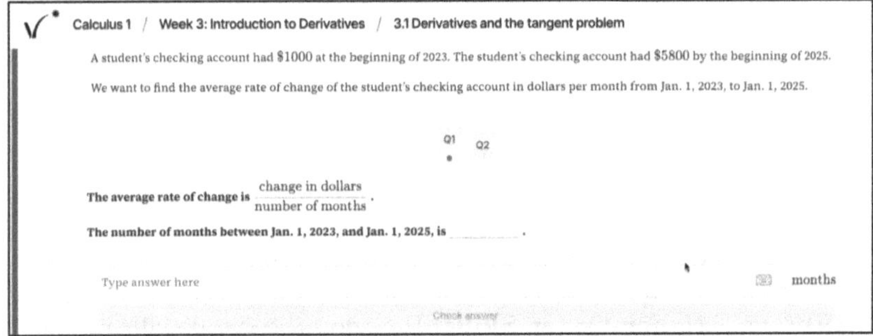

Fig. 2. A scenario problem in Calculus I.

2. **AI Student** (teachable agent): Attempts to solve the problems that may make different mistakes (e.g., common mistakes can be adopted from existing datasets such as Datashop, like "applying chain rule incorrectly").
3. **AI Tutor**: Generate feedback on the quality of the problem and the completeness of reasoning and evaluations, using rubrics on whether key variables, relationships, and conditions are specified.

There will be scaffolding mechanisms to support novice learners through the cognitively demanding tasks, such as using multiple-choice questions instead of asking students to construct calculus problems from scratch.

Illustrative Example. For a concrete example, students may see an average rate of change unit question in their regular Calculus I class (Fig. 2). For the alternative version in our teachable agent, students may receive a realistic bank balance table and be asked to author a problem based on the dataset (Table 1).

Table 1. Example Dataset for Problem Authoring

Date	Jan23	Apr23	Jul23	Oct23	Jan24	Apr24	Jul24	Oct24	Jan25
Balance ($)	1000	1300	2600	3000	3900	4600	5200	5600	5800

Table 2. Example AI Student Solutions for Average Rate of Change

AI Student 1 (Linear Assumption)	**AI Student 2 (Wrong Denominator)**	**Correct Solution**
From Jan 2023 to Apr 2023, the balance increased by $300 in 3 months, so $300 \div 3 = 100.$ Since savings increase monthly, the average rate of change is $100/month.	There are 9 data points, so 9 intervals. The change in balance is $5800 - 1000 = 4800.$ Average rate of change is $4800 \div 9 = 533.3.$	Average rate of change = $\frac{\Delta \$}{\Delta t} = \frac{4800}{24} = 200.$

The AI student may produce multiple solution attempts (Table 2), such as incorrectly dividing total change by the number of data points rather than elapsed time, or assuming local linearity. Humans are then required to design rubrics to grade these solutions and provide feedback by explaining errors. The rubrics function as mathematical test cases, which may include explicitly specifying quantities, plugging in values (defining the function, input, and expected output), and checking units. For this example, the rubric may include three criteria:

$$(1)\ \Delta \$ = 5800 - 1000 = 4800, \quad (2)\ \Delta t = 2 \text{ years} = 24 \text{ months}, \quad (3)\ \frac{4800}{24} = 200.$$

These rubrics then help human students explain which criterion an incorrect solution violates. In this way, calculus becomes an exercise in reasoning, validation, and communication rather than mere computation.

3 Methodology

The proposed project proceeds through a sequence of phases to iteratively refine the system and evaluate its impact on learning.

System Design and Task Refinement. We are currently developing the Calculus Teachable Agent by adapting our prior LLM-based teachable-agent infrastructure to calculus contexts. Tasks will be aligned with existing introductory calculus units such as derivatives, related rates, and optimization, ensuring that conceptual coverage remains constant while the structure of practice changes. In parallel, we will conduct small-scale pilot sessions and think-aloud studies with students to refine problem prompts, rubric scaffolds, AI-generated misconception variants, and feedback mechanisms.

Randomized Controlled Study. We will conduct a randomized controlled experiment comparing the teachable-agent intervention with traditional procedural practice on a unit (one week) of instruction on a Calculus topic (Fig. 3). Instructional explanations and conceptual materials will remain identical across conditions; only the practice question format differs.

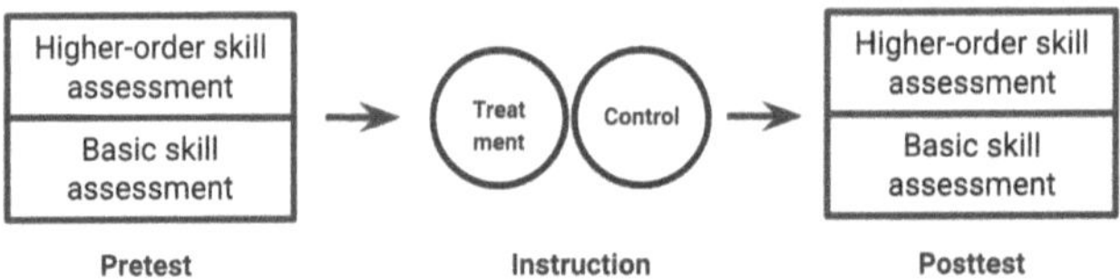

Fig. 3. Randomized controlled study design.

Evaluation and Analysis. Higher-order reasoning learning gains will be measured using isomorphic tasks that require students to construct and evaluate mathematical formulations in novel contexts. Procedural fluency gains will be assessed through quizzes drawn from standard coursework. Pre- and post-tests will allow examination of whether focusing on reasoning influences procedural learning. To examine transfer beyond instructional tasks, students will complete problem-solving activities using an LLM, such as modeling an epidemic or financial scenario. Prompts and solutions will be analyzed to assess the quality of human-AI collaboration. In addition, surveys will measure motivation, engagement, and perceived relevance of calculus before and after the intervention.

4 Expected Contributions

Our prior work deploying LLM-based teachable agents in computer science demonstrated that students who taught or debugged AI agents developed stronger debugging skills [10]. These are preliminary findings that learning-by-teaching could cultivate higher-order reasoning. In this work, we aim to extend the approach to quantitative reasoning domains in college mathematics instruction. Theoretically, this work seeks to operationalize higher-order calculus reasoning in the context of AI collaboration and clarify the relationship between procedural fluency and model specification and evaluation skills. Practically, we hope to provide a pathway for integrating AI-supported reasoning activities into existing calculus curricula without disrupting topic coverage, thereby preparing students for AI-mediated quantitative work.

Acknowledgments. This proposed study is funded by Learnvia. Published works of the author were partially supported by the National Science Foundation (award CNS-2213791, 2414915) and the Google Academic Research Award.

References

1. Bernacki, M.L., Walkington, C.: The role of situational interest in personalized learning. J. Educ. Psychol. **110**(6), 864–881 (2018). https://doi.org/10.1037/edu0000250
2. Biswas, G., Segedy, J.R., Bunchongchit, K.: From design to implementation to practice a learning by teaching system: Betty's brain. Int. J. Artif. Intell. Educ. **26**(1), 350–364 (2016). https://doi.org/10.1007/s40593-015-0057-9
3. Buentello-Montoya, D.A.: Computers as a tool to empower students and enhance their learning experience: A social sciences case study. Educ. Sci. (Basel) **13**(9), 886 (2023). https://doi.org/10.3390/educsci13090886
4. Callahan, J., Cox, D., Hoffman, K., O'Shea, D., Pollatsek, H., Senechal, L.: Calculus in Context (2008). https://textbooks.aimath.org/textbooks/approved-textbooks/callahan/
5. Christ, B.R., Kropko, J., Hartvigsen, T.: MATHWELL: generating educational math word problems using teacher annotations. In: Al-Onaizan, Y., Bansal, M., Chen, Y.N. (eds.) Findings of the Association for Computational Linguistics: EMNLP 2024, PA, USA, pp. 11914–11938. Association for Computational Linguistics, Stroudsburg (2024). https://doi.org/10.18653/v1/2024.findings-emnlp.696
6. Da, N.T.: Approach to realistic mathematics education in teaching calculus for high school students: a case of the application of derivatives. Int. J. Prof. Dev. Learn. Learn. **4**(1), ep2203 (2022). https://doi.org/10.30935/ijpdll/11832
7. Holdener, J.A., Jones, B.D.: Calculus homework: a storied approach. Primus **29**(1), 21–42 (2019). https://doi.org/10.1080/10511970.2017.1394946
8. Ma, Q., Koedinger, K.R., Wu, T.: Not everyone wins with LLMs: behavioral patterns and pedagogical implications for AI literacy in programmatic data science. In: Proceedings of the 2026 CHI Conference on Human Factors in Computing Systems. CHI '26, New York, NY, USA, pp. 1–22. Association for Computing Machinery (2026). https://doi.org/10.1145/3772318.3791283
9. Ma, Q., Peng, W., Yang, C., Shen, H., Koedinger, K., Wu, T.: What should we engineer in prompts? Training humans in requirement-driven LLM use. ACM Trans. Comput. Hum. Interact. **32**(4), 1–27 (2025). https://doi.org/10.1145/3731756
10. Ma, Q., Shen, H., Koedinger, K., Wu, S.T.: How to teach programming in the AI era? Using LLMs as a teachable agent for debugging. In: Olney, A.M., Chounta, IA., Liu, Z., Santos, O.C., Bittencourt, I.I. (eds.) AIED 2024. LNCS, vol. 14829, pp. 265–279. Springer, Cham (2024). https://doi.org/10.1007/978-3-031-64302-6_19
11. Matsuda, N., et al.: Tuning cognitive tutors into a platform for learning-by-teaching with SimStudent technology. In: International Workshop on Adaptation and Personalization in E-B/Learning using Pedagogic Conversational Agents (APLeC), pp. 20–25 (2010). https://ceur-ws.org/Vol-587/paper4.pdf
12. Roschelle, J., et al.: Integration of technology, curriculum, and professional development for advancing middle school mathematics: Three large-scale studies. Am. Educ. Res. J. **47**(4), 833–878 (2010). https://www.jstor.org/stable/40928357
13. Torres-Peña, R.C., Peña-González, D., Chacuto-López, E., Ariza, E.A., Vergara, D.: Updating calculus teaching with AI: a classroom experience. Educ. Sci. (Basel) **14**(9), 1019 (2024). https://doi.org/10.3390/educsci14091019

Exploring GenAI-Enabled Multimodal Feedback Processing in Collaborative Language Learning

Xinyu Guo and Yun Wen(✉)

National Institution of Education, Nanyang Technological University, Singapore, Singapore
yun.wen@nie.edu.sg

Abstract. Advances in GenAI-enabled multimodal feedback have shown promising potential for supporting second language learning. However, empirical research remains limited regarding how students interact with and process such multimodal feedback in collaborative group settings. To address this gap, this study investigates how feedback processing patterns are associated with learning outcomes and further explores how cognitive and socio-emotional interactions, as well as feedback uptake, emerge during learners' engaging with GenAI-enabled feedback in collaborative learning. This exploratory mixed-methods study was conducted using a self-designed AI-powered vocabulary learning system for Primary 2 students learning Chinese as a second language. A total of 83 students from four classes used the system for over 1 year. By extending the student–feedback interaction model from an individual to a group-level perspective in GenAI-promoted collaborative learning, this study aims to advance a process-oriented understanding of multimodal feedback processing and provide practical implications for educators and learning designers regarding the effective integration of GenAI-enabled feedback in collaborative language learning contexts.

Keywords: Generative AI · Multimodal Feedback · Collaborative Learning · Second Language Learning

1 Introduction

Studies have increasingly recognized feedback as a process through which learners make sense of information from various sources and use it to enhance their work or learning strategies [4]. Accordingly, feedback is conceptualized as a dynamic interaction rather than a static transmission of information about strengths, weaknesses, and ways to improve [10]. This perspective emphasizes the central role of the learner in engaging with feedback to improve subsequent learning performance. The rapid development of artificial intelligence (AI) has further reinforced this shift by enabling instant, adaptive feedback tailored to the diverse needs of students [17]. In particular, generative AI (GenAI) technologies, incorporating text, audio, visuals, gestures, and spatial elements, enables multimodal feedback to provide richer and more engaging support for learners [8]. Several studies have investigated GenAI-enabled multimodal feedback in language

E. G. Blanchard et al. (Eds.): AIED 2026, CCIS 3033, pp. 294–299, 2026.
https://doi.org/10.1007/978-3-032-29794-5_45

learning and have shown that such feedback can effectively promote the learning process by stimulating students' interest and affective engagement, guiding them to express intended meanings more clearly [1], and fostering deeper cognitive engagement and metalinguistic awareness [12], particularly in second language (L2) writing tasks [13]. These findings highlight that multimodal feedback offers both cognitive and affective affordances that enhance language learning engagement [11].

However, existing studies largely focus how individual learners cognitively and affectively engage with GenAI feedback [6], with limited attention to how L2 students process such multimodal feedback in collaborative settings. In group contexts, feedback effectiveness depends not only on its design or learners' characteristics, but also on how members collectively interpret, negotiate, and act upon it during interaction. Therefore, empirical research is needed to examine how feedback processing unfolds in authentic collaborative learning. To address this gap, this study investigates how feedback processing patterns relate to learning outcomes and how cognitive and socio-emotional interactions emerge during engagement with GenAI-enabled feedback.

This study was conducted using ARCHe 2.0, a self-designed AI-powered multimodal feedback system developed for lower-primary students learning Chinese in Singapore. In Singapore, students learning Chinese as an L2 come from diverse cultural backgrounds and display varying levels of language proficiency, posing challenges for teachers in providing timely and personalized feedback. In this context, GenAI-enabled feedback offers a scalable approach to addressing learner diversity and supporting differentiated instruction. In classroom implementation, students collaboratively constructed sentences as group artifacts to practice target vocabulary. The system generated multimodal feedback—including scoring, audio-supported grammar and content feedback, and image-based feedback—to support reflection and revision. By integrating multimodal feedback into collaborative tasks, the study seeks to connect feedback research with collaborative learning and provide practical insights for classroom integration.

2 Theoretical Foundations

2.1 Feedback-Students Interaction Model

Effective feedback processing has been shown to relate to improved learning outcomes. However, its effectiveness depends not only on how feedback is delivered but also on how it is interpreted and enacted by learner. Lipnevich et al. conceptualized feedback as a dynamic system involving the feedback itself, learner characteristics, processing mechanisms, and learning outcomes [10]. Central to this model is the feedback processing phase—the period between receiving feedback and taking action.

Specifically, feedback must be comprehensible and appropriately designed to enable uptake. At the same time, learner characteristics—such as prior knowledge, self-efficacy, and motivation—influence how feedback is evaluated and acted upon [2]. Upon receiving feedback, learners engage in interdependent cognitive and affective processing, and these appraisals shape subsequent actions and learning outcomes [14]. Importantly, feedback effectiveness extends beyond immediate task revision. It involves internalization that supports enduring learning and transfer to future contexts [18]. From this perspective, the present study examines not only how GenAI-enabled feedback improves immediate group performance but also how group-level cognitive and socio-emotional processing serves as a pathway to feedback internalization and longer-term learning gains.

In sum, the present study draws on Lipnevich et al.'s feedback-student interaction model and adapts it to the context of GenAI-enabled multimodal feedback for collaborative L2 learning. Figure 1 shows the research framework for guiding this study.

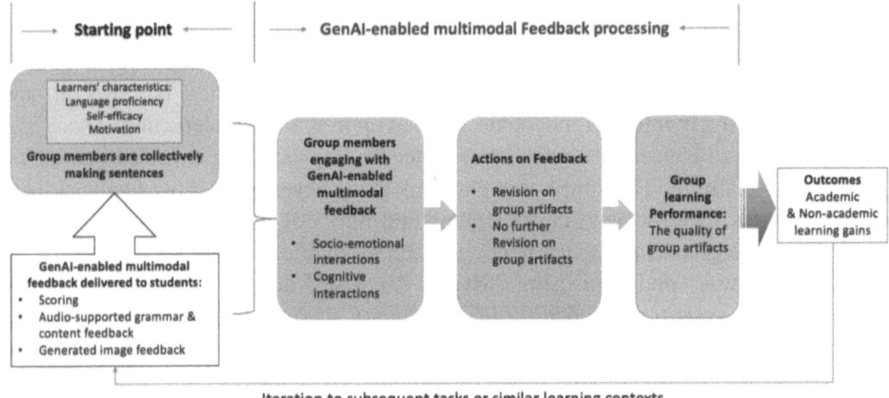

Fig. 1. Research Framework

2.2 GenAI-Enabled Multimodal Feedback in Language Learning

In AI-supported vocabulary and writing tasks, text-based automatic evaluation remains the most common form of feedback, providing direct corrective suggestions to improve language accuracy [5]. However, its effectiveness depends on learners' goals and proficiency. For young beginners, explicit feedback may be less accessible and may not sufficiently sustain positive academic emotion. Moreover, overly explicit corrections can encourage surface-level adoption without deeper cognitive engagement, limiting long-term learning benefits [3].

In contrast, within process writing approaches, indirect feedback is often preferred [7]. GenAI-enabled multimodal feedback can promote learners' interest and enjoyment, particularly among young learners, and may encourage self-correction and meaning-making rather than simple correction uptake [1]. Nevertheless, processing such feedback may also generate confusion or anxiety, especially in collaborative contexts where learners must interpret, negotiate, and apply feedback through peer discussion [9]. Conflicts between expectations and feedback may undermine productive cognitive engagement.

Taken together, building on the feedback–student interaction model, this study adopts a both product- and process-oriented approach to examining GenAI-enabled feedback in collaborative learning. The research questions are as follows:

RQ1. How are different group feedback processing patterns associated with group task performance and individual learning gains?

RQ2. How do socio-emotional and cognitive interactions emerge and coordinate within groups demonstrating different learning gains?

3 Methodology

3.1 Participants and Intervention

A total of 83 Primary Two students (aged 7–8) from four classes across two Singapore primary schools participated in the study. All classes used ARCHe 2.0 throughout 2025. Prior to the intervention, students attended a 60-min technical training session, and the four Chinese language teachers received professional training.

ARCHe 2.0 is a GenAI-enabled vocabulary learning system aligned with Singapore's Chinese language curriculum. In each 60-min session, students worked in groups of three to four (29 groups) to construct sentences based on sample pictures and revise them using AI-generated multimodal feedback. Upon submission, the system generated AI-based scoring to indicate overall quality, audio-supported grammar and content feedback to guide improvements in form and meaning, and image-based feedback derived from the submitted sentence (Fig. 2). Comparing the generated image with the original picture prompted reflection on semantic precision and further collaborative revision. Teachers concluded each lesson with comments and highlighted exemplary group work.

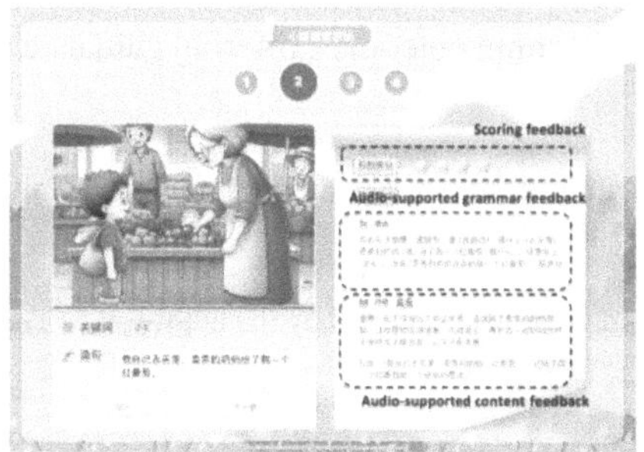

(a) scoring feedback & audio-supported grammar and content feedback

(b)generated image feedback

Fig. 2. ARCHe2.0 learning system with AI-promoted multimodal feedback.

3.2 Data Collection and Analysis

Five types of data will be collected: (1) individual pre- and post-tests on Chinese vocabulary aligned with ARCHe sentence-making tasks; (2) pre- and post-surveys on motivation and self-efficacy; (3) synchronized video and screen recordings of each group's collaborative process to capture interactions with GenAI-enabled multimodal feedback; (4) group artifacts evaluated using a rubric on grammatical accuracy and content richness; and (5) post-intervention semi-structured focus group interviews with selected groups.

Data analysis will follow an explanatory mixed-methods design. Quantitative analyses will examine associations between group feedback processing patterns and learning outcomes (academic and non-academic gains), using group artifact quality and individual test/survey gains as outcome indicators. Qualitatively, fine-grained content analysis will be applied to group utterances and observable actions to code cognitive and socio-emotional interactions and feedback uptake. To compare interactional patterns across groups, cluster analysis will be used to identify group profiles based on feedback processing patterns and learning gains. The resulting profiles will then be examined using ordered network analysis (ONA) to investigate the structural and temporal dynamics of cognitive and socio-emotional interactions. Micro-genetic analysis will also be considered to trace how these interactions evolve during conflict episodes. Finally, focus group interviews will be used to interpret group learning experiences with GenAI-enabled multimodal feedback.

4 Current State of the Research and Expected Contributions

I am currently finalizing data collection and have completed the cleaning and preprocessing of all quantitative data, as well as the transcription and coding of qualitative interaction data. However, further refinement of analytical strategies and theoretical framing is ongoing. This study contributes theoretically and practically to GenAI-enabled language learning. Theoretically, it advances a process-oriented view of feedback–student interaction by conceptualizing feedback processing as a socially situated, interactionally shaped phenomenon in collaborative contexts. Practically, the findings inform the design of GenAI-enabled multimodal feedback by identifying interactional conditions that support effective processing and improved learning outcomes, offering guidance for sustainable classroom integration.

Acknowledgments. This study is funded by Education Research Funding Programme, Ministry of Education (MOE), Singapore, with project nos. ERFP 05/23 WY.

Disclosure of Interests. No potential conflict of interest was reported by the author(s).

References

1. Aslan, S., et al.: An early investigation of collaborative problem solving in conversational AI-mediated learning environments. Comput. Educ. Artif. Intell. **8**, 100393 (2025). https://doi.org/10.1016/j.caeai.2025.100393
2. Bai, B., et al.: Self-efficacy, task values and growth mindset: what has the most predictive power for primary school students' self-regulated learning in English writing and writing competence in an Asian Confucian cultural context? Camb. J. Educ. **51**(1), 65–84 (2021). https://doi.org/10.1080/0305764X.2020.1778639
3. Cárcamo, B.: Classifying Written Corrective Feedback for Research and Educational Purposes: A Typology Proposal. Profile: Issues Teach. Prof. Dev. 22, 2, 211–222 (2020). https://doi.org/10.15446/profile.v22n2.79924
4. Carless, D.: Differing perceptions in the feedback process. Stud. High. Educ. **31**(2), 219–233 (2006). https://doi.org/10.1080/03075070600572132
5. Chen, Q., Su, W.: Comparing students' reception of AI-based video feedback and written feedback: a Q methodological study. Innov. Educ. Teach. Intl. 1–16 (2025). https://doi.org/10.1080/14703297.2025.2530770
6. Dang, B., et al.: Human– AI collaborative learning in mixed reality: examining the cognitive and socio-emotional interactions. Brit. J. Educ. Tech. **56**(5), 2078–2101 (2025). https://doi.org/10.1111/bjet.13607

7. Ferris, D.R.: Second language writing research and written corrective feedback in SLA: intersections and practical applications. Stud. Second. Lang. Acquis. **32**(2), 181–201 (2010). https://doi.org/10.1017/S0272263109990490
8. Hamid, S.: Integrating artificial intelligence and multimodality in language education: a systematic review of emerging trends and practices. JSOM **4**(2), 400–416 (2025). https://doi.org/10.56976/jsom.v4i2.253
9. Huang, L., et al.: Regulation of emotions in project-based collaborative learning: an empirical study in academic English classrooms. Front. Psychol. **15**, 1368196 (2024). https://doi.org/10.3389/fpsyg.2024.1368196
10. Lipnevich, A.A., Smith, J.K.: Student – feedback interaction model: revised. Stud. Educ. Eval. **75**, 101208 (2022). https://doi.org/10.1016/j.stueduc.2022.101208
11. Liu, Z. et al.: Scaffolding language learning via multi-modal tutoring systems with pedagogical instructions. https://arxiv.org/abs/2404.03429 (2024). https://doi.org/10.48550/ARXIV.2404.03429
12. Musk, N.: Correcting spellings in second language learners' computer-assisted collaborative writing. Classroom Discourse. **7**(1), 36–57 (2016). https://doi.org/10.1080/19463014.2015.1095106
13. Ozan, O., Azap, S.: Employing ChatGPT to improve high school students' writing skills by providing feedback on topic-specific writing tasks. Comput. Assist. Lang. Learn. 1–23 (2026). https://doi.org/10.1080/09588221.2026.2613219
14. Pekrun, R.: The control-value theory of achievement emotions: assumptions, corollaries, and implications for educational research and practice. Educ. Psychol. Rev. **18**(4), 315–341 (2006). https://doi.org/10.1007/s10648-006-9029-9
15. Wiliam, D.: Assessment for learning: meeting the challenge of implementation. Assess. Educ. Princip. Pol. Pract. **25**(6), 682–685 (2018). https://doi.org/10.1080/0969594X.2017.1401526
16. Winstone, N.E., et al.: Supporting learners' agentic engagement with feedback: a systematic review and a taxonomy of recipience processes. Educ. Psychol. **52**(1), 17–37 (2017). https://doi.org/10.1080/00461520.2016.1207538
17. Zhuang, Y., et al.: Enhancing language learning through generative AI feedback on picture-cued writing tasks. Comput. Educ. Artif. Intell. **9**, 100450 (2025). https://doi.org/10.1016/j.caeai.2025.100450

ProFeed: Designing Scaffolded Learning in the Age of AI

Mona Münstermann(✉)

University of Duisburg - Essen, Duisburg, Germany
mona.muenstermann@uni-due.de

Abstract. This research explores the design of an adaptive, theory-driven feedback framework for programming education. Although feedback is known to support learning, providing personalized guidance on a large scale can be challenging. To that end, we aim to develop ProFeed, a rule-based feedback framework combining insights from Contingent Tutoring and the Assistance Dilemma with AI-supported feedback mechanisms. The framework incorporates a student model that adapts the types of feedback provided, such as textual hints and worked examples, based on learner characteristics, including prior knowledge and perceived self-competence. By using mixed-methods studies in real programming environments, we will examine the effectiveness of this approach and refine and evaluate the feedback rules accordingly. Our contribution comes in two parts: First, we provide a structured, theory-informed rule-based framework that aligns feedback types with learner characteristics and pedagogical principles. Second, we present empirical evidence that demonstrates the effectiveness and scalability of AI-driven feedback in programming education.

Keywords: Automated Feedback · Human-Centered Computing · Personalized Learning

1 Introduction

Feedback can significantly affect learning outcomes [4], either positively or negatively. Nowadays, the need for well-designed feedback is greater than ever: Large Language Models (LLM) are being used more and more for learning and can generate personalized responses in real time [1]. Their ability to provide personalized, automated feedback to large groups of learners is promising, especially in programming education, where providing individualized guidance on a large scale is often difficult [11]. However, most LLM-based feedback systems are implemented without considering feedback theories. Consequently, while these systems can generate responses that appear personalized, there is no guarantee that the feedback is aligned with principles that support learning. This research aims to address the aforementioned gap, thus contributing to the field, by developing and evaluating ProFeed, a theory-driven, rule-based framework for adaptive feedback in programming education. The goal is to answer the following questions:

E. G. Blanchard et al. (Eds.): AIED 2026, CCIS 3033, pp. 300–305, 2026.
https://doi.org/10.1007/978-3-032-29794-5_46

How can we use AI to design and implement a framework (ProFeed) for delivering personalized and adaptive feedback in programming education?

- *RQ1:* Is rule-based, theory-driven feedback (like the one to be delivered by ProFeed) more effective in improving performance than LLM-generated feedback that is not grounded in feedback theory?
- *RQ2:* In what ways do learner characteristics, such as prior knowledge and perceived competence, affect the effectiveness of feedback and how can such characteristics be used to personalize and adapt feedback?

To answer these questions, I investigate how to design feedback that supports individual learners using feedback approaches such as Contingent Tutoring [15], and the Assistance Dilemma [6]. To that end, I consider various feedback types, such as textual hints and worked examples, and explore the use of LLMs for automated feedback generation to provide scalable, real-time guidance. For example, the ProFeed framework could look like this: A student attempts a programming exercise and makes a series of errors. The student model then estimates their level of mastery based on prior knowledge and performance. Since their mastery of the concept is below a certain threshold, the framework selects a high-support feedback type, such as a worked example. This decision is encoded in a prompt for the LLM, which generates a tailored explanation that addresses the student's specific error. If the student had a higher level of mastery, they might receive a different hint instead.

2 Related Work

Feedback is defined as *"information provided by an agent (e.g., teacher, peer, [...]) regarding aspects of one's performance or understanding"* [4]. In general, feedback can be divided into formative and summative types. Formative feedback is provided during the learning process to guide improvement, whereas summative feedback primarily evaluates performance for grading purposes [10]. According to [4], effective feedback can operate at three levels: feed-up clarifies learning goals ("Where am I going?"), feedback evaluates current performance ("How am I going?"), and feed-forward guides strategies for future tasks ("Where to next?"). Building on this, research shows that the impact of feedback varies by type: Simple reinforcement (right/wrong) is the least informative, while elaborated feedback that addresses task strategies, processes, and self-regulation is the most effective [14]. This reflects a shift from information-based to process-based feedback, which emphasizes offering guidance on learners' strategies and thought processes [8]. Research provides insights and guidance for designing effective feedback. For example, the Assistance Dilemma discusses how too much guidance fosters passive learning, while too little can cause frustration [6]. Similarly, the concept of Contingent Tutoring specifies how feedback should adapt across temporal, instructional, and domain dimensions [15].

In this research, I focus on feedback provided in Intelligent Learning Environments (ILEs), that is "*digital educational interactive applications equipped with features that enable the provision of personalized, adaptive support to students*" [7]. These systems maintain dynamic student models to track progress and adapt feedback in real time [12]. The recent incorporation of LLMs has made scalable, individualized feedback feasible even in large classrooms [1]. Such intelligent and adaptive learning environments have demonstrated that personalized feedback can produce significant learning gains, often approaching the effectiveness of feedback from human tutors [5,13]. Developing a framework that systematically integrates these theories with adaptive feedback mechanisms could provide both theoretical grounding and practical guidance, directly addressing the research question.

3 Methodology

3.1 Method of Research

To address the research question, I follow a mixed-methods design including exploratory and experimental studies with computer science students in higher education. This approach enables me to examine both measurable learning outcomes and the processes that influences learner interaction, feedback usage, and perception. Mixed-methods designs reveal mechanisms, contextual factors, and implementation processes that single-method studies often overlook [3]. Combining quantitative data, such as performance measures, with qualitative insights, like students' perceptions of feedback, offers a comprehensive understanding of how and why educational interventions are effective [2]. Previous studies have shown that combining qualitative and quantitative data improves the refinement and validation of feedback mechanisms in AI-supported tutoring systems [9].

3.2 Research Plan

Phase 1: Rule Generation. The first phase (see Fig. 1) focuses on deriving initial feedback rules that incorporate different types of feedback (e.g., worked examples and textual hints), learner characteristics, and feedback strategies, discussing learning with assistance in the context of programming education. To inform this process, we conducted a systematic literature review to map existing practices and identify research gaps. The review revealed that feedback theories are not commonly used to guide feedback in ILEs for programming. Then, we conducted an exploratory study with 50 participants who learned Python to examine the role of feedback types and learner characteristics, such as prior knowledge, gender and perceived self-competence. The study was facilitated by a custom-built learning environment that enabled participants to request on-demand feedback. Depending on the condition, participants received textual hints, worked examples, or no feedback. A pretest assessed prior knowledge, and learner characteristics were collected. Additionally, qualitative interviews captured learners' experiences and perceptions. The results indicated that learner

Research Phase 1: Rule Generation	Research Phase 2: Rule Refinement	Research Phase 3: Rule Evaluation
Systematic Literature Review Exploratory study to examine role of feedback types and learner characteristics in programming education Exploratory study examining the impact of different types of feedback generated by LLMs Exploratory study using JupyterLab to examine differences in Feedback types and learner characteristics from LLM generated feedback	Comparative simulation to examine the interaction of feedback types and learner characteristics Exploratory study which integrates a student model to automate level of support (feedback type) Exploratory study to validate student model and feedback rules	Experimental study to evaluate effectiveness of automated feedback system Comparative simulation to further analyze the impact of different learner characteristics and feedback types

Fig. 1. Research Plan indicating the current phase (Phase 1).

characteristics did not significantly affect performance, but learners performed significantly better with worked examples than with textual hints.

Following, we conducted two exploratory studies using a LLM-enhanced JupyterLab environment to examine differences in feedback types and learner characteristics.

- Quasi-experimental Study: This study was conducted across two different courses within the same university and included an exploratory and experimental phase. During the exploratory phase, students could prompt the LLM when they encountered errors. During the experimental phase, participants received support according to their assigned condition: no support, generic support, or support tailored to their specific error.
- Exploratory Study: Participants received a different type of feedback each week: worked examples, textual hints, or no feedback. The feedback became progressively more specific with repeated errors. Pre- and post-tests were used to assess learner characteristics (e.g., perceived self-competence and prior knowledge).

Currently, we are analyzing the collected data from the three studies to identify potential patterns in the effectiveness of feedback types. These insights will form the basis for an initial set of feedback guidelines formulated using an if-then-else pattern.

Phase 2: Rule Refinement. The second phase focuses on validating and refining the initial feedback rules derived in Phase 1 using empirical evidence. Therefore, we will introduce a student model to determine the level of support that should be provided to each learner. The student model will consider learner characteristics, such as prior knowledge and perceived self-competence, to adapt feedback. For instance, learners with low prior knowledge or low self-competence will receive detailed worked examples, while learners with high prior knowledge will receive textual hints and minimal guidance. To further investigate these patterns, we will conduct the following studies to refine the rule-based framework:

- A comparative simulation to examine the interaction of feedback types and learner characteristics.
- An exploratory study that will test the performance of the student model in realistic settings.

Phase 3: Rule Evaluation. The third phase focuses on exploring the generalizability of the rule-based framework derived from the previous phases. While Phase 1 and Phase 2 provide initial indications regarding the feedback effectiveness, this phase aims to investigate how the feedback rules and student model perform across different cohorts and over multiple years in programming education.

We will repeat the comparative simulation study from Phase 2, aiming to extension and diversification of the dataset. The goal of this replication is to examine the interaction between different feedback types and learner characteristics across cohorts closely and to determine if the patterns observed in Phase 2 remain stable when applied to a new cohort. An experimental study will follow to validate the simulation's findings under realistic conditions and strengthen the findings regarding the effectiveness of the automated feedback framework.

4 Contribution

This research designs ProFeed, a modular, extensible framework for adaptive feedback in programming education. ProFeed establishes a rule-based framework aligning feedback types with learner characteristics, drawing on the Assistance Dilemma [6] and Contingent Tutoring [15] to inform AI-supported feedback design. We expect two main contributions: (a) a structured, theory-informed framework that systematically connects feedback types, learner characteristics, and theories of assisted learning; and (b) empirical evidence on the effectiveness and generalizability of this approach across different programming education cohorts. By incorporating learner characteristics such as prior knowledge and perceived self-competence, ProFeed aims to deliver pedagogically grounded, personalized instructional support. Findings are expected to inform the design of intelligent adaptive learning environments in programming education and potentially other STEM fields. Future work will explore expanding the framework to additional domains and refining the student model's adaptive mechanisms.

References

1. Barros, J., Moraes, L.O., Oliveira, F., Delgado, C.A.D.M.: Large language models generating feedback for students of introductory programming courses. In: Cristea, A.I., Walker, E., Lu, Y., Santos, O.C., Isotani, S. (eds.) AIED 2025. LNCS, vol. 15878. Springer, Cham (2025). https://doi.org/10.1007/978-3-031-98417-4_30

2. Fetters, M.D., Molina-Azorin, J.F.: Utilizing a mixed methods approach for conducting interventional evaluations. J. Mixed Methods Res. **14**(2), 131–144 (2020). https://doi.org/10.1177/1558689820912856
3. Fàbregues, S., Sáinz, M., Romano, M.J., Escalante-Barrios, E.L., Younas, A., López-Pérez, B.S.: Use of mixed methods research in intervention studies to increase young people's interest in stem: A systematic methodological review. Front. Psychol. **13**, 956300 (2023). https://doi.org/10.3389/fpsyg.2022.956300
4. Hattie, J., Timperley, H.: The power of feedback. Rev. Educ. Res. **77**(1), 81–112 (2007). https://doi.org/10.3102/003465430298487
5. Kochmar, E., Vu, D.D., Belfer, R., Gupta, V., Serban, I.V., Pineau, J.: Automated personalized feedback improves learning gains in an intelligent tutoring system. In: Bittencourt, I.I., Cukurova, M., Muldner, K., Luckin, R., Millán, E. (eds.) AIED 2020. LNCS (LNAI), vol. 12164, pp. 140–146. Springer, Cham (2020). https://doi.org/10.1007/978-3-030-52240-7_26
6. Koedinger, K.R., Aleven, V.: Exploring the assistance dilemma in experiments with cognitive tutors. Educ. Psychol. Rev. **19**(3), 239–264 (2007). https://doi.org/10.1007/s10648-007-9049-0
7. Mavrikis, M., Holmes, W.: Intelligent learning environments: design, usage and analytics for future schools. In: Yu, S., Niemi, H., Mason, J. (eds.) Shaping Future Schools with Digital Technology. PRRE, pp. 57–73. Springer, Singapore (2019). https://doi.org/10.1007/978-981-13-9439-3_4
8. Ryan, T., Henderson, M., Ryan, K., Kennedy, G.: Designing learner-centred text-based feedback: a rapid review and qualitative synthesis. Assess. Eval. Higher Educ. **46**(6), 894–912 (2021). https://doi.org/10.1080/02602938.2020.1828819
9. Schmohl, T., Schelling, K., Go, S., Thaler, K.J., Watanabe, A.: Development, implementation and acceptance of an AI-based tutoring system: A research-led methodology. In: Cukurova, M., Rummel, N., Gillet, D., McLaren, B., Uhomoibhi, J. (eds.) Proceedings of the 14th International Conference on Computer Supported Education (CSEDU 2022), Vol. 2. pp. 179–186. SciTePress (2022). https://doi.org/10.5220/0011068500003182
10. Shute, V.J.: Focus on formative feedback. Rev. Educ. Res. **78**(1), 153–189 (2008). https://doi.org/10.3102/0034654307313795
11. Strickroth, S.: Scalable feedback for student live coding in large courses using automatic error grouping. In: Proceedings of the 2024 on Innovation and Technology in Computer Science Education. ITiCSE 2024, New York, NY, USA, vol. 1. p. 499–505. Association for Computing Machinery (2024). https://doi.org/10.1145/3649217.3653620
12. Thomas, D.R., et al.: Improving student learning with hybrid human-ai tutoring: A three-study quasi-experimental investigation. In: Proceedings of the 14th Learning Analytics and Knowledge Conference, pp. 404–415. ACM (2024). https://doi.org/10.1145/3636555.3636896
13. VanLehn, K.: The relative effectiveness of human tutoring, intelligent tutoring systems, and other tutoring systems. Educ. Psychol. **46**(4), 197–221 (2011). https://doi.org/10.1080/00461520.2011.611369
14. Wisniewski, B., Zierer, K., Hattie, J.: The power of feedback revisited: a meta-analysis of educational feedback research. Front. Psychol. **10**, 3087 (2020). https://doi.org/10.3389/fpsyg.2019.03087
15. Wood, H., Wood, D.: Help seeking, learning and contingent tutoring. Comput. Educ. **33**(2), 153–169 (1999). https://www.sciencedirect.com/science/article/pii/S0360131599000305

Chatbot Personalisation and Transparency for EFL Learning

Steve Woollaston[1(✉)], Brendan Flanagan[2], and Hiroaki Ogata[3]

[1] Graduate School of Informatics, Kyoto University, Kyoto, Japan
s.m.woollaston@gmail.com
[2] Center for Innovative Research and Education in Data Science, Institute for Liberal Arts and Sciences, Kyoto University, Kyoto, Japan
[3] Academic Center for Computing and Media Studies, Kyoto University, Kyoto, Japan

Abstract. Many Japanese EFL learners struggle with limited opportunities for authentic language use and a pedagogical focus on rote-learning for examinations. While Generative AI (GenAI) chatbots offer a flexible solution, existing tools are often non-personalised and fragmented, failing to track longitudinal progress across different learning contexts. This research proposes a unified personalisation framework that integrates interaction data from a suite of task-specific EFL (English as a Foreign Language) applications into a single learner model. Our methodology utilises Bayesian Knowledge Tracing (BKT) aligned with the Japan-centric CEFR-J framework to dynamically model vocabulary and grammar proficiency. By conducting semantic analysis of task contexts, the system identifies and injects learning items within a student's Zone of Proximal Development (ZPD) directly into chatbot prompts, personalising responses to each learner's individual learning needs. To ensure transparency and build trust, we provide an interactive dashboard for students and teachers to query progress in natural language and suggest actionable next steps. This work contributes to a scalable model for cohesive, data-driven language learning ecosystems.

Keywords: Chatbots · EFL · Language learning · Personalisation · Dashboard · LLM · GenAI

1 Introduction

Many Japanese learners of English face ongoing challenges: large class sizes, exam-focused rote-learning and teaching, and limited chances to use English in authentic contexts. Chatbots using GenAI offer a flexible way to practise English, but many are not personalised and do not track learner progress. Systems that are personalised often work in isolation, leading to low quality feedback. We propose combining data from existing tools into a unified learner model to inform personalisation. Further, we will make learning and next steps visible with a clear dashboard; boosting trust and engagement.

E. G. Blanchard et al. (Eds.): AIED 2026, CCIS 3033, pp. 306–312, 2026.
https://doi.org/10.1007/978-3-032-29794-5_47

This work investigates these research questions:

1. What is the impact of a personalised chatbot system (integrating individual proficiency and specific task context) on EFL learners' vocabulary and grammar mastery compared to non-personalised chatbot versions?
2. How does transparent access to proficiency data and suggested next steps for both learners and teachers affect learning outcomes, feedback uptake, and overall trust in the system?

2 Related Work

Despite substantial investment in English education, Japanese learners continue to face significant hurdles in developing functional communication skills, largely due to limited opportunities for authentic interaction [5]. While GenAI chatbots offer flexible, low-pressure environments for language practice, current tools typically lack personalisation [8], treating all learners identically and retaining no memory of past interactions.

This personalisation gap stems primarily from fragmented data. Most chatbots operate in isolation, ignoring learning data from other platforms and creating incomplete pictures of student progress. Consequently, they deliver generic feedback lacking the nuance required for effective EFL instruction. Furthermore, the opaque reasoning behind AI-generated responses undermines the transparency necessary for building learner trust. As Hattie [3] emphasises, effective learning must be visible; without understanding *why* a chatbot makes specific suggestions, students may find the technology unreliable.

True personalisation, shown to improve both engagement and outcomes [1], requires more sophisticated data integration. Kay et al. [4] highlight the necessity of robust pipelines that aggregate information across digital tools to construct "richer learner models" that accurately represent student knowledge.

Implementing such personalisation introduces technical challenges, particularly regarding LLM context management. Expanding chat logs can cause "context rot," where models lose focus or increase hallucinations [2]. Moreover, how LLMs prioritise past interactions remains opaque. Addressing these transparency and integration issues is essential for AI to evolve from simple conversational tools toward more trustworthy, explainable personalised learning systems [6].

3 Proposed Solution and Methodology

This research proposes a unified, task-contextualised personalisation framework (Fig. 1) coupled with a dashboard showing students and teachers interaction history, the learner model, and suggested next steps.

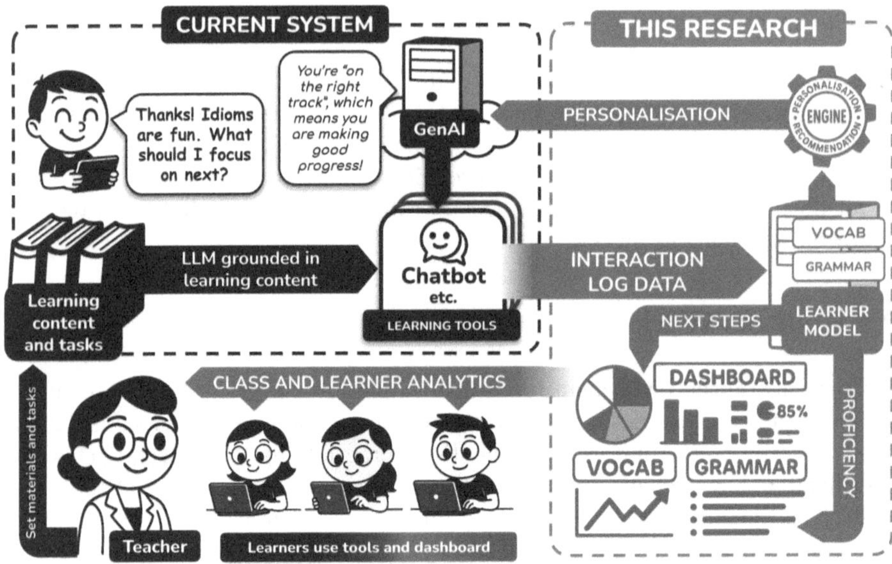

Fig. 1. Proposed personalisation architecture

3.1 Unified Personalisation Framework

The proposed system aggregates learner interaction data across a suite of task-specific EFL learning apps created by the author, including TAMMY (translation practice), ARCHIE (active reading), and Penny (diary writing) currently deployed in several Japanese high schools. By centralising log data into a unified backend, the system overcomes the limitations of isolated tools and constructs a holistic representation of the learner's evolving English vocabulary and grammar proficiency.

The dynamic adaptation of the chatbots is driven by a three-stage contextualised recommendation pipeline (Fig. 2):

1. **Proficiency Modelling:** The system utilises Bayesian Knowledge Tracing (BKT) to continuously monitor and update a learner's mastery of specific vocabulary and grammar items. This is aligned with the CEFR-J framework [7]—a localised adaptation of the Common European Framework of Reference for Languages (CEFR), specifically designed for Japanese EFL learners. It provides a more granular scale for lower proficiency levels (splitting A1 into sub-levels: A1.1, A1.2) to better track progress and aligns with commonly used English textbooks. To ensure accuracy over time, the learner model incorporates memory decay through the BKT+F algorithm, which adjusts proficiency levels based on how recently and frequently a learner has encountered specific material. To overcome cold-start limitations, BKT parameters are initialised by pooling historical interaction data across all users while grounding guess and slip probabilities at 10%. Individual mastery estimates

are subsequently validated using an observation-based confidence heuristic, ensuring the system only targets learning items with mathematically stable proficiency scores. Every interaction with the chatbot is logged and analysed to provide the data necessary for these estimations. Individual vocabulary proficiency is determined by evaluating correct spelling and contextual usage, while grammar is assessed by identifying a learner's intended linguistic structure and comparing it against their actual output. This comparative analysis provides the precise correctness data required for the BKT model to generate a reliable, dynamic map of student progress.

2. **Task Context Analysis:** When a learner engages in a specific activity, the system conducts a semantic analysis of the task context (e.g., a reading passage, diary prompt, initial student input). Word embeddings (`text-embedding-3-small`) are utilised to compute the semantic similarity between the task elements and the CEFR-J dictionary and grammar list, ensuring linguistic relevance of the recommended vocabulary and grammar items.
3. **ZPD Filtering:** To optimise learning, the system cross-references the contextual analysis with the learner's BKT profile, filtering for items that fall within the learner's ZPD, which we operationalise computationally as a mastery probability near 0.5. This threshold is used as a practical proxy for knowledge that is not yet mastered but also not entirely unfamiliar—that is, words and grammar structures that are neither too easy nor entirely novel. These targeted items are seamlessly injected into the LLM's prompts to shape real-time chatbot dialogue, scaffolding, and error correction.

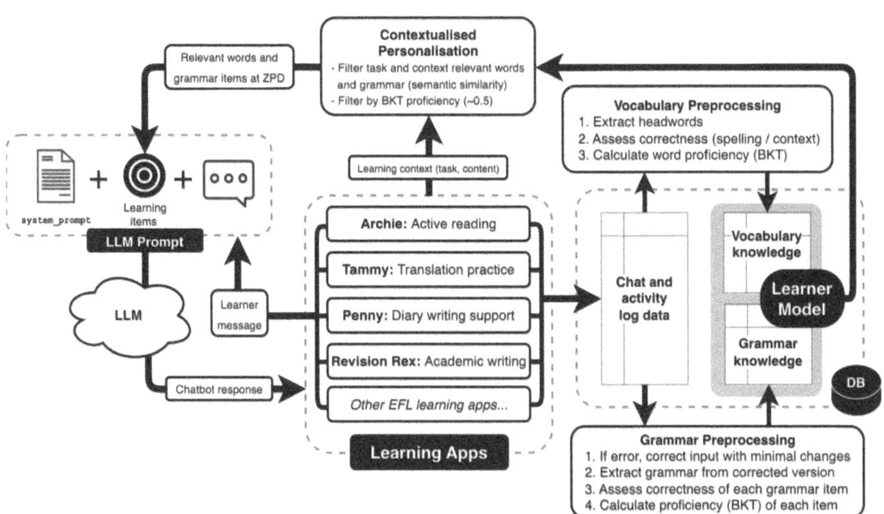

Fig. 2. Implementation of contextualised personalisation using BKT and ZPD filtering

3.2 Learner Model Dashboard

To foster transparency and trust, the framework includes a co-designed dashboard for both learners and teachers. Following feedback that the initial dashboard's exhaustive metrics were overwhelming, we developed an AI-powered natural language interface that allows instructors to query student performance data flexibly. Teachers can ask questions like *"Which grammar items are students struggling with this week?"* A natural language-to-SQL engine converts this to database queries using a curated semantic schema. Results return as interactive tables and visualisations. Queries are logged to identify which metrics are most relevant to practitioners. The dashboard incorporates automated anonymisation to maintain privacy when required.

A student-centered version is under development to support learner metacognition and autonomy. Students can view their longitudinal progress in vocabulary and grammar mastery alongside clear feedback on areas needing improvement. Closing the feedback loop, GenAI analyses current proficiency gaps and provides personalised next study sessions, such as specific grammar drills or targeted conversation topics.

4 Preliminary Results

Initial evaluations of the individual chatbots have yielded promising insights that establish the technical feasibility of the tools and inform the proposed integrated framework.

- **ARCHIE:** Epistemic and Transition Network Analyses of reading and chatbot interaction showed high-proficiency learners used more sophisticated strategies, while the chatbot effectively re-engaged off-task students [9,10].
- **TAMMY:** Achieved 96.5% chatbot response validity and 63.9% success guiding students to accurate translations over four months [11].
- **Penny:** Collected four months of daily writing feedback interaction data from 120 students for feedback uptake analysis *(submission pending).*

These foundational studies validate the pedagogical utility of the isolated chatbots, paving the way for the cross-tool, personalised learner modeling proposed in this research.

5 Contributions and Impact

This research unites fragmented educational chatbots through a cross-tool learner model. Our fundamental novelty is a bidirectional data flow: the ecosystem continuously updates a centralised proficiency profile from isolated apps while dynamically injecting that aggregated intelligence into LLM prompts in real-time. Methodologically, we advance AIED by integrating BKT and semantic analysis to tailor feedback directly to a learner's ZPD. Practically, by adopting CEFR-J standards and providing a transparent dashboard, this framework builds trust, supports student self-regulation, and delivers a scalable, data-driven ecosystem for EFL education in Japan.

6 Current State and Future Directions

The primary chatbot personalisation experiment is currently underway, utilising a randomised control design to evaluate impacts on learning outcomes. Concurrently, the teacher dashboard has been deployed; its reliability and pedagogical usefulness will be assessed via natural-language query success rates (log analysis), and questionnaire, and qualitative interviews. To bolster BKT accuracy, we introduced "Grammar Gretel," a targeted drill application that feeds objective performance data directly into mastery profiles, bypassing complex LLM-based correctness evaluations. Finally, we acknowledge limitations: BKT mastery provides a proxy rather than capturing holistic communicative competence, and future work should validate generalisability beyond the Japanese CEFR-J context.

Acknowledgments. This research is supported by Council for Science, 3rd SIP JPJ012347, and JSPS Grant-in-Aid for Scientific Research (B) JP23H01001, (A) JP23H00505, and KAKENHI Grant Number 26KJ1488.

References

1. Bartle, E.: Personalised learning: An overview. Tech. Rep., The Institute for Teaching and Learning Innovation. The University of Queensland, Brisbane, Australia (2015)
2. Danyaro, K.U., Abdullahi, S., Abdallah, A.S.: Hallucinations in large language models for education: challenges and mitigation. Indonesian J. Electric. Eng. Comput. Sci. **35**(2), 1054–1062 (2024). https://doi.org/10.11591/ijeecs.v35.i2.pp1054-1062
3. Hattie, J.: Visible Learning for Teachers: Maximizing Impact on Learning. Routledge, London, England (2012). https://doi.org/10.4324/9780203181522
4. Kay, J., Bartimote, K., Kitto, K., Kummerfeld, B., Liu, D., Reimann, P.: Enhancing learning by open learner model (OLM) driven data design. Comput. Educ. Artifi. Intell. **3**, 100069 (2022). https://doi.org/10.1016/j.caeai.2022.100069
5. Morita, L.: Why Japan needs English. Cogent Soc. Sci. **3**(1), 1399783 (2017). https://doi.org/10.1080/23311886.2017.1399783
6. Slamet, J., Basthomi, Y.: Examining the challenges and opportunities of ChatGPT in EFL education: a systematic literature review. J. Univ. Teach. Learn. Prac. **22**(2) (2025). https://doi.org/10.53761/deezkh88
7. Tono, Y.: Coming full circle – from CEFR to CEFR-J and back. CEFR J. Res. Practice **1**, 5–17 (2019). https://doi.org/10.37546/jaltsig.cefr1-1
8. Woollaston, S., Flanagan, B., Ogata, H.: Chatbots and EFL learning: a systematic review. In: Joint Proceedings of the 14th LAK Workshops. CEUR Workshop Proceedings, vol. 3667, pp. 89–98 (2024)
9. Woollaston, S., Flanagan, B., Ocheja, P., Toyokawa, Y., Ogata, H.: ARCHIE: exploring language learner behaviors in LLM chatbot-supported active reading log data with epistemic network analysis. In: Proceedings of LAK '25, pp. 642–654. ACM, New York (2025). https://doi.org/10.1145/3706468.3706556

10. Woollaston, S., Flanagan, B., Ocheja, P., Ogata, H.: ARCHIE: EFL learning processes in chatbot-supported active reading using transition network analysis. In: Proceedings of ICLEA 2025. APSCE (2025)
11. Woollaston, S., Flanagan, B., Ocheja, P., Dai, Y., Ogata, H.: TAMMY: usability and effectiveness of a translation practice chatbot for Japanese EFL learners. Res. Practice Technol. Enhanced Learn. **22** (2026). https://doi.org/10.58459/rptel.2027.22003

Pedagogically Steered LLM-Based Teachable Agents for Scaffolding Tutor Learning in Learning-by-Teaching

Lingxi Jin and Hyo-Jeong So(✉)

Department of Educational Technology, Ewha Womans University, Seoul, South Korea
{jinlingxi,hyojeongso}@ewha.ac.kr

Abstract. This AIED Doctoral Consortium paper presents an ongoing study on pedagogical steering of large language model (LLM)-based teachable agents for Learning-by-Teaching (LBT). Tutor learning in LBT depends on whether teaching elicits reflective knowledge-building processes rather than superficial knowledge telling. However, current LLM-based teachable agents rely on unconstrained generative behavior and lack explicit instructional control to systematically scaffold reflective tutor learning. We propose a pedagogical steering framework that models LBT tutoring strategies as explicit instructional states organized within a transition graph. The framework guides the agent to follow a formalized tutoring strategy during interaction instead of relying solely on generative dynamics. This study will examine whether pedagogical steering enables the agent to follow the LBT tutoring strategy and how tutors' reflective knowledge-building behaviors are associated with improvements in post-task performance. The work contributes a structured approach to regulating LLM-based educational agents to support tutor learning.

Keywords: Learning-by-Teaching · Teachable Agents · Large Language Models · Pedagogical Steering · Reflective Knowledge Building

1 Problem Statement

Learning-by-Teaching (LBT) has been widely studied as an instructional approach that promotes tutor learning by positioning individuals in the role of a teacher [1,10] However, research has consistently shown that tutor learning does not automatically arise from explaining content. Rather, it depends on engaging in reflective knowledge-building processes such as elaborative reasoning, monitoring of understanding, and explanation repair [13]. Empirical findings indicate that tutors frequently default to surface-level knowledge telling unless interaction structures actively elicit reflection and revision. Designing environments

E. G. Blanchard et al. (Eds.): AIED 2026, CCIS 3033, pp. 313–318, 2026.
https://doi.org/10.1007/978-3-032-29794-5_48

that reliably scaffold reflective tutor learning therefore remains a central challenge.

Prompt-based scaffolding has been widely used to support reflective learning processes. While prompts can guide knowledge construction, prior research has also documented potential limitations. Overly structured prompts may encourage procedural, step-by-step responding rather than deep conceptual integration [3], and learners may overlook broader problem-solving structures when guided by rigid prompt sequences [4]. In Learning-by-Teaching environments, both self-reflection prompts and agent-initiated question prompts have been explored as mechanisms to stimulate tutor reflection [8]. Although these approaches demonstrate the potential of prompts to enhance reflective interaction, they are typically implemented as fixed or stage-based scaffolding interventions without explicit regulation of multi-turn instructional progression.

Recent advances in large language models (LLMs) have enabled the development of LLM-based teachable agents that simulate novice learners in multi-turn dialogue [2,6,7,14]. Despite their conversational fluency, these agents generally rely on unconstrained generative behavior and lack explicit pedagogical control. Alignment methods such as reinforcement learning with human feedback optimize models for perceived helpfulness rather than for eliciting reflective tutor learning [11,12]. In tutoring contexts, this may lead to premature solution disclosure or over-resolution of uncertainty, reducing opportunities for elaboration and monitoring. Taken together, existing work highlights both the promise and limitations of prompt-based scaffolding and LLM-based teachable agents. However, there remains a lack of approaches that formalize reflective Learning-by-Teaching processes as explicit multi-turn instructional control structures governing agent behavior. This study addresses this gap by modeling LBT tutoring strategies as discrete instructional states organized within a transition graph and steering LLM-based teachable agents to follow this structured pedagogical plan during dialogue. To evaluate the proposed framework, this research addresses the following questions:

RQ1. To what extent will pedagogical steering enable the LLM-based teachable agent to follow the LBT tutoring strategy during multi-turn interaction?

RQ2. How are tutors' reflective knowledge-building behaviors during interaction with a pedagogically steered LLM-based teachable agent associated with improvements in tutors' post-task performance?

2 Proposed Methodology

2.1 Overview

This study will operationalize Learning-by-Teaching processes as an explicit pedagogical control architecture for LLM-based teachable agents. The proposed framework will consist of three interconnected components: (1) formalizing the dialogue tutoring task, (2) modeling the LBT tutoring strategy as a structured state-transition system, and (3) implementing tutor state tracing to determine state-contingent strategy progression. The LBT tutoring strategy will be represented as a transition graph whose nodes correspond to instructional states and whose edges encode permissible transitions conditioned on tutor interactional features. By separating pedagogical control from language realization, the framework will steer multi-turn dialogue according to an explicit instructional plan rather than relying on unconstrained generative behavior.

2.2 Formalism

Dialogue Tutoring Task. We model Learning-by-Teaching as a multi-turn dialogue between a human tutor T and an LLM-based teachable agent A. Our formulation builds upon prior dialog tutoring task definitions [9,12] by introducing an explicit tutoring strategy state to regulate instructional progression. Let the dialogue history up to turn t be $H_{\leq t} = (u_1, \ldots, u_t)$, where each turn is $u_t = (y_t, x_t)$, with y_t denoting the tutor utterance and x_t the agent utterance. The agent generates its next utterance conditioned on dialogue history, grounding information K, and an explicit tutoring strategy state c_{t+1}:

$$x_{t+1} \sim p(x \mid H_{\leq t}, K, c_{t+1}) \quad (1)$$

The grounding information K includes domain materials and task context relevant to the tutoring activity. A key design decision is that the teachable agent is not optimized to provide maximal instructional assistance. Instead, it is constrained to function as a simulated novice whose responses are regulated by explicitly modeled tutoring strategy states designed to elicit tutor elaboration, justification, monitoring, and explanation repair. The agent's response is generated conditioned on the selected tutoring strategy state.

Tutoring Strategy Modeling.

Formative Study. Prior to full system implementation, we will conduct a formative study to empirically ground the tutoring strategy model. Participants will engage in structured Learning-by-Teaching activities in which they explain domain-specific problems to a simulated novice. Tutor utterances will be coded to identify interactional moves such as direct explanation, elaborative reasoning, misconception repair, and monitoring statements. Sequential transition patterns across turns will be analyzed to characterize how reflective knowledge-building processes unfold over time. Following empirical coding, we will collaborate with learning sciences experts to refine operational definitions and consolidate the emerging taxonomy of tutoring strategy categories.

Strategy State Construction. Based on formative analysis, we will define a discrete set of tutoring strategy states:

$$C = \{c_1, \ldots, c_m\} \quad (2)$$

Each state c_i will represent a distinct instructional function (e.g., elaboration elicitation, misconception surfacing, monitoring). Instructional progression will be governed by the transition function:

$$c_{t+1} = \phi(s_t, c_t) \tag{3}$$

where s_t denotes the inferred tutor interactional state and c_t the prior strategy state. The function ϕ will be implemented as a transition graph encoding permissible multi-turn instructional trajectories. In this way, reflective Learning-by-Teaching processes will be operationalized as an explicit instructional control structure.

Pedagogical Question Prompt Design. Prior research on prompt-based scaffolding in learning environments has yielded mixed findings. While prompts can guide reflection and support knowledge construction, they may also unintentionally encourage procedural, step-by-step responding rather than deep conceptual integration [3]. Similarly, [4] noted that overly structured prompts may lead learners to overlook the broader problem-solving context. Studies on scaffolding strategies further suggest that students may omit or superficially respond to prompts unless appropriately regulated [4,5]

Within Learning-by-Teaching contexts, prior work has explored both self-reflection prompts and agent-initiated question prompts to stimulate tutor reflection [8]. These studies suggest that agent tutee question prompts may enhance reflective tutoring interaction compared to purely metacognitive self-reflection prompts. However, prior implementations have largely treated prompts as fixed or stage-based scaffolding interventions. In contrast, the present study formalizes pedagogical question prompts as state-conditioned realizations within an explicit transition-based pedagogical steering framework, enabling dynamic regulation of multi-turn interaction. Pedagogical question prompts realize the selected LBT tutoring strategy state. For each strategy state $c_{t+1} \in C$, we define a structured question prompt $\Pi(c_{t+1})$ that instantiates its instructional objective.

$$x_{t+1} = \text{LLM}(H_{\leq t}, K, \Pi(c_{t+1})) \tag{4}$$

When an elaboration-oriented state is selected, the prompt requests justification or clarification of conceptual relations. Misconception related states introduce plausible misunderstandings to elicit explanation repair. Monitoring-oriented states prompt evaluation of coherence and completeness. Question prompts enact the selected LBT tutoring strategy state, while state transitions remain governed by the transition functionϕ.

Tutor State Tracing. Tutor State Tracing estimates the tutor's interactional state:

$$s_t = \psi(H_{\leq t}, K) \tag{5}$$

where $s_t \subseteq S$ denotes inferred tutor-state features. These features include indicators of elaboration, knowledge telling, conceptual inconsistency, and monitoring. The inferred state s_t determines which tutoring strategy state should follow according to the LBT tutoring strategy.

2.3 Learning Algorithm

At each dialogue turn, the system will first infer the tutor interactional state s_t. Together with the prior strategy state c_t, it will determine the next instructional state c_{t+1} according to the transition function ϕ. The teachable agent will then generate its response using the pedagogical prompt associated with c_{t+1}. This procedure separates state inference, instructional decision-making, and language realization, ensuring that multi-turn interaction follows the predefined LBT tutoring strategy.

2.4 Empirical Study

To evaluate the proposed pedagogical steering framework in an authentic learning environment, we will conduct a controlled study with students engaged in Learning-by-Teaching activities. Students will be assigned to one of two conditions: (1) interaction with a pedagogically steered LLM-based teachable agent, or (2) interaction with a baseline LLM-based agent without strategy control.

For RQ1, we will assess tutoring strategy fidelity by measuring the extent to which the agent's responses align with the intended LBT tutoring strategy states defined in the transition graph.

For RQ2, students' tutoring dialogues will be coded for reflective knowledge-building behaviors, including elaboration, monitoring, and explanation repair. Following the tutoring session, students will complete a post-test assessing problem-solving and conceptual understanding of the instructional content. We will analyze both differences in learning outcomes across conditions and the association between reflective knowledge-building behaviors and post-test performance.

3 Expected Contributions

This study will contribute a formalized pedagogical steering framework for LLM-based teachable agents in Learning-by-Teaching contexts. First, it will operationalize Learning-by-Teaching processes as explicit instructional strategy states organized within a transition graph, bridging learning science theory with computational modeling of dialogue-based learning environments. Second, it will demonstrate how LLM-based teachable agents can be systematically guided to follow a structured tutoring strategy, introducing an explicit layer of pedagogical control beyond unconstrained generative behavior. Third, through a controlled student study, the research will provide empirical evidence linking tutoring strategy fidelity, reflective knowledge-building behaviors, and post-task learning outcomes. By examining these relationships, the study will contribute methodological insights into how pedagogical steering mechanisms can be evaluated within authentic learning environments. Finally, the work will offer design implications for integrating theory-informed instructional control into AI-powered educational systems, informing future development of LLM-based learning technologies.

References

1. Biswas, G., Leelawong, K., Schwartz, D., Vye, N., at Vanderbilt, T.T.A.G.: Learning by teaching: a new agent paradigm for educational software. Appl. Artifi. Intell. **19**(3–4), 363–392 (2005)
2. Chen, A., Wei, Y., Le, H., Zhang, Y.: Learning by teaching with Chatgpt: the effect of teachable Chatgpt agent on programming education. Br. J. Edu. Technol. **57**(1), 163–184 (2026)
3. Davis, E.A.: Scaffolding students' knowledge integration: prompts for reflection in KIE. Int. J. Sci. Educ. **22**(8), 819–837 (2000)
4. Ge, X., Chen, C.H., Davis, K.A.: Scaffolding novice instructional designers' problem-solving processes using question prompts in a web-based learning environment. J. Educ. Comput. Res. **33**(2), 219–248 (2005)
5. Greene, B.A., Land, S.M.: A qualitative analysis of scaffolding use in a resource-based learning environment involving the world wide web. J. Educ. Comput. Res. **23**(2), 151–179 (2000)
6. Jin, H., Lee, S., Shin, H., Kim, J.: Teach ai how to code: using large language models as teachable agents for programming education. In: Proceedings of the 2024 CHI Conference on Human Factors in Computing Systems, pp. 1–28 (2024)
7. Jin, L., Lin, B., Hong, M., So, H.J., Zhang, K.: Learning by teaching: enhancing music learning through LLM-based teachable agents. In: International Conference on Artificial Intelligence in Education, pp. 148–155. Springer (2025)
8. Looi, C.K., Wu, L.: Design of agent tutee's question prompts to engage student's role-playing as tutor in a learning-by-teaching agent environment (2008)
9. Macina, J., et al.: Opportunities and challenges in neural dialog tutoring. In: Proceedings of the 17th Conference of the European Chapter of the Association for Computational Linguistics, pp. 2357–2372 (2023)
10. Matsuda, N., Cohen, W.W., Koedinger, K.R.: Teaching the teacher: tutoring simstudent leads to more effective cognitive tutor authoring. Int. J. Artif. Intell. Educ. **25**(1), 1–34 (2015)
11. Ouyang, L., et al.: Training language models to follow instructions with human feedback. Adv. Neural. Inf. Process. Syst. **35**, 27730–27744 (2022)
12. Puech, R., Macina, J., Chatain, J., Sachan, M., Kapur, M.: Towards the pedagogical steering of large language models for tutoring: a case study with modeling productive failure. In: Findings of the Association for Computational Linguistics: ACL 2025, pp. 26291–26311 (2025)
13. Roscoe, R.D., Chi, M.T.: Understanding tutor learning: knowledge-building and knowledge-telling in peer tutors' explanations and questions. Rev. Educ. Res. **77**(4), 534–574 (2007)
14. Xing, W., Song, Y., Li, C., Liu, Z., Zhu, W., Oh, H.: Development of a generative AI-powered teachable agent for middle school mathematics learning: a design-based research study. Br. J. Edu. Technol. **56**(5), 2043–2077 (2025)

Analysis of Learner Interactions in Metaverse Learning Environments Using Artificial Intelligence

Akhil Hothi(✉) and Syaamantak Das

Centre for Educational Technology, IIT Bombay, Mumbai, India
{akhilhothi,syaamantak.das}@iitb.ac.in

Abstract. Metaverse Learning Environments (MLEs) generate rich, high-volume multimodal interaction data (e.g., gaze, gesture, speech, movement) that can reveal complex learner behavior. Yet, instructors lack tools that can cluster and visualize these data in an actionable, real-time manner. Furthermore, the scarcity of large-scale immersive datasets creates a bottleneck for algorithm development. This doctoral research addresses these challenges by developing an Artificial Intelligence analytics and visualization framework. The study proceeds in three phases: (1) generating hybrid synthetic interaction data via physics simulations and Generative Adversarial Networks (GANs) to overcome data scarcity; (2) designing an unsupervised machine learning pipeline for clustering multimodal learner behaviors; and (3) prototyping immersive, Generative AI-adapted dashboards that reduce cognitive load for data analysis and enhance instructional responsiveness. Preliminary outcomes include a Unity-based data capture prototype and a scoping review of 233 academic sources. This work advances Artificial Intelligence in Education (AIED) and immersive analytics by linking embodied learner behaviors to adaptive visual feedback.

Keywords: Artificial Intelligence · Learning Analytics · Data Visualization · Generative AI · Metaverse Learning Environments · Immersive Analytics · Synthetic Data

1 Introduction

The rapid adoption of extended reality (XR) technologies has enabled the creation of Metaverse Learning Environments (MLEs), distinguishing themselves from single-learner, fragmented virtual or immersive platforms by emphasizing persistent, interoperable, and collaborative spatial interactivity, thereby offering shared, embodied, multi-sensory educational experiences [5,6]. The high-dimensional data streams due to interactions through multimodal inputs offer unprecedented potential for multimodal learning analytics and AI in education [7].

E. G. Blanchard et al. (Eds.): AIED 2026, CCIS 3033, pp. 319–325, 2026.
https://doi.org/10.1007/978-3-032-29794-5_49

Despite this potential, current analytics systems for immersive learning remain limited by several major bottlenecks. First, there is a lack of utilization of rich interaction data; most dashboards reduce complex spatial and temporal behaviors to simplistic 2D metrics, ignoring embodied nuances. Second, there is a lack of adaptive visualization. Existing interfaces fail to align with the 3D, embodied nature of MLEs, leading to increased instructor cognitive load and reduced pedagogical responsiveness [2,3,5]. Third, there is a scarcity of large-scale interaction datasets. Collecting multimodal data from hundreds of real learners is logistically prohibitive, stalling the training and benchmarking of machine learning models.

This research addresses these challenges by leveraging Artificial Intelligence (AI) to synthesize scalable datasets, cluster embodied interaction logs, and design adaptive immersive dashboards grounded in human-computer interaction (HCI) principles.

2 Research Problem and Identified Gaps

MLEs can transform education through embodied and spatial learning, but their full potential is constrained by analytics systems designed for 2D, click-stream based platforms [7]. Rich interaction data remain under-exploited in real-time pedagogical decision-making. A synthesis of prior work across AI, XR, HCI, and educational technology reveals several key research gaps and challenges, summarized in Table 1.

Table 1. Key Challenges and Research Opportunities in Immersive Analytics

Gap or Challenge	Current Limitation	Research Opportunity (AI Solution)
Conceptual	MLEs lack a unified schema for data analysis.	Mapping Operational MLE definition to data types & interaction behavior.
Engineering	Resource constraints of collecting large-scale multimodal datasets.	Hybrid synthetic data generation via Simulation + GAN architectures.
Methodological	High-volume heterogeneous data lacks structured clustering methods.	Adapt unsupervised clustering algorithms to embodied immersive data.
Design	Dashboards ignore 3D spatial contexts and embodied interaction.	Create Generative AI-adapted dashboards for dynamic, localized feedback.
Empirical	Few evaluations in real-world teaching lack evidence of cognitive impact.	Test adaptive dashboards on usability, cognitive load, and responsiveness.

Addressing these gaps via AI pipelines will improve real-time pedagogical responsiveness and learner self-regulation, bridging the divide between raw immersive interaction data and adaptive visual feedback [2,7].

3 Research Goals and Methodology

Guided by the identified gaps, this research follows a Design-Based Research (DBR) approach [7] structured around three overarching Research Goals (RGs):

- **RG1:** Synthesize scalable, pedagogically valid multimodal interaction data by defining, designing and developing MLEs and developing hybrid AI pipelines (physics simulation + GANs).
- **RG2:** Translate raw, multimodal spatial telemetry into interpretable learner behavior patterns by combining generative AI (LLMs) and unsupervised clustering algorithms (e.g., DBSCAN, HMMs).
- **RG3:** Evaluate how AI-driven immersive dashboards compare to traditional 2D interfaces in reducing instructor cognitive load and enhancing real-time pedagogical decision-making.

3.1 Phase 1: MLE Development and Synthetic Data Generation (RG1)

RQ1: How can MLEs be operationally defined and equipped with scalable, AI-ready data pipelines?

- RQ1.1: What are the core characteristics (e.g., embodiment, synchronicity, persistence) that define MLEs? [6]
- RQ1.2: How can MLEs be designed to ensure cross-platform interoperability and high-fidelity interaction logging?
- RQ1.3: To what extent can a hybrid approach (physics simulation + GANs) generate synthetic datasets that accurately mirror real learner interaction patterns?

We are developing a set of interconnected MLEs, inspired by the foundational concept of computational microworlds [8], covering science and mathematics topics. To ensure interoperability, the environments are implemented across three game engines (Unity, Unreal, Godot), targeting various platforms.

To overcome the data scarcity bottleneck, we implement a synthetic data pipeline:

1. Physics Simulation: Using Meta Habitat 3.0 [9] and principles from GTA-Synth [1], we script heuristic agents that perform goal-directed actions within the MLEs, generating base interaction logs (3D coordinates, object states).

2. GAN Refinement: Generative Adversarial Networks are applied to introduce stochastic, human-like variability, such as saccadic eye movements, hand-tremor jitter, and non-linear gaze shifts, improving the ecological validity of the synthetic data and preventing algorithms from overfitting to perfectly linear simulated paths.
3. Scale: The pipeline targets 150 to 450 unique interaction instances, providing the necessary volume to train robust unsupervised clustering models.

3.2 Phase 2: Data Processing and Machine Learning (RG2)

RQ2: How can learner interaction data from MLEs be effectively processed, analyzed, and transformed into an actionable form using AI?

- RQ2.1: What role does each data type play in characterizing learner behavior within MLEs?
- RQ2.2: What combination of feature engineering and unsupervised clustering algorithms (e.g., DBSCAN, HMMs) provides optimal interoperability and accuracy for behavioral pattern detection in MLEs?
- RQ2.3: How can generative AI techniques be leveraged for the pre-processing, augmentation, and semantic enrichment of interaction data prior to analysis?

The synthetic and real interaction (as per availability) logs will be processed through a machine learning pipeline. First, Large Language Models (LLMs) will semantically enrich the data by parsing 3D telemetry serialized into text-based event logs (e.g., JSON sequences of gaze raycasts and coordinates), translating raw geometry into contextual pedagogical actions. Following this, feature engineering will extract relevant spatial and behavioral metrics. Unsupervised algorithms are selected specifically for embodied, multimodal data: DBSCAN maps arbitrarily shaped 3D interaction zones while filtering erratic movement noise, whereas Hidden Markov Models (HMMs) capture the temporal sequence of hidden cognitive states underlying observable actions. These will be evaluated using the Silhouette score and Davies-Bouldin index, followed by expert validation of the resulting behavior taxonomies.

3.3 Phase 3: Adaptive Visualization and Dashboard Evaluation (RG3)

RQ3: How can the resulting data clusters be visualized in adaptive immersive dashboards to support real-time teaching?

- RQ3.1: What design principles support cognitive alignment between immersive dashboards and instructor decision-making?
- RQ3.2: How do immersive analytics dashboards compare to traditional 2D interfaces in supporting awareness, reflection, and pedagogical action?
- RQ3.3: How can generative AI be employed to create context-aware data visualizations within MLEs?

- RQ3.4: What are the key contrasts in applying these visualization techniques to metaverse interaction data versus non-metaverse educational data?

The resulting data clusters will be visualized through two prototypes: a baseline 2D web dashboard and an adaptive 3D immersive dashboard implemented within the Unity environment. Generative AI will be employed to translate raw clustering output into localized, natural-language pedagogical cues (e.g., 'Group B exhibits high frustration'). The immersive visualization dynamically maps behavior patterns onto the virtual learning floor, directly supporting teacher-AI complementarity [3]. A controlled study with instructors will assess:

- Detection Accuracy: Success rate in identifying pedagogical events (e.g., student frustration, collaborative blocks).
- Response Time: Latency between event occurrence and instructor awareness.
- Cognitive Load: NASA Task Load Index (TLX) comparing the 3D immersive system against the 2D baseline.
- Usability: System Usability Scale (SUS) and qualitative interviews.

4 Expected Contributions

The anticipated outcomes extend beyond technical implementations to include theoretical, methodological, and design-oriented contributions for the AIED community (Table 2).

Table 2. Research Contributions and Their Significance

Contribution	Scholarly Significance	Practical Significance
Operational Definition of MLE	Integrates technological and pedagogical dimensions for ML.	Guides platform design and data standardization.
Synthetic Data Pipeline	Demonstrates SIM+GAN approach for scalable data synthesis.	Enables algorithm benchmarking without large participant pools.
Multimodal Clustering	Adapts unsupervised ML to embodied immersive data.	Delivers interpretable behavioral insights to educators.
Adaptive Immersive Visualization	Extends HCI and AI theory to immersive learning analytics.	Enhances data-informed decisions in MLEs.
Empirical Evaluation	Evidence of immersive analytics effectiveness.	Informs real-world classroom adoption.

5 Feedback Sought from the AIED Community

As this doctoral research integrates synthetic data generation with immersive learning analytics, feedback from the AIED community is particularly sought on the following methodological and theoretical challenges:

1. How can the pedagogical validity of behavioral clusters derived from synthetic interaction data be rigorously evaluated to ensure these patterns accurately reflect real-world learner behaviors?
2. How can GAN be effectively used to synthesize deep cognitive and learning-oriented behaviors, ensuring that generated human-like variability (e.g., saccadic movements, hand tremors) represents true pedagogical states rather than mere surface-level biomechanical mimicry?

6 Current Progress and Future Work

An earlier formulation of this doctoral research, focused on data visualization for metaverse-based learning environments, was presented at the ICCE 2025 Doctoral Consortium [4]. The present work substantially extends that contribution by introducing an AI-driven synthetic data pipeline, LLM-based semantic enrichment, and cross-platform MLE development. The literature scoping review [5] and the development of preliminary multimodal data capture modules within a standalone VR environment were completed during the 2024–2025 academic year. The MLE definition was developed through a systematic literature review & industry discourse, and has been accepted for publication [6]. Currently, the research is focused on the design and development of interconnected, cross-platform Metaverse Learning Environments (MLEs) across multiple game engines. Once these environments are deployed, work will proceed on the synthetic data generation pipeline. Future work (2026–2027 and beyond) will focus on feature engineering and unsupervised clustering of interaction data (RG2), followed by the prototyping and empirical evaluation of immersive visualization dashboards (RG3) with instructors. Thesis writing and dissertation submission are expected by mid-2029.

References

1. Curnis, G., Fontana, S., Sorrenti, D.G.: GTASynth: 3d synthetic data of outdoor non-urban environments. Data Brief **43**, 108412 (2022)
2. Dwyer, T.: Immersive analytics: an introduction. In: Immersive Analytics, pp. 1–23. Springer (2018)
3. Holstein, K., McLaren, B.M., Aleven, V.: Student learning benefits of a mixed-reality teacher awareness tool in ai-enhanced classrooms. In: International Conference on Artificial Intelligence in Education (AIED), pp. 154–168. Springer (2019)
4. Hothi, A.: Understanding learner interaction analytics through data visualization in metaverse-based learning environments. In: Proceedings of the 33rd International Conference on Computers in Education. Asia-Pacific Society for Computers in Education (2025)

5. Hothi, A., Das, S.: Learning analytics for the metaverse: a review of descriptive analytics and visualization tools for metaverse-based learning environments. In: Proceedings of the 33rd International Conference on Computers in Education. Asia-Pacific Society for Computers in Education (2025)
6. Hothi, A., Das, S.: A conceptual framework to define metaverse aligned learning environments. In: Proceedings of the IEEE International Conference on Advanced Learning Technologies (ICALT) (2026)
7. Ochoa, X., Worsley, M.: Editorial: augmenting learning analytics with multimodal sensory data. J. Learn. Anal. **3**(2), 213–219 (2016)
8. Papert, S.: Mindstorms: Children, Computers, and Powerful Ideas, Basic Books (1980)
9. Puig, X., Undersander, E., Szot, A., Cote, M.D., Batra, D., Rai, A.: Habitat 3.0: a co-habitat for humans, avatars and robots (2023). arXiv preprint arXiv:2310.13724

AI and Human Peer Feedback in Introductory Programming: A Mixed Methods Study

Ezgi Çallı(✉) and Erkan Er

Department of Computer Education and Instructional Technology, Middle East Technical University, Ankara, Turkey
ezgiecalli@gmail.com

Abstract. This doctoral study examines AI-generated formative feedback by positioning AI as a peer within a feedback process in an introductory Python course and comparing it with human peer feedback in supporting revision quality and learning outcomes. The study builds on a systematic literature review (SLR) of empirical work on AI-generated formative feedback in higher education, which identified theory-informed design principles that guide the present study. Students engage in a system-supported revision process involving submission, feedback (human or AI peer), revision, and dialogic interaction with the feedback source across multiple stages. An explanatory sequential mixed methods design is employed, combining a quasi-experimental phase examining differences in revision quality and learning outcomes with qualitative analysis of feedback uptake using chat logs, revision traces, and interviews. The study aims to advance process-level understanding of how learners interpret and act upon feedback across successive revisions and interactions.

Keywords: AI feedback · peer feedback · programming education · mixed methods

1 Introduction

Recent research in the AIED community has increasingly examined the use of large language models (LLMs) for formative assessment and feedback generation [8]. Particularly, LLM-based systems have been leveraged to generate formative feedback, including automated comments [10], rubric-aligned suggestions [3], and conversational guidance [5]. While current research shows that AI-driven advancements can facilitate scalable and timely feedback, there is a lack of focus on peer feedback. Therefore, a key pedagogical question remains regarding how

E. Çallı—PhD candidate; doctoral consortium submission.
E. Er—Supervisor.

E. G. Blanchard et al. (Eds.): AIED 2026, CCIS 3033, pp. 326–331, 2026.
https://doi.org/10.1007/978-3-032-29794-5_50

to leverage AI in the design of (formative) peer feedback that supports meaningful learning interactions and processes.

Peer feedback is widely used in higher education, particularly in writing [6] and programming contexts [7], to support learning through revision and reflection. It involves students generating and exchanging feedback based on shared criteria, shifting feedback from a teacher-directed activity to a more participatory, student-centered process. When a dialogic component is incorporated that builds on feedback exchanged, peer feedback can more effectively foster critical thinking, self-reflection, and evaluative judgement [9].

However, these benefits are not consistently realized in real-world contexts. In practice, peer feedback is often limited by students' varying ability to provide effective feedback, which in turn may yield low feedback uptake (the extent to which learners interpret and act upon feedback) [1]. Thus, peer feedback presents a dual challenge: generating feedback of sufficient quality, and ensuring that such feedback is meaningfully interpreted and enacted during revision.

This challenge is particularly pronounced in domains requiring iterative refinement, such as programming courses [4], where learning depends on cycles of feedback and revision. While such a constant feedback iteration is infeasible for instructors to sustain, relying on peer feedback to fill this gap requires careful reconsideration. This is particularly important in light of emerging AI affordances that may help address both the quality and uptake limitations inherent in traditional feedback processes.

One relevant affordance of AI might be to act not only as a feedback generator but as a peer-like participant capable of providing and receiving feedback. This offers a potential way to address key limitations of human peer feedback, particularly inconsistencies in feedback quality and limited uptake, by introducing more consistent and guided feedback interactions. However, prior research has largely treated AI as a feedback tool rather than as a participant in peer feedback processes. Consequently, it remains unclear how effectively peer feedback functions when feedback is generated by an AI peer compared to a human peer, or how learners interpret and act upon such feedback during revision.

Accordingly, this doctoral study positions AI as a peer within the feedback process, one that provides feedback, and investigates how this compares to human peers in an introductory Python course. Rather than relying on students' perceptions of feedback quality, in this comparison, the study examines how feedback is actually enacted in revisions and its effect on learning outcomes. The study builds on findings from a systematic literature review (SLR) of 103 empirical studies (2020–2025) on AI-generated formative feedback in higher education, which informed the design principles and analytical focus of the present study [11].

2 Research Questions

1. How does AI peer feedback compare with human peer feedback in promoting revision quality and learning outcomes in introductory programming?

2. How do students engage with and act upon AI peer feedback during a structured revision process?
3. How do learner characteristics (e.g., prior performance and feedback literacy) relate to differences in feedback uptake and learning gains?

3 Insights from the Systematic Literature Review

The SLR identified four design gaps: (1) programming studies largely emphasize automated grading and correctness feedback rather than theory-grounded, peer-style formative feedback; (2) evaluation focuses primarily on final outcomes or perceptions, with limited analysis of revision processes; (3) adaptivity is typically limited to generic prompt variation without systematic use of learner performance indicators; and (4) explicit integration of feedback literacy and dialogic principles into LLM feedback design is uncommon.

The present study addresses these gaps by situating the investigation in a programming context that enables traceable revision analysis. It incorporates process-level measures of feedback uptake through alignment of feedback, revision traces, and interaction data. It also operationalizes theory-informed, performance-informed feedback through structured prompt templates and rule-based variation in scaffolding based on prior performance indicators.

4 Conceptual Framework

The study operationalizes aligned formative feedback through three integrated layers [11].

Foundational Layer. Feedback is conceptualized as a revision-oriented, self-regulatory process. This is operationalized through prompt templates structured around the feed up, feedback, and feed forward model (i.e., clarifying goals, evaluating current performance, and guiding next steps) [4]. Feedback is designed to reduce the discrepancy between current understanding and desired performance rather than provide direct corrections. Prompt design will be refined through iterative testing and informed by feedback literature.

System Layer. A locally deployed, closed LLM-based chatbot developed within a TÜBİTAK-funded project provides a controlled research infrastructure. The system is implemented as a standalone web-based platform supporting both human peer and AI-generated feedback within a unified environment. It enables code submission, feedback exchange, and dialogue between students and feedback providers. AI-generated feedback is controlled through system-level prompt templates that translate pedagogical principles into structured outputs such as issue identification, explanation, and revision-oriented guidance. The system allows configurable feedback behavior while maintaining consistency across participants. All interactions, including submissions, feedback, and dialogue, are logged to support analysis of feedback uptake and revision processes.

Rather than implementing a dynamic learner model, the study adopts a rule-based approach in which feedback is differentiated based on observable prior performance. This allows controlled variation in the level of guidance and supports a focused examination of feedback design.

Interaction Layer. Feedback is enacted through system-mediated interaction in which the feedback source (human or AI) functions as a peer-like co-participant. After receiving feedback, students engage in guided dialogue with the feedback source to clarify, interpret, and extend feedback. Interactions are logged, and an instructor dashboard enables monitoring and alignment with the intended feedback design. This setup supports analysis of how feedback is interpreted and enacted during revision.

Together, these layers align theoretical grounding, system configuration, and learner interaction within a platform-mediated environment that enables analysis of feedback uptake.

5 Methodology

5.1 Mixed Methods Design

This study employs an explanatory sequential mixed methods design (QUAN → qual), in which a quasi-experimental phase is followed by qualitative analysis to explain observed outcome patterns [2]. Integration occurs at the interpretation stage.

5.2 Context and Experimental Phase

The study will be conducted in an introductory Python course with approximately 60 undergraduate students. A quasi-experimental design with two conditions is implemented:

- Human peer feedback
- AI-generated feedback (framework-aligned configuration)

Students submit an initial solution (T1), receive feedback (human or AI peer, anonymized), and submit a revised version (T2). This is followed by a guided interaction phase in which students engage in dialogue with the feedback source before producing a final revision (T3). Programming tasks consist of short problems aligned with course content and designed to allow multiple solution strategies and common error patterns.

Within the AI condition, feedback is performance-informed: students are grouped based on prior assessment scores, and feedback is differentiated accordingly, e.g. providing more guidance for lower-performing students and more concise prompts for higher-performing students. In the human peer condition, feedback is provided through system-supported peer interaction. Peer matching strategies will be informed by pilot findings and relevant literature to ensure comparable feedback exchanges across conditions.

5.3 Quantitative Measures

Programming submissions will be evaluated using an analytic rubric. The rubric criteria will be embedded within the system to ensure consistency across conditions.

Students will also be informed that the quality of the feedback they provide will be evaluated using a separate rubric, encouraging more deliberate feedback contributions.

Revision gains are examined across three stages: T1 (initial), T2 (post-feedback), and T3 (post-dialogue). Outcome measures include initial uptake (T2-T1), dialogue-supported gain (T3-T2), and overall improvement (T3-T1). A subset of submissions will be double-scored for reliability.

Prior performance and feedback literacy are included as covariates or moderators.

5.4 Qualitative Phase

Qualitative data include chat logs, revision artifacts (T1-T2-T3), and semi-structured interviews. The study adopts a system-logged, multi-source approach combining revision data, interaction logs, and interviews to examine how feedback is interpreted, evaluated, and enacted across successive revisions and interaction phases.

Analysis focuses on revision types, alignment between feedback and code changes, and patterns of interaction in dialogue. Interview data support interpretation of learners' reasoning in accepting or rejecting feedback. These findings explain quantitative differences across conditions and stages.

6 Progress and Timeline

The SLR has been completed and the conceptual framework finalized. A pilot study will be conducted in Spring 2026, followed by full implementation in Fall 2026.

7 Expected Contributions to AIED

This study contributes to both learning sciences and computer science. From a learning sciences perspective, it examines AI-supported formative feedback by analyzing how feedback is taken up across successive revisions and interaction phases using system-logged data. It brings feedback literacy and dialogic principles into AI feedback design and advances process-level understanding of feedback use.

From a computer science perspective, the study outlines a method for translating pedagogical principles into structured LLM prompt configurations and investigates how locally deployed AI systems can support controlled experimentation. It further examines performance-informed and rule-based feedback scaffolding as a transparent alternative to complex adaptive modeling.

Acknowledgments. This work is supported by the Scientific and Technological Research Council of Turkey (TUBITAK).

Disclosure of Interests. The authors declare no competing interests.

References

1. Ardill, N.: Peer feedback in higher education: student perceptions of peer review and strategies for learning enhancement. Eur. J. High. Educ. **15**(4), 696–721 (2025). https://doi.org/10.1080/21568235.2025.2457466
2. Creswell, J.W., Plano Clark, V.L.: Designing and Conducting Mixed Methods Research. Sage, 3 edn. (2018)
3. Er, E., Akçapınar, G., Bayazıt, A., Noroozi, O., Banihashem, S.K.: Assessing student perceptions and use of instructor versus AI-generated feedback. Br. J. Edu. Technol. **56**, 1074–1091 (2025). https://doi.org/10.1111/bjet.13558
4. Hattie, J., Timperley, H.: The power of feedback. Rev. Educ. Res. **77**(1), 81–112 (2007). https://doi.org/10.3102/003465430298487
5. Holderried, F., et al.: A language model-powered simulated patient with automated feedback for history taking: prospective study. JMIR Med. Educ. **10**(1), e59213 (2024)
6. Huisman, B., Saab, N., Van Den Broek, P., Van Driel, J.: The impact of formative peer feedback on higher education students' academic writing: a meta-analysis. Assess. Eval. High. Educ. **44**(6), 863–880 (2019)
7. Indriasari, T.D., Luxton-Reilly, A., Denny, P.: A review of peer code review in higher education. ACM Trans. Comput. Educ. **20**(3), 1–25 (2020)
8. Narreddy, C., Joordens, S., Prompiengchai, S.: Harnessing large language models for scalable and effective formative assessment in higher education: a review. Trends High. Educ. **4**(4), 65 (2025)
9. Nicol, D., Thomson, A., Breslin, C.: Rethinking feedback practices in higher education: a peer review perspective. Assess. Eval. High. Educ. **39**(1), 102–122 (2014). https://doi.org/10.1080/02602938.2013.795518
10. Palahan, S.: Pythonpal: enhancing online programming education through chatbot-driven personalized feedback. IEEE Trans. Learn. Technol. **18**, 335–350 (2025). https://doi.org/10.1109/TLT.2025
11. Çallı, E., Er, E.: When technological momentum overshadows pedagogical alignment: a systematic review of AI-generated formative feedback in higher education. Assess. Eval. High. Educ., 1–24 (2026). https://doi.org/10.1080/02602938.2026.2674230

Enhancing Climate Education Through Microclimate-Aware Learning Technologies: A GenAI and IoT Powered Approach

Imran S. Afizullah-Khan, Emmanuel G. Blanchard(✉), and Sébastien George

Le Mans Université, LIUM, F-72000 Le Mans, France
{imran.khan,emmanuel.blanchard,sebastien.george}@univ-lemans.fr

Abstract. Climate education is an urgent global priority, yet many existing approaches remain abstract and disconnected from learners' local experiences. This study explores the potential of microclimates within local nature parks as an observable context for place-based climate education. Addressing the limited research on leveraging microclimatic conditions for instructional purposes, we propose an approach that integrates IoT sensors-based microclimatic data such as ambient temperature, humidity and light, with Generative AI to create contextualized and personalized learning experiences. By situating climate concepts within learners' immediate surroundings, the study aims to enhance relevance, engagement, and overall learning outcomes for climate education.

Keywords: Climate Education · Place-based learning · Microclimate-aware learning · Generative AI in education · Educational Chatbot

1 Problem Statement

Climate education is widely recognized as an urgent global priority. Reports from international organizations like OECD [7] emphasize the far-reaching impacts of climate change on daily life, public health, economic stability, and environmental sustainability. Existing approaches often emphasize abstract explanations and global phenomena while neglecting how climate change is experienced in learners' local context. Place-based learning [12] is an approach that situates learning within learners' local environments and real-world contexts to enhance relevance and understanding. In this regard, places such as local nature parks, zoos, and reserves are directly affected by climate change and therefore offer significant potential for place-based climate education. While this approach has been explored through outdoor summer programs, classroom-based local climate instruction, and place-based film-making projects [12]. In this study, we leverage the microclimate notion because they make climate change concepts more concrete and locally observable [4], thereby supporting clearer and more meaningful understanding.

A microclimate refers to the localized climate conditions of a specific area that differ from the surrounding environment [4] for example, a shaded forest may be cooler and more humid than a nearby open field. Its definition varies depending on ecological perspective and spatial scale. In nature parks, microclimates can be understood as localized

E. G. Blanchard et al. (Eds.): AIED 2026, CCIS 3033, pp. 332–337, 2026.
https://doi.org/10.1007/978-3-032-29794-5_51

atmospheric conditions that differ across areas due to vegetation, terrain, water bodies, and exposure. These small-scale variations shape ecosystem functioning and influence how organisms respond to broader climate change, making them a valuable context for place-based climate education. In this study, we specifically focus on microclimatic conditions such as temperature, humidity, and light intensity. In educational settings, microclimates have primarily been studied in relation to learning environment enhancement [10] and their influence on learners' cognitive and affective states [5]. However, their use as an instructional context for place-based climate education remains under-explored, likely due to the complexity of implementation through traditional methods. Recent advances in Generative Artificial Intelligence (GenAI) and the Internet of Things (IoT) offer new opportunities to integrate real-time environmental data into learning experiences, a potential elaborated in the proposed solution section.

2 Theoretical Background

Our research is grounded in place-based education [12] and is further focused on five principles discussed below:

Domain-Guided Content Generation [3]. This principle emphasizes that instructional guidance should be grounded in structured and validated domain knowledge. Rather than relying solely on open-ended information generation, effective learning design integrates clearly defined concepts, established learning objectives, and curated knowledge sources.

Contextualized Instructions [7]. This principle emphasizes designing learning experiences that ground instructional content in the learner's immediate physical and environmental context, including the spaces where they live, study, and belong. By linking concepts to real-time, observable conditions rather than presenting them abstractly, it enhances relevance, reduces abstraction, and supports deeper conceptual understanding.

Instructional Scaffolding [11]. This principle refers to structured guidance that supports learners in progressively understanding complex concepts. Rooted in scaffolding theory, it involves introducing ideas step by step, using guiding questions, breaking content into manageable parts, and providing clear explanations. Such adaptive support fosters deeper and more independent understanding.

Adaptive Personalized Learning [9]. Effective instructional design recognizes that learners vary in their prior knowledge, experiences, and cognitive readiness. Since new information is processed in relation to existing knowledge, teaching strategies should be responsive to these individual differences. Adapting content and guidance to learners' levels supports clearer understanding, increases relevance, and facilitates meaningful knowledge construction.

AIED Unplugged [2] is an emerging framework within Artificial Intelligence in Education (AIED) that emphasizes leveraging the pedagogical strengths of AI-driven tools while minimizing reliance on advanced infrastructure or complex technical requirements. Supporting accessible learning experiences that can extend to remote and under-served regions worldwide. Grounded in the above principles, we developed a microclimate-aware learning technology (discussed in proposed solution) powered by

GenAI and IoT, using a design-based research approach. Aiming to answer the below research questions.

RQ1: To what extent do educators and other stakeholders perceive the microclimate-aware learning approach as acceptable and valuable?
RQ2: Does the contextualization of learning content enhance learners' overall learning outcomes?
RQ3: How can the key components of a microclimate-aware learning system be identified and integrated in alignment with the principles of AIED Unplugged?

3 Proposed Solution

The proposed solution is based on the theoretical principles outlined above and implemented as an educational chatbot due to its ability to provide contextualized instruction, interactive dialogue, and adaptive personalization in a scalable format. The chatbot follows a structured instructional approach, introducing predefined concepts through guided explanations based on human-designed learning plans and pedagogical rules. While the instructional sequence remains fixed, the explanations are dynamically adapted to the learner's current microclimatic conditions, ensuring contextualized delivery within a stable pedagogical framework.

Figure 1 illustrates chatbot dialogue flows under two different microclimate scenarios: Scene 1 (22 °C, 50% humidity, cloudy, winter) and Scene 2 (32 °C, 45% humidity, sunny, summer). Both scenes in Fig. 1 depict microclimate-aware interactions, each reflecting different environmental conditions to illustrate how the system adapts. Across both scenes, the chatbot follows a consistent yet contextually adapted learning sequence: it begins by introducing a concept, poses a guiding question to prompt reflection, responds to the learner's input, and then elaborates on the next concept, all while explicitly weaving in the current microclimatic conditions as part of the explanation. This cycle continues until all planned topics have been addressed, after which the learner is invited to ask further questions.

Technical Architecture. This section outlines the backend architecture, designed to support contextualized and adaptive learning beyond a chatbot interface and applicable to other instructional formats. The system is based on a Retrieval-Augmented Generation (RAG) [3] framework, grounding responses in verified knowledge sources while adhering to predefined pedagogical rules. By combining retrieval and generation, the architecture improves factual accuracy and enables the use of resource-efficient models, supporting scalability and alignment with AIED Unplugged principles. Figure 2 illustrates the overall system architecture.

Client. A web app that serves as the user interface, allowing learners to interact with the system, receive adaptive instructional content, and submit queries. *Atmo-Station.* A microcontroller-based device equipped with sensors that capture microclimatic data and transmit it to the server. The *Retriever* coordinates learner input, contextualization, personalization, domain knowledge, and knowledge interpretation in alignment with an educator-defined learning plan.

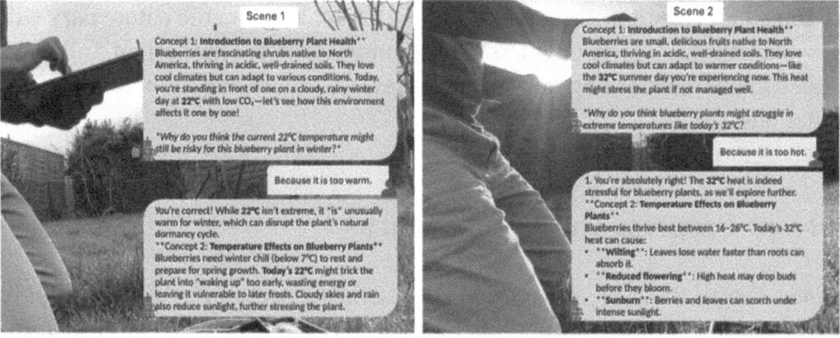

Fig. 1. Dialogue flow examples between the learner and microclimate-aware educational chatbot in two different scenarios.

This plan includes predefined pedagogical rules and instructional sequences, implemented through a context-engineering [1] approach. It then constructs a structured prompt aligned with the defined learning plan and instructional framework before forwarding it to the Generator. *The Generator.* A small language model [3] that processes the structured prompt to produce contextually adapted instructional content, which is then returned to the Client.

The process begins when the learner submits a query via the Client (a), which is sent to the Retriever (b). The Retriever also receives microclimatic data from the Atmo-Station (c), retrieves relevant knowledge from the KB (d), and forwards the structured prompt to the Generator (e). The generated, context-aligned instructional response is then returned to the Client for presentation to the learner (f), as illustrated in Fig. 2.

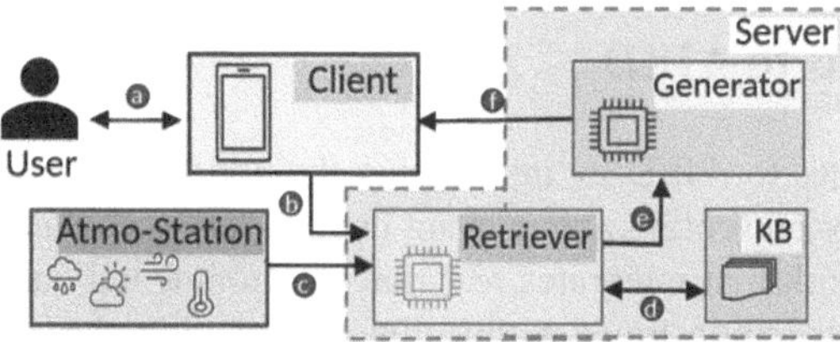

Fig. 2. Core architecture for a microclimate-aware learning system. (KB = Knowledge Base)

4 Methodology

To assess educational impact and practical feasibility, mixed-method evaluation will be conducted, comprising a learner-based experiment and an expert assessment.

Learner-Based Evaluation. A controlled study with two randomly assigned groups will be conducted on-site at a nature park. Participants will test either a microclimate-aware chatbot or a non-microclimate-aware control version. After consent and a demographic survey (GDPR-compliant), participants will complete a pre-test, a 15-min interaction, an immediate post-test, and a delayed post-test after two weeks. Interaction logs (clicks, time, chat data) will be recorded to examine engagement and usage patterns.

Expert-Based Evaluation. Mediators and professionals from the nature park will evaluate the system through a live or video-based demonstration of the system, followed by an online questionnaire assessing educational relevance, motivational potential, strengths, and limitations.

5 Current Progress and Future Works

As outlined above, the system has been successfully developed and deployed on low-resource hardware, specifically the NVIDIA Jetson Orin Nano [6], enabling fully local operation and supporting one or two learners simultaneously. To evaluate its feasibility in constrained environments, the system was tested with multiple SLMs. The results showed that, when appropriate context engineering strategies were applied, their performance was comparable to that of LLMs in generating contextual and accurate responses. Furthermore, a preliminary online video-based evaluation conducted with mediators and professionals from the local nature park yielded predominantly positive feedback, particularly regarding the system's contextual relevance and educational potential.

As a next step, further consultations with mediators and in-person system demonstrations are planned to collect localized, place-based knowledge for integration into the chatbot, ensuring alignment with the ecological and contextual characteristics of the nature park. Multiple large-scale evaluations with participants will then assess learning outcomes by comparing microclimate-aware system with non-aware control conditions. Future research could further investigate the impact of personalization and explore alternative pedagogical strategies, such as inquiry-based learning, as well as different interpretive approaches like modelling, to assess their comparative effectiveness.

6 Contributions to AIED

This study contributes to AIED by introducing the notion microclimate adaptation in learning contexts, by presenting one relevant use cases (i.e. climate education), and by providing a framework that integrates real-time environmental data into AI-supported instruction. Although demonstrated within climate education, the framework is domain-agnostic and transferable to other areas such as urban development, marine biology, and environmental science, where localized contextual data can meaningfully enrich learning experiences.

The study further highlights the pedagogical value of integrating real-world data into AI-supported learning environments, demonstrating how contextually grounded instruction can reduce abstraction, increase relevance, and deepen conceptual understanding. It further proposes an empirical evaluation framework combining controlled comparisons, learning outcome measures, interaction log analysis, and stakeholder assessment. Additionally, it examines stakeholder perceptions and advocates for their active involvement in the design and evaluation process to promote context-sensitive and collaboratively developed AI-supported educational systems. Finally, the research advances the principles of AIED Unplugged [2] by demonstrating how adaptive and context-sensitive learning can be implemented using resource-efficient architectures, including RAG, microcomputers [6] and SLMs. This design supports scalability and enables deployment in remote or technology-constrained regions, expanding the reach of AI-enhanced learning opportunities.

Acknowledgment. This doctoral research is supported by joint funding from Le Mans University, France, and the Pays de la Loire Region, France.

References

1. Context Engineering. https://www.philschmid.de/context-engineering. Accessed 23 Feb 2026
2. Isotani, S., Bittencourt, I.I., Challco, G.C., Dermeval, D., Mello, R.F.: AIED unplugged: leapfrogging the digital divide to reach the underserved. In: Wang, N., et al. (eds.) Artificial Intelligence in Education (AIED 2023). CCIS, vol. 1831. Springer, Cham (2023). https://doi.org/10.1007/978-3-031-36336-8_118
3. Liu, S., Yu, Z., Huang, F., Bulbulia, Y., Bergen, A., Liut, M.: Can small language models with retrieval-augmented generation replace large language models when learning computer science? In: Proceedings of the 2024 on Innovation and Technology in Computer Science Education, Milan Italy, vol. 1. pp. 388–393. ACM (2024). https://doi.org/10.1145/3649217.3653554
4. Mislan, K.A.S., Helmuth, B.: Microclimate. In: Fath, B. (ed.) Encyclopedia of Ecology, 2nd edn., pp. 472–475. Elsevier, Amsterdam (2008). https://doi.org/10.1016/B978-0-444-63768-0.00520-5
5. Nguyen, D.M.A., Nguyen, T.M.T., Lim, K.Y.T., Posada-Quintero, H.F.: Investigating effects of microclimate on stress and affect using low-cost wearables in quasi-formal academic contexts. AI Brain Child. **1**, 6 (2025). https://doi.org/10.1007/s44436-025-00007-1
6. NVIDIA Jetson Orin Nano Super Developer Kit, https://tinyurl.com/bdzy5558, last accessed 2026/02/27
7. Rivet, A.E., Krajcik, J.S.: Contextualizing instruction: Leveraging students' prior knowledge and experiences to foster understanding of middle school science. J. Res. Sci. Teach. **45**, 79–100 (2008). https://doi.org/10.1002/tea.20203
8. Nusche, D., Fuster Rabella, M., Lauterbach, S.: Rethinking education in the context of climate change: leverage points for transformative change. In: OECD Education Working Papers, No. 307, OECD Publishing, Paris (2024). https://doi.org/10.1787/f14c8a81-en
9. Sambrook, K., Konstantinidis, E., Russell, S., Okan, Y.: The role of personal experience and prior beliefs in shaping climate change perceptions: a narrative review. Front. Psychol. **12**, 669911 (2021). https://doi.org/10.3389/fpsyg.2021.669911
10. Strelets, K., Zaborova, D., Serbin, I., Petrochenko, M., Zavodnova, E.: Analysis of microclimatic comfort conditions in university classrooms. Sustainability. **16**, 3388 (2024). https://doi.org/10.3390/su16083388
11. Van De Pol, J., Volman, M., Beishuizen, J.: Scaffolding in teacher-student interaction: a decade of research. Educ. Psychol. Rev. **22**, 271–296 (2010). https://doi.org/10.1007/s10648-010-9127-6
12. Yemini, M., Engel, L., Ben Simon, A.: Place-based education – a systematic review of literature. Educ. Rev. **77**, 640–660 (2025). https://doi.org/10.1080/00131911.2023.2177260

Modeling Teacher-Student Co-regulation as a Relational Process in AI-Supported Learning

Valentina Scorza(✉) and Nicoletta Di Blas

Politecnico di Milano, Piazza Leonardo da Vinci 32, 20133 Milano, Italy
{valentina.scorza,nicoletta.diblas}@polimi.it

Abstract. In formal education, regulation is inherently relational: teacher and student continuously adapt to one another through dynamic interaction, responding to and shaping each other's actions over time. Despite its theoretical centrality in the learning sciences, teacher-student co-regulation has not yet been formalized as an explicit computational construct within AI-supported educational systems. AI in Education is evolving along two largely separate trajectories: student-facing systems that function as increasingly autonomous personalized tutors, and teacher-facing systems that position educators as recipients of analytics and performance indicators. This architectural divide is not merely technical. It implicitly reshapes the pedagogical relationship: learning becomes individually optimized, while teaching risks becoming observational rather than co-regulatory. This doctoral project investigates how teacher-student co-regulation can be formally represented and empirically studied as a relational process in AI-supported learning environments. It conceptualizes co-regulation as a dynamic coupling between student learning states and teacher instructional actions and examines how patterns of alignment and misalignment emerge over time using longitudinal digital trace data. A prototype system will be developed as a research instrument to operationalize this relational model and enable in-situ investigation of co-regulatory processes. By extending learner modeling from the individual to the relational level, the project introduces co-regulation as a unit of computational analysis in AI in Education and studies how its explicit representation shapes teacher-student coordination over time.

Keywords: Teacher-Student Co-Regulation · Relational Modeling · AI in Education (AIED) · Learner Modeling · HumanâĂŞAI Coordination

1 Introduction

Artificial intelligence in education has primarily focused on optimizing either the learner or the teacher, but rarely the relational processes that connect them [9,11]. Most existing approaches model regulation at the level of the individual: they either support students' self-regulated learning [6] or provide teachers

E. G. Blanchard et al. (Eds.): AIED 2026, CCIS 3033, pp. 338–344, 2026.
https://doi.org/10.1007/978-3-032-29794-5_52

with performance indicators to guide instructional decisions [10]. In both cases, regulatory processes are treated as located primarily on one of the two sides of the pedagogical relationship. In formal education, however, learning is shaped by ongoing interaction between teacher and student [4]. Goals are negotiated, progress is interpreted, and strategies are adjusted through a socially mediated process commonly described as co-regulation [1]. Although co-regulation is well established in the learning sciences, it remains largely implicit in digitally mediated environments and is rarely represented explicitly within AI-supported systems.

This doctoral project investigates how teacher-student co-regulation can be formally represented and computationally modeled in AI-supported learning contexts. The aim is to move beyond individual learner modeling by introducing a relational modeling layer that captures how student learning states and teacher instructional actions evolve together over time. Within this perspective, AI is conceptualized not as an autonomous tutor but as a coordination infrastructure that makes regulatory dynamics visible and supports alignment while preserving teacher and student agency. By positioning co-regulation as the primary unit of analysis, the project seeks to extend current AI in Education paradigms toward a relational understanding of regulation in digitally mediated learning environments.

2 Theoretical Foundations

Research on self-regulated learning (SRL) conceptualizes regulation as a cyclical and adaptive process through which learners set goals, enact strategies, monitor progress, and adjust their cognition, motivation, and behavior [13]. This perspective has strongly influenced research in the learning sciences and AI in Education, but it primarily locates regulation within the individual learner, even though it acknowledges the role of social influences.

In formal educational settings, however, regulatory processes are embedded within instructional structures shaped by teacher guidance, feedback, and pedagogical intentions [7,8]. Learners' goals, interpretations, and strategies are therefore influenced by interaction with others rather than formed in isolation.

Co-regulated learning (CRL) extends individual models of regulation by framing it as socially mediated and distributed across participants [3,5]. From socio-cognitive and socio-cultural perspectives, monitoring, interpretation, and adaptation emerge through relational processes in which regulatory responsibility shifts over time through ongoing reciprocal adjustment.

In digitally mediated environments, relational regulatory processes become observable through digital trace data rather than direct classroom observation [2]. This perspective is consistent with process-oriented SRL models that conceptualize regulation as a traceable process over time [12], enabling analytical and computational modeling of co-regulation within AI-supported systems.

3 Problem Statement and Research Gap

Prior research in the learning sciences emphasizes the importance of teacher-student co-regulation as a relational dimension of learning processes [3,8]. Co-regulation refers to reciprocal exchanges in which instructional actions and student responses shape each other over time. Research has increasingly examined its role in shaping engagement, collaboration, and learning outcomes [1,8]. However, despite this growing attention, the relational structure of co-regulation remains computationally under-specified in AI in Education [11].

Current AI-supported systems predominantly model regulation at the level of the individual [6,9]. Learner models infer student knowledge or behavioral states, while teacher-facing tools provide analytics to support instructional decisions [10]. In both cases, regulation is treated as residing primarily on one side of the interaction. The dynamic interdependence through which teacher and student mutually influence each other over time remains insufficiently modeled [11].

As a result, AI in Education lacks a computational framework capable of representing co-regulation as a dynamic process with identifiable states and transitions, including moments of alignment and breakdown. Addressing this limitation requires formalizing co-regulation in a way that preserves its pedagogical meaning while enabling systematic inference from interaction data.

This project addresses this gap by developing a computational formalization of teacher-student co-regulation as a dynamic process within AI in Education. The aim is to define how co-regulatory states can be inferred from interaction data, represented in computational models, and integrated into AI-supported systems in ways that preserve their pedagogical meaning while enabling systematic modeling and analysis.

4 Research Framework

The overarching goal of this doctoral project is to establish teacher-student co-regulation as a computationally formalizable and empirically investigable construct within AI in Education. To achieve this goal, the project is guided by the following research questions: **RQ1 (Computational Formalization)** concerns how teacher-student co-regulation can be defined and represented as a computational unit within AI systems; **RQ2 (Dynamic Characterization)** addresses which interaction patterns and temporal structures characterize the emergence, stability, breakdown, and repair of teacher-student co-regulation over time in AI-mediated educational contexts; and **RQ3 (Relational Consequences)** examines how explicit AI-based representation of co-regulation influences teacher-student coordination, instructional adaptation, and participants' perceptions of alignment and mutual responsiveness.

5 Proposed Approach

The project develops an AI-mediated framework that models teacher-student co-regulation as a shared and evolving regulatory state within a digital learning environment. AI functions as an intermediate computational layer embedded in the interaction workflow. On the student side, it infers latent learning states from longitudinal behavioral traces, including resource sequencing, revision patterns, and strategy changes. On the teacher side, it encodes instructional regulation through observable actions such as feedback timing, scaffolding intensity, and task adaptation. These perspectives are integrated into a dynamic co-regulatory representation capturing alignment between instructional actions and student learning behavior. StateâĂŞtransition dynamics inferred from interaction traces enable identification of alignment shifts, breakdowns, and regulatory repair.

AI operates as a relational layer that renders the co-regulatory state explicit within the interaction workflow and can intervene by signaling misalignments and proposing coordination actions. When discrepancies are inferred, the system generates candidate moves to support realignment. These proposals do not determine regulation but structure opportunities for adjustment requiring interpretation and decision-making by both teacher and student.

In this way, AI formalizes the teacher-student regulatory coupling as an analyzable and actionable construct: it makes relational dynamics computationally explicit, supports negotiated adjustment of the learning trajectory, and preserves the agency of both participants in shaping how regulation unfolds.

6 Methodology

The empirical context consists of a video-centered online learning platform used in secondary or higher education, serving as a testbed for developing and evaluating the proposed framework. The research unfolds in three phases. The first two adopt an iterative design-based approach to refine the framework in authentic educational settings, followed by a third experimental evaluation phase.

Initially, fine-grained interaction data (e.g., pausing, rewinding, revisions, timing patterns), together with session-level indicators such as delayed starting and study persistence, will be analyzed to operationalize student learning states and identify recurring regulatory patterns. In parallel, semi-structured interviews and workshops with teachers and students will examine how study behaviors, feedback exchanges, and moments of difficulty are interpreted. These qualitative insights will ground the definition of co-regulatory states and ensure the model reflects pedagogically meaningful constructs rather than behavioral signals.

Subsequently, a computational model will represent co-regulation as a dynamic relationship between inferred student states and teacher instructional actions. State-based or temporal modeling approaches will estimate transitions between alignment, misalignment, and repair. Model validity will be assessed not only through predictive performance, but also through teacher validation to assess interpretability and plausibility.

In the final phase, the model will be integrated into a prototype embedding explicit co-regulatory mechanisms within the learning workflow. A controlled classroom experiment will compare an experimental group (with AI-based co-regulation support) and a control group using AI-supported self-regulated learning tools without relational modeling. The study will examine the construct validity of the co-regulatory representation and differences in co-regulatory trajectories, alignment dynamics, and instructional adaptation across conditions. Evaluation will combine quantitative analyses of longitudinal interaction data with qualitative evidence from teachers and students to assess both modeling validity and its impact on regulatory coordination.

7 Current Progress

To date, the work has focused on the student-side modeling component within a video-centered online learning platform. The current objective is to identify observable interaction signals during video study that meaningfully indicate states related to self-regulated learning.

Preliminary analyses examine fine-grained behavioral traces, including pausing frequency, rewinding and rewatching patterns, skipping behavior, playback speed variation and session timing. These signals are analyzed to determine their correspondence to regulatory processes such as monitoring, persistence, strategy adjustment, or disengagement. Unsupervised clustering and temporal sequence analysis are used to identify recurrent behavioral configurations and transition patterns across learners.

The results reveal distinct behavioral clusters corresponding to different study patterns, suggesting that video interaction traces can be structured into interpretable learning state representations. The goal of this phase is to formalize these patterns into a computationally tractable representation of student learning states. This student-layer model will serve as the foundation for the subsequent integration of teacher instructional actions within a broader co-regulatory framework.

8 Expected Contributions and Impact

The primary contribution of this project lies in formalizing teacher-student co-regulation as a computationally tractable relational process within AI-supported learning environments. Although co-regulation is theoretically central in the learning sciences, it remains computationally under-specified in AI systems, which mainly focus on individual learner modeling or teacher-facing analytics. This research extends AI in education by formalizing co-regulation as a relational unit of analysis defined by observable states, temporal transitions, and alignment patterns inferred from longitudinal interaction data.

Methodologically, the project introduces a structured procedure for translating pedagogical constructs, such as instructional moves, strategy adjustments, and regulatory breakdowns, into computational representations grounded in interaction traces. Technically, it develops a dynamic state-based model linking inferred student learning states and teacher regulatory actions. Empirically, it examines how making co-regulatory dynamics explicit through AI-supported representation influences teacher-student coordination over time.

The broader impact lies in extending AI in Education beyond individual optimization toward relational regulatory modeling. By establishing co-regulation as a computationally representable and analytically tractable process, the project contributes a new perspective on learner modeling and informs the design of AI systems that support pedagogically aligned teacher-student interaction in digitally mediated contexts.

References

1. Allal, L.: Assessment and the co-regulation of learning in the classroom. Assess. Educ. Princi. Policy Pract. **27**(4), 332–349 (2020). https://doi.org/10.1080/0969594X.2019.1609411
2. Dillenbourg, P.: What do you mean by collaborative learning? In: Dillenbourg, P. (ed.) Collaborative-Learning: Cognitive and Computational Approaches, pp. 1–19. Elsevier, Oxford (1999)
3. Hadwin, A.F., Järvelä, S., Miller, M.A.: Self-regulated, co-regulated, and socially shared regulation of learning. In: Zimmerman, B.J., Schunk, D.H. (eds.) Handbook of Self-Regulation of Learning and Performance, pp. 65–84. Routledge, New York (2011)
4. Hattie, J.: Visible Learning: A Synthesis of Over 800 Meta-analyses Relating to Achievement, 1 edn. Routledge, London (2008). https://doi.org/10.4324/9780203887332
5. Järvelä, S., Hadwin, A.F.: New frontiers: regulating learning in CSCL. Educ. Psychol. **48**(1), 25–39 (2013). https://doi.org/10.1080/00461520.2012.748006
6. Jin, S.H., Im, K., Yoo, M., Roll, I., Seo, K.: Supporting students' self-regulated learning in online learning using artificial intelligence applications. Int. J. Educ. Technol. High. Educ. **20**, 1–21 (2023). https://doi.org/10.1186/s41239-023-00406-5
7. van de Pol, J., Volman, M., Beishuizen, J.: Scaffolding in teacher–student interaction: a decade of research. Educ. Psychol. Rev. **22**, 271–296 (2010). https://doi.org/10.1007/s10648-010-9127-6
8. Saariaho, E., Toom, A., Soini, T., Pietarinen, J., Pyhältö, K.: Student teachers' and pupils' co-regulated learning behaviours in authentic classroom situations in teaching practicums. Teach. Teach. Educ. **85**, 92–104 (2019). https://doi.org/10.1016/j.tate.2019.06.003
9. Sharma, K., Nguyen, A., Hong, Y.: Self-regulation and shared regulation in collaborative learning in adaptive digital learning environments: a systematic review of empirical studies. Br. J. Educ. Technol. **55**, 1398–1436 (2024). https://doi.org/10.1111/bjet.13459
10. Sušnjak, T., Ramaswami, G., Mathrani, A.: Learning analytics dashboard: a tool for providing actionable insights to learners. Int. J. Educ. Technol. High. Educ. **19** (2022). https://doi.org/10.1186/s41239-021-00313-7
11. Wang, S., Wang, F., Zhu, Z., Wang, J., Tran, T., Du, Z.: Artificial intelligence in education: a systematic literature review. Expert Syst. Appl. **252**, 124167 (2024). https://doi.org/10.1016/j.eswa.2024.124167

12. Winne, P.H., Hadwin, A.F.: Nstudy: tracing and supporting self-regulated learning in the internet. In: International Handbook of Metacognition and Learning Technologies, pp. 293–308. Springer, New York, New York (2013). https://doi.org/10.1007/978-1-4419-5546-3_20
13. Zimmerman, B.J.: Becoming a self-regulated learner: an overview. Theory Into Pract. **41**(2), 64–70 (2002). https://doi.org/10.1207/s15430421tip4102_2

Supporting Question-Asking in Early Science Learning with AI

Sunhyo Oh[1(✉)], Lauren Girouard-Hallam[1,2], Rotem Landesman[3], and Ying Xu[2]

[1] University of Michigan, Ann Arbor, MI 48109, USA
sunhyoh@umich.edu
[2] Harvard University, Cambridge, MA 02138, USA
[3] University of Washington, Seattle, WA 98195, USA

Abstract. Children's ability to ask questions is central to science learning. While generative AI has expanded opportunities for curiosity-driven learning, it also places new demands on children to formulate effective questions and critically interpret information provided by AI. To address this challenge, this study designs a voice-driven, LLM-based chatbot that supports children's learning-by-questioning through motivational, metacognitive, and cognitive scaffolding. An initial field study with 10 children aged 6 – 10 demonstrated the feasibility of these support mechanisms, revealing emerging improvements in inquiry skills and science learning outcomes. Building on these insights, the next phase will involve an efficacy study with 240 children to compare scaffolded AI interaction with unguided AI interaction and direct instruction. This study aims to examine how AI scaffolding shapes children's inquiry skills, science learning, and motivational engagement, thereby contributing to the design of AI systems that foster scientific curiosity while accounting for developmental considerations.

Keywords: Generative AI · Question-Asking · Child-AI Interaction · Science Learning

1 Introduction

Children's questions are widely regarded as a cornerstone of learning. In STEM subjects in particular, children's ability to recognize gaps in their understanding and articulate them as questions is central to initiating investigations and constructing knowledge over time [2]. These curiosity-driven skills become increasingly important in the age of generative AI. While AI has expanded the resources children can access, it can also give rise to a new digital divide, in which children's ability to ask good questions (i.e., "prompts") and to use the information they receive directly shapes how much they benefit from AI.

These interactional dynamics of AI are particularly consequential for children, whose developing language, metacognitive skills, and domain knowledge

E. G. Blanchard et al. (Eds.): AIED 2026, CCIS 3033, pp. 345–350, 2026.
https://doi.org/10.1007/978-3-032-29794-5_53

may constrain their ability to formulate effective questions. While children are capable of asking questions to acquire information from relatively early ages [3], their question-asking should yet be structurally guided to proceed with conceptual understanding [10].

Given both challenges and opportunities for children's learning-by-questioning in the age of AI, we aim to address the following overarching research question: *How can we design an AI agent that fosters children's scientific curiosity and directs it toward meaningful learning?* To achieve this aim, this study will design a voice-driven LLM-based chatbot that provides multidimensional scaffolding to guide children in asking focused, investigative questions. The following research questions will guide this project:

- **RQ1**: How do children ask AI questions to understand science phenomena?
- **RQ2**: How should AI be designed to support children's learning-by-questioning?
- **RQ3**: What are the effects of AI-powered scaffolding on children's inquiry skills and science learning?
- **RQ4**: How do those effects vary by children's age, scientific curiosity, and science knowledge and motivation?

2 Theoretical Framing and Related Work

This study is grounded in the intersection of cognitive development, learning sciences, and human-computer interaction, and proposes solutions informed by scholarship across these three domains. Curiosity is a foundational cognitive skill that supports lifelong learning [14], and question-asking represents one behavioral expression of curiosity [10]. Although children's questions have been recognized as central to active learning [3,8], most prior work has relied on constrained paradigms, such as twenty-questions game, with limited empirical investigation in authentic educational settings [15,20].

Children's questions now extend to engagements with conversational technologies, ranging from smart speakers [17] to generative AI [16]. Generative AI can facilitate children's questions, as it mimics human conversation and the interaction is solely initiated by child-driven questions. Drawing on distributed intelligence, it can also be beneficial as it reorganizes the cognitive process within which curiosity unfolds by lowering epistemic barriers and expanding accessible domains of knowledge [18]. From our recent study, we found that children indeed ask many factual questions to AI across different domains [16].

At the same time, it may also disrupt sustained inquiry. AI responses are often verbose and include unsolicited information [11], making it difficult for children to distinguish essential from peripheral content. Moreover, advances in prompt engineering demonstrate that certain inquiry formats yield higher-quality responses [12,21], yet such optimization strategies remain largely inaccessible to children. These uncertainties obscure what constitutes a good question for AI and what forms of guidance are necessary.

This system-level unpredictability is compounded by children's ongoing cognitive development. Effective learning in AI-rich environments is shaped by how cognitive effort is regulated between children's own reasoning and reliance on AI support [6,13,19]. However, this becomes a developmental challenge, as children must decide whether and how to offload cognitive processing to AI, while their metacognitive skills are still developing [5,7]. Taken altogether, these intersecting considerations highlight the need for guidance to support children's effective and sustained question-asking with AI.

3 Proposed Solution

3.1 Initial Work

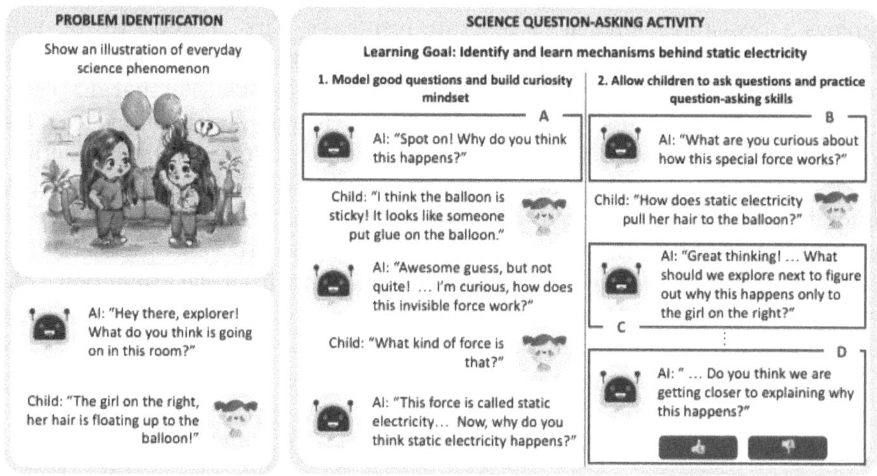

Fig. 1. The example interaction flow with two conversational stages

AI Chatbot Development. We have developed a voice-driven, LLM-based chatbot designed to facilitate children's question-asking by modeling curiosity questions and providing concrete scaffolding. Based on the 5E instructional model [1] and the PACE framework of curiosity [9], it integrates three supporting mechanisms to guide children's learning-by-questioning practices.

- **Motivational support**: The chatbot employs two key tactics to motivate curiosity by increasing uncertainty. **(1)** It situates children as problem-solvers in everyday science scenarios and **(2)** deliberately provides partial information in responses.
- **Metacognitive support**: The chatbot provides metacognitive prompts in two stages. **(1)** Before initiating inquiry, it prompts children to reflect on their prior knowledge. **(2)** During a series of inquiries, it provides periodic checkpoints that encourage them to monitor and evaluate their progress.

- **Cognitive support**: The chatbot augments children's inquiry processes by scaffolding both the conceptual scope and depth of subsequent questions, based on the real-time evaluation.

Throughout the interaction, the chatbot plays two complementary roles: as a question-asker that models good questions and builds a curiosity mindset, and as a question-answerer that leaves space for child-initiated inquiry. As illustrated in Fig. 1, the session unfolds in two stages. In the *Problem Identification* stage, the chatbot shows images of everyday science phenomena, and prompts children to identify a problem to explore (**Motivational support (1)**; see the left panel in Fig. 1). It then invites children to the iterative *Science Question-Asking*, where they are asked to first connect the problem to their prior knowledge (**Metacognitive support (1)**; see A in Fig. 1).

Once children start asking questions based on initial hypotheses, the chatbot employs a two-step approach to generate responses. First, it retrieves relevant knowledge components from an NGSS-aligned knowledge graph and classifies children's questions into six levels (Irrelevant, No Question, Factual, Explanatory, Causal, Experimental), developed based on the middle school science question rating scale [4]. Second, according to this evaluation, the system generates an explanation to the child's question and the adaptive scaffolding. The explanation is deliberately prompted to provide partial information to leave space for continued exploration (**Motivational support (2)**). To generate scaffolding questions, the prompt incorporates two inputs derived from the evaluation—the next relevant knowledge component and a higher-level question stem—so as to guide children toward more investigative inquiries (**Cognitive support**; see B, C in Fig. 1). Over the course of interaction, the system periodically provides a summary and prompts children to evaluate their progress and adjust their questioning strategies (**Metacognitive support (2)**; see D in Fig. 1).

Preliminary Findings. We have field-tested the usability of the chatbot with 10 children aged 6–10 to understand how they actually engage with the instructional materials. The field test results have suggested the feasibility of the three supporting mechanisms. Motivational support helped sustain their engagement throughout a 1-hour session. Given metacognitive prompts, children are observed to continuously reflect on gaps in their understanding. Additionally, children's questions became more relevant and focused over time in response to the cognitive scaffolding provided turn by turn. Children also demonstrated learning of science concepts through their interaction with AI. They correctly answered more than half of the post-test items assessing both comprehension and transfer. Notably, the knowledge components children asked about largely aligned with those they later answered correctly, despite AI introducing additional concepts, which suggests inquiries may play a key role in shaping the knowledge they retain and consolidate.

3.2 Planned Next Steps

Based on insights from the field study, the instructional materials and AI scaffolding mechanisms have been iteratively refined. To further evaluate their effectiveness on children's inquiry skills and science learning, this study will involve a between-subject, three-condition randomized controlled trial. A total of 240 children will be recruited and randomly assigned to one of three groups: (1) Scaffolded Interaction, in which the chatbot provides three supporting mechanisms; (2) Unguided Interaction, involving a baseline chatbot with minimal scaffolding (similar to standard LLM behavior); or (3) Direct Instruction. Each session will last 60 – 90 min with three parts: pre-test, interaction with AI, and post-test. We will collect baseline data on demographics, science knowledge and motivation, and science curiosity. The outcome data will include science learning achievement, inquiry skills, and science motivation and engagement. This evaluation will provide empirical evidence on the impact of AI-powered inquiry support on children's question-asking abilities and subsequent learning outcomes.

3.3 Expected Contributions

Our study aims to (1) develop a conversational AI agent that promotes children's scientific question-asking by motivating their curiosity and providing guidance for investigating concepts, (2) equip children with the skills to productively use AI by reflecting on the quality of their inquiries and the usefulness of the AI responses, and (3) identify key AI design features that can be broadly applied to support children's curiosity-driven learning across educational contexts.

Acknowledgments. This study is based upon the work supported by the Overdeck Family Foundation.

Disclosure of Interests. The authors have no competing interests to declare that are relevant to the content of this article.

References

1. Bybee, R.W., et al.: The BSCS 5E instructional model: Origins and effectiveness. Colorado Springs Co: BSCS **5**, 88–98 (2006)
2. Chin, C., Osborne, J.: Students' questions: a potential resource for teaching and learning science. Stud. Sci. Educ. **44**(1), 1–39 (2008)
3. Chouinard, M.M., Harris, P.L., Maratsos, M.P.: Children's questions: a mechanism for cognitive development. Monographs Soc. Res. Child Develop. i–129 (2007)
4. Cuccio-Schirripa, S., Steiner, H.E.: Enhancement and analysis of science question level for middle school students. J. Res. Sci. Teach. Official J. National Assoc. Res. Sci. Teach. **37**(2), 210–224 (2000)
5. Dicken, L., Suddendorf, T., Bulley, A., Irish, M., Redshaw, J.: Children's emerging ability to balance internal and external cognitive resources. Child Dev. **96**(2), 771–780 (2025)

6. Fan, Y., et al.: Beware of metacognitive laziness: effects of generative artificial intelligence on learning motivation, processes, and performance. Br. J. Edu. Technol. **56**(2), 489–530 (2025)
7. Gerlich, M.: Ai tools in society: impacts on cognitive offloading and the future of critical thinking. Societies **15**(1), 6 (2025)
8. Graesser, A.C., Person, N.K.: Question asking during tutoring. Am. Educ. Res. J. **31**(1), 104–137 (1994)
9. Gruber, M.J., Ranganath, C.: How curiosity enhances hippocampus-dependent memory: the prediction, appraisal, curiosity, and exploration (pace) framework. Trends Cogn. Sci. **23**(12), 1014–1025 (2019)
10. Jirout, J., Klahr, D.: Questions-and some answers-about young children's questions. J. Cogn. Dev. **21**(5), 729–753 (2020)
11. Kabir, S., Udo-Imeh, D.N., Kou, B., Zhang, T.: Is stack overflow obsolete? An empirical study of the characteristics of ChatGpt answers to stack overflow questions. In: Proceedings of the 2024 CHI Conference on Human Factors in Computing Systems, pp. 1–17 (2024)
12. Knoth, N., Tolzin, A., Janson, A., Leimeister, J.M.: Ai literacy and its implications for prompt engineering strategies. Comput. Educ. Artif. Intell. **6**, 100225 (2024)
13. Kosmyna, N., et al.: Your brain on ChatGpt: accumulation of cognitive debt when using an AI assistant for essay writing task. arXiv preprint arXiv:2506.08872 4 (2025)
14. McCoy, D.C., Sabol, T.J.: Overcoming the streetlight effect: shining light on the foundations of learning and development in early childhood. Am. Psychol. **80**(2), 135 (2025)
15. Mills, C.M., Legare, C.H., Grant, M.G., Landrum, A.R.: Determining who to question, what to ask, and how much information to ask for: the development of inquiry in young children. J. Exp. Child Psychol. **110**(4), 539–560 (2011)
16. Oh, S., et al.: Hey curio, can you tell me more?: Children's information-seeking and trust in AI. In: Proceedings of the 24th Interaction Design and Children, pp. 545–555 (2025)
17. Oranç, C., Ruggeri, A.: Alexa, let me ask you something different children's adaptive information search with voice assistants. Human Behavior Emerg. Technol. **3**(4), 595–605 (2021)
18. Pea, R.D.: Practices of distributed intelligence and designs for education. Distributed Cogn. Psychol. Educ. Considerations **11**, 47–87 (1993)
19. Risko, E.F., Gilbert, S.J.: Cognitive offloading. Trends Cogn. Sci. **20**(9), 676–688 (2016)
20. Ruggeri, A., Lombrozo, T.: Learning by asking: how children ask questions to achieve efficient search. In: Proceedings of the Annual Meeting of the Cognitive Science Society. vol. 36 (2014)
21. White, J., et al.: A prompt pattern catalog to enhance prompt engineering with chatgpt. arXiv preprint arXiv:2302.11382 (2023)

Weighted Allocation Probability Thompson Sampling for Response-Adaptive Learnersourcing

Haochen Song[1(✉)], Ilya Musabirov[2], Ananya Bhattacharjee[3], Audrey Durand[4], Meredith Franklin[1], Anna Rafferty[5], and Joseph Jay Williams[1]

[1] University of Toronto, Toronto, ON, Canada
fred.song@mail.utoronto.ca, meredith.franklin@utoronto.ca, williams@cs.utoronto.ca
[2] University of British Columbia, Vancouver, BC, Canada
ilya.musabirov@ubc.ca
[3] Stanford University, Stanford, CA, USA
ananyabh@stanford.edu
[4] Université Laval, Québec City, QC, Canada
audrey.durand@ift.ulaval.ca
[5] Carleton College, Northfield, MN, USA
arafferty@carleton.edu

Abstract. Learnersourcing platforms ask learners to contribute explanations, hints, answers, or feedback that may later support other learners. In these settings, the platform must decide which learner-generated content to retain, surface, revise, or remove while limiting exposure to lower-quality content during evaluation. Because learnersourcing can generate many candidate contents for the same task, the platform must decide how to reduce learners' exposure to clearly weak content during evaluation while still collecting enough evidence to identify strong content by the end. To address this, we study Weighted Allocation Probability Thompson Sampling (WAPTS), a response-adaptive framework for many-arm learnersourcing problems. WAPTS introduces a weighting layer between posterior information and final assignment, aiming to concentrate more quickly on early promising contents while still supporting identification of strong candidate contents by the end of the experiment.

Keywords: Adaptive experiment · Learnersourcing · Bandit algorithm

1 Introduction

Educational platforms increasingly support *learnersourcing* [2], in which learners generate content that can later support future learners. Examples include peer-written explanations, questions, worked examples, feedback, and candidate solutions. Learnersourcing can expand content supply and increase relevance, but

E. G. Blanchard et al. (Eds.): AIED 2026, CCIS 3033, pp. 351–356, 2026.
https://doi.org/10.1007/978-3-032-29794-5_54

it also creates an important decision problem: platforms must determine which learner-generated content should be retained, promoted, revised, or removed. A natural way to address this problem is through online experimentation. Rather than evaluating all candidate content in a fixed manner, an adaptive system can assign more learners to content that appears promising and fewer learners to content that appears weak. In principle, such adaptivity can improve learner outcomes during experimentation while also helping the platform identify useful content for future use.

However, learnersourcing changes the structure of the experimentation problem. Unlike a standard A/B test, where only a small number of fixed contents are compared, learnersourcing may produce many candidate contents for the same task. In other words, learnersourcing naturally creates a many-arm setting in which numerous explanations, hints, or solutions compete for limited learner traffic. In such settings, some candidate contents may be clearly poor, while others may perform similarly well [1]. This means that the practical goal is often not only to identify a single optimal content, but also to reduce exposure to clearly weak content and move learners more quickly toward *near-optimal* alternatives. This perspective motivates an experiment design that emphasizes lenient regret [4], where assigning learners to contents that are close in quality is treated as less costly than assigning them to truly poor ones.

This research presents a response-adaptive experimentation framework for learnersourcing in education. In particular, we investigate *Weighted Allocation Probability Thompson Sampling* (WAPTS), a modification of Thompson Sampling (TS) [3] designed for many-arm learnersourcing settings. The central motivation is that, as the number of candidate contents increases, standard TS may offer less useful control over how learner traffic is distributed across many competing options. This raises a natural design question: how can an adaptive method reduce exposure to truly weak content, concentrate more quickly on strong or near-optimal contents, and still preserve enough evidence to support final content decisions? WAPTS is proposed as one possible answer to this question. A broader goal of this research is to develop adaptive methods and practical guidance that are both statistically considerate and useful for experiment designers in AIED learnersourcing settings.

2 Problem Setting

For clearer communication of the proposed method and results, we formulate the learnersourcing problem as a multi-arm bandit problem with K candidate contents (or **arms**) [3], where each arm $k \in \{1, \ldots, K\}$ corresponds to a learner-generated explanation, hint, or solution. At each time $t = 1, \ldots, T$, the platform assigns one learner to one arm A_t, and then observes an outcome $Y_t \in \{0, 1\}$, where $Y_t = 1$ denotes a desirable learner-level evaluation signal after exposure to that content (for example, a correct response, successful task completion, or a positive signal used to assess content quality). Conditionally on the selected arm, outcomes are modeled as

$$Y_t \mid A_t = k \sim \text{Bernoulli}(\theta_k),$$

where $\theta_k \in (0, 1)$ denotes the true success probability associated with arm k.

To study this setting, we consider a *Unique Optimal Arm* scenario in which there exists a single best arm,

$$k^\star = \arg\max_{1 \le k \le K} \theta_k,$$

with expected reward $\theta_{k^\star}$.

To evaluate policies in a way that matches the practical goal of learnersourcing, we use ε-lenient regret [4]. For a tolerance level $\varepsilon > 0$, the ε-lenient regret at time t is

$$r_t^{(\varepsilon)} = \max\{(\theta_{k^\star} - \theta_{A_t}) - \varepsilon,\ 0\},$$

so assignments to arms within ε of the optimal arm incur no regret. Thus, regret is accumulated only when the selected content is meaningfully worse than the best available option.

We therefore define a *true bad arm* as any arm outside the ε-optimal set:

$$\theta_k < \theta_{k^\star} - \varepsilon.$$

Such an arm yields positive ε-lenient regret when assigned. This distinction is useful in learnersourcing because it separates clearly weak contents from near-optimal contents that may still be acceptable in practice.

3 Related Work

Adaptive experimentation has been widely studied in education as a way to improve learner outcomes through sequential assignment, and learnersourcing introduces a particularly challenging version of this problem by creating many candidate learner-generated contents that must be evaluated under limited traffic [2]. Related work on bandit strategies and many-arm settings highlights the difficulty of identifying strong arms when the number of candidate arms is large relative to the available data [5], while recent work on satisficing and lenient regret suggests that, in such settings, moving learners toward near-optimal options may be more practical than focusing only on exact best-arm identification [1,4]. However, there remains limited work on a response-adaptive strategy designed specifically for learnersourcing settings that simultaneously addresses the many-arm, data-sparse nature of the problem and the practical goal of favoring near-optimal over clearly poor content. This gap motivates the present work on WAPTS, which studies whether a weighted response-adaptive strategy can better support many-arm learnersourcing under a lenient, near-optimal decision objective.

4 Weighted Allocation Probability Thompson Sampling

The idea behind TS is to maintain a posterior estimation based on past observations of the trial, and select an arm at each time based on the posterior sample [3]. In contrast, WAPTS applies an additional weighting rule $w_k^{(t)}$ to each posterior sample, and the arm with the largest weighted score is chosen. As shown in Algorithm 1, the core idea of WAPTS is to modify the arm-selection step of TS through an explicit weighting step. In standard TS, one posterior sample is drawn for each arm, and the arm with the largest sampled value is selected. Although WAPTS does not explicitly compute assignment probabilities, this weighting changes the induced probability that each arm is selected at time t. In this sense, the method modifies the allocation probabilities implied by TS while preserving its Bayesian updating mechanism.

For this work, we focus on a simple weighting rule based on the posterior mean. Let $\hat{\mu}_k^{(t)}$ denote the posterior mean for arm k at time t. We define the arm weight as:

$$w_k^{(t)} = (1 + \hat{\mu}_k^{(t)})\hat{\mu}_k^{(t)}.$$

This weighting increases monotonically with the posterior mean and places greater emphasis on arms that currently appear stronger.

Algorithm 1. Weighted Allocation Probability Thompson Sampling (WAPTS)

Require: Number of arms K, horizon T, prior for each arm
1: **for** $t = 1, 2, \ldots, T$ **do**
2: **for** each arm $k = 1, \ldots, K$ **do**
3: Compute posterior mean $\hat{\mu}_k^{(t)}$ from history $\mathcal{H}_{t-1}$
4: Sample $\tilde{\theta}_k^{(t)} \sim p(\theta_k \mid \mathcal{H}_{t-1})$
5: $s_k^{(t)} \leftarrow w_k^{(t)} \cdot \tilde{\theta}_k^{(t)}$ $\leftarrow$ *WAPTS differs from TS here*
6: **end for**
7: $A_t \leftarrow \arg \max_{k \in \{1,\ldots,K\}} s_k^{(t)}$ $\leftarrow$ *TS uses* $\arg\max_k \tilde{\theta}_k^{(t)}$
8: Observe outcome Y_t and update the posterior of arm A_t
9: **end for**

5 Methodology for Experiment and Preliminary Results

At the current stage, we focus on the simulation component in order to study the behavior of the present WAPTS formulation under controlled conditions. Specifically, we consider a unique-optimal-arm setting in which the optimal arm satisfies

$$\theta_{k^\star} = 0.5 + \delta,$$

where $\delta > 0$ is an effect-size parameter controlling the gap between the optimal arm and the baseline level. Within this setup, we consider a *random sub-optimal arms* setting in which the remaining arms satisfy

$$\theta_k \overset{iid}{\sim} \text{Uniform}(0.5,\ 0.5 + \delta - \rho), \qquad k \neq k^\star,$$

for a small constant $\rho > 0$ (e.g., $\rho = 10^{-6}$) to ensure uniqueness of the optimal arm.

This setting emulates the learnersourcing scenario described earlier, where multiple candidate contents may be reasonably strong and some may be near-optimal. Because the sub-optimal arm parameters are drawn from a uniform distribution beginning at 0.5, the setting also allows substantial variation among non-optimal arms while allowing the possibility that several arms perform similarly well in practice.

The total number of time steps is $T = 1000$, with a burn-in period of 100 observations. The number of arms varies from $K = 2$ to $K = 50$, and the effect size parameter takes values $\delta \in \{0.05, 0.10, 0.20, 0.30\}$. For each combination of K and δ, we simulated 500 independent experiments and averaged the resulting performance metrics. The simulations compare WAPTS against two baseline policies: uniform random allocation (UR) and standard TS (Fig. 1).

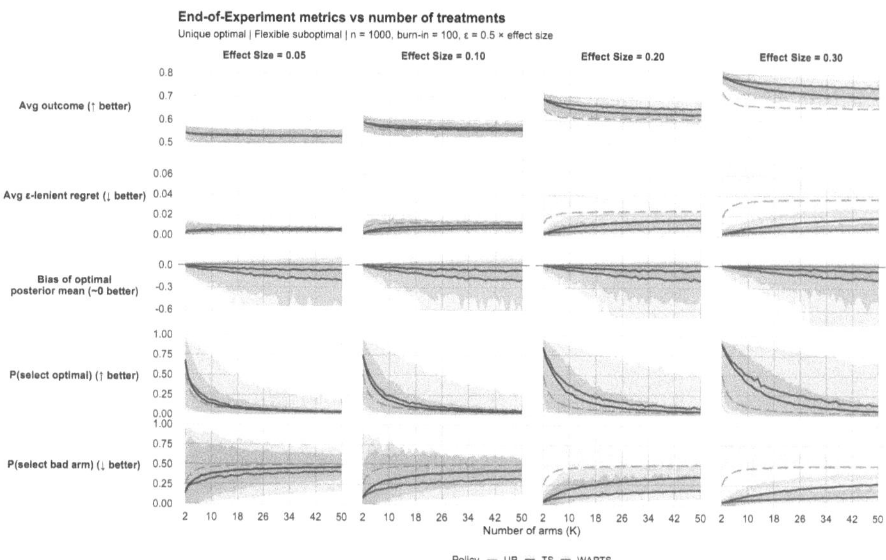

Fig. 1. End-of-experiment performance of WAPTS, UR, and TS across many-arm settings. The panels summarize average outcome, average ε-lenient regret, bias in the posterior mean estimate of the optimal arm, probability of selecting the optimal arm, and probability of selecting a truly bad arm.

The current results suggest that the present WAPTS weighting rule changes the allocation trade-off. Relative to standard TS, WAPTS tends to achieve higher end-of-experiment average outcome, lower ε-lenient regret, a higher probability of selecting the true optimal arm, and a lower probability of selecting a truly bad arm across many of the simulated many-arm settings. These patterns are more visible as the number of arms increases, which is the setting most relevant to learnersourcing. At the same time, these gains are not free. Under the current weighting rule, WAPTS also produces greater bias when performance is judged only through the posterior mean estimate of the optimal arm at the end of the experiment. In addition, the results exhibit higher variability, indicating that the more aggressive concentration induced by the current weighting rule can make performance less stable across runs.

Taken together, these results suggest that the current WAPTS formulation improves several decision-focused outcomes that are meaningful in learnersourcing, especially when the practical goal is to move learners away from clearly weak content and toward strong or near-optimal alternatives. However, these gains appear to come at the cost of increased estimation bias for the optimal arm and greater variability. Ongoing work focuses on clarifying when this trade-off is desirable, how sensitive it is to the choice of weighting rule, and how it should be tuned for different many-arm educational settings.

6 Expected Contributions and Next Steps

This research is expected to contribute to response-adaptive experimentation in learnersourcing settings. By introducing a weighting layer between posterior information and final assignment, WAPTS aims to concentrate more quickly on promising arms while reducing exposure to truly weak content. In future work, we plan to study the theoretical properties of weighted allocation rules in many-arm settings and expand the empirical evaluation to more realistic learnersourcing scenarios.

References

1. Bayati, M., Hamidi, N., Johari, R., Khosravi, K.: Unreasonable effectiveness of greedy algorithms in multi-armed bandit with many arms. In: Larochelle, H., Ranzato, M., Hadsell, R., Balcan, M., Lin, H. (eds.) Advances in Neural Information Processing Systems. vol. 33, pp. 1713–1723. Curran Associates, Inc. (2020)
2. Khosravi, H., Denny, P., Moore, S., Stamper, J.: Learnersourcing in the age of AI: student, educator and machine partnerships for content creation. Comput. Educ. Artif. Intell. **5**, 100151 (2023)
3. Lattimore, T., Szepesvári, C.: Bandit Algorithms. Cambridge University Press (2020)
4. Merlis, N., Mannor, S.: Lenient Regret for Multi-Armed Bandits. In: AAAI Conference on Artificial Intelligence (2020)
5. Rafferty, A., Ying, H., Williams, J.: Statistical consequences of using multi-armed bandits to conduct adaptive educational experiments. J. Educ. Data Min. **11**(1), 47–79 (2019)

A Human–AI Partnership Framework for Multimodal Analysis in Embodied Learning Environments

Joyce Horn Fonteles(✉) and Gautam Biswas

Vanderbilt University, Nashville, TN 37235, USA
{joyce.h.fonteles,gautam.biswas}@vanderbilt.edu

Abstract. Embodied learning environments produce rich multimodal data as students engage in learning through movement, gesture, speech, and social interaction. Interaction Analysis (IA) is a qualitative micro-analytic method that examines how learning develops through moment-to-moment embodied interactions. Although IA provides deep insights, it is labor-intensive, challenging to scale, and cognitively demanding for analysts. Recent advancements in multimodal learning analytics and large language models present new opportunities for supporting this work, while also introducing challenges related to interpretability, trust, and epistemic validity. This doctoral research focuses on human0–AI partnerships for analyzing embodied learning by integrating multimodal machine learning, large language models, and theory-based visualization tools. The study investigates how AI can assist, rather than replace, expert interpretation of learning processes in classroom settings, using self-regulated learning, socially shared regulation, engagement, and computational thinking as illustrative cases within a broader codebook-driven framework.

Keywords: Human–AI Partnership · Multimodal Learning Analytics · Embodied Learning · Large Language Models

1 Introduction and Background

Understanding learning in collaborative, embodied, and physically interactive environments remains a complex challenge [5,13]. In mixed-reality classrooms, students use movement, gesture, and speech while interacting with computational representations of their actions, generating rich multimodal data on cognitive, metacognitive, and social dimensions of learning [1].

Interaction Analysis (IA) offers a theory-driven approach for examining such learning through close analysis of video and discourse [12]. Although IA provides deep insight into moment-to-moment learning, it is labor-intensive and difficult to scale. In parallel, advances in multimodal learning analytics (MMLA) and artificial intelligence have enabled automated analysis of video, audio, and system logs [14]. However, many systems prioritize predictive performance over

E. G. Blanchard et al. (Eds.): AIED 2026, CCIS 3033, pp. 357–363, 2026.
https://doi.org/10.1007/978-3-032-29794-5_55

interpretability, limiting theoretical alignment and human refinement [11]. Here, interpretability refers to whether AI-generated behavior interpretations can be traced to modality-specific evidence, linked to theory-based codebook categories, and revised by human analysts.

In AIED and related communities, multimodal systems commonly employ early or late fusion strategies. Early fusion integrates cross-modal features at the representation level but often reduces interpretability due to model complexity [2]. Late fusion preserves modality-specific evidence, yet often relies on rigid aggregation schemes that struggle to capture the context-sensitive reasoning of embodied classroom activity. As a result, automated systems may misrepresent ambiguous, overlapping, or temporally distributed behaviors.

Recent work on large language models (LLMs) in education has focused primarily on text-based tasks such as dialogue analysis and feedback generation [3,4]. Their role in interpretive multimodal analytics remains under-theorized, particularly regarding validation and epistemic authority. In this dissertation, LLM-generated reasoning is treated not as self-validating explanation, but as a hypothesis grounded in multimodal evidence and reviewed against analyst-defined codebooks.

This dissertation proposes a human-in-the-loop AI framework that integrates multimodal machine learning, learning-theoretic codebooks, interactive visualization, and LLM-based reasoning. The goal is not to replace expert interpretation, but to support scalable, transparent, and theory-grounded analysis in embodied learning environments. The central claim is that theory-grounded multimodal analysis can be made more scalable and reusable through a codebook-driven human–AI framework, with different learning constructs serving as instances of a common analytic architecture. By structuring AI outputs for inspection, disagreement, and refinement, the framework seeks to preserve the interpretive strengths of IA while addressing scalability constraints.

This work is guided by three research questions:

RQ1. How can human-in-the-loop multimodal learning analytics operationalize learning-theoretic constructs in embodied environments while preserving interpretability and contextual grounding?

RQ2. What roles can LLMs play in multimodal learning analytics beyond behavior classification, including reasoning, evaluation, and real-time scaffolded feedback?

RQ3. What trade-offs emerge when balancing scalability, interpretability, and human oversight in AI-assisted analytic tools for classroom research and practice?

2 Proposed Approach and Methodology

Our research adopts a design-based, human-in-the-loop methodology grounded in classroom deployments of embodied learning environments across age groups and domains. Students engage in activities that generate synchronized multimodal data, including video, per-student audio, motion tracking, and system logs [6]. These streams are temporally aligned and processed through modality-specific machine learning components.

The Human–AI framework assigns complementary epistemic roles across disciplines. Learning scientists define constructs, develop codebooks, and adjudicate ambiguous cases, while computer scientists design AI systems that process multimodal data and generate evidence-grounded interpretations. Human experts retain epistemic authority, with AI supporting scale by reducing search and synthesis burdens while improving temporal sensitivity and consistency. In practice, the AI system proposes segments, labels, and justifications that analysts inspect in the timeline, revise when needed, and use to refine codebook indicators or prompting strategies; disagreements are treated as cases for adjudication and refinement rather than simple model errors.

This partnership is operationalized through the Human–AI framework in Fig. 1. Modality-specific features are extracted and synthesized through late fusion to preserve provenance. Large language models operate at this stage, reasoning over structured multimodal representations and mapping low-level features to learning-theoretic categories defined in a shared codebook [7,8]. These justifications are treated as reviewable hypotheses tied to multimodal evidence, supporting inspection and refinement rather than one-shot classification.

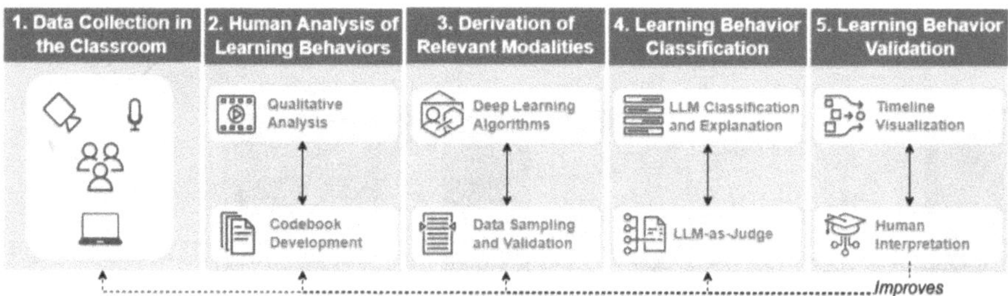

Fig. 1. Human–AI framework for theory-grounded multimodal learning analytics. Codebooks guide multimodal evidence synthesis, LLM-based interpretation, and evaluation, while the timeline supports human inspection and refinement. Outputs iteratively refine earlier stages, including codebooks, indicators, and prompting.

An AI-enhanced multimodal timeline serves as the primary analytic interface [10]. The timeline aligns synchronized video with multimodal signals and behavioral interpretations, enabling iterative validation consistent with interaction-analysis practices.

The codebook functions as the central abstraction layer [7]. Modifying it changes the target construct, relevant indicators, and prompting strategies without altering the underlying architecture. Recent extensions introduce LLM-based evaluators as triage mechanisms that assess whether predicted labels are supported by multimodal evidence before human review, thereby prioritizing analyst attention while preserving human judgment as the final authority.

3 Progress to Date

This research has progressed through a series of studies that collectively shape and test a common Human–AI framework across multiple constructs and settings. Early work examined how machine learning might support interaction analysis in embodied learning environments, highlighting opportunities for scalability alongside tensions with qualitative research traditions [6]. These studies showed that automated feature extraction could surface useful patterns, but meaningful interpretation required tools that preserved temporal context and human judgment.

Multimodal datasets have been collected across several authentic classroom settings that vary in domain, age group, and interactional structure. These include embodied collaborative science with middle school students (GEM-STEP), computer-based collaborative inquiry with high school students (Eco-Journeys), and embodied computational thinking activities in introductory computer science classrooms. Together, they provide a diverse empirical foundation for examining how a codebook-driven, human-in-the-loop framework supports multimodal analysis across contexts.

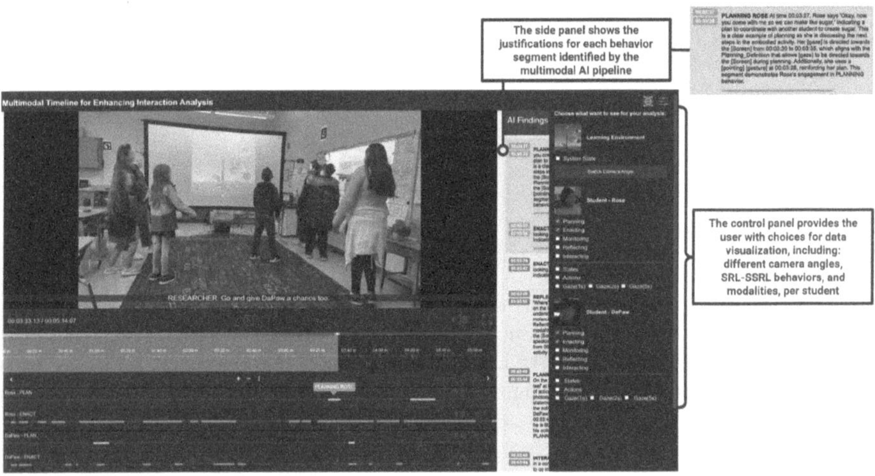

Fig. 2. Interactive multimodal timeline for human-in-the-loop analysis of embodied learning. It aligns classroom video, multimodal signals, and learning-theoretic interpretations to support inspection, validation, and refinement.

Subsequent work focused on the design and evaluation of the multimodal timeline as a core analytic artifact [10]. Through co-design with learning scientists, the timeline was refined to support replay from multiple perspectives, multimodal alignment, and comparison of interpretations across students and sessions. Case analyses showed that it improved the efficiency of identifying planning, monitoring, and collaborative behaviors while surfacing cases in which automated signals required expert revision (Fig. 2).

Building on this foundation, later studies introduced LLM-based late fusion to analyze self-regulated and socially shared regulation [7]. Results showed that LLMs could integrate modality-specific signals to generate behavior segments with explanatory justifications, which analysts then validated and refined using the timeline.

Parallel work applies the same framework to alternative constructs, including collaborative engagement, showing that modifying the codebook reconfigures analytic targets without altering the underlying architecture. This supports the claim that the dissertation's core contribution is a configurable, theory-driven framework rather than a separate system for each construct.

More recent extensions adapt the framework from post-hoc analysis to an online, agent-mediated setting in embodied computational thinking classrooms. Prototype classroom agents synthesize multimodal logs in near real time and compare enacted behaviors to stated strategies, providing bounded diagnostic feedback that supports refinement without automating solutions or foreclosing student sensemaking.

Recent studies also explore LLM-as-a-Judge mechanisms as triage tools for scalable evaluation of behavior interpretations [9]. While alignment with expert judgment is promising, findings raise questions about calibration, disagreement, and when cases should be escalated to human review.

Across studies, evaluation emphasizes alignment with expert interpretation, robustness under classroom conditions, and how analytic outputs and agent feedback support human sensemaking.

4 Expected Contributions and Open Questions

This dissertation contributes a general, codebook-driven Human–AI framework for theory-grounded multimodal learning analytics in embodied learning environments. Its primary contribution is an explicit and reusable model of human–AI collaboration in which learning scientists provide theoretical grounding and interpretive oversight, while AI systems support scale, temporal sensitivity, and multimodal evidence synthesis. Here, scalability does not imply removing human judgment, but reducing search and synthesis burdens while concentrating expert attention on ambiguous or theoretically significant cases.

A second contribution is the expansion of the roles of large language models in multimodal analytics. Beyond post-hoc classification, the framework positions LLMs as reasoning, evaluative, and feedback-generating agents operating across both analytic and online classroom contexts.

Finally, the work contributes design principles for building scalable, interpretable, and human-centered analytic systems that function as both research tools and bounded classroom supports. By integrating post-hoc analysis with real-time multimodal synthesis and agent-mediated scaffolding, the framework demonstrates how analytic systems can evolve without relinquishing human epistemic authority.

Open questions remain regarding generalizability across domains and age groups, calibration of agentic LLM authority in classroom settings, and the robustness required for real-time multimodal analytics to support bounded feedback without constraining learner agency, sensemaking, or pedagogical intent.

Acknowledgement. This work was supported by the National Science Foundation under Award DRL-2112635. Any opinions, findings, and conclusions or recommendations expressed in this material are those of the authors and do not necessarily reflect the views of the National Science Foundation.

References

1. Blikstein, P.: Multimodal learning analytics. In: Proceedings of the Third International Conference on Learning Analytics and Knowledge, ACM (2013)
2. Cohn, C., et al.: Multimodal methods for analyzing learning and training environments: a systematic literature review (2024). https://arxiv.org/abs/2408.14491. Submitted to ACM Surveys. Under Review
3. Cohn, C., Hutchins, N., Le, T., Biswas, G.: A chain-of-thought prompting approach with LLMs for evaluating students' formative assessment responses in science. In: Proceedings of the AAAI Conference on Artificial Intelligence (2024)
4. Cohn, C., Snyder, C., Fonteles, J.H., T. S., A., Montenegro, J., Biswas, G.: A multimodal approach to support teacher, researcher and AI collaboration in STEM+C learning environments. British J. Educ. Technol. (2024)
5. Danish, J.A., Enyedy, N., Saleh, A., Humburg, M.: Learning in embodied activity framework: a sociocultural framework for embodied cognition. Int. J. Comput.-Support. Collab. Learn. **15**(1), 49–87 (2020). https://doi.org/10.1007/s11412-020-09317-3
6. Fonteles, J., et al.: A first step in using machine learning methods to enhance interaction analysis for embodied learning environments. In: Proceedings of the 25th International Conference on Artificial Intelligence in Education (AIED 2024), pp. 3–16. Springer (2024)
7. Fonteles, J.H., et al.: Analyzing embodied learning in classroom settings: a human-in the-loop ai approach for multimodal learning analytics. Learn. Instruction (2026)
8. Fonteles, J.H., Cohn, C., Mereddy, D., Ashwin, T.S., Biswas, G.: Exploring agentic multimodal late fusion with LLMs for embodied learning. In: Proceedings of the EDM 2025 Workshop: Multimodal Multiparty Learning Analytics (2025). https://sites.google.com/colorado.edu/edm2025-mmla-workshop/accepted-papers
9. Fonteles, J.H., et al.: A novel approach to evaluating the effectiveness of large language models for multimodal analysis of embodied learning in classrooms. In: Proceedings of the 16th International Learning Analytics and Knowledge Conference. ACM (2026). Accepted to LAK 2026. In press
10. Fonteles, J.H., Srivastava, N., Davalos, E., Ashwin, T.S., Biswas, G.: Designing an ai-enhanced timeline for monitoring multimodal interactions in embodied learning environments. In: Proceedings of the International Conference on Computers in Education (2024). https://library.apsce.net/index.php/ICCE/article/view/4907

11. Giannakos, M., Cukurova, M.: The role of learning theory in multimodal learning analytics. Br. J. Edu. Technol. **54**(5), 1246–1267 (2023)
12. Jordan, B., Henderson, A.: Interaction analysis: foundations and practice. J. Learn. Sci. **4**(1), 39–103 (1995)
13. Lindgren, R., Johnson-Glenberg, M.: Emboldened by embodiment: six precepts for research on embodied learning and mixed reality. Educ. Res. **42**(8), 445–452 (2013)
14. Zhou, M., et al.: Interaction analysis practice within computational trends: promises and challenges. In: Proceedings of the 19th International Conference of the Learning Sciences (2025)

Designing and Evaluating AI-Based Reflection Support Systems for Students

Seyed Parsa Neshaei(✉)

EPFL, Lausanne, Switzerland
seyed.neshaei@epfl.ch

Abstract. Metacognition, learners' ability to regulate their own learning, is considered central to effective learning. However, many struggle to engage in deep and structured reflections. Although AI-based writing assistants and chatbots have been increasingly used to support reflection, existing tools often rely on generic prompts, surface-level feedback, and static interaction modalities, with limited grounding in learning theories or contextualization in each learner's personal experiences. My research aims to investigate how AI-powered support modalities can be designed to support reflection. Drawing on principles and theories from learning sciences, HCI, and NLP, I design and evaluate AI-based paradigms that provide structured, theory-informed, useful, and personalized reflective support. In my ongoing thesis work, I plan to further investigate and refine AI-powered interaction modalities for reflection, and develop principled ways of integrating prior experiences of learners from different educational levels into reflective support.

Keywords: metacognition · reflection · writing assistants · LLMs

1 Introduction

AI- and LLM-based EdTech are increasingly used to support learning processes such as reflection and self-regulation [21]. This creates new opportunities for learners to make sense of their experiences and adapt their learning strategies, even when lacking direct traditional in-class support. However, while the opportunities provided by reflection tools have been shown to be beneficial across domains [14,22], recent research in this area suggests that many existing AI-based reflection tools rely on surface-level feedback by prompting LLMs out of the box, often without sufficient grounding in learning theories or consideration of learners' prior experiences. As a result, many AI support modalities, e.g., conversational interfaces, while being useful in helping users to *write* a better text, do not necessarily benefit reflective *learning*. Particularly, my own work suggests that in several cases, using a conversational agent (CA, i.e., chatbot) might be ineffective or even counterproductive compared to traditional interfaces.

Given these opportunities and limitations, I argue that supporting metacognitive reflection with AI requires moving beyond one-size-fits-all interaction

E. G. Blanchard et al. (Eds.): AIED 2026, CCIS 3033, pp. 364–370, 2026.
https://doi.org/10.1007/978-3-032-29794-5_56

designs, towards theory-informed and empirically validated modalities of support. Following this goal, my thesis investigates how to reframe AI-based reflection support as a *learning-oriented design problem*, investigating which interaction paradigms meaningfully foster metacognitive processes through designing and evaluating educational tools which can adapt to learners with different experiences and educational levels. In this proposal, I describe the background behind my research, completed works, ongoing thesis work, and current status.

2 Background

Student metacognition refers to the understanding and management of a student's thinking processes [11]. Being proficient in metacognition can positively influence academic progress and achievement [10]. Several strategies for improving metacognitive skills include using mind maps [3] or thinking aloud [19]. Particularly, reflective practices, e.g., journaling or guided reflection, help learners revisit past experiences, derive actionable insights, and inform their future behavior [6,7]. However, learning sciences research shows that reflection is not necessarily a spontaneous skill: novice learners, in particular, struggle to structure reflections, connect experiences to prior knowledge, and move beyond descriptive accounts toward deeper analysis and future planning in their reflections [1], which ultimately affects learning negatively. As a solution, prior works proposed structured reflection models (e.g., [4,6]). While effective, they are often difficult to scale, require sustained involvement of tutors, or rely on static materials that cannot adapt to individual needs and prior experiences.

Recent advances in AI and LLMs have enabled new forms of reflection support through writing assistants and conversational interfaces. Some works have explored how reflective writing instruction can improve cognitive and empathic abilities [12]. Also, they have investigated the effects of embedding reflection manuals [23] or guiding questions [13] in the journal writing process. Some others have investigated the effects of providing automated AI-based feedback on reflection [2]. Finally, some have also explored using CAs, suggesting they can encourage engagement and trigger reflection in vocational education [22].

Still, important gaps remain in how AI-based reflection support is designed and evaluated. Most current works A) lack extensive grounding in learning theories, and B) provide little empirical comparison across different support interfaces and reflection modalities. Thus, it remains unclear which and how AI-based interaction designs can meaningfully foster reflection. This motivates the need for empirically and rigorously validated user-centric reflection support systems. I aim to find design insights for reflection tools and evaluate them in real-world educational settings.

3 Published Work

During my PhD, I have conducted several studies on different interaction paradigms of reflection support to investigate how learners use reflection assistants in educational settings, with a particular focus on reflective writing. These led to first-authored papers accepted at, e.g., British Journal of Educational Technology [16], CHI 2025 LBW [17], and CHI 2024 LBW [18]. Below, I focus on two of these studies and their main takeaways.

Study 1 - Reflectium: Learning Reflection From Examples [16]. In this line of work, I investigated how AI-based reflection support can be grounded in established learning theories rather than using LLMs out-of-the-box. I designed an AI-supported reflective writing system structured around the Gibbs cycle [6], comparing two paradigms of *learning from examples*: (1) learning from *worked* examples (i.e., prepared annotated full examples) with adaptive AI feedback, and (2) learning from *modeling* examples through having an LLM act as an instructor providing step-by-step instructions. Results on N=100 showed that those learning with *worked* examples produced significantly higher quality reflections than the CA group. We surprisingly found that the CA led to limited interaction depth and occasionally excessive support, which might have harmed learning gains. The lack of effectiveness of CAs was also reflected in my other work [18]. Together, these highlight the need for empirically grounded, careful decisions about when and how CAs should be used in reflection support.

Study 2 - Memoire: Context-Aware Reflection Support [17]. In this line of work, I explored how AI-based reflection support can move beyond generic feedback through leveraging the learners' prior experiences. Inspired by prior works showing the benefits of "bridging the gap" between classroom concepts and hands-on application [20], I designed a reflective writing tool that uses a RAG-based pipeline grounded in each learner's past reflections. The system retrieves prior reflections semantically close to the current writings, and uses them to generate context-aware suggestions. It aims to support reflection as a task inherently connected with the ongoing student educational journey, rather than treating it as an isolated writing task. I evaluated Memoire in a classroom study with 100 vocational nursing students. I compared different types of RAG-based suggestions inspired by prior work: Socratic-like questioning, autocomplete suggestions, and summaries. Learners reported high perception metrics and found the critical questions helpful for deeper reflection, while the other types were perceived as less relevant and redundant. Also, they found suggestions confusing when retrieved text didn't align with their current writing, suggesting the need for transparent, interpretable, and controllable reflection retrieval.

4 Ongoing Thesis Work

From these studies, two main insights can be extracted. First, commonly assumed "natural" interaction modalities, such as typing messages to a CA for reflective learning or reflective writing, do not necessarily foster deeper reflection, and can in some cases discourage well-structured reflection compared to more traditional approaches. Second, while personalization through students' prior experiences showed a high potential, it only becomes educationally meaningful when combined with carefully-designed interaction mechanisms that instruct students on how to write a good reflection and bring transparency and controllability to the retrieval pipeline. My thesis will extend upon the challenges and opportunities found in my completed works, exploring two main research questions: **(RQ1)** *"What are the appropriate interaction paradigms that AI-based systems supporting reflective learning can provide to foster deep and well-structured reflection?"* **(RQ2)** *"Which interaction paradigms can improve how learners connect with prior experiences and help them integrate those experiences into their current practice?"* In the rest of this section, I describe my proposed research plan to answer the RQs, as well as the current status of my thesis.

Research Plan for RQ1. My completed studies have shown the relative ineffectiveness of CAs, when used either for learning how to write reflectively [16], or directly in the writing process [18]. However, this does not suggest that other formats of CAs don't support reflection well. I propose *moving* the timing of reflection support from the "writing and revision" stage to the "planning" stage, which occurs *before* writing begins. This is inspired by the Cognitive Process Theory of writing [5] and previous research on how people use LLMs for planning writing [9]. I design a tool that embeds a chat interface *before* students start reflecting, probing them with open-ended questions to think about their experience. This approach aims to foster deeper reflections, which was lacking in my previous work that focused solely on the reflection structure [16]. I conduct a classroom study over several weeks, comparing pre- and post-tests to assess learning the ability to reflect deeply through CA interaction. I analyze data using a mixed-method approach: quantitatively by scoring reflections and answers to perception questions, and qualitatively by the provided open feedback on tool perception and helpful functionalities for reflective writing. These findings will serve as a hint to whether using CAs earlier may reduce the chance of "excessive support" (as seen in [16]) and lead to deeper reflections. I have conducted an experiment in a vocational school on N=93 students, using the reflection procedure detailed by [8], and an agent to extract key concepts from their conversation as they moved forward, to support students in the Planning and Translation phases through a CA. I compared the treatment group versus a control group using static text boxes to plan their writing instead. Both groups later used a revision interface, getting feedback on adherence to the Gibbs reflective cycle [6]. While we found early indications of improvements in reflection depth based on a rubric extracted from [8], we found that the second-stage feedback received on the Gibbs cycle dominated what students remembered from the intervention, possibly *washing out* the effects from the CA. Several results we obtained in this study are currently included in my AIED 2026 paper [15]. I am currently in the process of further adapting the study design, with the aim of launching a larger-scale study in the current semester.

Research Plan for RQ2. My completed work on Memoire has shown that connecting learners to their prior reflections has the potential to support reflection, but that basic, naive retrieval of past content is not necessarily sufficient to improve reflective learning, and can lead to confusion about why certain experiences are presented, limiting their educational benefits and even distracting learners from the current reflection. To address this, I plan to study how the *form* and *timing* of presenting prior experiences affects the reflection process. For example, taking cues from the Cognitive Process Theory of writing again [5], previous reflections might be perceived as more helpful when introduced as prompts during *planning*, as comparative examples during *translating* thoughts to writing, or as reminders during *revision*. I will empirically compare these alternatives, extracted through formative interviews with students from different groups, through iterative design and classroom-based studies. This enables me to examine how different designs influence the ability of students to form connections across experiences in their reflection process.

5 Conclusion

My research explores how AI-based systems can support reflection as a metacognitive learning process. Through my completed studies, I have shown that commonly-assumed paradigms, e.g., CAs, may not foster reflection in the best way, and also personalizing reflection feedback based on prior experiences requires careful design to become educationally meaningful. To address these challenges, my thesis investigates how theory-informed and user-centered reflection support can be designed, implemented, and empirically validated across different interaction paradigms and student groups. Through this work, I aim to contribute empirical insights to education research for building AI-based systems that meaningfully support reflective learning of students. I believe getting feedback from the AIED community at this stage would be vastly valuable; it will enable me to adapt and refine the methodologies I will follow in the rest of my PhD, particularly with regards to capturing longer-term changes in learners' metacognitive awareness.

References

1. Adeani, I.S., Febriani, R.B., Syafryadin, S.: Using GIBBS'reflective cycle in making reflections of literary analysis. Indonesian EFL J. **6**(2), 139–148 (2020)
2. Alrashidi, H., Almujally, N., Kadhum, M., Daniel Ullmann, T., Joy, M.: Evaluating an automated analysis using machine learning and natural language processing approaches to classify computer science students' reflective writing. In: Pervasive computing and social networking: Proceedings of ICPCSN 2022, pp. 463–477. Springer (2022)
3. Astriani, D., Susilo, H., Suwono, H., Lukiati, B., Purnomo, A.: Mind mapping in learning models: a tool to improve student metacognitive skills. Int. J. Emerg. Technol. Learn. (iJET) **15**(6), 4–17 (2020)
4. Brookfield, S.D.: Becoming a critically reflective teacher. John Wiley & Sons (2017)
5. Flower, L., Hayes, J.R.: A cognitive process theory of writing. College Composition Commun. **32**(4), 365–387 (1981)
6. Gibbs, G.: Learning by doing: a guide to teaching and learning methods. Further Education Unit (1988)

7. Gibson, A., Aitken, A., Sándor, ., Buckingham Shum, S., Tsingos-Lucas, C., Knight, S.: Reflective writing analytics for actionable feedback. In: Proceedings of the Seventh International Learning Analytics & Knowledge Conference, pp. 153–162 (2017)
8. Glogger, I., Schwonke, R., Holzäpfel, L., Nückles, M., Renkl, A.: Learning strategies assessed by journal writing: prediction of learning outcomes by quantity, quality, and combinations of learning strategies. J. Educ. Psychol. **104**(2), 452 (2012)
9. Göldi, A., Wambsganss, T., Neshaei, S.P., Rietsche, R.: Intelligent support engages writers through relevant cognitive processes. In: Proceedings of the CHI Conference on Human Factors in Computing Systems, pp. 1–12 (2024)
10. Loksa, D., et al.: Metacognition and self-regulation in programming education: theories and exemplars of use. ACM Trans. Comput. Educ. (TOCE) **22**(4), 1–31 (2022)
11. Mani, M., Mazumder, Q.: Incorporating metacognition into learning. In: Proceeding of the 44th ACM Technical Symposium on Computer Science Education, pp. 53–58 (2013)
12. Misra-Hebert, A.D., et al.: Improving empathy of physicians through guided reflective writing. Depart. Psychiatry Human Behavior Faculty Papers. Paper 51 (2012). https://jdc.jefferson.edu/phbfp/51
13. Moussa-Inaty, J.: Reflective writing through the use of guiding questions. Int. J. Teach. Learn. Higher Educ. **27**(1), 104–113 (2015)
14. Nehyba, J., Štefánik, M.: Applications of deep language models for reflective writings. Educ. Inf. Technol. **28**(3), 2961–2999 (2023)
15. Neshaei, S.P., Davis, R.L., Käser, T.: Moving beyond review: applying language models to planning and translation in reflection. In: International Conference on Artificial Intelligence in Education. Springer (2026)
16. Neshaei, S.P., Mejia-Domenzain, P., Davis, R.L., Käser, T.: Metacognition meets AI: empowering reflective writing with large language models. British J. Educ. Technol. (2025)
17. Neshaei, S.P., Tashkovska, M., Mejia-Domenzain, P., Wambsganss, T., Käser, T.: User-centric reflective writing assistance: leveraging RAG for enhanced personalized support. In: Proceedings of the Extended Abstracts of the CHI Conference on Human Factors in Computing Systems, pp. 1–8 (2025)
18. Neshaei, S.P., Wambsganss, T., El Bouchrifi, H., Käser, T.: MindMate: exploring the effect of conversational agents on reflective writing. In: Proceedings of the Extended Abstracts of the CHI Conference on Human Factors in Computing Systems, pp. 1–9 (2025)
19. Raihan, M.A.: Think-aloud'techniques used in metacognition to enhance self-regulated learning. J. Educ. Res. **25**(2), 125–160 (2011)
20. Schwendimann, B.A., Cattaneo, A.A., Dehler Zufferey, J., Gurtner, J.L., Bétrancourt, M., Dillenbourg, P.: The 'Erfahrraum': a pedagogical model for designing educational technologies in dual vocational systems. J. Vocational Educ. Training **67**(3), 367–396 (2015)
21. Song, I., Park, S., Pendse, S.R., Schleider, J.L., De Choudhury, M., Kim, Y.H.: Exploreself: fostering user-driven exploration and reflection on personal challenges with adaptive guidance by large language models. In: Proceedings of the 2025 CHI Conference on Human Factors in Computing Systems, pp. 1–22 (2025)

22. Wolfbauer, I., Bangerl, M.M., Maitz, K., Pammer-Schindler, V.: Rebo at work: reflecting on working, learning, and learning goals with the reflection guidance chatbot for apprentices. In: Extended abstracts of the 2023 CHI Conference on Human Factors in Computing Systems, pp. 1–7 (2023)
23. Wong, Y.M., Mansor, R., Samsudin, S.: The use of critical reflection manual in writing reflective journal: a case study of Malaysian student teachers' perceptions. Geografia **12**(1) (2016)

LLM-Supported Disagreements

Mariah Bradford(✉) and Nikhil Krishnaswamy

Colorado State University, Fort Collins, CO 80521, USA
mbrad@rams.colostate.edu, nkrishna@colostate.edu

Abstract. Disagreement is an important but challenging aspect of small group learning. While we want to make room for multiple perspectives and allow students to develop debating skills, unproductive disagreements can risk derailing the group. Finding a balance is made even more difficult when teachers are expected to mediate but are often monitoring many small groups at once. Because of this, I propose investigating LLMs for potential application in these scenarios. I will evaluate LLMs' ability to detect disagreement, as well as their ability to reword disagreements to be more productive. A reworded disagreement can serve as immediate feedback via an example for students. Disagreement detection can serve educators by helping them monitor group states. These evaluations serve as an initial study into LLMs' potential role in assisting in small group disagreements.

Keywords: small group work · disagreement · large language models

1 The Problem

Small group learning is a common classroom tool, wherein students learn together and learn collaboration skills. One common ocurrence in collaboration is disagreement. While it is useful for reasoning and is an important skill to develop, it is also challenging and can become problematic if left unmanaged. This poses a dichotomous situation for educators: suppressing disagreement may result in lost learning opportunities, but letting it grow without intervention may hinder the learning process. This delicate balance is made even more difficult as classrooms scale up, and one teacher is left to monitor many groups simultaneously.

Disagreement is an important dialogue event in small groups [5,20]. It is a critical component in forming a *theory of mind* [15] to understand what a student knows, as well as for groups to form common ground [10,20]. Additionally, the way disagreement is expressed impacts the outcome of the conversation [8,17]. Disagreements are often indirect and exist implicitly in context rather than being direct and potentially socially jarring [11,13,19], making social skills an important factor in disagreement. This also makes them pragmatically nuanced, necessitating an in-context interpretation of utterances.

Disagreement naturally occurs during group learning as students navigate new and existing knowledge together, and it is an important skill to develop.

E. G. Blanchard et al. (Eds.): AIED 2026, CCIS 3033, pp. 371–376, 2026.
https://doi.org/10.1007/978-3-032-29794-5_57

Offering heterogeneous perspectives is often beneficial [9,16] but can also be challenging [6,11]. Because of this, I am pursuing a research direction which aims to help educators by automatically detecting disagreements, and to help students develop the skills needed to disagree by providing positive examples informed by previous related work [4,8,17]. The massive improvements in large language models (LLMs) in recent years offer a new opportunity to detect highly pragmatic dialogue moves and provide personalized, instant feedback, paving the way for my current research direction.

2 Theoretical Framing and Solution

Learning is often a social experience, and collaborative learning aims to leverage this by encouraging students to engage with each other on lesson topics. At the same time, students are learning critical skills for collaboration needed in the workforce. In these contexts, disagreement arises naturally. This can be beneficial to students, as they are exposed to new perspectives and are challenged to express their own reasoning. However, these same situations can lead to relational tension [7] and frustration [3], which can both hurt the learning process. In classrooms where there are many groups and only one teacher, this delicate balance is difficult to navigate because the teacher may not be immediately informed or available when it becomes harmful. Teachers may even be inclined to discourage and avoid it to reduce risk [5]. However, the opportunities in automatic dialogue tracking and personalized, real-time feedback materializing in recent years provides an opportunity to help teachers monitor this discourse and provide students with positive examples of debate.

My approach is to first automatically detect disagreement in small groups. This is especially interesting because disagreements are so often implicit [19]. I am interested in leveraging LLMs for this task and evaluating them against other machine learning techniques. This is valuable because an automated system can help notify teachers of disagreements, especially when they are prolonged or escalating.

The second portion of my approach involves rewording the expression of disagreements while maintaining the intended meaning [1]. LLMs provide a new outlet for immediate personalized feedback accessible to every student at every moment. The rewording process is grounded in prior work showing that characteristics of an utterance - such as offensiveness, hedging, reasoning, and receptivity [1,2,4,17] - impact the outcome of a disagreement. For real-time support, an AI assistant can provide a reworded example for students, showing them immediate feedback and a grounded, applicable example of disagreement aligning with the aforementioned traits. LLMs are particularly well-suited for this task because of their ability to modulate the tone of a statement while preserving meaning [1].

Identifying disagreement can help educators track group dialogue and build theory of mind for students, and teaching them how to reword their expressions to be more constructive can help improve group outcomes. However, these opportunities are idealistic and rest on an automated system's ability to achieve these goals sufficiently. Therefore, my goal is to evaluate existing systems on these proposed tasks.

For my study, I will use DeliData [9], a publicly available corpus of 500 online groups of 2–5 members solving the Wason card selection task [18]. This famous reasoning task asks participants to choose the minimum cards needed to turn over to test a rule. Because there is one correct answer and a select-all-that-apply format, groups can be evaluated for correctness and percent agreement. Additionally, this dataset includes labels for agreement, disagreement, and each group member's individual answer. The first step is to evaluate LLMs detecting disagreements. I will follow existing methods for automatic detection and labeling evaluation with F1 score and Cohen's κ as my main metrics.

Next, I will prompt models to reword utterances labeled as disagreement. The rewording will be based on existing empirical results on improving the results of disagreements [1,2,4,17]. In order to evaluate the outputs, I will follow established methods for LLM role-play [12,14], bridging AI for education with state-of-the-art natural language processing techniques. My proposed pipeline can be seen in Fig. 1.

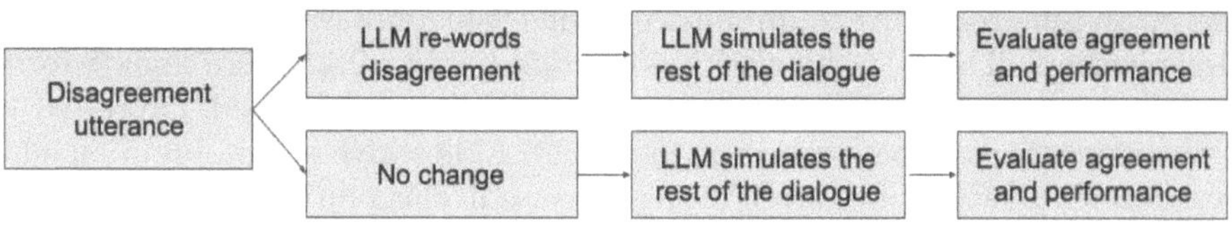

Fig. 1. Proposed LLM Role-Play Pipeline

LLM Role-Play. I will generate two role-play conditions. For my intervention condition, I will replace an utterance labeled as disagreement with the LLM-reworded output. I will then prompt a separate LLM - distinct from the LLM used for rewording - to continue the conversation from that dialogue step. As a control condition, I will utilize the original ground-truth disagreement utterance and again continue the conversation from the same dialogue step. The control condition allows me to explore the impact of the LLM in the intervention condition while controlling for LLM role-play.

Evaluation. I will evaluate the impact of the reworded disagreement by comparing the intervention condition to the control condition. The results will be evaluated by group performance and group agreement for each condition. Performance is calculated by averaging the score of the group members' answers compared to the correct answer. Group agreement is calculated using percent agreement between the group members.

For an additional analysis, I will utilize the control condition for comparison with the ground truth data. By doing so, I can observe patterns of variance between group outcomes in the real data and the LLM role-play. I will compare the control condition with the ground-truth data to evaluate the variance in predictions of group performance and group agreement. I will also evaluate whether the reworded utterances maintain intended meaning quantitatively (using embedding distance metrics) and qualitatively (using human evaluation). Finally, I will pilot small groups using the interventions and evaluate group perceptions using a scale following [17].

3 Contributions and Impact to Both AI and Education

This approach offers an exploration into new AI technology applied toward a well-known classroom phenomenon. From an AI perspective, I study the potential for LLMs to interpret multi-party dialogues and generate a theory of mind. By exploring disagreements between people, I can evaluate model performance in detecting conflicting propositions. This is a nuanced language task as well as a challenge using reasoning. Additionally, I will evaluate LLMs' ability to generate disagreements. This is particularly interesting because LLMs are known to be sycophantic, and conflict is known to be socially demanding. I am interested to see whether this will be a situation in which LLMs thrive or fail. From an educational perspective, this is interesting because it offers an evaluation toward a specific use case of LLMs in the classroom. If LLMs are able to achieve sufficient performance in detecting disagreement, this would be a useful feature to help teachers monitor many groups at once. While it is important to give students the opportunity to resolve conflicts on their own - both for reasoning and social skills - notifying a teacher of a prolonged or escalating conflict can help identify a group in need of facilitation. Additionally, if LLMs can reword disagreements to be better received by other group members, these examples can be used for real-time feedback for students. At the same time, it is critical that the examples are educational for students and don't become a crutch. If LLMs do showcase the necessary ability to perform these tasks, additional future work would still need to explore whether students' ability to express disagreement improves over time with this type of feedback, even when removed. One method of ensuring progress rather than reliance is a self-obsoleting design; success is defined by students needing the feedback less and less. This could be evaluated at the group level, such as performance; the individual level, such as team member evaluations; and even utterance level, such as containing the characteristics shown to improve disagreement outcomes in previous work.

The proposed approach leverages the interpretive power of LLMs and explores new applications of the technology. I will identify failure modes of existing LLMs, which can then be focal points of improvement in future versions. This will also advance our understanding of LLMs in small groups, such as whether they are capable of capturing separate representations of theory of mind at once. It also raises a specific reasoning challenge in identifying conflicting statements. For education, this approach is a method to automatically capture disagreements, theory of mind, and identify differences in understanding between students. It also creates a new opportunity to explore developing a nuanced social skill using LLMs for real-time feedback. Overall, I am interested in exploring small group disagreements - a known challenge in the classroom - with a new approach enabled by LLMs.

4 Preliminary Results

Preliminary results indicate that LLMs - specifically the Gemma-3 family - can capture agreements at moderate levels, but disagreements were uniquely challenging. I evaluated LLM performance in labeling DeliData [9]. The dataset includes labels for explicit agreement and disagreement. While the agreement labeling was a straightforward task, disagreement results had abysmal results. In my results, I saw that while recall was moderate, precision was extremely low. This showed the LLMs were largely overlabeling disagreements.

I explored false positive samples and found that disagreement labeling was unique because they were commonly implicit. The implicit disagreement events were not captured by labels provided in the dataset. However, the LLMs captured this disagreement, showcasing interpretive ability. Re-labeling for implicit disagreement is under way to further evaluate this observation. While LLMs captured implicit disagreement, this also left room for interpretation and hallucination. I identified specific failure modes of LLMs, including hallucinating a disagreement when participants engage in the process of elimination as well as asking questions. These results show potential in using LLMs for implicit detection - which will be evaluated next - and also the possibility of LLMs failing in reasoning and interpretation.

References

1. Atwell, K., Hassan, S., Alikhani, M.: APPDIA: a discourse-aware transformerbased style transfer model for offensive social media conversations. In: Proceedings of the 29th International Conference on Computational Linguistics, pp. 6063–6074 (2022)
2. De Kock, C., Vlachos, A.: I Beg to Differ: a study of constructive is agreement in online conversations. In: Proceedings of the 16th Conference of the European Chapter of the Association for Computational Linguistics: Main Volume, pp. 2017–2027 (2021)
3. D'Mello, S., Graesser, A.: Dynamics of affective states during complex learning. Learn. Instr. **22**(2), 145–157 (2012)
4. Farag, Y., et al.: Opening up Minds with Argumentative Dialogues. Findings of the Association for Computational Linguistics: EMNLP 2022, pp. 4569–4582 (2022). Publisher: Association for Computational Linguistics
5. Graesser, A.C., Fiore, S.M., Greiff, S., Andrews-Todd, J., Foltz, P.W., Hesse, F.W.: Advancing the science of collaborative problem solving. Psychol. Sci. Public Interest **19**(2), 59–92 (2018)

6. Hagvall Svensson, O., Johansson, A., Adawi, T.: How do students negotiate groupwork? The influence of group norm exercises and group development norms. J. Eng. Educ. (Washington, D.C.) **113**(3), 533–554 (2024). https://doi.org/10.1002/jee.20596. Place: Hoboken, USA Publisher: John Wiley & Sons, Inc
7. Jehn, K.A., Greer, L., Levine, S., Szulanski, G.: The effects of conflict types, dimensions, and emergent states on group outcomes. Group Decision Negotiation **17**(6), 465–495 (2008), publisher: Springer
8. Karadzhov, G., Stafford, T., Vlachos, A.: What makes you change your mind? An empirical investigation in online group decision-making conversations. arXiv preprint arXiv:2207.12035 (2022)
9. Karadzhov, G., Stafford, T., Vlachos, A.: DeliData: a dataset for deliberation in multi-party problem solving. In: Proceedings of the ACM on Human-Computer Interaction **7**(CSCW2), 1–25 (2023). Publisher: ACM New York, NY, USA
10. Khebour, I.K., et al.: Common ground tracking in multimodal dialogue. In: Proceedings of the 2024 Joint International Conference on Computational Linguistics, Language Resources and Evaluation (LREC-COLING 2024), pp. 3587–3602 (2024)
11. Lee, D., Huh, Y., Reigeluth, C.M.: Collaboration, intragroup conflict, and social skills in project-based learning. Instruct. Sci. **43**, 561–590 (2015). Publisher: Springer
12. Li, G., Hammoud, H., Itani, H., Khizbullin, D., Ghanem, B.: Camel: Communicative agents for "mind" exploration of large language model society. Adv. Neural. Inf. Process. Syst. **36**, 51991–52008 (2023)
13. McQuade, R., Wiggins, S., Ventura-Medina, E.: 'Doing' disagreement without being disagreeable: how students deal with conversational norms in group work. In: European Psychology Learning and Teaching Conference 2017: Evidence-based Improvement for Learning and Teaching Psychology (2017)
14. Nath, A., Graff, C., Krishnaswamy, N.: Let's roleplay: examining LLM alignment in collaborative dialogues. arXiv e-prints pp. arXiv–2509 (2025)
15. Premack, D., Woodruff, G.: Does the chimpanzee have a theory of mind? Behavioral brain Sci. **1**(4), 515–526 (1978)
16. Torrance, E.P.: Group decision-making and disagreement. Social Forces, pp. 314–318 (1957). Publisher: JSTOR
17. Tsai, M.H., Bendersky, C.: The pursuit of information sharing: expressing task conflicts as debates vs. disagreements increases perceived receptivity to dissenting opinions in groups. Organ. Sci. **27**(1), 141–156 (2016). Publisher: Informs
18. Wason, P.C.: Reasoning about a rule. Quarterly J. Exp. Psychol. **20**(3), 273–281 (1968)
19. Zhou, J., et al.: Disagreeing softly: supporting students in managing disagreement in peer critique: disagreeing softly: supporting students in managing disagreement in peer critique. Int. J. Comput.-Support. Collab. Learn. **20**(2), 249–282 (2025)
20. Zhu, Y., et al.: Modeling theory of mind in multimodal HCI. In: International Conference on Human-Computer Interaction, pp. 205–225. Springer (2024)

Supporting Data-Driven Mastery Learning at Scale

Yumou Wei[✉]

Carnegie Mellon University, Pittsburgh, USA
yumouw@andrew.cmu.edu

Abstract. An overarching goal of AI in education is to provide personal support for every student. This vision, however, is often obstructed by the lack of an integrated system that estimates a student's proficiency in real time and implements adaptive interventions at scale. My dissertation aims to delineate a research program to develop an AI-powered learning analytics platform that supports scalable mastery-learning strategies. Given a subject that one is interested in learning, the system will plan an adaptive curriculum by constructing a knowledge component (KC) model of the subject and generating relevant practice questions, and guide the student to mastery. The system tracks the student's proficiency in real time and uses data to optimize the learning experience. The core modules of this system include: (1) a real-time, longitudinal tracking engine to assess proficiency, (2) an automated method to extract KCs from unstructured questions, and (3) a question-generation pipeline to produce high-quality questions that assess specific KCs.

Keywords: Mastery Learning · Knowledge Tracing · Knowledge Component · Question Generation

1 Introduction

The theory of mastery learning posits that all students can achieve a high level of proficiency in any subject if provided with an appropriate level of instructional support [2], including personalized practice and targeted feedback. Providing personalized learning support has been a long-standing goal of AIED, which has motivated the development of dedicated educational technologies. Intelligent Tutoring Systems (ITS), for example, have demonstrated significant improvements in learning outcomes compared to traditional instruction [4]; however, the scalability of ITS remains a significant challenge.

The **vertical scaling** of ITS to cover a wide range of subjects is constrained by the need for extensive manual knowledge component (KC) modeling and question generation. An ITS typically requires a large collection of questions, each of which is labeled with the corresponding KCs, to provide adaptive practice opportunities; however, manual KC-labeling approaches are costly and difficult to scale [15]. Cognitive Task Analysis (CTA), for example, is the best manual approach to creating a detailed KC model for a domain, but it involves a

E. G. Blanchard et al. (Eds.): AIED 2026, CCIS 3033, pp. 377–383, 2026.
https://doi.org/10.1007/978-3-032-29794-5_58

laborious process of analyzing individual questions from a large collection [15]. Similarly, crafting high-quality practice questions that align with specific KCs is also time-consuming and reliant on the limited availability of domain experts.

The **lateral scaling** of ITS to serve a large and diverse student population also poses unique challenges. For example, the system must account for varying student backgrounds, learning styles, and motivation, which can complicate the design of effective instructional interventions. In addition, the system must be designed with thoughtful consideration of the ethical issues involved in AI use, such as data privacy [14], algorithmic bias [18], and inequitable access to educational technologies [17]. Providing accurate, personalized, and constructive feedback to guide students through the curriculum also requires estimating each student's proficiency in real time and adapting the instruction to their evolving needs, which requires sophisticated infrastructure and algorithms.

The **longitudinal scaling** of ITS to track a student's proficiency over an extended period remains an open research question. A truly personal ITS should not only provide real-time estimates of a student's proficiency during a tutoring session, but also account for the natural process of knowledge retention and decay over an extended period (the whole study program or lifetime), even when the student is not actively engaged. Existing student modeling techniques, such as Bayesian Knowledge Tracing (BKT) [5], primarily focus on short-term interactions and may not effectively capture long-term learning dynamics.

These challenges in scaling ITS create significant barriers to providing personal learning support at scale, motivating me to explore an important research question: **How can we build flexible AIED systems that use data to support personal mastery learning at scale for any subject?**

2 Research Goals and Questions

The overarching goal of my doctoral research is to develop an AIED system that supports data-driven implementation of mastery-learning strategies at scale. Given a subject that a student is interested in learning and that can be learned through practice, the system will automatically devise a practice-based curriculum by building a KC model of the subject and generating practice questions for each KC. As the student explores the curriculum, the system will track the student's proficiency in real time and use the data to optimize the learning experience. To support lifelong learning, where the student may interact with the system intermittently over an extended period, the system explicitly models the natural process of knowledge retention and decay, and accounts for the time elapsed when estimating proficiency between learning sessions.

The system will consist of two main components: a longitudinal proficiency tracker to assess student mastery in real time and an adaptive curriculum planner to optimize learning paths. The proficiency tracker (`Mod-1`) is a standalone module that continuously assesses a student's proficiency in each KC and works in synergy with the curriculum planner to provide adaptive practice opportunities. The curriculum planner is further composed of two complementary modules:

a KC-discovery module (`Mod-2`) that automatically constructs a KC model from an unstructured question collection and a question-generation module (`Mod-3`) that produces high-quality questions assessing specific KCs.

My dissertation will focus on the development and integration of these modules into a cohesive AIED system, which applies AI and machine-learning techniques to support data-driven mastery learning, followed by a rigorous evaluation of its effectiveness in improving student learning outcomes. The specific research questions (RQs) that I aim to address include:

- RQ-1: How can we effectively track a student's proficiency in real time, also accounting for knowledge growth and decay over an extended period?
- RQ-2: How can we discover accurate KC models from unstructured question banks using AI?
- RQ-3: How can we generate high-quality questions that align with specific KCs using AI?
- RQ-4: What is the overall impact of an AIED system that integrates these three modules on student learning outcomes, engagement, and satisfaction?

3 Existing Solutions

Central to supporting data-driven mastery learning at scale is the ability to track students' proficiency in real time. Common statistical approaches include BKT [5] and Additive Factors Modeling (AFM) [3]. More recent approaches, such as Deep Knowledge Tracing (DKT) [13] and Dynamic Bayesian Networks (DBN) [9], use machine learning to model complex relationships in student data. However, these approaches often focus on modeling student learning within a single session and do not account for the time elapsed between practice opportunities, leaving longitudinal proficiency tracking an open research question.

KC modeling complements proficiency tracking, as it defines the skills or concepts that students need to master. Traditional approaches often rely on expert knowledge or statistical methods [1]. More recent work has explored the use of machine learning techniques, such as clustering [10] and deep learning [12], to automate KC extraction from educational data. However, these methods often require expert-designed labels to create interpretable KCs, which limits the vertical scalability of ITS to new subjects.

Another key to vertical scaling is the ability to generate a large collection of high-quality practice questions. Automatic question generation has been an active area of research, with approaches ranging from rule-based systems [8] to neural-network models [7]. Recent approaches using large language models (LLMs) have shown promise in generating coherent and contextually relevant questions [6]. However, challenges remain in ensuring the quality, diversity, and alignment of generated questions with specific KCs.

4 Research Contribution

My research aims to develop an integrated AIED system that supports data-driven mastery learning at scale by combining longitudinal proficiency tracking (`Mod-1`) with automated KC modeling (`Mod-2`) and question generation (`Mod-3`). In this section, I describe my research conducted so far on the three modules, leaving the integration of the three modules for future work.

4.1 Longitudinal Proficiency Tracking (Mod-1, RQ-1)

Most existing solutions to track student proficiency, such as the original BKT model, do not account for the time elapsed between two learning opportunities. A consequence of this modeling assumption is that a student could be estimated to have the same level of proficiency in a KC whether they answered a relevant question yesterday or six months ago. This is problematic because it ignores the well-documented phenomenon of *forgetting*, which suggests that a student's proficiency in a KC may decrease over time if not reinforced through practice. Moreover, as advances in AIED provide growing opportunities for life-long learning, where students can interact with the system intermittently over an extended period, it becomes increasingly important to support longitudinal tracking of student proficiency that accounts for knowledge retention and decay over time, in addition to real-time tracking during a single learning session.

To address this gap, I plan to extend the BKT model with new modeling assumptions that incorporate the temporal dynamics of knowledge change. Specifically, instead of using the "slip" and "guess" parameters to describe the uncertainty around a student's proficiency p indirectly through the observed performance, I assume that p is a parameter following a Beta distribution: $p \sim \text{Beta}(\alpha, \beta)$. The parameters α and β represent the number of correct and incorrect responses that the student has given on a KC. An advantage of this Bayesian formulation is that α and β are not restricted to their physical interpretation, but can also be treated as "virtual counts" representing the evidence for and against the student's proficiency. This allows me to introduce time-dependent adjustments to α and β to model how the student reinforces or forgets a KC over time. For example, a model can exponentially reduce the mean $\mu = \frac{\alpha}{\alpha+\beta}$ and the "sample size" $\nu = \alpha + \beta$ of the Beta distribution after each time step to indicate decreased confidence in the student's proficiency. This approach allows the model to re-evaluate the evidence concerning a student's proficiency after each time step (rather than after each practice step), even if the student has not answered any questions during the preceding period.

4.2 Automated KC Modeling with KCluster (Mod-2, RQ-2)

In my recent work [16], I proposed `KCluster`, a novel approach that uses the probabilistic reasoning abilities of a small language model (SLM) to extract KCs from an unstructured collection of questions. As its name suggests, `KCluster` identifies **clusters** of questions that share the same **KC** by evaluating how much more likely the presence of one question makes another to appear. It uses an SLM called Phi-2 [11] to calculate the standalone probability of each question, $\Pr(q_i)$, and the conditional probability of the same question given another, $\Pr(q_i|q_j)$. A larger absolute difference in probabilities indicates a closer relationship between the two questions, since q_j significantly increases the likelihood of q_i. `KCluster` then applies a clustering algorithm to group the questions based on the strength of their pairwise relationships, forming clusters that represent distinct KCs. The evaluation showed that the KC model produced by `KCluster` led to more accurate predictions of student performance than the expert's KC model [16].

4.3 Question Generation Pipeline (Mod-3, RQ-3)

My recent work on using SLMs to generate questions was accepted at another conference [19]. I proposed a novel pipeline that first generates abundant questions corresponding to a given KC and then uses Phi-2's probabilistic reasoning to validate the generated questions to select high-quality ones. Experiments with seven teachers and one advanced LLM showed that the generated questions had clear answers and generally aligned well with the intended KC. This work marks another contribution to the use of SLMs for accessible AIED [17].

4.4 System Integration and Evaluation (RQ-4)

An important part of my dissertation research will be to integrate the three modules into a synergistic AIED system and conduct a rigorous evaluation of their combined effectiveness in supporting mastery learning at scale. This will involve designing a user-friendly interface that allows students to interact with the system and developing algorithms to orchestrate the interactions between the modules. Given the increasing popularity of agentic AI systems, I plan to integrate the three modules into an *Active Practice Agent* (APA) architecture that uses `Mod-1` to track a student's learning and actively adjust the curriculum for the best learning outcome. The APA will use `Mod-2` to build a KC model of the subject and `Mod-3` to generate practice questions for each KC. Depending on the pedagogical goal (which is determined by past data), the APA can select questions that the student is likely to answer correctly to build confidence and motivation or questions that the student has a moderate chance of succeeding in to create a productive struggle. The evaluation will involve controlled experiments, user studies, and analysis of learning data. The key metrics for evaluation are learning gain, efficiency, engagement, and student perceptions of the system.

5 Conclusion

I described my vision for an integrated AIED system that supports data-driven mastery learning at scale. I have made some progress for longitudinal proficiency tracking (`Mod-1`, RQ-1) and published a prototype for automated KC modeling (`Mod-2`, RQ-2) and question generation (`Mod-3`, RQ-3). The next steps involve integrating all three modules into a user-friendly platform, followed by a rigorous evaluation of the overall system's impact on student learning (RQ-4). I believe the system has the potential to advance AIED by collecting, analyzing, and integrating data to support personalized learning for every student and to improve the scalability of ITS in all three directions.

References

1. Barnes, T., Bitzer, D., Vouk, M.: Experimental analysis of the Q-matrix method in knowledge discovery. In: Hacid, M.S., Murray, N.V., Raś, Z.W., Tsumoto, S. (eds.) Foundations of Intelligent Systems, pp. 603–611. Springer (2005)
2. Bloom, B.S.: Learning for Mastery. Instruction and Curriculum. Regional Education Laboratory for the Carolinas and Virginia, Topical Papers and Reprints, Number 1. Tech. rep. (1968)
3. Cen, H., Koedinger, K.R., Junker, B.: Is Over practice necessary? –Improving learning efficiency with the cognitive tutor through educational data mining. In: Proceedings of the 2007 Conference on Artificial Intelligence in Education (2007)
4. Corbett, A.: Cognitive computer tutors: solving the two-sigma problem. In: Bauer, M., Gmytrasiewicz, P.J., Vassileva, J. (eds.) User Modeling. Springer (2001)
5. Corbett, A.T., Anderson, J.R.: Knowledge tracing: modeling the acquisition of procedural knowledge. User Model. User-Adapt. Int. **4** (1994)
6. Doughty, J., et al.: A Comparative Study of AI-Generated (GPT-4) and Human-crafted MCQs in Programming Education. ACE '24 (2024)
7. Du, X., Shao, J., Cardie, C.: Learning to ask: neural question generation for reading comprehension. In: Barzilay, R., Kan, M.Y. (eds.) Proceedings of the 55th Annual Meeting of the Association for Computational Linguistics (2017)
8. Heilman, M., Smith, N.A.: Good question! Statistical ranking for question generation. In: Human Language Technologies: The 2010 Annual Conference of the North American Chapter of the Association for Computational Linguistics, pp. 609–617. HLT '10, Association for Computational Linguistics, USA (2010)
9. Käser, T., Klingler, S., Schwing, A.G., Gross, M.: Dynamic Bayesian networks for student modeling. IEEE Trans. Learn. Technol. **10**(4) (2017)
10. Matsuda, N., Wood, J., Shrivastava, R., Shimmei, M., Bier, N.: Latent skill mining and labeling from courseware content. J. EDM **14**(2) (2022)
11. Microsoft Research: Phi-2: The surprising power of small language models (2023)
12. Pardos, Z.A., Dadu, A.: dAFM: fusing psychometric and connectionist modeling for Q-matrix refinement. J. Educat. Data Min. **10**(2) (2018)
13. Piech, C., et al.: Deep knowledge tracing. In: Advances in Neural Information Processing Systems, vol. 28 (2015)
14. Prinsloo, P., Slade, S.: An elephant in the learning analytics room: the obligation to act. In: Proceedings of the Seventh International Learning Analytics & Knowledge Conference, pp. 46–55. LAK '17 (2017)
15. Stamper, J.C., Koedinger, K.R.: Human-machine student model discovery and improvement using datashop. In: Biswas, G., Bull, S., Kay, J., Mitrovic, A. (eds.) Artificial Intelligence in Education, pp. 353–360. Springer (2011)
16. Wei, Y., Carvalho, P., Stamper, J.: KCluster: an LLM-based clustering approach to knowledge component discovery. In: Proceedings of the 18th International Conference on Educational Data Mining (2025)

17. Wei, Y., Carvalho, P., Stamper, J.: Small but significant: on the promise of small language models for accessible AIED (2025). arXiv:2505.08588
18. Wei, Y., Carvalho, P.F., Stamper, J.: Uncovering name-based biases in large language models through simulated trust game (2024). arXiv:2404.14682
19. Wei, Y., Stamper, J., Carvalho, P.F.: Generate-then-validate: a novel question generation approach using small language models (2026). arXiv:2512.10110

The Mediating Mirror: A Recursive Symbolic Production Model for GenAI-Mediated Language Learning

Jai Hong Lee(✉) and Cheolil Lim

Seoul National University, Seoul 08826, Republic of Korea
leejai@snu.ac.kr

Abstract. Generative AI has shifted the conditions of language learning from linguistic scarcity to abundance, where fluent output can be generated on demand, leading technical correctness to be increasingly commodified. Despite this shift, GenAI is rapidly being integrated into L2 education yet is still predominantly positioned as a tutor for accurate and efficient language performance. This orientation risks leaving learners' voice, stance, positioning, and accountability underdeveloped in an era of automated fluency. This research reframes the educational target of L2 education as symbolic competence and symbolic agency. To operationalize this shift, the study reconceptualizes GenAI as a "Mediating Mirror", a mediational partner that materializes learners' symbolic intent into inspectable representations for critical reflection. Learning is situated in Multimodal Artifact Production, with a focus on text-to-video synthesis. Central to the study is the development and validation of the Recursive Symbolic Production Model, which translates these commitments into a repeatable classroom procedure where learners iteratively notice and bridge gaps between their intended stance and the AI's materialization. Methodologically, the project adopts Design and Development Research Type 2 (Model Research), combining model development with internal and external validation.

Keywords: Generative AI · Symbolic Competence · Multimodal Artifact Production · Second Language Learning · Design and Development Research

1 Introduction and Problem: From Scarcity to Abundance

The trajectory of Artificial Intelligence in L2 education has evolved from early applications in computer-assisted learning in 1978 [1], to usage in formal education between 2000 and 2022 [2]. Earlier generations of L2 educational AI were often constrained by predefined, rules-based systems that could not flexibly adapt to unexpected learner interactions [3, 4]. Regardless, AI-based tools have long been utilized to support reading, writing, listening, and speaking activities [5, 6], while contributing to learner autonomy, reduced anxiety, and support for diverse proficiency levels [7–9]. Modern Generative AI, powered by Large Language Models, has rapidly entered language education, enabling

E. G. Blanchard et al. (Eds.): AIED 2026, CCIS 3033, pp. 384–389, 2026.
https://doi.org/10.1007/978-3-032-29794-5_59

contextually rich and coherent responses across diverse educational tasks [5, 10]. However, in many implementations, GenAI is positioned as a tutor, assistant, or feedback tool designed to optimize the accuracy and efficiency of language performance, still reflecting the educational paradigm that formed under conditions where linguistic production was relatively scarce and difficult to automate.

However, the rapid advancement of LLMs and GenAI has fundamentally altered the linguistic condition. As LLMs and GenAI systems generate linguistic work in multiple languages at a state-of-the-art-level [11], surface-level correctness becomes available on demand, reducing the historical scarcity of linguistic production which justified the instructional emphasis on language form production. With this shift, the question should no longer be whether learners can produce grammatically and communicatively acceptable language, but whether they can intentionally use language and other semiotic resources to frame meanings, relationships, and identities.

This introduces a serious educational problem as L2 education remains heavily centered on form-focused practices and test preparation [12, 13]. Furthermore, GenAI in L2 education is predominantly positioned as a tutor, assistant, or feedback engine oriented toward accuracy and efficiency. While traditional pedagogy remains useful and is not inherently invalid, this performance-centered paradigm risks leaving learners' voice, stance, positioning, and accountability underdeveloped in a world where AI can effortlessly produce "correct" language. The challenge for AIED, therefore, is not to simply integrate GenAI into existing instructional routines, but to redesign learning goals and activities so that human meaning-making remains central.

Looking at the historical expansion of language competence constructs, language education has repeatedly broadened what counts as meaningful competence, from linguistic competence (innate knowledge of grammar) [14], to communicative competence (appropriate use) [15, 16], to intercultural communicative competence (mediation between cultures) [17]. This leads to symbolic competence [18, 19], or the learners' ability to interpret and manipulate symbolic systems, resignify meanings, and construct legitimate subject positions. For this study, this orientation is further specified as symbolic agency, or the learners' capacity to intentionally use symbolic resources to frame reality, identity, and social positioning through accountable acts of meaning-making.

This research argues that a fundamental pedagogical shift is required. The central problem addressed is the lack of instructional models that move beyond treating GenAI as a tool for efficiency, pushing toward frameworks that cultivate symbolic agency through human-AI synergy. This research proposes a GenAI approach to a Multimodal Artifact Production (MAP) process and a Recursive Symbolic Production (RSP) Model, which conceptualizes human-AI interaction as a recursive cycle of mediated symbolic production, reflection, and revision. This study reframes GenAI as a mediational partner for developing learners' symbolic agency.

To guide this work, the following three research questions direct the inquiry. **RQ1** (Model Development): What design principles and instructional components should constitute the RSP Model for cultivating symbolic agency through GenAI-mediated multimodal artifact production? **RQ2** (Internal Validation): Is the RSP Model theoretically coherent, pedagogically appropriate, and usable, as determined by domain experts? **RQ3** (External Validation): How does RSP-guided MAP shape learners' enactment of symbolic agency in Korean-as-a-Second-Language (KSL) and English-as-a-Foreign-Language (EFL) contexts?

2 Theoretical Framing and Proposed Model: Recursive Symbolic Production (RSP) Model

As stated, the standards for what counts as "competence" in language have expanded through successive theoretical shifts. Moreover, as fluent language can be generated on demand, this study argues that L2 education must target symbolic competence as the primary educational goal. In this argument, language learning is the development of symbolic agency, or learners' capacity to intentionally frame reality, identity, and positioning through accountable semiotic choices.

Reframing GenAI as a mediational partner that materializes learners' symbolic intent in contrast to a tutor, assessor, or corrective engine implies a shift in how educational technology is conceptualized. Earlier paradigms were strongly influenced by information-processing views of learning [20], with emphasis on optimized sequencing and input efficiency [21], alongside multimedia traditions that optimize representations for comprehension and retention [22, 23]. While foundational, these approaches position learners primarily as recipients of designed representations. In contrast, this study is grounded in constructionist commitments that treat learning as strengthened when learners design and produce public artifacts [24]. This represents a shift from optimized presentation toward learner-driven multimodal expression where resources are tools for symbolic meaning-making rather than mere vehicles for clearer explanation.

Accordingly, this study conceptualizes Multimodal Artifact Production (MAP) as a synthesized pedagogical space, with an initial focus on text-to-video synthesis, where symbolic agency can be enacted, made visible, and refined. Multimodality theory emphasizes that meaning is designed through multiple modes, each with distinct affordances [25]. Multimodal composition is not merely additive but involves "braiding" or "orchestration", through which the resulting artifact produces a semiotic power that exceeds the sum of its parts [26]. Here, GenAI can reduce technical production barriers and accelerate iterative variation and transformation [27, 28], functioning as a "Mediating Mirror" – a mediational partner that externalizes learners' symbolic intent into external representations that can be inspected, critiqued, and revised.

This is the central motivation for this study's development and validation of the Recursive Symbolic Production (RSP) Model, the core objective for this study. The model seeks to translate these theoretical commitments into a repeatable classroom procedure. To elaborate, the RSP model governs the relationship between learners' internal intent and external production by structuring learning as a repeatable cycle of mediated symbolic work. This model would guide learners as they (1) externalize intended meanings through MAP, (2) use GenAI to materialize alternatives and perspectives, and (3) iteratively inspect, critique, and revise their semiotic choices to better align representations with intent.

Through this reflexive externalization loop, this research seeks to establish a framework for human-AI synergy that cultivates digitally literate, symbolically competent citizens, establishes a path that prioritizes human meaning-making over automated proficiency, and preserves learner agency. Operationalizing this framework, however, requires indicators that make symbolic agency observable in learner activity.

3 Methodology

Symbolic agency risks being mistaken for engagement (affective involvement) or creativity (novelty of output) in learner activity. Four indicators, derived from Kramsch's pillars and aligned with this study's data collection, operationalize the construct: (1) subjective reframing in the final artifact; (2) gap detection in prompt revision histories; (3) selection agency in adoption and rejection patterns; and (4) ownership-oriented justification in learner reflection, where choices are explained in terms of framing, stance, or identity rather than aesthetics or correctness. These indicators ground the rubric and log-analysis scheme that follow.

To systematically transition the Recursive Symbolic Production (RSP) Model from a theoretical construct into a repeatable classroom procedure, this research adopts a Design and Development Research (DDR) approach, specifically Type 2: Model Research [29]. DDR Type 2 is appropriate as it acts as a bridge between theory and practice by supporting the design, testing, and validation of instructional models that might otherwise remain conceptually persuasive but pedagogically under-specified. This study treats the RSP model as both a theoretical proposition (about GenAI-mediated symbolic agency) and a design object that will be progressively refined through cycles of conceptualization, expert feedback, and field-based implementation.

Following DDR, this research is structured into two phases: Model Development and Model Validation. The Model Development phase focuses on the conceptualization and initial model specification through literature review and synthesis across GenAI in language learning, applied linguistics, symbolic competence, sociocultural mediation, multimodal composition, and constructionist theories. Through the produced constructs and components – such as symbolic agency and mediated mirroring – and preliminary tasks for AI-mediated MAP, an initial instructional process is built.

Model Validation starts with a series of expert validations (with a panel of experts in language education, AIED, and the learning sciences) to review the model's theoretical coherence, pedagogical plausibility, and implementation feasibility. Feedback is then used to revise model components, refine design principles, and clarify boundaries of use. Following this, two field-based trials in two instructional contexts – Korean as a Second Language (KSL) and English as a Foreign Language (EFL) – are set to be conducted to generate implementation evidence regarding how learners engage in production and how proposed scaffolds support symbolic agency in practice.

Evidence is organized into streams prioritized by the study's research questions. For RQ1, evidence derives from literature synthesis. For RQ2, three Delphi rounds with a panel of 5–7 experts in educational technology, applied linguistics, and AIED provide internal validity evidence, judged on usability, appropriateness, completeness, clarity, and systemic logic. For RQ3, two field sites (KSL and EFL) generate the following triad of data: product evidence from rubric-based assessment (adapted from Kramsch) of final artifacts, process evidence from analysis of GenAI interaction logs, and perception evidence from in-depth interviews.

4 Expected Contributions & Impact

This study is expected to contribute to the AIED field by advancing a learning sciences and design-oriented account of GenAI-mediated learning that prioritizes human meaning-making, identity expression, and learner agency in conditions of linguistic abundance. This is accomplished as this study reframes language learning objectives in the age of GenAI by shifting the educational target from proficiency-oriented performance to symbolic agency through multimodal meaning-making.

By theorizing and operationalizing the Recursive Symbolic Production (RSP) Model, this research aims to provide a process-oriented account of how learners use GenAI to externalize, inspect, critique, and revise symbolic intent through iterative cycles of comparison and transformation. Doing so links symbolic competence with constructionist and multimodal learning traditions and offers an instructional model that supports teachers in moving beyond technical tool use toward meaningful classroom implementation. Overall, this research contributes not only a conceptual repositioning of GenAI but also a model for studying human-AI meaning-making as an accountable learning process rather than a purely output-based activity. From a computer science and AIED perspective, this study offers design implications for GenAI-supported environments that seek to preserve learner agency rather than maximize automation.

A further contribution is methodological. By employing DDR Type 2 to move from theoretical framing to iterative validation, this study offers a practical route for developing and testing instructional models in rapidly evolving GenAI contexts where pedagogical experimentation and practices often outpace stable evaluation frameworks.

Disclosure of Interests.. The authors declare no conflicts of interest.

References

1. Schulze, J.: AI in CALL – Artificially inflated or almost imminent? CALICO J. **25**(3), 510–527 (2008)
2. Ng, D.T.K., Lee, M., Tan, R.J.Y., Hu, X., Downie, J.S., Chu, S.K.W.: A review of AI teaching and learning from 2000 to 2020. Educ. Inf. Technol. **28**(7), 8445–8501 (2023)
3. Lee, S., Jeon, J.: Visualizing a disembodied agent: Young EFL learners' perceptions of voice-controlled conversational agents as language partners. Comput. Assist. Lang. Learn. **37**(5–6), 1048–1073 (2024)
4. Ji, H., Han, I., Ko, Y.: A systematic review of conversational AI in language education: focusing on the collaboration with human teachers. J. Res. Technol. Educ. **55**(1), 48–63 (2023)
5. Li, B., Lowell, V.L., Wang, C., Li, X.: A systematic review of the first year of publications on ChatGPT and language education: examining research on ChatGPT's use in language learning and teaching. Comput. Educ. Artif. Intell. **9**, 100445 (2025)
6. Liang, J., Hwang, G., Chen, M., Darmawansah, D.: Roles and research foci of artificial intelligence in language education: an integrated bibliographic analysis and systematic review approach. Interact. Learn. Environ. **31**(7), 4270–4296 (2023)
7. Ghafouri, M.: ChatGPT: the catalyst for teacher-student rapport and grit development in L2 class. System **120**, 103209 (2024)

8. Lee, J.H., Shin, D., Noh, W.: Artificial intelligence-based content generator technology for young English-as-a-foreign-language learners' reading enjoyment. RELC J. **54**(2), 508–516 (2023)
9. Li, X., Li, B., Cho, S.J.: Empowering Chinese language learners from low-income families to improve their Chinese writing with ChatGPT's assistance afterschool. Languages **8**(4), 238 (2023)
10. Schneider, J.: What comes after transformers? In: Rocha, A.P., Steels, L., van den Herik, J. (eds.) Agents and Artificial Intelligence, vol. 2, pp. 55–82. Springer, Cham (2025)
11. Kasneci, E., et al.: ChatGPT for good? On opportunities and challenges of large language models for education. Learn. Individ. Differ. **103**, 102274 (2023)
12. Hsu, W.H.: Transitioning to a communication-oriented pedagogy: Taiwanese university freshmen's views of class participation. System **49**, 61–72 (2015)
13. Jeon, J.: Key issues in applying the communicative approach in Korea: follow up after 12 years of implementation. Engl. Educ. **64**(4), 123–150 (2009)
14. Chomsky, N.: Aspects of the theory of syntax. MIT Press, Cambridge (1965)
15. Hymes, D.: On communicative competence. In: Pride, J., Holmes, J. (eds.) Sociolinguistics, pp. 269–283. Penguin Books, Harmondsworth (1972)
16. Canale, M., Swain, M.: Theoretical bases of communicative approaches to second language teaching and testing. Appl. Linguis. **1**(1), 1–47 (1980)
17. Byram, M.: 'Cultural awareness' as vocabulary learning. Lang. Learn. J. **16**(1), 51–57 (1997)
18. Kramsch, C.: From communicative competence to symbolic competence. Mod. Lang. J. **90**(2), 249–252 (2006)
19. Kramsch, C.: The multilingual subject: What language learners say about their experience and why it matters. Oxford University Press, Oxford (2009)
20. Atkinson, R.C., Shiffrin, R.M.: Human memory: A proposed system and its control processes. In: Spence, K.W., Spence, J.T. (eds.) The Psychology of Learning and Motivation, vol. 2, pp. 89–195. Academic Press, New York (1968)
21. Gagné, R.M.: The conditions of learning and theory of instruction, 4th edn. Holt, Rinehart & Winston, New York (1985)
22. Clark, J.M., Paivio, A.: Dual coding theory and education. Educ. Psychol. Rev. **3**(3), 149–210 (1991)
23. Mayer, R.E.: Multimedia learning, 2nd edn. Cambridge University Press, New York (2009)
24. Papert, S.: Mindstorms: Children, computers, and powerful ideas. Basic Books, New York (1980)
25. Kress, G.: Literacy in the new media age. Routledge, London (2003)
26. Hull, G.A., Nelson, M.E.: Locating the semiotic power of multimodality. Writ. Commun. **22**(2), 224–261 (2005)
27. Wu, J., Chen, D.T.V.: A systematic review of educational digital storytelling. Comput. Educ. **147**, 103786 (2020)
28. Xu, A.O.Z., Hashim, H.: Digital storytelling's impact on ESL learners' speaking skills (2019–2023): a systematic review. Int. J. Acad. Res. Bus. Soc. Sci. **13**(12), 947–962 (2023)
29. Richey, R.C., Klein, J.D.: Design and development research. Routledge, New York (2007)

Evaluating Pedagogical Styles of LLM-Generated Hint Sets

Matthew Kalarickal(✉), Eamon Worden, and Neil T. Heffernan

Worcester Polytechnic Institute, Worcester, MA 01609, USA
{mkalarickal,elworden,nth}@wpi.edu

Abstract. Intelligent tutoring systems rely on hints to support learning, but authoring high-quality hint sets is costly and limits scalability. Large language models (LLMs) offer a potential alternative, though rigorous evaluation of their pedagogical effectiveness remains limited. This study conducts a randomized experiment within ASSISTments comparing three theoretically grounded LLM-generated hint styles—Scaffolding, Socratic, and Teacher-style—to both no-hint and teacher-authored baselines. Randomization occurs at the student-problem level. The primary outcome measures short-term transfer via next-problem correctness, and hint usage is modeled to assess engagement. Results aim to identify whether LLM-generated hints improve performance and which instructional framing is most effective.

Keywords: Intelligent Tutoring Systems · Large Language Models · Instructional Scaffolding · Socratic Questioning

1 Introduction

Intelligent tutoring systems (ITS) aim to provide scalable, individualized instruction by offering on-demand support to students who request it. One mechanism for such feedback is hints: providing guidance to support students without revealing solutions. Prior research has shown that well-designed hints can improve student performance. Overly directive hints, however, may reduce learning by encouraging superficial task completion [2,9,17].

Traditional ITS often rely on manually authored hint sets, designed by domain experts, to provide assistance [12]. While effective, this approach requires time and effort, limiting scalability to large problem sets [12,20].

Recent advances in large language models (LLMs) suggest a scalable alternative to manual hint authoring. LLMs have been explored for explanation and hint generation in educational contexts [5,11,21], but controlled comparisons against teacher-authored hints under identical conditions remain limited [13,14].

This research investigates the utility of LLMs as an authoring tool for hint generation in ITS, addressing the gap in comparisons between LLM-authored and teacher-authored hint sets. This study evaluates pre-generated hint sets

E. G. Blanchard et al. (Eds.): AIED 2026, CCIS 3033, pp. 390–395, 2026.
https://doi.org/10.1007/978-3-032-29794-5_60

fixed for each problem, enabling isolation of hint style and direct comparison to teacher-authored hints under identical conditions.

Specifically, this work addresses three questions:

1. Do students perform better with LLM-generated hints compared to no hints?
2. Do students perform better with LLM-generated hints compared to teacher-written hints?
3. How does hint style (Scaffolding, Socratic, Teacher-style hints) affect student problem-solving performance?

2 Background

2.1 Hints and Instructional Scaffolding in ITS

As our study compares different hint sources and styles, we first review foundational work on hint design and instructional scaffolding in ITS. Hints are a central mechanism in ITS, usually implemented as sequences from general guidance to bottom-out hints, hints ultimately providing the final answer [3]. Research on the "assistance dilemma" highlights the focus of providing support and preserving learning effort [9]. Empirical studies have shown that over-reliance on hints can undermine learning, even when short-term performance improves [2,4].

2.2 The Authoring Bottleneck

Developing high-quality ITS requires substantial domain modeling and manual authoring of feedback and hints. The demand for specialized expertise slows the scaling of ITS platforms, often described as the "authoring bottleneck" [16]. Data-driven approaches have reduced some development costs [10]. However, scalable generation of pedagogically sound hint sets remains challenging, particularly in open-ended domains.

2.3 Large Language Models for Educational Support

As a potential remedy to the authoring bottleneck, LLMs have been proposed as scalable tools for producing explanations and tutoring feedback [1]. Early evaluations suggest that LLMs can generate coherent instructional responses, but emphasize the need for empirical validation of their effectiveness [7,18].

2.4 Hypotheses

- H1: Students receiving LLM-generated hints will demonstrate higher next-problem correctness than those receiving no hints, consistent with prior work on instructional support [2,17].
- H2: Different LLM-generated hint styles will produce differing effects on next-problem correctness due to their distinct pedagogical mechanisms.

- H3: Scaffolding hints will lead to higher next-problem correctness than Socratic hints, as they provide more structured guidance.
- H4: Teacher-style LLM hints will perform comparably to teacher-authored hints, as they emulate their structure and diversity.
- H5: Hint usage will vary across conditions, reflecting differences in how students interact with different pedagogical styles.

3 Proposed Methodology

3.1 Experimental Platform

This study will be conducted using the ASSISTments[1] online learning platform, which delivers mathematics problems to students and supports student learning with hints among other methods. ASSISTments includes a large collection of problems, some with teacher-authored hints and many without, reflecting the ongoing cost of manual hint authoring. In preliminary testing, we found that the hallucination rate of LLMs on image-based problems was high; therefore, we exclude such problems in this initial study.

3.2 Hint Styles

We collaborated with educators, learning scientists, and prompt engineers at The ASSISTments Foundation to design three LLM-generated hint styles.

The scaffolding template follows instructional scaffolding principles, progressing from high-level conceptual guidance to more focused task guidance without revealing answers [15,19]. The Socratic template uses structured questioning to induce self-explanation, shown to support transfer [6,8].

The teacher-style LLM hints do not follow a predefined pedagogical framework. Instead, the LLM is prompted with examples of teacher-authored hints from ASSISTments to emulate their overall style, tone, and structure.

3.3 Treatment Construction

For each eligible problem, we will generate three types of LLM-authored hints: Scaffolding, Socratic, and Teacher-style. Students are randomly assigned to one of four conditions:

- Control condition
  - If no hint exists: control = no hint set
  - If a teacher-authored hint set exists: control = teacher hint set
- LLM Scaffolding hint set
- LLM Socratic hint set
- LLM Teacher-style hint set

[1] https://assistments.org.

At the current time, some problems in ASSISTments contain teacher-authored hint sets and some do not. The control condition differs depending on problem type, so analyses will be stratified by original hint availability.

Teacher-authored hints encompass a wide range of styles, having been authored by many teachers across many years. Thus, this control group reflects authentic pedagogical diversity, and the teacher-style LLM hint style is designed to emulate this diversity rather than a single instructional strategy.

Randomization occurs at the student-problem level. For each problem with generated LLM hints, students are independently assigned to one of four conditions. This ensures within-problem comparability and unbiased estimation of treatment effects.

3.4 Outcome Measures

Our primary outcome measure is next-problem correctness, which captures short term transfer. Next-problem correctness is defined as a student answering the following problem correctly without requesting any hints.

This outcome is evaluated for all students in all treatment groups, regardless of whether they used a hint or not. This metric captures if exposure to a given hint style improves independent performance immediately afterward.

We will also measure the number of hints used on each problem. The average number of hints used per problem across treatment conditions will be analyzed to understand engagement and potential over-reliance. Differences in hint usage are interpreted as indicators of engagement and reliance on support, providing insight into how different pedagogical styles influence student interaction.

All outcome analyses will follow an intent-to-treat (ITT) framework, with students analyzed according to their randomized hint assignment regardless of actual hint usage.

3.5 Statistical Models

To estimate the effect of hint condition on next-problem correctness, we fit a mixed-effects logistic regression:

$$\begin{aligned}\operatorname{logit}\left(\Pr\left(Y_{i,p}=1\right)\right) = \beta_0 &+ \beta_1\,\text{Scaffold-LLM}_{i,p} + \beta_2\,\text{Socratic-LLM}_{i,p} \\ &+ \beta_3\,\text{Teacher-LLM}_{i,p} + \gamma_p + u_i\end{aligned} \tag{1}$$

where i indexes students and p indexes problems, Control is the omitted baseline category, and γ_p and u_i are random intercepts for problem and student, respectively. Coefficients β_k represent the log-odds difference in correctness relative to control. Models are estimated separately for (i) problems without original hints (LLM vs. no hints) and (ii) problems with teacher-authored hints (LLM vs. teacher). Re-parameterization allows direct comparison across LLM styles.

To model hint usage, we fit a mixed-effects negative binomial regression:

$$\log\left(E\left[H_{i,p}\right]\right) = \alpha_0 + \alpha_1\,\text{Scaffold-LLM}_{i,p} + \alpha_2\,\text{Socratic-LLM}_{i,p} + \alpha_3\,\text{Teacher-LLM}_{i,p} + \gamma_p + u_i \quad (2)$$

Given overdispersion in count data, this models expected hint counts as a function of treatment condition with the same random-effects structure. Coefficients α_k represent log differences in expected hint counts relative to control.

4 Expected Contributions

This work provides causal evidence on the pedagogical impact of LLM-generated hints in authentic classroom settings. By isolating hint source and instructional style within a randomized design, the study enables direct comparison of pedagogical framing effects.

Beyond evaluating LLM hints as a single intervention, this research experimentally compares three distinct hint styles: scaffolding, Socratic, and teacher-style explanation. This design allows us to test hypotheses about how different forms of guidance influence short-term transfer and productive struggle.

The study demonstrates a scalable framework for embedding multi-arm randomized experiments into live educational platforms. The findings aim to inform integration of LLM-based instructional support in K-12 systems by identifying not only whether LLM-generated hints are effective, but which instructional framing is most beneficial.

The study was anonymously preregistered on OSF[2]. It is currently anonymous until the embargo period has passed.

5 Limitations

This study focuses on next-problem correctness as a measure of short-term transfer and does not capture longer-term learning outcomes such as retention or error patterns. Additionally, while teacher-authored hints represent diverse instructional approaches, they are treated as a single condition. Future work could further analyze and cluster teacher-authored hints into pedagogical subtypes.

References

1. Al Faraby, S., Romadhony, A., et al.: Analysis of LLMs for educational question classification and generation. Comput. Educat. Artif. Intell. **7**, 100298 (2024)
2. Aleven, V., Mclaren, B., Roll, I., Koedinger, K.: Toward meta-cognitive tutoring: a model of help seeking with a cognitive tutor. Int. J. Artif. Intell. Educ. **16**(2), 101–128 (2006)
3. Anderson, J.R., Corbett, A.T., Koedinger, K.R., Pelletier, R.: Cognitive tutors: lessons learned. J. Learn. Sci. **4**(2), 167–207 (1995)

[2] https://osf.io/q2zx6/overview?view_only=5f8c2aa00ad54680b39ffc5890fafba1.

4. Baker, R.S., Corbett, A.T., Koedinger, K.R.: Detecting student misuse of intelligent tutoring systems. In: International Conference on Intelligent Tutoring Systems, pp. 531–540. Springer (2004)
5. Cedric Tonga, J., Clement, B., Oudeyer, P.Y.: Automatic generation of question hints for mathematics problems using large language models in educational technology. arXiv e-prints pp. arXiv–2411 (2024)
6. Chi, M.T., De Leeuw, N., Chiu, M.H., LaVancher, C.: Eliciting self-explanations improves understanding. Cogn. Sci. **18**(3), 439–477 (1994)
7. Dai, S.C., Xiong, A., Ku, L.W.: LLM-in-the-Loop: leveraging large language model for thematic analysis. In: Findings of the Association for Computational Linguistics: EMNLP 2023, pp. 9993–10001 (2023)
8. Graesser, A.C., Chipman, P., Haynes, B.C., Olney, A.: Autotutor: an intelligent tutoring system with mixed-initiative dialogue. IEEE Trans. Educ. **48**(4), 612–618 (2005)
9. Koedinger, K.R., Aleven, V.: Exploring the assistance dilemma in experiments with cognitive tutors. Educ. Psychol. Rev. **19**(3), 239–264 (2007)
10. Koedinger, K.R., Brunskill, E., Baker, R.S., McLaughlin, E.A., Stamper, J.: New potentials for data-driven intelligent tutoring system development and optimization. AI Mag. **34**(3), 27–41 (2013)
11. Macina, J., Daheim, N., Hakimi, I., Kapur, M., Gurevych, I., Sachan, M.: MathTutorBench: a benchmark for measuring open-ended pedagogical capabilities of llm tutors. In: Proceedings of the 2025 Conference on Empirical Methods in Natural Language Processing, pp. 204–221 (2025)
12. Murray, T.: An overview of intelligent tutoring system authoring tools: updated analysis of the state of the art. In: Authoring Tools for Advanced Technology Learning Environments: Toward Cost-effective Adaptive, Interactive and Intelligent Educational Software, pp. 491–544 (2003)
13. Pardos, Z.A., Bhandari, S.: ChatGPT-generated help produces learning gains equivalent to human tutor-authored help on mathematics skills. PLoS ONE **19**(5), e0304013 (2024)
14. Phung, T., et al.: Automating human tutor-style programming feedback: leveraging GPT-4 tutor model for hint generation and GPT-3.5 student model for hint validation. In: Proceedings of the 14th Learning Analytics and Knowledge Conference, pp. 12–23 (2024)
15. Van de Pol, J., Volman, M., Beishuizen, J.: Scaffolding in teacher-student interaction: a decade of research. Educ. Psychol. Rev. **22**(3), 271–296 (2010)
16. Suraweera, P., Mitrovic, A., Martin, B.: Widening the knowledge acquisition bottleneck for constraint-based tutors. Int. J. Artif. Intell. Educ. **20**(2), 137–173 (2010)
17. VanLehn, K.: The relative effectiveness of human tutoring, intelligent tutoring systems, and other tutoring systems. Educat. Psych. **46**(4), 197–221 (2011)
18. Wang, B., Yue, X., Sun, H.: Can chatGPT defend its belief in truth? Evaluating LLM reasoning via debate. In: Findings of the Association for Computational Linguistics: EMNLP 2023, pp. 11865–11881 (2023)
19. Wood, D., Bruner, J.S., Ross, G.: The role of tutoring in problem solving. J. Child Psychol. Psych. **17**(2), 89–100 (1976)
20. Woolf, B.P.: Building Intelligent Interactive Tutors: Student-centered Strategies for Revolutionizing E-learning. Morgan Kaufmann (2010)
21. Worden, E., Vanacore, K., Haim, A., Heffernan, N.: Scaling effective AI-generated explanations for middle school mathematics in online learning platforms. In: Proceedings of the Twelfth ACM Conference on Learning@ Scale, pp. 40–49 (2025)

A Near-Peer Reflective Agent for K-12 Collaborative Problem-Solving

Toni Earle-Randell(✉)

University of Florida, Gainesville, FL, USA
tearlerandell@ufl.edu

Abstract. Collaborative problem-solving (CPS) is a critical 21st-century skill. Despite evidence from a decade ago highlighting a global deficiency in collaborative problem-solving ability among K-12 students, there remains a shortage of structured approaches to develop effective CPS skills. Prior work has established virtual agents as effective tools for scaffolding interpersonal skills such as collaboration. However, a systematic review of 55 studies revealed that agent-based support for reflection is underexplored. This proposed doctoral research addresses this gap by designing, developing, and evaluating a novel near-peer virtual agent to facilitate individual weekly reflective sessions with K-12 students on robotics teams. Grounded in Experiential Learning and Self-Regulated Learning theories, the agent will guide students through structured reflection after collaborative work. This dissertation begins with a co-design think-aloud study to iteratively refine the agent's visual design, conversational architecture, and reflective protocol before longitudinal deployment. In doing so, this research investigates how the agent's design shapes students' reflective practice and its longer-term impact on collaborative dialogue patterns and overall collaborative competence.

Keywords: Collaborative Problem-Solving · Virtual Agent · Reflection

1 Background and Motivation

Collaboration is essential for success in both academic and professional settings [10]. Primary and secondary education are crucial for developing CPS skills, as the K-12 Years are a critical developmental period when social-cognitive abilities and collaborative behaviors are most malleable [3]. However, students often face challenges such as unequal participation, unproductive conflict, and a lack of shared understanding [7]. Intelligent virtual agents have emerged as powerful tools to scaffold learning and collaboration, with studies demonstrating their ability to model desirable behaviors, improve negotiation skills, and support students' metacognition [1,2,20]. Despite these advances in agent-based collaborative support, a blind spot persists. A recent systematic review of 55 studies on agent-supported human-human collaboration published in AIED revealed that

E. G. Blanchard et al. (Eds.): AIED 2026, CCIS 3033, pp. 396–401, 2026.
https://doi.org/10.1007/978-3-032-29794-5_61

only four studies focused on reflective support, which involves students assessing their own performance and learning process, as virtual agents predominantly focus on synchronous, in-the-moment interventions [7]. This omission is significant: without structured reflection, students may not connect their actions to outcomes or develop the capacity to independently improve their collaborative practices over time. Self-Regulated Learning research establishes that effective learners actively evaluate and adapt their own processes, and that metacognition is central to this capacity [9,21]. Kolb's Experiential Learning Theory [11] further posits that meaningful learning occurs and unfolds through a cycle of concrete experience (CE), reflective observation (RO), abstract conceptualization (AC), and active experimentation (AE), which students may struggle to complete without structured and intentional support [13]. Reflection compels students to practice this metacognitive regulation, preparing them to improve independently when a tutor is no longer present [18].

2 Research Goals

Acknowledging the gap, my dissertation explores how a near-peer virtual agent can influence K-12 students' collaborative skills through individual reflective sessions. Specifically, this study will be guided by the following questions:

- RQ1: What are the core themes in students' perceptions of and experience with a reflective, collaboration-focused near-peer agent, and how can these insights inform the agent's design?
- RQ2: How does longitudinal engagement with an agent-facilitated reflective process influence K-12 students'collaborative dialogue patterns, particularly their navigation of cycles of confusion and Disputational Talk?
- RQ3: To what extent does sustained interaction with a reflective virtual agent lead to measurable improvements in students' overall collaborative problem-solving competencies?

3 Related Work and State-of-the-Art

Current research demonstrates that virtual agents can effectively scaffold human-human collaboration [7]. These agents typically serve as in-the-moment coaches or models, intervening during a collaborative task to provide hints, prompt discussion, or model ideal behaviors like *Exploratory Talk* in which students critically and constructively engage with each other's ideas [12]. My previous research has shown that near-peer agents (positioned as relatable classmates rather than expert tutors) modeling Exploratory Talk are particularly effective for younger learners, fostering positive attitudes toward computer science and encouraging productive collaborative dialogue patterns, such as higher-order questioning [5]. Furthermore, my work using hidden Markov models [6] has identified distinct dialogue states in elementary students' collaborative dialogue. A key finding was that when students encounter a problem and enter a state of Confusion, they rarely return to productive *Exploratory Talk* without first passing through states such as *Disputational Talk*, characterized by frequent disagreements and competing assertions, where learners fail to share knowledge or build a shared understanding. Existing solutions are primarily designed to detect and correct unproductive behaviors like these as they occur [7], which does not explicitly empower students to recognize and regulate these behaviors themselves. The current state-of-the-art in collaborative learning lacks systems that leverage delayed feedback, a practice shown to be effective in digital learning contexts for problem-solving skill development [8] and essential for deep, transferable learning [4] and long-term skill development.

4 Contributions and Impact

Unlike most systems that intervene during a task, this proposed virtual agent interacts with students after their collaborative sessions. Positioned as a knowledgeable near-peer rather than an expert or teacher, this agent leverages the established benefits of near-peer agents in a reflective, collaboration-focused role [5]. By delaying the feedback and engaging students in reflection after collaborative sessions, the agent aims to develop the self-regulatory and metacognitive habits students need to independently navigate from *Disputational* to *Exploratory* Talk.

Additionally, the virtual agent will serve as a bridge between individual and collective growth. Because students may be reluctant to voice concerns about team dynamics in a group setting, individual sessions are designed to surface honest self-assessment that group reflection may not capture, counteracting the biased self-perceptions that can otherwise go unexamined [14]. Drawing on research suggesting students desire group discussion opportunities [19], the agent translates individual insights into team action. At the end of the reflection protocol, the agent helps students formulate their reflections into actionable items for team discussion, transforming individual learning into team-wide improvement.

This project also makes technical contributions to the design of LLM-powered educational agents. By establishing a 'blueprint' for the different phases of the interaction and using the LLM as a tool for naturalistic dialogue generation rather than the guiding force of the interaction [15], this approach will ensure predictable behavior that aligns with our research goals. This deterministic LLM approach offers a practical strategy for researchers developing virtual agents that require repeated interactions. Additionally, an exploratory evaluation of LLM-assigned collaborative dialogue codes will contribute empirical findings to ongoing AIED work on automated discourse analysis.

5 Methodology

5.1 Co-design Think-Aloud Study

Before the semester-long deployment, I will conduct a co-design think-aloud study to refine the agent and establish a structured reflection protocol that is meaningful and engaging for students. The students participating in the co-design study will be the same students who will participate in the dissertation study, and they will interact with a working prototype of the agent in individual 10-Min think-aloud sessions, verbalizing their thoughts to provide insights into the visual design and reflective prompts. Sessions will be followed by a semi-structured interview probing students' perceptions of the agent's trustworthiness and credibility as a near-peer, the clarity and usefulness of the structured reflection protocol, and moments where the interaction felt unnatural or unhelpful. While using the same students for both phases may influence their engagement and perceptions during the longitudinal study, this decision will ensure the agent's design reflects the needs and expectations of the team. Findings will directly inform revisions to the agent's prompt architecture, dialogue scaffolding, and visual design before the longitudinal study. This process will also produce a set of transferable design principles for reflective near-peer agents, addressing RQ1.

5.2 Longitudinal Study

This dissertation study will focus on a K-12 competitive robotics team (FIRST Tech Challenge). This context provides an authentic, long-term collaborative environment where teams of 10–15 students work together on complex engineering challenges, which is ideal for studying CPS skill development over time. Participants will include approximately 12 students in grades 7–12 from an established after-school robotics club in the Southeastern United States, reflecting the natural mixed-age composition of competitive robotics teams. To accurately assess the impact of the agent-guided reflections, this study will employ a longitudinal, qualitative multiple-case study design, following each student on one robotics team through a full semester (approximately 12 Weeks).

5.3 Procedure

Weekly Intervention: Each week after regularly scheduled robotics meetings, students will participate in a 10–15-minute individual session with the agent. The agent's conversational architecture follows a structured reflection protocol grounded in the four phases of Kolb's Experiential Learning Theory: students first recall a specific collaborative event (CE), then analyze what happened and why (RO), identify what they would do differently (AC), and finally formulate a concrete goal to bring back to their team (AE) [11]. To operationalize the architecture, a deterministic engine controls the LLM workflow by executing a predefined blueprint for these phases, invoking the LLM only for naturalistic dialogue generation within each phase [15]. This approach will also allow us to control the positivity bias that is present in most off-the-shelf LLMs. To supplement data collected from agent interactions, teamwork sessions will be video and audio recorded bi-weekly as they work on their robotics tasks.

Pre/Post-Assessment: Students will complete a quantitative assessment before and after the study to establish a baseline of collaborative competence and measure their change in collaborative problem-solving skills. This assessment will be based on the *PISA Collaborative Problem-Solving Assessment* [16] and the matrix of collaborative competencies, with particular focus on questions relevant to the Disputational Talk cycle [6].

5.4 Analysis

After the think-aloud study, survey and interview data will be analyzed qualitatively using thematic coding to understand student perceptions of the agent and identify design principles for reflective virtual agents, addressing RQ1. To observe longitudinal shifts in collaborative behavior within the team's dialogue and address RQ2, recorded dialogue will be transcribed and human-coded using the CPS framework by Sun et al. [17], which operationalizes collaboration into three facets: constructing shared knowledge, negotiation/coordination, and maintaining team function. An exploratory evaluation of LLM-assigned codes may supplement this analysis. Additionally, chat logs between the student and agent will be analyzed to identify longitudinal shifts in thinking, and pre/post assessment scores will be used as supplementary data to measure changes in collaborative competencies for each student and address RQ3. This research will be conducted under IRB approval with informed parental consent and student assent from all participants.

6 Current Status and Preliminary Results

I have completed and presented a comprehensive systematic review of 55 studies on agent-supported collaboration at AIED in 2025, which identifies the critical research gap in agent-supported reflection [7]. I have publications on designing and evaluating near-peer virtual agents for K-12 collaboration and on modeling the dialogue patterns that this project targets [5,6]. Co-design think-aloud studies are planned for Summer 2026 before deployment in the fall.

Acknowledgments. This research was supported by the National Science Foundation and the Institute of Education Sciences under grant DRL-2229612. Any opinions, findings, and conclusions or recommendations expressed in this material are those of the author(s) and do not necessarily reflect the views of the National Science Foundation or the U.S. Department of Education.

References

1. Azevedo, R., Wiedbusch, M.: Theories of metacognition and pedagogy applied to aied systems. In: Handbook of Artificial. Edward Elgar Publishing, Intelligence in Education, pp. 45–67 (2023)
2. Breideband, T., et al.: The community builder (CoBi): helping students to develop better small group collaborative learning skills. In: Companion Publication of the 2023 Conference on Computer Supported Cooperative Work and Social Computing, pp. 376–380 (2023)

3. Choudhury, S., Blakemore, S.J., Charman, T.: Social cognitive development during adolescence. Soc. Cognit. Affect. Neurosci. **1**(3), 165 (2006)
4. Coulson, D., Harvey, M.: Scaffolding student reflection for experience-based learning: a framework. Teach. High. Educ. **18**(4), 401–413 (2013)
5. Earle-Randell, T.V., et al.: The impact of near-peer virtual agents on computer science attitudes and collaborative dialogue. Int. J. Child-Comput. Int. **40**, 100646 (2024)
6. Earle-Randell, T.V., et al.: Confusion, conflict, consensus: modeling dialogue processes during collaborative learning with hidden Markov models. In: International Conference on Artificial Intelligence in Education, pp. 615–626. Springer (2023)
7. Earle-Randell, T.V., Zhang, S., Schroeder, N., Boyer, K.E., Dorley, E.: How virtual agents can shape human-human collaboration: a systematic review. In: International Conference on Artificial Intelligence in Education, pp. 468–486. Springer (2025)
8. Fakhri, M.M., Ahmar, A.S., Rosidah, R., Fadhilatunisa, D., Tabash, M.: Barriers to effective learning: examining the influence of delayed feedback on student engagement and problem solving skills in ubiquitous learning programming. J. Appl. Sci. Eng. Technol. Educ. **6**(1), 69–79 (2024)
9. Flavell, J.H.: Metacognition and cognitive monitoring: a new area of cognitive-developmental inquiry. Am. Psychol. **34**(10), 906 (1979)
10. Green, B.N., Johnson, C.D.: Interprofessional collaboration in research, education, and clinical practice: working together for a better future. J. Chiropr. Educ. **29**(1), 1–10 (2015)
11. Kolb, D.A.: Experiential Learning: Experience as the Source of Learning and Development. FT Press (2014)
12. Mercer, N.: Words and Minds: How we Use Language to Think Together. Routledge (2002)
13. Morris, T.H.: Experiential learning-a systematic review and revision of Kolb's model. Interact. Learn. Environ. **28**(8), 1064–1077 (2020)
14. Phielix, C., et al.: Enhancing Collaboration Through Assessment & Reflection. Unpublished PhD Thesis, Utrecht University, Utrecht, The Netherlands (2012)
15. Qiu, L., et al.: Blueprint first, model second: a framework for deterministic LLM workflow. arXiv preprint arXiv:2508.02721 (2025)
16. SOLVING, C.P.: Pisa 2015 results
17. Sun, C., Shute, V.J., Stewart, A., Yonehiro, J., Duran, N., D'Mello, S.: Towards a generalized competency model of collaborative problem solving. Comput. Educ. **143**, 103672 (2020)
18. VanLehn, K.: The behavior of tutoring systems. Int. J. Artif. Intell. Educ. **16**(3), 227–265 (2006)
19. Webb, L.A., Scoular, T.: Reflection on reflection on reflection: collaboration in action research. Educ. Action Res. **19**(4), 469–487 (2011)
20. Wiggins, J.B., et al.: Building the dream team: children's reactions to virtual agents that model collaborative talk. In: Proceedings of the 22nd ACM International Conference on Intelligent Virtual Agents, pp. 1–8 (2022)
21. Zimmerman, B.J.: Becoming a self-regulated learner: an overview. Theory Pract. **41**(2), 64–70 (2002)

Seeing Like a Student: Difficulty and Error Alignment of MLLMs on Visual Math Problems

Ethan Croteau(✉) and Neil Heffernan

Worcester Polytechnic Institute, Worcester, MA, USA
{ecroteau,nth}@wpi.edu

Abstract. Multimodal Large Language Models (MLLMs) are increasingly proposed for AI in Education (AIED), including automated feedback, formative assessment, and tutoring for mathematics problems that depend on diagrams, graphs, or other figures. For AIED uses that rely on interpreting learner behavior (e.g., misconception diagnosis or student modeling), it is unclear whether MLLMs behave in ways that align with real middle-school students on curriculum-authentic, image-dependent items. We investigate model–student alignment along two dimensions: *difficulty alignment*—whether per-item model accuracy tracks student difficulty—and *error/misconception alignment*—whether model wrong answers overlap with the three most frequent student wrong answers on the same items. Using 376 image-Required middle-school mathematics items from Illustrative Mathematics delivered in ASSISTments, paired with large-scale student response histograms and multi-run MLLM outputs, we find modest positive difficulty correlations but limited error alignment: when models make at least one error on an item, they match common student wrong answers on only a minority of items. We outline next steps to refine these alignment measures, develop a qualitative taxonomy of *aligned* vs. *alien* errors, and explore implications for AIED tasks such as misconception mining and using MLLMs as proxies for learner behavior.

Keywords: AIED · multimodal LLMs · mathematics education · difficulty · misconceptions · error analysis · validity

1 Problem and Motivation

Visual representations are central to middle-school mathematics and often encode essential quantitative information that must be interpreted alongside text [1,7,11]. AIED systems that support learners on such items must reason about both correctness and systematic error patterns, especially for targeted feedback and misconception diagnosis [2,14,15].

MLLMs could be used in these pipelines—as explainers, hint generators, or even as "simulated students" for stress-testing tutors [5]—but only if their behavior meaningfully reflects learner performance on authentic items. Our recent prior

E. G. Blanchard et al. (Eds.): AIED 2026, CCIS 3033, pp. 402–407, 2026.
https://doi.org/10.1007/978-3-032-29794-5_62

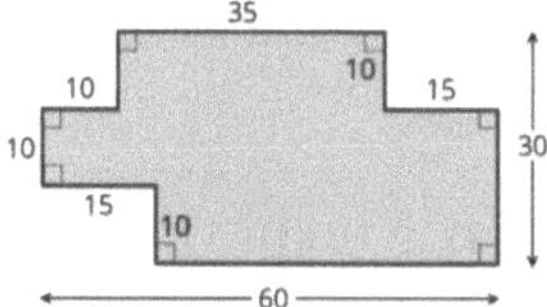

Fig. 1. Example image-Required problem: "Find the area of the shaded region. All angles are right angles."

work studied MLLM solvability, refusal, and failure modes on image-dependent math problems [3]; here, we shift focus to model–student alignment in difficulty and wrong-answer patterns (Fig. 1). We work with middle-school problems from the Illustrative Mathematics curriculum [10], delivered through ASSISTments, which supports classroom-authentic experimentation and fine-grained logging of student responses at scale [4].

2 Related Work

Multimodal reasoning benchmarks for visual mathematics (e.g., MathVista, MathVerse) show that even strong models struggle with quantitative visual interpretation, such as reading scales, matching corresponding parts, and counting objects in diagrams [9,13,16], suggesting that adding vision does not automatically yield robust visual-math understanding on curriculum-authentic items.

AIED has a long tradition of modeling student errors and misconceptions—for example, through knowledge tracing, distractor analyses, and item-response distributions—to support diagnosis and adaptive instruction [2,14,15].

Recent work also explores LLMs as educational agents and as proxies for student behavior, including using their output probabilities or choices to approximate which distractors confuse learners [5,8]. Liu et al. [8] study multiple-choice questions and find moderate alignment between LLM preferences over distractors and real student selection patterns, but focus on MCQs rather than short-answer numeric or algebraic responses and do not specifically target image-dependent items.

Our work extends this line of inquiry to short-answer, image-Required mathematics items, connecting modern MLLMs to classic AIED concerns about validity, misconceptions, and learner modeling in visually grounded mathematics.

3 Research Questions

RQ1 (Difficulty Alignment). How aligned are item difficulty patterns for middle-school students and MLLMs on image-Required math problems, and how does alignment vary by model family and student coverage?
RQ2 (Error/Misconception Alignment). When MLLMs answer incorrectly on these problems, to what extent do their wrong answers overlap with students'

most frequent wrong answers, and how does this overlap vary by model family and student item difficulty?

4 Proposed Evaluation Methodology

4.1 Items and Student Response Distributions

We analyze $N = 376$ image-Required items from the Illustrative Mathematics middle-school curriculum [10] as delivered in ASSISTments, an online homework platform for classroom-authentic experimentation and minimally invasive learning research [4]. Required items are those where key solution information is only available in the image, so visual perception and interpretation are genuine bottlenecks.

For each item, we obtain an aggregate summary with the proportion of student responses that are correct and a frequency distribution over distinct student answers. We treat these histograms as empirical approximations to student error patterns [15]. Because histogram quality depends on exposure, we conduct analyses on coverage-filtered subsets and treat items with at least 50 student answers as the primary analysis set.

4.2 MLLM Outputs and Correctness

For each model m and item p, we collect three with-image attempts under a fixed prompt template, prompting models as competent solvers rather than explicitly asking them to emulate a seventh-grade student. Each attempt yields an extracted final answer, which is scored correct when it is algebraically equivalent to the item's reference answer under a SymPy-based normalization and equivalence procedure [12]. Reference answers in this filtered dataset are unitless, and correctness scoring is fully automated. Per-item model accuracy is the fraction of correct attempts, $\mathrm{Acc}^{\mathrm{img}}_{m,p}$.

4.3 Alignment Metrics

We treat these alignment measures as proxies for aspects of student understanding and error structure, not as direct observations of underlying misconceptions.

Difficulty Alignment (RQ1). For each model, we compute Pearson and Spearman correlations between student difficulty (proportion correct for an item) and $\mathrm{Acc}^{\mathrm{img}}_{m,p}$ across items, echoing classical item-level analyses in AIED and educational measurement [2,14].

Error/Misconception Alignment (RQ2). For each item, we consider the three most frequent student wrong answers and the set of wrong answers produced by a model across its three attempts. An item counts as aligned for that model if at least one model wrong answer is algebraically equivalent (under the same SymPy-based normalization [12]) to one of the three most common student wrong answers. We report both the overall proportion of aligned items and the proportion restricted to items where the model makes at least one error.

Table 1. Difficulty alignment between students and models on Required items (with images; min-50 coverage set). Correlations are computed between student percent correct StudAcc_p and per-item model accuracy $\text{Acc}_{m,p}^{\text{img}}$ across Required items.

Model	Pearson r	Spearman ρ
Non-reasoning		
gpt-4.1	0.29	0.32
gpt-4o	0.30	0.32
grok-2-vision	0.38	0.41
Reasoning		
grok-4	0.15	0.16
o3	0.24	0.25
o4-mini	0.26	0.27

5 Progress and Preliminary Results

5.1 Coverage and Primary Analysis Set

Student coverage is high for most items but skewed: across the 376 items, the median number of answers per item is $\approx$ 496, and 329 items meet the min-50 threshold (used below as the primary set). Items with higher coverage yield more stable response histograms, which we treat as higher-confidence estimates of student wrong-answer modes [15].

5.2 RQ1: Difficulty Alignment

Table 1 reports correlations between student accuracy and $\text{Acc}_{m,p}^{\text{img}}$ on the min-50 set. Observed correlations (Pearson $r \approx 0.15$–0.38 across models) fall in the small-to-moderate range, indicating that models partially track which items students find difficult but do not closely match the student difficulty landscape.

5.3 RQ2: Error/Misconception Alignment

On the same min-50 set, per-model top-3 alignment is limited. Conditional on making at least one error on an item, models overlap with the top-3 student wrong answers on roughly 19%–34% of items (depending on the model). Aggregating models within each family shows a consistent pattern: non-reasoning models are less accurate overall but exhibit higher top-3 overlap when wrong, whereas reasoning models are more accurate overall but their residual errors overlap less with the most frequent student wrong answers. These results complement multiple-choice findings that LLMs sometimes select the same distractors that commonly mislead students [8], while highlighting that alignment is far from perfect on short-answer, image-Required problems (Table 2).

Table 2. Family-level accuracy and error-alignment on Required items (using the min-50 student coverage set). "% correct" is mean model accuracy across problems. "% align-top3" is the unconditional probability that at least one model wrong answer matches one of the top-3 student wrong answers on an item. "% align-top3|error" conditions on items where the model is wrong at least once.

Model family	n_{models}	% correct	% align-top3	% align-top3|error
Non-reasoning	3	38.2	21.9	31.4
Reasoning	3	50.7	13.6	23.4

6 Planned Work and Next Steps

The current pipeline provides a structure for measuring model–student alignment; next we will strengthen validity and explain *why* alignment succeeds or fails. For difficulty alignment (RQ1), we plan to test robustness of correlations across coverage thresholds using bootstrap confidence intervals, summarize alignment at the model-family level, and introduce item features such as figure type and visual bottlenecks to examine whether alignment differs for specific visual skills, informed by perception-focused diagnostics [13]. For error alignment (RQ2), we plan to develop a qualitative taxonomy for model and student errors (e.g., misread scale, correspondence error, counting error, algebraic slip, hallucinated constraint, refusal/hedge) with inter-rater reliability [6], characterize "aligned" versus "alien" errors on items with strong student modes and relate alien errors to explanation patterns that could affect feedback quality [5], and perform sensitivity analyses by varying the number of student wrong answers considered and exploring weighted overlap. We also plan to extend the same alignment analyses to text-only and image-Not-Required/image-Useful items to compare trends for all problems against the image-Required subset and clarify which patterns are specific to genuine visual bottlenecks. Together, these steps will yield an empirical validity analysis of MLLMs as proxies for student difficulty and misconceptions on curriculum-authentic visual math items, an alignment methodology and artifact set (items, aggregates, scripts, tables) to support future AIED evaluations of multimodal agents [4], and design implications indicating when MLLM errors are student-like (potentially useful for misconception mining and automated distractor generation [8]) versus alien (risk for feedback generation and assessment validity).

Acknowledgments. We would like to thank NSF (e.g., 2118725, 2118904, 1950683, 1917808, 1931523, 1940236, 1917713, 1903304, 1822830, 1759229, 1724889, 1636782, and 1535428), IES (e.g., R305N210049, R305D210031, R305A170137, R305A170243, R305A180401, and R305A120125), GAANN (e.g., P200A180088 and P200A150306), EIR (U411B190024 and S411B210024), ONR (N00014-18-1-2768), NIH (R44GM146483), and Schmidt Futures. None of the opinions expressed here are those of the funders.

Disclosure of Interests. The authors have no competing interests to declare that are relevant to the content of this article.

References

1. Ainsworth, S.: DEFT: a conceptual framework for considering learning with multiple representations. Learn. Instr. **16**(3), 183–198 (2006)
2. Corbett, A.T., Anderson, J.R.: Knowledge Tracing: modeling the acquisition of procedural knowledge. User Model. User-Adap. Inter. **4**(4), 253–278 (1994). https://doi.org/10.1007/BF01099821
3. Croteau, E., Heffernan, N.: Seeing is solving: MLLMs, reasoning, and refusal in visual math. J. Educ. Data Min. **18**(1), 244–285 (2026). https://doi.org/10.5281/zenodo.19420820
4. Heffernan, N.T., Heffernan, C.L.: The ASSISTments ecosystem: building a platform that brings scientists and teachers together for minimally invasive research on human learning and teaching. Int. J. Artif. Intell. Educ. **24**(4), 470–497 (2014). https://doi.org/10.1007/s40593-014-0024-x
5. Kasneci, E., et al.: ChatGPT for good? On opportunities and challenges of large language models for education. Learn. Individ. Differ. **103**, 102274 (2023)
6. Krippendorff, K.: Computing Krippendorff's Alpha-Reliability. Working Paper 43, University of Pennsylvania, Annenberg School for Communication, Philadelphia, PA (2011). https://repository.upenn.edu/handle/20.500.14332/2089, postprint version
7. Larkin, J.H., Simon, H.A.: Why a diagram is (sometimes) worth ten thousand words. Cogn. Sci. **11**(1), 65–100 (1987)
8. Liu, N., Sonkar, S., Baraniuk, R.: Do LLMs make mistakes like students? Exploring natural alignments between language models and human error patterns. In: International Conference on Artificial Intelligence in Education, pp. 364–377. Springer (2025)
9. Lu, P., et al.: MathVista: evaluating mathematical reasoning of foundation models in visual contexts (2023)
10. Mathematics, I.: Illustrative Mathematics, grade 6–8. Available at https://illustrativemathematics.org/ (2019). authored by Illustrative Mathematics
11. Mayer, R.E.: Multimedia Learning, 3rd edn. Cambridge University Press, Cambridge, UK (2020)
12. Meurer, A., et al.: SYMPY: symbolic computing in Python. Peer J. Comput. Sci. **3**, e103 (2017)
13. Sun, Y., et al.: Math Blind: failures in Diagram Understanding Undermine Reasoning in MLLMs (2025). https://doi.org/10.48550/arXiv.2503.20745
14. VanLehn, K.: The relative effectiveness of human tutoring, intelligent tutoring systems, and other tutoring systems. Educat. Psychol. **46**(4), 197–221 (2011)
15. Weitz, R., Heffernan, N., Kodaganallur, V., Rosenthal, D.: The distribution of student errors across schools: an initial study. Front. Arti. Intel. Appl. **158**, 671 (2007)
16. Zhang, R., et al.: Mathverse: does your multi-modal LLM truly see the diagrams in visual math problems? In: European Conference on Computer Vision. pp. 169–186. Springer Nature Switzerland, Cham (2024)

Modeling Embodied Collaborative Problem-Solving Dynamics in Immersive Virtual Reality

Xinyue Jiao(✉) and Xavier Ochoa

New York University, New York, NY, USA
{xj2320,xavier.ochoa}@nyu.edu

Abstract. Understanding how multimodal behaviors shape collaborative problem solving (CPS) in immersive environments is critical for designing AI-supported collaborative learning systems. Prior work has primarily examined verbal interaction patterns, leaving the role of embodied gestures in shaping collaborative dynamics underexplored, particularly in virtual reality (VR) collaborative games. In this study, we investigate dyadic collaboration processes in a VR problem-solving game. Multimodal behavioral data, including speech, gestures, and task-related actions, were collected and analyzed. We will construct joint verbal – gesture – action interaction tokens and apply multichannel Hidden Markov Models (HMMs) to identify latent collaborative states and their temporal transitions. This work contributes a multimodal modeling framework for uncovering embodied collaborative states in immersive collaborative learning environments.

Keywords: Collaborative problem-solving · Virtual Reality · Collaboration modeling

1 Introduction

Collaborative problem solving (CPS) is widely recognized as a core competency in contemporary education and a central focus within Artificial Intelligence in Education (AIED) [3,7]. As immersive technologies such as virtual reality (VR) become increasingly integrated into learning environments, they offer new opportunities to support CPS by enabling learners to engage in embodied interaction, share spatial representations, and coordinate actions in real time [4]. However, while VR enables rich multimodal interactions, including speech, gesture, and coordinated manipulation of shared virtual objects, there remains limited understanding of how learners' verbal and gestural behaviors unfold jointly over time, and how these multimodal processes relate to collaborative effectiveness and learning outcomes in VR [1,5,8].

Existing studies of collaborative learning in VR have often relied on aggregate indicators (e.g., task completion time, frequency counts of verbal moves)

E. G. Blanchard et al. (Eds.): AIED 2026, CCIS 3033, pp. 408–413, 2026.
https://doi.org/10.1007/978-3-032-29794-5_63

or examined single interaction channels in isolation, most commonly verbal discourse [5]. Such approaches risk oversimplifying collaboration by overlooking how learners dynamically coordinate speech, gesture, and action in real time. From a Learning Sciences perspective, CPS is a socially and temporally evolving process involving shared understanding, regulation, and coordination [3]. Yet the computational modeling of these intertwined multimodal processes in a principled and interpretable manner remains challenging.

Recent advances in multimodal learning analytics enable the capture of fine-grained behavioral data in immersive environments [6]. In parallel, probabilistic sequential modeling approaches, such as Hidden Markov Models (HMMs), provide a mechanism for distinguishing observable behaviors from latent collaborative states [2]. However, prior applications have often relied on coarse state definitions or single-modality inputs, limiting their ability to capture the embodied and situated nature of VR collaboration.

To address this gap, the present study aims to model embodied CPS dynamics in immersive VR by jointly analyzing sequences of coded verbal behaviors, gesture types, and task-related actions. Through multichannel modeling, the study seeks to identify latent collaborative states and examine how collaboration evolves over time via state transitions, thereby capturing the temporal structure of embodied CPS processes.

The overarching research question guiding this research is: How can embodied collaborative problem-solving dynamics in immersive VR environments be theoretically conceptualized and computationally modeled? To address this question, the study explores three interrelated sub-questions:

RQ1: How can multimodal behavioral indicators (verbal acts, gestures and movement) be modeled to capture embodied CPS interactions in VR?
RQ2: What latent collaborative states and temporal transition patterns emerge from multichannel modeling of multimodal interaction sequences?
RQ3: How are these latent CPS patterns associated with collaborative quality, learner experience, and performance outcomes?

2 Methodology

2.1 Research Context and Participants

This study aims to recruit 60 undergraduate students (aged 18–25) to participate in a VR collaborative puzzle-solving task. Participants will be paired into dyads and engage in the cooperative VR game *Carly and the Reaperman*[1]/, which requires two players to assume complementary roles and solve spatial puzzles through communication and coordinated action. The selected VR task will require participants to coordinate spatial movements in real time, thereby naturally eliciting joint planning, directive communication, embodied referencing,

[1] https://carlyandthereaperman.com/.

object manipulation, and repair behaviors. The immersive environment ensures that collaboration extends beyond verbal exchange and involves continuous spatial alignment and embodied coordination within a shared virtual space, leveraging the embodied interaction affordances of VR. Each session will involve two participants wearing Meta Quest 2 headsets, supervised by a researcher. A 360° camera will capture upper-body movement and gestures, while screen-recording software will document in-game actions and audio communication (Fig. 1).

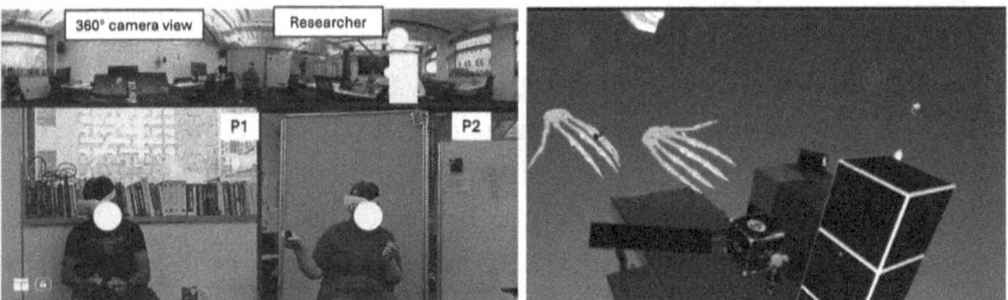

Fig. 1. VR collaborative game setup.

2.2 Multimodal Data Collection and Analysis

A multimodal analytic framework will be adopted in this study to model embodied CPS dynamics in immersive VR environments, as shown in Fig. 2.

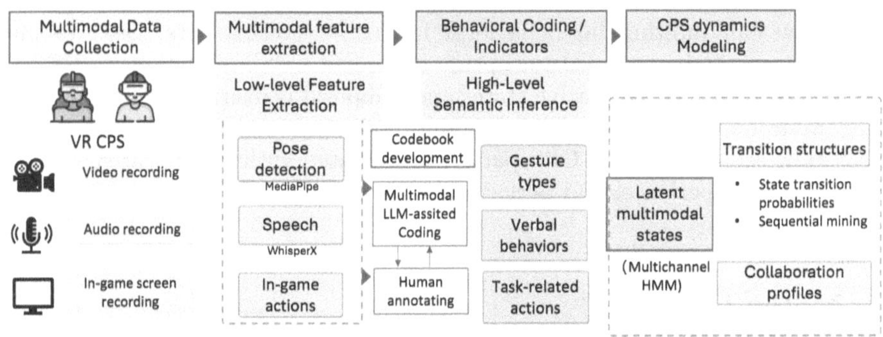

Fig. 2. Multimodal analytic framework.

Multimodal Data Collection. Multimodal interaction data will be collected through synchronized audio recordings, 360° video capturing upper-body movement and gesture, and in-game screen recordings documenting object manipulation and task events. All data streams will be temporally aligned and discretized into one-second intervals to preserve sequential structure while enabling computational modeling. This procedure will result in parallel time-series sequences for verbal, gesture, and task-related action channels for each dyad.

Multimodal Feature Extraction and Behavioral Coding. Gestures. Video data will be processed using MediaPipe[2] to extract structured human pose keypoints representing major upper-body joints (e.g. shoulders, elbows, wrists, and hips). Each detected keypoint will be characterized by two-dimensional spatial coordinates (x, y) within the image frame, along with an associated confidence score indicating detection reliability. These frame-level keypoints will be aggregated into temporally continuous motion trajectories for each participant. Based on these trajectories, movement-based indicators will be computed, including gesture amplitude, velocity, directional vectors, spatial proximity between collaborators, and inter-participant movement synchrony.

To complement geometric features with contextual interpretation, multimodal LLM (Gemini) will be employed to analyze video segments and generate structured semantic descriptions of gesture events. A predefined gesture codebook will be provided to the LLM to classify meaningful gesture types, such as *Pointing (Referential/Directive), Tracing (iconic gestures), Manipulating, and Beat* gestures. Human researchers will manually annotate a subset of gesture data to validate AI-generated outputs, refine classification criteria, and iteratively improve the gesture coding scheme.

Verbal Behaviors. Audio recordings will be processed using WhisperX to generate time-aligned transcripts with speaker diarization. The transcribed utterances will be segmented and coded into speech-act categories reflecting cognitive and regulatory processes in CPS, including *sharing information, questioning, explaining, directing, confirming, and proposing ideas.* LLM will be used to generate preliminary speech-act labels based on the verbal coding framework. Human annotators will then review, correct, and validate these classifications to ensure theoretical alignment and coding reliability.

Task-Related Actions. In-game screen recordings will be parsed to extract task-related behavioral events, including *object manipulation, spatial movement, puzzle interaction*, and *task progression milestones.* These events will be converted into structured, time-stamped action logs aligned with verbal and gesture channels. The task-related actions will be temporally synchronized with gesture and verbal behaviors.

Modeling CPS Behavioral Dynamics. After coding the three modalities of CPS behaviors in VR, a multichannel Hidden Markov Model (HMM) will be employed to model collaborative dynamics. Verbal behaviors, gesture types, and task-related actions will be treated as parallel observable channels, while latent states will represent probabilistic configurations of multimodal indicators corresponding to distinct collaborative modes. Models with varying numbers of hidden states will be compared using the Bayesian Information Criterion (BIC), and the selected model will estimate emission probabilities and transition matrices. State transitions will be analyzed to characterize the stability and flexibility of collaboration and to identify distinct collaboration profiles across dyads.

[2] https://ai.google.dev/edge/mediapipe/solutions/vision/gesture_recognizer.

Finally, regression analyses will examine associations between state distributions and measures of task performance, collaborative quality, and learner experience, linking latent multimodal dynamics to educational outcomes.

3 Current Progress and Preliminary Results

To date, 22 undergraduate students (11 dyads) have participated in the study, and all multimodal interaction data have been collected and preprocessed for exploratory analysis. To support gesture coding, we have developed an AI-assisted "Gesture Analyst" powered by Gemini 2.5 (see Fig. 3). The tool extracts video segments and generates structured gesture descriptions, predicted gesture types, and associated confidence scores based on predefined categories. AI-generated gesture labels are subsequently reviewed and validated by human annotators. In parallel, verbal behaviors are coded into speech-act categories, while in-game recordings are parsed to extract task-related actions.

A preliminary multichannel Hidden Markov Model (HMM) was conducted to explore latent collaborative structures. Model comparison indicated that a four-state solution provided the most parsimonious and interpretable fit. The identified states correspond to distinct multimodal configurations, including task execution (None veral + Munipulating), verbal directing (Directing + None gestures), shared understanding (Sharing + None gestures), and embodied coordination (Directing + Pointing). Notably, embodied coordination emerged as a distinct collaborative mode characterized by tightly coupled gesture and speech. Exploratory comparisons further suggest that higher-performing dyads enter embodied coordination states more frequently and exhibit more flexible transitions across states.

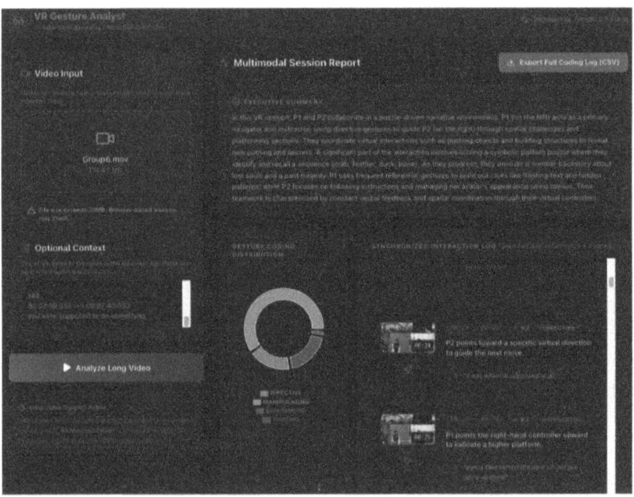

Fig. 3. Gemini powered AI gesture analyst.

4 Expected Contributions and Impact

This study extends CPS research by systematically mapping CPS constructs onto multimodal behavioral indicators. By operationalizing embodied coordination processes through synchronized gesture, verbal, and task-related actions, the study provides a more comprehensive understanding of how collaboration unfolds in immersive environments. In particular, leveraging embodiment affordances in VR, this study will demonstrate how gestures and spatially grounded actions jointly shape collaborative problem-solving.

Methodologically, this research advances multimodal learning analytics by modeling collaboration in VR as a temporally evolving process across synchronized behavioral modalities. The use of multichannel modeling preserves temporal structure and captures probabilistic transitions between collaborative modes. In addition, the integration of LLM-assisted gesture analysis with human validation establishes a scalable and theoretically aligned workflow for multimodal behavioral coding. More broadly, this work contributes to ongoing efforts in AIED to integrate rich multimodal data with interpretable AI models, supporting a deeper understanding of complex collaborative learning processes in immersive VR environments.

References

1. Graesser, C., Foltz, A., Rosen, P.W., Shaffer, Y., Forsyth, D.W., Germany, C., M.L.: Challenges of assessing collaborative problem solving. In: Assessment and teaching of 21st century skills: Research and applications, pp. 75–91. Springer (2017)
2. Earle-Randell, T.V., et al.: Confusion, conflict, consensus: Modeling dialogue processes during collaborative learning with hidden markov models. In: International Conference on Artificial Intelligence in Education, pp. 615–626. Springer (2023)
3. Graesser, A.C., Fiore, S.M., Greiff, S., Andrews-Todd, J., Foltz, P.W., Hesse, F.W.: Advancing the science of collaborative problem solving. Psychological Sci. Public Interest **19**(2), 59–92 (2018). https://doi.org/10.1177/1529100618808244
4. Johnson-Glenberg, M.C.: Immersive vr and education: embodied design principles that include gesture and hand controls. Frontiers Robot. AI **5**, 375272 (2018)
5. Van der Meer, N., van der Werf, V., Brinkman, W.P., Specht, M.: Virtual reality and collaborative learning: a systematic literature review. Front. Virtual Reality **4**, 1159905 (2023)
6. Ochoa, X., Worsley, M.: Augmenting learning analytics with multimodal sensory data. J. Learn. Anal. **3**(2), 213–219 (2016). https://doi.org/10.18608/jla.2016.32.10
7. OECD: PISA 2015 Results (Volume V): Collaborative Problem Solving. OECD Publishing, Paris (2017). https://doi.org/10.1787/9789264285521-en
8. Stancek, M., Polasek, I., Zalabai, T., Vincur, J., Jolak, R., Chaudron, M.: Collaborative software design and modeling in virtual reality. Inf. Softw. Technol. **166**, 107369 (2024). https://doi.org/10.1016/j.infsof.2023.107369, https://www.sciencedirect.com/science/article/pii/S0950584923002240

Teachers Personalizing Lesson Plans and Tasks Using GenAI

Theodora Beauchamp(✉) and Candace Walkington

Southern Methodist University, Dallas, TX 75205, USA
theob@smu.edu

Abstract. Teachers are using Generative artificial intelligence (GenAI) to create various items to be utilized for learning, yet limited research examines how mathematics teachers develop the knowledge and epistemic orientations necessary to use these tools critically and effectively. This pilot study, which will develop into a dissertation, investigates how teachers build intelligent technological pedagogical content knowledge (I-TPACK) and utilize epistemic agency when integrating GenAI into lesson planning and instructional design. Drawing on the conceptual framework, Interactive Styles of Learning, the study frames teacher-AI collaborations as a dynamic interaction shaped by teacher knowledge and their observable design behaviors. Preliminary findings from a pilot study of mathematics teachers engaged in AI-supported lesson planning reveal distinct interaction patterns that are dependent upon teachers' pedagogical decision making, iteration, and reflective processes. Research will continue to evolve as the data is analyzed through thematic coding. This work will contribute a teacher-centered framework for understanding GenAI integration and offer design implications for mathematics teacher education.

Keywords: Intelligent TPACK · epistemic agency · lesson design

1 Research Problem and Motivation

Teachers are in a position to change how they build instructional design, which could have a direct impact on student learning. Key potential affordances of GenAI for teachers include improved efficiency, higher student engagement, and better differentiation to student needs. Recent students highlight both the transformative potential and pedagogical challenges of LLM-based systems used in a K-12 mathematics education context [1]. Teachers increasingly use GenAI tools to generate context-specific math problems, differentiate instruction, and design lesson plans. Early research has emphasized tool affordances [2], but as this area of research matures, more attention needs to be devoted to understanding how teachers develop an epistemological stance on using GenAI.

Personalization of instructional content to individual students' interests has long been recognized as a powerful mechanism for increasing engagement and achievement in mathematical learning [3, 4]. GenAI tools appear to offer scalable personalization by creating different versions of learning tasks that correspond to students' fine-grained

E. G. Blanchard et al. (Eds.): AIED 2026, CCIS 3033, pp. 414–418, 2026.
https://doi.org/10.1007/978-3-032-29794-5_64

interests; however, effective implementation depends on teachers' ability to evaluate and adapt AI-generated content. Teachers who use generative AI output as-is, with little reflection or modification, engage in static forms of usage, which demonstrates a "one-size-fits-all" model of tool usage rather than one that is highly adapted to student needs. Such static usage of AI offers a fixed instructional style that focuses on what the AI is trained on. Dynamic usage of AI, on the other hand, offers teachers an iterative process that can provide personalization at scale. As a result, teacher decision-making and epistemic stance become central to instructional quality.

This work shifts the focus from what teachers produce with GenAI to how they interact with AI systems during instructional design, positioning their interactions as the critical focus of teacher learning and knowledge development. This dissertation investigates how K-12 mathematics teachers develop I-TPACK and enact epistemic agency when integrating GenAI into instructional design. Central to this work is the development of an Interactive Style of Learning framework,

2 Literature Context

2.1 Technology Integration and I-TPACK

The Technological Pedagogical and Content Knowledge (TPACK) framework pinpoints the knowledge needed by teachers to effectively integrate technology into their practice [1]. The convergence of teachers' Pedagogical Knowledge (PK), Content Knowledge (CK), and Technological Knowledge (TK) allow teachers to effectively create learning opportunities for students, and Pedagogical Content Knowledge (PCK), which combines PK and CK, makes teaching possible.

Recent scholarship argues that AI integration requires expanded forms of Technological Knowledge. Intelligent Technological Pedagogical Content Knowledge (ITPACK) extends TPACK by including prompt engineering, output critique, and the ethical dimensions of AI [5].

2.2 Epistemic Agency in Human-AI Systems

Epistemic Agency [6] in AI is described as a dynamic back-and-forth interaction in which the teacher guides and refines AI-generated outputs while maintaining instructional understanding. Teachers in a continuous process decide when to rely on AI models for support, when to set boundaries around AI outputs, and when revision or a restart is needed altogether, which describes these steps in the iterative process as a decision-shaping tool to maintain realism and meaningful content [6].

2.3 Interaction Teaching Styles

Teachers who engage in questioning of AI outputs and iterative co-design with AI are more likely to ensure that generated tasks align with instructional goals. The conceptual framework of interaction teaching styles conceptualizes three preliminary interaction patterns that teachers use when engaging with AI [7]. The first is a "teacher-dominated" style, in which the teacher constrains the degree to which the AI is involved in the design, supplies the AI with low amounts of context, gives the AI little corrective feedback, and engages in little reflective feedback of their own use of AI. The second is the "AI-Dominated" style- which teachers delegate substantial design decisions to AI systems-they give the system few constraints, give it little contextual guidance, and give minimal corrective feedback. The third is "Human-AI" Partnership, where teachers engage in iterative prompting and negotiated refinement. They give the AI moderate constraints, provide substantial contextual elements to the AI, and offer high levels of corrective and other feedback to the AI. These interaction styles represent observable teacher moves that demonstrate a structured lens for examining teachers' Intelligent TPACK within their subject area.

Dissertation focus and research question:

1. How do teachers' interaction styles influence their practices of personalization, specifically, and their instructional decision making generally?

3 Methodological Approach

3.1 Phase 1: Systematic Literature Review

A systematic synthesis of research on GenAI in mathematics teacher instruction examines how studies conceptualize teacher knowledge, epistemic stance, and instructional integration. This phase identifies theoretical gaps and informs refinement of the Interaction Styles conceptual framework.

3.2 Phase 2: Interaction Analysis Study

A qualitative interaction analysis of teacher-AI collaborative lesson design will be implemented to analyze the epistemic positioning of teachers, the revision patterns of teachers, and will result in a close analysis of teachers' prompt refinement to identify themes within these teacher moves. Video data will be segmented into interaction episodes with attention to prompting, AI responses, and teachers' revisions. A coding scheme will be developed iteratively which will combine the deductive categories from the Interactive Styles framework along with the inductive codes that emerge from the data. Multi-modal data (e.g., screen recordings, teachers' verbalizations, and text inputs) will be synchronized to trace how teachers negotiate instructional decisions over time.

Data sources include: screen recordings of lesson design sessions, chat transcripts documenting prompting and AI responses, instructional artifacts like lesson plans and rubrics, teacher reflections on using different AI tools and processes, and the analytic memoing from the researcher of observations in an AI course for teachers.

3.3 Phase 3: Framework Refinement

Findings will be used to refine the Interactive Styles taxonomy and examine its explanatory power for understanding teacher AI-instructional design.

4 Progress so Far

A pilot study has been conducted to explore initial patterns of teacher-GenAI interaction during lesson design tasks using AI tools: Colleague AI, MagicSchoolAI, and Khanmigo [8–10]. Participants (n = 15) engaged in AI-supported lesson planning and instructional design over a 14-week course titled "Generative AI for Teachers. "Teachers engaged with these AI tools while working individually or in groups during structured class time, cataloguing their prompts and intermediate versions of products and reflecting on their usage. They also used these AI tools independently for several course projects, developing classroom-ready AI-enhanced instructional resources or reflecting on potential AI use in their classrooms. Preliminary analysis revealed variation in structural control and evaluative judgement: Teacher-Dominated Styles- teachers asserting pedagogical authority; AI-Dominated Styles- teachers offered minimal critique; and Human-AI partnership- multiple iterations or revisions to create a usable lesson plan.

Key tensions were between efficiency and pedagogical depth as well as trust and skepticism toward AI output. These findings provide a firm foundation and further refinement of the Interaction Styles conceptual framework, which will be continued through the analysis.

5 Expected Contributions & Impact

5.1 Theoretical Contribution

This study aims to demonstrate the value of multimodal interaction data (screen recordings, chat logs, reflection notes) for analyzing teacher-AI collaboration.

5.2 Methodological Contribution

This study aims to design principles for teachers' professional development in AI contexts. It offers guidance for AI tool developers seeking to support teacher agency. Lastly, it contributes to the responsible integration of teacher usage of GenAI in K-12 education.

6 Feedback Requested

Through this doctoral consortium, I seek mentorship on several aspects of my research. I am to refine the conceptual integration of I-TPACK, epistemic agency, and the interactive styles of learning conceptual framework to ensure theoretical coherence. Secondly, I would benefit from guidance on the methodological design for analyzing teacher-AI interactions, particularly working with multimodal data such as screen recorders, chat logs, and artifacts. Lastly, I seek support to fully integrate ethical considerations related to GenAI use in both my research design and conceptual framework.

7 Disclosure of Interests.

The authors have no competing interests to declare that are relevant to the content of this article.

Acknowledgments. This pilot study was conducted within a graduate-level course on generative AI integration for in-service teachers at Southern Methodist University. The authors gratefully acknowledge the participating teachers for their engagement and contributions to this research.

References

1. Walkington, C.: The implications of generative artificial intelligence for mathematics education. Sch. Sci. Math. (2025). https://doi.org/10.1111/ssm.18356
2. Beauchamp, T., Walkington, C.: Mathematics teachers using generative AI to personalize instruction of students' interests. AMTE Connections (2024). https://amte.net/connections/2024/05/connections-thematic-articles-artificial-intelligence-mathematics-teacher
3. Walkington, C.A.: Using adaptive learning technologies to personalize instruction to student interests: the impact of relevant contexts on performance and learning outcomes. J. Educ. Psychol. **105**(4), 932 (2013)
4. Bernacki, Walkington, C.: The role of situational interest in personalized learning. J. Educ. Psychol. **110**(6), 864 (2018). https://doi.org/10.1037/edu0000250
5. Chiu, T.K.F.: Developing an intelligent-TPACK (I-TPACK) framework from unpacking AI literacy and competency: implementation strategies and future research direction. Interact. Learn. Environ. **33**(7), 4192 (2025).https://doi.org/10.1080/10494820.2025.2545053
6. Wu, J.-Y., Lee, Y.-H., Chai, C.S., Tsai, C.-C.: Strengthening Human Epistemic Agency in the Symbiotic Learning Partnership With Generative Artificial Intelligence. Educational Researcher (2025). https://doi.org/10.3102/0013189X251333628
7. Beauchamp, T., Walkington, C., Pruitt-Britton, T.: Mathematics teacher interaction styles with generative AI. In: Proceedings of the American Educational Research Association (AERA) Annual Meeting. To appear (2026)
8. Colleague AI: AI-Powered Education Platform for K-12. Available at https://www.colleague.ai/ (accessed Feb. 2026)
9. Khanmigo: AI-Powered Teaching Assistant by Khan Academy. Available at https://www.khanmigo.ai/ (accessed Feb. 2026)
10. MagicSchool: AI Platform for Schools, Teachers, and Students. https://www.magicschool.ai/. Accessed Feb 2026

Academic Practice and Generative AI: Configurations of Work in Two Mexican Universities

Yanahui Anaid Caletti González(✉) and Luis Antonio Mata Zúñiga

Universidad Iberoamericana, Mexico City, Mexico
{yanahui.caletti,luis.mata}@ibero.mx

Abstract. This doctoral research investigates how academic practice is configured in its encounter with Generative Artificial Intelligence (GenAI) in two Mexican universities with contrasting institutional conditions. GenAI has arrived to stay, and understanding how academics engage with a technology that will not disappear is critical to comprehend the reconfiguration of their professional practice. Drawing on Latin American configurational theory, the study conceptualizes academic work as an articulation of three inseparable dimensions: structural conditions, concrete actions, and processes of subjectification. Through a comparative case study at UAM-Cuajimalpa (public) and IBERO-CDMX (private), combining narrative interviews, participant observation, and artifact analysis, the research reconceptualizes the GenAI debate from the standpoint of academic work. An initial empirical exploration (n = 49 questionnaire respondents, four in-depth interviews) reveals that structural conditions, autonomous learning patterns, and ethical ambivalence constitute axes configuring this encounter. The study contributes an analytical framework that moves beyond adoption–resistance binaries, articulating three analytical levels (structure, action, subjectivity) to examine how labor conditions shape the ways university faculty adopt, negotiate, or resist GenAI.

Keywords: Academic practice · Generative AI · Configurational theory · Higher education · Working conditions · Sociology of work

1 Introduction and Problem Statement

Although there is abundant research on AI in higher education, it centers primarily on benefits, risks, and ethical dilemmas, overlooking how AI configures academic work itself [5, 21]. Research examining the relationship between working conditions and GenAI use in Mexican higher education is notably absent. This gap is significant: without analyses that overcome technological determinism and individual voluntarism, the instrumental logic of technology becomes naturalized, reducing academic practice to mere adaptation.

This research analyzes how academic practice is configured in its encounter with GenAI under specific working conditions. Adopting an interpretive-critical approach, it rejects the notion that technology is neutral or deterministic [10, 17], recognizing it as

E. G. Blanchard et al. (Eds.): AIED 2026, CCIS 3033, pp. 419–424, 2026.
https://doi.org/10.1007/978-3-032-29794-5_65

part of historical, institutional, and disciplinary configurations where it reorders practices and is simultaneously resignified by its users [7, 8]. It articulates three analytical levels (structure, action, and subjectivity) to examine how labor conditions shape the adoption, negotiation, or rejection of GenAI. Facing inevitable technological transformations in higher education, the study provides conceptual tools to understand these dynamics and preserve margins of professional autonomy within contexts of labor intensification.

2 Theoretical Framework and Research Questions

This research is grounded in Latin American configurational theory [8], analyzing practice as a contingent articulation between three inseparable dimensions. Structure refers to objective conditions (temporal, organizational, economic, social, normative-disciplinary) that constrain practice through institutionalized "objectifications" (regulations, policies, disciplinary criteria) [8]. Subjectivity encompasses the processes through which academics produce meanings about their practice, including underlying logics, emotions, and senses of identity; these are polysemic, allowing multiple meanings to coexist in tension [8, 9]. Action refers to the repertoires academics deploy in their encounter with GenAI, including practices, decisions, negotiations, and resistances. Following De Certeau [6], academics operate through "tactics" that adapt, resist, or subvert technology within imposed systems [15].

For example, an academic with a temporary contract and large class groups faces reduced margins for exploring GenAI (structure). Yet this does not mechanically determine practice; they simultaneously attribute contradictory meanings to the tool—useful for saving time but threatening to disciplinary identity—and this tension orients their decisions (subjectivity). Both dimensions are expressed in their actual practices: they neither fully adopt nor reject GenAI, but develop situated tactics, such as using it discreetly in class preparation (action).

The research integrates contributions from the sociology of work [7, 13, 18, 19] and Dubet's [9] logics of experience (integration, strategy, and subjectification), which coexist in tension. Following Anaya Torres [2], labor precariousness in higher education constitutes a structural configuration that shapes how academics encounter and negotiate emerging technologies; this analytical lens is useful to understanding the structural dimension of academic practice in this research.

The study addresses the general question: How is academic practice configured in its encounter with GenAI in situated contexts of academic work? Through four specific inquiries: (1) How do structural conditions participate in this configuration? (2) How do academics make sense of their encounter with GenAI? (3) How do forms of action unfold in teaching, research, engagement, and management? (4) How is difference between academics configured in this encounter?

3 Methodology

This research adopts a qualitative interpretive-critical approach through a multiple case study design with comparative logic [20]. The cases are two Mexico City universities with differentiated labor contexts: UAM-Cuajimalpa (public) and IBERO-CDMX (private).

Two disciplines are studied—Communication and Computer Engineering—presenting different relationships with technology and disciplinary quality criteria.

Comparison serves to reconstruct how GenAI and academic practice manifest under differentiated structural conditions [20]. UAM-C (public, full-time faculty, stronger union tradition) and IBERO-CDMX (private, Jesuit, majority temporary faculty) offer contrasting institutional configurations. In Communication, AI relates to writing and content production, raising authorship and ethics concerns; in Engineering, it links to assisted programming and problem-solving. This institutional and disciplinary contrast allows analyzing how the same technology participates in configuring academic practices governed by different criteria, as well as the strategies of appropriation, resistance, and negotiation academics deploy in contexts marked by productivist pressure and structural inequalities [1, 11].

Participant selection follows theoretical intentionality and analytical pertinence criteria. Academics affiliated with the institutions and disciplines who perform substantive university functions and have situated GenAI experience are included, with willingness to narrate concrete practice episodes. The number of participants remains open to adjustment as fieldwork develops.

Data collection techniques include: (1) Semi-structured narrative interviews as the central instrument, oriented toward reconstructing professional practice through situational narratives [3]; (2) Participant observation to capture what academics do in concrete situations, when field access permits, for instance, in departmental meetings, class sessions involving GenAI, or shared workspaces; (3) Digital trace analysis, adopting Hine's [14] proposal in which digital traces (prompts, conversations, produced materials) function as analytical equivalents of direct observation, enabling triangulation of accounts; (4) Contextualization questionnaire addressing labor trajectory, contract type, workload, access to resources, frequency of GenAI use by substantive function, and perceptions of institutional policies; and (5) Institutional documentary analysis of policies and regulations on AI use. The analysis employs a thematic and abductive approach [4], in constant dialogue between empirical data and the configurational theoretical framework.

4 Preliminary Empirical Findings

An initial empirical exploration was conducted to assess the pertinence of the data collection tools. While not constituting the definitive data collection phase, this exploration yielded findings that inform instrument refinement. The following results are drawn from this preliminary phase.

4.1 Contextualization Questionnaire (N = 49)

The questionnaire was administered to 49 academics between January 30 and February 1, 2026. The sample was gender-balanced (51% male, 49% female) with diverse academic profiles: 51% hold a Master's degree and 40.8% a doctorate. Engineering and Technology (34.7%) and Social Sciences (24.5%) were the most represented areas. A critical finding is that 73.5% hold hourly or adjunct contracts, and 46.9% work at multiple institutions, indicating some of the elements of the precariousness documented in the literature [12,

13, 16]. Teaching (69.4% weekly or daily) and research (61.2%) are the functions where GenAI is most frequently incorporated. Item-total correlation analysis identified the need to refine the instrument for the definitive data collection; this was only a contextualizing exercise.

4.2 In-Depth Interviews (N = 4)

Four semi-structured interviews were conducted with academics at a major public Mexican university, using pseudonyms to protect identity. Three articulating axes connecting the configurational dimensions were identified in this exploration: (1) Precariousness – Instrumental use – Survival logic: structural labor conditions constrain faculty toward GenAI as a "survival tool," generating subjective tension between efficiency and loss of professional autonomy; (2) Normative vacuum – Tactical autonomy – Ambivalence: the absence of institutional policies leaves faculty to define their own boundaries, producing ethical ambivalence and concealment tactics; (3) Disciplinary norms – Functional differentiation – Authorship resignification: disciplinary expectations configure differential GenAI use across substantive functions, leading to rethinking of authorship and knowledge validity criteria. This was an exploratory exercise.

From a configurational-abductive analytical logic, episodes such as that of a lecturer holding hourly contracts across multiple institutions, who turns to ChatGPT to develop rubrics due to workload overload, yet does so discreetly because she considers it "not what a good professor should do," are interpreted as concrete configurations in which structure, action, and subjectivity are articulated within a single practice. In the initial exploration, this type of situation made it possible to identify analytical axes such as workload overload, tactical appropriations of GenAI, and ethical ambivalence; however, this was only a preliminary approximation. The subsequent analysis will seek to reconstruct patterns of articulation among these three levels, understood beyond correlations between variables and oriented toward identifying configurations in which each element acquires its specific meaning in relation to the others. Thus, the same structural condition may articulate with different meanings and give rise to different forms of action. This does not reduce the analysis to isolated individual trajectories; rather, it guides the comparative reconstruction of recurrent patterns that help explain how particular articulations between structural conditions, processes of subjectivation, and forms of action configure differentiated academic practices. Read in light of Marcuse, such cases also show how technological rationality reorganizes academic practice in terms of efficiency and instrumental problem-solving, making the technical resource appear necessary even when it comes into tension with ethical, authorial, and professional criteria.

5 Expected Contributions and Next Steps

The preceding exercises suggest the pertinence of the configurational approach; structure, action, and subjectivity can be empirically reconstructed as articulated configurations. From this perspective, the analysis moves beyond the descriptive level of narrated situations and follows what De la Garza conceptualizes as an articulated reconstruction, starting from the real concrete expressed in interviews, artifacts, and documents, passing through an analytical moment of abstraction, and moving toward the concrete as thought; a theoretically reconstructed totality in which structural conditions, forms of action, and subjective meanings are understood in their interrelations. In the initial exploration, this logic made it possible to recognize that elements of labor precariousness, tactical GenAI use, and ethical ambivalence converge in concrete configurations of academic practice.

Next steps. The remaining phases include ethical approval, participant selection across both universities and disciplines, and definitive data production through interviews, situated observation, artifact analysis, and institutional documents. The subsequent analysis will identify the relevant conditions in each narrated situation, examine how structure, action, and subjectivity articulate, compare these articulations across cases, and reconstruct configurational patterns. Analytical closure will depend on the explanatory capacity of the reconstructed configuration; whether it makes intelligible why academic practice takes one form rather than another in its encounter with GenAI.

This research contributes to AIED by shifting attention from adoption-centered narratives toward the academic as worker and by showing that GenAI use cannot be understood apart from the working conditions under which academic practice unfolds. Its main contribution lies in introducing a configurational framework grounded in articulated reconstruction, one that moves beyond adoption–resistance binaries and makes it possible to analyze how structural conditions, subjective processes, and forms of action jointly shape the encounter with GenAI. For tool design and higher education policy, this perspective highlights that meaningful GenAI integration requires attention not only to training and access, but also to the structural conditions of academic labor that shape how these technologies are interpreted, negotiated, and used in practice.

References

1. Abbott, A.: The System of Professions: An Essay on the Division of Expert Labor. University of Chicago Press, Chicago (1988)
2. Anaya Torres, E.D.: Las voces de los nadies. Precariedad laboral en docentes universitarios. Revista Latinoamericana de Estudios Educativos **55**(1), 277–302 (2025). https://doi.org/10.48102/rlee.2025.55.1.666
3. Bertaux, D.: Les récits de vie: Perspective ethnosociologique. Bellaterra, Barcelona (2005)
4. Braun, V., Clarke, V.: Using thematic analysis in psychology. Qual. Res. Psychol. **3**(2), 77–101 (2006)
5. Crompton, H., Burke, D.: Artificial intelligence in higher education: the state of the field. Int. J. Educ. Technol. High. Educ. **20**, 22 (2023)
6. De Certeau, M.: The Practice of Everyday Life. University of California Press, Berkeley (1984). Original work published 1980
7. De la Garza Toledo, E.: Subjetividad, cultura y estructura. Iztapalapa **50**, 83–104 (2001)
8. De la Garza Toledo, E.: La metodología configuracionista para la investigación social. GEDISA/UAM, Barcelona (2018)
9. Dubet, F.: Sociologie de l'expérience. Seuil, Paris (1994)
10. Feenberg, A.: Transforming Technology: A Critical Theory Revisited, 2nd edn. Oxford University Press, New York (2002)
11. Freidson, E.: Professionalism, the Third Logic: On the Practice of Knowledge. University of Chicago Press, Chicago (2001)

12. Galaz Fontes, J.F., Gil Antón, M.: La profesión académica en México: Un oficio en proceso de reconfiguración. Revista Electrónica de Investigación Educativa **11**(2), 1–20 (2009)
13. Gill, R.: Breaking the silence: The hidden injuries of neo-liberal academia. In: Ryan-Flood, R., Gill, R. (eds.) Secrecy and Silence in the Research Process: Feminist Reflections, pp. 228–244. Routledge, London (2010)
14. Hine, C.: Virtual Ethnography. SAGE, London (2000)
15. Karam, T.: Tácticas cotidianas en entornos digitales: Creatividad, negociación y micro-resistencia. Comunicación y Sociedad (in press, 2026)
16. Kezar, A., DePaola, T., Scott, D.T.: The Gig Academy: Mapping Labor in the Neoliberal University. Johns Hopkins University Press, Baltimore (2019)
17. Marcuse, H.: One-Dimensional Man: Studies in the Ideology of Advanced Industrial Society. Beacon Press, Boston (1964)
18. Musselin, C.: The Transformation of Academic Work: Facts and Analysis. Research & Occasional Paper Series, CSHE.4.07. Center for Studies in Higher Education, UC Berkeley (2007)
19. Slaughter, S., Rhoades, G.: Academic Capitalism and the New Economy: Markets, State, and Higher Education. Johns Hopkins University Press, Baltimore (2004)
20. Yin, R.K.: Case Study Research and Applications: Design and Methods, 6th edn. SAGE, Thousand Oaks (2018)
21. Zawacki-Richter, O., Marín, V.I., Bond, M., Gouverneur, F.: Systematic review of research on artificial intelligence applications in higher education – where are the educators? Int. J. Educ. Technol. High. Educ. **16**, 39 (2019)

Diagnosing When to Trust AI Coding of Student-Generated Text: A Committee-Based Framework for Characterizing Uncertainty in LLM Annotation Systems

Fanjie Li(✉)

Vanderbilt University, Nashville, TN, USA
fanjie.li@vanderbilt.edu

Abstract. This paper operationalizes a committee-based performance diagnostic framework that combines inter-model agreement, consensus entropy, and borderline rate to support interpretable monitoring of AI coding of student text without ground truth. In a pilot application to nursing simulation reflections, these complementary metrics revealed distinct ensemble patterns, including stable consensus and divergence between agreement and decisiveness. The results illustrate how committee diagnostics can support ongoing oversight of AI coding as systems encounter new learners, contexts, and language use at scale. Building on this framework, future work will develop interpretable approaches to decomposing LLM coding uncertainty into its underlying sources, such as underspecified prompts, input ambiguity, and model limitations, to support more trustworthy AI coding systems.

Keywords: Automated Coding · LLMs · Uncertainty Quantification

1 Introduction

AIED systems increasingly rely on automated interpretation of student-generated text such as written explanations, short responses, and dialogue to deliver adaptive support [1]. Recent advances in large language models have lowered the barriers to large-scale automated text analysis; but the value of such systems depends on maintaining coherent behavior beyond training and testing as models encounter new learners, contexts and forms of expression. In practice, however, such AI coding pipelines rarely include systematic mechanisms for ongoing post-deployment validation or monitoring. Even when methods such as confidence monitoring or drift detection [2] are employed, these techniques typically focus on changes in individual predictions or input distributions, offering limited visibility into whether models continue to produce consistent, aligned interpretations of target constructs once deployed. In educational settings, this

E. G. Blanchard et al. (Eds.): AIED 2026, CCIS 3033, pp. 425–431, 2026.
https://doi.org/10.1007/978-3-032-29794-5_66

can result in misleading feedback, inappropriate agent responses, or misaligned system actions. As the use of LLM-based coding rapidly expands, ensuring that AIED systems continue to respond appropriately to the constructs they are intended to detect across learners, contexts, and time requires new approaches to monitoring automated AI analysis of student-generated text throughout the system lifecycle. To address this gap, this paper introduces a committee-based diagnostic framework that integrates measures of inter-model agreement and decisiveness to support interpretable monitoring of automated coding on unlabeled data. A related paper presenting this framework and its pilot evaluation has been accepted as a short paper at AIED 2026 [6]. The present DC paper extends this work by articulating a broader doctoral research agenda focused on interpretable uncertainty decomposition for trustworthy AI coding.

2 AI Coding Approach and Monitoring Diagnostics

To provide visibility into the behavior of LLM-based coding systems on unlabeled data, we develop a committee-based diagnostic framework with mechanisms to surface uncertainty at three levels: within individual judgments of code presence (via guided chain-of-thought with explicit uncertainty flagging), across each AI coder's repeated inference attempts (via decision stability quantification [7,8]), and among multiple LLMs (via committee agreement [2]). Together, they provide the foundation for detecting when and where model outputs may be unstable or deviate from ensemble behavior established during calibration and testing.

2.1 AI Coding System Elements

Guided Reasoning with Uncertainty Flags. When LLMs are used for automated coding, they are typically prompted to produce label predictions with little visibility into decision confidence. Prior work has shown that chain-of-thought prompting, where models articulate step-by-step reasoning before reaching conclusions, can improve both performance and interpretability [1]. We extend this approach by embedding explicit uncertainty signaling within the reasoning process. Specifically, the AI coder is prompted to: (1) reason through the application of the codebook to a data instance, (2) note any moments of decision difficulty (e.g., competing interpretations) and (3) flag cases where code presence or absence cannot be determined with confidence. The output includes both a binary judgment (code present/absent) and an uncertainty flag (raised or not), which together can be used to derive an uncertainty-adjusted score (see Sect. 2.2).

Repeated Inference for Decision Stability. Beyond single-shot inference, each AI coder processes every data item through multiple independent runs (e.g., $N = 10$) with a non-zero temperature (e.g., temperature $= 1$), following prior work using repeated inference to examine LLM decision stability [7,8]. This approach draws on the self-consistency hypothesis [10], which posits that, when a construct is well operationalized, multiple valid reasoning paths should converge on the same coding decision. In contrast, variability across repeated inferences signals intra-coder decision instability, often reflecting latent ambiguity or competing interpretations that warrant closer human inspection.

Committee-Based Coding with Multiple LLMs. As a single AI coder's uncertainty estimate may reflect model-specific biases or overconfidence, the system employs a committee of three AI coders, each using a different LLM. This ensemble approach follows Query by Committee method from active learning [2], which use disagreement among diverse models to identify ambiguous cases near the decision boundary. When multiple models independently flag uncertainty or disagree, the ensemble provides more robust signals of collective uncertainty that are not subject to a particular model's training bias.

2.2 Instance-Level Scoring

For each data instance, run-level outputs are aggregated within each AI coder to produce a single coder-level score ($LLMq{-}c \in [0, 1]$ described below) that summarizes decision stability and uncertainty across stochastic runs. The resulting set of coder-level scores is then used to derive committee-level decisions per data instance and compute diagnostic measures of agreement and decisiveness across the dataset: **(1) Certainty-Weighted LLMq (*LLMq-c*):** At the individual coder level, we build on Tai et al. [8]'s Large Language Model quotient (LLMq), which measures model confidence in code presence by averaging binary codes across repeated LLM queries. Our certainty-weighted variant extends LLMq by down-weighting uncertainty-flagged outputs toward the neutral midpoint (0.5), then averaging these uncertainty-adjusted scores across runs, preventing hesitant decisions from artificially inflating or deflating the confidence score. **(2) Ensemble Consensus Score ($\hat{p}$):** Consistent with prior work demonstrating improved robustness through ensemble aggregation [2], we compute the committee's collective judgment as mean of the three AI coders' *LLMq-c* scores; applying a 0.5 threshold produces the final binary decision for downstream analysis.

2.3 Performance Monitoring Metrics

On unlabeled data, traditional metrics (e.g., F1) are unavailable. However, the committee-based, uncertainty-aware framework allows system health to be diagnosed through three complementary metrics that require no ground truth labels.

Inter-Model Agreement (α_{AI}). Krippendorff's α [3], a robust and widely used measure of inter-rater reliability, is used to assess inter-model agreement. Based on the three models' thresholded decisions derived from binarized *LLMq-c*, this metric indexes how often the model committee converges on the same coding decision (α>0.67 considered as moderate agreement; α>0.80 as strong agreement [3]). High agreement indicates consistent codebook application across models, while declining α_{AI} signals potential drift, suggesting models begin to diverge in how they interpret the codebook when applied to new data.

Consensus Entropy (H). This metric is computed as the Shannon entropy $H \in [0,1]$ over the instance-level, cross-model consensus score ($\hat{p}$) [15], where: $H = -[\hat{p} \times \log_2(\hat{p}) + (1-\hat{p}) \times \log_2(1-\hat{p})]$. Following [2], average consensus entropy across items serves as a summary indicator of ensemble decisiveness on unlabeled data. Lower H indicates more decisive ensemble judgments (consensus near 0 or 1); higher H indicates greater indecisiveness ($\hat{p}$ near 0.5) which can occur when models confidently disagree or are uncertain or unstable across runs.

Borderline Rate (B). While consensus entropy summarizes overall decisiveness, it does not distinguish between pervasive uncertainty versus uncertainty concentrated on a small number of items. Following prior work that distinguishes aggregate uncertainty from a concentration of ambiguous instances [2], we formalize borderline rate (B) as the percentage of items for which $L \leq \hat{p} \leq U$ denote lower and upper probability bounds defining a region of decisional ambiguity.

In the following section, we first provide an initial proof-of-concept demonstrating how these diagnostics characterize ensemble behavior in practice. We then outline a broader research agenda aimed at developing approaches to decompose AI coding uncertainty into interpretable and actionable components tied to its underlying sources, supporting more informed human oversight and targeted interventions to improve system reliability.

3 Proof-of-Concept Pilot

To illustrate the use of the proposed diagnostics in a real-world AIED setting, we draw on data from the *Reflect* system, a post-simulation reflection platform for nursing education. Simulation-based education is central to nursing preparation, supporting the development of clinical judgment and reflective practice. Guided written reflection on simulation experiences further supports this process by prompting deeper sensemaking, yet in practice these reflections are rarely reviewed beyond the learners themselves. Automated coding of student reflections offers a scalable way to support reflective skill development and provide instructional insight into students' clinical judgment across contexts and time. However, without mechanisms for ongoing monitoring, such systems may produce inconsistent or misleading interpretations as they encounter new cohorts and simulation contexts beyond those involved in initial testing.

The pilot uses an event-level Reflect corpus of 213 reflections from 16 students reflecting on key moments from a range of adult and pediatric simulations. A nine-activity coding scheme aligned with models of clinical judgment [9] and self-regulation [4] was developed through iterative refinement with input from nursing education experts. The codebook was applied by three researchers to double code 60 reflections (IRR: $0.63 < \alpha < 0.91$), after which data were split into training (N=36) and test sets (N=24). Three LLM-based coders were calibrated through iterative prompt refinement using a shared system prompt template and dynamically inserted codebook. Data instances with high uncertainty triggered targeted human review and prompt refinement until human-AI

Table 1. Performance metrics for Test Data and Unlabeled Data.

Activity Code	Test Data				Unlabeled Data		
	F1	α_{AI}	H	B	α_{AI}	H	B
GATHER	0.966	0.942	0.295	4.17%	0.885	0.275	7.69%
IMPLMT	0.941	1.000	0.322	0.00%	0.951	0.218	5.13%
T-COMM	0.923	0.877	0.295	8.33%	0.946	0.230	2.56%
P-COMM	0.923	0.944	0.214	8.33%	0.917	0.131	3.42%
INTRPT-SIT	0.770	0.683	0.344	8.33%	0.756	0.276	9.40%
INTRPT-VLDT	0.947	1.000	0.321	0.00%	0.837	0.343	9.40%
INTRPT-EVAL	1.000	0.844	0.195	0.00%	0.532	0.163	1.71%
GOALS	0.824	0.698	0.506	25.00%	0.719	0.456	12.82%
TIME	1.000	0.735	0.379	4.17%	0.644	0.309	11.11%

agreement stabilized after which performance was evaluated on held-out data. Full details of the prompt engineering and training workflow are reported in [5].

Here we characterize model behavior on both the test set and unlabeled data using the three diagnostic metrics introduced above: inter-model agreement (α_{AI}), consensus entropy (H), and a borderline rate (B) of $0.35 \leq \hat{p} \leq 0.65$ (Table 1). The goal is to illustrate how complementary diagnostic signals can be jointly interpreted to reveal patterns of ensemble behavior in the absence of ground truth. Table 1 shows that interpreting agreement (α_{AI}) together with decisiveness (low entropy H and low borderline rate B) reveals recurring ensemble patterns. The behaviorally explicit codes (GATHER, IMPLMT, T-COMM, P-COMM) fall into the high-agreement/high-decisiveness region, indicating stable ensemble behavior and consistent construct interpretation across models. In contrast, several interpretive codes sometimes exhibit moderate/high agreement yet low decisiveness (elevated H/B), suggesting ambiguities in construct operationalization that can benefit from prompt/code-definition refinement (see [5]). Finally, INTRPT-EVAL shows low agreement despite high decisiveness on the unlabeled set (α_{AI} drops while H/B remain low), a pattern consistent with low-prevalence codes where models confidently predict negatives but disagree on rare candidate positives, motivating selective human audit of high-disagreement cases. Together, these patterns demonstrate how α_{AI}, H, and B can be jointly interpreted to distinguish stable versus problematic ensemble behavior and guide actionable next steps, such as targeted data review or construct refinement.

4 Future Work: Toward Interpretable Uncertainty in AI Coding

The diagnostics presented in this paper identify when AI coding outputs are unstable, but they do not yet explain the sources of that uncertainty. In LLM-based coding, output variability may arise from multiple factors, including under-specified coding criteria, limitations in model knowledge, or legitimate data ambiguity due to vague or partial evidence. Distinguishing among these sources is critical for determining appropriate interventions, such as refining prompts, fine-tuning or selecting models, or deferring ambiguous instances for human judgment.

This doctoral research aims to develop a framework for interpretable uncertainty decomposition in LLM-based coding systems, building on the committee-based framework introduced in this paper. The first line of work examines how uncertainty arising from underspecified coding criteria can be reduced through iterative prompt refinement. Using a committee-based active learning approach [5], high-disagreement instances are selectively reviewed to clarify coding criteria, refine construct boundaries, and improve prompts. By comparing uncertainty patterns before and after active learning, this study evaluates whether prompt refinement reduces disagreement attributable to task under-specification while isolating uncertainty associated with data ambiguity or model limitations. The second line of work focuses on interpreting where in the reasoning process models diverge. Using structured reasoning outputs, this study analyzes model-generated reasoning chains to identify divergence points, such as differences in evidence extraction, construct interpretation, or decision thresholds. Instances with high inter-model disagreement (epistemic uncertainty) are expected to exhibit early divergence in reasoning, reflecting differences in interpretation, while cases with high intra-model variability (aleatoric uncertainty) are expected to show convergent reasoning with explicit uncertainty flags, indicating shared recognition of ambiguity. Together, this research advances a framework for interpreting uncertainty in AI coding systems, supporting more informed decisions about when to trust, re-evaluate, or reject automated categorizations. In AIED contexts, this work addresses the challenge of maintaining robust and reliable AI coding of complex, open-ended student work as systems encounter new populations, contexts, and patterns of expression at scale.

References

1. Cohn, C., Hutchins, N., Le, T., Biswas, G.: A chain-of-thought prompting approach with LLMs for evaluating students' formative assessment responses in science. In: Proc. AAAI Conference on Artificial Intelligence, pp. 23182–23190 (2024)
2. Herrera-Poyatos, D., et al.: An overview of model uncertainty and variability in LLM-based sentiment analysis: challenges, mitigation strategies, and the role of explainability. Front. Artif. Intell. **8**, 1–24 (2025)
3. Krippendorff, K.: Content analysis: An introduction to its methodology (2019)
4. Lajoie, S.P., Gube, M.: Adaptive expertise in medical education: Accelerating learning trajectories by fostering self-regulated learning. Medical Teacher **40**(8) (2018)
5. Li, F., Mason, M.L., Levin, D., Wise, A.: Using RE-LLM coding uncertainty to resolve codebook ambiguities: An example of the CLARIFY toolset and workflow in action. In: Joint Proceedings of LAK 2026 Workshops, pp. 1–10 (2026)
6. Li, F., Mason, M.L., Levin, D., Wise, A.: When can we trust AI coding of student-generated text? a committee-based approach to diagnosing agreement and uncertainty at scale. In: Proceedings of the 27th International Conference on Artificial Intelligence in Education (AIED'26), pp. 1–9 (2026)

7. Ramanathan, S., et al.: When the prompt becomes the codebook: Grounded prompt engineering (GROPROE) and its application to belonging analytics. In: LAK'25 Proceedings, pp. 713–725. ACM (2025)
8. Tai, R.H., et al.: An examination of the use of large language models to aid analysis of textual data. Int J Qual Methods **23**, 1–14 (2024)
9. Tanner, C.A.: Thinking like a nurse: a research-based model of clinical judgment in nursing. J. Nurs. Educ. **45**(6), 204–211 (2006)
10. Wang, X., et al.: Self-consistency improves chain of thought reasoning in language models (2023). arXiv:2203.11171 [cs.CL]

Contingent Support with LLM-Based Scaffolding for Collaborative Problem Solving in an Inquiry-Based Game Environment

Daeun Hong[1](✉), Yeojin Kim[2], and Cindy E. Hmelo-Silver[1]

[1] Indiana University, Bloomington, IN 47405, USA
dh37@iu.edu
[2] North Carolina State University, Raleigh, NC 27606, USA

Abstract. Drawing on sociocultural perspectives, this study investigates whether and how LLM-based scaffolding—beyond mere technical adaptivity—provides contingent support for middle school students' collaborative problem solving (CPS) in a collaborative game environment. For CPS tasks, we introduce two LLM-based scaffolds: Discussion Tips, triggered by real-time indicators to promote productive CPS practices, and Response Feedback, delivered after students submit their responses to provide feedback on their written work. Using trace logs and focal-group video, we examine (a) pre–post changes in CPS practices and learning performance using learning analytics, (b) interaction patterns through which the scaffolds provide contingent support using interaction analysis, and (c) cases that disrupt or limit the scaffolds' contingent support using thematic analysis. The study is expected to yield actionable design and evaluation principles for LLM-based scaffolding that is demonstrably aligned with students' evolving CPS needs in computer-supported collaborative learning settings.

Keywords: Scaffolding · Large Language Model · Collaborative Problem Solving · Computer-Supported Collaborative Learning

1 Introduction

Rapid advancements in large language models (LLMs) have accelerated educational technology innovations and the adoption of LLMs in learning contexts. LLMs are generative AI systems that produce human-like text in response to natural language prompts and are trained on massive datasets with large numbers of parameters [12]. A key affordance of LLMs is adaptivity: they can analyze students' learning processes at scale and provide real-time support—such as feedback, hints, resources, and recommendations—tailored to learners' actions, potentially improving engagement and learning outcomes [3]. This technical adaptivity can enable support that is contingent on learners' evolving needs within their zones of proximal development (ZPD), helping learners accomplish more than they could with assistance [11]. However, integrating LLMs into classroom learning also raises concerns. LLMs can struggle to interpret complex, nuanced, context-specific, and time-sensitive information and may respond inappropriately [7]. In addition,

E. G. Blanchard et al. (Eds.): AIED 2026, CCIS 3033, pp. 432–437, 2026.
https://doi.org/10.1007/978-3-032-29794-5_67

insufficient validation of LLM-based systems may reduce transparency and introduce inaccuracies [9], which can mislead learners or shape their practices in ineffective ways. These opportunities and risks underscore the need for rigorous design and evaluation of LLM-integrated learning supports.

Building on these affordances, recent studies have explored LLM-based supports for developing critical competencies such as collaborative problem solving (CPS). CPS is inherently demanding, requiring learners to integrate knowledge, regulate processes, and coordinate tasks toward shared goals [5], and these demands are often amplified in computer-supported collaborative learning (CSCL) environments [4]. Prior work has used LLMs to provide contingent feedback to support discussion and argumentation in computer-mediated settings [1] and to generate context-sensitive reflective prompts based on learners' actions and performance [6]. Yet, whether LLM-based scaffolding can provide truly contingent support for CPS remains an open question. CPS is dynamic and distributed across teammates; learners' needs shift rapidly as groups negotiate meaning, coordinate roles, and regulate progress, making it difficult for an LLM to (a) accurately diagnose evolving group needs and (b) deliver support that is appropriately targeted and timed. Consequently, LLM-based scaffolding designed specifically to support CPS in CSCL settings remains underexplored. Addressing this gap, the present study will introduce two LLM-based scaffolds designed for middle school students and examine how these scaffolds contingently mediate learning in a CSCL game environment. Specifically, in this study, the following research questions will be addressed:

RQ1. What changes, if any, do students show in CPS practices and learning performance after exposure to LLM-based scaffolds?
RQ2. How, if any, do LLM-based scaffolds provide contingent support for students' CPS practices and learning performance?
RQ3. What cases might disrupt or limit the contingent support provided by LLM-based scaffolding as students' needs evolve during CPS tasks?

2 Theoretical Background and Framework of CPS

Drawing on sociocultural approaches to learning, social interactions play a critical role in mediating learning processes [11]. Collaborative problem solving (CPS) refers to situations in which two or more individuals work together to solve a shared problem by pooling, coordinating, and integrating their knowledge, skills, and efforts toward a common goal. CPS integrates cognitive and social dimensions that are tightly intertwined: the cognitive dimension concerns problem-solving processes, whereas the social dimension concerns coordination and collaboration processes [5].

Andrew-Todd and Kerr proposed a framework that provides a theory-driven representation of CPS subskills and their interrelationships, linking each subskill to observable behaviors in computer-mediated tasks [2]. Their framework differentiates social and cognitive dimensions. The social dimension includes four subskills: (a) maintaining communication, (b) sharing information, (c) establishing shared understanding, and (d) negotiating. The cognitive dimension comprises five subskills: (a) exploring and understanding, (b) representing and formulating, (c) planning, (d) executing, and (e) monitoring. Notably, the framework connects CPS constructs not only to verbal indicators (e.g., discourse) but also to non-verbal indicators (e.g., in-game actions), both of which can serve as evidence of CPS performance [2].

3 Learning Context

3.1 Crystal Island: EcoJourneys

CRYSTAL ISLAND: ECOJOURNEYS is a scaffolded, collaborative inquiry-based game environment designed to support middle school students' disciplinary learning in life science and their collaborative problem-solving (CPS) practices. In the game, students work in teams of three to four to investigate why tilapia fish at a local farm became sick across four quests. At the start of each quest, students individually gather and examine information related to water quality and fish ecosystems. They then participate in CPS activities in which they use the information they have collected to develop explanations and make decisions collaboratively. One focal CPS activity is TIDE (Talk, Investigate, Deduce, Explain). During TIDE, students evaluate whether the information they collected (i.e., notes) supports a given claim using the TIDE board (Fig. 1, left), a real-time collaborative whiteboard. Students construct arguments for or against the claim by placing relevant notes as evidence in the appropriate columns and explaining their reasoning to one another. Students may also indicate agreement or disagreement with a peer's note placement. Through discussion, the team reaches consensus on whether to keep a note in its current column, move it to a different column, or remove it. At the end of each TIDE activity, teams collaboratively generate an open-ended question (Fig. 1, right) that reflects the main idea of the quest.

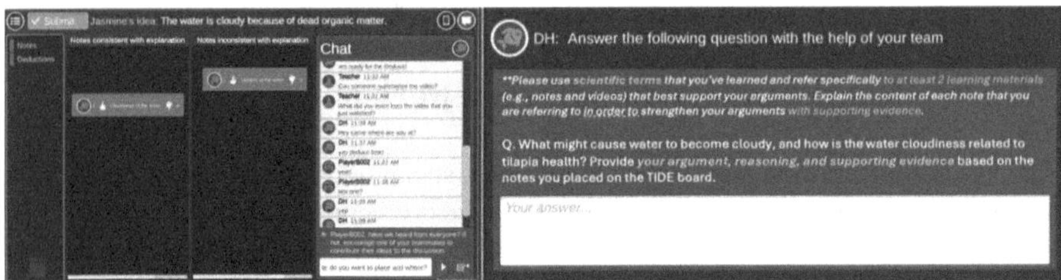

Fig. 1. The left figure shows the TIDE board with the hypothesis, chat, and notes, while the right figure shows an example of the open-ended question students answer.

3.2 Embedded LLM-Based Scaffolding During TIDE

While working on the TIDE tasks, students receive two LLM-based scaffolds to support their CPS practices: Discussion Tips (Fig. 2, left) and Response Feedback (Fig. 2, right). Discussion Tips promote productive CPS discourse and are triggered when real-time chat indicators suggest a need for additional support; Response Feedback, delivered by a non-player character after students submit their written responses, provides formative feedback on response quality (e.g., correctness and areas for improvement) tailored to students' answers. The scaffolding system uses the Llama-3.1-8B-Instruct model [10] with an error-augmented prompting approach. The prompt template included CPS label definitions, behavioral markers, expert-curated representative and near-miss dialogue examples, and the focal dialogue context [8]. To construct the near-miss examples, we split the dataset into training and test sets, ran classification on the training set, and identified error cases for inclusion in the prompt. We then evaluated different numbers of near-miss examples, selecting four as the optimal value based on training-set performance [8]. Rather than generating suggestions directly, the LLM classifies the most recent 20-line chat segment into predefined CPS discourse categories at 2.5-min intervals, grounded in the CPS model [2]; these classifications then determine whether support is needed and, when warranted, the system adaptively assembles and delivers expert-authored suggestions mapped to each category. To guide the design of Discussion Tips, we defined CPS discourse categories based on the CPS model and prior CPS discourse data. We assessed the contextual appropriateness of these classifications using a 2.5-min context window and an LLM-as-a-judge (GPT-4o-mini). Across the categories, the alignment rate was 0.88, suggesting that the scaffolding was generally contextually appropriate. In parallel, students' written responses were evaluated using a multi-component rubric assessing Argument, Reasoning and Evidence, and Use of Scientific Terms. Using quest-specific context and expert-defined criteria, the LLM assigned qualitative ratings (Emerging, Developing, Exemplary), after which expert-authored feedback was delivered. Agreement between LLM-generated and human-assigned labels was moderate but varied by dimension: 65% for Argument, 68% for Reasoning and Evidence, and 58% for Use of Scientific Terms.

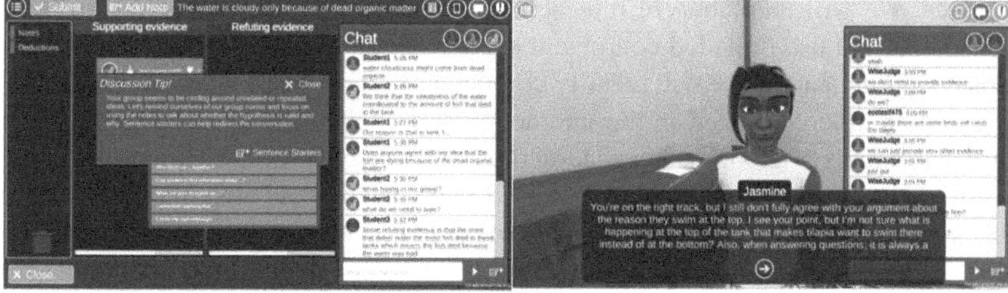

Fig. 2. The figure on the left shows an example of a Discussion Tip. The figure on the right shows an example of Response Feedback delivered by a non-player character.

4 Methods

4.1 Data Collection

Middle school students aged 12 to 14 from six to eight science classes will participate in the study. Working in teams of three to four, students will be organized into multiple groups and will use individual laptops to engage in the collaborative gameplay. In each class, two to three groups will be selected as focal groups, and their small-group interactions and screens will be video-recorded during the classroom implementation. In total, data will be collected from approximately 60 consenting students across 14 to 18 focal groups. Students will engage with the game for an average of 50 min per class session and will complete the full gameplay over 8 to 10 days.

4.2 Data Sources and Analysis

During the data collection period, two primary data sources will be gathered to address the research questions: (a) game trace logs capturing students' in-game actions, in-game chat, and written responses, and (b) video recordings of focal groups during gameplay, capturing in-person talk, gestures, and their engagement with the game.

To examine the efficacy of the LLM-based scaffolds (RQ1), we will use learning analytics combining in-person discourse and trace-log data from TIDE sessions. Two researchers will code students' utterances using an adapted CPS framework [2] and establish inter-rater reliability on 20% of the dataset; relevant in-game actions will be mapped to the same CPS framework and synchronized with the coded discourse. We will segment the synchronized data into 60-s windows before and after scaffold delivery and compute the frequency of CPS labels for each TIDE session. Learning performance will be operationalized using ratings of students' written responses across three quests. We will then test pre–post changes using paired-samples t-tests for CPS indicators following Discussion Tips and Wilcoxon signed-rank tests for changes in written-response quality following Response Feedback.

To address RQ 2 and 3, we will conduct interaction analysis and thematic analysis using video, discourse, and log data, including the scaffolds and students' written responses. For RQ2, we will iteratively review TIDE videos and write analytic memos to characterize students' responses to scaffolds and how these interactions shaped CPS processes. We will then analyze representative episodes for each pattern to examine whether scaffold use provided contingent support aligned with students' needs. Using adapted CPS indicators, we will identify contingent support based on whether a scaffold addressed an emergent need in the interaction and elicited the targeted CPS process, rather than simply aligning with a general discourse category. For RQ3, we will analyze episodes in which the scaffolds were not used as intended or did not effectively mediate CPS, and two researchers will iteratively develop and refine themes capturing conditions and reasons for limited support, reaching agreement through discussion.

5 Expected Contribution and Impact

As LLMs advance, adaptive learning environments can provide increasingly sophisticated forms of scaffolding. Yet adaptivity alone is not sufficient: effective support must be contingent—timely, appropriately targeted, and aligned with learners' evolving needs within their ZPD. Building on this premise, the present study examines how LLM-based scaffolding can support productive CPS practices when it is contingently aligned with students' moment-to-moment collaborative engagement. The study also identifies conditions under which LLM-based support is limited, clarifying when and why adaptivity becomes constrained. By empirically distinguishing adaptivity from contingency in an LLM-supported CSCL context, this work helps narrow the conceptual and practical gap between these constructs. Further, it illustrates how theory-driven LLM scaffold designs can mediate specific CPS processes by grounding support in observable collaborative engagement. These contributions offer actionable design for LLM-based scaffolding in CSCL, enabling researchers and practitioners to develop supports that are not only adaptive in name but demonstrably aligned with students' dynamic, real-time needs. Ultimately, this work can strengthen the rigor and effectiveness of classroom integration of LLM-based supports in CSCL contexts.

Acknowledgments. This work was supported by the National Science Foundation under Award No. DRL-2112635. The views expressed are those of the author(s) and do not necessarily reflect those of the National Science Foundation.

References

1. An, S., Zhang, S., Guo, T., Lu, S., Zhang, W., Cai, Z.: Impacts of generative AI on student teachers' task performance and collaborative knowledge construction process in mind mapping-based collaborative environment. Comput. Educ. **227**, 105227 (2025)
2. Andrews-Todd, J., Kerr, D.: Application of ontologies for assessing collaborative problem solving skills. Int. J. Test. **19**(2), 172–187 (2019)
3. Ba, S., Zhan, Y., Huang, L., Lu, G.: Investigating the impact of ChatGPT-assisted feedback on the dynamics and outcomes of online inquiry-based discussion. Br. J. Edu. Technol. **56**(5), 1710–1734 (2025)
4. Cress, U., Rosé, C.P., Law, N., Ludvigsen, S.: Investigating the complexity of computer-supported collaborative learning in action. Int. J. Comput.-Support. Collab. Learn. **14**(2), 137–142 (2019)
5. Hesse, F., Care, E., Buder, J., Sassenberg, K., Griffin, P.: A framework for teachable collaborative problem solving skills. In: Griffin, P., Care, E. (eds.) Assessment and Teaching of 21st Century Skills: Methods and Approach, pp. 37–56. Springer, Dordrecht (2014)
6. Hu, W., Tian, J., Li, Y.: Enhancing student engagement in online collaborative writing through a generative AI-based conversational agent. The Internet High. Educ. **65**, 100979 (2025)
7. Ji, Z., et al.: Survey of hallucination in natural language generation. ACM Comput. Surv. **55**(12), 1–38 (2023)
8. Kim, Y., et al.: Collaborative dialogue analysis for productive problem solving. To appear in: Proceedings of the Fifteenth International Learning Analytics and Knowledge Conference (LAK 2026), Bergen, Norway (2026). in press
9. Sahoo, N.R., Saxena, A., Maharaj, K., Ahmad, A.A., Mishra, A., Bhattacharyya, P.: Addressing bias and hallucination in large language models. In: Proceedings of the 2024 Joint International Conference on Computational Linguistics, Language Resources and Evaluation (LREC-COLING 2024): Tutorial Summaries, pp. 73–79 (2024)
10. Touvron, H., et al.: LLaMA: Open and efficient foundation language models. arXiv 2302.13971 (2023)
11. Vygotsky, L.S.: Mind in Society: The Development of Higher Psychological Processes. Harvard University Press, Cambridge, MA (1978)
12. Xu, Y., Hu, L., Zhao, J., Du, W., Wang, W.: Technology application prospects and risk challenges of large language models (in Chinese). J. Comput. Appl. **44**(6), 1655–1662 (2024)

From Competence Structures to Formative Feedback: A Knowledge Space Theory Pipeline for Evaluating and Enhancing LLM-Based Learning Recommendations

Peter Steiner(✉) and Jan Hochweber

Gallen University of Teacher Education, Notkerst. 27, 9000 St. Gallen, Switzerland
peter.steiner@phsg.ch

Abstract. Formative assessment that identifies a learner's current competence state and next feasible learning steps is essential for adaptive instruction, yet difficult to implement at scale in everyday teaching. Emerging digital tools, particularly intelligent tutoring systems combined with generative AI, offer promising avenues to make such support feasible, but only if they are grounded in statistically valid and psychometrically sound models. In educational measurement, Item Response Theory (IRT) remains the dominant framework, although its outputs are often considered too coarse to support individualized next-step recommendations. This motivates alternative approaches that model learning as graphical structures rather than unidimensional scales, which are particularly promising for generating learning recommendations. However, their practical usability remains limited due to challenges in identifying the underlying structures.

Consequently, this work proposes Competence-based Knowledge Space Theory (CbKST) as a statistical framework to inform LLM-based learning recommendations by investigating four research questions. The first two research questions lay the theoretical foundation by examining (1) the validity of purely LLM-based learning recommendations, given their potential to replace traditional statistical learner models, and (2) which structure-based statistical frameworks have already been successfully implemented in educational practice. The second category focuses on practical validation and establishes a proof of concept by investigating (3) how data-driven methods, expert ratings, and LLMs can be integrated into a coherent pipeline for the statistically valid derivation of competence structures, and (4) to what extent CbKST-based learning recommendations are statistically valid in real-world classroom settings, based on a competence structure developed for the domain of linear functions.

Keywords: Student Assessment · Knowledge Space Theory · Formative Assessment

E. G. Blanchard et al. (Eds.): AIED 2026, CCIS 3033, pp. 438–443, 2026.
https://doi.org/10.1007/978-3-032-29794-5_68

1 Motivation

Formative competence assessment that identifies a learner's current competence state and next feasible learning steps is widely regarded as a cornerstone of adaptive and individualized mathematics instruction. Such information enables instruction to be tailored to learners' current needs and supports individual learning trajectories. In everyday classroom practice, however, providing this level of fine-grained, individualized feedback remains difficult for teachers, particularly when teaching heterogeneous groups of students and working under time constraints. As a result, the potential of formative assessment is often only partially realized in practice.

Recent advances in digital technologies offer promising opportunities to address this challenge. Intelligent tutoring systems and, more recently, tools based on generative artificial intelligence have the potential to provide individualized feedback and learning recommendations at scale. However, for such systems to be educationally meaningful and trustworthy, their recommendations must be grounded in statistically valid and psychometrically sound models of learning and assessment.

2 Theoretical Background

In educational measurement, Item Response Theory (IRT) continues to be the dominant statistical framework underlying many digital assessment tools. While IRT provides robust and well-established methods for estimating learner proficiency on latent scales, its outputs are often considered too coarse to support fine-grained formative feedback, particularly with respect to identifying individual next learning steps [2, 5]. In contrast, approaches based on hierarchical competency structures—such as Competence-based Knowledge Space Theory (CbKST, [1]), Hierarchical Diagnostic Classification Models [12] and Dynamic Bayesian Networks [7]—offer richer diagnostic information by modelling the prerequisite relations among skills and competencies.

Despite their theoretical advantages, the practical usability of structure-based approaches remains limited. A central challenge lies in identifying and validating the underlying competence structures that capture prerequisite relations within a domain. Deriving such structures typically requires either substantial domain expertise [6] or empirical response data [4]. Although methods for both approaches are well established in theory, their practical applicability is often constrained by real-world data conditions. In particular, the standard data-driven method, Inductive Item Tree Analysis (IITA) [10], generally assumes large, complete response datasets without missing values—conditions that are rarely met in authentic educational settings. Moreover, existing approaches based on expert elicitation and those based on empirical data have largely been developed in isolation, and systematic procedures for integrating both sources of information into a unified pipeline are still lacking. Finally, the potential of generative AI to support the elicitation and validation of competence structures has not yet been systematically explored.

Nonetheless, structure-based approaches have already been implemented in practical educational settings. For example, the commercial learning platform ALEKS is based on Knowledge Space Theory [3]. While these applications of state-of-the-art statistical frameworks offer valuable insights, there is currently no systematic overview of existing implementations, their effectiveness, and their limitations.

In recent times artificial intelligence plays an increasing role in student assessment [11]. While generative AI offers clear advantages in language production and conversational support, its didactic and, in particular, psychometric capabilities have not yet been sufficiently evaluated. Although first benchmarking approaches for didactic capabilities have begun to emerge [8], there is still a lack of conceptual frameworks for evaluating AI systems' ability to infer a learner's competence state and derive appropriate learning recommendations.

3 Research Questions

The resulting overarching goal of this work is to establish structure-based psychometric frameworks as a necessary foundation for LLM-based learning recommendations and to demonstrate and support the practical implementation of CbKST in this context. In the light of this, the four research questions will be investigated:

1. To what extent do purely LLM-based learning recommendations align with psychometrically grounded models of learning? (RQ1)
2. What assessment methodologies based on hierarchical structures have been implemented in practical educational systems such as intelligent tutoring systems, and how do they compare in terms of diagnostic information, scalability, and practical requirements? (RQ2)
3. How can hierarchical competency structures be derived from a combination of empirical data, expert knowledge and the use of LLMs? (RQ3)
4. Does the CbKST-based assessment tool developed in the SaTiM project provide valid and usable formative feedback in authentic classroom contexts?

4 Methods

To investigate the validity of purely LLM-based learning recommendations (RQ1), a controlled simulation study will be conducted in which LLM-generated recommendations are compared to psychometrically grounded recommendations derived from Competence-based Knowledge Space Theory (CbKST). In this framework, next feasible learning steps are defined as outer fringes, which serve as the reference standard. Multiple knowledge spaces from different mathematical content domains will be constructed, varying systematically in size and subject characteristics, and simulated learners will be generated by sampling knowledge states from these structures. For each simulated learner, LLM-based recommendations will be elicited using standardized prompts that are systematically varied (e.g., prompt format, amount of contextual information), while also comparing models of different sizes. The resulting recommendation sets will then be compared to the corresponding CbKST-derived outer fringes using set-based similarity and distance measures (e.g., Jaccard distance, F1-score), allowing for a systematic evaluation of how closely LLM-based recommendations align with psychometrically grounded next-step suggestions across conditions.

To address RQ2, a systematic literature review will be conducted following the PRISMA guidelines [9] for reporting systematic reviews. Relevant studies on hierarchical assessment frameworks implemented in educational systems (e.g., Knowledge Space Theory, CbKST, hierarchical cognitive diagnostic models, Dynamic Bayesian Networks) will be identified through structured database searches and screened using predefined inclusion criteria. The selected studies will be analyzed with regard to their diagnostic information, scalability, practical requirements, and reported effectiveness, enabling a structured comparison of existing implementations and their strengths and limitations.

To address RQ3, methods for deriving hierarchical competence structures will be extended and integrated into a unified pipeline. Expert-based procedures, such as the QUERY method, will be translated into accessible software tools to facilitate structured expert elicitation. Data-driven approaches, in particular Inductive Item Tree Analysis (IITA), will be adapted to handle incomplete response data, enabling their use in realistic educational datasets with missing values. In addition, the potential of generative AI to support structure elicitation and validation will be systematically investigated. Finally, these three components—expert input, empirical data, and AI support—will be combined into a coherent pipeline, which will be evaluated in a controlled simulation study with respect to its ability to recover and validate underlying competence structures.

Finally, the diagnostic tool developed within the SaTiM project will be evaluated in terms of its psychometric validity in real-world classroom settings.

5 Preliminary Results

Preliminary results have been obtained for RQ1 and RQ3. A completed pilot study established Knowledge Space Theory (KST) as a viable benchmark for evaluating LLM-based learning recommendations. Six LLMs (GPT-4o, GPT-4o-mini, Claude 4.5 Sonnet, Claude 3 Haiku, Gemini 2.5 Pro, and Gemini Flash) were evaluated across two domains of linear functions—linear modelling and slope identification from graphs—each represented as KST knowledge spaces with expert-derived prerequisite structures. For 1,000 simulated learners per domain, the recommendations generated by each LLM were compared with the KST-derived outer fringes using normalized symmetric difference, Jaccard distance, F1-score, and perfect-match rate. Using a naïve prompt to reflect realistic usage, all models showed non-negligible deviations from the KST benchmark (mean relative errors: 18–47%). Friedman tests revealed significant differences between models (Kendall's $W = 0.25$–0.37), with smaller models consistently performing worse than larger ones. These results validate the proposed benchmarking approach and provide a baseline for subsequent investigations of prompting strategies.

With respect to RQ3, prior work has advanced both empirical and theory-based approaches to deriving competence structures. On the empirical side, a new software implementation of Inductive Item Tree Analysis (IITA) was developed and extended to handle missing data; a simulation study showed that the true structure could still be recovered at average missing-data proportions of up to.21. On the theory-driven side, the QUERY procedure was implemented as an accessible software tool to support structured expert elicitation. In addition, a data-informed query-ordering method was developed to reduce the number of required expert judgments. Finally, a prototype for eliciting LLM-based prerequisite queries was created. Together, these developments provide the methodological foundation for integrating empirical data, expert knowledge, and AI support into a unified pipeline for competence structure derivation.

6 Expected Contributions to the Field

This work establishes structure-based psychometric frameworks as a foundation for LLM-based feedback in educational assessment. By using Competence-based Knowledge Space Theory (CbKST) as a formal reference model, it provides a principled way to evaluate and guide AI-generated learning recommendations with respect to their diagnostic validity. In addition, the dissertation introduces a benchmarking framework based on KST outer fringes, enabling systematic comparison of LLM outputs with psychometrically grounded next-step recommendations. Methodologically, it contributes a practical pipeline that combines data-driven methods, expert knowledge, and generative AI to derive competence structures under realistic data conditions. Finally, the classroom-based validation within the SaTiM project demonstrates the feasibility of integrating psychometrically grounded models and LLMs into real-world adaptive learning environments. Together, these contributions support the development of trustworthy, AI-driven formative assessment systems grounded in sound statistical principles.

Acknowledgments. This work is part of the SaTiM project, funded by the Swiss National Science Foundation (SNSF), grant number 100019_219884.

Disclosure of Interests. The authors have no competing interests to declare that are relevant to the content of this article.

References

1. Albert, D., Lukas, J. (eds.) Knowledge spaces: theories, empirical research, and applications. L. Erlbaum (1999)
2. Bez, S., Burkart, F., Tomasik, M.J., Merk, S.: How do teachers process technology-based formative assessment results in their daily practice? results from process mining of think-aloud data. Learn. Instruct. **97**, 102100 (2025). https://doi.org/10.1016/j.learninstruc.2025.102100
3. Cosyn, E., Uzun, H., Doble, C., Matayoshi, J.: A practical perspective on knowledge space theory: ALEKS and its data. J. Math. Psychol. **101**(2021), 102512 (2021). https://doi.org/10.1016/j.jmp.2021.102512
4. De Chiusole, D., Spoto, A. Stefanutti, L.:. Innovative methods for building knowledge structures. Advanced Series on Mathematical Psychology, pp. 87–104. World Scientific (2024)
5. Huff, K., Goodman, D.P.: The demand for cognitive diagnostic assessment. cognitive diagnostic assessment for education. In: Leighton, J., Gierl, M. (eds.), pp. 19–60. Cambridge University Press (2007)
6. Kambouri, M., Koppen, M., Villano, M., Falmagne, J.-C.: Knowledge assessment: tapping human expertise by the QUERY routine. Inter. J. Hum.-Comput. Stud. **40**(1), 119–151 (1994). https://doi.org/10.1006/ijhc.1994.1006

7. Käser, T., Klingler, S., Schwing, A.G., Gross, M.: Dynamic bayesian networks for student modeling. IEEE Trans. Learn. Technol. 10(4), 450–462 (2017). https://doi.org/10.1109/TLT.2017.2689017
8. Macina, J., Daheim, N., Hakimi, I., Kapur, M., Gurevych, I., Sachan, M.: MathTutorBench: A Benchmark for Measuring Open-ended Pedagogical Capabilities of LLM Tutors. arXiv (2025)
9. Page, M.J. et al. 2021. The PRISMA 2020 statement: an updated guideline for reporting systematic reviews. BMJ, n71 (2021). https://doi.org/10.1136/bmj.n71
10. Schrepp, M.: Extracting knowledge structures from observed data. British J. Math. Stat. Psychol. **52**(2), 213–224 (1999). https://doi.org/10.1348/000711099159071
11. Swiecki, Z., et al.: Assessment in the age of artificial intelligence. Comput. Educ. Artifi. Intell. **3**(2022), 100075 (2022). https://doi.org/10.1016/j.caeai.2022.100075
12. Templin, J., Bradshaw, L.: Hierarchical diagnostic classification models: a family of models for estimating and testing attribute hierarchies. Psychometrika **79**(2), 317–339 (2014). https://doi.org/10.1007/s11336-013-9362-0

Automating the Identification of the Triggers of Socially Shared Metacognitive Regulation in Ill-Structured Collaborative Problem-Solving: A Multimodal Analysis Approach

Vishwas Badhe(✉) and Ramkumar Rajendran

Centre for Educational Technology, Indian Institute of Technology Bombay, Mumbai, India
{vishwasbadhe,ramkumar.rajendran}@iitb.ac.in

Abstract. Socially Shared Metacognitive Regulation (SSMR) is central to effective collaborative problem-solving (CPS), yet its automatic identification remains a significant challenge. In a prior study conducted in a 12-week Human-Computer Interaction course, we developed a machine learning (ML) model using verbal discourse and Conditional Random Fields (CRFs) to identify SSMR triggers from team transcripts, achieving a moderate accuracy of 56%. While promising, this unimodal approach is inherently limited. This paper reports the completed work and proposes a multimodal extension incorporating video-based analysis of posture and head movement alongside verbal interactions to substantially improve trigger identification accuracy. By leveraging recent advances in Multimodal Large Language Models (MLLMs) and multimodal learning analytics (MMLA), the proposed approach aims to deliver richer, context-sensitive detection of SSMR episodes in CPS. This work contributes to the AIED community by advancing automated methods for understanding and supporting group-level regulatory processes in authentic learning environments.

Keywords: Socially Shared Metacognitive Regulation (SSMR) · Triggers of SSMR · Multimodal Learning Analytics · Multimodal Large Language Models

1 Introduction: Problem, Educational Relevance, and State of the Art

Socially Shared Metacognitive Regulation (SSMR) the group-level, cyclical process by which learners collectively monitor, evaluate, and redirect shared metacognitive activity [1, 3] is critical in ill-structured CPS contexts prevalent in higher education. Yet identifying SSMR episodes and their triggering moments currently relies on time-consuming, subjective manual analysis of verbal interactions [2, 4], making it impossible to scale or deliver real-time support to learners. The AIED community has addressed related challenges through NLP, ML, and more recently GenAI. Speech-based analytics [5] and MMLA approaches [7] have shown that both verbal and non-verbal signals (posture, gaze) carry rich regulatory information [4, 6]. MLLMs now enable scalable extraction of such non-verbal features from video [8]. However, automated multimodal detection of SSMR triggers specifically in CPS remains unexplored.

E. G. Blanchard et al. (Eds.): AIED 2026, CCIS 3033, pp. 444–449, 2026.
https://doi.org/10.1007/978-3-032-29794-5_69

This doctoral work directly addresses this gap. In a completed prior study conducted within a 12-week HCI course (HCI22), we developed and evaluated the first known automated system for identifying SSMR triggers from verbal discourse using speaker diarization, automatic speech recognition (ASR), and a CRF-based ML model. The model identified 1,396 SSMR episodes from 21,256 conversational turns across four CPS teams, achieving a 56% accuracy upon manual validation. While this is a meaningful proof-of-concept, the moderate accuracy underscores the limitations of unimodal text-based approaches. The proposed doctoral research extends this work by incorporating video data specifically posture and head movement features extracted using MLLMs (extracted postural and head-movement features) to develop a multimodal SSMR trigger identification system capable of greater accuracy, scalability, and contextual sensitivity.

2 Theoretical Framing and Proposed Solution

2.1 Study Design Theoretical Framework: SSRL, SSMR, and Regulatory Triggers

SSRL encompasses all forms of intentional group-level regulation, including co-regulation and socially shared regulation [1]. SSMR, as a subset, specifically concerns shared metacognitive activity: the negotiation and exercise of collective monitoring, evaluation, and control over cognitive processes [2, 3]. Within CPS, SSMR episodes are typically initiated by regulatory triggers specific verbal or behavioral cues that signal a transition into shared metacognitive activity [2, 4]. These triggers may manifest as expressions ('I think…', 'why did we…'), calls for re-planning ('we need to…'), or shifts in task understanding. Identifying these triggers is theoretically significant.

Sobocinski [4] demonstrated, using video and physiological data, that non-verbal behaviors particularly postural shifts and movement changes, are temporally aligned with regulatory transitions during CPS. This provides the theoretical basis for our multimodal extension: if SSMR triggers are manifested not only in what learners say but also in how their bodies respond, then combining verbal and non-verbal signals should yield substantially better detection accuracy.

2.2 Proposed Solution: Multimodal SSMR Trigger Identification

We ground the proposed solution in Ochoa's [7] MMLA construct-mapping framework, which links theoretical constructs (SSMR triggers) to observable behavioral markers (verbal cues, postural changes, head movements) and then to multimodal data traces. Whitehead [8] validated that MLLMs can reliably annotate posture from collaborative learning video (test-retest reliability M = 0.944), confirming technical feasibility. Our pipeline fuses: (1) CRF-based verbal trigger detection; (2) MLLM-based non-verbal feature extraction; and (3) a multimodal fusion layer combining both streams.

3 Research Questions

The following research questions guide this doctoral work:

RQ1: To what extent can verbal discourse features, processed using speaker diarization, ASR, and CRF-based machine learning, automatically identify SSMR triggers in ill-structured CPS environments?

RQ2: How can non-verbal behavioral features (i.e. posture and head movement extracted from video data) improve the accuracy of automated SSMR trigger identification when integrated with verbal discourse analysis?

RQ3: What are the key design considerations, including methodological, ethical, and practical factors, for developing a reliable and scalable multimodal system for detecting SSMR triggers in authentic CPS environments?

4 Methodology

4.1 Study Context, Participants, and Data

HCI22 (face-to-face) involved 15 first-year graduate students (9 PhD, 6 Master's; mean age = 25, SD = 1.77; 47% male) in a 12-week online HCI course, divided into four CPS teams of 3–4. Teams worked on an open-ended design challenge. Verbal interaction and video data were collected across all team sessions with informed consent.

4.2 Verbal Analysis Pipeline (Completed)

Speaker diarization (Pyannote) attributed turns to individuals; ASR (Whisper) generated manually validated English transcripts from multilingual audio (Hindi, Marathi, Telugu, English). A CRF model trained on theoretically grounded trigger criteria (Table 1) capturing lexical cues like 'I think,' 'we need to,' 'why' identified and segmented SSMR episodes using weak supervision. CRFs were chosen over LLMs for this task due to their sequential dependency modeling, feature integration (keywords, speaker changes, sentiment), and precision—LLMs tend to hallucinate or rephrase original discourse, which is unsuitable for contextual qualitative validation.

Table 1. The sample criteria derived from literature to identify triggers of SSMR episodes

Heading level	Example
What	**What** I have to do on the screen. Just give me a pen
Why	**Why** did you do that? Should I put the vlog in this?
I think	**I think** I have issues. I forgot also to ask before. That's how
I should	No, no. **I should** have gone to the cultural one too
We need to	So, first **we need to** define the problem. We need to include the issue, not just work on it
We should	Yeah, for now **we should** keep it cool, later if we come again
Instead of	**Instead of** using the word reward, we should use something

4.3 Proposed Multimodal Analysis Pipeline

To address RQ2 and RQ3, the pipeline is extended with three stages: (1) Non-verbal feature extraction YOLOv8 crops individual participants per video frame; GPT-4o (via Azure OpenAI) classifies posture categories and head movement states per second using MLLM prompt engineering with a codebook-aligned coding scheme [8]; (2) Temporal alignment and fusion non-verbal features are aligned with verbal trigger windows by participant-level timestamp and fused via late fusion (ensemble ML) and early fusion (feature concatenation into CRF/transformer); (3) Validation SSMR trigger identifications are validated against expert human annotations (Cohen's Kappa), with accuracy compared directly against the 56% verbal baseline. Ethical safeguards mirror Whitehead [8]: privacy-preserving API settings, restricted data access, and bias-aware codebook design.

5 Preliminary Findings

The CRF model analyzed 21,256 turns across four teams, identifying 1,396 SSMR triggers (Table 2).

Table 2. Number of Triggers of SSMR Episodes Identified by ML Model in Each Team

Team	Number of Turns Analyzed	Episodes	Total Number of Turns Involved in Identified Episodes
Team 1	6481	387	5539
Team 2	3769	350	3231
Team 3	7667	422	6854
Team 4	3339	237	2878
Total	21256	1396	18502

Manual validation of a 25% random sample yielded 56% accuracy above chance and confirming sensitivity to the trigger criteria, but clearly limited by the unimodal verbal signal. Speaker diarization reliably attributed turns in most sessions. These results establish a meaningful baseline and directly motivate the multimodal extension.

6 Proposed Multimodal Analysis: Design and Rationale

The 56% verbal-only accuracy reflects a fundamental limitation: lexical cues alone cannot reliably distinguish SSMR-relevant moments from routine conversation. Non-verbal signals postural shifts, leaning forward, head orientation toward teammates are temporally correlated with regulatory transitions [4, 6] and can disambiguate genuine SSMR moments. The MLLM-based posture annotation validated by Whitehead [8] (test-retest M = 0.944; substantial inter-rater agreement for key categories) confirms scalable extraction is feasible.

The non-verbal feature set for fusion will include: posture categories (sitting, leaning forward, engaged with peripherals, arms resting on table); hand indicators (hands near face, task-object manipulation); and head movement features (nodding, head direction relative to screen/teammates). Two fusion strategies will be evaluated: late fusion (combining CRF verbal predictions with MLLM non-verbal predictions via weighted ensemble) and early fusion (concatenating feature vectors at turn level for a unified BiLSTM-CRF or transformer classifier). Both will be benchmarked against the verbal-only baseline to quantify accuracy gains.

7 Expected Contributions and Impact

7.1 Contributions to Learning Sciences

This doctoral work makes several contributions to the Learning Sciences. First, it advances the empirical understanding of SSMR triggers in authentic ill-structured CPS by providing the first large-scale automated analysis of trigger occurrence patterns across teams. The identified trigger profiles which verbal and behavioral markers co-occur at regulatory moments will enrich theoretical models of SSMR, particularly regarding the conditions under which groups transition into shared metacognitive activity. Second, by demonstrating that non-verbal behavioral cues complement verbal triggers in identifying regulatory moments, the work contributes to a more holistic understanding of SSMR as an embodied, multimodal process not merely a linguistic one.

7.2 Contributions to Computer Science and AIED

From a technical standpoint, this work contributes a validated multimodal pipeline for SSMR trigger detection, integrating speaker diarization, ASR, CRF-based sequence labeling, and MLLM-based non-verbal feature extraction. This pipeline is modular, scalable, and designed for deployment in real-world educational settings a significant advance over manual or lab-constrained approaches. The demonstrated application of MLLMs for educationally relevant non-verbal feature extraction extends the methodological toolkit available to the MMLA community. The work also generates design guidelines for multimodal AIED systems that operate on authentic, noisy, and multilingual data knowledge that is directly transferable to broader AIED system development.

8 Limitations, Scalability, and Generalizability

The primary limitations of the current work are: (1) small dataset (4 teams, 15 students, single institution, single course); (2) verbal-only detection with known false-positive risk for planning talk; (3) validation on a 25% sample rather than full expert annotation. Plans to address these in the doctoral work include: expanding data collection to HCI23 (in progress, 4–6 additional teams) and to a second course context to test cross-context generalizability; developing a full expert-annotated gold standard on at least one team's complete data to enable rigorous comparison; and releasing the codebook and anonymized dataset to support replication. The pipeline's modular design (diarization $\rightarrow$ ASR $\rightarrow$ CRF/transformer $\rightarrow$ MLLM fusion) is inherently scalable to larger datasets without architectural changes.

References

1. Hadwin, A., Järvelä, S., Miller, M.: Self-regulation, co-regulation, and shared regulation in collaborative learning environments. In: Handbook of Self-regulation of Learning and Performance, pp. 83–106. Routledge, New York (2017)
2. Vauras, M., Volet, S., Iiskala, T.: Socially-shared metacognitive regulation in collaborative science learning. In: Trends and Prospects in Metacognition Research across the Life Span: A Tribute to Anastasia Efklides, pp. 83–102. Springer, Heidelberg (2021). https://doi.org/10.1007/978-3-030-51673-4_5
3. Järvelä, S., Järvenoja, H., Malmberg, J., Hadwin, A.F.: Exploring socially shared regulation in the context of collaboration. J. Cogn. Educ. Psychol. **12**(3), 267–286 (2013)
4. Sobocinski, M., Malmberg, J., Järvelä, S.: Exploring adaptation in socially-shared regulation of learning using video and heart rate data. Technol. Knowl. Learn. **27**(2), 385–404 (2022); Automating the Identification of Triggers of SSMR in CPS 51
5. Pugh, S.L., Rao, A., Stewart, A.E.B., D'Mello, S.K.: Do speech-based collaboration analytics generalize across task contexts? In: LAK22: 12th International Learning Analytics and Knowledge Conference, pp. 208–218 (2022)
6. Radu, I., Tu, E., Schneider, B.: Relationships between body postures and collaborative learning states in an augmented reality study. In: Bittencourt, I., Cukurova, M., Muldner, K., Luckin, R., Millán, E. (eds.) AIED 2020. LNCS, vol. 12164. Springer, Cham (2020). https://doi.org/10.1007/978-3-030-52240-7_47
7. Ochoa, X.: Multimodal learning analytics: Rationale, process, examples, and direction. In: Handbook of Learning Analytics, 2nd ed., pp. 54–65. SoLAR (2022)
8. Whitehead, R., Nguyen, A., Järvelä, S.: Utilizing multimodal large language models for video analysis of posture in studying collaborative learning: a case study. J. Learn. Analy. **12**(1), 186–200 (2025)

From Assessment to Tutoring: Evidence-Led Faithfulness for Goal-Oriented Singing Practice

Tengteng Cheng and Zitao Liu(✉)

Guangdong Institute of Smart Education, Jinan University, Guangzhou, China
chengt19980421@stu2024.jnu.edu.cn, liuzitao@jnu.edu.cn

Abstract. Singing practice for beginners is driven by many goals, such as pitch accuracy, vocal stability, and expressive control. It also changes across stages, from warm-up drills to phrase practice and full song performance, so tutoring feedback needs to shift in focus and detail over time. Recent audio and language models can generate critiques for singing performance, but these critiques are not always accurate and may not be effectively supported by the input audio. This paper studies evidence-led faithfulness for singing tutoring, where feedback stays tied to verifiable acoustic evidence and remains consistent across repeated attempts. We introduce an Evidence Ledger that stores a persistent state of key evidence and intermediate judgments, and we use a faithfulness contract that requires each diagnosis and recommendation to cite ledger entries. We then outline an evaluation plan with counterfactual faithfulness tests, robustness analysis under timbre shift, and a minimal causal study to test whether evidence-constrained feedback leads to measurable short-horizon improvement on the same practice goal.

Keywords: Singing tutoring · Faithfulness · Evidence grounding · Multi-agent systems · Singing assessment

1 Motivation for Research

Singing is a natural entry point to music learning, yet effective practice is hard for beginners. A novice singer often needs to manage several targets at once, including pitch accuracy, stability, timing, and basic technique. These targets also evolve during practice. Early stages benefit from simple drills and coarse feedback, while later stages require more focused guidance at the phrase level and more holistic feedback at the song level. Although automated assessment can provide practical value in education, singing practice requires a tutor that supports stage-wise practice and repeated attempts [6,8].

Recent cross-modal audio-language models support joint modeling of acoustic signals and text, and many systems can therefore judge performance and generate natural language feedback [5]. This is useful, but it creates a key reliability risk. A critique can sound clear and consistent, while still being weakly

E. G. Blanchard et al. (Eds.): AIED 2026, CCIS 3033, pp. 450–455, 2026.
https://doi.org/10.1007/978-3-032-29794-5_70

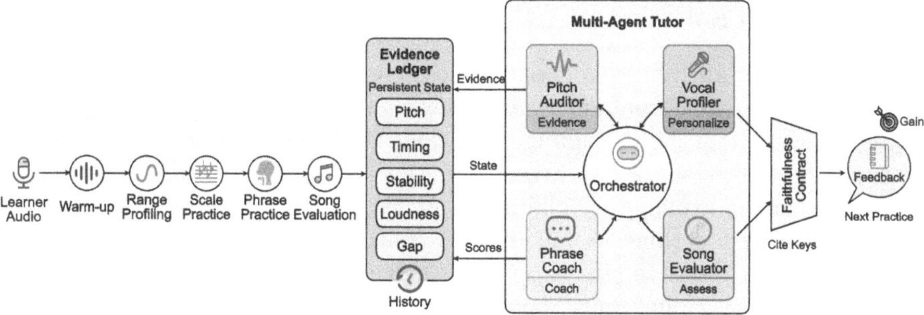

Fig. 1. Stage-wise singing tutoring as an evidence-to-action loop. A persistent Evidence Ledger stores verifiable acoustic evidence across attempts, and a faithfulness contract requires each diagnosis and recommendation to cite ledger keys before feedback is shown.

supported by the input audio [3,9]. When this happens, the tutor may suggest the wrong next practice, or it may focus on the wrong problem. In tutoring, this is more than a reporting issue. It can change the learner's actions, which can slow progress or even build bad habits. For this reason, we focus on evidence-led faithfulness. We define it as a property of tutoring feedback where each diagnostic claim can be traced back to verifiable acoustic evidence, and where the feedback stays stable under small changes in wording but changes when the underlying evidence changes.

Figure 1 summarizes the stage-wise tutoring loop. Building on our prior stage-wise multi-agent tutor for singing practice, we focus here on making tutoring feedback explicitly traceable to evidence. Rather than redesigning the tutoring architecture, we study how evidence should be represented, cited, and used in tutoring decisions. We therefore study three linked questions: how to represent persistent and verifiable evidence from learner audio, how to constrain diagnoses and recommendations so that they remain traceable to that evidence, and whether such constraints improve robustness and short-horizon learning. This shifts the focus from fluent critique generation to evidence-led, traceable tutoring decisions.

2 Proposed Solution and Practical Concerns

Our solution is designed around a simple principle. Tutoring should be driven by evidence that can be checked rather than by free-form critiques that only sound plausible, consistent with recent work on structured, task-aligned signals in other domains [2]. To support this principle, we propose an evidence-led tutoring loop with two main elements, a persistent Evidence Ledger and a faithfulness contract. The ledger acts as the shared state that accumulates verifiable acoustic evidence across attempts. The contract acts as a gate that constrains what the system can claim and what it can recommend.

2.1 Proposed Solution

The core state is an Evidence Ledger whose entries are structured as key-value tuples with unit, scope, confidence, and provenance. In the current design, entries may encode pitch stability, timing deviation, loudness, goal gap, and attempt history. The ledger supports three claim types: diagnostic claims about current performance, explanatory claims about likely causes, and recommendation claims about next actions. A faithfulness contract requires each diagnostic or recommendation claim to cite supporting ledger entries. When the evidence is weak, explanatory claims must be framed as tentative rather than definitive. Unsupported claims are removed, softened, or converted into requests for additional evidence. The multi-agent tutor reads from and writes to this ledger, while the Orchestrator uses the current evidence state to decide what to practice next, what to correct now, and when to advance, retry, or roll back. This design is also consistent with recent work showing that intermediate step-level signals can guide multi-step reasoning more effectively than relying only on final outcomes [7].

2.2 Practical Concerns

Although an evidence-led design is appealing, it raises practical concerns that matter in real tutoring settings. First, the quality of tutoring depends on the quality of the underlying evidence. If the pitch backend makes octave or voicing errors, or if timing estimates shift under different recording conditions, the ledger may store misleading signals and propagate them into downstream routing and feedback. This is especially relevant under timbre shift, where unusual vocal tone or synthetic-like signals can break assumptions of standard pitch extraction. A reliable tutor should therefore not treat all extracted evidence as equally trustworthy, but should attach confidence to the evidence state and allow the system to request another attempt or a more controlled rendition when the signal is unstable.

Second, a strict faithfulness contract may make feedback too cautious. If the system rejects too many claims, it may produce vague advice or repeatedly ask for more evidence, which can frustrate learners and reduce motivation. Third, the right level of evidence granularity is not obvious. Fine-grained evidence can support precise diagnosis, but it can also make feedback harder to act on and the overall system less stable. Coarser evidence is easier to communicate, yet it may hide the cause of a problem. For this reason, the ledger must balance diagnostic precision, stability, and usability, rather than maximizing detail alone.

These concerns are pedagogical as well as technical. Evidence-based feedback mainly focuses learner attention on the dimensions that the system can track, such as pitch and timing, and may give less attention to broader musical expression and self-monitoring. We therefore view the tutor as a support tool rather than a replacement for human teachers, especially because higher-level musical judgment cannot be fully captured from acoustic evidence alone. Finally, deployment must also respect privacy and usability constraints, because audio recordings may be sensitive and classroom devices and network conditions can vary. For these reasons, our evaluation plan will examine uncertainty handling, safe fallback behavior, and human-facing usefulness alongside faithfulness itself.

3 Research Questions

We study faithful singing tutoring as an evidence-to-action problem in which acoustic evidence must support both what the tutor says and what it asks the learner to do next. This perspective raises three linked questions: whether diagnoses and recommendations are genuinely supported by evidence, whether evidence-driven decisions remain reliable under variation, and whether tighter evidence grounding leads to measurable short-horizon improvement in practice.

Context and Current Status. Building on prior stage-wise singing tutoring work, we focus on three open questions. First, improved prediction and critique consistency do not guarantee that individual diagnoses and recommendations are truly supported by acoustic evidence derived from learner audio. Second, even if feedback is tied to evidence, errors in the evidence state under timbre shift and other non-target variation may still distort downstream tutoring decisions. Third, it remains unclear whether making feedback more tightly grounded in acoustic evidence leads to measurable short-horizon improvement in practice. These questions motivate our study of faithfulness, reliability, and learning efficacy.

RQ1 (Faithfulness): How can we ensure that individual diagnoses and recommendations are genuinely supported by acoustic evidence derived from learner audio? We hypothesize that faithful tutoring requires both explicit evidence citation and explicit control over unsupported content. We will therefore examine whether citation constraints improve claim traceability and whether unsupported claims can be reliably filtered, softened, or revised before feedback is shown to the learner.

RQ2 (Reliability): How can we make evidence-driven tutoring decisions robust to errors in the evidence state, especially under timbre shift and other non-target variation? We hypothesize that reliability depends on uncertainty-aware evidence modeling and conservative decision rules rather than treating all extracted signals as equally trustworthy. We will therefore test whether confidence-annotated evidence states and safe fallback actions reduce routing instability and limit the propagation of evidence errors into feedback and next-step recommendations.

RQ3 (Learning Efficacy): Does feedback that is more tightly grounded in acoustic evidence lead to measurable short-horizon improvement on the same practice goal? Here, acoustic evidence provides the basis for feedback, while faithfulness constraints determine how tightly diagnoses and recommendations are tied to that evidence. We focus on adjacent attempts on the same phrase because this design keeps the practice goal fixed and makes the effect of evidence-grounded feedback easier to observe.

4 Evaluation Plan

Datasets and Evidence Extraction. We will use controlled singing recordings from VocalSet [10] and task-oriented evaluation data from recent multimodal singing assessment work, including the Sing-MD dataset and VocalVerse [9]. Because claim traceability is meaningful only when the underlying evidence is sufficiently reliable, we will first validate the core evidence extractors, especially pitch-related cues, against benchmark references and, where necessary, expert judgments [1]. Pitch-related evidence will then be extracted with a robust pitch tracker such as CREPE [4], together with additional checks for octave and voicing failures. This validation step is especially important under timbre shift, where non-target variation can distort the evidence state and mislead downstream tutoring decisions.

Protocol A: Counterfactual Faithfulness Tests (RQ1). We will construct controlled perturbations and compare feedback before and after the perturbation. We use two complementary interventions: (i) evidence-level edits that directly modify selected evidence entries, and (ii) audio-level edits (small pitch shift or mild time-stretch) that change evidence through the extractor. We will report three metrics. The first is citation coverage, defined as the share of diagnostic and recommendation claims that cite evidence keys. The second is directional sensitivity, which tests whether changed evidence yields changed recommendations in the expected direction. The third is unsupported-claim rate, estimated through human judgment on a sampled subset. We will also examine how unsupported claims are handled, including whether they are filtered, softened, or revised into evidence-seeking feedback before being shown to the learner. Explanatory claims will be evaluated together with their uncertainty markers.

Protocol B: Policy Reliability Under Variation (RQ2). We treat the tutor as an action policy conditioned on confidence-annotated evidence states, and record routing decisions, selected practice types, and focus dimensions. We test stability under minor prompt paraphrases and non-target audio variation, and measure safe fallback rate, defined as the frequency with which the system requests additional evidence when inputs are unreliable. For ablations, we compare: no persistent state, persistent state only, and persistent state plus citation constraints. We also draw inspiration from evidence-table style orchestration used in music generation and editing systems [11], while adapting the idea to tutoring actions.

Protocol C: Short-Horizon Learning Study (RQ3). We propose a within-subject cross-over design at the phrase level. Each participant practices the same phrase under two conditions in randomized order: evidence-accountable feedback with evidence citations, and unconstrained feedback with the same surface format but without a citation rule. Primary outcomes are evidence-level improvements from attempt 1 to attempt 2 (pitch stability, off-pitch frame ratio, timing deviation), computed from the same extraction pipeline [4]. Secondary outcomes are short self-reports on perceived usefulness, effort, and calibrated trust.

5 Expected Contributions and Roadmap

This work contributes a compact path toward faithful AI music tutoring through a persistent evidence state, an evidence-conditioned view of tutoring actions, and an evaluation suite spanning faithfulness, reliability, and short-horizon learning. In the near term, we will finalize the evidence schema and complete Protocols A–C.

References

1. Alanko, A.J., Nie, P., Wang, C., Du, B., Tao, S., Tervaniemi, M.: Developing and testing an analysis system to assess singing-pitch accuracy of Chinese children. J. New Music Res. **54**, 34–46 (2025)
2. Chen, Z., Liu, T., Tong, Q., Tian, M., Luo, W., Liu, Z.: Advancing mathematical reasoning in language models: the impact of problem-solving data, data synthesis methods, and training stages. In: Proceedings of the Thirteenth International Conference on Learning Representations. Singapore (April 2025)
3. Ji, Z., et al.: Survey of hallucination in natural language generation. ACM Comput. Surv. **55**, 1–38 (2023)
4. Kim, J.W., Salamon, J., Li, P., Bello, J.P.: CREPE: a convolutional representation for pitch estimation. In: Proceedings of the 2018 IEEE International Conference on Acoustics, Speech and Signal Processing. Calgary, AB, Canada (April 2018)
5. Li, H., Ding, W., Kang, Y., Liu, T., Wu, Z., Liu, Z.: CTAL: pre-training cross-modal transformer for audio-and-language representations. In: Proceedings of the 2021 Conference on Empirical Methods in Natural Language Processing. Online and Punta Cana, Dominican Republic (November 2021)
6. Liu, Z., et al.: Dolphin: a spoken language proficiency assessment system for elementary education. In: Proceedings of The Web Conference 2020, Taipei, Taiwan (April 2020)
7. Ma, Y., et al.: What are step-level reward models rewarding? counterintuitive findings from mcts-boosted mathematical reasoning. In: Proceedings of the 39th Annual AAAI Conference on Artificial Intelligence, Philadelphia, PA, USA (February 2025)
8. Piao, Z., Xia, G.: Sensing the breath: a multimodal singing tutoring interface with breath guidance. In: Proceedings of the International Conference on New Interfaces for Musical Expression, Auckland, New Zealand (June 2022)
9. Wang, Z., et al.: Singing timbre popularity assessment based on multimodal large foundation model. In: Proceedings of the 33rd ACM International Conference on Multimedia, Dublin, Ireland (October 2025)
10. Wilkins, J., Seetharaman, P., Wahl, A., Pardo, B.: VocalSet: a singing voice dataset. In: Proceedings of the 19th International Society for Music Information Retrieval Conference, Paris, France (September 2018)
11. Zhang, Y., Maezawa, A., Xia, G., Yamamoto, K., Dixon, S.: Loop copilot: conducting AI ensembles for music generation and iterative editing. arXiv preprint arXiv:2310.12404 (2023)

A Case Study with an Intelligent Tutoring System for Active Study of Worked Examples in Introductory JAVA Programming

Arun Balajiee Lekshmi Narayanan(✉), Mohammad Hassany, Rully Hendrawan, Kamil Akhuseyinoglu, and Peter Brusilovsky

School of Computing and Information, University of Pittsburgh, Pittsburgh, USA
arl122@pitt.edu

Abstract. Worked examples are step-by-step solutions to problems in a specific domain, offered to students to acquire domain-specific problem-solving skills. We could magnify the power of worked examples by combining them with self-explanations, a strategy in which students explain each problem-solving step rather than passively studying it. In this work, we improve an existing system for automatically assessing student explanations to support the active study of worked examples. In particular, we use LLMs to address the limitations of semantic similarity methods for automatically assessing student explanations. We compare several methods based on semantic similarity with directly prompting LLMs. We showed that LLMs achieve an F1 score of 0.98, outperforming all semantic similarity baselines (F1 = 0.94). Our proposed work will improve the automated assessment and evaluate the system in a user study.

Keywords: Programming · Self–Explanations · Evaluation · Feedback · LLMs

1 Introduction

In the domain of programming, worked examples (WE) are offered as "explained code" where the lines or fragments of a program (code) solving a problem are augmented with expert explanations [2,9]. Although these interactive tools demonstrated their positive impact on learning in several studies [2,7], reading or listening is classified as *passive learning*, which is not the most efficient way to learn. Summarizing multiple years of learning science research, ICAP framework [5] argues that active learning promotes greater comprehension than passive learning. Several researchers demonstrate the critical role that self-explanations (active reflections on the content students process during learning) play in making passive learning more active [3,19].

Oli and Colleagues [15] comprehensively evaluated different LLM-based approaches for assessing students' line-by-line explanations of code. Denny and

E. G. Blanchard et al. (Eds.): AIED 2026, CCIS 3033, pp. 456–461, 2026.
https://doi.org/10.1007/978-3-032-29794-5_71

colleagues [6] use code explanations as a technique to evaluate code understanding and writing skills. In our work, in addition to assessment, we also focus on improving code comprehension skills [17] with a focus on enhancing the process of reading worked examples itself in the context of reading worked examples.

So, our primary research question is the following: *How can we automate the assessment of student explanations using LLMs and integrate the implementation into a system for active study of worked examples*?

2 Preliminary Findings

2.1 Dataset

To answer our research question, our first step was to use the recently released SelfCode2.0 dataset [4], which included explanations produced by 60 students and 2 experts for individual lines of four code examples. In the dataset, each student's explanation is labeled by annotators as correct or incorrect. In total, the dataset included 3019 pairs of student and expert explanations for the same code lines. For our study, we used a subset of these pairs (1854 out of 3019) in which both a student and an expert explained the line using a single statement. This selection was made to facilitate the exploration of modern semantic-similarity approaches that focus on complete sentences. In these 1854 pairs, 1794 student explanations were labeled as correct (positive examples) and 60 as incorrect negative examples.

2.2 Method

Large Language Model (LLM) Based Evaluation Approaches. Our LLM-based approaches for evaluating student explanations are based on treating an LLM as an "oracle" that directly predicts the *correctness* of student explanations. We prompt the LLM with the context that included the problem statement of the explained WE, the code line to explain along with the line number, and the associated student explanations from the data set (Fig. 1). In all prompts, we use the same section headings in capital letters, such as "PROGRAM DESCRIPTION", "LINE NUMBER" and so on (Fig. 1). We use the prompts with GPT-3.5-Turbo-16k for the automated assessment task. We define correctness in the prompt by focusing on the behavior-based approach to explain a code line, i.e., the result of executing this line.

Semantic Similarity Based Evaluation Approaches. We use the original Deep-Tutor (DT) toolkit that adopted the algorithm described to evaluate correctness in the DT-GRADE corpus [1] and was use in process of data collection of our dataset [4]. The method generates similarity scores using Support Vector Regression with a feature set combining SentenceBERT and DeepTutor similarity scores [18]. To assess student explanations as correct or incorrect, this approach employs a decision threshold. We iterated over a range of thresholds from 0 to 1 with a step size of 0.05 and selected the threshold that achieved the

```
Determine the correctness of the student's explanation based on a given source code, specific line number.

"Correctness" A correct STUDENT EXPLANATION explains the code behavior using the code syntax.
ONLY set "Correctness". DO NOT PROVIDE REASON.
PROGRAM DESCRIPTION
{program desc}
SOURCE CODE
{source code}
LINE NUMBER
{line num}
STUDENT EXPLANATION
{student explanation}
CODE
{line content}
Correctness:
```

Fig. 1. Prompting LLM to evaluate students' explanations. "OR" notation is used in this to indicate only one of the 3 possibilities were used to define "Correctness" to the model.

best F1 score, a harmonic mean of precision and recall. We determined that the optimal threshold for Deep Tutor is 0.2 to obtain correctness predictions with the optimal F1 score.

2.3 Results

In this analysis, we compare each approach with the label (correct/incorrect) assigned by the annotators to that pair in the dataset. For each approach, we calculated the True Positives (TP), False Positives (FP), False Negatives (FN), and True Negatives (TN). TP cases are those in which students write correct explanations, and the evaluation algorithm judges them as correct. FN cases are those in which the student's answers are accurate, but the algorithm judges them as incorrect. Using these key parameters, we generate F1 and accuracy scores (see Table 1). As the data shows, the LLM-Behavior prompting emerges as the clear winner with the best F1.

Table 1. Comparing All Methods on Correctness for Top & Bottom Similar Students Separated using METEOR similarity scores between expert and student explanations

	F1	Acc	TP	FP	FN	TN
Deep Tutor	0.94	0.89	1619	37	175	23
LLM-Behavior	0.98	0.96	1774	46	20	14

3 System Implementation

The original system provides students with the option to adaptively and selectively navigate the code in worked examples, line by line, and read expert-provided explanations for those lines. Our preliminary results showed that we could replace a semantic similarity method with an LLM-powered automated assessment.

We will deploy the Example Study with Self-Explanations (ESSE) system in a semester-long course hosted on MasteryGrids [10]. Students will work through an in-class activity using the tool to learn programming by practising the active study of worked examples with self-explanations. The integrated "LLM-as-a-Judge" [8] paradigm evaluates student explanations for correctness and completeness, without ground-truth expert explanations (see Fig. 2).

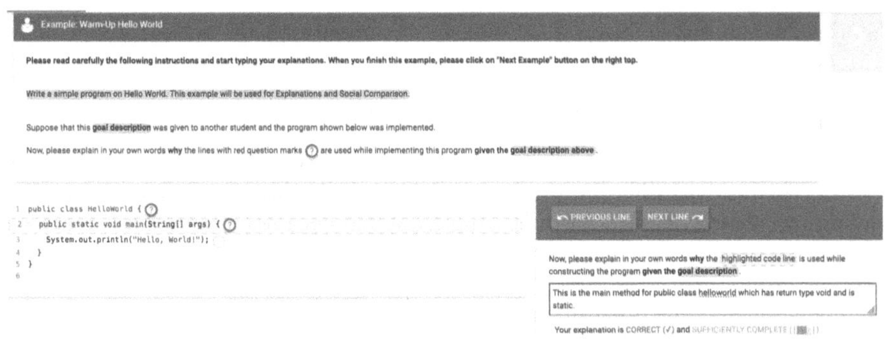

Fig. 2. ESSE accepts a student explanations by providing feedback to the student (green) (Color figure online)

4 User Study

With the instructor's permission, we will ask students to practice using ESSE during a lab recitation rather than regular instructor-created homework. ESSE will include four intermediate-level Java programming examples for students to explain, covering topics such as conditions, loops, and object-oriented programming. Participants will be students enrolled in an CS1 JAVA programming course at a large US-based university. We will provide incentives for participating students to earn extra credit. The ESSE system will log student interactions in a database which we will use to measure the changes in quality of student expalanations to address our research questions.

5 Expected Contributions

We expect this work to yield a few indicators to further explore the already established connections between student explanations and program comprehension [3,19]. Firstly, the work will highlight the use of automated approaches that differentiate student explanations from instructor expectations, presenting a diversity of explanations that can be provided for a particular line of code. Secondly, the work will provide further evidence of the effectiveness of students' learning through writing explanations. As they read more code and actively explain their code comprehension and writing skills may improve [11]. To the best of our knowledge, no current work enhances the use of existing AI tools with interfaces that promote critical thinking for code comprehension and code writing skills using self–explanations as mechanism for reflection. Next, general experiments on sense-making used step–wise self–explanations [14,16] to promote code comprehension. So, our experiments with a line–level self–explanation assessement system will provide additional support to existing theories and insights into the mechanism for learning with self–explanations. Finally, theories on self–explanation [12] suggest 3 dimensions for self–explanations – bridging, paraphrasing and elaboration – which can be tested and applied flexible using our tool unlike existing available AI tools. When students are allowed to work with free–text AI tools and LLMs, instructors leave a lot of agency with the learner [13]. Students learning with AI tools could instead be scaffolded by offering them with different methods to learn with interfaces like ours, while leaving the choice of the tool in the hands of the learner.

Acknowledgments. This work is partially supported by PreDoctoral Fellowship from the Intelligent Systems Program and NSF Awards 1822842 & 1822816.

References

1. Banjade, R., Maharjan, N., Niraula, N.B., Gautam, D., Samei, B., Rus, V.: Evaluation dataset (dt-grade) and word weighting approach towards constructed short answers assessment in tutorial dialogue context. In: Proceedings of the 11th Workshop on Innovative Use of NLP for Building Educational Applications, pp. 182–187 (2016)
2. Brusilovsky, P., Hsiao, I.H., Yudelson, M.: Annotated program examples as first class objects in an educational digital library. In: Joint Conference on Digital Libraries, JCDL 2008, pp. 337–340 (2008)
3. Caughey, M., Muldner, K.: Investigating the utility of self-explanation through translation activities with a code-tracing tutor. In: International Conference on Artificial Intelligence in Education, pp. 66–77. Springer (2023). https://doi.org/10.1007/978-3-031-36272-9_6
4. Chapagain, J., Narayanan, A.B.L., Akhuseyinoglu, K., Brusilovsky, P., Rus, V.: Selfcode 2.0: an annotated corpus of student and expert line-by-line explanations of code examples for automated assessment. The International FLAIRS Conference Proceedings, vol. 38(1) (May 2025). https://doi.org/10.32473/flairs.38.1.138727, https://journals.flvc.org/FLAIRS/article/view/138727
5. Chi, M.T., Wylie, R.: The icap framework: linking cognitive engagement to active learning outcomes. Educ. Psychol. **49**(4), 219–243 (2014)
6. Denny, P., Smith IV, D.H., Fowler, M., Prather, J., Becker, B.A., Leinonen, J.: Explaining code with a purpose: An integrated approach for developing code comprehension and prompting skills. arXiv preprint arXiv:2403.06050 (2024)
7. Hosseini, R., et al.: Improving engagement in program construction examples for learning python programming. Int. J. Artif. Intell. Educ. **30**(2), 299–336 (2020)

8. Li, D., et al.: From generation to judgment: Opportunities and challenges of llm-as-a-judge. In: Proceedings of the 2025 Conference on Empirical Methods in Natural Language Processing, pp. 2757–2791 (2025)
9. Linn, M.: Can experts' explanations help students develop program design skills. Inter. J. Man-Mach. Stud. **36**, 511–551 (1992)
10. Loboda, T.D., Guerra, J., Hosseini, R., Brusilovsky, P.: Mastery grids: an open-source social educational progress visualization. In: Proceedings of the 2014 Conference on Innovation & Technology in Computer Science Education, pp. 357–357 (2014)
11. Lopez, M., Whalley, J., Robbins, P., Lister, R.: Relationships between reading, tracing and writing skills in introductory programming. In: Proceedings of the Fourth International Workshop on Computing Education Research, pp. 101–112 (2008)
12. McNamara, D.S., Newton, N., Christhilf, K., McCarthy, K.S., Magliano, J.P., Allen, L.K.: Anchoring your bridge: the importance of paraphrasing to inference making in self-explanations. Discourse Process. **60**(4–5), 337–362 (2023)
13. Nieto-Cardenas, J., Kramer, E.J., Kurto, P., Dickey, E., Bejarano, A.: Owlgorithm: supporting self-regulated learning in competitive programming through llm-driven reflection. In: Proceedings of the 57th ACM Technical Symposium on Computer Science Education, vol. 1, pp. 757–763 (2026)
14. Oli, P., Banjade, R., Chapagain, J., Rus, V.: Automated assessment of students' code comprehension using llms. arXiv preprint arXiv:2401.05399 (2023)
15. Oli, P., Banjade, R., Chapagain, J., Rus, V.: Automated assessment of students' code comprehension using llm. In: Ananda, M., et al. (eds.) Proceedings of the 2024 AAAI Conference on Artificial Intelligence. Proceedings of Machine Learning Research, 26–27 Feb, vol. 257, pp. 118–128. PMLR (2024), https://proceedings.mlr.press/v257/oli24a.html
16. Oli, P., et al.: Improving code comprehension through scaffolded self-explanations. In: International Conference on Artificial Intelligence in Education. pp. 478–483. Springer (2023). https://doi.org/10.1007/978-3-031-36336-8_74
17. Oli, P., Banjade, R., Narayanan, A.B.L., Brusilovsky, P., Rus, V.: When is reading more effective than tutoring? an analysis through the lens of students' self-efficacy among novices in computer science. Grantee Submission (2023)
18. Rus, V., D'Mello, S., Hu, X., Graesser, A.: Recent advances in conversational intelligent tutoring systems. AI Mag. **34**(3), 42–54 (2013)
19. Shareghi Najar, A., Mitrovic, A.: Examples and tutored problems: how can self-explanation make a difference to learning? In: Lane, H.C., Yacef, K., Mostow, J., Pavlik, P. (eds.) AIED 2013. LNCS (LNAI), vol. 7926, pp. 339–348. Springer, Heidelberg (2013). https://doi.org/10.1007/978-3-642-39112-5_35

Comparing Multimodal Learning Analytics Pipelines and Multimodal Large Language Models for Detecting Collaborative Engagement in Science Simulations

Chris Palaguachi(✉)

University of Illinois Urbana-Champaign, Urbana, IL 61820, USA
cwp5@illinois.edu

Abstract. Collaborative engagement in immersive science simulations emerges through intertwined verbal, behavioral, and regulatory processes. Multimodal learning analytics (MMLA) has enabled fine-grained modeling of these processes through engineered features and supervised pipelines, but such approaches are technically demanding, context-sensitive, and difficult to scale. Advances in multimodal large language models (MLLMs) offer an alternative paradigm, enabling prompt-guided semantic interpretation across modalities without task-specific feature engineering. However, systematic comparisons between these paradigms under shared theoretical constructs remain limited. This dissertation proposes a comparative benchmarking framework to evaluate MMLA pipelines and MLLM-based approaches for detecting collaborative initiative, awareness, breakdowns, and persistence regulation in HoloOrbits. The project will (1) develop a theory-grounded collaborative engagement codebook, (2) implement parallel analytic pipelines using shared datasets and constructs, and (3) evaluate tradeoffs in detection quality, robustness, interpretability, analytic agency, and scalability. By providing empirical evidence and methodological guidance, this work advances theory-aligned, trustworthy AI-driven collaboration analytics in AIED.

Keywords: Collaborative Problem-Solving · Multimodal Learning Analytics · Multimodal Large Language Models

1 Background and Motivation

Collaborative engagement is central to inquiry-based learning and long-term academic success [5]. Through science simulations, learners coordinate ideas, negotiate meaning, regulate frustration, and persist through difficulty while interacting with peers and digital tools. These processes unfold across discourse, gesture, posture, and task actions, making collaboration inherently multimodal. Multimodal Learning Analytics (MMLA) addresses this complexity by integrating

E. G. Blanchard et al. (Eds.): AIED 2026, CCIS 3033, pp. 462–467, 2026.
https://doi.org/10.1007/978-3-032-29794-5_72

heterogeneous data streams like logs, transcripts, and video to map theoretical constructs to observable indicators [1,4]. Through engineered features and supervised modeling, MMLA enables fine-grained detection of collaboration and regulation [2]. However, these pipelines require substantial feature engineering, preprocessing, and contextual tuning, limiting portability and interpretability [8]. Recent multimodal large language models (MLLMs) introduce an alternative paradigm based on prompt-guided semantic reasoning. When paired with structured codebooks, MLLMs have demonstrated reliable multimodal annotation without task-specific feature engineering [13,14]. However, there are limited benchmarks that compare the MMLA and MLLM approaches under shared constructs and validation protocols. This dissertation addresses this gap by implementing parallel pipelines for detecting collaborative engagement in HoloOrbits, evaluating tradeoffs in precision, interpretability, robustness, and scalability.

2 Research Goals

Acknowledging the methodological gap between feature-engineered MMLA pipelines and emerging MLLM approaches, this dissertation investigates how these paradigms compare in detecting collaborative engagement within immersive science simulations. Rather than treating MLLMs as incremental tools within existing pipelines, this work positions MMLA and MLLMs as distinct analytic approaches that must be evaluated under shared theoretical constructs and empirical conditions. Specifically, this study is guided by the following research questions:

- **RQ1:** How do feature-engineered MMLA pipelines and prompt-based MLLM coding approaches compare in detecting collaborative behaviors and persistence regulation in HoloOrbits?
- **RQ2:** How do MMLA and MLLM approaches differ in interpretability, auditability, and the distribution of analytic agency across stages of construct mapping, behavioral interpretation, and validation?
- **RQ3:** To what extent do the two paradigms differ in scalability, including human annotation demands, computational requirements, engineering effort, and portability to new learning contexts?

3 Related Work and State-of-the-Art

MMLA research has demonstrated that multimodal data can detect socially shared regulation, engagement, confusion, and collaboration quality by integrating discourse, gaze, posture, and log data [1,2,4]. These systems rely on structured construct mapping and engineered feature pipelines to estimate theoretically grounded behaviors. While precise, such approaches require extensive preprocessing and domain-specific tuning, limiting rapid deployment and generalization [9]. LLMs and MLLMs introduce prompt-based semantic coding. Prior work shows LLMs can support deductive discourse coding [12,14], and MLLMs can interpret visual inputs without task-specific training [13]. However, these models have primarily been used within existing pipelines rather than evaluated as alternative analytic paradigms. More work is needed to systematically compare MMLA and MLLM approaches under shared constructs. This dissertation takes a step in that direction.

4 Contributions and Impact

Unlike prior work that incorporates MLLMs within existing MMLA pipelines, this dissertation positions MMLA and MLLMs as distinct analytic paradigms and evaluates them under shared theoretical constructs and empirical conditions. Rather than asking whether MLLMs can assist feature extraction, this project investigates when, why, and under what constraints different analytic approaches are preferable for detecting collaborative engagement in digital learning environments [7]. Through a structured head-to-head comparison, this work advances the methodological foundations of AI-driven collaboration analytics in AIED. This dissertation makes three primary contributions. First, it develops and validates a unified, theory-grounded collaborative engagement codebook operationalizing constructs such as collaborative initiative, awareness, breakdown-related behaviors, and persistence regulation in digital learning environments, strengthening theoretical coherence across analytic approaches. Second, it introduces a systematic benchmarking framework comparing feature-engineered MMLA pipelines and prompt-based MLLM coding under identical datasets and validation protocols, extending evaluation beyond accuracy to include robustness, interpretability, analytic agency, and scalability. Third, it provides technical guidance for designing trustworthy, theory-aligned analytics pipelines by clarifying engineering tradeoffs in MMLA and advancing structured, codebook-based prompting strategies for MLLMs. The broader impact of this work lies in enabling scalable, interpretable, and theory-driven detection of collaborative engagement in digital learning environments. By clarifying the strengths and limitations of competing paradigms, this dissertation informs the design of adaptive collaboration supports and contributes to the development of transparent, evidence-based AI in education.

5 Methodology

5.1 Codebook Development and Validation

Before implementing the comparative benchmark, this dissertation will develop and validate a unified collaborative engagement codebook grounded in CSCL and persistence theory. This process begins with construct mapping, aligning theoretical definitions of collaborative initiative, collaborative awareness, breakdown-related behaviors (e.g., confusion and disagreement), and persistence regulation with observable multimodal indicators in the HoloOrbits environment found in previous collaborative problem solving literature [3,6,10]. For preliminary testing, a subset of collaborative sessions (20% of total video clips) will be selected for human annotation. Multiple trained coders will independently label temporally segmented interaction windows using the structured codebook. Inter-rater reliability will be assessed using Cohen's kappa and Krippendorff's alpha to ensure construct clarity and operational precision. This validation phase ensures that both analytic pipelines operate under identical theoretical constructs and provides a gold-standard dataset for subsequent benchmarking, supporting RQ1.

5.2 Parallel Analytic Pipeline Implementation

Following codebook validation, the dissertation will implement two parallel analytic pipelines using identical segmented data windows and evaluation splits.

Feature-Based MMLA Pipeline: The MMLA approach will involve temporal segmentation of multimodal data streams, engineered feature extraction across transcripts, simulation logs, and video-derived behavioral indicators, and supervised or sequential modeling to predict collaborative engagement constructs. Feature selection will align directly with the construct mapping stage to maintain theoretical coherence. Model performance will be evaluated using cross-validation and event-level detection metrics.

Prompt-Based MLLM Pipeline: The MLLM approach will convert each segmented interaction window into a structured multimodal prompt including transcript excerpts, salient log events, and selected visual summaries. Prompts will incorporate explicit codebook definitions and require structured JSON outputs. Deterministic configurations will reduce stochastic variation, and both zero-shot and few-shot settings will be examined to assess sensitivity to exemplar inclusion. By keeping segmentation strategies, datasets, and construct definitions constant, the study isolates differences attributable to the analytic paradigm rather than data variation, addressing RQ1 and RQ2.

5.3 Robustness and Interpretability Analysis

To evaluate robustness, both pipelines will be systematically stress-tested under analytic variations, including segmentation granularity, transcript noise, and input framing perturbations. For the MLLM pipeline, prompt rephrasing and contextual framing will be varied to assess sensitivity. These analyses address RQ2. Interpretability and analytic agency will be examined through feature importance transparency (MMLA) and rationale grounding (MLLM), alongside human audit sessions measuring the time and effort required to interpret and verify outputs. This stage examines how analytic control is distributed across construct mapping, behavioral interpretation, and confirmation, addressing RQ3.

5.4 Evaluation Metrics and Scalability Analysis

Detection performance will be evaluated using macro F1, event-level F1, confusion matrices, and calibration analysis. Scalability will be assessed through engineering effort, annotation demands, computational cost, and portability to new datasets, addressing RQ3 by quantifying human and computational trade-offs across paradigms. All studies will be conducted under IRB approval with appropriate consent procedures. Together, these analyses provide a structured comparison of MMLA and MLLM approaches for detecting collaborative engagement.

6 Current Status and Preliminary Results

Data collection within HoloOrbits is largely complete, and analytic pipeline development is well underway. We have begun human annotation of collaborative problem-solving behaviors with an initial focus on non-verbal indicators, including gaze, tool usage, gesture, and lean-in/lean-away behaviors. These annotations are aligned with collaborative constructs and serve as preliminary ground truth for benchmarking analyses.

On the MMLA side, multimodal feature extraction pipelines have been developed across audio, video, and log data. For video data, we have extracted facial action unit and pose estimation, with manuscripts submitted examining non-verbal collaborative indicators [11]. For audio and text data, recorded interactions have been transcribed using a combination of automated speech recognition and human verification. We have established natural language processing pipelines for topic modeling, sentiment analysis, and clustering of collaborative discourse. For log data, we have extracted collaborative initiative behaviors within HoloOrbits. For log data, we also conducted sequential pattern mining to model strategy usage and persistence behaviors in a different science simulation. Collectively, these pipelines provide a robust foundation for feature-engineered collaborative behavior detection.

On the MLLM side, we have conducted preliminary analyses using a subset of data consisting of one group and approximately twenty minutes of interaction with established non-verbal ground truth. Using a MLLM, we prompted the system to extract non-verbal collaborative behaviors directly from 360-degree video inputs. Initial findings are promising, particularly in detecting gaze direction, body orientation, and lean behaviors, suggesting that MLLMs may be viable codebook-aligned annotators in group settings.

At this stage, the pipeline for multimodal feature extraction is in place. The next phase involves expanding manual annotation to additional collaborative constructs, integrating lexical indicators of collaboration into the codebook, and systematically evaluating MLLMs as structured codebook annotators. During the upcoming semester, I will complete feature extraction across modalities and begin formal benchmarking between MMLA and MLLM pipelines.

Acknowledgments. The materials used in this study are based upon work supported by the National Science Foundation and Institute of Education Sciences under Grant 2229612.

References

1. Blikstein, P., Worsley, M.: Multimodal learning analytics and education data mining: using computational technologies to measure complex learning tasks. J. Learn. Analy. **3**(2), 220–238 (2016)
2. Cukurova, M., Giannakos, M., Martinez-Maldonado, R.: The promise and challenges of multimodal learning analytics. Br. J. Edu. Technol. **51**(5), 1441–1449 (2020)
3. Dey, I., Ko, M.L.M., Puntambekar, S.: Visualizing collaboration using multiple modalities. In: Proceedings of the 18th International Conference on Computer-Supported Collaborative Learning-CSCL 2025, pp. 664-666. International Society of the Learning Sciences (2025)
4. Di Mitri, D., Schneider, J., Specht, M., Drachsler, H.: From signals to knowledge: a conceptual model for multimodal learning analytics. J. Comput. Assist. Learn. **34**(4), 338–349 (2018)
5. Dillenbourg, P.: Collaborative learning: cognitive and computational approaches. Advances in learning and instruction series. ERIC (1999)
6. Fonteles, J.H., et al.: Analyzing embodied learning in classroom settings: a human-in-the-loop ai approach for multimodal learning analytics. Learn. Instruct. **103**, 102274 (2026)
7. Hur, P., et al.: A framework for considering exploration, interpretation, and confirmation during data analysis: Computationally assisted analysis of teacher-group interactions. J. Educ. Data Mining **18**(1), 180–207 (2026)
8. Martinez-Maldonado, R., et al.: Lessons learnt from a multimodal learning analytics deployment in-the-wild. ACM Trans. Comput,-Hum. Interact. **31**(1), 1–41 (2023)
9. Radu, I., Tu, E., Schneider, B.: Relationships between body postures and collaborative learning states in an augmented reality study. In: Bittencourt, I.I., Cukurova, M., Muldner, K., Luckin, R., Millán, E. (eds.) AIED 2020. LNCS (LNAI), vol. 12164, pp. 257–262. Springer, Cham (2020). https://doi.org/10.1007/978-3-030-52240-7_47
10. Rajarathinam, R.J., Kang, J.: Taking the lead: exploring collaborative initiative in cscl contexts. In: Proceedings of the 18th International Conference on Computer-Supported Collaborative Learning-CSCL 2025, pp. 608-610. International Society of the Learning Sciences (2025)
11. Rajarathinam, R.J., Kang, J., Palaguachi, C.: 360-degree cameras vs traditional cameras in multimodal learning analytics: comparative study of facial recognition and pose estimation. J. Educ. Data Mining **17**(1), 157–182 (2025)
12. Suraworachet, W., Seon, J., Cukurova, M.: Predicting challenge moments from students' discourse: a comparison of gpt-4 to two traditional natural language processing approaches. In: Proceedings of the 14th Learning Analytics and Knowledge Conference, pp. 473–485 (2024)
13. Whitehead, R., Nguyen, A., Järvelä, S.: Utilizing multimodal large language models for video analysis of posture in studying collaborative learning: A case study. J. Learn. Analy. **12**(1), 186–200 (2025)
14. Xiao, Z., Yuan, X., Liao, Q.V., Abdelghani, R., Oudeyer, P.Y.: Supporting qualitative analysis with large language models: combining codebook with gpt-3 for deductive coding. In: Companion Proceedings of the 28th International Conference on Intelligent User Interfaces, pp. 75–78 (2023)

Generative AI in Secondary Education Across Diverse Populations

Tamara Dalki(✉), Miri Yemini, and Ido Roll

Technion-Israel Institute of Technology, 3200003 Haifa, Israel
tamara.dalki@campus.technion.ac.il

Abstract. Generative Artificial Intelligence (GAI) is reshaping educational environments and intensifying debates regarding its potential to mitigate or reproduce sociocultural inequalities in learning. This study examines how adolescents' AI literacy and engagement with GAI vary across sociocultural backgrounds within Israel's stratified education system. Adopting a mixed-methods design, Study 1 employs a quantitative questionnaire (N = 500 middle-school students) to identify AI literacy profiles and examine variation across social and cultural groups. Preliminary pilot findings suggest that adolescents demonstrate qualitatively distinct literacy profiles rather than linear differences in competence, and that frequency of AI use does not necessarily predict conceptual understanding. Study 2 combines qualitative inquiry with computational analysis (N = 50) to examine adolescents' real-time interactions with GAI during authentic curricular tasks. By triangulating AI literacy assessment, observed engagement, and learner attitudes, the study aims to advance theoretically grounded, equity-oriented approaches to AI integration in education.

Keywords: Generative Artificial Intelligence · Adolescents · Sociocultural Gaps · Educational Gaps · AI Literacy · Performance Measures

1 Introduction

The rapid spread of Generative Artificial Intelligence (GAI) in education has raised opportunities and concerns related to learning and equity [1, 12]. While GAI may support personalized learning, unequal access, algorithmic bias, and differences in engagement may reproduce educational inequalities [8, 12]. Increasingly, scholars argue that the educational value of GAI depends not only on access but also on students' AI literacy; their ability to engage with AI critically and strategically [9]. These issues are especially important during adolescence, when academic identities and learning behaviors are still developing [14]. Yet research rarely examines how adolescents from different sociocultural contexts develop AI literacy or how it is reflected in observable engagement, relying instead on self-reported perceptions [16]. This gap is particularly relevant in Israel, where disparities between Jewish and Arab education systems shape educational opportunities and digital experiences [20]. This study addresses these gaps by investigating adolescents' AI literacy and real-time engagement with GAI during authentic learning tasks, conceptualizing AI literacy as a contextually situated construct emerging through interaction across sociocultural settings.

E. G. Blanchard et al. (Eds.): AIED 2026, CCIS 3033, pp. 468–473, 2026.
https://doi.org/10.1007/978-3-032-29794-5_73

2 Background

Educational outcomes are shaped not only by individual ability but also by socially and culturally distributed forms of knowledge and practice, as emphasized in Bourdieu's theory of cultural capital [5]. These gaps carry forward from school into higher education [19]. Similarly, Van Dijk's multidimensional model of the digital divide highlights that technological inequality extends beyond access to include differences in skills and meaningful use [21]. From this perspective, emerging technologies such as GAI operate within existing social structures rather than independently of them. Within Israel's stratified educational landscape, disparities between Jewish and Arab schooling contexts- including differences in infrastructure, resources, and learning opportunities- may shape students' experiences with digital technologies [20]. Consequently, variation in GAI engagement likely reflects broader sociocultural differences in knowledge, confidence, and strategic use rather than simple access disparities. Understanding these mechanisms requires a clearer conceptualization of AI literacy and its relationship to social context.

AI literacy refers to the ability to understand AI systems, critically evaluate outputs, recognize societal implications, and use AI responsibly [9]. Contemporary frameworks conceptualize AI literacy as multidimensional, encompassing operational, sociocultural, and critical dimensions [3]. Emerging research further suggests that learners may display distinct literacy profiles reflecting different forms of knowledge rather than varying along a single continuum [15]. For adolescents, such differences may shape trust in AI-generated information and influence engagement strategies. Despite conceptual advances, most empirical work relies on self-report instruments that capture perceived rather than demonstrated competence [16]. Performance-based approaches offer more objective assessment; however, research examining how adolescents enact AI literacy during authentic interaction with GAI remains limited. As a result, the relationship between literacy profiles and real-time engagement across sociocultural contexts remains underexplored.

Research on students' use of GAI has mainly focused on attitudes, intentions, and patterns of use, emphasizing factors that shape adoption and frequency of engagement [7, 13]. Although recent studies have begun to examine differences in usage across student groups and interaction patterns, the literature remains largely descriptive and centered on self-reported behaviors rather than deeper learning processes or competencies [10, 14]. This gap is particularly significant within stratified educational systems, where differences in prior digital experiences may influence both literacy development and engagement patterns [20, 21]. Examining AI literacy as an enacted phenomenon in authentic learning contexts is therefore essential for understanding whether GAI supports educational empowerment or reinforces existing inequalities. This study addresses three research questions:
RQ1: How do adolescents' AI literacy profiles vary across sociocultural backgrounds?
RQ2: How do adolescents from different sociocultural backgrounds engage with GAI in learning contexts?
RQ3: To what extent does AI literacy explain differences in observed GAI engagement across sociocultural backgrounds?

3 Methodology

This research employs a mixed-methods design comprising two complementary studies. Deliberate triangulation integrates multiple data sources to strengthen validity and deepen interpretation [17]

Study 1: Quantitative Questionnaire of AI Literacy Profiles

Methods. Study 1 examines adolescents' AI literacy by employing a performance-based questionnaire that emphasizes demonstrated understanding and assesses three AI literacy dimensions: Understanding How AI Learns (How-AI), measuring conceptual knowledge through tasks such as predicting AI classification based on training data; AI Recognition (With-AI), assessing the ability to identify AI-enabled technologies; and Non-AI Recognition (Without-AI), assessing the ability to distinguish AI from non-AI tools. The questionnaire also includes a self-report measure of GAI usage experience, in which students report frequency of use from unfamiliarity to daily engagement. The questionnaire is adapted from a validated instrument for adults [15].

Participants. The sample will include approximately 500 middle school students recruited through purposive stratified sampling to ensure meaningful variation across Arab-Israeli and Jewish-Israeli students, religious backgrounds, socioeconomic levels, school sectors, and geographic regions.

Data Collection and Research Procedure. The researcher will obtain a consent form from the participants' parents. An online questionnaire will be sent to the head teacher, who will administer the questionnaire along with the researcher. The questionnaire will include an informed consent form, the questionnaire questions, and a demographic questionnaire.

Data Analysis. Study 1 will use psychometric and statistical analyses, including reliability and validity checks, factor analyses, regressions, group comparisons, and clustering, to examine AI literacy, related attitudes, and differences across student groups.

Study 2: Observed Engagement with Generative AI in Learning Contexts

Methods. Study 2 investigates how adolescents from different sociocultural backgrounds engage with GAI during authentic academic tasks and explores how observed engagement relates to AI literacy profiles identified in Study 1.

Participants. Approximately N = 50 students will be purposively selected to enable focused within- and between-group comparisons across sociocultural backgrounds.

Data Collection and Research Procedure. The study will begin with a participatory co-design phase in which the researcher will collaborate with teachers to develop 2 curricular and pedagogically coherent tasks across four subjects (mathematics, sciences, humanities, and social sciences) and one grade level. Students will complete these tasks using a dedicated AI system in a closed, anonymous digital environment in Hebrew or Arabic according to each participant's choice. Full interaction logs will be collected. Following task completion, semi-structured interviews (40–60 min) and focus groups will be conducted to explore perceptions, trust, emotional responses, and contextual influences shaping AI use.

An informed consent form will be distributed to participants at the beginning of the interviews and the focus groups. The researcher will conduct the interviews and the focus groups frontally in schools. The interviews will be recorded and transcribed by the researcher. In order to maintain the rules of ethics, participants will be informed that their real names will not appear in the study.

Here is an Example of a Task Inspired by Potter et al. [18]. Use AI for one hour to investigate this question: If people in Israel used public transportation instead of private cars, what would be the estimated impact on CO2 emissions? *Data Analysis.* Student–GenAI interactions in Study 2 will be analyzed using a combined inductive and deductive approach. ChatGPT will support the initial generation of preliminary codes, which will then be manually refined by the research team, in line with Barany et al. [4]. In parallel, interaction data will also be automatically annotated according to predefined dimensions such as Bloom's taxonomy and conversational context [2]. Qualitative materials (in-depth interviews and focus-group recordings) will be analyzed using thematic analysis [6].

4 Preliminary Results from a Pilot Study

Preliminary findings informing Study 1 derive from a pilot phase conducted in collaboration with other researchers [11]. The pilot included two phases: an initial administration of the questionnaire ($N = 82$) to examine item performance and factor structure, followed by a larger-scale implementation ($N = 295$) used to refine the instrument through confirmatory factor analysis and identify preliminary AI literacy profiles via clustering analyses. The pilot examined the feasibility of a performance-based AI literacy assessment for middle-school learners and identified early patterns in adolescents' understanding of AI.

The instrument demonstrated acceptable internal consistency across three factors—How-AI, With-AI, and Without-AI ($\alpha > .50$). CFA led to the removal of three poorly fitting items, resulting in a refined structure with sufficient reliability. K-means clustering ($k = 5$), selected via the elbow criterion, identified five relatively balanced profiles: All-is-AI, AI-Absence, Guessers, Conceptual-only, and Transitioning. Internal validation indicated moderate but meaningful structure (Silhouette = 0.313; Davies–Bouldin = 1.063; Calinski–Harabasz = 123.67), with significant between-cluster differences (PERMANOVA, $p = .001$) and moderate stability (mean ARI = 0.558). A chi-square test revealed a significant association between cluster membership and generative AI usage frequency ($\chi 2(8, N = 285) = 28.99$, $p < .001$; Cramér's $V = .226$). Post-hoc analysis showed that only the Transitioning group was overrepresented among frequent users ($z = 4.35$, $p < .001$), while no other clusters showed significant deviations.

These findings indicate that the instrument captures differentiated patterns of AI literacy and the complexity of learners' understanding. The five profiles—AI Absence (learners claiming AI is not anywhere), All-is-AI (learners overestimating AI presence), Guessers (learners randomly selecting responses), Transitioning (learners showing an emerging ability to understand AI mechanisms), and Conceptual-only (learners demonstrating stronger understanding of learning mechanisms but weaker identification of

AI in everyday contexts)—reflect qualitatively different configurations rather than a simple progression. The association between clusters and usage further suggests that increased exposure to AI tools does not necessarily correspond to improved AI knowledge, as deeper understanding—rather than frequency of use—appears to drive meaningful engagement. The moderate reliability and need for item refinement point to the ongoing development required in performance-based AI literacy assessment for younger learners.

5 Expected Contributions

This study makes three contributions to research on GAI in school education, relevant to AI in Education and the Learning Sciences. First, it examines adolescents' AI literacy and knowledge, offering insight into how learners understand AI. Second, it explores how demographic and sociocultural differences shape students' use of, attitudes toward, and behaviors related to GAI, addressing equity issues. Third, by foregrounding students' perspectives in authentic school contexts, it supports learner-centered AI design, classroom integration, and inclusive educational policy. Although grounded in the Israeli education system, the study also speaks to broader AIED contexts by showing how AI literacy and GAI use are shaped by sociocultural and structural inequalities.

Acknowledgments. This study is funded partially by the Chief Scientist in the Ministry of Education in Israel.

Disclosure of Interests. The authors declare that they have no known competing financial interests or personal relationships that could have appeared to influence the work reported in this paper.

References

1. Akgun, S., Greenhow, C.: Artificial intelligence in education: addressing ethical challenges in K-12 settings. AI Ethics **2**(3), 431–440 (2022)
2. Anonymous Author(s).: AI in the wild: A large scale analysis of authentic interactions of college students with generative AI. In: Proceedings of the 13th ACM Conference on Learning @ Scale (L@S 2026), 6 pages, ACM, New York (2026)
3. Atias, O., Mawasi, A.: Conceptualizing AI literacies for children and youth: a systematic review on the design of AI literacy educational programs. Comput. Educ. Artifi. Intell. **9**, 100491 (2025)
4. Barany, A. et al.: ChatGPT for education research: exploring the potential of large language models for qualitative codebook development. In: Olney, A.M., Chounta, I.-A., Liu, Z., Santos, O.C., Bittencourt, I.I. (eds.) Artificial Intelligence in Education, pp. 134–149. Springer Nature Switzerland, Cham (2024). https://doi.org/10.1007/978-3-031-64299-9_10
5. Bourdieu, P.: The forms of capital. In: Richardson, J.G. (ed.) Handbook of Theory and Research for the Sociology of Education, pp. 241–258. Greenwood Press, New York
6. Braun, V., Clarke, V.: Using thematic analysis in psychology. Qual. Res. Psychol. **3**, 77–101 (2006)
7. Bueie, A.A., Skar, G.B., Graham, S.: High school students' use and beliefs about generative artificial intelligence and writing in school. Reading and Writing (2025)

8. Capraro, V., et al.: The impact of generative artificial intelligence on socioeconomic inequalities and policy making. PNAS Nexus **3**(6), 191 (2024)
9. Chiu, T.K.F., Ahmad, Z., Ismailov, M., Sanusi, I.T.: What are artificial intelligence literacy and competency? a comprehensive framework to support them. Comput. Educ. Open **6**, 100171 (2024)
10. Dong, T. et al.: Identifying secondary school students' patterns in prompting generative artificial intelligence in AI education. In: 2025 International Symposium on Educational Technology (ISET), pp. 129–133 (2025)
11. Gabbay, H., Halstuch, R., Ston, R., Roll, I., Shwartz, Y., Alexandron, G.: Revisiting the role of learning AI principles in moving students beyond anthropomorphic thinking. To appear in Proceedings of the First International Workshop on Advancing AI Literacy with Learning Analytics (AI-LIT), LAK 2026 (2026)
12. Hadar Shoval, D.: Artificial intelligence in higher education: bridging or widening the gap for diverse student populations? Educ. Sci. **5**(5) (2025)
13. Ismail, A.F., Almughyirah, S.M., Zaky, Y.A.M., Alfadil, N.H., Shahpo, S.M., ALSaadi, O.: Exploring sociocultural patterns in evolving educational practices: Arab students' use of generative AI in accomplishing academic assignments. J. Cultural Analy. Social Change **10**(2), 397–410 (2025)
14. Klarin, J., Hoff, E., Larsson, A., Daukantaitė, D.: Adolescents' use and perceived usefulness of generative AI for schoolwork: exploring their relationships with executive functioning and academic achievement. Front. Artifi. Intell. **7** (2024)
15. Klein-Avraham, I., Ston, R., Atias, O., Roll, I., Baram-Tsabari, A.: Measuring different types and domains of AI knowledge: developing and validating a performance-based scale. Comput. Educ. **247**, 105573 (2026)
16. Lintner, T.: A systematic review of AI literacy scales. npj Sci. Learn. **9**(1), 50 (2024)
17. Patton, M.Q.: Enhancing the quality and credibility of qualitative analysis. Health Serv. Res. **34**(5 Pt 2), 1189–1208 (1999)
18. Potter, T., Englund, L., Charbonneau, J., MacLean, M.T., Newell, J., Roll, I.: ComPAIR: A new online tool using adaptive comparative judgement to support learning with peer feedback. Teach. Learn. Inquiry **5**(2), 89–113 (2017)
19. Ram, I., Shwartz, A., Roll, I.: Minding the gender gap in advanced STEM courses: effects of student preparedness and activity level. Instr. Sci. **53**(6), 1457–1478 (2025)
20. Saffuri, R.: Arab and Jewish education systems in Israel: differences, disparities, and challenges. a comparative review of structure, funding, and outcomes in local authorities. SEA-Pract. Appli. Sci. **13**(39), 159–168 (2025)
21. Van Dijk, J.: The Digital Divide. Polity Press, Cambridge, UK; Medford, MA (2020)

Author Index

E. G. Blanchard et al. (Eds.): AIED 2026, CCIS 3033, pp. 475–478, 2026.
https://doi.org/10.1007/978-3-032-29794-5

G

H

I

J

K

L

M

Zeitfracht Medien GmbH
Ferdinand-Jühlke-Straße 7
99095 Erfurt, Deutschland
produktsicherheit@kolibri360.de